European Intellectual History Since 1789

Sixth Edition

Roland N. Stromberg

University of Wisconsin–Milwaukee

Prentice Hall

Englewood Cliffs, New Jersey 07632

Library of Congress Cataloging–in–Publication Data

Stromberg, Roland N.
 European intellectual history since 1789 / Roland N. Stromberg.—6th ed.
 p. cm.
 Includes bibliographical references and index.
 ISBN 0–13–105990–4
 1. Philopsophy—Europe—History—19th century. 2. Philosophy—Europe—
History—20th century. 3. Europe—Intellectual life—19th century. 4. Europe—
Intellectual life—20th century.
I. Title.
B803.S85 1993
940.2—dc 20   93–10201
                                                                          CIP

Editorial/production supervision, interior design,
  and electronic page make up: Marielle Reiter
Cover design: Maureen Eide
Manufacturing buyer: Mary Ann Gloriande
Prepress buyer: Kelly Behr
Acquisitions editor: Steve Dalphin
Editorial assistant: Caffie Risher
Copy editor: Jeannine Ciliotta

 © 1994, 1990, 1986, 1981, 1975, 1966 by Prentice-Hall, Inc.
A Simon & Schuster Company
Englewood Cliffs, New Jersey 07632

Printed in the United States of America
10 9 8 7 6 5 4 3 2 1

ISBN 0-13-105990-4

PRENTICE-HALL INTERNATIONAL (UK) LIMITED, *London*
PRENTICE-HALL OF AUSTRALIA PTY. LIMITED, *Sydney*
PRENTICE-HALL CANADA INC., *Toronto*
PRENTICE-HALL HISPANOAMERICANA, S.A., *Mexico*
PRENTICE-HALL OF INDIA PRIVATE LIMITED, *New Delhi*
PRENTICE-HALL OF JAPAN, INC., *Tokyo*
SIMON & SCHUSTER ASIA PTE. LTD., *Singapore*
EDITORA PRENTICE-HALL DO BRASIL, LTDA., *Rio de Janeiro*

Contents

Preface

For this edition of a book first written two decades ago, I have undertaken probably the most thorough revision of any of the five it has undergone. The intellectual landscape of the present, of course, constantly changes in our volatile society, and this inevitably affects our perception of the past. (Marx suddenly looks much less important than he once did!) New fashions in ideas emerge every season, it seems, and the awesome volume of scholarship and commentary in the manifold regions of literature and thought multiplies like Malthus's population. When I first wrote this book, it was possible virtually to ignore feminism, while terms like "deconstuction" and "postmodernism" had not even been invented. Moreover, the book in all previous new editions underwent a procedure perhaps not inaccurately described as scissors-and-paste alteration: This time I have totally rewritten it. Even if some passages survive intact, they have all been looked at and many changed in some way. The urge of every author to rewrite his book constantly (Karl Marx as well as James Joyce expressed this desire) has become almost realizable with the aid of computer technology.

Wihtal, I have tried not to interfere too much with a book that has been successful. Some parts of it at least have pleased many people. The book may appeal to those who want some sort of a grasp, however tenuous, on the totality of the intellectual world. We all must live schizophrenically in several divided and distinguished realms: private life (family, friends, love, marriage, career included); public life (politics—local, national, international); and the realm of ideas or discourse, of what Teilhard de Chardin named the noösphere—the world of literature, books, music, art, to some a more vividly real as well as more interesting world than the others. But this cultural realm is itself incredibly vast and diverse. How to find one's way around in it?

Some further reflections on the nature and value of intellectual history will be found in the Introduction. Here is the place only to acknowledge debts. I owe a great debt to those who have read and criticized the book, often on the basis of classroom use. Among these helpful critics are, recently, Thomas W. Judd of SUNY College at Oswego and James E. Young of San Bernadino Valley College. Above all, I am profoundly grateful for help and encouragement from all the many students whom I have taught (and who have taught me), or who have written to me over the years.

Roland Stromberg

Introduction

INTELLECTUAL HISTORY AS A DISCIPLINE

"It is better to know how men thought in former times than how they acted," Voltaire declared. This is not only because such a story is more pleasant, contrasting with the rather gloomy recital of wars and famines and revolutions that passes as "action" history—a kind of City of God compared to the City of Man, in St. Augustine's famous dualism—but also because it seems to represent a higher level of achievement. Human thought has contained its share of grievous error; yet Plato, Michelangelo, Galileo, and Freud stand up well against the Caesars and Napoleons and Bismarcks who are featured in most general histories. Given that we do not have time to learn everything, it is better to encounter the great works of art, literature, philosophy, and science than to spend limited resources on the soldiers and politicians, or even the farmers and workers. (This recently fashionable type of history, as one of its critics has written, shows us "people who produce, eat, pay, and die, but not ones who play, pray, dream, and love.")

Additionally, we may argue that in fact the ideas stand behind the events, or at least are a vital part of them. "The actual world is the result of men's thoughts," J. N. Figgis claimed; "all human history is fundamentally a history of ideas," H. G. Wells thought. To be sure, others like Karl Marx have declared that the "real world" of human actions comes first, ideas being a by-product. "Not ideas, but

1

material and ideal interests directly govern man's conduct," the great sociologist Max Weber wrote, but then immediately added that "very often the world images created by ideas have, like switchmen, determined the tracks along which action has been pushed by the dynamics of interest." This seems to be one of those chicken-and-egg disputes, in the end irresolvable; we can only affirm a close connection and constant interplay between the two realms, which are "the two faces of reality." We may well wonder whether the economic thought of Adam Smith and his successors was less important in the so-called Industrial Revolution than the coal or climate of the British Isles; it is hard to deny that both were important, and equally hard to prove that one was primary and the other derivative.

In a celebrated statement, John Maynard Keynes remarked that "madmen in power" seize on the ideas of some defunct economist to justify their actions. The men and women who made the great French Revolution appropriated slogans from the eighteenth-century "philosophers," Montesquieu and Voltaire and Rousseau, usually misunderstanding or at any rate oversimplifying them. Historians today, looking at the social background of the great French Revolution with the aid of immensely more data than anyone then possessed, do not find a picture much like that seen by the men and women who made that Revolution. But obviously what counts most in explaining that event is what moved people to action then.

Many historical studies, comparing the ideas with the reality, find large discrepancies. The nobles of pre-1789 France shared a perception of themselves that did not at all coincide with fact—they thought, for example, that they were descended from the Frankish conquerors of the fifth century. Yet it is obvious that this perception of themselves largely determined how they acted, by defining their identity and underscoring their pride. Thus the "idea" can be the decisive factor in history. Long ago John Locke, the philosopher who most influenced the eighteenth-century Enlightenment, observed that "In truth the ideas or images in men's minds are the invisible powers that constantly govern them." Or, as Schopenhauer put it, "Opinion rules the world." People can probably only act, in any way beyond the simplest sort of a response to immediate external stimulus, in terms of some perception or idea they hold in their minds. And history may be best understood as a collection of ideas.[1]

This debate might be pursued indefinitely, and probably without any change in tempo. But it does provide a good reason for anyone interested in general history to know something about the history of ideas. The intellectual historian is fascinated by the interplay between ideas and human behavior in causing great happenings.

---

[1] This may even be true of something as personal as love. Romantic love with all its overtones, as still celebrated in fiction and cinema, is a literary, artistic, and philosophical creation. A character in George Gissing's "realistic" novel *The Odd Women* remarked impatiently that "in real life" men and women seldom "fall in love"; "Not one married pair in ten thousand have felt for each other as two or three couples do in every novel."

This is to say nothing about where these "ideas" that take shape within human minds come from, how they are formed—an issue the historian is well advised to leave to others.[2] Democritus in ancient times thought they came from outside, like atoms bombarding the skull, a view John Locke evidently shared in the seventeenth century: ideas are learned from experience, registered somehow in the human brain. But Plato thought they came from another world, and rendered this one intelligible; definitely not from sense experience, more nearly the reverse, they enable us to make sense of the chaotic impressions that bombard us. Immanuel Kant, as we shall see, partly agreed. René Descartes started a long debate in the seventeenth century, not yet finished, when he upheld the view that soul and body are entirely separate principles. We can leave this to the philosophers and psychologists or "cognitive scientists," accepting as given the human ability—probably unique among all living creatures— to manufacture "an interior world confronting, separate from, and opposing the exterior world" (Ortega y Gasset).

Granted that university students will profit from knowing the "great ideas," which ones should they know? Today these "ideas" are divided up among numerous departments of knowledge. Arthur O. Lovejoy, a pioneer in the history of ideas, began by being dismayed at the dissection of the living body of thought into at least twelve "disciplines," each carting away a piece of the dismembered body to study it in isolation— the various sciences, philosophy, religion, several branches of literature, sociology, economics, and so on. It has occasionally occurred to literary critics that they ought to know something about history, or to scientists that they might profit from some philosophy, but in general they ignore what goes on in the other departments. Sometimes they try to do their own internal history, usually badly.

The historian of ideas or intellectual historian is committed to the belief that at any given time (varying from generation to generation) there is a certain spirit of the age affecting all branches of thought and expression. "Such is the existing spirit of speculation," Coleridge wrote, "during any given period, such will be the spirit and tone of the religion and morals, nay even of the fine arts, the manners, and the fashions." "The primary function of the intellectual historian," a more recent practitioner declared, "is to delineate the presuppositions of thought in given historical epochs and to explain the changes which these presuppositions undergo from

---

[2] "What went on in No. 1's brain?...What went on in the inflated gray whorls? One knew everything about the far-away spiral nebulae, but about this nothing. That was probably the reason history was more an oracle than a science. Perhaps later, much later, it would be taught by means of tables of statistics, supplemented by such anatomical sections. The teacher would draw on the blackboard an algebraic formula representing the condition of life of the masses of a particular nation at a particular period.... And, pointing with his ruler to a grey foggy landscape between the second and third lobes of No. 1's brain: "Now here you see the subjective reflection of these factors. It was this which in the second quarter of the twentieth century led to the triumph of the totalitarian principle in the East of Europe." (Arthur Koestler, *Darkness at Noon*). One wonders.

epoch to epoch."[3] Structuralist theorists like Michel Foucault and Julia Kristeva have postulated an *episteme* or mode of discourse or system of signs characteristic of an era, which may change abruptly.[4] More popularly, we are likely to say that the decade of the 1960s had its special flavor or style, which changed sharply in the following decade. The intellectual historian, according to Hayden White, "attempts to write the history of consciousness in general," rather than separate histories of the various branches of knowledge. He/she searches "to find the word, the feeling, the concepts that are the infrastructure of the thought" of an era (Lucien Febvre).

Even if there is no neatly defined total Zeitgeist, there are lots of interactions reaching across departmental boundaries. The great philosopher Immanuel Kant received a decisive influence from the novelist and essayist Jean-Jacques Rousseau. The poet T. S. Eliot, a philosophy student, got much from philosophers like Henri Bergson and F. H. Bradley. The psychologist Sigmund Freud exerted probably his most important influence on literature, besides finding much of his inspiration there. Such examples are innumerable.

We have, then, several possible models for our study of ideas. We could select a number of thinkers who by consensus represent pinnacles of human achievement —the Darwins and Einsteins, Marxes and Nietzsches. Or we could isolate not individuals but important ideas. Mortimer Adler in his study of Great Ideas chose six largish ones—like Justice and Equality— that echo down the cen-

---

[3]John C. Greene, "Objectives and Methods in Intellectual History," *Mississippi Valley Historical Review*, June 1957. The following is a selection of other discussions about the nature of intellectual history: Franklin L. Baumer, "Intellectual History and Its Problems," *Journal of Modern History* September 1949; Arthur O. Lovejoy, "The Historiography of Ideas," *Essays in the History of Ideas* (1948); Hayden White, "The Tasks of Intellectual History," *Monist*, vol. 53 (1969), 600–30; Quentin Skinner, "Meaning and Understanding in the History of Ideas," *History and Theory*, vol. 8 (1969), 3–53; Norman Hampson and Betty Bahrens, "Cultural History as Infrastructure," *Studies in Voltaire and the Eighteenth Century*, vol. 86 (1971); Joseph Anthony Mazzeo, "Some Interpretations of the History of Ideas," *Journal of the History of Ideas*, July–September 1972; Leonard Krieger, "The Autonomy of Intellectual History," *Journal of the History of Ideas*, October–December 1973; Roland N. Stromberg, "Some Models Used by Intellectual Historians," *American Historical Review*, June 1975; Jaakko Hintikka, "Gaps in the Great Chain of Being: An Exercise in the Methodology of the History of Ideas," *Proceedings of the American Philosophical Association*, vol. 49 (1975–76), 22–38; Nils B. Kvastad, "Semantics in the Methodology of the History of Ideas," *Journal of the History of Ideas*, January–March 1977; essay by Paul K. Conkin in Charles Delzell, ed., *The Future of History* (1977); Dominick LaCapra, *Rethinking Intellectual History*, and, with Steven L. Kaplan, eds., *Modern European Intellectual History: Reappraisals and New Perspectives* (1982); Preston King, ed., *The History of Ideas: An Introduction to Method* (1983); Martin Jay, "Two Cheers for Paraphrase: The Confessions of a Synoptic Intellectual Historian," in his *Fin de Siècle Socialism and Other Essays*; Isaiah Berlin, *Against the Current: Essays in the History of Ideas* (1980).

[4]Foucault, who seemed to think of himself primarily as an intellectual historian, arbitrarily rejected other kinds of intellectual history in favor of an "archeology of ideas" that uncovers the various "modes of discourse" in a society at any given time, and explores the relations between these various modes. All of these together constitute an "epistemological field" or *episteme*, which sets the terms of knowledge in any given epoch. At bottom this fashionable French theorizing seems to do little more than endow the old *Zeitgeist* with a novel set of terms.

turies. "The cardinal controversies of human society are few, and they remain curiously fixed," John Morley claimed. The terms change but the basic ideas are constant. Such a "the more things change the more they are the same" view contrasts with a model of progress in which "successive steps…each adds something to the thoughts of predecessors" (Ludwig von Mises). But both can be true.

We might choose some slightly less abstract but quite pertinent nineteenth-century ideas: nationalism, socialism, liberalism, democracy, words that dominated the epoch. The pioneer historian of ideas Arthur O. Lovejoy picked out key structuring conceptions like "the great chain of being" and "primitivism." Alternatively, we could concentrate on showing that the acknowledged grand events of history, the French Revolution and Industrial Revolution and Russian Revolution, even the two world wars, derived at least in part from pure thinkers or writers. Or we could search for the *Zeitgeist* or *episteme* of each era, noting how this crossed lines to affect all the separate branches of thought. Romanticism provided such a theme for the early years of the last century.

This book attempts to do something of each of these. Intellectual history should provide an introduction to the most important systems of thought within our Western, European tradition; introduce the student to some great minds, which hopefully he and she will pursue further; relate these ideas to the social and political background; indicate the continuity and lineage of thought; and show how these ideas are connected within the general cultural context. Probably no one book is going to accomplish all these ends, but it ought at least to point the way.

Students may not be greatly interested in these methodological problems. If they are, they can look into the works cited in footnote 3. It is more practical to ask, of what value is this subject? And is it enjoyable? The answer lies partly in one's temperament. Some people find ideas interesting. "There is but one thing more interesting than the intellectual history of a man, and that is the intellectual history of a nation," the historian Moses Coit Tyler once wrote. Dr. Samuel Johnson wrote scornfully of "wretched un-idea'd" people; to him a person without thoughts was unspeakably dull. An idea need not be ponderous, totally abstract; it can be about love, war, romance, animals, anything. To enrich our minds with ideas is to become a civilized person able to live more fully. And, as Dr. Johnson added, "There is no part of history so generally useful as that which relates to the progress [?] of the human mind, the successive advances of science, the extension and resuscitation of the arts and the revolution of the intellectual world."

This attempt to learn something of all thought is admittedly an ambitious one. "Read the great authors whole," Walter Pater advised his students. "Read Plato whole; read Kant whole; read Mill whole." Excellent advice, no doubt, but a little impractical for most people. Aldous Huxley, himself an admirable historian of ideas via the novel, mused that "Science is not enough, religion is not enough, art is not enough, politics and economics are not enough, nor is action, however disinterested, nor, however sublime, is contemplation. Nothing short of everything will really do." But is it possible? "Learn everything" was the advice of Hugh of

St. Victor in the twelfth century. We can hardly succeed; but striving to learn as much as possible of the whole structure of knowledge is what drives the intellectual historian.

THE INHERITANCE

Our narrative begins in 1789 (a conventional turning point), but no one would make the mistake of supposing that significant thought began at that time. In the background of European civilization, reaching back to the ancient Greeks and Romans and Christians, lay a rich intellectual tradition. We may imagine that only a few simple ideas existed before the modern explosion, but it hardly seemed that way to our ancestors. A very sophisticated seventeenth-century Frenchman, La Rochefoucauld (a psychologist who influenced Nietzsche and Freud) sighed that "Everything has been said, and we come too late after more than 7,000 years in which man has existed and thought!" Like almost everyone else, he supposed that Plato, Aristotle, Euclid, Ptolemy and the other great ancient philsophers and scientists had forever defined the realm of knowledge, just as Homer and Aeschylus and Virgil had set the limits of art. In fact, the ancients did define the genres much as we still use them today, with terms such as physics, philosophy, poetry, politics, economics—and history (from the Greek *'istoria*, an inquiry). And the ancients defined our very modes of thought, through their logic, their rhetoric, tropes, genres, categories. When we classify or compare we still think much as they taught us, and when we talk or write we use metaphor, simile, and metonymy.

A Renaissance in the twelfth and thirteenth centuries, and then the more famous one of ca. A.D. 1450–1600, had been proud simply to rediscover and restore the great works of the Greco-Roman period which had flourished more than a thousand years earlier. Few thought more could be added. But in fact an outburst of original genius marked these years, not only in the arts but in literature and, finally, in science.[5] At the end of the sixteenth century the genius of an obscure Englishman, William Shakespeare, produced dramatic works that in a strange way were to haunt the imagination of Europe through all the centuries and from one end of the continent to the other (the Stratford bard was as well known in Catherine the Great's Russia as he was in England.) Hardly less universal was the Spaniard Cervantes, whose *Don Quijote* has been called the first modern novel. Shakespeare borrowed his plots and his themes —universal, timeless ones—from the ancient classics, but he endowed them with unrivaled gifts of imagery and language.

Writing in the eighteenth century D'Alembert, an editor of the famous French *Encyclopédie*, engaged in reevaluating the intellectual inheritance, saw three "revolutions of the spirit" as he looked into the recent past: the renaissance of

---

[5]In trying to reproduce the ancient musical drama the Italians unintentionally invented a new form, the *opera*.

the arts after (he says) 1453, mainly in Italy; the religious Reformation stemming from the German Martin Luther in the sixteenth century; and then the advent of modern scientific philosophy, which D'Alembert associated with the great seventeenth-century French philosopher and mathematician René Descartes. This scientific revolution in fact extended from Copernicus to Newton, from 1543 to 1687, and overthrew the authority of the ancients in basic conceptions of the material universe, from astronomy and physics to anatomy and physiology. (The chemistry revolution lay ahead, a work of the later eighteenth and early nineteenth centuries.)

The startling moment that alerted Europe to the collapse of the old order of nature came from Italy in 1610, when Galileo observed through his telescope phenomena such as the moons of Jupiter and the phases of Venus that were wholly incompatible with the Ptolemaic model of astronomy. He was to show, additionally, that a sun-centered system, using the elliptical orbits of the planets that Johannes Kepler had discovered, accounted for the observed movements of the planets better than the old earth-centered one. The earth had been displaced from its proud spot as center of the universe. This was about the date of Shakespeare's retirement; the cosmology in his plays is still thoroughly medieval. The earth stood solidly at the center of the universe, while around it in circular spheres revolved the planets, including the sun, made of a different, weightless substance and carried on crystalline spheres. The last outlying circle of heavenly bodies carried the fixed stars. This old cosmology was tied to an Aristotelian philosophy that blended with medieval Christianity. As the earth was a unique physical body forming the center of the cosmos, so man as lord of the earth was a unique being. Everything in the universe was made for him.

Today, as we contemplate a universe consisting of billions upon billions of stars like our own solar system, which is situated somewhere on the edge of one of a million or so galaxies, we may well smile at the earth-centered and man-centered outlook of our ancestors of only a few hundred years ago. But the laughter is a little hollow. The universe was then a friendlier place. To the ancients anything that happened in the physical universe was connected with human affairs. Correspondences between the macrocosm and the microcosm, the heavens and the humans, were seen everywhere. As the plotters prepare Caesar's assassination in Shakespeare's *Julius Caesar*, strange portents abound; lightning flashes and wonders are seen. "The heavens themselves blaze forth the death of princes." To Shakespeare's audience this was literal reality; nature and humanity were so closely tied together that anything that happened in one arena could not fail to affect the other. Ficino, notable Renaissance philosopher, founder of the Florentine Academy, advised the wearing of talismans to ward off evil and believed in astrology.

Though the authority of the ancients was being overthrown in these important areas of natural science, the power of classical literature remained. Seventeenth-century scientists did seek to establish a new kind of discourse, plainer and clearer, avoiding the traditional devices of rhetoric, "these specious Tropes and Figures," as Thomas Sprat, the historian of the Royal Society, called them. But at Darwin's Cambridge as late as the 1820s, education was almost exclusively a matter of Greek and Latin. The French Revolution itself was heavily influenced by classical motifs, and the eighteenth century Enlightenment with little exaggeration has been called a revival of ancient paganism. Certainly it was accompanied by a strong wave of neo-classicism. Among the less orthodox Greeks of the sixth to the fourth century B.C. Athens were atomists and materialists and sceptics, including that Cynic and dropout Diogenes. Some of them had anticipated Darwin's theory of evolution. Karl Marx wrote his doctoral dissertation on the ancient materialists, by whom he was obviously greatly influenced, and declared that the historian Thucydides was the father of us all.

One of the avant-garde artists of the early twentieth century, Ludwig Meidner, included a chapter in his memoirs which consisted solely of hailing all the "thunderers down the millennia" beginning with Homer and Pindar, totaling over a hundred individuals. Such an imposing inheritance continued to exert its power. In his book about the continuing influence of the classics in the nineteenth century, *Blood for the Ghosts*, H. Lloyd-Jones has chapters on Goethe, Coleridge, Marx, Wagner, Nietzsche, and Gladstone—quite a cross-section of the century's thought. That Sigmund Freud found his key terms in ancient Greek literature and myth is well known. So much for alleged modernity! It is true that in the second half of the nineteenth century classicism came under increasing attack from the scientists; this was the great power struggle of the century in the universities.

We might single out two features of this past inheritance that were quite different from the modern outlook into which it would evolve in the nineteenth century and after. First, it was a Church-centered culture. Christianity's dominant role in culture was reflected in the clerical monopoly of cultural and intellectual institutions. The universities, a creation of the Middle Ages, were staffed by clergy and organized around a synthesis of Christianity and classical philosophy. Almost all important art of any sort was Church art: the majestic cathedrals of Europe dominated architecture, while painting, sculpture, and music were overwhelmingly used to adorn the churches and embellish religious services.[6] As late as the early eighteenth century, a large majority of published books dealt with theology or practical piety. Insofar as there were welfare services such as health, education, even psychiatry,[7] also inns and hotels, friars or monks or priests performed these functions.

This primal situation in which the whole of society was almost one great religious communion had begun to change, with an increasing momentum. The world was being *secularized.* A noted historian has observed that "The progressive secularization of the religious quest for truth forms the mainstream which governs the flow of intellectual currents in Europe over the last three centuries." The Reforma-

---

[6]Julian Rushton, *Classical Music* (London 1987) says: "in the late 18th century for the first time in the Christian era, secular music completely outstrips sacred music in its importance."

[7]One Elizabethan parson developed a national reputation for treating mental disturbances, including the numerous cases he classified as "mopishness," which seems as good a diagnosis as our present "depression."

tion as well as the scientific revolution assisted this process. By secularization we mean the transfer of scholarship, literature, serious thought, education, artistic expression, as well as human services and government, from the Church to non-Church, "lay" personnel and institutions. Many of these belonged to the State, rapidly cutting loose from religious domination; others came from private sources including the new scientific societies. A recent scholarly study of Oxford in the nineteenth century (mostly after 1847) is called *From Clergyman to Don*, its title indicating the process in which professional university education replaced Church of England religious training, previously the sole object of higher learning. The European nineteenth century was probably the first predominantly secularist century in the history of human culture.

Earlier, the Enlightenment's self-appointed elite of "philosophers" had conducted a sharp attack on the clergy. One may read in most of the nineteenth century's serious intellectual enterprises the search for a nonclerical substitute for religion. The quasi-religious "ideologies" of nationalism and socialism were filled with symbols of belief and regeneration through struggle. Economic and political ideas cut loose from their position as branches of Christian ethics to develop independent "scientific" status. Resistance to this came not only from the old faith, but from others shocked by the loss of authoritative moral guidance and cultural unity. The great debates of the century revolve around attacks on religion, from Bentham, Marx, and Darwin to Nietzsche and Freud.

The other thing worth noting as a general quality of the older intellectual world is its static and absolutist nature. The world was regarded as unchanging, truth therefore being fixed and certain. Plato's realm of eternal Ideas expressed this, no less than Aristotle's belief that the world had had no beginning in time but was always as it is now. The rules of art according to the classical and neo-classical esthetic (never stronger than during the seventeenth and eighteenth centuries) remained the same for all times and places, rooted as they were supposed to be in a single unvarying Reason. That the Christian revelation stood forever valid was of course doubted by Protestants no more than by Catholics. The great Puritan revolution of seventeenth-century England did not claim to discover new principles of government but sought rather to restore the ancient ones, just as the Protestant Reformation had professed to return to the uncorrupted purity of the early Church. It was generally agreed that there was mutability in the real world, because it imitated the ideal one only imperfectly; things decayed, but there was also recovery. In human affairs as well as in nature, the cycle oscillated around a permanent center that scarcely changed. "To Platonism," a classical scholar remarks, "man was a fallen spirit; to modern science he is a risen animal" (F.M. Cornford). As a fallen spirit the human creature would eventually return to the pure realm from which it had come, a kingdom of unalterable perfection.

Human nature did not change; as Bakhtin (*The Dialogic Imagination*) observes, literary forms such as the chivalric romance and the baroque novel assume the inborn and statically inert nobility of its heroes: "To this the modern novel opposes the process of a man's becoming." Rather than the testing of an

already preformed and predetermined hero, nineteenth-century novels told the story of the development of a person through his education, his experience. The *Bildungsroman* became a norm. In his study of *The Idea of History*, R. G. Collingwood noted that historical work has flourished more in modern times than in ancient because the ancients saw peoples as having a given inherent nature, which their actions illustrated; we have learned to see them as shaped by their history.

The stupefying achievement of Isaac Newton at the end of the seventeenth century in discovering the laws of gravity and motion, climax of the scientific revolution, tended to reenforce this bias toward immutability. The new science had indeed overthrown truths long regarded as unalterable, but it had not suggested a model of endless revision; it had found a new basis for timeless certainty. The eighteenth-century Enlightenment tended to be dominated by the model of a great world machine. This world existed as an objective entity; human intelligence had not yet fathomed all its secrets, but there was no scepticism about the possibility of attaining knowledge of it. It did not evolve.

Before Darwin, the image of biological nature was the Great Chain of Being, a classical idea revived by Pope in his rhymed *Essay on Man*. An unbroken ladder of ascent linked the crudest stones and the loftiest angels, with Man as the middle term, one foot in both camps. The ladder did not change, though along it creatures strove upward, seeking vainly to reach a rung higher than their appointed one. It was an eternal perfection. Discovery of extinct species dealt it a mortal blow at the end of the eighteenth century, for no species could ever cease to exist on the Great Chain. (For this reason Thomas Jefferson insisted there must be mastadons alive somewhere.)

A futuristic utopia written in 1763 in Great Britain pictured what life would be like in the reign of King George VI, 1900 to 1925. Chronologically the projection was not too far off (George V actually was the British monarch 1910–35). The author was also rather prescient in foreseeing a great war in 1917, though he had Britain fighting *on the side of* Germany and against France and Russia. What is striking is his assumption that nothing has changed in the mode of living. Not only is war still being fought with the weapons and tactics of Frederick the Great, but Alexander Pope still dominates literary taste. Moreover the political order seems much the same, though English freedom overthrows Continental despotism as the grand climax of this early adventure in futurism. "Everything from poetry to architecture exists in a Newtonian universe of unalterable and unerring laws," remarks the author of an article about this literary curiosity (in *History Today*, December 1963). The point of any such sci-fi excursion today, needless to say, would be to imagine all the extraordinary changes certain to occur, especially in technology and science. Then, it was much more to show that *plus ça change, plus c'est la même chose.*

That this belief in an essentially unchanging world now seems distinctly odd to us is a measure of the intellectual revolution of the last two or three centuries. Many were at first shocked at the rapidity of change in the nineteenth century. Some tried to hold back the flood that swept aside familiar landmarks and

[handwritten top margin: This is change over time. Current diversity is multiplicity even within the instant,]

cast doubt on long accepted certainties. Others made an idol out of Change, projecting visions of a better world to come further down the temporal road. The dialectic of movement and order, progress and reaction, is another key to nineteenth-century thought, permeating almost all its chief intellectual systems as well as popular ideas. *[handwritten: X]*

THE GREAT DIVORCE

Shakespeare's unique achievement seems to relate among other things to his standing halfway between an oral and a literate culture. His plays, spoken to a live audience and often written out, it seems, just before performance, have something of the quality of improvisation. They stand in the tradition of medieval morality plays and religious drama of the sort still preserved in the celebrated Passion Play performed at Oberammergau in Bavaria. This in turn had roots in tribal religious ceremonies. The bards of primitive society declaimed from memory the epics of the tribe to a congregation of the people. But Shakespeare's plays were written, and that he was a conscious and sophisticated artist his sonnets above all reveal. *[handwritten: oral not sophisticated artists?]*

In Shakespeare's day high and low culture had not yet separated. It seemed amazing to later generations that common people as well as the upper classes joined in understanding Shakespeare's plays. Just after his time, partly as a result of the scientific revolution, the new urban intellectual elite divorced itself from the masses. Educated people would begin to ridicule the old village culture of unlettered people, with its magic potions and witches and folk medicine. These ancient folkways seemed ignorant and superstitious to the new scientist, as well as to the devout Christian. It has remained for recent social historians to rediscover and value the old village peasant culture with its basis in oral lore. The eighteenth century Enlightenment was inclined to think it a menace to civilization. Robespierre, the future French Revolution leader, made his reputation arguing against villagers who refused to put up Franklin's lightning rods. Voltaire and Rousseau both felt strongly that the uneducated masses should be kept from power, even that they were incapable of rational thought. *[handwritten right margin: no, this was going on by 1500 in Italy or indeed in Aristophanes & the like]*

Such data as are available indicate that literacy rose rapidly in western Europe in the seventeenth and eighteenth centuries. Shakespeare's own father was unable to read or write, but in 1750 two-thirds of the men and half the women in an English rural community could write at least their names. In 1790, 80 percent of the men and 64 percent of the women in a French village were apparently literate. The rapid expansion of the book trade is considered to be one of the prime causes of the French Revolution; a crowd of ambitious would-be authors in Paris supplied some of the revolution's leaders, as well as reading material for an increasing number of people. They followed in the footsteps of Voltaire and Jean-Jacques Rousseau, who were among the first authors to gain fame and fortune solely by their literary efforts. In 1761 the latter's "novel" *La nouvelle Héloïse* became "the biggest best-seller of the century," going through seventy editions in the four decades after its publication in 1761 and being translated into every European language. It reduced all Europe to tears. Children were named Juliette, and later Emile after another Rousseau creation. People wrote to Rousseau from all over Europe, sometimes bringing him their real life problems; he was the first Dear Abby.

The success of Rousseau's story was part of a "reading revolution" that occurred in the middle to later eighteenth century. Samuel Richardson achieved a similar success in England with his novel *Pamela*. Books were not new, of course, but they now changed into something like a mass media, no longer just rare objects treasured by a small elite. They became available to a far wider audience through cheaper production and extensive distribution. (Rousseau's novel was rented out by the hour as well as bought.) The seventeenth century had produced a large number of pamphlets, and the first newspapers. Now the extensive printed book, available in numerous copies, began to appear—even if the numbers were small by comparison with the present.

Rousseau and the reading revolution were associated with a new kind of individual consciousness. With only slight exaggeration Rousseau, author of what has been called the first autobiography (his "Confessions" were certainly a new *kind* of autobiography) has been credited with inventing the self, or self-consciousness. Modern literature, whether poetry or prose, has typically been written in private by an individual author, printed in a book, then read in isolation by readers. Readers identified closely and passionately with the characters in the novel (people wrote to Rousseau from all over asking him to assure them that Julie really existed.)

His famous heroine raised the question of individual versus social duties. Julie conquers her own passionate indiscipline to accept social order at the price of marriage to a man she does not really love—a rather unromantic message in the work that supposedly started romanticism. In this work Rousseau rejected the claims of the emancipated individual ego, yet he raised the question of its conflict with society. This exciting ambivalence was the key to much of Rousseau's strange power, whether as social theorist or novelist.

So the divorce was not merely between city and country, literate and folk cultures, but between the individual and society. This tension will appear in almost every one of the great nineteenth-century novels, whose authors were leading figures of their times—Balzac, Dickens, Flaubert, George Sand, George Eliot, and others. Their widely read tales present the drama of individuals, of both sexes, seeking to find their identity and define their relationship to society as they grow up.

Throughout the nineteenth century and after, powerful forces were transforming the social structure in which ideas operate—vast processes of population growth, urbanization, technological change, and new social stratification. "The concentration of population in cities," a British student of urbanization, A. F. Weber, noted near the end of the nineteenth century, had been "the most remarkable social phenomenon" of that century. The teeming urban masses were uprooted from their traditional folk cultures to become consumers of ideas and values supplied by urban intellectuals. "What bonds link the two million inhabitants who crowd into Paris?" asked Baron Haussmann, the redesigner of Paris, in 1864. "For them Paris is a great consumers' market, a vast workshop, an arena for ambitions." A place of marvelous stimulation where keenness of mind fed on rapid communications and the competition for prizes, the metropolis was also a place of restless discontent. And it was where an essentially new class, the intellectuals, specialists in ideas, sellers of dreams and ideological wares, flourished as never before. It is to this extraordinary century that we now turn.

It falls rather naturally into three parts, from the vantage point of intellectual ages. The first was the Romantic and revolutionary era, lasting from about 1789 to 1832 or perhaps 1848, marked by much storm and stress, the creation of new social doctrines, and a powerful revolution in language and taste as well as society. It was a time when people felt old moorings give way and wondered where the storm would blow them, but also entertained high hopes for some wonderful destination. Then during the noonday of the century calm returned; the Victorian era was marked by relative stability and some remarkable efforts at synthesis of social doctrine. Realism replaced romanticism in literature, and science came to the front of the stage. After the failure of the 1848 revolutions there was some disenchantment, but also practical success.

The evening of the century brings an increasing estrangement of the intellectual and artist from the mainstream society, and a turn toward irrationalism. If the average man remained complacent and hopeful, post-Darwinian and post-Marxist Europe produced a crop of amazingly insightful thinkers who were exploring domains never heretofore much known, zones of fearful nonsymmetry. The "modernist" mood and movement began. "The first half of the nineteenth century considered itself the greatest of all centuries," George Bernard Shaw wrote with only a little of his customary exaggeration. "The second half discovered that it was the wickedest of all the centuries." In terms of individual thinkers, we will have passed from Kant and the Romantic poets through Marx, Mill, Comte, and Darwin down to Nietzsche, Freud, and Bergson.

1

Romanticism and Revolution

THE FRENCH REVOLUTION

Ideas played a vital part in the coming of the great French Revolution that began in 1789 and dominated the European scene for some years. It had been preceded by the remarkable *philosophe* movement, featuring a celebrated gallery of intellectual leaders who after emerging in the late 1740s reached the peak of their fame and influence in the 1760s and 1770s just in time to indoctrinate the future leaders of the revolution. "It is by *words* that they accomplish their ends; *words* did everything," a recent historian quotes from a Frenchman of the revolutionary years. These were the words of Voltaire, Diderot, Montesquieu, Rousseau, and their disciples, who were constantly quoted and enshrined in the pantheon of heroes the revolutionary government created. The leading factions or parties of the revolution were defined much more by ideas than by membership in social classes. *Sans culottism*, the outlook of revolutionary Paris, was "more a state of mind than a social, political or economic entity," a leading student of it finds. Jacobins, as the group dominant from 1792 to 1794 were called, came from every social class. The revolutionary leaders tended to see the revolution as the fruit of Enlightenment thought. Brissot boasted in September 1791 that "Our revolution is not the fruit of an insurrection. It is the work of a half century of enlightenment." "Philosophy has directed a great revolution in France," a leading journal declared in April 1793.

Unfortunately the ideas of the *philosophes*, usually rather vague on social-political matters, proved inadequate to guide the revolution. That after a brave start it degenerated into bitter and bloody internal strife, leading to the Reign of Terror of 1793–94, some blamed on the confusions and inconsistencies in Enlightenment thought, or on its lack of applicability to the real world. The conservative manifesto of Edmund Burke, the Anglo-Irish statesman-philosopher whose *Reflections on the Revolution in France* became the bible of France's enemies, indicted the revolution for having based itself on abstract ideas in an area where only concrete human ties and rooted traditions can work. It must be admitted that, in the words of a recent careful student of their thought (John Lough),"The search for the views of the Philosophes on the future government of France brings very little reward."

In fact, almost all the surviving representatives of the *philosophe* persuasion (most of the great generation had passed on)[1] were horrified by the revolution almost from the start. After all, they stood for reasoned progress through intellectual enlightenment, not violent revolution; most of them despised the mob and hoped for some kind of enlightened despotism. They were believers in a rational order and a scientific method which the disorders and wild rhetoric of the revolution affronted. The word "revolution," it has been pointed out, is almost entirely absent from the writings of the *philosophes*. The creation of a better world they expected to be the result "not of angry revolution but of gradual, controlled, and maximally predictable reform." Baron d'Holbach, one of the more radical of the philosophers (atheist, at least when the servants were absent, "the personal enemy of God") had written in his political magnum opus (*La politique naturelle*, 1773) that "In revolutions, men, guided by fury, never consult reason. "Rhetorically hostile to the Church, most of the *illuminés* (they were not all of the same mind) wanted to replace the Christian clergy with a priesthood of Reason, and in general they did not wish to abolish the monarchy but use it as a means of enlightenment.

The so-called Girondin faction harbored most of the Enlightenment intellectuals. The Jacobin followers of Robespierre and Saint-Just, who sent the Girondists to the guillotine or to suicide in 1793–94, bitterly denounced the *philosophes* and Encyclopedists. "Men of letters" became almost synonomous with traitors. The radical Jacobins saw their enemies as "the most educated, the most scheming, the cleverest," who, Robespierre declared, "favor with all their power the rich egoists and the enemies of equality." The Jacobins did use one major Enlightenment thinker, Rousseau, extensively and even obsessively. "Divine man," Robespierre called him. But the Rousseau whom they made their patron saint was the enemy of Voltaire and Diderot; he was the anti-*philosophe* who had rejected sophisticated reason in favor of natural feelings. Had Rousseau lived to see the revolution, Robespierre declaimed, "who can doubt that his generous soul would have embraced the

---

[1]Voltaire and Rousseau, the rival giants, both died in 1778; David Hume in 1776, Denis Diderot in 1784, d'Alembert in 1783, Condillac in 1780, Frederick the Great in 1786. Buffon and Franklin were octogenarians. This had been the incomparable Enlightenment *philosophe* generation. But their immediate disciples, such as the Marquis de Condorcet amd Manon Roland, carried on the tradition.

cause of justice and equality with transports of joy?" But the moderates Brissot and Mme. Roland were equally devotees of Rousseau; they drew on different interpretations and different writings, which still give rise to considerable differences of opinion among scholars. In contradiction to Robespierre, Buzot, Mme. Roland's lover, wrote from his death cell that if the *philosophes*, including Rousseau, had been alive, "they would have experienced the same fate. Like us, if they had not emigrated...Montesquieu, Rousseau, Mably would have been condemned to death; they would all have perished on the scaffold."

The Girondists, the party of the rationalistic intellectuals, revealed their temperament in their aversion to bloodshed and mob violence, forces their enemies used to destroy them. The concrete issue on which the factions broke apart—and which in the end broke the Girondins—found the latter unwilling to condemn King Louis XVI to the guillotine (1792–93) because they shrank from the implications and consequences of so drastic a deed. Yet it was under Girondist leadership in 1792 that France embarked upon war with Prussia and Austria that led to more than two decades of almost incessant European conflict, causing the French Revolution to become something like a world one. The Girondist segment included some of the most militant enemies of "priestcraft" and "superstition" in the best, or worst, spirit of the Encyclopedists, deists, anti-clerics. They supported, indeed created, the controversial Civil Constitution of the Clergy, a kind of nationalization of the Church, which some of them saw as a reformed Christianity, and others as a non-Christian cult.

The left-wing Jacobins developed a conception of democracy based on their reading of Rousseau's "general will." Their goal was equality, and the idea of the general will together with the mass or mob action on which their power often depended caused them to glorify the people *en masse*. This strain of thought had little regard for individual rights or parliamentary institutions, which seemed to it selfish and corrupt. The Jacobin constitution of 1793 provided for no separation of powers, no guarantees of individual liberties. It sanctioned a plebescitary dictatorship based on the popular will, but with power delegated to a small number of people. "I speak for the people," Robespierre claimed. At times democratic in a deep sense, with a feeling for the common people, a passion for equality, and a desire to bring the people directly into government (Robespierre wished to build a stadium holding twelve thousand people to allow the crowd to watch the legislators), this "totalitarian democracy" disregarded legal process and individual rights; its consequence was the Reign of Terror, under conditions of extreme war emergency in France in 1792–93.

Maximilien Robespierre was the great ideologist of the revolution and leading political personality during the hectic days of the Republic of Virtue. As a child of the Enlightenment he disbelieved in Christianity but demanded the worship of a Supreme Being, a goddess of Reason; atheism, he declared, is aristocratic. His god was a kind of abstract embodiment of the people. Effective mass orator, he was coldly unhappy in most of his relationships with real people. Doctrinaire, sincere, rhetorical, a man of words and not of action (Robespierre almost never did anything; he made speeches), the self-righteous Robespierre was above all an actor, a totally political man with no private self, inventing himself as the incarnation of the spirit of history. With a sensitivity that caused him to tremble at the sight of blood, he could order the death of thousands in the name of humanity. All that Edmund Burke meant when he accused the revolution of abstract theorizing and a want of practical judgment seemed embodied in Robespierre, the man of austere principle who became a bloody dictator, before he himself perished by the revolutionary machinery he had used to destory his enemies.

Robespierre was not the most radical product of the French Revolution. Jacobinism was not socialistic, though it accepted the supremacy of community over individual in the spirit of Rousseau's social contract. Robespierre and his friends assumed a right to regulate property in any way necessary to the public welfare, but the social order they believed to be best was one in which every citizen held a little property, as Rousseau had proposed. This might well be designated as a petty-bourgeois or artisan-worker utopia. Socialism did appear in the revolution, but it did not get very far. In the desperate days of 1795, when the revolution seemed to be falling apart, a small band of socialists attempted an insurrection. This Conspiracy of the Equals, led by Babeuf and Buonarrotti, failed badly, but it left behind a strong tradition. Somewhat inarticulately these pioneer socialists, who took their inspiration also from aspects of Rousseau's writings, hated property, commerce, and luxury, and extolled the virtues of poverty, honest labor, the simple life. Buonoarrotti survived to become a link with the socialism of the 1840s. This *sans culotte* socialism spread over Europe, making an appeal to the doctrinaire representatives of the poorer classes. It was close to elemental Christianity. Russo, the Italian Bebeuvist, echoed Savonarola's medieval call to the rich to throw away their jewels.

Its extremes tended to discredit the revolution. The initial joy with which it was greeted all over Europe turned to disillusion as civil war, persecution, terror, and international war swept the Contintent in the 1790s. At first most of the intellectuals of Europe were enchanted by it, including many who later became its bitter foes. "Bliss was it in that dawn to be alive," as the young Wordsworth sang. Not only he but Maistre, Chateaubriand, Kant, Fichte, Novalis, Goethe, and many others felt the initial thrill. Rousseau had passionate admirers in England, like the father of Thomas Malthus, who asked only to be known as "the friend of Rousseau." Gilbert Wakefield, a Rousseau disciple, was imprisoned in 1799 for allegedly expressing a wish that the French would invade and conquer Britain. Everyone was reading Edward Gibbon's *Decline and Fall of the Roman Empire*, which he had finished in 1787 after more than twenty years of labor; it radiated a republican spirit, or so it seemed in the atmosphere of 1789. The ancient Roman state had begun its collapse with the first emperor, and Christianity had finished it off, the great historian seemed to be saying.

But the French Revolution lost its way and turned to violence, rapine, and injustice. It ended with the awesome spectacle of the revolution devouring its own children. The result was a reexamination of the premises of the Age of Reason and a rejection of them that aided the turn toward romanticism. After 1794 a former *philosophe*, Saint-Martin, became the leader of a new mystical religion associated with occult branches of Freemasonry. Rousseau's influence here extended in the direction of intuition and imagination.

THE ATTACK ON THE REVOLUTION

Ideological responses to the French Revolution were not slow in appearing. Among these the leading one came from England, in the form of Burke's 1790 *Reflections on the Revolution*. Burke claimed that the revolution went wrong because its leaders tried to scrap an entire political system and overnight install a new one; he related this mistake to the outlook of the *philosophes*, the political rationalists whose methods were those of abstract theory in an area where abstractness is fatal. There was some truth in the charge. "Abbé Sieyes has whole nests of pigeon-holes full of constitutions ready made," Burke wrote scornfully, "ticketed, sorted, and numbered"; but constitutions are not to be selected from the wares of political theorists, they have to grow like a great tree from the soil of a country over many centuries.

Burke's style lent to his book a dazzling sense of the subtle texture of actual politics. As a piece of literature, the *Reflections* was one of the major prose works of the new Romantic style. The leading idea emerging from this eloquence was that society is a vast and complicated historical product that may not be tinkered with at will like a machine; it is a repository of human wisdom to be regarded with reverence, and if reformed at all it must be with due respect for the continuity of its institutions. There were other related ideas: that a political community is shaped by history to make an unanalyzable bond between people which makes free government possible; that the social organism has its hierarchy, so that in a healthy society the common people respect the "natural aristocracy"; that general rules and abstract principles are of no help in politics. He distrusted the restless innovators who had not the patience to draw out the wisdom of their ancestors but must draw blueprints for the total reconstruction of society as if they were the first to think.

Disdaining the "abstract rights" proclaimed by the French, Burke tried to make clear the real rights of man; he certainly believed in such rights, though he stressed the degree to which those entering civil society must give up some of their liberties to gain the advantages of government. Such rights were based on Christian foundations in Western political society and rooted in history. A social animal, the human being would be no more than a beast if cut off from the sustaining fabric of ancient custom and tradition. And the human being is a religious animal who, without Christianity, would turn perforce to some other and probably less satisfactory faith. Reverence toward God and the social order are therefore the two great duties, and they are linked, for history is the revelation of God's purpose. Burke was accused of valuing the old Church just because it was old, but his piety was certainly genuine.

The Irish orator deeply influenced all subsequent conservative thought. Edition followed edition of the *Reflections*, all over Europe. Louis XVI personally translated it into French. It owed this popularity not only to the richness of the style, but to what seemed an uncanny prophetic quality, for Burke announced the inevitable failure of the French Revolution soon after it began. Burke's treatise, many have thought, rose above conservative factionalism to make a real contribution to political thought, and even to the science of social reform. He was certainly not opposed to change, if properly managed, and his own career, that of a person of humble birth, consisted of one passionate crusade after another—on behalf of American independence, Ireland, and India,[2] as well as against the French Revolution. Temperamentally this Irishman was as little a conservative as it is possible to conceive; "the most urgent need of his nature was always some great cause to serve, some monstrous injustice to repair," one of his biographers observes. A great deal of Burke has been regarded as essential wisdom for anyone who wants to participate effectively in politics as it is. One twentieth-century socialist, Harold Laski, declared that "the staesman ignorant of Burke is lost upon a stormy sea without a compass." Still, there were positions in Burke that came to be associated with modern conservative ideology: the feeling of piety for the social order, the mistrust of hare-brained reformers with a one-shot plan, the organic conception of social growth.

Burke's style deeply influenced his generation and contributed not only to the antirevolutionary cause but to romanticism. In his youth, in the 1750s, a struggling young lawyer turned literary man, Burke had written a treatise called *The Sublime and the Beautiful* which has often been seen as landmark in the evolution of taste from neoclassical to romantic. He argued that while the realm of the "beautiful" is indeed subject to the classical rules of harmony, proportion, and elegance, there is another realm of sensibility, "the sublime," which inspires fear and awe, which does not civilize and socialize us as does the classical, but makes us feel alone while exalting and exhilarating us. Burke was always a little romantic, his career very much so, and his last great work was, perhaps paradoxically, as romantic in style as it was conservative in content. So in a way the great advocate of the counterrevolution was a revolutionary too.

Burke's *Reflections* did not lack answers. In 1794 Tom Paine's reply to it, *The Rights of Man*, sold like hot cakes in London. William Godwin's *Enquiry Concerning Social Justice* was very much in the French spirit, a rationalist utopia based on the ideal perfection of individuals. Godwin, father-in-law of the poet Shelley and husband of the women's rights advocate Mary Wollstonecraft—a group around which much of the political left in England revolved—was a philosophical anarchist, hostile to the state and indeed to all forms of institutional orga-

---

[2]In the celebrated Warren Hastings trial, which stretched over the years between 1785 and 1795, ending in acquittal, Burke spoke long and bitterly against the first governor-general of British India, accused of arbitrary and illegal actions against Indian natives.

nization (he attacked public education, for example.) "Government, like dress, is a badge of lost innocence," Paine had written; "the common consent of society, without government" ought to be able to perform all the necessary social functions government power has usurped. This was one possible derivation from Rousseau. That society will run itself if free from governmental interference was an idea associated with political economists of the Adam Smith school. It sounded more radical in Godwin's mouth: "Did we leave individuals to the progress of their own minds," he declared, "without endeavoring to regulate them by any species of public foundation, mankind would in no very long period convert to the obedience of truth."

Godwin's admiration for Rousseau became highly unpopular as Britain moved toward mortal conflict with revolutionary France. A mob destroyed Joseph Priestley's laboratory, for the famous chemist was politically pro-French. In Scotland a storm of criticism forced Dugald Stewart to retract a favorable opinion he had written about Condorcet, the relatively moderate French political leader. Coleridge, who along with his friend Wordsworth had at first sympathized with the revolution, "threw away his squeaking baby-trumpet of sedition" to combat the revolutionary heresy. Coleridge ranks with Burke, to whom he owed much, as a founding father of British conservatism. But the radical journalist William Cobbett also joined the anti-Jacobin cause. The Evangelical movement within the Church of England, led by William Wilberforce, arose to combat the deistic laxities of the eighteenth century Church and thus reproach the infidel French.

THE BONAPARTE ERA

Insofar as he was trying to defend tradition and "prescription" as the "guardians of authority," Burke was swimming against the tide. Despite its excesses, the French Revolution happened and, as the great British historian Lord Acton later remarked, "it taught the people to regard their wishes and wants as the supreme criterion of right"; it accustomed men and women[3] to change and swept away the old order beyond hope of recovery. Even Burke, realist that he was, did not imagine that it would be possible to restore the *status quo ante* in Europe. Soon French troops spread the revolution all over Europe. The dictatorship of Napoleon Bonaparte (1800–1814) turned much of thinking Europe against the revolution, but Napoleon's victories continued to overturn the old arrangements, and he found distinguished intellectual supporters for his campaign to unite Europe under a new order of legal equality and an end to "feudalism."

Benjamin Constant, Mme. de Staël, and René Chateubraind headed a bril-

---

[3]The revolution in its Jacobin climax was quite antifeminist; it sent Mme. Roland and Olympes Gouges (who sought to establish the "Rights of Woman" alongside the "Rights of Man") to the scaffold and banned females from public meetings unless they brought their knitting and sat quietly. The deposed Girondists led by Condorcet had been somewhat feminist.

liant crowd of French refugees who fled from what they regarded as tyrannical rule. There were other Europeans like Goethe, the greatest figure of German literature, who never lost faith in Napoleon, seeing in him the man of destiny whose mission it was to unite Europe under a single progressive law. Others retreated to positions of neutrality. In France the so-called Ideologues, intellectual offspring of the former *philosophe* Destutt de Tracy (saved from the guillotine by a matter of minutes), reacted against political failure and disillusion by becoming severely objective, seeking to study the human mind as strict scientists: "bridging the gap between animate and inanimate nature" by developing Condorcet's "social mathematics." (Destutt's influence on Auguste Comte links him to the rise of modern sociology.)

A distinguished group of French scientists, including the biologists Lamarck and Cuvier, showed that the more detached sciences could flourish under Napoleon, who also shared the historical and orientalist interests of his time; on his military expedition to Egypt in 1798 he took along two hundred scholars to investigate that fascinating but still largely unknown land of antiquity. Laplace crowned the "classical mechanics," perfecting Newton's physical laws, and was the author of a famous *Système du monde*, which undertook to explain the operations and evolution of the universe without recourse to Newton's *deus ex machina*. ("Sire, I have no need of that hypothesis," he responded when Napoleon asked him about God.)

Personally, Napoleon was the most emancipated of thinkers, delighting in shocking people in private conversation with his atheism and cynicism. But believing that "only religion gives the state firm and lasting support," he would not tolerate any public irreligion and healed the revolution's quarrel with the papacy. Privately Napoleon might call adultery "a mere peccadillo, an incident at a masked ball," but the Code Napoleon, the great legal code drawn up under his supervision to install the new equalitarianism, was severe on adultery, since "the stability of marriages serves the interest of social morality." He was antifeminist, speaking of women as "mere machines to make children," and affected to despise intellectuals and artists, as well as "what is called [literary] style." The most enjoyable literary works in his library, he claimed, were the statistics of his army! Yet he was an omnivorous reader, missing little that went on in the world of art, science, and philosophy, as well as politics, and often commenting on it shrewdly. He did not admire the new literary fashion of romanticism that was adopted by his foes, Staël and Chateaubriand. Speculative thought and letters did not on the whole flourish in France in the years of Napoleon, though he was no Stalin or Hitler.

Bonaparte did not see himself as a tyrant and affected to be shocked that he was widely so regarded. On his deathbed in exile on the remote island of St. Helena, he declared that his mission had been to extinguish feudalism, reunite the continent, and "secure the dignity of man" by just and impartial laws. He had organized the revolution and made it practical, pacified turbulent France, and opened up opportunities for the common man by his "career open to talents" principle. He had exported liberty and equality under the law to Germany and Italy. The restorer of

Polish independence, he always had friends there and in other parts of Europe; the war he waged almost constantly during the fifteen years of his rule resembled a European civil war, though many outside France came to see it as French imperialism. Some who had cheered him early, like the poet Shelley, finally rejected him as a betrayer of the cause of liberty. The story that Beethoven first dedicated his great Eroica symphony to Napoleon but then tore it up when the First Consul had himself crowned emperor has been questioned, though it may have been true. Among other major thinkers, the German philosopher Hegel was always a staunch Bonapartist. The jury is still out on the great man; it always will be, according to the classic historical work by the Dutch historian Pieter Geyl, *Napoleon: For and Against*. It is certain that the little Corsican who rose from obscurity to become for a moment almost master of the world left it forever changed; he expressed and embodied forces far larger than his own outsize personality.

There was much millennial excitement in Europe in these epochal years, which saw the extinction of ancient landmarks such as the Holy Roman Empire, the deposing of kings and installing of new rulers. Bonaparte was as good a candidate for the role of Antichrist as had come along in many a moon. Estimates of the number who followed the prophet Joanna Southcott in London from 1803 to 1814 ranged as high as a hundred thousand. This unlettered Devonshire countrywoman who announced the second coming of Christ became a sensation; her message fitted the unsettled times, when fears of a French invasion combined with economic distress from rising prices and unemployment. Thomas Macaulay was amazed: "We have seen an old woman, with no talents beyond the cunning of a fortune teller, and with the education of a scullion, exalted into a prophetess and surrounded by tens of thousands of devoted followers; and all this in the nineteenth century, and all this in London." An outcropping of millenarian cults also appeared in the traditional Reformation country of southern Germany and Switzerland at this time.

Controversy about Napoleon remained to the end. William Hazlitt, the English essayist and literary critic, was described by a friend as "prostrated in mind and body" when he learned of Bonaparte's final defeat; "he walked about unwashed, unshaven, hardly sober by day, and always intoxicated at night" for weeks, until one day he awoke as if from a stupor and never touched alcohol again. His friend Haydon, author of this description, believed that Napoleon had criminally betrayed the true cause, and yet on the great man's death in 1821 he reflected in his diary that "posterity can never estimate the sensations of those living at the time" about Bonaparte—how his rise, his glory, and his fall affected people. These were exciting times. It is not surprising that romanticism arose in the twenty-five years between the first dawn of revolution in 1789 and the final defeat of Napoleon in 1815.

The most obvious political impulse that emerged from the reaction to Napoleon was nationalism. It is often dated in Germany from humiliation at the Prussian defeat in 1807 at the battle of Jena. Fichte and Herder, giants of German thought, preached it, along with humbler writers and organizers of youth. The Enlightenment had been cosmopolitan. Fichte became convinced that this was another of that now discredited era's mistakes. The French had led the Enlightenment; now Germany, in the time of Goethe, Beethoven, Schiller, Kant, was assuming the cultural and intellectual leadership of Europe. Germany must wake up politically as she had done culturally and intellectually, Fichte declared in his popular *Addresses to the German Nation* (1807). Equal rights for all, the revolution's goal, is a worthy one; but rights need to be rooted in a specific human family not a vague universality of mankind. The revolution itself contained a strong nationalist component. It was a *French* revolution, in the sense of happening to the whole land, drawing together the various provinces of that once highly feudalized country. (If Paris was the revolution's headquarters, many provincial cities copied the scenario, and the war against the revolution's enemies drew the country together.) It was accompanied by a drive to centralize the government and unify the culture, forming a single French language out of the many local dialects, for instance.

The revolution implied nationalism in its very nature. Once the old order of social hierarchy was dissolved, the nation became the natural focus of the new social equality. As what were people equal? As *enfants de la patrie*, children of the fatherland. Redeemed from domination by the privileged orders, the state became the possession of everyone and stood as the guarantor and the symbol of equal rights. "*Freies Reich! Alles gleich!*" sang the German nationalists. The *Volksstaat*, or people's state, knew no privileged orders, only equal citizens in the one nation.

As a prominent nineteenth-century ideology, nationalism will be discussed again in the next chapter. Meanwhile Napoleon's armies had thoroughly uprooted the old monarchies and they could hardly be restored as they were. The statesmen who gathered at Vienna in 1815 to put Europe back together after Bonaparte's final defeat tried to establish monarchical "legitimacy" as the guiding principle of political authority, but it did not work. Before long the Italians, to take the leading example, were up in arms at the attempt to return much of the peninsula to Austrian control. The Carbonari followed by Young Italy were the most "romantic" movements of revolutionary nationalism from 1820 on.

As a movement of the mind, nationalism was closely bound up with romanticism, the dominant spirit of the post-Enlightenment age. We may approach romanticism by way of the great philosopher who influenced it.

IMMANUEL KANT AND THE REVOLUTION IN PHILOSOPHY

"As clear a case of a violent break in the history of thought as history records" (J. H. Randall), romanticism was certainly a part, if not the whole, of the revolution of 1780–1815. There would seem to have been at least three revolutions in this approximate time frame, coinciding and overlapping, mutually influencing one another, yet essentially separate, and sometimes even at odds: the French, the Kantian, the Romantic. To these, general history must add the so-called Industrial Revolution.

There are connections among all of them. Writing in 1816, Francis Jeffrey, who didn't like either, attributed "the revolution in our literature" to "the agitations of the French Revolution." Some scholarly studies of romanticism have supported this verdict. The excitement engendered by the tumultous history of this generation ruled out any tame response; Napoleon's career was melodramatic beyond anything the wildest imagination could conceive. On the other hand Napoleon, a child of the eighteenth-century Enlightenment, hated romanticism; the revolution itself had been bathed in classicism—which is usually considered to be the style romanticism negated and supplanted. And one kind of romanticism grew to be associated very closely with a conservative reaction against the revolution; we have seen the germs of this in Edmund Burke. (It quickly becomes clear that we must discriminate between types of romanticism.)

Romanticism obviously came from sources other than the French Revolution. It arrived most clearly, perhaps, around 1781 in the writings of Schiller and the young Goethe, in a context that was not at all politically revolutionary. The young Goethe was mostly interested in mystical religion. Goethe described how he and his friends began to weary of the dry rationalism of Voltaire's age; they found it simply boring. The future master of German literature wrote his early *Sorrows of Werther* as an exercise in sentimentality that rivaled Rousseau's in reducing all Europe to tears. Schiller's *William Tell* was indeed to inspire many a revolutionary, but it was not written until 1804.

These uncertain connections between revolution and romanticism may be duplicated in the relation of both to the revolution in philosophy associated with Immanuel Kant. Karl Marx once declared that Kant was the intellectual counterpart of the French Revolution, a point repeated by his friend the poet Heinrich Heine, who remarked that with the publication of Kant's *Critique of Pure Reason* (1781), "an intellectual revolution began in Germany that offers the strangest analogies with the material revolution in France." But Kant knew nothing of French politics; he was working on problems bequeathed to philosophy by the British empiricists, John Locke, Bishop Berkeley, and especially David Hume, as well as his own countryman Leibniz. The quiet philosopher of Königsberg wrote his chief books just before the French Revolution, and his basic position does not seem to have been affected by that event, though it stirred him deeply (he expressed a desire to be warmed by it but not burnt up). The French revolutionaries certainly had not read these difficult works by an east German professor. But a common denominator was Rousseau, who influenced both Kant and the revolution. There is a story that the only time Kant missed his famous morning walk, by which the natives could set their watches, was to read the last episode of *Nouvelle Héloise*! The Rousseau influence appeared in Kant as a limitation on scientific reason, which in its own domain can attain exact knowledge, but which needs to be supplemented by a realm of essences and purposes approachable only through other ways of knowledge.

The same ambivalent association exists between Kant and romanticism. Fichte and Schelling, the disciples of Kant, pushed his thought in that direction, but Kant did not much approve of their interpretation of his ideas. Clearly he had so searchingly criticized the Enlightenment's assumptions that nothing could be the same thereafter in the house of reason, and he left the door open for other and much different avenues to truth. But Kant's was not a very romantic temperament. Born in 1724, he was for a long time a rather typical *philosophe*, brought up in the philosophical school of Leibniz as systematized (and simplified) by Christian Wolff, and showing strong scientific interests. It was only in middle age that David Hume and Jean-Jacques Rousseau combined to shock him out of his "dogmatical slumber." His main goal, however, was to defend scientific reason from the skeptical attacks of Hume.

That eighteenth-century Scottish philosopher and historian had taken his departure from Locke's empiricism, which held that sense experience is the only real source of knowledge; the role of mind is a passive one, simply to absorb these external stimuli. Hume demonstrated—and Kant accepted his demonstration as "irrefutable"—that through the senses alone the human mind cannot encounter reality at all, nor can it have a science founded on anything but "opinion." We experience only an unrelated sequence of sense impressions. The principle of cause and effect cannot be derived from experience alone; we simply assume it arbitrarily. How can I say that A "causes" B, when I only experience A and B, not "cause"? I do not see the cause, for example, when A strikes B causing it to move; I see the events and the sequence. In Kant's mind this raised the question of the possibility of a valid science, and he sought by overcoming this Humean skepticism to ground scientific knowledge on unshakable foundations. Stated more technically, the problem was the status of "synthetic *a priori* judgments," synthetic being the factual as opposed to the strictly logical or "analytic." Are the observed relationships in nature as certain as mathematical truths, or are they, as Hume suggested, accidental, contingent, uncertain?

Kant's reply was basically as follows: The mind or intellect, far from being passive, contains the organizing principles that impose order on experience. The mind contains forms and categories which are the concepts that give meaning to experience. These "fundamental conditions of thought itself" are *a priori*—that is, not derived from experience, but present independently or in advance of it. Kant specified these forms and categories: the forms of perception, space, and time; and twelve categories of the understanding, for example, cause and effect. These correspond to the types of judgment of Aristotelian logic—quantity, quality, relation, and modality with their subdivisions. All minds contain these categories, and thus mind is a fundamental unity—reason is "transcendent."

Our minds condition and, indeed, determine knowledge. Agreeing with Leibniz against Locke, Kant denied that there is nothing in the mind except what the senses bring in; there is the mind itself, an organizing agent that sorts out and classifies sense data, thus rendering them intelligible. We will not here, of course, attempt to follow all of Kant's arguments, which have attracted the attention of skilled philosophers from that day to this. From his powerful analysis, it is enough to say, emerged a picture of mind as creative, not passive, and of reason as a priori, thus rescued from the skepticism of an empirical approach. Goethe interpreted

Kant to mean that "had I not borne the world within myself to begin with, I would have remained blind even with eyes that see." In other words, sense impressions would be senseless—"a great blooming buzzing confusion," as William James once said—if we did not have a preformed structure within the mind capable of giving them meaning. These "solid" sense data of science would be a hopeless jumble without the inner structure of mind.

A debate arose about whether Kant was an "idealist," by asserting that reality is a creation of the mind. Some of his followers went that far, but Kant does not seem to deny that things have an independent existence, and in striking our senses provide the indispensable primary data of knowledge. (His "critical philosophy" was not concerned to make metaphysical statements, but to analyze the way we know.) The point is that we could not make sense of the external world unless we had a rational structure in our minds. Experience would be senseless without mind. But the external world exists, and is equally necessary to the rational process; mind without data to classify would be futile. As someone put it, percepts without concepts are blind, but concepts without percepts are empty. The computer must have data to work on.

It must be added immediately that the sort of knowledge we have been talking about, scientific knowledge, exact knowledge of the external world, was not to Kant the only kind of knowledge. It is not in fact knowledge of ultimate reality. The domain of science is perfectly valid; he wished to rescue it from what he thought was a doubtful foundation, and to represent him as a foe of science is gross error. He himself made some contributions to the sciences, in which he was always interested. But scientific knowledge is a particular kind of knowledge, appropriate to the practical or useful side of life. It is knowledge of appearances, not of substance; in the famous Kantian terminology, it is *phenomenal* as opposed to *noumenal*. It relates to the properties of things, not to the "thing in itself." As we observed, Rousseau's influence helped form his other great objective, to rescue the realm of value from the scientists. Thus he set up two (or perhaps three) sharply different realms of knowledge. Science, which is useful knowledge, deals with the world of appearances, the phenomenal world. Religion is intuitive and deals with the realm of substantive reality. Kant thinks these two realms must not be confused; they are different categories. One of his achievements was to criticize the proofs of God's existence derived from the facts of physical nature—traditional arguments, very popular in the eighteenth cntury still, especially the "argument from design" (which got him into some trouble with the Prussian authorities). Kant so devastated these venerable "proofs" that few have ever dared revive them. The proofs appropriate to science have nothing to do with God, Kant believed. God's existence cannot be "proved," but in moral experience we find strong hints of it.

The noumenal realm nevertheless exists, but Kant was not sure whether we can know it at all. The nature of the transcendental reason that is in our minds, and that enables us to make sense of the world, Kant regarded as a mystery, itself noumenal. Reason can analyze itself, he said, but it cannot explain itself—explain why it is. Questions of this sort exceed the limits of reason. I can know that I have it, and see what it can do, but what it essentially is I cannot know. That would be like jumping out of our skin. Questions about ultimate purposes or origins reveal their inaccessibility to reason by the "antinomies" or contradictions we encounter when we attempt to reason about them: apparently opposing propositions that seem equally true or equally false, like whether the world had a beginning in time or not, whether there can be an uncaused cause, whether God exists.

In moments of moral or esthetic experience, Kant suggests, we can glimpse the noumena, but only fleetingly. The human soul, a thing-in-itself, may make contact with other things-in-themselves by means other than analytical reason. Kant seems ambiguously poised between the Enlightenment and romanticism here. On the one hand he said that "he had to deny knowledge to make room for faith." His most widely quoted sentence is the one in which he declared the equal wonder of the two realms, the starry heavens and the moral law. On the other hand Kant was no mystic by temperament, and was not at all sure about our being able to make contact with the noumena. Evidently we are condemned to live divided lives, each of them flawed. Phenomenal, scientific knowledge is exact but superficial. Noumenal, spiritual knowledge is profound but we can never reach it. This conclusion was not satisfactory to the scientists or to the romanticists.

Kant's writings on ethics were among his most celebrated. Consistent with his general point of view, he argued that valid rules of conduct cannot be found in experience but must be sought in pure reason. The "categorical imperative," the basic moral principle, cannot be found in circumstances, but is in the moral agent, the person. That which is good in itself is the good Will; and a will is good when it is rational. The moral worth of an action is determined by the motive, not (as the Utilitarians argued) the result; it is Duty, the rational resistance to evil impulses, that is the highest moral faculty. In the end Kant reached his famous statement of the moral imperative: Act so that your action is one you would want to be a universal law; or, in his other version of it, Always treat people as ends, not means. (If you act in a way you would *not* want everyone else to act, you are selfishly using them as means for your ends.)

Kant's influence on esthetic theory was equally great. In giving autonomy to the realm of art, it coincided with a Romantic thrust. According to the Königsberg sage, beauty is not in the object, as classicism claimed, it is in the eye of the beholder. The standards that determine what we regard as beautiful are in our minds, a given or *a priori* part of our intellectual equipment. Kant did not regard these standards as arbitrary, or determined by some particular cultural circumstances, as we might do today; he thought they were rooted in transcendental reason as much as scientific knowledge and moral values are. They must be the same for everybody everywhere at all times—though this judgment lies in the realm of the noumena and thus cannot be known for certain. In any case the esthetic realm is autonomous; it joins the moral and the scientific as one of the diverse ways of looking at things, each yielding its separate kind of truth.

Some saw Kant as the destroyer, blasting holes in traditional certainties, undermining objective truth by making everything depend on the subject; or, in a "decadent" way, being more interested in form than content, in consciousness than in its objects. (See Leon Daudet's diatribes against Kant as the "evil genius" responsible for the whole "stupid nineteenth century.") But in Kant's own view he had tried to save reason from an arbitrary subjectivism. There is truth in each of these verdicts. Kant is a figure of transition between two world views, as one gave way to another in this great intellectual revolution of modernity. As every great thinker does, he left puzzles for his successors to work on.

Most were dissatisfied with his unresolved dualism, leaving the world as it were split in two. His "critical philosophy" (which, we should again stress, was just that, a critical analysis, not the creation of a "system") might be made the foundation for several different systems. Some Kantians forgot about the thing-in-itself and became either idealists, arguing that the world is completely a mental construct, or positivists (phenomenalists), urging that we cannot know what ultimate reality is and should therefore remain content with the orderly arrangement of our observations. Others developed Kant's noumenalism in a romantic or mystical direction, stressing the role of religious or poetic intuition in reaching the deepest reality by nonrational methods. If Kant himself was hardly a romantic, the movement of romanticism was beginning as he wrote and tended to blend with versions of his thought. Fichte and Schelling, his immediate successors in German philosophy, sought for a unifying principle that would bring together the separated worlds of thought, the pure and the practical reason (see further below).

Most people, of course, could not follow the great philosopher in all the subtleties of his thought. Many have always regarded him as fiendishly difficult, if not incomprehensible. And yet Kant, who honestly wanted to write so that ordinary people could understand him (it was part of his Rousseauism), left a deep if fuzzy impression on countless people who were not technical philosophers.[4] He became the archetypical example of Man Thinking. There was something wondrous about this humble, modest man of quiet habits, living in an obscure university town from which he never ventured, yet changing the course of human thought and hence human history. Near the end of the century South African General Jan Smuts, having made his fortune and reputation by the age of thirty, decided to retire. "I prefer to sit still, to water my orange trees, and to study Kant's 'Critical Philosophy,' "he said. It was any thinking man's dream.

Kant was not wrong in saying of *The Critique of Pure Reason* that "my book can produce nothing less than a total change of outlook in this area of human knowledge." His "Copernican revolution" consisted basically in shifting the main arena from outside the mind to inside. The human mind is creative, not passive; it is not the wax of Condillac, but an active agent imposing rules on nature. The creative mind is as much a necessity in science as in literature. It

---

[4]Wilhelm Busch, the popular children's poet whose *Max and Moritz* (1865) is the German equivalent of *Alice in Wonderland*, wrote in his autobiography that he was fascinated by Kant though he could not understand him. Kant's writings, he said, left him with a delighted interest in the secret places of the mind "where there are so many hiding places."

must, for example, frame hypotheses, ask questions of nature; pure empiricism is poor scientific method. And as a noumenal thing the human person is a creature of great dignity; Kant's political thought, though not perhaps his strongest suit, contributed much to nineteenth-century liberalism (and socialism) by its stress on the dignity of the autonomous moral agent, who must be free and must be treated as an end, not a means.

POST-KANTIAN PHILOSOPHERS

The golden age of German philosophy began with Kant and ended a half-century later with Hegel. In between lay several other notable thinkers, most significantly Johann Gottlieb Fichte and Friedrich Wilhelm Joseph von Schelling. Fichte, who became tremendously excited on reading Kant and appointed himself chief expounder of the Kantian philosophy, had more popular flair than the Königsberger. Dismissed from the University of Jena in 1799 for his excursions into religion, he wrote the widely read *Addresses to the German Nation* we have mentioned as a landmark in the idea of nationalism. Fichte was not exactly a romantic; philosophy, he thought, should be an exact science. But he preached a philosophy of idealism, turning Kant's ambivalent position in that direction. The universe consists of an absolute Ego of which our own consciousness is a part—a unique, free activity that strives to realize itself in perfect self-awareness and is the foundation of all nature.

Though couched in the usual opaque terminology of German metaphysics, this vision of reality compelled attention by its dramatic picture of human will or consciousness as the hub of the universe, an expression of the absolute spirit of which the cosmos consists. We begin with our consciousness, an intuitively certain thing that escapes thought because it cannot be objectified (try thinking about your consciousness as an object of your thought). Reason itself has to be an invention of this human subjectivity, which Fichte saw as an active imagination. Curing Kant's dualism by subsuming everything under Spirit, Fichte much more than his master saw the world as nothing but man's soul or imagination writ large. He also formulated the famous dialectical principle, the means by which spirit develops, of thesis/antithesis/synthesis, for which Hegel has sometimes wrongly been given credit. The pure subjective self begins by establishing a Not-self and thus begins the dialectical process. There is much in Fichte of what has passed for novelty among ego psychologists in recent times. He was a fiery and persuasive if somewhat loose thinker—Hegel was to subject him to ridicule—who probably did more than anyone else to popularize the romantic vision of the free creative imagination.

Schelling, a disciple of Fichte and friend and collaborator of Hegel, whom he influenced, produced a stream of writings between 1797 and 1802 setting forth what he called Transcendental Idealism. He put greater stress than Fichte on physical nature as the objective form of the Absolute and pointed out the road Hegel was to follow in many respects. Perhaps the most striking feature of his thought, especially with regard to romanticism, was his representation of artistic creation as the supreme human achievement. In it the two forms of the Absolute, the conscious and unconscious forces, are fused in synthesis; it is in art that the infinite manifests itself in finite form. When the artist shapes something from nature, as when Michelangelo carves a statue, the subjective spirit (Michelangelo) and objective nature (the marble) meet to become one. The Romantic poets for understandable reasons absorbed Schelling eagerly; he provided a metaphysical basis for art such as had never been heard before. Romanticism's glorification of the poet as seer, in Shelley's phrase "the unacknowledged legislator of the human race," relates closely to Schelling's thought. Coleridge and later Thomas Carlyle imported this German metaphysics into British poetry. Much later in his career, Schelling opposed Hegel's excessive rationalism by offering a kind of foreshadowing of Existentialism; he influenced Kierkegaard, who came to his lectures at Berlin in the 1840s. He came to reject all abstract, conceptual thought as "negative philosophy," inferior to concrete, existent realities. He showed a keen interest in religious mythologies, like Carl Jung and others in our time.

This extraordinary spate of German philosophizing continued with the great G. W. F. Hegel, consideration of whom we postpone until the next chapter. The whole of it cut a wide swath through intellectual Europe in the nineteenth century, especially the first half. Professional philosophy fell almost exclusively under its domination, about the only choice being between Kant and Hegel until near the end of the century. But German philosophy had a much broader appeal; it had not been aimed at gaining tenure in a department of philosophy. Professionalization of such subjects indeed barely began until after mid-century. German philosophy offered a kind of philosophical alternative to religion, substituting its Absolute for the Christian God. This religion was more humanistic than Christianity. Humanity's place in it was almost the equivalent of God. The Absolute seemed almost to be the human ego writ large. The human consciousness reflects and participates in the divine. Human art and moral experience are in effect cosmic forces working in and through him/her. German idealism united with romanticism to produce that strain of "titanism" so prominent in the nineteenth century and, according to some, so dangerous. "Glory to Man in the highest," the poet Swinburne exclaimed.

THE ORIGINS OF ROMANTICISM

Romanticism is often said to have begun with Rousseau. Certain romantic affinities have been found in other eighteenth-century writers who departed in various ways from the classical qualities of reason, moderation, and order. They played with the grotesque, the primitive, and the mysterious, invoking the Sublime against the Beautiful. Rich folk built themselves artificially wild ruins; the Noble Savage, whether from North America or the South Seas, found himself lionized in European drawing rooms. The "Gothic novel," with its eerie abodes and sinister spooks, made its debut. There was a good deal of this "wildness" in the eighteenth century, as perhaps there always had been. (The Middle Ages loved to fantasize about monsters in the woods or across the unknown seas.) The gentler poets Thomas Gray and William Cowper have been classified as "pre-Romantics" because of their sensitive introspection, at a time when "the man of feeling" was in vogue. We have mentioned the young Goethe's sentimental *Sorrows of Werther*, rivaling Rousseau's novel in its ability to reduce people to tears. The *Sturm und Drang* plays of the early Schiller included that glorification of the outlaw life, *The Robbers*, written in 1781.

In France, Enlightenment rationalism persisted more strongly; as we know, Napoleon was its friend, encouraging the Ideologues until eventually he became as contemptuous of them as of other intellectuals. But French romanticism asserted itself strongly with the powerful figure of Chateaubriand, the leading literary personality of his day. With his *Atala* and *René*, novels set in the forests of the New World, and his deeply religious spirit, he introduced a new mode of literature. Chateaubriand's life itself was romantic in its sheer energy and scope, as he moved from literature to politics amid memorable love affairs. He was the father, as Rousseau was the grandfather, of all subsequent French Romantic literature.

Meanwhile in England the young poets Samuel Taylor Coleridge and William Wordsworth were experimenting with a poetry they rightly felt to be revolutionary. They, along with the poet-seer William Blake, began British romanticism just before the turn of the century, but it remained obscure for some time. Blake printed his own books, *Songs of Innocence* and *Songs of Experience* (1789, 1794) but they were unnoticed for a number of years. He was known as a designer and engraver, but hardly at all as a poet, until well into the nineteenth century. The Napoleonic wars interrupted literature; Coleridge and Wordsworth took up political pampleteering, while Chateaubriand went into exile. But in Germany romanticism flourished. A group that included Friedrich Schlegel and his brother August in Berlin, and Novalis and Schelling at Dresden and Jena, called themselves Romantics and emitted the philosophical ideas so important to the movement. The theology of Schleiermacher (1799) and the music of Beethoven (1800 on) marked this moment of romanticism's creative young adulthood. German romanticism, always basic to the movement, flourished not only in philosophy, but in a stream of literature that fascinated a generation. Jean Paul Richter, a German Rousseau, became a cult figure.

Romanticism's greatest triumphs lay ahead. Its maximum influence came from about 1810 to 1830. Wordsworth and Coleridge began to achieve fame and were joined by Shelley, Byron, and Keats to make up the most renowned group of English poets since Shakespeare's time. They were all labelled Romantic. Lord Byron became an incredible culture hero. It was in 1812 that he "awoke to find himself famous." Napoleon's invasion of Russia scarcely held a candle that year in London to the publication of the first two cantos of *Childe Harold's Pilgrimage*. After he left the England he had scandalized (adding incest to adultery) in 1816, Byron's fame spread to the Continent; a few years later Karl Marx was as familiar with him in Germany as Pushkin was in Russia. That after a life of immense dissipation in Italy he died fighting for Greek independence, everybody knew if they

The Romantic poet Lord Byron, in Albanian dress, 1813. (London, National Portrait Gallery. Portrait by T. Phillips)

knew no other facts of modern history. His death came in 1824 at the age of thirty-six. Tennyson said the whole world seemed darkened by Byron's death. But how romantic to die young, after exhausting oneself in a frenzy of living and loving! Better, as Pushkin said, to be an eagle for an hour than a crow for centuries.

The Swiss-born Germaine de Staël, a glamorous figure who wrote, made love, and fought Napoleon with equal verve, popularized the German Romantics in France with her *D'Allemagne* in 1813. France succumbed to romanticism after Napoleon's downfall, between 1820, when Schiller's *Maria Stuart* (composed in 1801) took Paris by storm, and 1830, when Victor Hugo's play *Hernani* caused the wildest turmoil in the history of French theater. Hugo and Lamartine, who along with the novelist Alexander Dumas were the avowed leaders of the Romantic movement, were the most popular as well as the most distinguished writers of their age. At the same time the painter Eugene Delacroix headed a school calling itself Romantic. Add Stendhal, Musset, Nerval, Sand, Vigny, Balzac, with Chopin and Liszt also in Paris, and "the dozen years from about 1823 to 1835 are a cultural apocalypse" in France (Geoffrey Hartman). The strength of French romanticism is sometimes underestimated. In that land of a strong classical tradition there was always opposition. Hugo was five times denied admission to the exclusive French Academy, the last time in 1836, and warfare between Classical and Romantic never ceased to enliven the theatrical season. In 1829 the Academy denounced romanticism as that which "puts in disorder all our rules, insults our masterpieces, and perverts mass opinion." Eighteenth-century classical and rococo taste remained popular even at the high tide of romanticism.

In England, embittered literary conservatives helped bring on Keats's early

death, his friends believed. The greatest of German literary figures, Goethe, who
contributed to romanticism early in his career, eventually declared that classicism
is healthy and romanticism diseased. ("What is the good of curbing sensuality,
shaping the intellect, securing the supremacy of reason? Imagination lies in wait as
the most powerful enemy.") Unconverted classicists always existed and, indeed,
there was something of a classical revival in the era of romanticism. If we grant
that the Romantics had borne off most of the prizes by 1830, they were soon to
come under withering attack from a new generation in the 1840s and 1850s, who
accused the writers of excessive sentimentalism and pomposity.

Yet between 1760 and 1840, to take the widest time span, Europe had been
hit by something new, exciting, and controversial. We have yet to define what this
was, though in naming its landmarks we have suggested some qualities. In fact, a
definition of romanticism proved elusive; someone declared that the inability to
define it was the scandal of the century. The word took on many meanings, some
of them apparently contradictory. The romanticism of Chateaubriand was Catholic
and Royalist, but the romanticism of Victor Hugo (though he began as a conservative) became republican, liberal, even revolutionary. It was romantic to fight, as
Byron did for Greece and Giuseppe Mazzini was soon to do for Italian nationalism,
but also to withdraw to a quiet life of communing with nature. It was romantic to
love passionately and transcend the conventional moral boundaries, but the eighteenth century had done that too, like all the other centuries. It was romantic to
read about the Middle Ages, now rescued from the Enlightenment's scorn, but also
to adore the days of classical antiquity—"fair Greece, sad relic."

From this confusion some thought to rescue the question by proposing that
there was not a single romanticism; the term "has become a label for half a dozen
things that have only an accidental connection" (Christopher Dawson). Love of
nature, intuition as the source of truth, expressing the emotions, the view of society
as an organism—these ideas or fashions bobbed up about the same time and got
squashed together under a single vague rubric, but have no necessary connection. *but an actual one?*
The founding father of intellectual history, Arthur Lovejoy, wrote one of his best
known essays in support of the view that we must speak of romanticisms, not
romanticism; the latter "has come to mean so many things that, by itself, it means
nothing." From this degree of nominalism one might go further, as many literary
scholars in our highly specialized present era do, and give up everything except the
individual author, or the individual text; no time to dither about "romanticism"
when there is more than enough to do explicating a single poem by Coleridge.

On the other hand, the mood of an age may be nonetheless real for being
illogical, and there was undoubtedly a common feeling among people all over
Europe in this generation that one needs a word for. It is possible that "the indefin-
able word is the essential one" (G. K. Chesterton). Irreducible entities, such as
love, good, blue, cannot be defined, only pointed to. If we seek too narrow a definition of romanticism we are in danger of losing sight of an important if imprecise
reality, the spirit or language of this age, which signified a deep change in human
consciousness. Comparable problems arise with any general term used to cover an

entire era, terms such as Renaissance, Enlightenment, Victorianism, Modernism. Yet we need such terms to give unity to cultural phenomena; even if it is in part a specious unity, as an ideal type it enables us to understand history.

VARIETIES OF ROMANTICISM

Romanticism may be understood in part as a simple reaction against the Enlightenment. The latter, a powerful, extended movement of the mind and spirit, finally wore out its welcome and induced a countermovement. Rationalist, classicist, and materialist, the Enlightenment had feared strong passion, subjectivity, and disorder. In its passion for clarity it tried to banish mystery. In the end it became unexciting, dull, and unadventurous. Its ethic of hedonism and self-interest seemed cravenly unheroic. (Voltaire said he didn't like heroes, they made too much noise.) So the Romantic era is filled with cries of rejection. "I, for my share, declare the world to be no machine!" exclaimed Carlyle; the eighteenth century had said it was. Against Enlightenment rationalism, Burke declared that reason is "but a part, and by no means the greatest part" of human nature; Coleridge added that the mere "calculating factor" is inferior to the "creative faculty." (Indebtedness to Kantian and post-Kantian philosophy was of course involved here.) The *philosophes* had assailed traditional Christianity in favor of a "deism" or rational religion, making God in effect the master mechanic; in reply, romanticists now delighted in the mysteries. Nothing, said Chateaubriand, is pleasing except the mysterious. (Romantic religion did not escape its own version of heresy, which was a tendency toward pantheism or the worship of a great world-soul in place of the Christian deity.) Religion, as anything more than polite behavior, had slumbered during the Age of Reason; it was now back in favor.

Stylistically, romanticism rebelled against the rules imposed on drama and poetry; it was "an insurrection against the old traditions of classicism." Hugo's violations of the rules that were supposed to govern tragedy was what caused the furor over *Hernani*. Each piece can make its own rules, the Romantics declared, rather then follow a formula supposed to govern all compositions (the unity of time, place, action, for example; the nobility of heroes; the kind of poetic meter appropriate to each genre.) Less formally, romanticism encouraged a more personal, intimate tone, something Rousseau had started; as if speaking in confidence from one person to another, rather than declaiming in a public place. Eighteenth-century poetry had grown tame and feeble. "Crush'd by rules, and weakened as refined," this polite literature seemed unable to communicate sincere feeling, as Dr. Johnson (hardly himself a Romantic)[5] had noted:

---

[5]From his famous *Dictionary*, definition of "Romantick":
   1. Resembling the tales of romance, wild....
   2. Improbable; false.
   3. Fanciful; full of wild scenery....

From bard to bard the frigid caution swept,
While declamation roar'd and passion slept.

Though not uncritical of the new poetry, Hazlitt conceded that

> Our poetical literature had, toward the close of the last century, degenerated into the most trite, insipid, and mechanical of all things....

So the Romantic poets were determined to bare their souls, the prose writers to cultivate eccentricity, perhaps too much so.

Along the same lines, folk themes attracted the Romantics, largely because the neo-classical canon had frowned on the serious treatment of vulgar subjects. The term romanticism itself derived from the medieval romances, so-called because they were written in the vernacular speech rather than in Latin. For centuries all serious composition was supposed to be in Latin; anything else was stigmatized as lowbrow. Now, folklorists like Herder went seeking "the simple roundelays of the peasant folk." Wordsworth thought he was writing poetry in the speech of plain countryfolk. As we noted, this was also an aspect of the French Revolution–democratic nationalism complex. In some important ways, romanticism was a democratic response to aristocracy. The Old Regime was permeated by that sense of hierarchy that the classical rules of composition reflected. Everything had to be in its exact place in a perfect scheme of things, the essence of which was unequal roles. "Take but degree away, untune that string," as a famous Shakesperian passage warned, and the whole structure would come unraveled. To put a comma in the wrong place could entail the ruin of the state. The fall of neo-classicism was connected to the fall of the whole (in theory) highly structured old social regime.

The eighteenth century, in striving for common sense and moderation, seemed to have lost touch with ideals, and the Romantics typically disparaged its ethic as a crass, materialistic one. "Soul extinct but stomach well alive," as Carlyle sneered, it had been an age of gluttony (Thackeray). Everyone now scorned "the man of Locke," a prudent citizen whose goal had been a rather ignoble "pursuit of happiness." The reaction in favor of heroism pushed the Romantics into some lofty poses, though Byron in *Don Juan* could simultaneously laugh at his hero's wild adventures.

The Middle Ages were back in style, because the rationalist, neo-classical age just ended had despised that era of priestcraft and Gothic architecture. Edward Gibbon said that the Piazzo San Marco in Venice contained "the worst architecture I ever saw"; John Ruskin, a few decades later, pronounced it the most beautiful of human creations (*The Stones of Venice*). The French Revolution started to pull down Gothic cathedrals, "piles of monkish superstition"; the Romantic period featured a Gothic revival in architecture. In the eighteenth century the poet Thomas Warton had called Dante's *Divine Comedy* "disgusting," and a follower of Voltaire pronounced it the worst poem in all the world. In England Dante's reputation was made by Blake, Byron, Shelley, and Coleridge, enthusiastically seconded in the next generation by the great Victorians.

In a similar way the taste for wild nature, for mountains and deep forests, was a Romantic reaction to the neo-classical distaste for such irregularities (the Alps were regarded as hideously unkempt). Rousseau's *Reveries of a Solitary Walker* passed down to Byron, to Chateaubriand, and to Lamartine's *Meditations*. Everyone knows how important nature was to Wordsworth and to Henry David Thoreau. This attachment to nature leads us to the more positive side of romanticism; it had a metaphysical foundation in the philosophical idealism born in Germany. Wordsworth expressed this pantheistic spirit in his poetry, when he felt

> ...a sense sublime
> Of something far more deeply interfused,
> Whose dwelling is the light of setting suns
> And the round ocean and the living air,
> And the blue sky, and in the mind of man;
> A motion and a spirit that impels
> All thinking things, all objects of all thought,
> And rolls through all things.

This vision of reality as basically spiritual, and basically one, filtered down from German philosophy. The poets Novalis and Richter and Hölderlin transformed the abstractions of philosophy into concrete poetic symbols in Germany. Coleridge brought them to Britain. Many people came to hold, more or less loosely, something like this idealist-Romantic position, meaning that we can see God or some higher reality in nature and commune with it, feeling its basic kinship to our own souls. Nontechnical, semi-popular Romantic idealism can be found in Thomas Carlyle's first book, *Sartor Resartus*, wherein this vivid writer gave expression to the idea that "the external world known to our sense and explored by our sciences is mere Appearance. Reality is its divine, unseen counterpart, standing to Appearance as Soul stands to Body."

Transcendentalism became a byword among the literati of both France and America from 1820 to 1840; the American sage Ralph Waldo Emerson was associated with it. This heady doctrine might persuade people that all the "appearances," for example, social conventions, are a fraud, and that each of us can be godlike if only we dare to search our own selves and act accordingly. It was close to mystical pantheism, a heresy long known to Christianity, wherein the god-intoxicated felt they might communicate directly with deity. Often it had roots in neo-Platonism; Blake's mysticism has been traced to this source, and Coleridge claimed he had found mysticism in the ancients before he read the Germans. There was also the important discovery of the Indian religio-philosophical tradition at this time. "The pantheism of the Orient, transformed by Germany," Edgar Quinet wrote in 1841, was responsible for what he called a *renaissance orientale*. (The discovery and translation of the Hindu classics owed most, in fact, to an Englishman, Sir William Jones, and a Frenchman, Anquetil-Duperron.)

It is above all the artist, the poet, who feels the Infinite Spirit when creating. Working intuitively, the artist "elicits truth as at a flash" (Coleridge), truths deeper than the experimental or analytic. Poetic images are symbols of nature, keys to reality. This visionary-religious element in romanticism is found in the works of William Blake, the English artist-seer-poet. Taking quite seriously the identification of his own thoughts with the soul of the universe,[6] Blake believed it was the mission of the poet and artist to be a religious prophet, to endow the old religious truths with fresh meaning. A "symbolist" before the school that was to bear this name later in the nineteenth century, a discoverer of "the archetypes of the unconscious" before Carl Jung, Blake gave new names to the gods and spoke of building a "new Jerusalem" in England. His haunting, childlike songs touch closely on perennial religious and moral experience.

Romantic religion appeared not only in Burke, but in the Swedish seer Emanuel Swedenborg, who had lived in the eighteenth century (d. 1772) and left behind disciples of the Church of New Jerusalem. There is still a Swedenborgian society in England; there was considerable interest in it in the United States also. The German Romantic theologian Friedrich Schleiermacher (*Discourses on Religion*, 1799) sought to transpose Christianity from dogma to interior experience, to transform literal faith into concrete human terms. Through the nineteenth century this idea merged with the "liberal" Christianity that dismissed biblical literalism, arguing that the essential truths of Christianity are deeper and broader. Romantic theology stressed inward emotional experience as the criterion of faith, and interacted with a revival of evangelical, pietistic Christianity. That the older sects remained important is suggested by the fact that Alexander I, the tsar of Russia, turned to religion under the influence of German Moravians and English Quakers.

John Wesley's Methodism and German Pietism had begun in the eighteenth century, but now became more influential. The Evangelical movement within the Church of England, a reaction against the laxities of the eighteenth-century church, began just before the turn of the century and greatly affected the whole Victorian era. The Oxford movement a little later (dominant at Oxford University in the 1830s until John Henry Newman's famous "apostasy" to Rome in 1845) was intellectually distinguished, esthetically fastidious, and totally reactionary. Its romanticism appeared in a love of ceremony, mystery, and historic tradition. The Tractarians' warfare against the by then dominant secular liberalism stemmed from their dislike of its shallow materialism. John Keble, E. B. Pusey, and others who rallied to Newman's standard wrote much poetry as well as the tracts that gave the movement its name. Some Oxonians followed Newman to Catholicism, but most

---

[6]Compare Gerard de Nerval, the French romantic poet: "The human imagination has invented nothing that is not true, either in this world or the next."

stayed to support the "high church" faction within the Church of England. Romantic religion thus came in various packages; the common denominator was a desire to make religion fervent and personally meaningful, something experienced as a living reality. On this subject the Catholic Newman was as "existentialist" as any Protestant evangelist or Swedenborgian pantheist.

ROMANTIC POLITICS

Romanticism was politically ambiguous. Coinciding with the French Revolution, it could not help but interact with that great event. At first most Romantics hailed the revolution with delight, joining figuratively with the young Wordsworth as he danced in the streets with the French people. Then they turned against it, listening to Burke's great indictment, which is charged with many feelings close to the heart of romanticism. The revolution had failed, perhaps, because it was too closely bound to the reactionary creed of eighteenth-century rationalism. Most Romantics distinguished between the French Revolution as a particular historic event and the broader movement of history it imperfectly embodied. They did not doubt that humanity was on the march, seldom wanted to go back to the prerevolutionary regime, but agreed that the revolution had degenerated into a cynical materialism because of its false groundings in Enlightenment materialism. Thomas Carlyle, who wrote a famous history of it, regarded it as having failed because it did not (at least until Bonaparte) produce any "great man." But the advocate of hero worship condemned the Ancient Regime also for having failed to provide inspiring leadership, a sure sign of decadence. Romantics might, like Wordsworth, retain a rather naive Godwinian faith in human perfectability, but believe that the utopia would not come until people realized their *inner* powers of consciousness, something not to be attained by mere changes in forms of government.

Coleridge's political odyssey was not untypical. Interested in politics (Britain on the eve of 1789 was full of plans and hopes for political reform) and at first enthusiastic for the French Revolution, he wrote an ode on the storming of the Bastille, but by 1798 his *Ode to France* records his disillusion. "In Mr. Burke's writings the germs of almost all political truths may be found," he thought, but he also thought that Burke had gone too far in his hatred for the revolution. Coleridge found in Kant's categorical imperative, that persons are not to be treated as things, a firm moral foundation for public policy. He was a foe of economic individualism and political economy, which he regarded as "solemn humbug." Society is sacred, held together by mystic bonds; Coleridge embraced this organic conception of society that was so prominent in Romantic political thought.

Here Romantic political ideas blended with the conservative ideology, an enemy of liberal individualism and constitutionalism in the earlier nineteeenth century; this will be discussed further in the next chapter. Others in the galaxy of great English Romantic poets illustrate the political ambiguity of romanticism. If Wordsworth and Coleridge ended as Tories, Byron, by far the most popular poet of his day, was an aristocratic revolutionary who defended the machine-smashing

Luddites, wrote much about rebels, and died fighting in the Greek rebellion. But in view of Byron's life, we cannot but feel that he more nearly spoke his mind when he asked for "wine and women, mirth and laughter." The Byronic rebel, in any case, was a proud and moody soul who preferred solitude and did not love his fellow man—we have to wonder how successful he could have been in any kind of practical politics. Shelley, whom Matthew Arnold called a "beautiful and ineffectual angel" (some recent biographers have questioned this view), was also full of rhetorical revolt at times:

> Men of England, wherefore plough
> For the lords who lay ye low?

But more full of poetry and love of beautiful women. The greatest of these poets, John Keats, simply had no discernible politics; nightingales interested him far more.

"Romanticism," the authors of a book about it assert, "fostered sympathy for the oppressed...and looked forward to a new social system, a Utopia" (W. V. Moody and R. M. Lovett). No doubt it did, or some Romantics did. But another authority (C. Grana) tells us, with equal accuracy, that "romanticism included a revival of political traditionalism, neo-feudal at times, decrying social fragmentation and exalting a sense of unspoiled community, born of spontaneous loyalty to ritualized customs." And we should have to take account of others like Keats or Alfred de Musset, who said nothing about either of these things.

How are we to reconcile these differences? Between Coleridge opposing the English reform bill of 1832 and Hugo on the barricades there seems a decided gulf.[7] We can say that all these diverse political directions shared a common exaltation of consciousness born of this exciting era. Even Keats felt a sense of impending climax or apocalypse ("great spirits now on earth are sojourning") though he identified it with no particular political creed. Stendhal, in his essay "Racine and Shakespeare," remarked that those who had experienced the Terror and marched with bloody feet through Russian snows with Napoleon (as in fact this great French writer did), could no longer be moved by the sober and restrained tragedies of classicism. Whatever the choice, for people of the Romantic generation it was likely to be a stirring one.

The relationship between romanticism and politics finds a striking example in the extraordinary Russian emperor who died just a year after Byron and who, with the burning of Moscow and the retreat of Napoleon, had leapt to fame in the same year as the British poet. Educated in the Enlightenment mold under the supervision of his remarkable grandmother Catherine the Great, Alexander I followed the trend toward romanticism after 1800. The fearful burden of leadership, thrust upon a sensitive man who never had much taste for politics, pushed him in a

---

[7]A Russian Communist historian once resolved the issue by alleging there were two romanticisms, one good and one evil—one progressive, revolutionary, proletarian, the other escapist or reactionary. This does not help much.

mystical religious direction during the terrible days of 1812. After consulting with Moravian and Quaker brethren he changed his dissolute lifestyle and became almost obsesssively pious in a most unorthodox way (from the viewpoint of his Russian Orthodox Church). Then in 1814–15, as the great war wound to a close and the victors assembled to dictate the future shape of Europe, the most powerful man in Europe became involved romantically with some women who were both beautiful and mystically religious. Julie de Krüdener, widow of a Baltic baron, had in her youth been both a writer and something of a *femme fatale*; she was a friend of Mme. de Staël, Jean-Paul Richter, and others of the literary world. At the age of forty she turned to religion, and interacted with such prominent philosophers of the new mysticism as Saint-Martin and the Munich seer Franz von Baader. She met Alexander early in 1815 and swept him off his feet by a combination, it seems, of prophetic eloquence and sex appeal. Together they devised the Holy Alliance, intending it as a new principle of statecraft based on genuine spiritual Christianity. This utopia did not survive the realities of postwar politics, becoming a symbol of reaction in a way Julie and Alexander had not intended.

Soon separating from the tsar, Julie threw herself into helping the poor and downtrodden in a way that earned her the enmity of authority all over southern Germany. She, at least, thought spiritual Christianity capable of profound social applications. But the tsar drifted into inertia and despair. His apparent death in 1824 (rumors circulated of a counterfeit death and reappearance as a Siberian holy man, a romantic story indeed, which Leo Tolstoy later believed) was the signal for an attempted revolution by some young army officers, moved partly by the French Revolution and partly by Byronic romanticism. The Decembrist revolt failed, of course. But it left behind a legend on which future Russian revolutionaries down to Lenin would build.

In a country such as Russia with an uncertain sense of identity, romanticism was especially close to nationalism. Peter the Great had forced Russia to westernize; in St. Petersburg people spoke French or German, not Russian. The implication was that Russia was miserable and savage, and must be made over in the image of foreigners. Catherine had imported French culture and ideas, though in her later years she became deeply interested in Russian folk culture and tried to develop the Russian language. The first of those later to be called Slavophiles had already appeared in the eighteenth century. Not the artifical city St. Petersburg but Moscow is the real heart of Russia, they said. In this debate Rousseau's glorification of popular culture and the countryside, romanticism's delight in folklore and folk identity, reenforced the Slavophiles against the westernizers—a perennial debate that split the Russian personality at all times.

THE MEANING OF ROMANTICISM

More than a century of scholarship and criticism has sought in vain for a single definition of romanticism. From this some have drawn the conclusion that the term is useless. (They have often drawn similar conclusions about terms such as liberalism, democracy, socialism, fascism, terms which nevertheless persist because they are needed, even if imprecise.) The term romanticism survives despite all efforts to kill it because it is a useful term to cover a number of striking cultural phenomena of the period from about 1780 to 1830. Possibly we should use several terms; but we can, if we like, choose to subdivide the one term, qualify it, mark the exceptions, but retain it for heuristic purposes.

The Romantic revolution is linked to Kant and to the French Revolution as a vital aspect of what was perhaps the most exciting and creative period of modern times. Probably the basic factor in this revolution was subjectivism, by which is meant, first, the Kantian point that mind participates in shaping reality; it is not just a passive observer. The knowing process had previously been conceived in terms of the object known; now the emphasis shifted to the subject. Coleridge declared that in the Newtonian system "mind is always passive—a lazy looker-on" of the external world. But "any system built on the passiveness of mind must be false," this leading expounder of Romantic philosophy in Great Britain added, underscoring the words for emphasis. This was the central insight of romanticism. The mirror and the lamp, as one critical study put it—the mind lights the way to truth rather than merely reflecting it. Possessing the gift of imagination, the creative mind can actually shape external reality.

In this many were to see a destructive principle, a mark of "decadence"; the healthy society does not so relativize truth. In the end, we reach Nietzsche's insight that there are as many truths as there are individual viewpoints. The economic and political individualism that began to grow at this time (this is treated more fully in the next chapter) also fragmented the unity of society, something that has been going on ever since with increasing momentum. The literature of the eighteenth century had been a social literature that sought not to express the personal soul but to communicate common ideas. The outsider, the misanthrope (see Molière), the *Sonderling* or unusual person, generally was ridiculed, not applauded. Now came the Byronic hero, lonely and moody, a person who "did not love the human race." Romanticism ushered in the modern fate of loneliness in the crowd, or the privilege of individual self-development, as one may choose to put it. Romantics made legends of poets destroyed by an unfeeling society (Chatterton, Chénier); persecuted by the "philistines," they "perished in their pride" but were admired for their courageous independence. The Thoreauvian individualist who marches to his own drum entered history.

Nothing, Wordsworth wrote in a characteristically Romantic way, "can breed such fear and awe" as to look

> Into our minds, into the mind of man—
> My haunt, and the main region of my song.

The Romantic poets began a long exploration of ever more mysterious landscapes of the inner consciousness. The seeds of what later became depth psychology are strewn among their writings. Freud named Goethe (as well as Shakespeare) among the creative writers he said were the sources of his psychoanalysis. He

"Songs of Innocence & Experience" as Superego & id

could well have added William Blake, often seen today as Freud's precursor. How differently men would behold the world, Byron mused in 1820 (and "how much would novels gain")

> If some Columbus of the moral seas
> Would show mankind their souls' antipodes.

The stanzas that follow in *Don Juan* hint at dark secrets that if uncovered could lead to new understanding of human creative powers. Thus began a long, perhaps dangerous, certainly difficult quest for the springs of human action.

Many of the great Romantic poems use the play of memory across time to narrate the process of growing out of childhood into maturity, a voyage of the self. The *Bildungsroman,* the novel of self-discovery and education, was a Romantic genre that stretched all the way down the century. Stendhal, anticipating Freud, tried to recover the full memory of his past in order to "divine what kind of man I have been." This novelist, whose real name was Beyle, and who wrote his memoirs under the name of Brulard, gave up before the bottomless well of memory, forced to admit "I do not know what I am." The search for a secure ego, an "identity," had begun; its foundations had been called into question by Romantic subjectivity. The conflict of the individual with society became the other great theme of the nineteenth-century novel.

Thus, as Hegel put it in his early work *The Phenomenology of Mind,* "the spirit passes over into another region, the land of the inner subjective moral consciousness." Lovejoy found the fundamental Romantic trait to be diversity or pluralism, as opposed to Enlightenment standardization and simplification—a search for, and delight in, unique particulars rather than universals and generals. "We are not to number the streaks of the tulip," Dr. Johnson had pronounced in the name of classicism. Romantics wanted to do just that. The nineteenth century was to be eclectic in its architecture, pillaging the past for its borrowed styles; it was to offer a "generous confusion" of modes in the arts and ideas; it divided into separate national cultures to a considerable extent. Man was parceled out in men, as the poet Rossetti put it—he took it to be a sign of Europe's decadence. In this sense romanticism predicted the fragmentation of thought and society that was to go on with ever increasing momentum through the next two centuries. Yet we cannot be entirely content with this definition. Romantics held on to unity in their transcendental philosophy and their fierce quest for ideal truth. Most of them would have been shocked at recent "postmodernist" celebrations of chaos in the realm of values.

They were, after all, despite lapses into modish *Weltschmerz* or Byronic *Menschenhass,* on the whole optimistic. Their note was an enthusiastic love of life and art. The critic Lionel Trilling remarked that nothing today can compare with the exhilarating effect of Keats's letters. The renewal of language was partly responsible for this effect, but deeper than that was a new inspiration and hope. The poetic impulse swept into the other arts. "In 1813 music had newly become the most astonishing, the most fascinating, the most miraculous art in the world,"

George Bernard Shaw wrote. The marvelous energy of Beethoven and Schubert would carry on in their successors, Chopin, Schumann, Berlioz, whose lives were as Romantic as their music. The visual arts, despite a Blake, a Delacroix, or a Caspar David Friedrich (who declared "the artist should paint not only what he sees before him, but what he sees within him") seemed less affected, probably because painting and sculpture are more classical in spirit, best at depicting repose and equilibrium rather than—as in a Beethoven sonata—the ongoing rush of powerful emotion.

Whatever its confusions of thought, the Romantic era saw an outburst of creative energy not matched since the Renaissance and hardly equaled since. It revitalized language and, among other things, brought poetry to the people. Musset and Hugo in France, Byron and Wordsworth in England, Goethe and Kleist in Germany, Emerson and Longfellow in the United States, Bobbie Burns in Scotland, Pushkin and Lermontov in Russia—all these names are connected with a literature that reached deeply into the popular consciousness, providing images for speech and culture second only in English to the Bible and Shakespeare. In the case of the Russians, this early nineteenth-century generation virtually created a national literature where none had existed before.

The popular side of romanticism includes vampires (a recent history of vampire literature, by Christopher Frayling, begins with Lord Byron), Frankenstein's monster, and the fairytales of the Grimm brothers. Charles Dickens and the other great Victorian writers are inconceivable without the Romantic inheritance they were born into.

If we attempt to tie the great writers and artists of the Romantic era to any one social class, we fail; they were a diverse group in terms of social origins. Keats was the son of a livery stable manager, Blake the offspring of a haberdasher, Tom Moore the child of a grocer, John Clare a farm laborer. Victor Hugo's father, on the other hand, had been a Napoleonic general. Lord Byron of course was high born, though not of a wealthy branch of the family. Balzac, actually of bourgeois origin, added a "de" before his last name to make himself sound aristocratic. "George Sand," offspring of an aristocratic father and a low-born mother, was raised in a convent and first donned her male attire as a farmworker, not a feminist; she then married a country squire before fleeing to Paris with her two children to write eighty novels and become famous. Her story is a microcosm of the era. The ability to find fame and fortune in the new urban market for literature was a factor of increasing importance. Writers became glamorous figures, the culture heroes and heroines of their day. They came from all classes and every sort of background, united only by their talent and by their enthusiasm for romanticism—whatever it was. In the end it was the artist's credo of self-expression:

> Weave a circle round him twice
> And close your eyes with holy dread
> For he on honey-dew hath fed
> And drunk the milk of paradise.
>
> (Coleridge)

2

The Age of Ideologies, 1815–1848

THE EUROPEAN SITUATION 1815–1848

A profusion of political and social "isms" in Europe after 1815 resulted from the crucial situation after the defeat of Napoleon: one world was dying and the next struggling to be born. Carrying the principles of the French Revolution, Bonaparte had shattered the old order in much of Europe and installed sweeping innovations. Now the revolution and its great leader were washed away. Though most thoughtful people were glad that the upstart Corsican's wild ride was over, not even the most reactionary thought it was possible to go back to the pre-1789 regime. What lay ahead? Everywhere people felt the need to take soundings and mark out a new course. Having laid waste the old Europe, the revolution had failed to establish a new one. It had failed morally and now physically, from the Reign of Terror to Napoleon's dictatorship and so to his military defeat after a dreadful war. "The people who have gone through 1793 and 1814 bear two wounds in their hearts," wrote Alfred de Musset, attributing to these wounds "all the sickness of the present century." What could cure the sickness?

Those who had lived through the revolution, the wars, the Bonapartist regime, and its defeat might land on the shoals of cynicism, with Stendhal's young hero of *The Charterhouse of Parma*. They might take refuge in the delights of Romantic literature and try to escape from the public world to a purely personal one. But the need to search for new principles of social order could hardly be avoided. In all parts of Europe political and social ideologies constituted the leading intellectual interest of the years between 1815 and 1848: socialism, liberalism, conservatism, and in some places nationalism, stronger in Germany and Italy as these areas struggled to liberate themselves and achieve national identity.

A number of ideas or systems of thought devoted to economic and political theory leaped to the front. Even in pure philosophy, the political impulse was evident, for although the philosopher Hegel devised a system many found too metaphysical, his chief interest was in human history and its political order; those he influenced included critical historians such as David Strauss and social economists such as Karl Marx, as well as nationalists.

The peace settlement at Vienna in 1815 tried to reorganize Europe politically and morally, but it mostly failed. Uprisings against its dispositions of peoples and governments soon broke out, notably in northern Italy. That area is a good case study for the restlessness of post-Congress Europe. Italy had strongly felt the influence of Rousseau and the French Revolution. Not a few Italians contributed to the Enlightenment (a good example is the criminologist Beccaria), and the revolutionary society that preceded Mazzini's Young Italy had its roots in the Masonic lodges so widespread in the eighteenth century. Napoleon Bonaparte, born in Corsica, was more Italian than French in ancestry, and his thoroughgoing reorganization of Italy around the Code Napoleon, abolishing feudal privilege, found much support there. With Napoleon's final defeat all this disappeared, replaced by a substantial return to the old order under Austrian control. The principle of "legitimacy" adopted by the Congress of Vienna restored most of the old rulers to their thrones; this included the House of Savoy in northern Italy. The Grand Duke of Tuscany relied on the Austrians to keep him in power, while the Austrians governed directly in Venice and Lombardy. Nowhere was there more discontent with this reactionary peace settlement than among the young idealists of Italy. Nationalism, which in Germany dates from the humiliating Prussian defeat at Jena, thrived in Italy on hatred of an alien ruler.

In return for remarkably lenient peace terms based on Tsar Alexander's distinction between the French people and Napoleon (in fact most of the French always supported Napoleon), France was restored to the Bourbon monarchy in the person of Louis XVIII. For the moment royalism reigned; even Victor Hugo was a monarchist in 1820. But a liberal opposition soon emerged and so did socialists, or "associationalists," who by the 1830s were a significant influence on the intellectuals. The next French revolution was only a few years away; it came in 1830, forcing Charles X to abdicate. The ambiguous regime that ensued sought to combine royalism (though not "legitimacy") with liberal constitutionalism; this July Monarchy too was doomed to fall after eighteen uneasy years. Neither the pure conservatives nor the socialists accepted it. Its main support came from the upper bourgeoisie, an elite of merchants and bankers and industrialists.

Great Britain too had its revolution in 1832, a peaceful one though not without some riotous rumblings before Parliament passed the great Reform Bill of

1832. It is commonly said to have marked the victory of the "middle classes" over the old aristocracy, though in fact the political leadership of the House of Commons continued to come from the landed aristocracy long after 1832. Far from establishing democracy, the reform left a majority of Englishmen without the vote, just as did the 1830 revolution in France. But together with the beginning of Queen Victoria's reign a few years later it provided a basis of social stability in England for the rest of the century. It had admitted the new manufacturing entrepreneurs of a rapidly industrializing country to a share of political power, its chief reform being a reapportionment to provide equal representation for the rapidly growing industrial midlands region.

So there are some grounds for saying that the first half of the nineteenth century saw the victory of the middle classes or industrial bourgeoisie, and of the social theory associated with them. Broadly speaking it may be said that the French Revolution led to three main streams of nineteenth-century social thought, conservative, liberal, and socialist, as a natural result of its outcome. The revolution had established the principle of formal or legal equality of individuals as the basis of society. The Old Regime it overthrew had been organic, corporative, and hierarchical; that is to say it had not treated people either as equals or as individuals, but as members of groups that performed different functions in a total structure. It might be compared to the outlook still prevalent in groups like sports teams, where it would seem ridiculous for the substitute lineman to claim equality with the star quarterback. Though an unequal place, there was a place for all in theory within this society, the poor man having as much right to his hovel as the lord did to his mansion. Within fifty years of the French Revolution, a thinker as radical in some ways as Thomas Carlyle could develop a considerable nostalgia for the old order, where the poor peasant, unlike the factory hand, at least had a protector.[1]

The revolution proclaimed equality and freedom. People were free to make their own way; they were also free to starve. The medieval peasant held land by custom (status); the nineteenth-century mill worker had no such security, he could rise but if he fell there was no one to rescue him.

The three positions resulted from varying reactions to this situation. There were those who thought the whole change a ghastly mistake and wanted to restore the pre-1789 order, as far as possible; they hated industrialism and despised the new middle classes, they thought the ordered society of the countryside best, they resisted equality of status and of political rights, written constitutions and contractual relations.

If these conservatives stood on the right, they agreed in some ways with those on the left, the socialists, who also opposed the liberal order of individual competition. "The Revolution ended one inequality only to give birth to another,"

---

[1]In *Past and Present* Carlyle asked his readers to consider "Gurth, born thrall of Cedric the Saxon," who, though not exactly "an exemplar of human felicity…to me seems happy, in comparison with many a Lancashire and Buckinghamshire man, of these days, not born thrall of anybody!" The argument was congenial to both American slaveowners and Russian owners of serfs.

the socialists asserted. The new inequality was even more intolerable than the old. Plutocracy had replaced aristocracy. Legal, juridical equality meant a race in which the more energetic and less scrupulous ground the weaker or unluckier into the dirt. The new ruling class of money was worse than the old one. Socialists held, as G.K. Chesterton wrote in his poem "The Secret People,"

> They have given us into the hands of the new unhappy lords
> Lords without anger or honour, who dare not carry their swords.

Socialists disagreed with conservatives in desiring not to go back to the old regime but to go forward another step to a society that would achieve real (economic) equality rather than a merely formal kind. Their suggestions about the exact nature of this society and how it might be attained were varied.

Those who were content in the main with what the revolution had achieved (legal equality and free competition) were the (bourgeois) liberals. They were mainly on top in the nineteenth century, for if the dream of restoring the old days was an impossible one, socialism was almost equally utopian. So the "middle classes" came into their own, despite a great deal of grumbling about the kind of society they dominated. It may be a mistake to tie this so closely to social classes, a model Marx and the socialists largely imposed on our vocabulary. After all, a good many workers, farmers, and even aristocrats approved of the liberal model, while the socialists were almost all discontented sons of the bourgeoisie. But in fact there was considerable class consciousness among those who arose at this time to make their fortunes as entrepreneurs.

Power must be transferred from the landed oligarchy to "the intelligent middle and industrious classes," said Richard Cobden, English manufacturer who was an oracle of British liberalism. These new men making their fortunes via the new manufacturing processes using steam power, especially Cobden's textile industry, distinguished themselves from the "mob" below as carefully as from the aristocracy above—from both of which they differed in possessing industriousness, efficiency, and morality, they thought. (The upper classes and the lower, someone said, were united by the bond of a common immorality, especially in sexual matters, the former having advanced beyond morality, the latter having not yet encountered it.)

The new bourgeoisie were serious, frugal, upright, hardworking and, according to their critics, hardhearted. Certainly they were builders of wealth in this vigorous morning of the Industrial Revolution, proud of their achievements, inclined to be scornful of those they believed contributed less. Distinctions must be noted within the "bourgeoisie," the term being too broad to be meaningful. In France, the "grande bourgeoisie" was a coterie of rich bankers and notables who were "political liberals and social conservatives," having little esteem for their social inferiors and absolutely no taste for democracy. After the 1830 revolution, perhaps one in 40 French males voted compared to one in 75 before. In Great Britain after the 1832 reform, one in five had the vote. In the revolutions of 1848 on the Continent a lower bourgeoisie joined with workers in demanding universal suffrage. Britain escaped that revolution because to a much greater extent its lower as well as upper bourgeoisie were enfranchised.

The word "bourgeois" became an epithet in two circles: that of the socialists and the literary circle. The stereotype of the bourgeois (as depicted in a Daumier caricature, for example) had some basis in reality. The Benthamite *Westminster Review* regarded literature as unnecessary to civilization, while the liberal *Economist* considered it better to starve the poor than administer public charity. But one must grant the strength of this "industrious and intelligent" element in society. By and large they *were* in possession of those not altogether contemptible characteristics, industry and intelligence. Nor were they so far from the world of literate culture as they would be later in the century. They were creating wealth as it had never been created before. If their natural habitat was the bourse or the factory rather than the university or parliament, they did produce powerful voices in this era. Not least of these were the political economists, authors of a new, acute, and powerful science.

Balzac, the great French novelist and observer of the "human comedy," once made the point that if the bourgeoisie destroyed the nobility, a combat would ensue between the bourgeoisie and the people beneath them in the social scale. The weapons with which the bourgeoisie had destroyed the aristocracy—charges of special privilege and unearned income, demands for more democracy and equality—could obviously be turned against them. Coleridge, opposing the extension of the suffrage in 1832, warned the middle class that it would be unable to stop at giving the vote just to itself, but would eventually have to give it to all. Carlyle warned employers that by refusing to look after their workers, they would drive them to social revolution. So the "social question" arose early. Few serious thinkers were ever happy with the new organization of society, or lack of it, under middle-class liberal auspices.

Despite the socialist allegation, it is not true that the new bourgeoisie entirely neglected the welfare of the poor. They could hardly deny that their maxim of free competition, "a fair field and no favors" required some social services. Education was the leading case of this sort. "The schoolmaster was abroad" in these years. Guizot, who scorned the multitude, nevertheless put through the French educational reform of 1833, called the charter of French primary education. It fell well short of installing free and universal elementary education, but by requiring every commune to maintain a public primary school, it began the movement that led in this direction. The German system of education from *kindergarten* to *gymnasium* became a widely imitated model. German and also French bourgeois nationalists regarded public education as the leading means of inculcating civic consciousness as well as teaching sober work habits to the underclass.

Writing in 1831, on "The Spirit of the Age," young John Stuart Mill declared that "a change has taken place in the human mind.... The conviction is already not far from universal that the times are pregnant with change, and that the nineteenth century will be known to posterity as the era of one of the greatest revolutions of which history has preserved the remembrance, in the human mind, and in the whole constitution of human society." Everybody felt an almost dizzying sense of change. "We have been living the life of 300 years in 30," Matthew Arnold's father, a famous schoolmaster, remarked. "Can we never drop anchor for a single day/ On the ocean of the ages?" Lamartine wondered. An unprecedented ferment of social and political thought reflected this concern, and prepared the way for the revolutions of the year 1848, hardly less earthshaking than that of 1789. Various kinds of socialism, democracy, social democracy, and liberalism mingled in another apocalyptic moment, when many expected the deferred social millennium. Again came apparent failure followed by disillusion. But in fact democracy and socialism persisted after 1848; the political ideas created between 1815 and 1848 are those the world has been living with ever since.

CONSERVATISM

As noted in Chapter 1, the conservative ideology virtually began with Edmund Burke, and all subsequent members of this school were indebted to his *Reflections on the Revolution*. Some found a contradiction in the very idea of a conservative "ideology." The term suggests a political doctrine deliberately manufactured by some theorist and imposed on real life. But conservatives usually held that human society does not work this way; its values and institutions are not manufactured in the study, but grow from the soil as rooted, historical things. Constitutions ought not to be written out as formal rules; they exist in the hearts of people or they are no good. Leadership should emerge not from some formal process of election, but as spontaneous recognition. Rights in the abstract are worthless or pernicious; real rights are products of a people's history and are embedded in its customs. Nevertheless, the natural state of things having been interrupted by parties and creeds, conservatives had to reply to these novelties, and so in spite of themselves were forced to produce writings, arguments, doctrines. As Joseph De Maistre wrote, "the intellectual principle has taken priority over the moral principle in the direction of society."

Coleridge built on Burke's foundations in England. He did not go as far as Burke in rejecting rationalism in politics, but he joined him in the respect for tradition, the organic sense of society, and the feeling for a moral order in history. His influence flowed through the nineteenth century as a philosophic source of enlightened Toryism. British and European conservatism, it should be noted, was generally an enemy of *laissez-faire* individualism and the negative state, principles associated with their foes the liberals (in the nineteenth-century sense). Coleridge believed in government regulation of manufacturers, government aid to education, and the duty of the state to enhance the moral and intellectual capacities of its citizens in many positive ways. It was even possible in England to speak of a "tory socialism." Coleridge's later thought also featured the idea of a new kind of national church led by prominent people from all areas of life and thought—not just a separate caste of clergymen but a "clerisy" composed of all the best and the brightest, to provide national direction. Coleridge's Christianity was liberal in being based on individual conscience rather than dogma or ceremony; it was a legacy of his romanticism. It was conservative in the sense of seeking to combat anarchic individualism and materialism. His Broad Church within the Church of England appealed chiefly to intellectuals.

Conservatism was more likely than liberalism in nineteenth-century Britain to support government welfare measures for the poor. Related to the rural squirearchy, it was certainly not equalitarian or leveling. Coleridge opposed the reform bill of 1832. But the leading hero of factory reform and other humanitarian measures in early industrial England was a Tory, Lord Shaftesbury. The Coleridge tradition passsed to John Ruskin, who described himself as "a violent Tory of the old school" while castigating the materialistic and unprincipled society of industrial England. It also influenced Benjamin Disraeli, perhaps the most truly literate prime minister Britain ever had, who championed a democratized Conservative party leading the way in social reform.

Ruskin and Disraeli, like many others, had felt the influence of Thomas Carlyle, probably the most influential social and political ideologist of the 1830s and 1840s. It is difficult to know where to place Carlyle in the ideological constellation; he was either Tory or Socialist, but certainly never Liberal. The Scottish essayist and historian was a prominent spokesman of what has been called "social romanticism." On its politicoeconomic side romanticism sometimes glorified the free spirit, the rebel; it also showed a Rousseauist tendency to deplore urbanism and industrialism. Few friends were found among the Romantics of the "dark Satanic mills" or their owners, one of whom Carlyle caricatured as "Plugson of Undershot." Organic human communities dissolved under the impact of this inhuman system of production, they thought. In an eccentrically romantic, highly charged, enormously effective prose style Carlyle announced the urgency of the "social question," thundering against "the gospel of Mammon," the economics of irresponsibility, the substitution of a "cash nexus" for real human ties. His ties to conservatism included the strong sense of organic community, the call for strong leadership ("captains of industry"), the hatred of selfish individualism.

The world needed a renewal of faith, the faith that binds people together in a common cause. The old faith of Christianity was dying, mortally wounded by the Enlightenment. That "chilled age," with its cold rationalism, had been able only to destroy, not to create. The task of their age, Carlyle and his friend the Italian nationalist Mazzini thought, was to rescue humanity from Enlightenment materialism by producing a new religion, one appropriate to the postrevolutionary era. "Life without a noble goal, life not devoted to the pursuit of a great idea, is not life but vegetation," Mazzini pronounced. The French socialist prophet Henri Saint-Simon, a strong influence on both Carlyle and Mazzini, had written of a *Nouveau Christianisme*. Carlyle's religion was hero worship, the inspiration that comes from imitating the best examples of human achievement.

It was in France that a conservative ideology developed most strongly, from the emigrés who returned in glory after 1815 to dominate intellectual fashions for a few years at least. There were a few French liberals of great distinction, including Bonaparte's enemies Constant and Staël, who stressed constitutionalism, civil liberties, a limited monarchy, a strong parliament. In this camp too one might put the formidable figure of Chateaubriand, who turned from literature to political leadership. But both conservative and socialist thought was more significant in France. The chief conservative theoreticians were Joseph de Maistre and the Comte de Bonald.

Born in 1753 of an aristocratic Savoyard family, Maistre was early a follower of Rousseau. In the 1780s he became interested in occult religion, but dropped this when the Church pronounced against it. (Many ideas of this sort appeared in that decade, including esoteric versions of Freemasonry; Mozart's late, great opera *The Magic Flute* is an example.) A provincial senator, happily married, Maistre would never have become celebrated in the history of thought had it not been for the revolution. Initially he supported it, but after falling afoul of the Jacobin regime in the stormy year 1793 he chose exile, as many others did. At Lausanne in Switzerland he frequented the society of former French government leader Necker, along with Necker's famous intellectual daughter, Germaine de Staël. There he met the historian Edward Gibbon. At that time he began to put together his thoughts on the origins of the revolution, the reasons for its failure, and the means of reconstructing France.

Bonald was in exile in Heidelberg at the same time, and Maistre wrote to him in 1796 that "your spirit and mine are in perfect accord." They had to wait out the Napoleonic years, though Bonald returned to live in France. Maistre went to Russia as ambassador from the kingdom of Sardinia, and wrote his chief works in St. Petersburg. He returned to France after the fall of Napoleon to receive considerable acclaim; he was considered to be the chief theorist of the Restoration. He died in 1821, but Bonald, whose ideas were similar, lived on to reign as the high priest of the legitimists, joined among others by the youthful and fiery La Mennais, who would later turn to the left. But of these Maistre's writings were the best known.

Maistre's writings were marked by a strong dislike of the whole *philosophe* school. He wished "absolutely to kill the spirit of the eighteenth century." The *philosophes* had introduced the poison that caused the sickness of revolution; it must be purged from France before the nation could be restored to health. Locke, Hume, Voltaire, Rousseau were all evil men; the very visage of Voltaire bespoke his service of the Devil. But Maistre went on to try to show on what basis society could be reconstructed on proper principles. Here Maistre and especially Bonald proved stimulating, and influenced many who did not share their conservatism. They combined insights into the weakness of a democratic or liberal order with some fruitful ideas about social science methodology. Maistre was a writer of genius and a scholar of great learning.

The two so-called reactionaries were aware that one could not go back to 1788, much though they may have regretted the revolution, which Maistre could only explain as having been sent by God to punish France for its sins. Maistre was not simply "the prophet of the past," as a wit dubbed him. It was necessary to establish a new political philosophy. The conservative argument made much of the idea that the natural order of human society is historical and traditional, while individualism and democracy are diseases resulting in—or the products of—social anarchy. There are no universal rules; each nation has a form of government suitable to it, a civic culture worked out through long centuries. Ignorance of and contempt for history was the prime source of political error. Abstract theorizing about politics had caused much damage. Society is a living body. To supplant the natural, organic relationship between social elements with egalitarian rhetoric is madness. Contractual agreements, paper constitutions, legal regulation of social relations are false and alienating—as if a family had to have elections, printed rules, contracts between children and parents.

The conservatives argued that only monarchy (at least in France) can provide political security. Their arguments in favor of absolute monarchy may now make tedious reading, but the conservative school had a considerable influence on nineteenth-century thought. Bonald has been called the founder of sociology; he certainly influenced Auguste Comte, who is more frequently granted that title. Alexis de Tocqueville's *Democracy in America*, a pioneer work of social analysis, owed much to these writers. Tocqueville was evidently testing the hypotheses of La Mennais, in his 1825 *De la religion considerée dans ses rapports avec l'ordre politique et civil*, that democracy leads to despotism, enshrines mediocrity, and causes people to be rootless, godless, and materialistic. Whereas the conservative theorists' recommendations for the good society came to little, their investigations of such matters as this, the relationship between religion and society or politics, were stimulating. The historical school of jurisprudence, led in Germany by Savigny, stressed the law's evolution and its relation to society.

Otherwise, a deep awareness of the tragic features of the human situation marked Maistre's writings. History is a sea of blood, the hangman is the epitome of government; some primeval curse must lie on the human race. It is this savagery that demands submission to authority and dooms any liberal democracy. But Maistre was in a sense not illiberal; he wanted the monarch checked by tradition, the nobility, and by local institutions in a decentralized society, much as in the Old Regime. Such pessimists as Maistre are kept from belief in despotism by the same mistrust of human nature that prevents them from accepting democracy; you can't trust the powerful any more than the masses. He distinguished an "absolute" monarchy from an unlimited or despotic one. In a notable argument set forth in his work *On the Papacy*, Maistre argued that the popes might mediate between state sovereignty and individual liberty. The argument impressed few, least of all the pope, but it indicates Maistre's desire to limit the power of the state. He did not think parliamentary democracy was the answer for France, but he conceded that it might be for England. In France it would only lead to a new Bonaparte. How accurate that prophecy was the events of 1848–1851 revealed. Too much the polemicist and marred by corroding hatreds, Maistre remains a major figure because of his flashes of rare insight.

The deepest insight of the conservative school was undoubtedly its conviction that human society is doomed if it loses its primeval, tribal ties of community. "A society founded on sheer egoism...will undergo atomization, anomic loss of sense of belonging," Benjamin R. Nelson observed more recently. As the next section points out, schools of individualism such as utilitarianism and political economy were beginning to dominate the scene as the conservatives wrote. Free self-reliant individuals, these liberals asserted, are "the mainsprings of social progress." Their energies released by the knowledge that what they gain will be their own, they enrich themselves and thereby enrich the nation as a whole. But this doctrine entailed loss of the social sense. Society became a collection of individuals, their relations regulated by the impersonal force of the market, a "cash nexus." Such atomization destroys a sense of community and personal ties necessary to human life.

Conservative thought produced a strong vein of social criticism, since their foes the liberals had seized the heights, leaving them to defend "lost causes and impossible loyalties," as was said of the Newmanites at Oxford. They disliked bourgeois commercialism as well as mass democracy, and upheld the ideal of a society that was aristocratic but not socially irresponsible. The prominent socialist Henri Saint-Simon acknowledged a debt to Bonald, who taught him that society is "an organic machine whose every part contributes to the movement of the whole," not a mere collection of individuals. Much though they might differ in other respects, the conservatives and the socialists held in common the social principle, against the nineteenth-century liberals. Socialists held to an Enlightenment faith that reason might invent a new and better form of social organization. Conservatives held this to be impossible and, if tried, disastrous. No opinion lay closer to the heart of conservative doctrine than a mistrust of what Burke had called "the fallible and feeble contrivances of our reason." The liberals and radicals believed that people could do better; conservatives feared they might well do worse. They would rely on an allegedly natural social order, which often seemed to mean just the status quo. Their problem was that the age was seething with change, and there was no longer a stable order of things.

LIBERALISM

Though conservatives tried to put down an anchor against the currents of change, no task was less promising in the dynamic first half of the nineteenth century. And their cultural pessimism was at odds with the generally hopeful mood of the times. There is an exuberance that reflects this basic optimism in the titanic creative energies of a Dickens or Balzac, as well as in the explosion of hopeful solutions for all the problems of humanity. "The period was full of evil things, but it was full of hope," Chesterton wrote in his book about Charles Dickens. Its typical giants, like Victor Hugo, dreamed romantic dreams of progress and threw themselves furiously into the task of transforming them into reality. So it was not, on the whole, a good time for conservatives, except for a few years just after the fall of Napoleon. They would make a comeback after 1848.

Liberalism was a term like romanticism, broad and vague, and still is. By general agreement it was strongest in Great Britain, which had an ancestral form of liberalism (though that term was not used in any systematic way until the 1830s) reaching back to the seventeenth-century revolutions and embracing parliamentary government and civil liberties. The English had not known absolute monarchy since 1688, if ever, and fondly recalling such landmarks as Magna Carta and the Bill of Rights, considered themselves freer than any other people; this conviction amounted virtually to a national religion. The storms of the French Revolution caused some curtailment of this liberty between 1795 and 1820, producing toward the latter date what has been called the ugliest estrangement between government and people since 1688.

After a bloody clash between police and a crowd being addressed by radical orators in Manchester in 1819, the repressive Six Acts clamped down on freedom of speech, press, and assembly, suspending habeas corpus. But this repression did not last, and under Whig auspices a series of parliamentary measures between 1825 and 1840 registered the victory of a liberalism marked by commercial freedoms (removal of tariffs, monopolies, other restrictions on trade), personal freedoms (of press, religion), and political reform (the 1832 Reform Bill which, as we noted, extended voting rights to the middle class and redistricted for more equitable representation of regions according to population). In 1829 the Catholic Emancipation Act and repeal of the Test Acts removed political discrimination against non-Anglican Christians, though the Established Church remained and Jews were not similarly relieved for thirty more years.

All this stood in contrast to much of the Continent, where the "Metternich system" reigned. Count Metternich, the Austrian statesman who tended to control policy in the German world, considered freedom of the press "a modern scourge." Seven Göttingen professors became martyrs to the censorship of ideas even in the traditionally free German universities, and the leader of Young Italy, Mazzini, after being hounded even from Switzerland, found refuge in England in 1837; London became a place of refuge for all sorts of people fleeing from political intolerance on the Continent.

The limits of British liberalism did not escape notice. Liberals also enacted the harsh Poor Law of 1834 and fought the Ten Hour Bill, introduced by a Tory, to forbid inhumanly long hours for women and children in the new mechanized factories. One of the most radical of the liberals, Francis Place, felt that granting any great amount of welfare relief to the poor would "encourage idleness and extinguish enterprise." A courageous band fought to abolish slavery within the British Empire, but most of them were Tories. All in all, early nineteenth-century liberalism was a somewhat curious thing as we see it today.

It was closely connected to two notable intellectual systems of the period, themselves closely connected: utilitarianism and political economy. The former was the offspring of a strange genius, Jeremy Bentham. Bentham had been writing as early as the 1770s and was an old man in 1810 when his school began to become prominent; he was essentially a child of the Enlightenment, betraying that as much by his scoffing at religion as by his attempt to establish a social science on a simplified theory of human behavior. The Romantics hated him; he was the only person ever known to cause Coleridge to lose his temper. John Stuart Mill, son of Bentham's leading disciple, described in his autobiography the inhuman regime of mental training under which he was raised, and which finally caused him to have a breakdown; Dickens parodied this ruthless suppression of the imagination in the character of Thomas Gradgrind in *Hard Times*. Mill's relief came only when he found consolation in poetry. After this dramatic and symbolic experience Mill wrote a series of essays in which he presented Bentham and Coleridge as the two seminal and rival influences of the century. The two lines of thought, romantic-conservative and rationalist-liberal, sent forth two different strains which even Mill's wise and generous mind could not quite reconcile, but which taken together sum up much of the English nineteenth century.

The lineage of utilitarianism can be traced back to various earlier sources, especially, in the eighteenth century, the French *philosophe* Helvetius's *Treatise on Man*, and to Francis Hutcheson and David Hume of the Scottish school. Helvetius

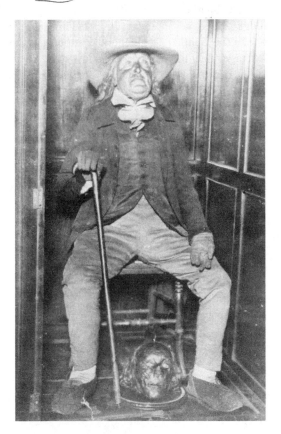

Jeremy Bentham's body, as he requested, still sits in the board room of University College, London. The real head is the one on the floor. (The Bettman Archive/BBC Hulton)

had defended the proposition that the best government is that which secures the most "happiness" for its people. He also agreed with the Physiocrats, early economic theorists, that probably the best thing government could do would be to get off their backs, and leave them alone to pursue their own interests. Hutcheson used the phrase "the greatest happiness of the greatest number." Hume, in criticizing the social contract, that political myth beloved of the eighteenth century, had concluded that "it is on opinion only that government is founded"—that is to say, there is no sanction for government except its usefulness in the eyes of its citizens. William Paley, in his influential textbook *Principles of Moral and Political Thought* (1785), accepted this and defined utility as the sum of happiness. A law is good or bad as it increases or lessens this total of well-being.

The best known of Bentham's immense body of writing was perhaps his 1789 *Principles of Morals and Legislation*. But the hermit of Queen's Park Square, able through an inheritance to indulge his taste for social engineering, poured forth a stream of proposals for the reform of practically everything. Laws and institutions must justify themselves on the grounds of practical welfare provided. Here was the perfect example of systematizers who demanded total and immediate reform on theoretical principles, as such arousing the rage of Burkean conservatives. Utilitarianism was also based on individualism, each person being the best judge of his own interests. In calculating the sum of welfare, "each is to count as one." The Benthamites generally supported the democratic principle of universal suffrage, including, at least at times, votes for women as well as men.[2]

They proposed numerous other breathtaking changes in government. Instead of two houses of Parliament there should be just one; aristocracy as well as monarchy must go; the common law should be replaced by a codified one. Prisons should be reformed, schools should be reformed, virtually everything should be reformed. Here was a revolutionary doctrine demanding that every institution and policy appear before the bar of reason and defend itself at the cost of being abolished or altered if it failed to pass the test of its usefulness. It only remained, of course, to provide some plausible formula by which utility could be measured. It only partly comforted members of the status quo to know that Bentham thought violent revolution likely to create more unhappiness than it eliminated.

To further this ambitious program, the followers of Bentham, including James Mill and others, wrote pamphlets, edited magazines, tried to elect members of Parliament, sought to enlist converts. The movement reached its peak as an organized movement in the 1820s, but continued to have an influence throughout the century. They called themselves Philosophical Radicals, and obviously in demanding the sweeping reform of practically all public institutions they were

---

[2]Bentham changed his mind several times, and his final inclination was evidently to restrict suffrage not only to adult males but to literate ones, although "every individual of the human species" should be a part of the "public opinion tribunal." For a tribute to Bentham's feminism see Miriam Williford, "Bentham on the Rights of Women," *Journal of the History of Ideas*, January–March 1975.

indeed quite radical. On the other hand, they were in other ways less than radical. Apart from being peaceful reformers seeking to convert rather than to destroy, they defended private property, resting their case on the self-interest of free and assertive individuals. Especially after an initial phase of reformist enthusiasm, the utilitarians tended to accept the minimal government position, adopting the views of the political economists (James Mill was himself a charter member of this group too) and opposing socialism. Bentham wrote that "The request which agriculture, manufacturing, and commerce present to governments, is modest and reasonable as that which Diogenes made to Alexander: 'Stand out of my sunshine!' We have no need of favor—we require only a secure and open path."

Still, Benthamites never made *laissez faire* into a dogma; the question always was, on any particular policy, whether it did or did not increase the sum of happiness or well-being. In the 1840s Edwin Chadwick undertook the sanitary reform of the city of London as a utilitarian disciple. A late nineteenth-century political writer, A. V. Dicey, alleged that utilitarianism really undermined property and other individual rights by basing them on expedience, not principle. If you could persuade a utilitarian that collectivism or a rigid despotism would produce more happiness, he would have to agree to it. "I never had, nor ever shall have, any horror...of the hand of government," Jeremy had declared.

Within the camp of liberalism, Bentham and his followers differed from many in rejecting the natural rights school, a distinguished source of English liberalism reaching back to John Locke and the Glorious Revolution of 1688. Such alleged rights, standing above positive law, are either meaningless or false, Utilitarian theory held. ("Nonsense," Bentham barked; if called "imprescriptible" rights, nonsense on stilts!) There is no absolute "liberty"; concrete liberties must be embodied in legislation to be meaningful, and the nature of such legislation should be determined by investigation into real circumstances. (There was a certain affinity here between Bentham and Burke, in most ways so opposed.) Free speech, for example, on Benthamite terms is desirable (if it is) not because we have a sacred right to it, but because, on balance, it has more practical advantages than disadvantages for the whole society. Obviously natural law, or any higher law by which particular acts might be judged, was in conflict with Bentham's principle of judgment, that of utility. In ethical theory Kant's principle of Reason, which judged actions by their intrinsic quality, stood opposed to Bentham's Utility, which judged actions by their consequences, not their intent.

The goal at which legislation should aim is the sum total of individual happiness units. Attempts to provide an exact calculus of this essential entity involved difficulties. A "felicific calculus," a scientific measurement of welfare, had to be found. The search for this exact science of human welfare was a long one. As late as 1920, the British economist A. C. Pigou claimed to have solved the problem in his *The Economics of Welfare.* Meanwhile post-1860 economic theory made notable use of "marginal utility" as the determinant of prices and regulator of production (see further below, pp. 96–97). Pleasure and pain, the two sovereign mas-

ters: I will work and spend for a commodity up to the point where a further increment of it will not satisfy me enough to justify the additional expenditure.

Objections to Benthamism were numerous. It seemed, for one thing, to rule
out any discrimination in the quality of satisfaction or happiness; "pushpin is as
good as poetry," a pig in ecstasy is as good as Socrates in anguish (is happiness
really the highest value?), John Stuart Mill protested. "Let Benthamism reign, if
men have no aspirations," Newman exclaimed. Selfishness and hedonism seemed
enshrined in this utterly unheroic ethic. This was particularly offensive to the
Romantics who were also on the rise about the same time, and led to some classic
confrontations. The Utilitarians were as much a radical minority as Romantic
poets; "in their religion intolerable atheists, in their politics bloody-minded repub-
licans," as Lord Brougham asserted in 1827, they affronted most respectable Englishmen and never had more than a small number in Parliament. One of them was
sent to the Tower in 1809.

Critics noted that utilitarian principles, followed literally, might lead to evident injustice; for example, killing an old man whose death would make his sons
and daughters very happy, or doing away with minorities. If a law discriminating
against blacks makes the white majority very happy, it should presumably be
enacted, according to Utilitarian principles. A distinction was drawn between act-
utilitarianism and rule-utilitarianism: judging according to their consequences not
separate acts, but acts complying with a rule that has the best consequences. These
and other arguments must be referred to the philosophers. It may be presumed that
Bentham, whose embalmed body in accordance with one of his wishes still sits
today in a room at University College, London, had not fully reasoned out all the
implications of his exact science of government. Students have usually concluded
that it contained too many admixtures of ideology and bias to be as pure a science
as he claimed.

In the last analysis, Bentham takes his place in that gallery of ambitious
utopists whose prescriptions failed to bridge the gap between theory and practice.
But he had far more impact than most of them. The utilitarians' influence worked
steadily down through the century, giving rise to numerous reforms, if nothing like
the major restructuring of political institutions they initially hoped for. Their
method was most important: thorough factual investigations by parliamentary
commissions. Investigate, legislate, inspect, report was the Bentham program. The
Fabian Socialists would later take it up. Benthamites had little feeling for the reality of politics, critics complained; but they pointed to evils and insisted on improvement. Utilitarianism spread far beyond its native shores to Russia, Spain, and Latin
America. It offered a simple and rational rule for reform and had the merit of
avoiding nebulous sloganizing and revolutionary rhetoric; its method seemed scientific. When Lord Byron, dreaming that Greece might still be free, became com-
mander-in-chief of the Greek rebel army in 1823, he found another Englishman
there in charge of a rival Greek resistance faction. This was Charles Stanhope, the
Earl of Harrington, and he was a Utilitarian as well as a soldier who had previously
tried to reform the British government in India.

POLITICAL ECONOMY

Closely allied to Utilitarians in the camp of British liberalism were the political economists. Political economy was not absolutely new. The term itself was evidently coined in 1615 by a French writer, Antoine de Montchrètien. Historians of economic thought find practically all the key ideas of nineteenth- and even twentieth-century economic analysis foreshadowed in one place or another during the previous several centuries. What was new was their systematic development and integration into a collective enterprise, something that was happening to the natural sciences in the nineteenth century too.

Certainly the eighteenth century had made brilliant contributions to the study of economics. The French called this new science physiocracy, and contributed a considerable body of writing on the subject, which strongly influenced *philosophe* and revolutionary thought. They were overshadowed by the famous Scotsman Adam Smith, whose *Wealth of Nations*, published in 1776, has been recognized as a landmark in human thought hardly less momentous than Newton's *Principia Mathematica* or Darwin's *Origin of Species*. It owed, in fact, a considerable debt to the former. Newton's friend John Locke had written a little on economic as well as political theory. Growing up in the shadow of Newton, the Scotsman Adam Smith as a student in the 1740s was keenly interested in physical science, and once embarked upon a history of astronomy. In *Wealth of Nations* we meet a conception of society as a collection of individuals whose rational pursuit of their own interests leads to a society in which wealth is maximized. The writer Bernard Mandeville had already presented in less rigorous form the thesis that "Private vices equal public benefits." And Smith was preceded by the great Scottish philosopher David Hume in showing that the actions of individual human agents, based on self-interest, add up to a social order governed by general laws. In such an idea one might see an analogy with Newton's separate atoms obeying a general rational law.

The Newtonian analogy was ever-present in the eighteenth-century mind. Thus, one of the intellectual leaders of the French Revolution of 1789, the Abbé Sieyes, saw the legislative process as one in which "all particular interests must be allowed to jostle and collide with one another," after which "they finally come together and fuse into a single opinion, just as in the physical universe a single and more powerful force can be seen to result from a mass of opposed ones."

A brilliant group of theorists followed up this promising lead in the nineteenth century. J. B. Say and J. C. Sismondi kept up the French contribution, but in the main it was the British who took over the subject, now designated political economy. Perhaps this was because its determined individualism suited the English temperament; perhaps because economic growth was taking place uniquely in Great Britain, forming a laboratory for the testing of economic ideas. But the Napoleonic years with their abrupt changes and painful readjustments also provided a laboratory for the testing of economic theories. It may be significant that Sismondi defected to socialism, while in Germany "romantic" economists like List and Mueller rejected the individualist, Utilitarian premises of the "classical"

British school. In Britain too, to be sure, the great Scottish writer Thomas Carlyle joined Coleridge in deploring the "dismal science"; the economists dismissed them as mere amateurs and sentimentalists.[3]

The new science flourished and became exciting. Ricardo's 1817 *Principles of Political Economy* was a high point, followed in 1821 by the translation of Say's *Treatise*. Popularizations appeared such as that of Mrs. Marcet (1816), a talented woman who turned from explaining chemistry to economics, and Harriet Martineau's stories in the later 1820s illustrating the ideas of the new economic science. It was the fashion of the hour; it became "high fashion with the blue ladies to talk political economy." This ascendancy continued, on the whole, with a growing number of incisive contributions by Thomas Malthus, Nassau Senior, J. R. McCulloch, the Mills father and son. In 1856 a distinguished member of Parliament remarked that "Political Economy is not exactly the law of the land, but it is the ground of that law." Leaders of government sought the advice of the economists— as they still do—and parliamentary committees turned to them for guidance. As the historian of economic thought Eric Roll observes, "The corpus of classical theory had become an accepted part of the mental equipment of those classes of society from whom political leaders and administrators were drawn."

What advice did this powerful oracle give out? The economists were not by any means in complete agreement. They have always had heated debates, the discipline being characterized by gurus as proud as they are keen-minded. In the "classical" period from about 1810 to 1845 it is possible to identify a left wing and a right, led, respectively, by James Mill and J. R. McCulloch. Malthus and Ricardo engaged in a memorable debate about effective demand, to which John Maynard Keynes returned a century later to judge Malthus right, though it had always been thought otherwise. Ricardo, the Dutch Jew who made a fortune on the stock market before retiring at the age of twenty-five to devote himself to purely theoretical problems, has often been considered the greatest of all economists, or next perhaps after his master, Adam Smith. The ambivalence of the message may be illustrated by Ricardo. Though often associated with the most brutally pessimistic of those who spoke of an "iron law" keeping wages close to the sustenance level ("the natural price of labour is that price which is necessary to enable the labourers, one with another, to subsist and perpetuate their race, without either increase or diminution"), his work led to a kind of socialism and he was best known for denouncing the landlords as virtually the enemy of society.

Ricardo evidently believed less than Adam Smith that there is natural harmony in economic affairs, assured by a providential "unseen hand." He saw the landlord and the factory owner as natural foes. Rents raise the price of food, which forces wages up, which causes profits in manufacturing to fall. It was also difficult on Ricardo's terms to avoid the conclusion, which many of the socialists were

---

[3]John Stuart Mill, in his discriminating and appreciative essay on Carlyle, said that "in political economy he writes like an arrant driveler, and it would have been well for his reputation had he never meddled with the subject." In return, Coleridge regarded political economy as "solemn humbug."

quick to draw, that the wage worker is at war with the employer, since the latter must keep wages low in order to keep profits high. The long struggle in British politics over repeal of the Corn Laws, or protective quotas on grain, during which liberal manufacturers like John Bright attacked Tory landlords as parasites, sprang in good part from Ricardo's theory about rents. Owenite socialists took their inspiration from his labor theory of value, and Karl Marx built a system on it.

Yet of course the main message, especially in the popular versions of political economy, was that of individualism and free enterprise, delivered from the heavy hand of government. Competition and the profit incentive operate to secure the most efficient production and most equitable distribution of wealth. "The whole art of government," Smith and the Physiocrats had thought, "lies in the liberty of men and things." His successors may have moralized less, but they continued to assume that the free competitive system is the best and that state intervention seldom serves a useful purpose; it is either harmful or redundant. Political economy based itself on an assumption of human selfishness or self-interest. Smith had posited the "economic man," seeking his own advantage. That everyone wishes to obtain additional wealth, as efficiently as possible, Smith's successors took as their starting point. A directed economy, they noted, must burden itself with an expensive bureaucratic system, whereas the undirected one is largely self-running.

Even if the major political economists never dreamed of eliminating all government—they assumed a strong infrastructure, and in fact paradoxically the state grew along with private enterprise in the nineteenth century—they preached the doctrine of free trade. "Mercantilist" regulations of it via protective tariffs and chartered monopolies were rapidly consigned to the dark ages of economic ignorance. (One of the great early victories, engineered by Ricardo, freed the currency from government management to allow the money supply to be decided by the market in gold.) Say's law of the market posited automatic adjustment in a free market between production and consumption. The wage fund theory asserted the futility of "artificial" attempts, such as by trade unions, to alter the sum available for wages. In one of Mrs. Martineau's little tales, a strike takes place and some wage increases are granted, but then the owner informs the workers that some of them must be fired. If some workers get more than their share, others will get less. If the total sum of wages were increased, the manufacturer would lose business to others and everybody would lose their jobs.

In another of her stories, it is explained how public expenditure on the poor raises tax rates, which discourages capital and thus intensifies unemployment. By this time the Reverend Thomas Malthus had deeply affected many with his famed tract on population, arguing that population always tends to increase up to the limit of sustenance, thus ensuring perpetual poverty unless something really heroic is done to break the gloomy cycle. The "hard line" Poor Law of 1834, written by the economists, aimed at deterring rather than relieving poverty by making welfare relief both hard to get and unpleasant.

The view that the poor would not work unless forced to by the threat of starvation had been widespread in the eighteenth century. That "The poor have nothing to stir them to labour but their wants, which it is wisdom to relieve but folly to cure," the view of Arthur Young, was shared by Bernard Mandeville, Daniel Defoe, Turgot the physiocrat, and most other eighteenth-century writers on the problem of poverty. In general, to the *philosophes* equality meant equality before the law, not equality of condition, "an impossible chimera." Anatole France parodied equal submission to the laws as the equal right of rich and poor to sleep in the streets, or (Blake) one law for the lion and the lamb. The *Encyclopedia* article "Mendiant" says the more deserving poor (including children) should be set to work in workhouses, the others exported to the colonies. The prestigious teachings of political economy now lent support to this belief.

James Mill observed that capital tends to increase less rapidly than population, and the growth of capital cannot be forced. The classical economists would have listened with bewilderment or perhaps amusement to recent debates about how to go about "creating economic growth" by the activities of various government agencies. Their world was strictly bounded by the limitations of nature; they saw the law of diminishing returns (each successive application of more capital yields decreasing gains in productivity) and increasing population as probable barriers to any great improvement in the overall lot of the human race. They permitted themselves only an occasional hint of a brighter future. This habitual pessimism of "the dismal science" stands in sharp contrast to the excitement of sustained economic growth that was then going on, perhaps for the first time in human history, in Great Britain from about 1780 on. This was a triumph of hard work and austerity. Classical political economy appealed to the Puritan spirit of the industrious small manufacturers and entrepreneurs who were climbing from poverty to riches in the favorable climate of England during and soon after the Napoleonic wars.

Their slogan was self-help. The creed which Carlyle thought a monstrous "gospel of Mammon" seemed to them the way to progress. It was the presence and power of this industrial middle class more than any other factor that was responsible for the success of Britain as it assumed the leadership of the industrialization process. They had energy and hope, the system of competitive capitalism provided them with incentive, the credo of political economy lent a scientific sanction to their efforts.

Of course, the economists did not wish to be known as the ideological apologists for a single class or viewpoint; they declared that they were creating a neutral science, which anyone could use or ignore at their peril. And indeed they began the development of an imposing body of thought that continued down the century and continues, still amid many debates and disagreements, but with an authority that derives from its obviously high intellectual quality. To this body of thought others than the British contributed; French, German, Austrian theorists joined in what became an international scientific community, similar to others that were developing in the nineteenth century.

The British economists were cordially disliked as well as much admired in their time, and excited a vigorous countermovement. Socialism took its point of departure from the economic inequalitarianism as well as the economic individualism of their teachings. Bentham, who had supported political and legal equality, accepted economic inequality as their result. There must be equality in that each is entitled to the just fruits of his or her own labor. But since people have unequal talents and energies, this will mean unequal rewards. Compelling people to share the fruits of their labor with others, the only practical way of attaining economic equality, not only violates justice but by destroying incentive will prove disastrous to the economy. Coleridge reached the same conclusion, an example of agreement between the leaders of rival schools of social thought. One must choose between civil and economic equality, one cannot have both; as students of ethics would put it, the problem is personal versus distributive justice. Bentham admitted that on other grounds equal distribution of wealth was desirable as contributing to the greatest happiness of the greatest number. The principle of diminishing utility, he pointed out, means that the addition of a unit of wealth to one who already has a good deal of it brings less pleasure than it does to one with less of it. Thus was posed the dilemma: in the name of social justice and economic efficiency, one sanctioned inequality and hence unhappiness.

Into the making of British middle-class liberalism, expressed in the Manchester School headed by John Bright and Richard Cobden, went some other ingredients, in addition to the intellectual systems of utilitarianism and political economy. Bright was a Quaker; Manchester was a provincial town growing into a great city. The rising capitalists of the Midlands were typically nonconformist in religion, "new men" from outside the old aristocratic establishment. As Dissenters they had fought discrimination; Bright said he had to be a liberal because of the persecutions his people had endured. Scripture played as much part in the Manchester School as economic theory. The Bright-Cobden group went into the great crusade against the Corn Laws, symbol of a hated landed aristocracy, with Bible phrases on their lips. Tennyson ridiculed Bright as "This broad-brimm'd hawker of holy things," but the charge of hypocrisy will not really stick against Bright. Self-interest was there along with political economy, but so was a Puritan conscience. A part of the liberal creed was a hatred of militarism and war that led Bright to stand out courageously against the Crimean War of 1854–56. Religion and economics joined to create an antiwar ideology: free trade would do away with war, the liberals believed, bringing the nations together in a single economic community, as the peaceful competition of trade replaced the aristocratic game of honor and war.

Thus there were several strains in early modern liberalism. They were not always in exact agreement, as we noted in the case of utilitarian and natural-law views about the source of individual rights. But they came together on a negative conception of the state, a defense of the individual against government, a belief in private property as the foundation of society.

The liberal position was to come under attack from critics who saw it as extending benefits only to a minority of the people. Socialism, Harold Laski wrote, was based on "the realization that the liberal ideal secured to the middle class its full share of privilege, while it left the proletariat in its chains." With allowance for rhetorical embellishment, this statement came close to expressing the paradox that did exist—namely, that equality under the law, equality of opportunity, might mean an inequality of condition. Liberty—the liberty of all citizens to prosper or fail in accordance with their energies, abilities, and luck, the law keeping the rules of the game the same for all and the state refusing to intervene to protect the weaker or less fortunate—meant inequality and even injustice. It meant that those who succeeded had both the protection of the law and the accolades of society, while those who failed, for whatever reason, might expect to hear only that most ancient of cries, *vae victis.*

SOCIALISM

Socialism came on the scene about the same time as conservatism and liberalism. The word "socialism" does not seem to have come into use until the 1830s, but the idea itself was forming earlier; "associationalism" was a term used in the 1820s. In 1822 Charles Fourier, son of a Besançon merchant and a retired civil servant, published his *Traité de l'association,* and about the same time the eccentric Count Saint-Simon was sending forth a spate of writing that supported his claim to be the first important socialist. Neither Fourier or Saint-Simon was a modest man. Each claimed to be the modern Newton, and predictably they quarreled jealously with each other. Meanwhile in Britain a successful capitalist, Robert Owen, was popularizing his plan for a more social organization of industry; thousands came to New Lanark to inspect it.

Premonitions of socialism may be found in the Enlightenment, though far weaker than the dominant strain of individualism among the *philosophes.* Rousseau sometimes called private property "sacred," but in one notable passage, which shocked Voltaire, he located the root of all subsequent evil in the initial act of usurpation when somebody said "This is mine" and got away with it. The happier stage that preceded "civilization" with its greed and corruption had been one of primitive communism. Friedrich Engels once remarked that Rousseau's *Essay on the Origin of Inequality* contained all the seeds of Marxism. Rousseau's concept of the General Will—the will of society as a whole, superior to the sum of individual wills—was a source of statism. His *Social Contract* taught that all rights are derived from society; private property exists not as an absolute right, but as a convenience permitted by society. If Rousseau was an influence on some socialists, they were not the kind who stressed greater productivity and wealth, for he thought the good life was one of Spartan simplicity. The socialist element in Rousseau, and more explicitly in the rather obscure writer Morelly, who has been called "the only consistent communist among the eighteenth-century thinkers," was an echo of the mythic Golden Age, embodied in Christianity as the prelapsarian Garden of Eden. In transferring original sin to the invention of private property, Rousseau was not so far from primitive Christianity, which some radical Protestant sects revived during the Reformation. The historian of socialism J. H. Noyes called the Shakers and Rappites, religious communitarian sects, "the real pioneers of modern socialism."

"Gracchus" Babeuf and his rather pathetic Conspiracy of the Equals in the latter days of the French Revolution (1795) has been mentioned. "Nature has given every man an equal right to the enjoyment of all goods," Babeuf argued, advocating a "distributive socialism." Taking from the rich and giving to the poor, the Robin Hood principle, may seem simpleminded, but even today it still seems to have considerable electioneering appeal. The influence of the Equals carried on into the nineteenth century, joining a profusion of schemes and plans. The eagerness with which socialist ideas were produced in this period reflects the general feeling that some new plan of social reorganization was desperately needed, and the discontent with a liberalism that seemed to mean inequality and exploitation under another name.

In seeming to support a principle of universal selfishness, political economy outraged the morally sensitive. "There is a coldness in their principles and opinions that I hate," William Cobbett wrote. Others found it lacking in orderliness, "a mere congeries of possessors and pursuers" as the great twentieth-century economist John Maynard Keynes once called the capitalist "system." Surely the human intellect could devise something worthier than this selfish scramble. The telling reply of the liberals was that the free competitive system governs itself by laws of the market which operate automatically, and basically reflect the wishes of the people, while any planned economic order requires some self-appointed elite making arbitrary decisions about what to produce and how to distribute it. But the fact of ongoing poverty and lower-class misery lent urgency to the search for a better system.

France gave birth to most of the socialist doctrines. When in 1842 young Friedrich Engels, a German then living in industrial England, became interested in socialism, an interest he was soon to communicate to his friend Karl Marx, he began to study the French social thinkers and identified no fewer than eight important ones. Marx came to Paris in 1843 to meet as many of these French socialists as he could. Among them the disciples of Fourier and Saint-Simon were prominent, joined by more recent prophets such as P. J. Proudhon and Etienne Cabet.

George Orwell once remarked that the socialists, who claimed to speak for the working class, in fact all came from the upper class, and Claude Henri de Rouvroy, Comte de Saint-Simon (1760–1825) seemed to begin this tradition. He was a French aristocrat who traced his ancestry back to Charlemagne. He fought in the American Revolution and narrowly escaped the guillotine during the French Revolution before making a fortune in financial speculation. Then, like the manufacturer Robert Owen, he poured all his fortune into publicizing his schemes for a new moral and social world, dying in dire poverty. Between 1802 and 1825 he produced a stream of writings and left behind a cult. A remarkable group of these "apostles" formed a community in Paris in the early 1830s, before dispersing to carry the message into the world; one of them ended up engineering the Suez Canal.

Saint-Simon's vision of socialism was marked by order and organization, efficiency and elite rule; a governing class of social engineers would plan and run society on rational principles as one great workshop. His new religion, a "new Christianity," also was to be presided over by a priestly elite. In calling for "captains of industry" to rescue society from leaderless drift and the gospel of mammon, Thomas Carlyle betrayed the influence of Saint-Simon, a powerful one in its day. Saint-Simon's was probably the most influential socialist voice before Marx, who himself was deeply indebted to the French sage. The Marxist rulers of Soviet Russia later enshrined Saint-Simon as a founding father of communism. It may be noted that Saint-Simon's socialism was neither democratic nor proletarian, though he is credited with coining the latter term as a description of the modern industrial working class. Its stress was on the planning and engineering side; a new economic system should substitute rational order for chaos and in so doing abolish poverty through increased production and more equal distribution.

Hardly less renowned than the French technocrat was Robert Owen, to whom a kindly employer introduced Rousseau, Godwin, and other Enlightenment thinkers when Owen was a child. One of thirteen children, he started work at the age of nine and went into business for himself at eighteen, in the burgeoning cotton textile industry. After buying the mills at New Lanark, Scotland, Owen set to work reforming the ignorant, degraded mill hands (largely children); he reduced the long working hours, improved housing, banned alcohol, established schools, and set up communal stores where goods were sold at fair prices. He was the benevolent dictator of a model community to which visitors came from all over the world. Owen's fame as a model employer was such that when he visited the United States in 1829 he was invited to address a joint session of Congress. He was at this time a respectable example of enlightened capitalism, but he soon embarked upon much more daring schemes for the total reformation of society. He attempted to found a highly unorthodox Rational Religion, which may be compared with Saint-Simon's New Christianity. But most of Owen's enormous energy went towards efforts to plant other socialist communities modeled after New Lanark. Though the community at New Harmony, Indiana (which Owen bought from the religious Rappites), was the best known of these, there were numerous others of varying sizes in the United States and the British Isles. They invariably failed, but attracted thousands of eager experimenters enchanted by the idea of helping to found what Owen called a New Moral World, to be marked by the spirit of community rather than selfishness. In England Owen at one time had a tremendous following; "In the peak years 1839–41," writes the historian of his movement J. F. C. Harrison, "two and a half million tracts were distributed; 1,450 lectures delivered in a year, Sunday lectures attended by up to 50,000 weekly."

The Owenite communities, like the later Fourierist ones, seemed, alas, to prove not the workability of socialism, but rather the validity of the liberal-utilitarian claim that people are moved primarily by self-interest. The Owenites adopted a simple form of Ricardian socialism in which they attempted to devise a medium of exchange based on labor power, to escape capitalistic exploitation of the worker. They tried to abolish the family, that bastion of private interest, in favor of some form of communal living arrangements—a feature which, along with religious unorthodoxy, generally shocked and alienated the neighboring populace. In this respect the followers of Charles Fourier, who also went in for experimental communities (of which Brook Farm in New England was the most celebrated) were even more daring, at least in their attitude toward sexual morality. A bachelor himself, Fourier saw in the monogamous family the root institution of bourgeois selfishness. In his utopia there would be instant divorce, total promiscuity, complete sexual "emancipation." There is some anticipation of Freud in Fourier's "passional attractions." More than Owen or Saint-Simon, he was a psychologist who tried to base his social system on a proper combination of human passions as well as interests. His blueprint for the ideal community was more exact than Owen's. Science, speaking through Fourier, had determined the organization of the communities down to the last detail.

This was utopian socialism. The fad for socialist communities took on fresh life under Fourier's influence, and then that of Etienne Cabet. Harriet Martineau had written that the principle of cooperation "will never rest till it has been made a matter of experiment." Experiment seemed to tell against it, and yet Fourierist ideas spread all over the world. Traces have been found as far afield as Scandinavia, China, and Latin America. In Russia, between 1845 and 1849, Petreshevsky spread the ideas of "Sharlia Fure" by connecting them to the Russian peasant village, the *mir*, with its medieval communal practices. Via eastern Europe the present-day Israeli *kibbutz* is said to owe something to Fourier.

Cabet, author of the 1839 utopian romance *Voyage to Icaria*, was a "communist" in the sense of vesting total ownership and absolute power in the community; Karl Marx probably learned this term from Cabet. The Icarians joined the Owenites and Fourierists in establishing communities in the New World (Illinois, Iowa, Texas), one of which survived until 1898, though in general the utopian ideal failed in practice. The aggressively capitalistic atmosphere of the United States was hardly a propitious environment for these dreamers. They were nonviolent and nonrevolutionary, hoping to spread socialism or communism by the force of example. There was an insurrectionary tradition, stemming from the French Revolution, carried on in the 1830s by such as Blanqui in France; it was a different one.

In the 1830s other prophetic voices swelled the chorus of opposition to a dog-eat-dog social ethic. The most popular French political tract of that decade was probably the *Paroles d'un croyant* by La Mennais, or as he now called himself (the change had a democratic significance), Lamennais. Earlier a prominent reactionary, he now became an equally enthusiastic social democrat. The "words of a believer" came from a priest whose desire to democratize the Roman Church found little sympathy in the Vatican and got him expelled. The Breton priest felt "a tremendous revolution going on at the heart of human society," destined to produce a "new world." He denounced wage slavery and castigated the rulers of society for neglecting their responsibilities to society. His British counterpart was Thomas Carlyle, whose electrifying prose called attention to "the social question" in an enduring classic, *Past and Present*. This was the decade of Victor Hugo, Lamartine, George Sand, and Balzac in France, powerful novelists vividly describing society in a genre that has been called "social romanticism." These popular writers contributed to the sense of some apocalyptic event about to happen. When it came in 1848, the revolution exposed the vagueness of the socialist position.

Thus there were various kinds of socialism. Agreeing in their desire for some sort of social control over private property, the socialists differed in the degree of control they would exercise, in its manner, and in its institutionalization. They were much better at theorizing on paper than carrying out plans in practice, and their experimental efforts proved almost uniformly disastrous. For this reason they were not much of a threat to the established order. Yet they were a colorful crew whose ideas proved endlessly fascinating to a large supply of people uncomfortable with the status quo, which seemed hopelessly at odds with an ideal world. Romanticized intellectuals increasingly complained that action is not the sister of the dream (Dostoyevsky). Trying to square the philistine world with the visions of romanticism, Florestan with Eusebius, the great composer Robert Schumann became a schizophrenic.

With the aid of German philosophy and hard-headed British economics, Karl Marx would try to rescue socialism from its "utopian" false start. He always acknowledged a debt to the pioneer socialists for having created the idea of socialism, and reproached them only for being naive about how to achieve it and make it work.

NATIONALISM

Nationalism was an -ism that could unite all three of the sometimes bitterly divisive ideologies of left, right, and center. In one sense nationalism was conservative, stressing tradition, the spirit of community, the authority of the state. In another it was liberal-democratic, for it rested on the equality of all citizens, their equal rights to share in the national welfare and receive the protection of its laws. It could also be socialist, as nothing illustrates better than some of the leading political personalities of this era. To liberate oppressed peoples supposedly crying for their freedom from foreign rule went along with liberating oppressed classes.

In 1821, after a sixteen-year-old law student, the son of a Genoese doctor named Mazzini watched refugees fleeing through Genoa from an insurrection brutally suppressed by the Austrian army, he began a remarkable career as revolutionary that was to span almost a half century. Giuseppe Mazzini was hostile to liberalism because it was too negative and selfish; he affirmed the value of both democracy and "association," under the umbrella of nationalism. The people should stand unselfishly together in a folk community. Mazzini's socialism was a function of that selfless devotion to the whole national community which the religion of popular nationalism was supposed to inspire. Marx's class warfare was anathema to Mazzini, whose watchwords were harmony and cooperation.

Nationalism as discussed by the German philosophers (Fichte is the prime example) produced its own mystique which assigned to national peoples a special mission in God's plan for the progressive development of the human race. According to the Romantic nationalists, the nation is an organic growth which flowers in history and expresses the deepest potentialities of a people. The free individual realizes himself through this membership in an expanding group consciousness. As

Mazzini explained, "Nationality is the role assigned by God to each people in the work of humanity; the mission and the task which it ought to fulfill on earth so that the divine purpose may be attained in the world." Thus conceived, nationalism was not opposed to either individual fulfillment or internationalism.

The eventual goal of a universal brotherhood of man will come after each nation has been liberated and has flowered culturally. Persons must first find membership in their own national community. "He who wants humanity wants a fatherland." Just as individual people are fulfilled in finding a community, so the nations will blend together to form collective humanity. Each has its own special part to play in the symphony of humankind.

Usually led by intellectuals but finding some measure of popular response, such movements grew up all over Europe. The Slavophiles were the hit of the 1840s in Russia. Nationalism may be found in virtually every significant German writer and thinker of the times; a galaxy ranging from serious philosophers to popular organizers shared it. In 1848, when nationalism was the key component in the political explosions, possibly the most outstanding European figure was the Hungarian nationalist leader Louis Kossuth. Polish nationalism flared up in 1830 and 1863.

But Mazzini was the master spokesman. "Eloquent, repetitive, diffuse," his prose was a prize example of rhetorical excess such as romanticism produced at its high tide. He combined this verbal art with a considerable passion for organization; when not writing or orating, he spent his time creating "associations" and fomenting conspiracies. Though it seems a poor charge to level against a man with so much social conscience, one might accuse Mazzini of a basic egoism. What mattered to him at bottom, as he frequently said, was for people to choose a heroic mission and stick to it. Mazzini had chosen to unite the Italian people, this was what gave his life meaning and excitement. It was his religion.

It may later have seemed reactionary, but for at least the first half of the nineteenth century nationalism was liberal, progressive, and democratic. It meant the rights of peoples to be free and self-determined. It was not considered to be inconsistent with internationalism, since each people plays its special part in the great symphony of nations. Concretely speaking, it meant the struggles of countries like Poland and Italy to free themselves from foreign tyranny. The smaller peoples of Europe found a cause and identity by discovering, usually for the first time, that they were nations endowed with a special destiny. The Danes, who previously had had no inkling of their separate nationhood, sought to recover the ancient Danish tongue and old Danish customs. Gothicism in Sweden represents a similar impulse. The Belgians now found it demeaning to live under a Dutch king, no matter how beneficent his rule.

The shaping of a larger community, forged from local, regional loyalties, appealed to many in this historically minded age as a step forward on humanity's road to some future utopia of world unity. "The larger the fatherland becomes, the less one loves it," Voltaire had thought. "It is impossible to love tenderly an overly large family that one scarcely knows." That is why the eighteenth century philosophers doubted that democracy could exist beyond the village level. But now it was becoming possible to think of a nation as a single family because improved transportation and communications were breaking down provincialism. The age of Mazzini was also the age of the railroad. And with the weakening of traditional local communities, and an increasing population in large cities, the need for community became attached to the nation. In Old Regime France few people would have identified themselves primarily as Frenchmen; provincial identity was more important (Bretons or Provençards or Gascons). That social order belonged to the past; the movement of history, involving technological and economic factors, was toward centralization.

In this evolution the "reading revolution" that began in the later eighteenth century played no small part, for nationally circulated journals and books could break through the boundaries of local culture. Nationalism in this period was in fact something of a literary creation—found more often among poets and philosophers than among the "people" they glorified in the abstract. (This "people" is nothing but the great soul of Mazzini, someone observed.) It was found more among the intellectuals than the masses. Later it would seep down, especially among the urban populace. The nation was always an imperfect community. Modern nations, Michael Oakeshott observed, are too artificial, too lacking in common traditions, beliefs, purposes, too nonvoluntary to be a community. Nationalism was a negative thing, defined by relation to a rival or enemy in the outer world. The nation-states seldom corresponded exactly with ethnicity. Thus even in Great Britain the Scots retained a strong sense of separateness; there was hardly such a thing as "British" nationalism. (Compare the Basques in Spain, to say nothing of those parts of eastern Europe where peoples were hopelessly intermingled.) When one has entered all these caveats, it remains true that the sentiment of nationalism has been the most powerful political force in modern Europe, which exported it to the rest of the world. Of this more later.

DEMOCRACY

If both romanticism and nationalism contained elements of democracy, the latter idea produced no ideology in this period in the way that liberalism and socialism did. It crept in rather indirectly and found few committed supporters. It was backed by no imposing body of doctrine. The legacy of thought was mainly against it. Writing at midcentury, John Stuart Mill observed that the changes made in the direction of democracy "are not the work of philosophers but of the interests and instincts of large portions of society recently grown into strength."

The Enlightenment, to begin with, was rather strongly antidemocratic, in the sense, first, of doubting the wisdom of the masses and, second, of questioning the wisdom of deciding policies by majority vote rather than reason. The great bulk of humanity was sunk in "passion and superstition," John Locke confided to his journal. Another great forerunner of the Enlightenment, Pierre Bayle, found "no counsel, no reason, no discrimination, no study or exactitude" in the common herd. The irrationality of the masses is a litany of the literate from Milton to Voltaire, who called them cattle and held they would always remain that. "The greater part of men, and still more of women [!] judge without reflecting and speak without thinking," the great iconoclast remarked. Voltaire doubted that the multitude should even be educated. (It was a later Voltairean who observed that attempting to instruct the masses was like building a huge fire under an empty pot!)

William Godwin in his well-known *Political Justice* (1793) referred indignantly to "that intolerable insult upon all reason and justice," the deciding of truth by the counting up of numbers, adding that truth "cannot be made more true by the number of its votaries." If we are as confident as the Enlightenment thinkers were that Reason exists, then it is absurd to suggest arriving at decisions by any other method. The test of truth cannot be popularity. Two plus two does not equal five (except in George Orwell's 1984 nightmare State) though an army be found to affirm it. If, as T. C. Hall once wrote in discussing the Puritans, "the sovereignty of God does not wait upon a majority vote," neither does the sovereignty of reason. *Vox populi*, Coleridge remarked, must be tried "by the prescript of reason and God's will." Social reformers of the doctrinaire variety held similarly based views; Robert Owen, from whom Karl Marx learned his socialism, thought government by a democratically elected parliament about the most absurd notion conceivable, likely to be as inefficient as it was turbulent. The prominent French socialist-anarchist Proudhon pronounced universal suffrage "the materialism of the Republic."

Though Rousseau has been called a source of democratic sentiment, and in some sense undeniably was, his kind of democracy (a term he did not use) was far different from the kind we are likely to think of today. If we could restore the purity of precivilized existence, Rousseau thought (and of course he knew we couldn't), we would live in a small community democratic in the sense that everyone is a part of the consensual group. Rousseau was not alone among eighteenth-century political writers in thinking democracy feasible, if at all, only in a small community. Representation, the election of delegates to represent individuals' views, seemed to them not democratic at all, as of course it isn't if we are thinking of a pure democracy.

The kind of Jacobin democracy practiced by Robespierre and the Terror during the French Revolution assumed that the General Will, far from being something one got by counting votes, was a mystic entity the dictator might embody and express. This "totalitarian" democracy, as it has been called, tended further to discredit democracy. When Robespierrian democracy came crashing down in July 1794, reaction set in and "democracy," the only kind identified during the revolution, came badly out of the whole experience. When the rural neighbors of the young poets Coleridge and Wordsworth wanted to express their disapproval of these strange urban intellectuals, they could think of no worse epithet to call them than "democrats."

Political economists as well as socialists, any who thought they knew the right answer *a priori*, were not likely to welcome democracy in the sense of leaving matters to a popular vote. They were democrats if at all only in the sense that they thought they knew what was best for the people: government for, but not by and of the people. The British historian and statesman Thomas Macaulay thought that universal suffrage would be "fatal to all the purposes for which government exists; utterly incompatible with the very existence of civilization," chiefly because only a few could understand the intricate science of political economy—"the most difficult of all the sciences," Nassau Senior thought. Ignorant voters were tempted to tamper with its often unpleasant prescriptions in the interest of some apparent short-term advantage. John Bright, leader in Britain of the fight against privilege and aristocracy, said "I do not pretend to be a democrat."

One of the greatest liberals of this liberal era between 1815 and 1848 made the contradiction between liberty and democracy the guiding theme of a memorable book. In his *Democracy in America* (1831–1835), Alexis de Tocqueville thought that mass culture blights individual creativity by imposing a "tyranny of the majority." Majority rule, whether of the mind or the body, oppresses the free individual, especially anyone not cut from the standard mold. Individual freedom requires protection against any external authority, and a democratic one can be as oppressive—more oppressive, indeed—than a monarchical one. Democracy, liberals often asserted, would lead to socialism, for the propertyless majority if given political power would certainly use it to dispossess those who held wealth. Or, employing an argument Aristotle had used, they held that democracy would lead through mob rule to a dictatorship. "Classical liberalism" presented itself as the triumph of individualism over both despotism and democracy. The nineteenth century is filled with books proclaiming the eternal opposition of democracy and liberty. (See the long history of this conflict written by the Irish Victorian W.E. H. Lecky.)

To the list of those who opposed or had severe doubts about democratic government or social leveling could be added the greatest philosopher of the age, Hegel (see the next chapter). He retained too much of the Enlightenment's belief in reason as "trained intelligence" rather than simply "a matter of people" to be a democrat. He tended to locate reason—the Absolute Spirit whose self-unfolding was the essence of history—in the ranks of the thinking portion of humanity, an intellectual elite whose wisdom stands in contrast to the hopeless ignorance and misjudgment of the toiling masses. To Hegel, democracy was a form that had become obsolete in the modern state, belonging to a bygone era of small communities. In the last year of his life the greatest thinker of his age wrote against the British Reform Bill, enacted in 1832 to extend the vote and make representation fairer.

We might add romanticism's tendency to admire the misanthropic Byronic hero who despises the crowd, or the soaring individual genius rising far above the "unforeseeing multitudes." Whatever attraction existed between some Romantics and an idealized "people" (not to be confused with any actual specimens of grubby humanity), their dominant interest hovered around the self, the unusual self. Such basic individualism clashed with democracy.

Though they might not welcome it, a host of observers noted, nevertheless, that democracy was the wave of the future; "the inexorable demand of these ages," Carlyle said; a "predestined evolution" it seemed to Count Cavour at about the same time, in 1835. Two years later Cardinal Manning reflected that "The course of Europe seems to be toward a development of national life and action by calling into political power large numbers of people." Tocqueville's great inquiry resulted from a conviction that it was vain to deplore the spread of democracy, it only remained to examine its consequences, and to learn to live with it.

In 1847 Mazzini, political orator of "social romanticism," declared that "By decree of providence, gloriously revealed in the progressive spirit of humanity, Europe is fast advancing towards democracy." If one believed in progress, as so many hopeful crusaders like Mazzini did, one was almost forced logically to accept an ultimate democracy. The best society will be one in which the good is extended to everybody. If we are to attain a perfect condition, obviously it is more perfect if all attain it—rather like the medieval ontological argument for God's existence, that there is a greater perfection in something that actually exists. As the idea of secular progress seized hold of the nineteenth-century mind and became its great principle of faith, it inevitably carried democracy with it. Writing about that emblem of Progress, the great 1851 Crystal Palace exhibition, Dr. Whewell, Master of Trinity College, Oxford, and schoolmaster to Victorian England, defined progress in the arts and sciences as their extension from the service of the few to the service of the many.

THE REVOLUTIONS OF 1848

These numerous ideas of political reform or social salvation that circulated from one end of Europe to the other (Byron and Bentham were as well known in Russia as they were in England) prepared the way for the revolutions of 1848. In the background was a messianic or apocalyptic mood. Surely Europe must come to some historical culmination. Historians like Michelet, Quinet, and the socialist Louis Blanc presented the French Revolution of 1789, heretofore unpopular, in a more favorable light; even Carlyle's famous history of the revolution saw something exciting and prophetic about its terrible turmoil. Humanity was on the march. The ideologists might disagree on its destination, but few doubted the existence of some goal.

The 1830s were a restive time; the Romantic youth who taunted the traditionalists over Victor Hugo's play *Hernani* soon aimed at bigger targets. "Bohemians" with long hair and bizarre clothing created a surrogate society in the 1830s featuring hard drugs, little magazines, unconventional morals, and much cursing of the bourgeoisie from which they sprang, much like radical youth 130 years later. In 1835, following an insurrection among the artisans of the Lyon silk industry, the French government held a "monster trial" of 164 radicals, mostly young, and convicted 121 of them. Adolphe Blanqui, who spent half his life in prison, became a revolutionary hero. Mazzini, as we have noted, had organized Young Italy and gotten expelled from Italy, then France, then Switzerland before coming to London in the late 1830s as the forerunner of many subsequent political refugees; there he became a close friend of the Carlyles and soon a well-known figure as he continued to write and conspire on behalf of Young Italy.

In England the Chartists produced an enormous petition for a democratically elected Parliament, which the House of Commons ignored. Working-class speakers such as the Irishman Feargus O'Connor frightened the men of property even more. Robert Owen in his later years turned his attention to the trade union movement, just getting under way. The popular novels of Charles Dickens and Mrs. Gaskell contained their share of social protest and social satire. It might even be said that the discovery of the urban poor belongs to this decade. Eugene Sue's *Mysteries of Paris* found an echo in the widely read reportage of Henry Mayhew in London's *Morning Chronicle*. Dickens published *Oliver Twist* in 1837.

The great debate of the 1840s in Britain turned on the issue of free trade versus protection, embodied in the struggle to repeal laws protecting agricultural products from foreign competition. The liberal manufacturers who demanded and won repeal organized the Anti-Corn Law League and carried political debate to the grassroots level. With this victory added to the 1832 reform of Parliament, Great Britain avoided revolution in 1848 and proceeded toward democracy at a more moderate pace.

New socialist voices of the 1840s in France included Pierre-Joseph Proudhon, an eloquent if inconsistent writer, himself from the artisan working class, who created a sensation by defining property as theft, and whose chief message was to abolish unearned income and unproductive property (*What Is Property?* 1841). Though Karl Marx later ridiculed Proudhon for the crudeness of his economic thought, Marx was anxious to meet him in 1843 when Proudhon was probably the best known of the radical theoreticians. An enemy of statism, Proudhon influenced the anarchist tradition; he suggested farmers' and workers' cooperatives as the answer to economic injustice. He laughed at the panacea of another prominent socialist of the 1840s, Louis Blanc, who advocated state-owned factories. To Proudhon the root of the matter was demand, not production. Leave the working class without adequate purchasing power and the state factories would stagnate quite as much as privately owned ones. Proudhon's was the classic statement of the underconsumption theory of economic depression. He supported currency reform of the sort being urged in England by "Ricardian socialists," among them the Owenites, who wished to base money on labor power in some way.

Proudhon seldom stayed long in one position, and the socialists in general were hardly a model of consistent and incisive thought. But they appealed to growing numbers discontented with the "bourgeois monarchy" of Louis Philippe, which had come into existence in 1830. Though liberal enough to permit free speech and encourage education, its constitution denied representation to all but a few and its social philosophy was *laissez-faire* liberalism, its motto "enrich yourself" the epitome of economic individualism. The king who had gained his crown

Marx's colleague and sometime rival, Pierre-Joseph Proudhon, as seen by the great French caricaturist Honoré Daumier. (National Gallery of Art, Washington, Rosenwald collection)

by a revolution was easily persuaded to give it back when violent protest spread early in 1848. What was remarkable was that Italy, Germany, and Austria responded to this signal from Paris, and for the next year and a half much of Europe seethed with discontent.

Milan rose up in March and drove out the Austrian garrison. Venice followed suit; King Charles Albert of Piedmont miraculously granted a constitution and declared war on Austria, which seemed to be falling apart. Mazzini hastened from his London exile to Paris to be received as a guest of honor by the poet Lamartine, leader of the newly proclaimed French Republic, and then, crossing the Alps on foot, received a roaring welcome in Milan. The great composer Giuseppe Verdi arrived at about the same time, and Mazzini commissioned him to write a battle hymn. This episode encapsulates the "revolution of the intellectuals," as it has been called.

From the first, however, there were seeds of dissent within the ranks of the revolutionaries; the more moderate ones feared Mazzini, who in turn mistrusted them. They wanted constitutional government, the rule of law, protection for property, but definitely not socialism or even democracy. The various states were going their own way, aiming at enlarging their own boundaries, jealous of each other. Little national consciousness yet existed. In Milan the conservative king of Piedmont deposed Mazzini's citizen's government, allowing the Austrians to move back in. The people, Mazzini lamented, had thrown the national flag not at the feet of a principle, but a wretch. In Naples King Ferdinand recovered his nerve and withdrew the constitution he had originally granted.

In Rome on November 15 a mob stormed the Capitol and assassinated the reactionary papal adviser Count Rossi, after which the pope fled from Rome in disguise! The ubiquitous Mazzini was soon heading a Roman Republic that lasted for three months before being overthrown by French troops, the newly established French republic having elected as its president (to the great disappointment of the radicals) another Bonaparte, Napoleon III, who had the support of France's conservative peasantry and Catholics. Meanwhile in Germany, where revolution also flared up only to die out in confusion, the Frankfurt Assembly labored on a long German constitution and found no one prepared to install it. The tsar of Russia, Nicholas I, younger brother of Tsar Alexander but no liberal, was more than eager to lend support to the reaction. There had been no revolution in St. Petersburg. Nor in London, despite a major Chartist rally. British opinion was largely sympathetic to the cause of Italy, thanks in good part to Mazzini, but all the British sent was sympathy.

The confusion of doctrines as well as the political ineptitude of intellectuals (though Mazzini in fact governed brilliantly in Rome) got blamed for the failure of 1848. It became known as the turning point when history failed to turn. Certainly 1848 was remarkable for the participation of poets, artists, and thinkers in politics, and for their seeming failure in this role. Lamartine was political leader of France before retiring in high disgust at the human race ("the more I see of people the more I like my dogs.") Richard Wagner was one of a revolutionary triumvirate ruling Dresden until he was forced to flee to Switzerland. The Frankfurt Assembly was filled with high-minded lawyers and professors. The experience had a devastating effect on confidence in visionaries, dreamers, and impractical men to act effectively in politics. They largely retreated, after 1848, to the ivory tower. Give me the highest one possible, cried Gustave Flaubert. Echoes of the disenchanting experience with revolutionary politics may be found in such places as Wagner's stunning operas and Baudelaire's invention of a new kind of poetry.

But like all great historic events, the 1848 revolutions left behind many permanent deposits. Universal suffrage, abruptly established in France in 1848, has never since ceased to exist in some form. A new realism resulted from the sobering experience of 1848. Romanticism went out of style, whether in the arts or in politics. Young Karl Marx, taking some part in the German '48 as a Rhineland newspaper editor, revised his views about the imminence of revolution after fleeing to London in 1849. Not for more than a decade did the socialist cause show signs of recovery. Mazzini went back to London and watched the unification of Italy take place, to his dismay, in a much less romantic way than he had envisioned. The ideologies and -isms did not die, but they were considerably transformed over the next half-century. Scientific positivism became the reigning system of thought, along with literary realism and political *Realpolitik*. The idle dreams of romanticists and the simplistic schemes of utopists seemed equally out of date.

3

Ideas of Progress: Hegel, Comte, Marx

HEGEL

G. W. F. Hegel, Kant's successor as the leading German philosopher, died in 1831 of cholera—a scourge of the times—at the age of sixty. Hegelian philosophy triumphed in academic circles all over Europe, so much so that by the end of the century, even in Great Britain and the United States (where there was some resistance to it as overly abstract and metaphysical), the leading university philosophers were largely of this school. But Hegel's thought was more broadly influential than that. Professionalism had not yet entirely taken over the realm of profound thought and deep learning. Though a university professor, Hegel was not highly specialized and not writing just for other professors. He had in fact been a *gymnasium* teacher and a private tutor before gaining the appointment at Berlin university as a result of his publications (he was a South German by birth). Hegel's influence is perhaps best known through its importance for Karl Marx, who came to Berlin as a student in 1836 and joined the group of leftwing interpreters of the master who called themselves Young Hegelians. Marx cut his teeth on Hegelianism and while much more than a disciple (he offered substantial criticisms of Hegel), his thought is hardly conceivable without the Hegelian component.

This was by no means the only example of Hegel's impact on important social or political ideas. Hegelianism in its popularized form figured almost as another ideology. Its strong elements of synthesis appealed to those baffled by the sudden changes and swirling controversies of post-French Revolutionary Europe. Belinsky, the Russian socialist, wrote that when he read Hegel he was overcome with emotion and the world took on a new meaning. History and human affairs were no longer chaotic; every event was seen to have its place in an unfolding plot. "For me there was no longer anything arbitrary or accidental in the course of history." The revelation had come from Hegel's argument that "the real is reasonable and the reasonable is real"; rightly understood, the course of human events shows a purposeful plan and is connected to the very nature of the universe.

"Historicism" of this sort was not born with Hegel. The root Western religions of Judaism and Christianity found meaning and purpose in human history. It might be said that Hegel only secularized this vision of human progress through time toward a final reunion with God. It was not characteristic of the anti-Christian Enlightenment; Voltaire, though much interested in history, found it in general a sad record of "crimes, follies, and misfortunes" without any coherent pattern, though with occasional inexplicable triumphs of reason. From Rousseau, however, had come what F. C. Lea has called "the romantic myth" of progression through history from alienation to reunion, through civilization to a higher perfection at the end of historic time. Socialists like Saint-Simon believed that a "supreme law of progress of the human spirit" determined the course of history; "men are but its instruments." The German Romantic folklorist Herder drew on the Neapolitan Giambattista Vico's hitherto obscure "New Science" to underpin a historicism that saw humanity creating its own destiny in the process of cultural development.

Hegel's inheritance was chiefly German philosophy, to be sure. The Critical Philosophy of Kant had left the world divided between subject and object, noumena and phenomena. Hegel aspired to a magnificent if obscure totalism that saw the universe as one great whole. The Absolute (a philosophical equivalent of God) is a single totality of all that is; it shows itself in and through the finite human mind developing through history. The Absolute seeks to complete itself via the evolution of this mind or spirit (*Geist*). The Absolute, Hegel explained, has three parts: pure Idea, the Absolute-in-itself, of which Logic is the science (a dialectical logic, a logic of the concrete, which Hegel offered as superior to the static formulations of traditional logic); Nature, the Absolute-for-itself, studied by philosophy of nature (the empirical sciences philosophically understood); and Spirit, the Absolute-in-and-for itself. Hegel's early *Phenomenology of the Spirit* was an attempt to show how human consciousness is linked with the outer pattern of social evolution, and how the dialectical interaction of inner and outer leads onward and upward in an endless process of change.

So the underlying ideal unity of things is nothing more or less than humanity making its own history via dialectical development—the interaction of the human mind with external circumstances. This self-realization of the Spirit in human history leads finally to, or ever more closely approaches, full self-consciousness in which the external, alienated realm of matter is progressively confronted, conquered, and absorbed into Spirit. The Hegelian dialectic is something more than the triad of thesis-antithesis-synthesis, which actually was first suggested by

Fichte, but this formula is often used to describe the process, which is the motive force of change: a condition or statement, its negation, then a restatement that contains and reconciles the two opposites, only to confront a new negation in an endless process. To Hegel, remember, this process was more than just the structure of a debate, it was the way the cosmos works. In the beginning, Being negated by Nonbeing found its synthesis in Becoming, and so the world began. It was a world in process, a dynamic not a static one; its proper logic had to be a dialectical not a static logic.

All this was bewilderingly abstract, perhaps, but Hegel did not entirely lack concreteness. The opinion of more down-to-earth historians that Hegel's history was all abstract theory is not quite correct. Hegel was a formidable polymath who lectured on science, the law, the state, politics, religion. He wanted to incorporate the solid realities of the material world into his ideal realm of spirit. Did he teach an idealism that assigned fundamental reality to a ghostly spirit? So his most famous disciple, Karl Marx, was to allege. Had not Hegel written that "History is mind clothing itself with the form of events"? Marx ridiculed Hegel for endowing metaphysical categories with physical or human existence. Marx thought Hegel had found the right method, but had the subject of the process wrong, seeing it as an abstract idea or consciousness rather than as flesh-and-blood people; he had "enveloped it in mysticism." One must begin with sentient human creatures realizing themselves in work rather than thought, engendering thought as they work.

But it is not certain that Marx correctly interpreted Hegel. Hegel seems to see the process as a struggle between spirit and matter, the former objectifying itself and then trying to recapture its alienation, a process in which humanity at least helps God or the Absolute Spirit achieve its ends. The difference between Marx and Hegel may be less than some have thought. They simply chose to stress different sides of the dialectic. The important point is that neither, unlike some of their disciples, held to a deterministic system, whether idealist or materialist; they both saw a genuine interaction between idea and matter. Lenin once remarked that "intelligent idealism is closer to intelligent materialism than is unintelligent materialism."

Hegel did not think, as some accused him of thinking, that the pattern of history can be determined by pure logic without reference to the events. We must study the actions, the empirical events, but then we must "think them through" to discover their inner logic. When we do, we do not always find a neatly logical plan to history. But we do discern larger patterns of meaning.

According to Hegel, the three main phases of history had been the Asiatic, characterized by absolute monarchy; followed by the classical Greco-Roman, marked by local freedom (the city-states); then the Germanic-European state synthesized these two as freedom in the context of a strong state. Hegel's disciple F. C. Baur applied the dialectic to New Testament studies by finding the thesis in Jewish nationalism, the antithesis in Pauline universalism, and the synthesis in the mature Christian church that emerged in the second century A.D. An eagerness to make the facts fit this framework led Baur into some serious mistakes.

Any historian who allows his thesis to run away with him is in danger. But

hypotheses are necessary. This was an era when professional, "scientific" historiography flourished, especially in Germany, and contemporaries of Hegel like
Leopold von Ranke and B. G. Niebuhr, using archival sources and carefully criticizing the documents, thought Hegel too speculative. But he aroused great interest
in history by endowing it with profound philosophical significance, and all historians probably owe their basic professional debt to Hegel. The past became not just a
pastime for antiquarians or a source of amusing or edifying stories, but an exciting
vision of human progress which, properly deciphered, tells us basic truths about
the ends of human existence.

Hegel defined his historical epochs in political terms. To Auguste Comte, the
key lay in modes of thought, while Marx located it in modes of economic production. Hegel's preoccupation with the political reflected the urgency of that problem
in the Germany of his day, disunited and seeking to find political unity. With some
justification Hegel felt that the master institution of the present age was the nation-
state. Most nineteenth-century historians believed, with the English master E. A.
Freeman, that "history is past politics." Rebellions against the narrowness of this
definition have been frequent since; but it might be defended on the grounds that
the political order has usually given epochs their distinctive stamp, from the Oriental despotisms of earliest times through the Greek city-states, the Roman Empire,
feudalism, down to the age of the territorial nation-state—and so to a federated
Europe. Politics is simply the way people organize themselves for cooperative life;
it is basic. There cannot be either effective economic production or cultural, intellectual life until the society has found a mode of government. In any case the nineteenth century was a great political age, whether in the United States of Jackson
and Lincoln, the England of Disraeli and Gladstone, or the Germany of Bismarck.

Hegel was accused of teaching that might makes right. Like all systems
declaring the universe to be rational, his seemed to require the belief that whatever
has happened is for the best; whatever is is right. The dominant theme at any particular moment in history is necessary and in the right. Whatever group represents
that theme is endowed with a mandate. "The hour strikes once for every nation,"
and some nations are "world-historical" ones destined to contribute more than others to the great design. Everything, including war, is a necessary part of the pattern.
Hegel at times declared that individuals are unconscious tools of the teleology of
history which the "cunning of reason" exploits for its own transcendent purposes.
In this metahistorical determinism, usually tied to nationalism as its means of operation, many critics discerned a dangerous invitation to imperialism and war. Certainly Hegel inspired or reinforced a large amount of nationalism of the messianic
sort. L. T. Hobhouse later accused him of causing World War I! As an example,
the Polish nationalist and Hegel disciple Count August Cieszkowski used Hegel as
well as Herder to support his vision of a great Slavic state that would adorn the
next and perhaps last stage in the evolution of humankind. Pan-Slavism, like other
nationalist myths, found congenial a thinker who seemed to teach that history has a
goal toward which all is tending, and that the vehicles of this historic progress are
"historic peoples."

If Hegel supported nationalistic causes, he looked in other directions as well. The totalist view that saw a necessary place for everything could obviously find room for all causes, provided only that they showed the necessary dynamism. Hegel's own politics were somewhat ambivalent. In some ways he was a man of the right. An ardent Bonapartist in his youth, Hegel's chief political work was a product of the reaction (*Philosophy of Right*, 1821); he preferred monarchy to democracy and opposed individualism. Hegel believed in freedom, but not in negative freedom—in just being left alone. His positive freedom was Rousseau's "forced to be free"; freedom is realization of possibilities, a point illustrated by the example of the child, whom we compel to go to school so that she can expand her possibilities of growth, though doubtless if given her way the child would prefer not to be educated. Ignorance is slavery; the savage who is "free" is really far less so than the modern individual who is bound by the rules of a state. No creature is absolutely free, but free only to realize its natural possibilities. A bird is free to fly, but not to swim. Human beings, as creatures of reason, realize freedom by developing their rational potential, and to do this may require sacrificing much liberty of action. We must live in an organized state, obey its laws, and serve the interests of the community.

But if Hegel was a conservative, or a kind of conservative liberal (nothing was more alien to his thought than arbitrary authority), many of his disciples failed to show it. While some went to the right (stressing order, discipline, national strength) and others to the center (emphasizing constitutional government and the rule of law), there were those "young Hegelians" of whom Karl Marx became the best known, who were atheists and communists. Belinsky also was a socialist or anarchist, Hegel influenced more moderate protesters against economic individualism such as the important English source of the welfare state in the 1880s, T. H. Green. When Hegel glorified the state, he used the term in a rather special way. In his system it is the dialectical synthesis of family and civil society, or the union of universal and particular in the "concrete universal." As always in the dialectic, the higher form does not abolish but rises above the earlier ones. "Civil society," meaning the economic realm of competing private interests—the world of the political economists—is necessary, but it is not enough. The state must correct its injustices and give it order. Hegel thought the state could stand above the private realm as a community, representing the whole society. It was a point on which Marx was to criticize Hegel, arguing that the state can only reflect the economic interests of a given stage of civil society; a capitalist economic order will have a capitalist state. You cannot combine a bourgeois economy with a true social state. Hegel thought you could.

Hegel did not conceive of the state as Proudhon and the anarchists did, as a leviathan standing against its subjects, a bully browbeating and intimidating people. It is more like Rousseau's General Will, the common rational spirit of the whole community made manifest. This view appealed to moderate liberals or social democrats because it allowed for the claims of the state while not ignoring those of the individual. According to Hegel, it is only as a citizen that the individual becomes wholly free and possessed of rights. This feeling for association against individualism, though with a conservative cast, made Hegel a favorite of the more moderate social reformers.

But of course what Marx found congenial in Hegelianism was the sense of constant progressive movement in history, via the revolutionary method implied by the dialectic. A moment comes when bottled-up change suddenly breaks through in an hour of rapid and drastic change. And we cannot really know what the unfolding process will bring; the owl of Minerva flies late, one of Hegel's most celebrated axioms declared—the historian never knows what will happen before it happens.

Hegel's ambivalent position between radicalism and conservatism appeared also in his view of religion, probably to his contemporaries the most urgent issue. Hegel was apparently a Christian, offering his philosophy as one compatible with and supportive of the orthodox creed. But Kjerkegaard, the Danish pastor who became the chief founder of religious existentialism, accused him of devitalizing Christianity by rationalizing it and making it abstract. So did Nietzsche. ("He who said that God is Mind took the longest step toward unbelief yet taken on earth.") Hegel's new version of scholasticism made reason and religion coincide, but the highest synthesis is philosophy. Christianity is the symbolic or mythical mode of expression suitable for minds incapable of philosophy. Christianity is done the honor of having its representations agree with Hegel's philosophy in a slightly inferior manner. If many Christians had their faith confirmed by finding that it agreed with the most advanced philosophy, others understandably resented the patronizing.

One could easily, with Marx and Feuerbach, forget about the religion, and take the philosophy alone, converting it into a purely secular and humanistic statement. The Young Hegelians showed a decided interest in biblical and religious studies. Marx began his radical career with atheism, not socialism. Close to this circle was David Strauss, whose critical biography of Jesus (1835) was one of the century's most sensational books; one of the first significant treatments of Christianity's founder as a historic, human figure, not a supernatural one. Strauss was able to argue that what really counted was not the mere facts, right or wrong, about Jesus; it was the Idea that his life expressed.

Taking the next step beyond Hegel in the progression his own ideas demanded, the post-Hegelians discovered that God was just a human invention, which now at a higher stage of mental evolution could be seen for what it was, a purely human aspiration. "Politics must become our religion," Marx's teacher Ludwig Feuerbach announced. In Italy, Hegelianism became the creed of anticlericals, who held that the state is above the church. When the Roman Catholic Church produced its list of modern heresies in the famous 1864 Syllabus of Errors, it included Hegelianism as a form of anticlerical liberalism. Actually, Hegel excluded religion from the historic sphere, regarding progress as social and political, not religious. In sharply separating private religion from public affairs, he took a traditional Lutheran position.

As a substitute religion itself, Hegelianism offered a picture of humanity on the march through the world in order to realize God's purposes, with each individual contributing a small share. Our soaring ambitions come to us from our membership in this great collective enterprise; if our limited achievements frustrate us, we can nevertheless do what our talents permit us to do confident in the knowledge that it does fit somewhere into the great plan.

Hegelianism exerted so strong an appeal because it was a complete system, an exceptionally unified total philosophy. It was the first of several in the nineteenth century. Only Comte's, Marx's, and Herbert Spencer's Darwinian synthesis competed with it, and of these Marx's owed its basic traits to Hegel. A generation confused by sudden change and a profusion of new ideas needed such integrating systems. Hegel offered an apparently satisfying unity that found a place for everything and discovered order behind the baffling façade of events. Faced with the question of whether liberals, conservatives, or socialists were right, the Hegelian could answer all of them are—each in its place and time, each a part of the ongoing dialogue leading ever forward. Confronted by revolutions and counterrevolutions, wars and political turmoil, the Hegelian could hold that all these occurrences are part of a necessary pattern. Hegel found a place for both reason and religion, which many saw locked in mortal conflict: they are just different ways of saying the same truth. This harmonizing synthesis was almost as impressive as that which Thomas Aquinas had offered at the peak of medieval civilization in the thirteenth century.

Hegel's influence extended all across Europe and influenced all kinds of people in addition to technical philosophers—a remarkable achievement.[1] His mode of thought made itself at home in the British universities, with F. H. Bradley and Bernard Bosanquet in the later nineteenth century; via T. H. Green the Hegelian view of the state became a leading source of the rebellion against *laissez-faire* individualism from the 1880s on. The Italian philosophers Benedetto Croce and Giovanni Gentile made Hegelian strains dominant in Italy. But at the end of the century there was a reaction against the rigid monism of Hegel; the American pragmatist William James thought it a stuffy house without enough air in it. Some twentieth-century positivists assailed it vigorously; in an important book, *The Open Society and Its Enemies*, the Viennese-born liberal Karl Popper attributed practically all the sins of a totalitarianized world to Hegel's baleful influence. (It seemed that Mussolini and Hitler as well as Lenin and Stalin were among his disciples.) But philosophers such as Alexander Kojève revived left-wing interest in Hegel, finding him more satisfactory than Marx.

And so Hegel remained an almost inexhaustible fountain. "All the great philosophical ideas had their origin in Hegel," exclaimed the twentieth-century existentialist, Maurice Merleau-Ponty. Certainly many existentialists went back to

---

[1] Such influence could be indirect. Hegel bowled over Mallarmé, but inspection of the great French poet's library after his death revealed that all the pages in his copy of Hegel's works were uncut. Compare the many Marxists who notoriously had never read Marx.

Hegel; Jean-Paul Sartre's vocabulary of being-in-itself and being-for-itself came from that source. It is an oddity that when the other great source of existentialism, Kierkegaard, stressed radically undetermined freedom in the human consciousness, he was reacting against what he conceived Hegel to represent.

Whatever else he meant, no one could deny that Hegel was the philosopher of movement and change, of an organic rather than a mechanistic universe, of things in process and development and evolution; not blindly or accidentally, as Darwin was soon to suggest, but purposefully, toward ever greater fulfillment.

COMTE

In Germany, a "back to Kant" movement—back to phenomenalism and away from the Hegelian metaphysical turn—played a role somewhat similar to positivism in France. It was the latter that tended to occupy the center of the intellectual stage from 1850 to at least 1880.

J. B. Bury in his classic study of the idea of progress chose Auguste Comte as his examplar of that nineteenth-century faith. Marx, who in his youth did constant battle with the ghost of Hegel and never did quite escape it, viewed the French founder of sociology as philosophically "miserable" compared to Hegel, and no doubt he was. The antimetaphysical spirit of the French Enlightenment notably inhabited Comte's "positivism," which advised sticking to the facts and avoiding futile metaphysical speculations. In French philosophy Victor Cousin produced something in the nature of Hegelianism in Restoration France, but was much more obscure. The tradition of the *philosophes* and the Ideologues was much stronger.

Comte's *Course of Positive Philosophy* appeared in six volumes between 1830 and 1842; it came into its own during the post-Romantic years after 1848, when positivism became the intellectual orthodoxy of the Second Empire period; it was closely associated with the prestige of natural science in this era of Louis Pasteur and Claude Bernard, avowed disciples of Comte. Positivism seemed a better philosophical foundation for the sciences than Hegelian idealism, and a better foundation for political order than Romantic utopias.

Aided by John Stuart Mill, who wrote a book about it, positivism spread to England. Charles Darwin encountered Comte about the same time as he received his notable influence from Malthus, in 1838, getting from the former a sense of the scientific study of life, divorced from theology—or rather, a new kind of scientific theology. A British Comtean, Professor E. S. Beesly, was a friend of Marx's and in fact chaired the first meeting of the workingmen's International in 1864. George Eliot and her husband admired and apostrophized Comte. Another British disciple was Richard Congreve, an Oxford don in the 1850s, one of whose students was the leading publicist of English positivism, the historian and essayist Frederic Harrison.

In the 1870s positivism had a vogue among Russian intellectuals, supplanting.

Hegel and preceding Marx as the favorite of those earnest seekers of light from the West. The Polish girl who as Marie Curie was destined to become the most famous woman scientist of all time in her youth in the 1880s frequented positivist circles which the tsarist police viewed with grave suspicion. In Italy, positivism reigned as the leading philosophical school in the later part of the century, its chief spokesman being Roberto Ardigo. All in all, Comte's positivism joins Bentham's utilitarianism and Hegelianism among the leading systems of the first half of the nineteenth century, an age of syntheses. If Hegel was called another Aquinas, Basil Willey applies the same term to Comte: a nineteenth-century schoolman basing his *Summa* "not on dogmatic theology, but on dogmatic science."

The same political ambivalence that we observed in Hegel may be seen in Comte, who (once the secretary of Saint-Simon) was a kind of moderate socialist, holding rather like Carlyle that economic individualism is irresponsible anarchy and a sound society places altruism above selfishness. The path of social evolution, Comte thought, is away from selfishness and toward altruism. Hostile to orthodox religion, Comte offered in its place a religion of science. Comte's Religion of Humanity offered an appealing channel for young idealism. The fearless scientist, a courageous benefactor of humankind, slays dragons in the form of superstition and error, challenging the Church and all who would trammel the inquiring mind.

At the same time, Comte was in favor in France during the regime of Napoleon III, who had overthrown the republic of 1848 and stressed authoritarian rule, though he did have some progressive programs. Disillusioned post-1848ers turned away from politics to cultivate art or science in the ivory tower. Comte disliked revolution as well as democracy, and favored a regimented and hierarchical society.[2] At the end of the century the fascist-like *Action Française* of Charles Maurras acknowledged a debt to him. John Stuart Mill, attracted to some features of positivism, pronounced Comte's social plan "the completest system of spiritual and temporal despotism which ever yet emanated from a human brain, unless possibly that of Ignatius Loyola." The French agnostic shared with the Spanish Jesuit a horror of intellectual anarchy and a belief in a hierarchy of priests; his church, however, would be directed by scientists.

According to Comte's famous "three stage" theory of human development, society passes from the theological to the metaphysical to the positive stage, based on the dominant mode of thought in each period. Comte's history was at least as speculative as Hegel's; it seems impossible to fit the facts into this scheme. For example, anthropologists no longer accept the progression within religion as postulated by Comte, from fetishism to polytheism to monotheism. Historians would have to point out, among other things, that science appeared as early as the ancient Greeks and metaphysics as late as Hegel, Comte's near contemporary. If the Comtean formula is reduced to the proposition that primitive peoples are not capa-

---

[2]Slaveholders in the South of the United States (like George Fitzhugh) made use of Comte to support their arguments for an organic, stable, and authoritarian society.

ble of modern thought, it becomes little more than a tautology. Objections may be raised to any such simplified periodization, including Marx's five economic stages and Hegel's three political ones. (Comte probably knew the great eighteenth-century Neapolitan philosopher of history, Giambattista Vico, neglected in his own time but resurrected by Herder; Vico found all civilizations to pass from the religious or theocratic through the heroic-aristocratic and then to the humane or democratic; each transition was abrupt, "a roll of thunder" ending one and inaugurating another epoch. This was, however, not a progress, apparently, but an endless cycle.) But so discriminating a critic as John Stuart Mill thought the Comtean three stages an illuminating key to the natural evolution of civilization.

Europe was now entering the positive stage and needed to reconstruct its civilization on that basis. *Positivism* Comte defined as the method of observed facts handled with the use of hypotheses but without drawing any conclusions about the substantive nature of reality. Comte agreed with Kant that science studies only phenomena. In his own words, "the human spirit, recognizing the impossibility of obtaining absolute ideas, renounces the search for origins and goals of the universe and the effort to know the innermost causes of things, in order to concentrate on discovery, by experiment combined with reason and observation, of the effective laws, that is, their unchanging relations of succession and similarity." This was not exactly new, and Ernest Renan, himself something of a disciple, reproached Comte with having said, "in bad French," what all scientists had known for two hundred years. This was not quite fair; it had really only been known clearly since Kant, and Comte revealed many of its implications. He was perhaps philosophically more acute than those Marxists and others who dogmatically assumed a materialism which Comte knew was untenable; we are not justified in saying what the essence of reality is. (Lenin would reject positivism or phenomenalism for a direct-copy theory of sense perception that is philosophically naive but permits a full-blooded materialism. Marxists seemingly felt there was something wishy-washy about positivism that was inappropriate to revolutionaries.)

By the same token Comte felt that atheism is not justified, either; we cannot have certain knowledge of either the existence or non-existence of God. Science is descriptive only; we should not even speak of "causes," only of "observable sequences." In his *Course of Positive Philosophy* Comte undertook to arrange the sciences in logical order. From the most abstract, mathematics, we proceed through astronomy, physics, chemistry, biology, and finally to the most concrete, which he called sociology. Of this last and greatest science Comte, of course, regarded himself as the discoverer. It included what we should now call psychology, economics, politics, history, and originally ethics; the human studies have grown a bit since Comte. Comte recognized that each of the sciences has to have its own methods; you cannot "reduce" social science to biological, or biological to mathematical. Sociologists who convert social phenomena into statistics are ignoring the warning of the founder of their science, that this sort of procedure often "disguises, under an imposing verbiage, an inanity of conceptions."

Later (after falling in love!) Comte put ethics and religion at the top, above even sociology, and gave the world the Religion of Humanity. A great sociologist of the next generation, Max Weber, treated with devastating irony those scientists who found new religions, and this obviously strikes home against Comte. He seems to have hopelessly confused his multiple roles as social scientist, social reformer, and prophet. Still, their apparent unity gave his system its popular appeal. His British disciple Frederic Harrison boasted that "Positivism is at once a scheme of Education, a form of Religion, a school of Philosophy, and a phase of Socialism." Could it be all of these things, effectively?

As a school of philosophy positivism managed to survive for a while by becoming more sophisticated (see further in Chapter 7 for logical positivism). Sociology survived as a discipline, but its scope is now much narrower than Comte conceived. The Religion of Humanity fits incongruously with both; but for a time it showed a surprising vitality. The intellectual world was eager for a new faith. There were Comtean churches as far afield as Brazil. (Positivism flourished surprisingly in Latin America.) Positivist societies were formed in England and France for the adoration of great people of the past, which Comte suggested as a substitute for the Christian saints. This was in George Eliot's mind when she expressed a poetic wish that she might "join the choir invisible"

Of those immortal dead who live again
In minds made better by their presence.

Comte worked all this out rather comically with scientific precision; there would be exactly 81 saints, from Archimedes through Newton, for people to adore.

This is rather like Thomas Carlyle's recommendation for a modern source of values, hero worship. And in fact their mutual indebtedness to Saint-Simon suggests an odd connection between the French rationalist and the Scottish thunderer. The student of Victorian England Walter E. Houghton noted a considerable vogue for hero worship as a substitute religion, "inheriting the functions once fulfilled by a living church"; at a popular level, Samuel Smiles' inspirational lives of successful capitalists and engineers supply an example. But the Positivist Church fell far short of its founder's expectations. Positivism served chiefly as a rallying point for the "rationalists," the militantly antireligious.

Extremely fashionable in Second Empire France, post-Comtean positivism was represented by such luminaries as Claude Bernard the psychologist, Emil Littré the lexicographer, Hippolyte Taine the historian, and Renan, one of the most brilliant and versatile French "men of letters" of the century. This group tended to reject Comte's dabbling in religion as an eccentricity and accepted only his scientific method. But they tended to make science a substitute religion. Most of them finally came to see that science itself cannot give us values, ideals, goals. Insofar as we have these, they must come from outside the empirical investigation of nature. The faith that they held, that science was a worthy vocation because it benefitted the human race, could hardly be proved by scientific methods.

Renan, a passionate seeker, looked long for a religion he could square with his scientific outlook. Like Matthew Arnold, his British contemporary and perhaps kindred spirit, Renan felt the need for religious experience, keenly regretting the ebbing of the sea of faith. He rejected Christianity on the grounds of evidence; his *Life of Jesus*, one of the best known popularizations of the "higher criticism" of the Bible, shocked orthodox Christians all over Europe by its critical handling of the supernatural claims. He rejected Hegelianism as too metaphysical. He came close to making a religion of art, as Baudelaire and Flaubert were doing. But a "religion of science" remained his lifelong quest and he failed to find it; he ended his life a skeptic.

He came closest to finding his faith in a positivist version of Hegelianism, a theme of progress running through history that gives evidence of God. "Science alone can lead the soul to God," Renan insisted near the end of his life. "My religion is still the religion of reason, i.e. of science." To multitudes of the less reflective, science in the guise of new technologies provided the most compelling reason for belief in progress; it stood behind that rise in living standards which by the 1880s had become startlingly evident to the average person. To some like Renan who understood the need for values, science could also supply these. But by the end of the century this view was less often found among the intellectuals. A rebellion against scientific materialism as the enemy of the spirit began among poets as well as the religious. That mood belongs, however, to a later era.

The later nineteenth century was a time of great scientific achievement. Western civilization was becoming positivistic in that metaphysical and religious modes were not congenial to it. Everyday life was so surrounded with the technological and scientific, so conditioned to mechanical models and explanations, that conscious mental life for the majority ran naturally in grooves that can be called "positivist," averse to any truths not immediately verifiable by experiment or demonstration. "What grows on the world is a certain matter-of-factness," the Victorian literary banker Walter Bagehot mused. He blamed it on business as well as science. "The world today is without mystery," the French writer Berthelot complained in 1885.

A recent philosopher, Kai Nielsen, remarks that the whole thrust of intellectual history since the Enlightenment "has made it second nature" to "accept the authority of science rather than that of religion or philosophy in fixing belief concerning what is and might become the case." "The steady demystification of the world" has been an irresistible trend. Metaphysics, the belief that pure philosophical reflection can work out the fundamental categories and constituents of the world, independent of and prior to experimental investigation, has become as obsolete as faith healing. Comte's positivism was taken up by the Logical Positivists of the next two generations, in a more sophisticated form but true to this bias against metaphysics.

It is true that in violent opposition to this "rationalization" of life, a marginal group of artists and poets proclaimed their defiance of scientific reason; all the more evidence of its strength. So Comte, though far from inventing this feature or being the only thinker to express it, identified himself with a basic trait of modern Western civilization.

MARX

Fitting this pattern in many ways was Karl Marx, who along with other Young Hegelians turned their master's thought away from idealism and toward materialism or phenomenalism. Hegel, they thought, in assigning the primary role to mind had inverted the proper order of things, putting the cart before the horse, making the son beget the father. He should be "set right side up." Reality is actually material, ideas are only a projection of physical being. In human history we begin with real, sentient human beings, not a ghostly idea. Ludwig Feuerbach, whose widely read *Essence of Christianity* George Eliot translated into English, argued that God was a human invention, a projection of human ideals. Another of the group at Berlin in the late 1830s, Marx's teacher Bruno Bauer, actually was the source of a quotation frequently attributed to Marx, that religion is the opiate of the people. Marx joined Bauer and Feurbach in creating the Archives of Atheism, a venture that cost the young scholar his chance at a university appointment.

The son of a Rhineland lawyer and public servant, Karl was an apostate from a long line of Jewish rabbis. Though his father was an admirer of Enlightenment deism, the young Marx got his militant antireligious ideas mainly from the Romantic poets and his own fiery temperament—or perhaps from those ancient Greek materialists about whom he wrote his doctoral dissertation. Initially he was attracted to Byronism and wrote some Romantic verses, not very successfully. The Romantic deep structure of Marx's thought may be seen in its themes of rebellion, Promethean defiance of the gods, sympathy for underdog, and hatred of the philistine businessman. Turning to philosophy after transferring from Bonn to Berlin university, Marx joined the Hegelian circle. He took up socialism under the influence of Moses Hess, the "communist rabbi," a fellow Young Hegelian, and then Friedrich Engels, son of a Rhineland cotton textile capitalist with a branch in Manchester, England. The young Engels, destined to be Marx's lifelong friend and supporter, published a book in 1844 on *The Condition of the Working Class in England*, based on parliamentary investigations into shocking factory conditions as well as on his own Manchester experiences.

It was another of the young Hegelians, the Pole Ciezskowski, who coined the aphorism that the next step after Hegel was to change the world, not merely understand it. Marx was a born activist, as well as a brilliant pamphleteer. He got a job as writer for and then editor of a Cologne newspaper, only to lose it when he defied the censorship. From his native Rhineland he looked westward to Paris, home of socialist ideas, as he also continued to conduct a critique of Hegel. In an article published in the only issue of a French-German magazine Marx tried to establish in Paris in 1843–44, the proletariat (a term used by the pioneer socialist Saint-Simon, with whom Marx was probably acquainted early) makes its appearance as the destined emancipator of the human race, expressing the next movement of the dialectic of history.

Marx struggled with Hegel through the vast and formless "Paris manuscripts" of 1844, long unknown and only published in the twentieth century; and with Feuerbach, Max Stirner, and others of his fellow Hegelians in books with

Karl Marx. (Washington, DC,
Library of Congress)

Engels (*The German Ideology* and *The Holy Family*), one of which was obscurely
published and the other consigned "to the criticism of the mice." Marx changed
Hegel's "alienation" from spirit externalizing itself in nature (and then reclaiming
the alienation), to something that happened to workers under capitalism, as excessive division of labor plus ownership by another of what they produce deprive
them of the satisfaction of creative labor. The early Marx put more stress on this
alienation concept than he did later. (He owed this idea in good part to another
member of the *Doktorclub*, Moses Hess.) Under capitalism, the workers are alienated not only from the products of their labor, but from themselves and from other
workers. This was a psychological critique of the mechanized and rationalized
society, operating with a "cash nexus" (a term Marx borrowed from Carlyle) rather
than human bonds.

Meanwhile, after marrying his childhood sweetheart, the daughter of a local
baron, Marx began a family while disappointing his mother and mother-in-law
with his choice of careers. The young radical managed to get himself thrown out of
both Germany and France by 1845. He moved to Belgium, where he satisfied his
urge to become actively involved by joining the Communist League. Marx thought
this group of artisans, led by Wilhelm Weitling, too moralistic and theoretically
naive; "a more scientific understanding" than their "unrealistic humanism" was
needed. They tended to think him an intellectual snob, but in 1847 he and Engels
wrote for them the famous "Communist Manifesto," an accessible if simplified
statement of their views, long treasured by disciples whom Marx's more esoteric
exercises mystified. History as class struggle, the sharpening of the conflict today
as capitalism reaches a crisis, criticism of other varieties of socialism as not

informed by enough theoretical understanding and knowledge of history—these themes accompanied a rousing call to proletarian revolution: "Let the ruling classes tremble at a communistic revolution."

In 1848, revolutions did break out all over Europe, though they were scarcely communistic. The thirty-year-old Marx returned to edit the newspaper in Cologne where he had worked five years earlier. The ruling classes may have trembled, but as we have already noted, they quickly regained their courage and profited from confusion and contradictions among the revolutionaries to regain control. By the middle of 1849 Karl and Jenny, who had another child on the way, pawned the family jewels as they fled to London, refuge of many other continental rebels in that year of reaction. They would live there the rest of their lives.

That life at first was hard, and three of Marx's six (legitimate) children (he had another one by the maid) died in infancy, should not obscure the fact that Marx usually lived as well as an improvident and generous nature allowed, for Engels and other friends provided subsidies that later became almost lavish. He had, however, to a considerable degree been marginalized. A foreign refugee in a London almost swarming with them, he would never be a professor or an established "man of letters." He did earn something by writing European reports for Horace Greeley's New York newspaper *The Tribune*. Some have found it piquant that the great anticapitalist was kept going by a capitalist press baron (though Greeley had an interest in socialism). Altogether between 1851 and 1862 his paper published 487 articles from Marx, and although Engels actually wrote more than a fourth of these, the output is impressive and many of these articles, written in a vigorous and interesting style, found their way into *Das Kapital*.

This latter book was the vast project on which Marx expended the bulk of his intellectual energy, laying the British Museum library under heavy contribution, and pausing only to dash off an occasional pamphlet or *pièce d'occasion*. He had lost his illusions about an immediate social revolution; he was forced to admit that capitalism had greater staying power than he had thought. Marx's first year in London saw preparations for the great Crystal Palace Exhibition of 1851, displaying products of the new technology, a landmark in the development of capitalist self-confidence. The hungry forties gave way almost miraculously to the stable and prosperous fifties. In France, a man Marx detested and scorned, Napoleon III, assumed control and presided over nearly two decades of political stability and economic progress. Left-wing causes were in sad decline; the Communist League to which Marx had belonged ceased to exist. Dropping out of political activism for more than a decade, he resigned himself to a long and careful study of the laws of economic development.

In 1857–58 he outlined an ambitious program for his inquiries into political economy. The spectacular success of Charles Darwin's *Origin of Species* in 1859 encouraged him in his ambition to become the founder of "the science of society," doing for humanity what Darwin had done for the lower forms of life. Like Darwin's, his would be an evolutionary scheme based on the realities of social existence. It would show how the struggle to wrest a living from nature had passed through several stages marked by changing social relations, reflecting material conditions.

But the first volume of *Das Kapital* did not come from the press until 1867. He had allowed himself again to be distracted by *praxis*, returning to the political arena in the 1860s as the atmosphere changed again. The decade of Garibaldi, Lincoln, Bismarck, the liberation of American slaves and Russian serfs, the unification of Germany and Italy, was hardly a quiet one. It was actually a revolution in Poland (soon suppressed) that precipitated the founding of the International Working Men's Association, with which Marx was long to be associated. In October 1863, he had attended a great rally of Londoners on behalf of the North in the American Civil War. (His rival socialist theoretician Proudhon opted for the South, as did Carlyle.) Garibaldi, the liberator of Italy, was about to have an enormous London reception, said to be the largest turnout for a foreign visitor in the history of the city. These were exciting times.

Marx labored for years as secretary of the First International, devoting endless hours of drudgery to it until its demise in 1874, victim chiefly of the Franco-Prussian War. It is doubtful if this attempt to realize his dream of a union of theory and practice fared any better than the first one twenty years before. It certainly delayed completion of his magnum opus. But the first volume of *Capital* did appear in 1867, giving Marx a measure of recognition, as did his brilliant pamphlet on the Paris Commune of 1871. Projected to cover a vast terrain of historical, social, and economic analysis, *Das Kapital* was never finished; three other volumes came out at various times after his death, edited from miscellaneous fragments by friends and disciples. Within a few years volume 1 was translated into Russian and then French, while a second German edition was issued, even though it had taken four years to sell the first edition of 1,000 copies. Aimed at showing the industrial workers, the modern "proletariat," their path to self-liberation, it was not pitched at the level of working-class understanding; one worker to whom Marx sent a copy said he felt like he had been handed an elephant. (In his preface Marx indicated rather scornfully that he was not writing for nincompoops.) Though at times deeply eloquent, the book was too abstruse and technical for all but a handful of experts.[3]

There was no English translation until 1887, four years after Marx's death. The rich mid-Victorian harvest of literature and ideas was at its peak. Not many in an England whose serious readers were absorbed in John Stuart Mill, John Ruskin, and Matthew Arnold paid heed to the often indigestible tome of a German refugee. Its socialist audience was intensely committed, but small and culturally isolated. And even among socialists Marx had many rivals. In time, the weight of *Das Kapital* was to overcome most of them.

The sources of Marx's thought, of which he made an original synthesis, were

---

[3]Vilfredo Pareto once remarked that people found in Marx and Engels "a happy combination of passion and reason, calculated to satisfy both the vulgar and the learned."

of course Hegel, the early socialists, and the political economists. His friend Moses Hess wrote a book about the European trinity of Germany, France, and Britain, each with its special aptitude in ideas, which he hoped might be brought together, and Marx seems to have striven to carry out this synthesis. He had divided his time as well as his residence between the three lands, as he studied German philosophy, French social ideas, and British economic theory. He criticized all three, yet made use of what he kept after the critique. Hegel was wrong in his idealism, right in the dialectical vision and totalist approach. Owen and Saint-Simon created the worthy socialist ideal but did not understand how to make it a reality. Adam Smith and his successors had contributed many insights to the world of actual economic relations but failed to see that economic laws were dynamic, not static. But Marx, unlike many of his disciples, was not a person who read just one book. He was deeply versed in the Western literary tradition, from Homer to Balzac; Shakespeare was "the Bible of our house," his daughter Eleanor reported.

Marx was more complex than his disciples, who made a dogmatic system out of him. Reading some of these, Marx once burst out "Thank God I am not a Marxist!" "He laughs at the fools who parrot his proletarian catechism," an acquaintance testified. Engels, a vigorous but less subtle writer, was the source of some of the simplifications; even Engels, however, lost patience late in his life with the "economic determinist" Marxists. Yet there must have been something in the master to invite this vulgarization. As many testified, Marx could be arrogant—"provoking and intolerable," the German-American statesman Carl Schurz declared; "vain, treacherous, and morose," Marx's rival revolutionary Mikhail Bakunin alleged. Nor could he easily repudiate popularizations of his thought, for it was his central conviction that thought must meet and influence social action, being modified in return by this practical experience. His mission was not to produce just another philosophical concoction smelling of the lamp or the seminar room, like Hegel's; it was to help change the world. Marx never resolved the contradiction between theory and practice, but he tried.

It was this dramatic, indeed romantic aura that provided Marxism with its mystique. Its simplest substructure was a kind of secular version of ancient messianic Christianity or Judaism. The exploited workers must break the mental as well as physical chains of their slavery, make a great revolution in which the last become first, and then usher in an ideal society marking the end of human history. From what they understood or misunderstood of Marx, however, the disciples of this religion added significant details. Semi-popular Marxism held that Marx had scientifically proved that capitalism digs its own grave, growing ever more monopolistic and exploitative, and becoming "a fetter on production" as well as a source of misery to the masses. In the end it collapses of its own weight. Marxists believed that history is a record of class struggle, class being defined by role in the processes of economic production; and that as the end of capitalism approaches, the modern proletariat or working class becomes ever more conscious of itself and its historic role. Social class is "the lever of social change," in one of Marx's many striking metaphors. Historical epochs are defined by the dominance of an economic class, first the slaveholders, then the feudal lords, now the capitalistic bourgeoisie.[4]

The Marxist claim that the mode of economic production largely determines social, political, and cultural forms meant, as a practical matter, that existing capitalist (bourgeois) values are not eternal, but only a smokescreen for class rule. Their allegedly timeless economic laws are really valid only for their own economic system. This subverting of established creeds became an attractive feature of Marxism to disgruntled intellectuals. Freud later joined Marx as a "master of deceit," one who shows us that proclaimed ideals conceal some secret, probably unworthy or shameful motive. W. H. Auden, recalling his undergraduate Marxism of the 1930s, said that "We were interested in Marx in the same way we were interested in Freud, as a technique of unmasking middle class ideologies...." As Marx had explained, "All the struggles within the State, the struggle between democracy, aristocracy, and monarchy, the struggle for the voting franchise, etc., are nothing but the illusory forms in which the real struggles of different classes are carried out one among another." What a manifesto for historians interested in revising the whole interpretation of the past! Not until feminism was anything like it seen.

This last is significant because Marx's appeal was mainly to the intellectuals. Singularly enough, it is doubtful if Marx ever had much relevance for the working class for whom he claimed to speak—or, indeed, that his fascinating analyses of history and society had much basis in reality. Thus, a recent carefully researched study of Victorian England[5] finds that "class" was quite insignificant as a factor in the lives of people. Class was a creation of Marx's imagination, a logical deduction, not an observed reality. He never actually wrote much about it in any detail; it functioned as a talisman of theoretical analysis. How many classes there are is a question to which Marx in different places gave varying answers; and at times the word "bourgeois" seems more like a principle of human nature than a social reality.[6] (Landowners are now capitalists, it seems.) Can a class exist without anyone knowing it, as Marx implies? ("Class consciousness" is something the workers are exhorted to have but evidently all too often lack.)

And indeed it could be said of Marx's whole imposing edifice of thought, which so many moderns adopted as a means of ordering a confusing world, that, even more perhaps than Hegel's, it was a "dance of categories," a model made up of abstractions. Anyone who mastered Marxian theory was in possession of a uni-

---

[4]To Marx the capitalist was the employer of labor and producer of commodities, the "manufacturer." Other economists have distinguished between the capitalist as one who supplies money for investment, and the entrepreneur who borrows this capital, rents land, and hires labor in order to create a production facility.

[5]Patrick Joyce, *Visions of the People: Industrial England and the Question of Class, 1840–1914* (1991).

[6]For a discussion, see P. N. Furbank, "Marx's Unwritten Chapter," in his *Unholy Pleasure: or the Idea of Social Class* (1985).

fying system of thought offering explanations for almost everything. He had a picture of the whole world. But facts or events in the real world had to be decoded, sometimes painfully, to make them fit into this structure of ideas. Their real meaning then became some symbol which had its place in the Marxist framework. Almost nothing, to the Marxist, was as it seemed. Marxism had the advantage of being largely unrefutable on its own premises. And any who questioned the premises could of course be dismissed as prisoners of bourgeois ideology, possessing a "false consciousness" that forced them to see as through a glass darkly.

Marx's chief assertions of fact were doubtful. "In proportion as capital accumulates, the lot of the labourer...must grow worse." In his major book Marx argued that the rate of profit under capitalism must in the long run steadily decline, driving the capitalists to seek an ever greater exploitation of their workers, trying to extract from them a "surplus value" the rate of which is threatened by increasing mechanization. (Human labor power, not machine power, is the only source of profit, Marx thought, relying on the labor theory of value he inherited from Smith and Ricardo.) In later editions of *Capital* Marx backed away somewhat from the idea that wages must fall toward the level of bare subsistence and stressed spiritual rather than economic impoverishment, or relative deprivation: workers may be better off but their employers are even more so. He spoke of the moral degradation of workers through being made appendages to the machine. But Marxism's essential claim remained that under capitalism workers become more and more miserable, the chief reason why "capitalism is doomed." Yet in fact the working class did not grow worse off under capitalism. The evidence indicates a rising standard of life through most of the century, even as population greatly increased—an almost miraculous success story. Though it might be a moral failure, capitalism was a material success.

Marx's attitude toward capitalism was in fact marked by a curious ambivalence that was responsible for his disciples going in two different directions. Running through Marx's writings about the existing social order of "capitalism" was a vacillation between the view that a contemptible system will soon be overthrown by a violent revolution of the oppressed, and the view that a progressive, productive system will peacefully die when it has given all that it has to give. At times Marx's idea of progress compelled him to recognize that capitalism is after all the next-to-last rung on the ladder of social ascent, far better than its preceding stage and containing many good things, which will survive under socialism. The dialectical negation does not cancel out what it reacts against, but preserves it in a higher form. Socialism emerges from the womb of capitalism, which therefore cannot have been altogether bad. Capitalism accomplished many progressive things, creating an advanced technology, breaking down parochial units to form the national and even international economy, and accustoming people to a rational, materialistic outlook. The socialist future will not destroy these things, but improve them. Even if unintentionally, the bourgeoisie raised the consciousness of workers and brought into existence potentially democratic political institutions. Capitalism had an indispensable historical role to play, and true socialism does not make its appearance on stage until this part of the play is over. A premature revolution such as Romantic insurrectionists called for would be futile or counterproductive. Only in the fullness of time will the new order be born, and its birth may be almost painless.

Marx always disparaged the Romantic revolutionaries who failed to study society scientifically. It is grotesque that Third World dictators and terrorists should invoke his authority as they have done in recent times. In Russia around 1890 Marxism was a relatively conservative alternative to the now discredited terrorists, and Leninism was heresy within Marxist circles there before 1917. In Germany the Social Democratic party, created in Marx's image if not entirely with his approval, devoted itself to peaceful educational work, abjuring violent revolution. The Social Democrats thought the revolution would come in due time via the ballot. It can be argued that Marx always believed in democracy, and that Lenin gravely misconstrued him in using the phrase "dictatorship of the proletariat" to mean arbitrary rule by a revolutionary elite.

On the other hand, Marx had a revolutionary temperament and never entirely abandoned a certain crusty hatred of the status quo. He retained to the end traces of his rebellious personality, rejoicing in the next to last year of his life that today's children "have before them the most revolutionary period with which men were ever confronted." He obviously relished the notoriety he had gained as a fierce and dangerous scourge of the bourgeoisie. He told the Russian revolutionaries that it might be possible for them to bypass capitalism and leap directly to socialism, using their peasant-village tradition—a rather startling heresy coming from Marx himself. Whenever conditions seemed to revive the radical cause, as in the 1860s for a time, or the 1870s in Russia, he eagerly welcomed this as a hopeful sign. But after the Paris Commune of 1871 disappointed him, Marx in his last years, beset by illness and flagging energies, seems to have lost hope in revolution again—except perhaps in a place as little suitable for his theories as Russia. He probably always looked back wistfully to the days of 1848 and the soaring hopes of his youth for a total Hegelian transformation.

It is vain to demand total consistency from Marx, something no great thinker ever exhibits. Would he have accepted the attack on his economics that appeared too late in his life for him to absorb? Marx based his analysis of capitalism on the labor theory of value. Stanley Jevons' *Theory of Political Economy*, which came out only four years after volume 1 of *Das Kapital*, was the first shot in the "marginal utility" school's war on the Ricardo-Mill tradition; by the end of the century it had gained the support of almost all professional economists. This "neo-classical" revolution, to which Alfred Marshall and the Continental economists Carl Menger and M. E. L. Walras also contributed, undermined the foundations of Marx's theory of value.

No metaphysical "value" consisting of labor power inheres in a commodity; value is just exchange value, and this is determined by how much people desire a certain commodity and how painful it is to produce it: a psychological equation more than a social one. The final increment, the marginal one, determines exchange value. Commodities exchange at ratios such that their marginal utilities are equal. Under the aegis of marginalism, economics became heavily mathematicized; the determination of prices under conditions of perfect competition became a study hardly matched for subtlety since Isaac Newton. And indeed Walras claimed that "economics is a mathematical science on a par with mechanics and astronomy." As such, it divorced itself from history as well as political morality.

This story was a part of the larger one of the professionalization of every study in the later nineteenth century. Marx was relegated to the status of an amateur, much as he had once laughed at the naiveté of Owen and Saint-Simon. Rhetorical, manipulative, using ideas as weapons for his passionately desired goals, Marx was at odds with scientific method despite his claim to have founded the "science of society." The universities largely ignored him, though Antonio Labriola lectured at the University of Rome in the 1890s on the materialist conception of history, and there were a few Marxist professors in Russia, the "legal Marxists." The great Neapolitan philosopher Benedetto Croce showed an interest in Marx, but his 1900 *Historical Materialism and the Economics of Karl Marx* rejected dogmatic Marxism. Marx retained his following in the European socialist movement, which made a comeback after 1890; Marx was its chief prophet. Of this, more later.

Meanwhile the sweeping scope of his synthesis, and its position as an alternative to the existing culture, made him attractive to intellectuals. This was a source of strength as well as weakness. One seemingly had to swallow Marxism as a whole, excluding any other approach. The theory of class cultures relegated all existing "bourgeois" thought to the status of "ideology" or "false consciousness," and claimed a monopoly of truth for the proletarian thought (Marxism) that replaced it. It was evidently all or nothing. Marxism was not just an idea that entered the house of knowledge to mingle with all the other guests; it occupied a wholly different building, and one had to choose which to live in.

In Great Britain, where he had lived the last half of his life, Marx's legacy was slight. His followers included his own brilliant daughter, Eleanor, a tragic suicide in her forties, and the eccentric H. M. Hyndman, accustomed to addressing the workers wearing full dress suit and top hat. Such major figures as William Morris and George Bernard Shaw appreciated Marx but were scarcely Marxists. British socialism owed more to John Ruskin than to Marx, and was in fact quite eclectic in the sources it drew on. In any case it was not much of a force before 1919; the Labour party born in 1900 was at first strictly trade unionist in its goals, while after 1885 welfare state ideas penetrated the Liberal party with the aid of Hegelian social thought.

This lively end-of-the-century scene will be reported on in a later chapter. Marxism, needless to say, had a powerful role to play in Russia as well as in Germany, with two different versions of it reflecting that ambivalence we have noted between evolution and revolution. French radical thought found some place for Marx, one of whose daughters married a prominent French socialist, but paid tribute also to his rival Proudhon as well as to others; the French left was notoriously much divided.

THE IDEA OF PROGRESS

Marx's was another version of the idea of progress. It was profoundly historicist, seeing human society as an evolution through successive stages, characterized in Marx's case by types of economic technology and ownership of "the means of production." The contradictions in each of these past epochs caused their downfall and planted the seeds of the next stage, from the slaveowning societies of ancient times through medieval "feudalism" and so to "capitalism." (Marx was never quite sure when this transition occurred, dating the origins of capitalism all the way from the eleventh to the seventeenth century.) Like Hegel's and Comte's, Marx's broad scheme of historical stages was vastly oversimplified yet stimulating.

It was more than a model for historical research; it was also a eschatological religion. The journey across time leads toward a final glorious climax. With the proletarian revolution comes at last the classless society, when distorting ideologies no longer muddy the images of truth, justice, and beauty, while material abundance for all accompanies the advent of true freedom. "Communism is the answer to the riddle of history"; Marx's own utopianism cannot be denied.

Marx's economic theory was not basic in his thought; Hegelianism was. In his most impressive book Marx tried to nail down the economic details, but his larger view of capitalism's inevitable transition to socialism was rooted in Hegelian historicism. The dialectic of change decreed the movement of humanity through different stages en route to some final destination. At bottom this was a kind of cosmic, ultimately mystical process. Marx tried to transform this idealistic or religious vision into concrete, material terms, but it seems evident that the model came to him in advance of his empirical investigations.

To believe that "history is on our side" is a powerful stimulus to any movement, and all the nineteenth-century ideologies, whether liberal, socialist, or nationalist, made use of it. Liberals like Benjamin Constant and John Bright, the Saint-Simonian socialists as well as the Marxists, preachers of national mission like the Russian Slavophiles, all claimed that successive ages of the past pointed toward their valued cause as the denouement of a long unfolding story.

In this age of the developing historical profession, historians less obviously partisan than Marx shaped their accounts around the making of the nation, which had grown over the centuries from small seeds into the great and powerful France or England or Germany. Such, for example, was Guizot's history of France, written by the scholar-statesman who was a leading figure of the July Monarchy period. A French rival was the more eloquent Romanticist Jules Michelet. Michelet's English counterpart was Thomas Babington Macaulay, essayist, poet, member of Parliament, and author of a history of England that became a best-seller in the 1850s; it told the story of the rise of liberty and defeat of royal tyranny with much use of rhetoric and scant effort to disguise its Whig bias. The historian Nikolai Karamzin probably had more to do with the growth of Russian national pride than any other writer—an urgent matter for a people groping to find identity.

Midcentury witnessed a proliferation of such histories, sometimes literary classics, usually with a concealed propaganda intent, all designed to uncover the teleology of the past. The 1850s was, of course, the decade of Charles Darwin and evolution, consideration of which we postpone to the next chapter. A number of writers attempted to apply Darwin's idea of natural selection to the history of human societies or institutions. His influence helped establish the feeling that all things are in process of change, and they must adapt or perish. It was not so clear that this was straight-line progress, yet it seemed that, however clumsily, higher forms did evolve. Darwin's friend Herbert Spencer produced an incredibly popular evolutionary ideology that saw a steady advance onward and upward. Romanticism had stimulated imaginative interest in the past; Burkeans saw it as the school of political wisdom, German philosophers as the unfolding of truth. The Carlyles and Macaulays and Michelets lent their powerful pens to serious history's popularization. There were others, such as the positivist Henry T. Buckle, whose multivolume history of England lined the shelves of many a Victorian library.

Meanwhile history as a profession was coming of age, with the Germans leading the way. The gathering of materials in the great national archives, libraries, and museums of Europe made possible their careful criticism and use as source materials in university seminars. The feeling grew that the study of the past was at last passing from the realm of conjecture and opinion to the status of a genuine science. "History was born from the womb of the archives," Michelet and Acton declared. The German professors, armed with scientific methods of criticism, did not doubt that their patient inquiries would someday reveal an important truth about humanity. "History is more than a mere record of the course of events and far more than a record of political events," said Lord Acton, the British liberal Catholic historian and activist. "It is a philosophy of origins and causes, the profound, spiritual origins that determine events."

Though sometimes accused of producing arid accounts of political minutiae, the German academics saw the larger patterns in history. Leopold von Ranke, the exemplar of the German scientific school, a historian of prodigious energy, wrote massive studies of the medieval, Reformation, and early modern periods, by today's standards impossibly broad in his subjects; at the age of ninety he thought he was ready to write his "universal history!"

Ranke was no historian of "progress" in the cruder sense, since he thought each epoch was "equidistant from eternity" and must be understood on its own terms. But he was sure that all these pieces would fit together somehow to form one great harmonious pattern. History follows a path traced for it by the hand of God, as the French socialist historian Louis Blanc said. Of the popular American historian George Bancroft, Russell Nye wrote that "He saw the American past as a great play, written by God and man together, moving toward a triumphant last act in which the promises of the Christian tradition and the Age of Reason came true."

In this era New England scholars like Bancroft tended to go to Germany for their advanced education. Lord Acton, together with his friend the Munich professor I. Döllinger, formulated a historical theology of Catholicism according to which the Christian truth gradually revealed itself in history through the mediation of the Church. This is an interesting example of the impact of history in this age, even though the Vatican balked at the implication that the past Church did not have the full truth. A student of Victorian love literature marks the way in which affairs of the heart became "events," things that happened in time, things that grew and developed; in every sphere of life, the framework of understanding changed from a static to a dynamic one.

All were at bottom convinced that the past was more than a repository of interesting or edifying tales. The great nineteenth-century theories posited an ascent from lower to higher, in one way or another. Bitter critic of capitalist society that he was, Marx was as optimistic as any Victorian in the long run. One more turn of the wheel of history and the goal would be reached.

A significant exception to this optimism was a French theorist of history and society who was almost exactly Marx's contemporary (1816–1881) and equally destined to great future influence. This was the Comte de Gobineau, called the father of racism. His magnum opus, *Essay on the Inequality of the Human Races*, appeared in four fat volumes during the 1850s, decade of historicism. A disenchanted scion of the French nobility, Gobineau attributed the sad decline of culture to the mixing of races. He thought there were pure races to which correspond certain qualities of character. Of these the Aryan, purest strain of the white race, he claimed to be the most creative. But in creating civilization it sowed the seeds of destruction by intermingling peoples.

The work of an amateur, almost valueless as science even in its own day, Gobineau's *Essay* possessed an imaginative appeal in its sweeping synthesis and provocative thesis. He eventually became a Wagnerian and passed the racial hypothesis on to Houston Stewart Chamberlain, an Englishman who directly influenced Adolf Hitler's National Socialism in post-1919 Germany. Actually Gobineau thought the German nation as mongrelized as any. He saw the path of history as a steady decline—a direction and a destiny, to be sure, only the opposite of the progressivists. The evolutionary sociologist Vacher de Lapouge, like Gobineau, saw degeneration more than progress; natural selection seems to result in the triumph of the worst, as the ignoble materialism and cheap culture of modern man indicates.

Oswald Spengler's *Decline of the West* took up this theme in the twentieth century, when it became more fashionable. It was an anomaly in the mid-nineteenth century. Toward the end of the century, talk about degeneration became somewhat more common. The disillusion of 1848 brought some doubts. What Georges Sorel later called "the illusions of progress" had already appeared in the Russian emigré Alexander Herzen's bitter reflections on the illusion:

> If progress is the end, for whom are we working? Who is this Moloch who, as the toilers approach him, instead of rewarding them, only recedes, and, as a consolation to the exhausted, doomed multitudes, can give back only the mocking answer that after their death all will be beautiful on earth?

But it remained largely for a later, post-World War I generation to reject the myth of progress thoroughly and indignantly. Emil Brunner called it "an axiomatic belief which needed no proof nor could be disproved.... a pseudo-religious creed, which to negate was a kind of blasphemy." As late as 1908 the British statesman-philosopher Lord Balfour was sure that "there are no symptoms either of pause or regression in the onward movement which for more than a millennium has been characteristic of Western civilization."

What seems remarkable now is that these beliefs in progress assumed not only a steady onward and upward movement, but a movement of the entire society. We would be inclined to say today that some things doubtless "progress," if we define the term in certain ways: technology becomes more efficient, scientific knowledge accumulates, communication speeds up. But other phases of life remain the same or deteriorate. Only a rash person would claim that art,[7] morality, or political wisdom have advanced. (A French poet at the time expressed doubts about whether the art of lovemaking had shown much progress over the centuries.) Our ability to integrate all these spheres has plainly gone downhill. Some of the technical advances create possible retrogression in other areas, causing, for example, mental stress and moral breakdown. The nineteenth-century optimists supposed that society is a unit that progresses as a whole, so that every part of it is engaged in constant improvement.

The temper of the first half of the nineteenth century, filled as it was with the excitement of meaningful change for perhaps the first time in human history, if also with the first painful decades of industrial growth and urbanization, was generally optimistic. In his book about Charles Dickens, G. K. Chesterton wrote that "the first period [of the nineteenth century] was full of evil things, but it was full of hope," while the reverse was true of the last part. If more doubts appeared after 1860, the reason must be sought in Darwinism and the decline of traditional religion.

Among the always eager Russian intelligentsia, made up of "repentant nobles," the *raznochintzny* of the 1860s resembled the equivalent of realists and positivists in being anti-Romantic, scientific, materialist, reductionist. They popularized the term "nihilism," meaning by it scorn for ancestral values, questioning of all authority. They are portrayed in *Fathers and Sons*. They constituted the second generation of Russian revolutionaries, and in Chernyshevsky produced the most committed and fanatical of all revolutionists, one who exerted a powerful influence on Lenin. The older gentry liberals seemed to them soft and ineffectual. Scientism, transferred to the explosive Russian scene, turned out to mean a tough-minded and violent social attitude.

The philosopher for this disenchanted post-1848 anti-romanticism was the

---

[7]Looking at the paintings by primitive people in a Spanish cave, a twentieth-century historian, Jaquetta Hawkes, was moved to exclaim that art is immemorial. Certainly twentieth-century artists returned to the primitive and found inspiration there.

brilliant misanthrope Arthur Schopenhauer. In his youth Schopenhauer had ventured to challenge the great Hegel but failed to gain any adherents; in his later years he became fashionable. Schopenhauer asserted that the universe is not Hegel's Reason but is Will, a blind amoral striving felt in human beings as wanting, desire, appetite. From this tyranny of the will, chaining us pointlessly to the wheel of life, Schopenhauer saw only art, especially music, as an antidote, other than that extinction of the will to which Oriental philosophy aspired as the ultimate wisdom. (Knowledge of the Hindu classics was just beginning to seep into Europe in the first part of the nineteenth century.)

In seeing the world as an arena of power without meaning or purpose and in seeing reason as a tool of instinct, Schopenhauer's vision, though expressed in quite different terms, resembled Charles Darwin's. It is to Darwin that we must turn next.

4

Darwin
and the Victorian Crisis
of Faith

DARWIN AND DARWINISM

No one did more than Charles Darwin to implant the characteristically modern idea that change is the law of life. If we did not include him in Chapter 3's discussion of ideas of progress, this is because a great many people received no notion of progress in the comforting sense from Darwin's message. Change, yes, but not necessarily improvement—or, if so, at an unacceptable price. Not only was Darwin's nature a scene of brutal struggle for survival, "red in tooth and claw," but the struggle was perhaps aimless; certainly it was untidy. Accident determined the outcome, dead ends adorned the tree of life. This apart from the immense shock given to traditional religious belief, threatening not only the biblical doctrine of creation but, more important, the uniqueness of the human soul. Winwood Reade told the story of a Victorian youth who brooded on the Book of Doubt (Malthus's *Essay on Population*) and the Book of Despair (Darwin's *Origin of Species*), then took his own life. It was hardly a unique case. Darwinian despair seemed at times to flow over the whole Victorian scene, spoiling its dreams of happiness.

A long and intense discussion followed publication of what was by pretty general agreement the century's most important book. (A poll of distinguished people taken at the end of the century to determine the ten most influential books of the century showed that *Origin of Species* was the only title on every list.) The debate might lead to such consoling conclusions as: (a) The struggle for survival is not always brutal; it takes place silently, and rewards efficiency and care more than ruthlessness or brute strength. The "strongest" did not necessarily survive, but the best adapted; the dinosaurs perished, the cockroach lived on. (b) If the Darwinian universe is full of suffering and death, no serious thinker had ever supposed life to be a perpetual bed of roses. Realism compels attention to the less pleasant aspects of life, but answers exist to the "problem of evil," an old question which Darwin essentially revived. (Eighteenth-century thinkers had worried about the Lisbon earthquake.) Perhaps evil was necessary to good; no omelet without broken eggs. (c) The purpose of all the struggle and pain must remain hidden from mere mortals, but one was free with Tennyson to "faintly trust the larger hope" that there is an ultimately beneficent purpose.

These and other points emerged during the long debate about Darwinism. They did not in the end dispose of an uncomfortable feeling that the world would never again be quite as happy a place. But neither did they do away with a generally optimistic Victorian outlook. Certainly the mental landscape was forever changed; everybody realized this, in one of history's most memorable intellectual revolutions. Change had taken over from stability. Darwin had made his presence known.

Like other great scientific discoverers, he was not the sole and miraculous producer of the new truth, but rather the beneficiary of a long process to which many had contributed. When in 1858 he decided to publish a shortened version of the manuscript he had been working on for more than twenty years, he did so because he knew that at least one other naturalist was about to present essentially the same thesis. A few scholars still think that Darwin and life were unfair to Alfred R. Wallace; additional candidates for the almost-but-not-quite role have found advocates. But the majority verdict has been that Darwin, like Einstein and Freud (to name two others who had rivals for an epochal theory that became attached to their names), deserved the credit. Not for the theory of evolution itself—that had been around for at least half a century—but for giving it a plausible explanation and making it convincing.

Evolution had a history. There were some suggestions of it among the ancient Greeks, such as Anaximander and Empedocles. Apart from that, evolution as a speculative idea had aroused interest for a century prior to 1858. The eighteenth century showed a great interest in biology. Buffon was one of the best-known writers of the French Enlightenment, and other distinguished *philosophes*, including Diderot and Maupertuis, speculated on the origins of life and the nature of species. Among others Charles Darwin's own grandfather, Erasmus Darwin, a doctor, in 1798 poetically supposed that original "forms minute"

> as successive generations bloom
> New powers acquire and larger limbs assume;
> Whence countless groups of vegetation spring
> And breathing realms of fin, and feet, and wing.

The eccentric Scottish jurist Lord Monboddo, an amateur anthropologist and prolific writer, held similar beliefs, and even claimed that some of his friends had tails. Of the widely ridiculed Monboddo Dr. Johnson remarked: "Other people have strange notions but they conceal them."

But none of these predecessors of Darwin defended the actual transformation of species. There seemed no convincing evidence for it, and the weight of Buffon was thrown against it. But the question had been raised, and for the next century a host of investigators groped for an answer as data poured in from many quarters. That the many pieces of evidence Darwin was to assemble came from so many different areas makes the evolution of evolution one of the most interesting of all studies in the history of ideas.

The chief of these sources was the new science of geology, together with the related subject of paleontology, the study of fossils. They came into their own in the closing years of the eighteenth century. The Genevan geologist de Saussure seems to have been the first to use the term, in 1779. In 1788 the Scotsman James Hutton presented his "uniformitarian" theory. All during the eighteenth century there had been speculation, often fanciful, about the meaning of fossils and about the age of the earth. In 1780 the German mineralogist A. G. Werner proposed the

Darwin and Evolution:
A contemporary view.
(Washington, DC, Library of
Congress)

hypothesis that the earth was originally engulfed in ocean waters that subsided, leaving behind the various minerals, fossils, and rock formations. This was the "catastrophist" or "neptunist" school, which squared well, it seemed, with biblical stories. Hutton challenged this orthodoxy by proposing to account for the phenomena by the steady operation of unchanging natural forces over what then seemed immensely long periods of time. "Uniformitarianism" stirred the wrath of some religious people because it could scarcely be adjusted to a literal reading of the Old Testament. A lively competition ensued between the two schools, which is good for any science.

We would say today that both were partly right, but concerning the time element Hutton clearly prevailed. The revolution in the age of the earth constitutes one of the great changes in our conception of the world. Coming between about 1780 and 1830, this geology-based revolution may be compared to the seventeenth-century revolution in astronomy. To the immensity of space was added the immensity of time. "Oh, how great is the antiquity of the terrestrial globe," exclaimed Lamarck, the great French paleontologist. "And how little the ideas of those who attribute to the globe an existence of six thousand and a few hundred years duration from its origin to the present!" (the prevailing orthodoxy based on Scripture).

As new data accumulated, especially the fossils, conservatism had to give way. The Reverend William Buckland, an Anglican clergyman (geology had become a favorite outdoor sport of the English countryside) devised a compromise between scriptural and geological views, saving the biblical Deluge but proposing a series of earlier floods.[1] In the 1820s Buckland claimed to have found evidence that there had been a flood about six thousand years ago, confirming the biblical one. But his modified catastrophism accommodated the accumulating paleontological evidence being collected by such masters of fossil analysis as William Smith and the French scientist Cuvier. Buckland thought there had been a series of floods, perhaps four, each of which wiped out existing life and was followed by a fresh divine creation of life. Why God should have chosen to achieve his work in several stages, punctuated by dramatic catastrophes, rather than all at once, was a mystery, but the catastrophists salvaged the biblical account at the cost of admitting a kind of creationist evolution.

It remained for another Englishman, Charles Lyell, to write the definitive geological synthesis in the early 1830s, a work of prime importance for the young Darwin; "I feel as if my books came half out of Sir Charles Lyell's brain," wrote the Cambridge scientist, a lifelong friend of Lyell's who kept a picture of him in his office. Lyell was a thoroughgoing uniformitarian, and he brushed aside religious objections as irrelevant. While increasing knowledge about fossils suggested its possibility of evolution, the time revolution helped the case for it by allowing

---

[1]The Bishop of Chichester paraphrased Pope on Newton:
  Some doubts were once expressed about the Flood:
  Buckland arose, and all was clear as mud.

enough time for a long, slow process. But the fossil record with its apparent great gaps and sudden interruptions made Buckland's thesis plausible. (Abrupt transitions after long periods of stability are still what we find today in our much more complete fossil record.) Lyell was not an evolutionist. He could not find in the fossils sufficient evidence for the transformation or progression of species—that is, one actually growing out of another. The biological evidence seemed to support the traditional notion of constancy of species, which other evidence, such as the apparent sterility of animal hybrids, also indicated. To be sure, evidence that some species became extinct now threatened the venerable "great chain of being."

Evolutionary ideas, as we know, were certainly in the air in a general way: the obvious presence of social change encouraged them. But neither Hegel nor Comte suggested the evolution of lower forms of life. "Nature and history are different things," Hegel held. "Nature has no history." There is a logical but not a temporal connection between humans and the lower forms. The cycle of nature is endless repetition from which nothing new evolves, contrary to the situation in human history. Hegel's very concern to make human history the unique arena of Providence kept him from an evolutionary view of nature. The Romantic approach to science known as *Naturphilosophie*, an interest of some German philosophers, was framed in evolutionary terms but was not "scientific"; the approach held that a spiritual force ran through nature.

Schopenhauer, the interesting German philosophical pessimist, believed that this life force appears in us as an instinct to live, which nature uses to trick us into striving so that the species may be reproduced; it is an outlook that may have worked its way into Darwinism. But while a few had mentioned evolution via the transformation of species as a speculative idea, proof of it was lacking. As early as 1800, Lamarck had proposed a theory to account for the evolution of species, one destined to a long life, but it failed to convince most thinkers. Lamarck believed that developed characteristics could be inherited. A giraffe stretches its neck a little by reaching and then hands on this gain to its offspring, who add their own cubits. But in actuality this does not happen; acquired traits are not inherited genetically. Darwin disparaged and ridiculed Lamarck, who had intruded a perhaps attractive but certainly fanciful desire or purpose into the picture, as if the bird's *wish* to fly enabled the species to stretch an organ into a wing. Darwin will claim that some birds happened to have more nearly winglike organs and these had better survival chances—a mechanical and accidental process, more scientific in not attributing will or desire to nature. At least, he argued, this "natural selection" is far and away the most important process in evolution, if not the only one.

Rapidly developing scientific knowledge in a number of fields and far-ranging scientific expeditions had produced much new data about life on earth. Darwin himself sailed on the famous *Beagle* voyage from 1831 to 1836, studying and collecting zoological evidence. A sickly youth, marked by few signs of genius, Darwin had tried and failed to follow his imposing father's profession of physician, then had his life changed by a teacher at Cambridge who got him to apply for the *Beagle* post. He had no notion of overturning long held and deeply cherished views when he set out; but as he gathered and observed specimens, questions formed in his mind. He became convinced that species are not immutable. Why should different subspecies appear in exactly the same environment?

In the main, however, Darwin in his memorable five years on the *Beagle* (of which he kept an elaborate journal) just eagerly observed and collected, dragging numerous specimens of all sorts—skeletons, rocks, fossils, rare plants and animals—back to England to join a growing collection in the museums that was to form the basis of new theorizing about the age and transformation of the earth, and the origin and nature of life forms. He would try to sort it all out at his leisure. Darwin was only one of a swarm of naturalists both amateur and professional who eagerly speculated about these matters. He was the greatest, or at least the most tenacious. With an independent income, he settled down in a Kentish village where he collected and experimented, and fought ill health as well as the distractions of Victorian family life—including ten children.

But it was from reading on another subject that Darwin got his theory about how transmutation might take place. Thomas Malthus and Herbert Spencer suggested "survival of the fittest" to him. Reading Malthus's well-known *Essay on Population*, which went through a number of editions in the first four decades of the century, Darwin said: "It at once struck me that under these circumstances favorable variations would tend to be preserved and unfavorable ones would be destroyed. The result would be the formation of a new species." The circumstances to which the gloomy parson had called attention was the tendency of population to increase faster than food supply. Many more human beings are born than will survive. How much more true this is in the plant and animal world. In 1837–38 Darwin made this his hypothesis, and spent the next twenty years patiently assembling evidence to support it. As early as 1844 he had a manuscript, but he would not publish it until he had made it entirely convincing. By nature conservative, Darwin was in fact reluctant to accept his own logic.

He learned this caution from others who had rushed in prematurely. The group numbered more than poor Lamarck. In 1844 the Scottish encyclopedist Robert Chambers, a famous polymath, published anonymously *The Vestiges of the Natural History of Creation*, a book that provocatively set forth the evolutionary hypothesis, though without enough clarity or evidence. The work caused a considerable stir. Fifteen years before anyone had heard of Charles Darwin, people were chattering about evolution, poets were being depressed (Tennyson's *In Memoriam* with its famous lines about "nature red in tooth and claw" long preceded Darwin's *Origin*), and scientists were arguing. In the end Chambers received a verdict of "not proven." It was all the more urgent to resolve the issue, but clearly necessary to do better than this amateurish effort. So Darwin and others worked away.

Origin of Species is a masterpiece of scientific argumentation, designed to make readers see that the notion of transformation of species, so long regarded as unthinkable, is really quite plausible. In addition to the fact that more offspring by far are produced than survive, of which Darwin provided striking examples (though the elephant is the slowest animal to reproduce, if all the elephant babies

survived, the earth would soon be overrun by them), he relied on the equally familiar fact that small variations do exist in every species. No two people are exactly
alike; some are taller, stronger, smarter, handsomer than others. So it is with all living creatures. Given the intense competition for survival, the variations that for
some reason have greater survival value must tend to live and reproduce themselves more often than others. Changing environmental conditions, in climate, say,
would provide the challenge to adapt.

The other factor Darwin made much of was the vast length of time that (from
geological evidence) we now know that the earth has existed. In Darwin's time this
was not as long as we would say today, but much longer than previously supposed—roughly from 6,000 years to Darwin's 500,000 to today's more than 4 billion years. Here, he argued, was enough time for an almost infinite number of tiny
cases of natural selection to add up.

On all these points Darwin argued lucidly and persuasively, with the aid of a
fine command of classical rhetoric. Darwin's book survived, we might say (turning
his own argument on him), because he was the fittest—not only in marshalling evidence but in presenting his case. Darwin was no elitist expert spouting incomprehensible jargon or using advanced mathematics; the book was thoroughly
comprehensible to almost any literate person, yet scientifically impressive. A few
noted the fact that it did not really prove its case; on the crucial question of exactly
how one species does turn into another, Darwin could not supply decisive evidence. But he drew on anatomy, experimental breeding,[2] and other fields, as well
as paleontology, to collate a large amount of evidence built around his hypothesis
of natural selection.

THE RECEPTION OF DARWINISM

Sold out on its first day of publication, Darwin's book was immediately controversial. Few areas were untouched by the Darwinian revolution. That is why it is the
classic study in intellectual history. Religion, philosophy, the social sciences, literature and the arts—none would be the same. The impact of evolution caused a
basic shift in the structure of all thought.

Most scientists were convinced of evolution, if less so of Darwin's chief
explanation for it, "natural selection." The situation varied somewhat from place
to place. Darwin himself commented that "it is curious how nationality influences
opinion." The French had their own hero of biology in Louis Pasteur, and tended
to look on Darwinism as an imperialistic Anglo-Saxon invader. Twelve years
after the publication of *Origin of Species*, a conference of French anthropologists
found "no proof or even presumption" in favor of natural selection as a cause of

---

[2]Darwin had joined workingmen in London pubs to learn how they bred their pigeons, a favorite
hobby of the lower class. It is a remarkable example of his scientific curiosity and of his common touch.

transformation. But by 1872 Darwin could write that "almost every scientist admits the principle of evolution" and most, he thought, of natural selection as its chief means of operation. A minority strenuously dissented; a good example of anti-Darwinism was the eminent American (Harvard) naturalist Louis Agassiz, who spent the rest of his life, and lost his scientific reputation, trying to disprove this "monstrous" theory.

In the long run Darwin was to keep his place as a great scientist while his theory underwent some modifications—a process that still goes on. Darwin had little understanding of the mechanism of heredity, which did not even begin to be grasped until 1900. (The Austrian monk Gregor Mendel published his pioneer findings in 1866, but science ignored them until 1900.) Today few biologists deny natural selection's importance, but the function of mutation, including macromutation or the accidental production of extreme variants, a factor unknown to Darwin, seems equally important. Insofar as he argued for slow and gradual evolutionary change, declaring that "nature makes no leaps," Darwin was mostly wrong. Modern theory stresses the sudden leaps. Later genetics established that heredity does not work simply by blending the parental traits, as Darwin supposed; in the genes all traits are preserved and may appear unimpaired in some later individual. Long periods of stability, then quick, sweeping change is the frequent pattern, and Darwin was wrong in arguing that this apparent discontinuity is due to an incomplete fossil record.[3] Needless to say biology has come a long way since Darwin; the subtleties of present-day evolution theory must be left outside our view here. The theory traveled along grooves Darwin started.

To a surprising extent, the morally more attractive Lamarckian explanation of evolution retained adherents until after the turn of the century. It enabled one to accept evolution but not natural selection. Samuel Butler, Victorian man of letters and free thinker, himself a critic of religious orthodoxy, after initially admiring Darwin came to think him a fraud and deceiver. Led back to Lamarck by the Roman Catholic biologist St. George Mivart (*The Genesis of Species*, 1871), whom Darwin regarded as a dangerous foe, Butler assailed the whole scientific establishment in *Evolution Old and New* (1879). He worked out an attractive evolutionary religion on Lamarckian principles. Each person makes his or her contribution to human knowledge and consciousness, passing this on to the next generation; we may all feel that what we have learned and created is not in vain, but a link in the chain of human progress. Unfortunately, this seems not to be true in a genetic sense. We can teach our children if we are able, but they do not inherit our knowledge biologically.

Though the evidence was less clear than it later became, the dismal implications of Darwin's true science was really why so many opposed him. Von Baer,

---

[3]Thus the present view is that a "Cambrian explosion" of some 500 million years ago produced most presently existing types of animal life in one sudden burst of creativity. Similarly, *homo sapiens* was born rather suddenly.

the distinguished German scientist, refused to believe in a theory that made humanity "a product of matter" and debased it to the level of animals. The professor of geology at Cambridge, Darwin's one-time friend Adam Sedgwick, declared that acceptance of Darwinism would "sink the human race into a lower grade of degradation" than it had ever known since the dawn of its history. George Bernard Shaw later wrote: "If it could be proved that the whole universe had been produced by such a selection [Darwin's "survival of the fittest"], only fools and rascals could bear to live."

Of course, some Christians were shocked at the refutation of Genesis and at the implication that there was no unique human soul (if such a thing existed, it was already there in the amoeba on Darwin's principles). But the dismay extended far beyond orthodox religious circles. Shaw and Samuel Butler, after all, were far from orthodox in their beliefs. Were any moral values possible in a Darwinian world? Perhaps the most disturbing feature was the apparently accidental and purposeless nature of the process. Chance determined the extinction of whole species, the rise of others for a moment of glory before some change in climate, perhaps, condemned them to death. No medieval reflection on the vanity and mutability of the things of this world could have been gloomier.

Darwin himself had lost his religion in studying nature (as well as in personal tragedies such as the death of a beloved daughter.) Lyell's geology first led him away from biblical Christianity; then natural selection destroyed in his mind the classical arguments for natural religion, drawn from the evidence of design and purpose in organisms. The textbook much used in early nineteenth-century England, William Paley's *Natural Theology* (1802), argued with a wealth of carefully observed detail that the marvelous adaptation of organisms to their environment proves deliberate contrivance by an "intelligent Creator." With a change in perspective, many of Paley's examples could be seen as adaptation via natural selection rather than providential design. And a closer look reveals cases of very imperfect design—what the present-day biologist Stephen Gould calls "odd arrangements and funny solutions," like the title of one of his books, the panda's thumb. A divine creator would surely have given the panda a good thumb rather than an improvised one (adapted wrist bone). Likewise revealing are vestigial remains: parts of the anatomy no longer useful but existing as evidence of an earlier state.

Darwin's concluding paragraphs in the *Origin* point toward a theism that was in fact quite widely adopted: It is not less wonderful but more so that God chose to plant the seeds of all life in a few simple forms rather than create each species separately. But, as his letters and subsequent published writings reveal, Darwin abandoned this position. He saw too much chance and too much evil in the biological world to permit him to believe in a benevolent divine plan. "I cannot persuade myself that a benevolent and omnipotent God would have designedly created the Ichneumonidae with the express intention of their feeding within the living bodies of caterpillars, or that cats should play with mice." The thought also struck him that the mind of humanity itself is a product of the evolutionary order, thus merely a tool of survival. Our ideas themselves exist because they enabled the species to cope, not because they are true or false.

The same thought was to jolt others. Oddly enough, this would seem to leave science along with theology as lacking any higher validity; everything would have to become just a weapon in the struggle for survival. Darwin's somewhat confused speculations mirrored those of many others thrown into disorder by this new knowledge. Unwilling to be dogmatic, Darwin called himself an "agnostic." But careful study of his religious views suggests that it would not be unjust to equate them with atheism. Darwin found absolutely no evidence for divine creation and providence.

Meanwhile the debate between shocked Christians and some of Darwin's more dogmatic followers enlivened the Victorian scene. Most famous was the encounter in 1860 between Bishop Samuel Wilberforce and Thomas Huxley, "Darwin's bulldog," a polemical scientist whose animus against the religious led him to assert that "extinguished theologians lie about the cradle of every science as the strangled snakes beside that of Hercules." According to the legendary account, "Soapy Sam," as his foes called him, observed that he would rather not have a monkey for an ancestor, to which Huxley made the crushing reply that he would rather be descended from an honest ape than from one who though endowed with brains refused to use them.[4] It is, however, not true that all clergymen rejected Darwin, and his foes included scientists and other nonclerical people. Nevertheless the conflict between science and religion became a standard Victorian set piece. We will refer to it again, for it included elements other than Darwinism.

There were those who sought to end the conflict by arguing that Darwinian evolution is consistent with divine purpose. Was there not something sublime in the ascent of life through the eons from primeval slime to an intelligent and spiritual being? (Henry Drummond) Admit the cruelty and suffering, one still had as an undeniable fact the grand result. "Red in tooth and claw" was somewhat overstated, students of Darwinism pointed out; survival depends more on the struggle with nature than on competition between organisms, and cooperation can be an aid to survival. Creatures who care for their offspring and help each other tend to survive. Strength is less important than energy and intelligence. Natural selection often operates silently and painlessly, via the nonreproduction of less efficient organisms. In the end, the more intelligent species win out, humans being the great example.

Asa Gray, the American naturalist, complimented Darwin for having *restored* teleology to nature. There was design, if "on the installment plan." As Mr. and Mrs. Carlyle pointed out, whether we are or are not derived from the

---

[4]Huxley's descendants continued to be militantly anti-theist. The distinguished twentieth-century biologist Julian Huxley, grandson of Thomas, called himself a "humanist" and declared that while Newton had disposed of the need for God to guide the stars in their courses, "Darwin's natural selection made it posssible and necessary to dispense with the idea of God guiding the evolutionary courses of life" (*On Living in a Revolution*, 1944).

amoeba is irrelevant to our spiritual life. Josiah Royce, the distinguished American philosopher, held to an evolutionary idealism and noted that the human spirit does seek values, is not animal-like: this fact is as incontrovertible as Darwin's, if puzzlingly different. Darwin had not and could not make us brutes. He had given us new and puzzling knowledge, but so long as human consciousness exists it will rise above matter to seek understanding and the good. Some of the most conservative theologians, the old-fashioned Calvinists, had the least trouble accepting Darwinism; they had always known that suffering and conflict, the consequence of original sin, are a part of life. Only the naively optimistic should be upset by the thought that the world, as Coleridge had put it, is not a goddess in petticoats but the devil in a straitjacket.

Vitalist approaches to evolution postulated a "life force" that is the basic cause of evolution, natural selection being only one means that it uses. This was Schopenhauer's "will"—an irrational "striving, persistent, vital force, a spontaneous activity, a will of imperious desire," which the offbeat German philosopher substituted for Hegel's Mind as the spirit that constitutes basic reality in the cosmos. Schopenhauer was a pessimist. This force torments us, tricks us into going through the toil and turbulence of life, and is the enemy of that tranquility the wise person will seek by suppressing desires. Others saw it more optimistically. Human intelligence is no less creative for being a part of the natural order. French vitalism culminated at the end of the century in the popular philosophy of Henri Bergson, discussed later in the book. Here was an evolutionist alternative or supplement to Darwinian mechanism and materialism, with some resemblances to Lamarck, who continued to find disciples, though seldom among the professional biologists.

But philosophically Darwinism helped discredit idealism or intellectualism. "Naturalism" saw mind as a product of evolution, ideas as the result of natural selection. Even the basic conviction that nature makes sense is because those of our ancestors who could not make sense of it failed to survive. Reason is a survival trait. A character in one of Shaw's plays remarked that the modern view is not "I think therefore I am," but "I am therefore I think." Reason is a product of the nature it purports to understand. Mind itself is an evolutionary product, as much as the monkey's tail or the giraffe's neck. Truth is just what works, or has worked through the ages of struggle. Mind no longer stands against the world seeking to understand it; it is a part of the world, a product of its processes. (Of course, this idea itself is presumably not timelessly true, but just a product of evolution.)

Bergson, Nietzsche, and American Pragmatists such as John Dewey would fall under the influence of this striking thought and puzzle over it. On any showing, the realm of thought had been changed. The vision of the universe had been transformed. To Anatole France this "revolution of modern times" was ambivalent, bringing both confidence and uneasiness, and most people probably would have agreed. Dewey in his assessment of *The Influence of Darwin on Philosophy* (1909) thought that by shattering the Platonic eternals and the closed metaphysical system of Hegel in favor of "the principle of transition," Darwinism encouraged pluralism and experimentation. Evolution seemed a fresh breeze blowing over the desiccated landscape of idealism, asking for ever new knowledge, and new forms of art; an architecture, for example, that was not based on the traditional styles but was something altogether different, a modern mode demanded by the modern age.

OTHER SCIENTIFIC INFLUENCES

The rise of science as the prevailing mode of thought owed more to Darwin than to any other one figure, but it was part of a larger pattern. Many noted this change about midcentury. The Oxford scholar Mark Pattison dated it between 1845 and 1850. Oliver Wendell Holmes, Jr., the great American jurist, thought that of all the intellectual gaps between generations, that between his own and his parents (about 1865) was the greatest: "It was the influence of the scientific way of looking at the world." He mentioned, in addition to Darwin and his *Origin of Species*, Herbert Spencer and Henry T. Buckle, two who were trying to apply scientific methods to the study of human affairs. Of Spencer and his "social Darwinism" more in a moment; there were other scientific advances and scientific heroes.

Having measured accurately the distance to the sun and moon and arrived at a notion of the fantastic distances of the stars, astronomers came upon the stunning fact of the existence of other *galaxies*. In 1796 Laplace's *System of the World* was an almost rhapsodic tribute to the orderliness of physical nature. But riddles of the sort that eventually brought physical science to its late nineteenth-century upheavals bobbed up earlier. In 1827 the French military engineer Sadi Carnot called attention to the apparently irreversible loss of energy, as heat, when bodies cool. Was the entire universe running out of energy as it approached an equilibrium temperature? (The famous British physicist Lord Kelvin dismissed Darwinism because he thought the laws of heat testified against the world's being nearly as old as the geologists claimed.) Thermodynamics here seemed to defy Newton's laws of physics, which assumed reciprocal relationships, not an irreversible one-way movement. It was a riddle scientists struggled with until the end of the century. Pessimists could find in the Second Law of Thermodynamics another argument against progress; in the long run, the direction was the reverse.

The young Polish girl Maria Sklodowska, better known later by her married name of Marie Curie, in her youth in the 1880s frequented Positivist circles (which the tsarist police regarded with grave suspicion) and found her idol in Louis Pasteur, called by Frenchmen "the Galileo of Biology" because of his contributions to bacteriology and medicine. She would go to Paris to study physics and chemistry. Already in Warsaw she had fallen in love with a chemistry laboratory. Her cousin had worked under the great Russian chemist Mendeleyev, who established the periodic table of the elements to which Mme. Curie was to add a few notable footnotes. The chemical revolution advanced parallel to biology in the nineteenth century. Chemistry had found its Newton late in the eighteenth century in a French banker and amateur scientist who became a victim of the Reign of Terror during the Revolution: Antoine Lavoisier. Chemistry was on the cutting edge of intellectual excitement; Coleridge, speculating about the influence of scientific ideas on other branches of knowledge, thought that the discoveries of Scheele, Priestley, and Lavoisier, "reducing the infinite variety of chemical phenomena to the actions, reactions, and interchanges of a few elementary substances," would affect philosophy and other fields of thought no less than Newton had done in the eighteenth century. It is significant that Friedrich Engels, when trying to illuminate the laws of dialectical materialism he claimed existed in nature, tended to use examples from chemistry.

In Britain there were interesting connections to Darwin's own circle. From John Dalton, disciple of Humphrey Davy, the picturesque Welsh friend of Charles's grandfather Erasmus Darwin, came the atomic theory and the electrical nature of chemical affinities: when "atoms" combine they exchange electrical impulses. Electricity, assimilated to magnetism, came together here also with chemistry. Atoms were thought of as hard, irreducible units of matter, which is what the Greek word meant; Newton's "solid, massy, impenetrable" particles.

The remarkable Scottish genius, James Clerk Maxwell, addressed himself to the apparently random and unpredictable behavior of gas molecules, still puzzling when Einstein confronted it in 1905. It was an example of uncertainty in nature that undercut scientism's faith in a completely orderly and totally explainable natural order. Maxwell's great contribution was the mathematical formulation of the laws of electromagnetism. The path of progress in electrical phenomena, from Volta and Galvani at the end of the eighteenth century to Michael Faraday's invention of the electrical generator in the 1830s, prepared the way for the mighty invasion of life by electricity within a few decades after that, as electrical power began to light cities, run trains, operate factories. Clerk Maxwell's theoretical prediction of various kinds of rays led to X-rays, radio waves, and other forms of radiant energy. His 1864 work was perhaps the beginning of the whole scientific revolution that burst out toward the end of the century, with Max Planck, Albert Einstein, Marie Curie, and others (see Chapter 7).

Overshadowed publicly at least by Darwin, these other areas of scientific inquiry, leading to increasing power over nature and also to some theoretical enigmas, were equally important. The last half of the century saw an unprecedented professional organization of science marked by numerous international meetings, journals, professional societies, collation of research. All the hard sciences progressed and, as they did so, illuminated amazing, and sometimes disconcerting, features of the universe.

Within the universities, scientists led the struggle to transform the basic principles of higher education. The metamorphosis its leading historian calls "from clergyman to don" in Oxford and Cambridge occurred after midcentury. It was a process of laicization, or secularization, as well as scientization; the new don was as likely to be a humanist as a scientist—what he was not was a clergyman. Many of the old clergy shared the fascination with science; some of the new dons deplored it. But in any case the Cambridge that Darwin had known in the 1820s, where science had scarcely any place and the purpose of university training was to produce priests for the Church of England, was no more. The goal became that of producing a man liberally educated for some secular career. The curriculum had expanded to include history, modern languages, and at least some science in addition to the old Greek-Latin-mathematics foundation. Much the same thing was happening in France, where the University of Paris abandoned its theology faculty in 1866—as its medieval founders, no doubt, spun in their tombs.

Nevertheless the chief leaders of thought continued to be "men of letters" who were not specialists and often not even from the universities. Herbert Spencer, architect of the most popular synthesis of all knowledge for the Victorians, came from well outside the Establishment. He was of lower middle-class background, and largely self-taught. A man of prodigious energy and memory, influenced by Lyell and von Baer, he had preceded Darwin in coining the phrase "survival of the fittest." The well-worn description of him as a "social Darwinist" overlooks the fact that he was actually more Lamarckian than Darwinian in his theory of evolution. Darwin called him "about a dozen times my superior," and indeed Spencer's range and speculative boldness far excelled that of the man who liked to call himself, perhaps with false humility, only a humble scientist, and who indeed preferred to write about the habits of barnacles and earthworms rather than philosophical theories. It remained for Spencer to stretch evolution over everything.

HERBERT SPENCER AND SOCIAL DARWINISM

Writing voluminously and with an encyclopedic knowledge few could match, Spencer tended to bowl over opposition by the sheer weight of his formidable erudition. He was close to being the most popular serious thinker of all time, to judge by the sale of his books. "Probably no philosopher ever had such a vogue as Spencer had from about 1870 to 1890," wrote the American publisher Henry Holt, who had the enviable privilege of selling Spencer's books in the United States. William James called Spencer's system "the most ambitious attempt at synthesis of all knowledge since St. Thomas or Descartes." People bewildered by the profusion of new knowledge and the collapse of old frameworks eagerly sought such a synthesis. Spencer has been called the Marx of the middle class; he could equally well be called the British Comte or Hegel.

Like those other ambitious system-makers, he tended to depreciate somewhat in value. Little remains of Spencer's effort to formulate a universal evolutionary theory. It was in connection with Spencer that T. H. Huxley spoke of "a beautiful theory slain by an ugly fact," and too many of these interfered with Spencer's scheme of the entire universe obeying the same laws of evolution—the physical world and human society reduced to the same principles. Spencer formulated these as an invariable evolution from homogeneous to heterogeneous, from undifferentiated to differentiated, and from unintegrated to integrated; "from a relatively diffused, uniform, and indeterminate arrangement to a relatively concentrated, multiform, and determinate arrangement." In other words, the cosmos began with simple atoms scattered through space, human society with unspecialized isolated individuals; each developed toward a complexly organized system with much division of labor or specialization. The student will probably think of lots of objections right away. The primeval atom exploding at the beginning of the universe (or this cycle of it) to disperse ever since, which is what scientists ask us to believe today, seems rather the reverse of Spencer's notion of dispersed cosmic dust gradually coming together. Primitive human societies are quite tightly organized.

Yet Spencer's later sociology exercised considerable influence on theorists in its stress on social change via unstable equilibria in a single complex social organism. Spencer's model differed from Marx's in being steady and gradual rather than sudden and revolutionary—an echo of the old debate between uniformitarians and catastrophists.

Unfortunately Spencer mixed his science as freely with ideology as did Marx. He became identified with the application of Darwinian struggle for existence or "survival of the fittest" to economic society. A one-time editor of *The Economist*, Spencer knew political economy before he turned to evolution and shows the intimate connection between the two. John Maynard Keynes once wrote that "the principle of the Survival of the Fittest could be regarded as a vast generalization of the Ricardian economics." Spencer freely mixed ideological elements into his science of society. He owed much to the tradition of English liberalism, reaching back beyond the Manchester School to John Locke, though he also borrowed from Edmund Burke the idea of society as a complicated organism. He was an aggressive "agnostic" whose scientific positivism resolutely rejected any other dimension than that of empirically verifiable facts. Essential natures, origins, ultimate causes belong to the realm of the "unknowable," about which it is futile to speculate. Spencer was a positivist like Comte, a phenomenalist like the Kant of *Critique of Pure Reason*. Believing Christians, in fact, thought him one of the age's leading infidels.

Spencer's liberalism appeared in his vision of the evolution of the individual toward greater freedom and less constraint. While society grows more complex and interdependent, it also grows more diverse and freer. Competition is the key to progress. Spencer at times complacently identified the poor with the unfit who may safely be left to die out. The often quoted passage in *Social Statics* was first published in 1851, but not significantly changed in the many later editions: "to prevent present misery would entail a greater misery on future generations," because "when regarded not separately but in connection with the interests of universal humanity," it is wiser and kinder to let the natural process of competition weed out the defective organisms. It is like a surgical operation, painful but necessary for the body's long-term interests. Spencer's apparently callous rejection of charitable concern for the weak and the poor caused a considerable reaction against him from the 1880s on.

At the very least, Spencer's argument was confused. Biological competition, affecting the sickly and the healthy, ought not to be equated with economic competition. Perhaps we should not keep alive the physically or mentally defective to reproduce themselves at the expense of future generations; yet a sickly person may be an intellectual or artistic genius of greater value to the human race than a healthy athlete. A person reduced to poverty may owe this to luck or circumstances, not to innate ability or character; it takes a great deal of gullibility to believe that those who lag behind in the race for economic success are the "unfit" who rightly perish.

Again, distinctions should be drawn between the various units of society that are subject to natural selection. Spencer sometimes mixed them up. Is it individuals that compete within a given society, or societies that compete with each other? Or social institutions such as the family? E. B. Tylor, a prominent social evolutionist, held that "the institutions which can best hold their own in the world gradually supersede the less fit ones." Spencer as well as Hegel thought that out of the competition between whole social units, like nations, we get increasing efficiency. Spencer stressed that societies are organisms akin to individual bodies, being functionally organized and experiencing growth; they are tested by the environment and evolve from small and simple to large and complex. He was a vigorous anti-imperialist, believing that one nation or race should not impose its rule on another. He also shared with Manchester School liberals the conviction that war had become obsolete in the modern world, replaced by economic internationalism. These were perhaps inconsistencies. And would not cutthroat competition within a society handicap that society in its own struggle for survival with other societies? Treating your poor with cruelty and neglect surely will not cause them to support your team when it comes up against another one.

These confusions apart, Spencer thought, more or less consistently, that free competition makes for the best society and the best humanity as well, "best" being defined as most efficient, best adapted to the challenge of the environment. Social anthropology, a science that owed its start as a professional discipline to Darwin and Spencer, assumed at first that there was an evolutionary ladder comparable to the biological one. For example, in religion animism comes first, monotheism last, in a straight-line path of development; "primitive" peoples existing in the world today are just late starters on a road that will eventually lead them to where Europe now is. Tylor declared that "human institutions like stratified rocks succeed each other in series substantially uniform over the whole globe." Skepticism about such laws of human development soon appeared, and by the end of the century practitioners of the new science or art of anthropology were finding that each primitive people is unique and can be fitted into no evolutionary pattern. Nevertheless the original impetus to sociology and anthropology came from the expectation of finding such laws.

Spencer's brand of social Darwinism, sanctioning a social ethic the American sociologist William Graham Sumner bluntly described as "root, hog, or die," did not please other Darwinists. A radical creed in many ways (anti-religious, for example), social Darwinism appealed to many socialists. Marx's editor and sometime son-in-law Edward Aveling even invented a letter tying Marx to Darwin. In Germany Darwinism and Marxism were closely associated (see Alfred Kelly, *The*

Descent of Darwin, 1981). The British socialist Ramsay MacDonald, in his preface to an 1894 book on socialism and science, wrote that Darwinism "is not only not in intellectual opposition to socialism, but is its scientific foundation." That struggle is the law of life, that conditions change and social institutions must change too were notions easily bent to radical usages. In "Why Darwin Pleased the Socialists," G. B. Shaw made the point, half-seriously as usual, that it took the capitalists down a peg to be told that they were rich not because they deserved it, but simply by accident. Research has established, in fact, that Darwinism was less a favorite of businessmen anxious to justify their rapacity than used to be said.

In 1893 Thomas Huxley, Darwin's aggressive champion against the churchmen, argued in a well-known series of lectures that in human affairs natural selection is *not* the rule to follow. In this sphere, unlike in lower nature, progress consists in working *against* nature and evolution, "checking the cosmic process at every step." He agreed with Matthew Arnold that

> Man must begin, know this, where nature ends;
> Nature and man can never be fast friends.

What surives may be the best in a practical sense, but not an ethical one. Unguided evolution may lead to moral regression and social failure. Or, as others put it, rational evolution for humanity consists in replacing crude physical conflict with the higher survival value of welfare and peace, organized through brain rather than brawn. Some pointed out that even in the subhuman realm conflict is not the only rule; cooperation also exists as a means of biological survival. (So argued a widely read book by the Russian anarchist, Prince Kropotkin.)

Here were interesting debates and abundant confusions. Darwin himself, in his later book *The Descent of Man* (1871), declared that it would be injurious to the human race to keep alive "the weak of mind and body" rather than eliminate them as he says "savage" tribes do, and also that "an endless number of lower races will be eliminated by the higher civilized races throughout the world." Darwin seemed to adopt Spencerism with a vengeance. Believing firmly in the separate nature of women, he has earned low marks from recent feminists too. Darwin's cousin, Francis Galton, in his book *Hereditary Genius* (1869) coined the term "eugenics" or the science of improving the human race by perpetuating the more intelligent genetic strains. For us, after Hitler, such ideas are decidedly uncomfortable.

Among the numerous Darwinian offshoots were the "social imperialists." In 1894 a thirty-five-year-old British civil servant and amateur biologist named Benjamin Kidd published a book called *Social Evolution* that became a best seller and was translated into ten languages including Chinese. Although Kidd's great reputation later sank almost entirely out of sight, he was then at least as famous a social thinker as Karl Marx. Kidd's social evolutionism mixed socialism and imperialism. Natural selection operates on groups, favoring the ones knit together most closely by habits of cooperation, which religious faith helps. Some of the irrationalism characteristic of the *fin de siècle* crept into Kidd's thought. He was a curiously reactionary kind of feminist who thought that in being less intellectual, women were ahead of men on the evolutionary ladder; feelings are more important than reason. Thus did the evolutionary idea continue to emit sparks, some of them rather garish.

Meanwhile the naturalist school of literature, much indebted to Darwin, seized the center of the literary stage for a while in the last third of the century. Emile Zola, Jack London, Gerhart Hauptmann and others of this sort wrote about the lower depths with brutal frankness. They sought a scientific detachment as well as realism that hovered on the edges of cosmic pessimism: fate is blind as well as usually cruel. Both Zola and Thomas Hardy, the great English novelist and later poet, were nineteen years old when *Origin of Species* appeared and thus belonged to the generation that felt its major impact. To the specific influence of the theory of evolution via natural selection was added that of science in general; of positivism, applying the scientific method to literature and philosophy; and of rapid change in society in general, especially technological and industrial. For Zola, a further stimulus came from the shocking defeat of France in the 1870 war with Prussia—evidence, it seemed, that a nation must adapt or perish, in a competitive and rapidly changing world. Everything conspired to drive home the lesson that stability was no longer the norm; the new god was change, and one failed to accept this fact at one's peril.

THE VICTORIAN CRISIS OF FAITH

The generation of the 1870s found parents and children torn apart by the new irreligion. Robert Louis Stevenson's father, dismayed at his son's seduction by Herbert Spencer, thought that anyone not a Christian was simply "a knave, a madman, or a fool." British Liberal Prime Minister William Gladstone did not think civilized society likely to survive the discrediting of the Bible's plenary inspiration. "The devil's dust of agnosticism fills our lungs," conservatives lamented. This crisis of faith owed more, probably, to the new historical criticism of the ancient sacred writings than to Darwin and science—even though, as French writer Jules Goncourt mused, each day science takes another bite out of God (*mange de dieu*). The two blows, one from history and the other from nature, came at about the same time. In England, *Essays and Reviews*, a landmark statement of the case against biblical literalism, followed Darwin's blockbuster by just a year, and made almost as great an impression. Both were part of the larger context of secularization.

Christianity was very much alive in the nineteenth century. Victorian England featured a religious revival that produced Oxford's Anglo-Catholicism, delighting in ancient mysteries and ceremonies, a conscious antidote to the pervasive positivism; and in another direction the more powerful Evangelical movement. All types of Christian evangelicalism stress complete commitment and practical changes in conduct after the conversion experience. British evangelicalism began as a reaction against the lax, merely nominal Christianity of the eighteenth-century Church of England—and also as a reaction against the godless French Revolution. Theologically simple, stressing will rather than elaborate doctrine, the Evangelicals were austerely moral and full of the work ethic. Their enemies, in the end numerous and vociferous, with much justification accused them of narrow-mindedness and philistinism, but Evangelical achievements in the area of personal behavior were impressive. A founding father of the movement, William Wilberforce (father of Huxley's opponent "Soapy Sam"), upon his retirement from the House of Commons after forty-five years of service, recalled that body's transformation over the century from an assemblage of drunken and brawling rakes to the sober chamber it had become.

This discipline and energy arguably had more than anything else to do with Britain's becoming the leading industrial nation of the world. What are often labeled "middle class" qualities—sobriety, diligence, frugality, intellectual seriousness, along with a mistrust of all idle amusements including the arts—actually derived from the evangelical spirit, or its equivalent in the nonconformist Protestant sects. Evangelical zeal for reform manifested itself in the antislavery cause, in overseas missionary activities, and to a degree in efforts to protect workers from gross abuse (an evangelical Tory, Lord Shaftesbury, was the most notable champion of legislation limiting hours of labor). But the Evangelicals did not challenge the existing social order; they counseled workers to eschew revolt, accept subordination, and pull themselves up by hard work. With their amazing energy and dedication, their narrowness and fanaticism—destined to drive many a Victorian youth to revolt—the Evangelicals have been a riddle to later generations. But of their influence there is no doubt. Queen Victoria herself was of their number. Evangelical Christianity was the strongest ideology among the reigning "middle classes." Did they create it, or vice versa? It is a question for Karl Marx. (Historian Boyd Hilton has recently asked about its relationship to social and economic thought.)

The third force in the Anglican Church was much smaller, though intellectually distinguished: the Broad Church deriving from Samuel Taylor Coleridge's "clerisy" concept. In effect surrendering to the secular spirit, Coleridge would keep a national institution embracing the best and the brightest and dedicated to excellence in all things. The Roman Catholic Church was scarcely less divided, confronting in the 1860s a crisis of liberalism versus conservative traditionalism that led through the 1864 Syllabus of Errors to the momentous ecumenical council of 1870 (see further below, p. 123).

All these differences within the much-divided Christian faith paled into insignificance compared to those stemming from the Higher Criticism. In *Essays and Reviews*, a group of leading churchmen and scholars declared, in effect, that the time had come to admit that educated people can no longer believe in the Bible as literal truth. They hoped to show what Coleridge and other Romantic theologians had argued earlier, that this abandonment of literal truth need not destroy Christianity, the validity of which rests on other grounds. But to the faithful the book was shocking, and it led to a trial for heresy within the Church of England. The 1860s brought other popularizations of the so-called Higher Criticism, such as

Ernst Renan's life of Jesus and J. R. Seeley's *Ecce Homo* (1865). Both were preceded, we will recall, by the Hegelian David Strauss's 1835 account of Christ's life. The Germans in fact led the way in this advance on the Old and New Testaments with the tools of modern historical research.

The issues were far from new. The famous philosopher Spinoza and the Oratorian priest Father Richard Simon had begun the critical examination of Scripture back in the seventeenth century (there were even earlier premonitions of it in Lutheran Germany). The eighteenth-century deists and skeptics made much of materials gleaned from these investigations; a furious debate raged throughout that century about the accuracy of accepted versions of the sacred scriptures, which presented formidable textual problems (no original text, innumerable faulty translations and copies, scores of conflicting renditions—matter enough to keep a horde of scholars employed down to the present.) Now, however, with the aid of new information and the critical scholarship for which German historians became renowned, a fresh phase of this inquiry emerged. The leading feature of the "higher" (historical) criticism as distinct from the "lower" (textual) was its awareness of an immense literary tradition among the other peoples of the ancient world, which bore on the Bible at many points. The Bible was no longer seen in isolation, as a unique document. It fitted into a larger context that was beginning to be recovered. Thus seen, it became a part of human history rather than the record of a divine miracle.

In 1878 J. Wellhausen offered persuasive support to a theory already advanced that a substantial portion of the early books of the Bible (the Pentateuch or Torah) was not written until much later than the events they describe, and indeed were not put into final form until about 400 B.C., nearly a thousand years after Moses. Wellhausen carried the day among scholars, especially the younger ones. A French scholar wrote in 1894 that "whoever is not totally prejudiced, whoever has not decided in advance that any kind of criticism is false, must accept the idea that the Priestly Code was not formed until after the Babylonian exile." The Ten Commandments, in brief, did not come from God by way of Moses but from fourth- or fifth-century scribes looking at several hundred years of uncertain sources and traditions.

To some of the pious, this was a shocking conclusion. It cast doubt on the Bible as revealed truth, divinely inspired, the root and foundation of Christianity. The arguments of liberal theologians, that the history of Israel and Judea in the broader sense justified the claim of a unique religious mission vouchsafed to the Jewish people, carried little conviction to those brought up to believe, as Gladstone, for example, did, that the literal truth of every line of Scripture was the impregnable rock upon which Christianity rested. Edmund Gosse marveled that his mother "had formed a definite conception of the absolute, unmodified and historical veracity, in its direct and obvious sense, of every statement contained within the covers of the Bible." She was surely more typical than her sophisticated son.

In 1872, George Smith called attention to a Babylonian version of the Flood—a shattering discovery. A good deal of the Old Testament has parallels in the sacred literature of the Babylonians and other ancient peoples with whom the Jewish people were in contact. Widening knowledge of other, non-Western cultures contributed to this de-centering of the traditional European religions. Popularized in books such as James Frazer's widely read end-of-the-century success, *The Golden Bough*, the fruits of anthropological research showed that even primitive religions make use of beliefs similar to those of Christianity and Judaism. Awareness of Indic thought advanced steadily in the nineteenth century, revealing a whole additional world of higher religion. All this further eroded the uniqueness of Christianity. Comparative religion discovered that the god who comes down to earth, is killed, rises again and redeems humanity appears in many traditions; it is seemingly a human archetype. Myths about the martyr, the miracle worker, the man of the people, the wanderer, and others found in the Christ saga belong to the storehouse of stories told by every people.

The originality of the Hebraic outlook perhaps remained—its determined monotheism, its messianic strain, its high ethical precepts—but in many details the biblical story lost its ability to pass as something quite outside the experience of the rest of the ancient world. The Jews could never again be quite the "peculiar people" in the old sense.

By the end of the nineteenth century, critical research into the New Testament was questioning whether the Gospels consist of four independent testimonies to Christ's life and death. The authors of Matthew and Luke leaned heavily on the Gospel of Mark, and even the latter contains interpolations not taken from Jesus himself. All the stories rest on oral traditions written down several decades after Jesus's death. All this was much disputed, yet the net result of intensive and interesting historical analysis was to cast doubt on the accuracy of the Gospels as accounts of the life of Jesus and of the attribution to him of various ideas and sayings. The more skeptical would say, as did Bertrand Russell, that there is not enough hard evidence to convince an unbiased person that Christ even existed. If some such person did exist, the accounts of his life are too garbled and confused to be relied on.

Opening up the question of the historical Jesus by no means meant destroying Christianity, but simple folk among the pious might understandably think so. A quarrel between "modernists" and "fundamentalists" soon divided most Christian churches. In 1864 an outraged Pope Pius IX, further embittered by the Italian liberal-nationalist attack on the papacy's temporal power, issued a Syllabus of Errors, placing the Roman Church at odds with much of nineteenth-century thought; liberalism and democracy, as well as modern science and Hegelian philosophy, were declared to be irreconcilable with Christianity and the Church. In 1870 the same pope summoned a great Ecumenical Council, the first since the sixteenth-century Council of Trent, chiefly to solemnize the doctrine of papal infallibility. The goal was not achieved without a severe struggle, in which many of the German, French, and English bishops opposed the papal party; after the decrees, some liberal Catholics left the Church.

Small wonder that Nietzsche soon announced the death of God, and Charles

Péguy viewed with alarm the coming for the first time in Western history of a world without Jesus. For many living in the last decades of the century the question was an agonizing one. A widely read novel of 1888 by Mrs. Humphrey Ward, *Robert Ellsmere*, is about an Anglican clergyman who confronts the Higher Criticism and finally becomes convinced that the supernatural claims about Christ's life cannot be verified; his conscience forces him to leave the Church and his vocation. For the Victorians this was high drama.

"Once vivid faiths are now very numb," John Morley observed. For such as Gladstone, the result would surely be "to snap utterly the ties which, under the still venerable name of religion, unite men with the unseen world, and lighten the struggles and woes of life by the hope of a better land." A famous popular novel imagined the discovery of a document that definitely disproved the story of Christ's resurrection, and then the aftermath: the collapse of all law and order, the total extinction of civilized life.

But in 1876 Leslie Stephen, father of the great novelist Virginia Woolf and a highly eminent Victorian scholar, announced in his "Agnostic's Apology" that he no longer believed in anything but nevertheless intended to go on being a gentleman. And a lively group of "rationalists" or "secularists" so rejoiced in the downfall of clericalism that they formed a kind of skeptics' church of their own. "There lives more faith in honest doubt" than in any religious creed, a poet quipped. Even the Victorian atheists were religious, Lytton Strachey said. Like Comte and Feuerbach, they would make a religion of humanity. In 1885 one of them created a sensation by being elected to Parliament and refusing to take the inaugural oath because it included "So help me God."

VICTORIAN WRITERS AND RELIGION: JOHN STUART MILL

The major writers of the latter part of the century tended in greater degree or less to share this pessimism or anxiety. Among the eminent Victorians, the most eminent thinker, all things considered, was probably John Stuart Mill. He had a wider range than probably any other British thinker of his time, extending from pure philosophy to political thought and economic theory, on which he wrote the definitive Victorian textbook. His many essays also touch literature and ethics. He entered politics, and together with his wife wrote the most celebrated document of nineteenth-century feminism, as he campaigned for women's rights among other unpopular causes.

John Stuart's father, James Mill, had carried on Bentham's scorn for Christianity as simply childish superstition. Raised in this anti-theist orthodoxy, John Stuart Mill found himself torn between austere rationalism and the needs of his spirit for something warmer and more consoling. As he told in his classic *Autobiography*, he found a counterweight in Coleridge. Poetry filled the place of religion; Mill until late in his life was consistently antireligious. Bertrand Russell was surely not the only one who lost his faith from reading Mill. In his youthful (1831) essay

John Stuart Mill in 1873, as seen by the famous *Vanity Fair* caricaturist "Spy." (*Vanity Fair,* March 1873)

on "The Spirit of the Age," Mill had noted that "the brightest ornaments" of society had quietly dropped their religious beliefs. Mill became interested in Comte, finding in the Frenchman's discipline and social sense a corrective to British individualism, though there was much in Comte he could not accept. Indeed, Mill, who lies buried with his wife Harriet Taylor at Avignon, always owed much to the French. He greatly admired Tocqueville's great book on democracy.

Mill read the novels of Dickens and formed a firm friendship with Thomas Carlyle, so much his opposite in many ways. This openness to many perspectives was a notable feature of Mill's mind. His thought has been described as a series of compromises. This may seem to sit oddly with his impassioned commitment to causes, but the chief of these causes for Mill was freedom of thought itself, on which he wrote the definitive statement. But he rejected Kant and Hegel, so far as he understood them; they were too metaphysical for his Anglo-Saxon mind. Empiricist and positivist in his philosophy, he refused to say with the Kantians that the laws of thought are merely mental constructs; he held them to exist objectively, and he prepared a systematic treatise of inductive logic—the scientific method.

A classic defender of the liberty of the individual, Mill showed sympathy with socialism up to a point, but he feared the element of compulsion lurking in every socialist scheme; cooperation would have to be voluntary. In his famous textbook *The Principles of Political Economy*, his foundation was individualistic capitalism, but he was prepared to entertain exceptions to the rule of unrestrained private enterprise whenever a sound case could be made. The exceptions, it was noted, grew with every edition of the book, so that Mill became an ancestor of English Fabian socialism. He was always willing to temper the narrower individualism of Benthamism with some of Coleridge's feeling for the community. He once burst out that "the restraints of communism would be freedom in comparison with the present condition of a majority of the human race." But while expressing sympathy for the ideal of socialism, Mill doubted that in the present state of human nature it could work without compulsion, and he was never prepared to abandon his belief in individual liberty.

His best-known work, in fact, was *On Liberty* (1859), a work to which his wife, Harriet, contributed much. It is the classic argument for the maximum of individual liberty, though in the end one is left wondering whether Mill did not allow too many loopholes. "The only purpose for which power can be rightfully exercised over any member of a civilized[5] community against his will is to prevent harm to others. His own good, either physical or moral, is not a sufficient warrant. He cannot rightfully be compelled to do or forbear...because in the opinion of others to do so would be wise or even right." [Our present-day welfare philosophy, obviously, totally rejects this principle.] Mill proceeds to make the case for maximum liberty of thought and discussion. The doctrine we suppress may be true, unless we arrogantly claim infallibility for our own opinion; or if not true it may contain some truth; even if it contains little or none, it is valuable in forcing us to show the reasons for our belief, thus preventing intellectual stagnation.[6]

Mill made it clear, however, that there are circumstances under which free speech must be checked, as when it is "a positive instigation to some mischievous act." Justice Oliver Wendell Holmes, Jr., later observed that there can be no freedom to cry "Fire!" in a crowded theater, and this is about what Mill meant. How far could people ever agree on the exact boundary here? Holmes used the principle to ban free speech in wartime by opponents of the war, a ruling some liberals thought to be an outrageous violation of civil liberties. Mill seemed to think that these boundaries can be made logically clear. Anyone who prefers to stress society's claims rather than the individual's can turn most of Mill's arguments against him. One such Victorian answer was James Fitzjames Stephen's *Liberty, Equality, Fraternity*.

Nevertheless, Mill's tract with its magisterial style and high seriousness is one of the great Victorian period pieces. Mill thought that the liberty necessary to

---

[5]Mill stressed the word "civilized"; barbarians, he said, would be better with an enlightened despot. The reign of liberty places heavy demands of self-control on the people who live under it.

[6]Mill's fellow Victorian, the great Roman Catholic John Henry Newman, adjusted his religion to liberalism by arguing, similarly, that heresy is necessary to faith. Unless error forces us to clear thinking, we do not perfectly know our creed.

human dignity was all too lacking in the modern world. He borrowed from his friend Tocqueville the sense of a danger from the "tyranny of the majority," which had replaced regal despotism as a threat to liberty; the democratic age produced its own kind of intolerance. "That so few now dare to be eccentric marks the chief danger of the time." Everything was becoming standardized, from shoes to ideas, and Mill complained, as so many have done since, of the mass culture that was promoting conformity and mediocrity. Mill fought for such unpopular causes as admission of Jews as members of Parliament, and freedom for the orators on soapboxes in Hyde Park, a famous symbol of British liberty that Mill once saved by a filibuster when he sat as an independent member of Parliament.

Probably Mill's best-known crusade was that indicated in his other famous essay, *On the Subjection of Women*. Written in 1861, it belongs to the same year as the emancipation of Russia's serfs, the beginning of the end for American black slavery, and Garibaldi's march toward Italian freedom from foreign rule. Emancipation was one of the great processes involved in modernization. The results of liberation were sometimes less exhilarating than expected, but the process was inevitable and irreversible. Mill's essay, written in collaboration with Harriet Taylor and her daughter by a previous marriage (a marriage that caused John and Harriet to wait many years for the consummation of their relationship, until the death of her husband, divorce being hardly thinkable) was not published until 1869, after unsuccessful efforts to include women in the voting reform of 1867. This suggests the depth of the opposition. The world was readier, it seemed, for the emancipation of slaves than of women. The movement Mr. and Mrs. Mill were instrumental in starting bore little fruit for many years.

The Mills argued, against the almost universally accepted opinion to the contrary, that sex differences are rooted in social usage, not innate psychology, and therefore women, having the same intellectual potential as men, should receive the same education. Other eminent Victorians, including John Ruskin and Thomas Carlyle, strongly disagreed. The latter sage, in many ways so unorthodox, married to a woman of strong intellect, believed that her role was to support and care for him, women being by nature "passive" rather than active. Darwin's opinion that they did not belong in the scientist's realm of creativity has been noted. James Bryce observed in 1864: "The notion that women have minds as cultivable, and as worth cultivating, as men's minds is still regarded by the ordinary British parent as an offensive, not to say revolutionary paradox." Elizabeth Barrett Browning reflected at length on the dilemma of the woman poet, condemned to be thought unnatural (unwomanly) if she was too intellectual, or assumed to be shallow because female.

Not that the Mills' tract, though it launched the women's movement in Britain, was the first to address the issue. Mary Wollstonecraft, Shelley's stepmother-in-law, wife of the left-wing Rousseauist William Godwin, had published her *Vindication of the Rights of Women* in 1792. A tradition of feminism came from the *philosophes*. Though the socialists offended many by advocating sexual freedom, they did keep alive the question of the emancipation of women. The

Saint-Simonian Disciples searched for a woman messiah. A significant group of feminists in the pre-1848 era included the celebrated George Sand. Living in London exile in the 1840s, Mazzini became friends with a family whose four daughters all smoked cigars like the famous French novelist! Oscar Wilde's mother, a mid-Victorian Irish lady, declared that in tracing the history of women from earliest times, "we have heard nothing through the long roll of the ages but the sound of their fetters."

England then produced its own female George; the woman who called herself George Eliot, scorning Mary Ann Evans, was perhaps the greatest Victorian novelist. If not she, then one of the remarkable Brontë sisters. Adored wife of the greatest Victorian poet, Elizabeth Barrett Browning was no mean poet herself. The notion that women were being held in intellectual if not actual servitude (they did have a separate and subordinate legal status, which the Mills assailed) is difficult to square with the large number of women writers of the first rank. The Brontës and Eliot, who followed in Jane Austen's distinguished footsteps, might occupy a niche long allowed to women. Women were permitted to write novels and almost held a monopoly of a certain kind of less than profound storytelling. But there were also imposing "bluestockings," from the redoubtable Harriet Martineau early in the century (and Mary Shelley, author of *Frankenstein*) to Beatrice Potter Webb at the end of it. Webb contributed notably to economics and political thought, if not science. John Stuart Mill himself owed much to the woman he married and worshipped, as did August Comte's religion of humanity.

In its attitude toward women as in other matters, the Victorian age stands between the traditional and the modern. Treatment of sex roles and sexual interaction form the interesting crux of most of the great Victorian novels, those of Dickens, Eliot, Thackeray, Hardy, Meredith, Butler, Gissing. A recent treatment of that archetypically Victorian novelist Anthony Trollope (by Jane Nardin) finds him changing in the direction of a more liberal feminism as he aged and moved with the times.

Indeed, the Victorians virtually made a religion of idealized womanhood. Later feminists objected to this; the angel in the house was treated as something too pure for the real world, purposefully kept apart as a symbol of virtue. George Bernard Shaw wrote that, needing something to adore, the Victorians "set up a morality and a convention that women were angels." Much of the alleged Victorian secretiveness about sex—Shaw claimed he never knew until well into young manhood that women had legs—grew out of the need to preserve the myth that some women belonged to a higher, more ethereal realm of being. From an all too obviously imperfect workday world, men could come home to something different and better. The notion that women might want to participate in the grubby marketplace or grimy factory, or in the tainted world of politics, would have astonished them. Mill, at any rate, was free from this patriarchal state of mind.

Near the end of his life he reconsidered his antireligious position. He felt the bankruptcy of scientism and edged toward belief in a finite God. God is not omnipotent; he (she) needs our help. Mill's concluding remarks in the essays called "Theism" seem to bring in all the forms of nineteenth-century faith. He salutes the Religion of Humanity, "that real, though purely human religion." And the spirit of Hegel seems to dwell in the statement that

> To do something during life, on even the humblest scale if nothing more is within reach, towards bringing the consummation ever so little nearer [the triumph of good over evil] is the most animating and invigorating thought which can inspire a human creature.

But perhaps, he added—quite a concession from the lifelong rationalist—supernaturalism may make its contribution too.

OTHER VICTORIAN SAGES

Matthew Arnold—poet, critic, essayist, satirist—spoke for the civilized tradition as no one else did. Too critical to accept fundamentalist Christianity, Arnold worried about the decline of religion. His best-known poem deplored the "melancholy, long withdrawing roar" of the sea of faith, leaving us here as on a darkling plain. His 1852 poem "Empedocles on Etna" was about the suicide of the ancient Darwin, who threw himself into the volcano after finding no meaning in life. Musing over "the strange disease of modern life," with its shallowness and nervous frenzy, Arnold reminded his progress-enchanted Victorian readers that civilization does not consist of material things and mere numbers of people; it is development of intellect and taste, a "certain temper of mind," broad, intelligent, critical, refined. No one felt more keenly than Arnold—earlier than most intellectuals—the decadence of modern life, with its "sick hurry and divided aims."

In *Literature and Dogma*, Arnold in his urbane way presented a plea to save the essence of religion from the dogmatists, to save Christianity from the Christians, as it were. The narrowmindedness of the Evangelical "philistines" repelled him. But he did not spare the materialistic scientists; both religious and scientific dogmatism are enemies of the spirit, which should be open, tolerant, humane. Basically Arnold's religion was like Comte's, a religion of humanity. He held up for adoration not so much lives as text, "the best which has been thought and said in the world." "The best poetry will be found to have a power of forming, sustaining, and delighting us, as nothing else can." The Bible would be included, of course—great literature, but hardly outranking Plato, Shakespeare, and all the other masters. In a celebrated dictum he declared that both Hebraism and Hellenism are integral parts of European civilization, but in evangelical England there was too much of the former.

Arnold's listing of dogmatic science and dogmatic religion as equally deplorable is similar to what Leo Tolstoy, the Russian giant, declared: "the two most terrible plagues of our time" were Church Christianity, the official religion of the State and its servants—of which he himself had so often been the adversary—

and "materialism," the crude dogma of the scientists, including Darwinists and historical materialists. The uncritical belief in science as a new god is quite analagous to dogmatic religion, Tolstoy thought.

The other leading Victorian sage, John Ruskin, offered a religion of social service. Ruskin began as a student of architecture, making himself the Victorian oracle on this subject at midcentury with *The Seven Lamps of Architecture* and *The Stones of Venice*; his remarkable descriptive powers owed much to Thomas Carlyle. And Ruskin carried on Carlyle's radical critique of economic individualism from a neo-medievalist point of view. All great art comes from a sound society, Ruskin held; the Gothic stemmed from the medieval craftsman, not yet a degraded appendage of the machine, but a creative artist. Ruskin thundered like a modern Jeremiah against the soullessness of industrial England, where "we manufacture everything but men." Division of labor had destroyed the integrity of the creative process. The result was that beauty had fled from building; London was "a ghastly heap of fermenting brickwork." Shaw said that Ruskin's jeremiads against capitalism made Marx sound mild. *Unto This Last* (1860) voiced protest against the economics of irresponsibility and the social creed of neglect, so eloquent that it became the leading Bible of British socialism. The historian of the Manchester School, W. D. Grampp, credits Ruskin with doing more than anyone else to discredit the *laissez-faire* doctrine.

William Morris, craftsman, poet, and socialist, the leading spirit in English socialism toward the end of the century, enlisted both Marx and Ruskin in his creed. But in fact the two brands of socialism were very different. Ruskin's was antimaterialist and antidemocratic (or antiequalitarian). The key to economic and moral renewal lay in a new attitude toward labor and art. Ruskin implied that the cause of ethical decline was esthetic. The puritanism and utilitarianism of the middle classes joined to make them shockingly indifferent to art, this son of a businessman alleged. Ruskin's early popularity with these classes faded as he increasingly assailed their values and lifestyle, and his sanity wavered late in his life. He always remained such a master of prose that his disciples included some of the greatest writers in all countries: Proust, Tolstoy, Gandhi, and Frank Lloyd Wright were among them. He tried to reestablish orders dedicated to service on the medieval pattern (the Peace Corps would have pleased him).[7] These met with doubtful success, but Ruskin left behind an Oxford college bearing his name and dedicated to bringing working-class people to the university.

With his love of the Middle Ages, Ruskin seems close to the Catholicism of John Newman's Oxford movement, traces of which were in fact to be found among the late-century esthetic school. Ruskin did not, however, take the road to Rome himself. He did believe in a transcendent God, but it was hardly the God of the Christians. He could agree with Arnold that what modern man needed above all was a faith, but like Arnold he wanted a humanistic one, derived from a sense of

---

[7]This attempt to enlist the spirit of medieval chivalry in the cause of modern reform has a long history. In 1810 the French emigré noble Ferdinand de Bertier founded the Chevaliers de la Foi, an offshoot of Enlightenment Freemasonry.

beauty and craftmanship. Through looking at great works of art and architecture, and above all in being an artist, which means creating beautiful objects in everyday life, human beings become whole again. "To see clearly," he wrote, "is poetry, prophecy, and religion."

So there were a number of competitors for the huge vacancy left by the decline of a believable Christian myth—something, Arnold mused, that we can neither live with nor without. The story of many a Victorian was like that of Arthur Clough, who spent his life in doubt but always searching. Made a skeptic by Mill, he turned to Carlyle for a faith, then complained that "Carlyle led us out into the wilderness and left us there." Like Matthew Arnold, he resigned his Oxford fellowship; the conflicting views at the university of Tractarians, Utilitarians, Unitarians, Positivists had only confused him. He was attracted to Coleridge's Broad Church, and then to the hope of revolution in 1848, but he never found the answer he was looking for. He became famous for never becoming famous, never realizing the hopes that had caused him to be considered the brightest of all the bright young men at Oxford. But it was Clough who wrote

> 'Tis better to have fought and lost
> Than never to have fought at all

and "Say not the struggle naught availeth." The Victorians at times seemed to relish their anguish.

Certainly the Victorians were not the complacent people they are often said to be. It is true that the reigning orthodoxy of free trade and self-help seemed dominant. Samuel Smiles's *Self-Help* was one of the century's best-sellers in England. George Orwell said his father had read only two books in his life, the Bible and *Self-Help*. Popular also was Smiles's *Lives of the Engineers*, telling of poor boys who made their way to wealth and glory. Faraday was a blacksmith's son, Stephenson a collier's. Based on individual initiative, the nation grew rich and powerful under the rule of minimum government and free trade. The powerful London *Economist* assumed without any question that the sum of private interests "is always the same as the public interest."

Queen Victoria's long reign (1837–1901) became a legendary symbol of British success. This was the heyday of the middle class, an "age of improvement." But protest was never absent among the leading writers. In *Hard Times* (1854), Charles Dickens, the age's chief literary figure, turned his powerful pen against the world of greedy capitalists and inhuman political economists, as he had already satirized the law and education, the cruelty of the poorhouses, the stupidity of the bureaucrats. Charles Kingsley's tract *Cheap Clothes and Nasty* exposed the exploitation of labor. Carlyle and Ruskin thundered away; the former became quite unbalanced in his hatred of the liberal orthodoxy. Kingsley along with Robert Browning's friend F. D. Maurice were Christian Socialists. To them, the right religion was a crusade for social justice and working-class amelioration. Socialism, by 1884, had become a substitute religion for the British intelligentsia.

5

From Naturalism to Modernism

LITERATURE AFTER MIDCENTURY

One of the great adventures of the nineteenth century lay in the realm of pure literature. It was a brilliant literary era, in all parts of Europe. In an "age of reading," writers become cultural heroes. They could rise from poverty and obscurity like George Sand to become famous; grow rich like Balzac and Dickens, sway the destinies of peoples like Victor Hugo. Poets and novelists took on the role once filled by priests. With the decline of the traditional Church and of any agreed-upon orthodoxy in either religion or philosophy, the great imaginative writers have supplied most of the values of the modern world. They served as sociologists and social historians as well as social critics, chronicling in a vivid way all the urgent issues that crowded this age, in both public and private life: urban society, working conditions, poverty, sex, marriage, women's role. Freud said they were the first psychoanalysts.

The novel, that "loose and baggy monster" with no confining structural rules, led the way; Stendhal, Balzac, Flaubert, Zola, Eliot, Thackeray, Dickens, Hardy rivaled the philosophers and scientists in intellectual importance in France and Great Britain. In Russia, which lacked a political culture, writers like Turgenev and Tolstoy assumed an even more important public role as prophets and teachers. But there were the great Victorian poetic voices, too, led by Browning and Tennyson, distinct both from what came earlier and later. More sober than the Romantics, more didactic than the esthetic rebels of the end of the century, they came closer than either to bridging the gulf between high and low culture. With Ibsen, Hauptmann, Wilde, Shaw, the theater flourished as well.

A growing alienation from public values marked the post-1848 literary generation, especially on the Continent. A group of post-Romantic writers called themselves "realists." Literature and art joined the reaction against Romantic dreams and postures. In France the "art for art's sake" school, disapproving of both their styles and subject matter, accused the Romantics of sentimentality and sloppiness. "Deliver us from the Middle Ages!" cried Théophile Gautier. The "flowing style" of his friend George Sand sickened Gustave Flaubert. *Art pour l'art* insisted upon more careful craftsmanship as well as less moralizing in literature. Disgusted with bourgeois society but disillusioned with socialist utopias, these writers withdrew to cultivate an ironic detachment, practicing a severely objective, "scientific" approach to literature as they dealt "realistically" with far from heroic people in their novels. The style was lean, spare, carefully crafted, rather a return to classicism. With *Luisa Miller* (1849), the great Italian opera composer Giuseppe Verdi turned from "the grandiose gestures of his youth to a simpler and quieter style, more suitable to the portrayal of ordinary human beings and human emotions" (Julian Budden); it was a path Dickens also followed and was characteristic of the time.

Flaubert provided the most famous French novel of the 1850s, *Madame Bovary*, a savage satire on romanticism. One of the most famous but most pathetic of all literary heroines, poor Emma Bovary is led to destruction by her inability to accept reality—though we may sympathize with her rebellion against a dull provincial existence. The amoralism of *Mme. Bovary* shocked the public and anticipated a slightly later (post-Darwinian) "naturalism" in its depiction of a world ruled by accident and blind chance. A bitterly alienated personality, Flaubert used his "realism" as a strategy for attacking the idols of the bourgeois tribe. Joining him in this was the Russian emigré writer Ivan Turgenev, whose birth and death dates exactly match those of Karl Marx and who probably knew Marx in Berlin in the late 1830s. Turgenev's *Fathers and Sons* was the classic account of the generation conflict at midcentury. Nor is Emma Bovary very far from young Leo Tolstoy's Anna Karenina, also destroyed by an adultery conceived in desperation. They are the forerunners of Hardy's Tess and Zola's Nana, tragic victims of fate.

Flaubert the realist joined the pioneer modernist poet Charles Baudelaire in achieving a *succès de scandale* as well as a genuine success of art when in 1857 both of them faced criminal prosecution, the former for his *Flowers of Evil* and the latter for *Madame Bovary*. In England the so-called Pre-Raphaelite painters and poets were criticized as immoral, and in the 1860s the deliberately provocative poet Algernon Swinburne stirred up a storm. These art-for-art's-sake writers were hostile to Christianity and conventional morality. In Swinburne's unpublished novel *Lesbia Brandon* the theme of homosexual love, handled also by Gautier and Baudelaire, accompanies an estheticism in which people cultivate their senses and live saturated in beauty. Baudelaire's "satanism," purveyed in the dazzling technique of a new kind of poetry, seemed to ask the poet to seek out morbid and abnormal themes.

Swinburne, John Morley wrote indignantly in 1866, was "the libidinous laureate of a pack of satyrs." And indeed Swinburne, whose alliterative verses enchanted a generation of esthetes (before he lost his creativity and settled into a placid old age) recommended trading "the lilies and languors of virtue" for "the roses and raptures of vice." His early enthusiasms also extended to revolutionary figures like the Italian Orsini, who tried to assassinate Napoleon III.

Harold Nicolson wrote that Swinburne's *Atalanta* appeared (1866) as "a blinding flash of lightning," to an "intelligentsia" (his term) willing and anxious to be startled. "The age was seeking for its heresies." The heresy was that the *frissons* of art, or of life lived for art, outranked virtue, and that private experience was worth more than public duty. If "the world of letters was shaken as though by an earthquake" by Swinburne's *Poems and Ballads,* this led on to Oscar Wilde and Walter Pater, aggressively preaching the new estheticism as an immorality, while making their lives a challenge hurled at respectability. Victorian respectability was indeed outraged. It blamed this diabolism on the French, leading to an attempt in 1887 to ban or censor literature from across the Channel. The whole mighty saga of this esthetic revolt against the norms of a business-oriented society—which itself came from very respectable sources (the Greek classics taught at Oxford and Cambridge being the prime agency of corruption)[1]—swept on into a Europe soon to be dominated by Wagner and Nietzsche, Ibsen and Dostoyevsky.

The new writers on the whole were apolitical. The reigning bourgeoisie, fat bankers or vulgar merchants, disgusted them hardly more than simple-minded socialist crusaders. No form of government has a place for the poet, Baudelaire declared, whether republic or monarchy. Before 1848 he had been a Fourierist, an admirer also of the socialists Blanqui and Proudhon; he mounted the barricades in '48. But the collapse of that episode left him like so many others in a mood of desperate isolation. His pessimistic withdrawal from society corresponded to his greatest literary period, before an early death from syphilis.

NATURALISM

"Every twenty years theories change," a Zola character observed. The modern era in literature and the arts has indeed been marked by a restless generation revolt every few years. The reasons are simple enough. Thrilled by the poetry of Yeats and Auden, the twentieth-century poet John Berryman remarked that he didn't want to write *exactly* like them, "since in that case where the hell was I?" Each

---

[1]*Marius the Epicurean* was a leading work of Walter Pater, the high priest of late-century estheticism.

generation, and at length each individual writer, wants to find his own voice. And the excitement that a new style, a new manner of writing provided soon wears off. If Sand came to nauseate Flaubert, the master himself eventually lost his ability to provide *frissons*.

The movements in the arts that followed midcentury "realism" and "art for art's sake" were naturalism and symbolism. These two important schools somewhat overlapped. The birth of symbolism in the 1880s was partly a reaction against naturalism; "away from Zola" in Paris, "los von Hauptmann" in Berlin were among the battlecries of symbolism and its close relative "decadence." Yet the sources of *fin de siècle* symbolism actually lay in Baudelaire and Rimbaud, writers of the 1850s and 1860s. And the powerful impulse stemming from Emile Zola and his cohorts was just reaching some parts of the world in 1890; Americans like Jack London and Stephen Crane only heard of naturalism around 1900. Major figures like Ibsen and Dostoyevsky felt influences from both naturalism and symbolism, sometimes simultaneously.

In France, generally the leader in launching esthetic novelties, naturalism was a word of the 1870s and Zola was its leading representative. An extension of the realism of the Flaubert era, naturalism was realism of a more brutal sort. The naturalists made a career of literary slumming, going into "the living, swarming streets" (Huysmans) to discover criminals, prostitutes, gin-soaked wretches; Zola also found depravity in the countryside (see *La Terre*). One motive was obviously to disturb the bourgeoisie by revealing the horrors of the society of which they were so proud. The scientific influence on naturalism, in this age of Darwin and Pasteur, appeared in Zola's claim (obviously dubious) that as novelist he was nothing but a scientific sociologist, going forth with notebook in hand to record the lives of people exactly as they were. Scientific determinism pervaded this literature. Zola's huge multivolume chronicle purported to trace the effects of heredity and environment in determining the lives of a series of descendants from the same woman by two different men.

In principle, naturalist writers upheld no ideals and found no values; their works exhibited the harsh realities of the world as it is, a world chiefly filled with brutalized or impoverished creatures. It is also a world where chance and accident rule. In practice, their books were likely to stir sympathy for the poor wretches they described. But Zola's novel of industrial strife, the widely read *Germinal*, did not condemn the mine owners for the misery and tragedy of the industry. (Compare Gerhart Hauptmann's famous play about the Silesian weavers.) Everyone is caught in the trap. As a Dickensian character was fond of saying, "It's nobody's fault." But such tracts did perform a social service in poignantly calling attention to grim conditions of life.

A deep pessimism, derived partly from Darwinism, could be found in Zola's British counterpart, the talented and controversial Thomas Hardy. Hardy's novels of the 1890s, especially *Tess of the d'Urbervilles* and *Jude the Obscure*, presented people as the helpless victims of an almost malignant deity. "The President of the Immortals had finished his sport with Tess," Hardy remarks at the end of her story.

Lives are ruined by the merest chance. Hardy's later novels so shocked the British public that he quit writing them altogether, turning to poetry after 1895. But the vogue spread widely. The Irishman George Moore, and in the United States such figures as London, Crane, Frank Norris, and Theodore Dreiser, exposed the grim underside of industrial society, the pathos of lives in the urban wilderness, while luxuriating in the fashionable atheism. Theodor Fontane led a notable Berlin school of naturalism, similarly based on a disgust with bourgeois culture.

Though Henrik Ibsen was too big a figure to be pigeonholed, the Norwegian dramatist's iconoclastic plays, which were the sensation of Europe in the 1880s, probably fit best into the naturalist-realist category. They certainly had the power to arouse intense public controversy by touching exposed social nerves. Upon the performance of Ibsen's *Ghosts* in London in 1891, a decade after its European debut, George Bernard Shaw wrote *The Quintessence of Ibsenism*, one of the major critical works of the era as well as a defense of the play. England vibrated to a theatrical controversy as France had often done; *Ghosts* was the modern *Hernani*. In his book Shaw asked why some hailed Ibsen as the greatest living dramatist, the modern Shakespeare, while others requested his suppression in the name of common decency and public order. The answer lay in Ibsen's shattering attacks on conventional morality. In *Ghosts*, an apparently model wife and mother is shown to be living amid lies, unfaithfulness, and corruption, much as Nora Helmer was in the famous *A Doll's House* (1879). In *The Enemy of the People* (1882), respectable society persecutes the honest person who would interfere with its material prosperity by telling the truth about the evil source of that prosperity. Hating *Pillars of Society* (the name of another of his plays), Ibsen followed the naturalist path in having little more regard for idealistic reformers. His *Peer Gynt* is a modern Don Quixote who makes himself ridiculous by pretending dreams are reality. A hero of the feminists because of *A Doll's House*, Ibsen disconcerted them by disclaiming any connection with the women's rights movement; he told the Norwegian feminists in 1898: "My task has been the portrayal of human beings."

SYMBOLISM

In his later plays Ibsen adopted symbolist ideas and techniques. Few serious writers (or musicians or painters) escaped the potent influence of the mood that suddenly invaded Europe's civilized consciousness in the mid-1880s. At this time the Symbolist Manifesto (written by Moreas), the appearance in Paris of the *Revue wagnerienne*, the poems of Stéphane Mallarmé, and the publication of the curiously significant book called *À Rebours (Against the Grain)* written by the ex-naturalist Joris Huysmans, were among the symptoms of a veritable revolution in esthetic consciousness, perhaps the most significant in modern history.

The hero of Huysmans' book, Des Esseintes, was the prototype of all the "super-esthetical young men" whom Oscar Wilde and *The Yellow Book* were soon to introduce to an amazed Victorian public. Emaciated, depraved, and sophisticated, the last pale but exquisite flowers of a decadent civilization, they amused themselves with art and vice. Picking up a copy of the notorious *À Rebours,* Oscar Wilde's hero in *The Picture of Dorian Gray* felt that "the heavy odor of incense seemed to cling about its pages and to trouble the brain." Cold, cruel, green-eyed *femmes fatales* filled "decadent" stories and novels. Homosexual perhaps like Wilde, the decadent type might shade into more sinister types representing what Mario Praz characterized as "the Romantic Agony." An exciting suspicion of nameless sins hung over this literary assault on respectability. The Russian symbolist Alexander Dobrolyubov drank opium, lived in a small attic papered in black, and practiced black masses; he was an example of the provocatively bizarre lifestyles of these *fin de siècle* artists-rebels.

The symbolist-decadent outlook spread rapidly from Paris to Vienna, to Italy, to Russia, all over Europe, becoming virtually the banner of those whom Nietzsche called "we homeless ones," a minority of the avant-garde artists and intellectuals. Hugo von Hofmannsthal, the Viennese dramatist and poet much affected by Mallarmé, wrote in 1893 of a "spiritual freemasonry" of a few thousand people strewn around the cities of Europe who represented the consciousness of this generation.

Symbolism certainly had earlier roots, not least in Baudelaire and Arthur Rimbaud, "damned poets" of the previous generation. Rimbaud believed that the poet has the power to penetrate a deeper reality, bypassing conceptual thought to make contact with a realm of symbols in a "reasoned disordering of the senses." A vision akin to religious mysticism was here presented by a man whose life was that of an alienated rebel, who fled Europe to wander over Africa. Some have made this strange genius the object of a veritable religious cult.

It was perhaps the leading principle of the symbolist school that poetry is totally different from prose. It should not argue or narrate or describe, but convey by means of images and symbols the subtle inner world of the mind which eludes rational description. This impulse to create a "pure" poetry came from the "Parnassian" school of Rimbaud's friend Paul Verlaine in the 1860s. The goal was to distinguish poetry from prose by its content as well as its form, a deviation from all previous literary doctrine, and from the long narrative poem such as Tennyson and Browning wrote. Poetry should not be an alternative mode of discourse, but an incantation that seeks to capture ineffable moods and impressions by a kind of mysticism of the Word; "an ingenious complicated style, full of shades and allusions, pushing back the boundaries of speech," Théophile Gautier called it.

The French symbolists regarded Richard Wagner as virtually the founder of symbolism. Wagner's conception of art, they declared, was "at the origin of Symbolism." Poetry should resemble music. From the great German composer turned prophet came the idea of a total art, fusing all the arts in one, and also the message of art as the salvation of a society in need of emotional and religious rejuvenation, the restoration of community feeling and cultural richness. But Wagner had had more faith in art's social function than did the French symbolists. A national musical theater could rescue the people from bourgeois philistinism and materialism.

Not even Karl Marx (almost his exact contemporary) had more scorn for the gospel of mammon; but Wagner's revolution would be based on a new art celebrating heroes dredged up from the folk unconscious. The greatest of nineteenth-century opera composers deeply influenced Freud, Jung, and Nietzsche. He is in many ways the central figure of the whole modern cultural movement. A successful entrepreneur as well as artist and prophet, Wagner raised enough money to build his theater at Bayreuth in Bavaria, where his operas were performed and where an international collection of disciples began to gather.

Ibsen, Wagner, Dostoyevsky, the French symbolists formed a brotherhood of the avant-garde stretching across Europe, from Rome to Stockholm and St. Petersburg. The Swede August Strindberg and the Italian Gabriele D'Annunzio were charter members. So was Oscar Wilde, possibly the movement's leading theorist as well as its most controversial personality.

So lines of influence led from London to Paris to Vienna and back, all over Europe. The French symbolists and decadents who founded the Wagnerian Review in 1884—just after the master's death—included Mallarmé and Edouard Dujardin, one-time music student, whose novel *The Laurels Are Cut Down* was to introduce the "stream of consciousness" to Sigmund Freud and psychoanalysis as well as to James Joyce and modern literature. (Wagner also deeply influenced Joyce directly.)

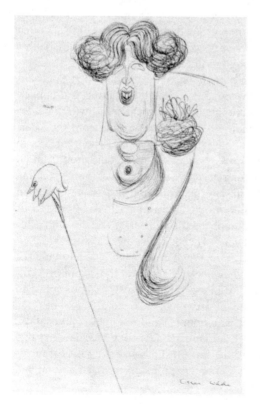

Caricature of Oscar Wilde.
(Ashmolean Museum, Oxford;
caricature by Max Beerbohm)

This revolution in language and life deeply stirred a creative minority of young Europeans at the end of the century. Some recent theorists, such as Michel Foucault and Julia Kristeva, have posited a sudden, drastic change in the *episteme* or the *idéologème* at about this time; a whole new universe of discourse replaced the old system. A sense of crisis was felt almost simultaneously all over Europe. At its root was a feeling of utter boredom, a sickness unto death with a "hideous society." Such a profound revulsion led the hero of *À Rebours* to cut all ties to the real world of men, and the realistic, scientific style that represented it. Theodore Fontane's "infinite loathing" of everything around him in imperial Germany, whether the court, the nobility, or the bourgeoisie (1896), was a typical reaction. The symbolists felt an intense indignation against a social order that was destructive of all beauty and integrity—"a hideous society," Des Esseintes exclaims.

Of the symbolists it was said that they could neither accept nor transform reality—they had given up on the dreams of socialist utopians—and so they made of their lives and works a negation of reality, the reality of existing mainstream society. They invented an imaginary world and called it reality. Wilde expressed symbolism's profound rebellion against external "reality," its vision of a new world created by the artist. "The first duty of life is to be as artificial as possible," Wilde wrote, adding that "what the second duty is no one has yet discovered." Nature is a poor thing, Oscar declared; let it imitate art. It does; the fogs of London imitate Impressionist paintings. Balzac and Dickens invented the nineteenth century. In the same spirit the master epigrammist remarked that "Any fool can make history, but it takes a genius to write it."

One of symbolism's most celebrated literary characters, the hero of Villiers de l'Isle Adam's *Axël* (*Axël's Castle* is the title Edmund Wilson gave to his classic study of this movement) lives alone in a Wagnerian castle studying occult philosophy; when he and a girl who has come to murder him fall immediately and sublimely in love, they decide to commit suicide because reality could not possibly measure up to the perfection of their love as they felt and experienced it at that moment. (Baudelaire had found each of his romances almost immediately disillusioning.) Living, Count Axël and Sara thought, is too vulgar; "our servants can do that for us." So too the hero and heroine of D'Annunzio's decadent novel *The Triumph of Death* plunge to their death as the ultimate thrill.

This intense idealism, based on total disgust with existing reality, might itself become a dead end, leading to suicide or immersion in drugs. But the positive side of symbolism was its undoubted success in creating a new kind of writing, one that poetically explored the strange world of the inner mind, struggling to suggest the incommunicable, including "the subtleties of neurosis, the dying confessions of passion grown depraved," which the French had been developing from Baudelaire and Rimbaud to Verlaine and Mallarmé. The young James Joyce, his brother said, preferred poems that "sought to capture moods and impressions...by means of a verbal witchery that magnetizes the mind like a spell, and imparts a wonder and grace...."

"The individual whose authentic life has been stolen from him seeks it elsewhere," Yeats declared. The "inward turn" stemmed from the alienation of consci

tive individuals from the body politic; it brought a new poetry, a new sense of language, a new European consciousness. It was the climax of a steady divergence of art and literature from society ("the noisy set of bankers, schoolmasters, and clergymen that passses as the world") going on over the whole nineteenth century. The symbolism of the 1880s was a total revolt not only against the mainstream society (socialists and naturalists had already done that), but against the previous generation of intellectuals and artists who had hoped to reform the society by criticizing it. It was a revolt against any conceivable society, indicated in Ibsen's switch in *Wild Ducks* from the attack on illusions to the necessity of illusions. Symbolism was the "move inside" of those who had given up hope of social change and become bored with the language of idealist escape that romanticism had tried. History is the successive exhaustion of options: "We are tired of the commonplace, the generally understood." The bourgeoisie had understood Goethe and Hugo!

A sign of the crisis was the sense of a split between reason and intellect, even "the intellect as the soul's enemy" (*Der Geist als Widersacher der Seele*, Ludwig Klages); "the revolt of the soul against the intellect" (Yeats, 1892). The symbolists had spoken of "a reasoned disordering of the senses," a mysticism of the Word, a new kind of poetry that had nothing to do with argument. The inner world, rich, subtle, as elusive as dreams, splits off from the external public self to become a realm of specialized interest with its own methods, entirely diffferent from those of the scientists and politicians. The symbolist search for a new kind of poetic language stemmed from the inability of ordinary discursive language to render the real flavor of experience. Robert Musil, the Viennese writer who turned from science to the novel, cited Maurice Maeterlinck, the Belgian symbolist: "We believe we have dived to the uttermost depth of the abyss, and yet when we return to the surface the drop of water on our pallid fingertips no longer resembles the sea from which it came."

Much of modern poetry lies under the influence of the great symbolist poets Verlaine and Mallarmé, followed by Jules Laforgue and Paul Valéry. T. S. Eliot brought symbolism's manner and mood into English poetry a few years later. Russian symbolism was more mystical and activist on the whole than its Western counterparts. According to the "mystical anarchism" of the poet Vyacheslav Ivanov, the special wisdom available to the artist as he penetrates arcane mysteries should be used to transform life and build a new world. But this hope of a political restoration via poetry was not entirely absent in Europe proper, as the example of Hugo von Hofmannsthal in Austria indicates.

ANTISYMBOLIST REACTIONS

The older realistic writers were often as shocked as the general public by this new kind of literature, which, they thought, emanated from depraved outcasts and seemed to border on madness. This was by no means true of the founders of the movement, of Mallarmé or Musil, who were serious writers and thinkers. Others, like Wilde and D'Annunzio and Strindberg, supply examples of something in between—decidedly outrageous personalities who were also dedicated artists. There is an enormous range of types among the end-of-the-century esthetic rebels and revolutionaries. They all had made a drastic break with literary tradition. In 1910 a leading English poet pronounced the verses of Thomas Stearns Eliot "insane." (The young American expatriate was importing the techniques and attitudes of French symbolism into English letters.)

A sane man has virtually no interior life, Max Nordau declared. This Jewish socialist wrote an attack on the new literature called *Degeneration* (*Entartung*, 1892), which may be compared to Tolstoy's philippic against the symbolists in *What Is Art?* (1897). Nordau saw nothing but "degeneration" in the new literature. He declared Nietzsche, Walt Whitman, Wagner, Ibsen, even Tolstoy (himself an opponent of the symbolists and decadents) as well as the French poets, to be so many morbid diseases. They were mad, they were antisocial, they were obsessed with sex (sexual overstimulation ruins civilization, Nordau believed). The German socialist was almost prepared to join Plato in banishing the artist from society in the interest of social stability. He did declare his respect for the "healthy art" of Dante, Shakespeare, and Goethe. (The almost universal worship of Shakespeare among the avant-garde writers might have caused him to reconsider.) Few of the moderns—Hauptmann's *The Weavers* was an exception—passed his critical inspection. He rejoiced that the average person remained immune to these siren calls, continuing to prefer music hall melodies to Wagner, farces to Ibsen.

The most famous of all writers, Leo Tolstoy, also condemned the new literature and art as elitist, antisocial, incomprehensible. Literature should speak the language of the common people, communicate important truths to them. These modern writers could hardly communicate with each other. Their motto was *odi profanum*, "I hate the rabble." Tolstoy thought that he could speak the language of the Russian peasant. In his later years (he died in 1910) Tolstoy wrote simple parables for the people. The author of *War and Peace*, after experiencing a profound spiritual crisis, turned to a kind of primitive Christianity and wrote powerfully moving religious tracts. He is an important figure in the late nineteenth-century "return to religion, " a rebellion against the domination of positivistic science. Neither the abstractions of the philosophers nor the facts and theories of the scientists helped him in his despair, and so he turned to Christianity—not the official Christianity of the Orthodox Russian Church, which he assailed and which tried to have his teachings condemned, but the original creed of the early Christians. Tolstoy thought that formal religion had falsified Christ's true message, which contained deep spiritual truths no mere dogma could express. The Russian Church excommunicated him for denying original sin, the divinity of Christ, and all the church sacraments, which he called "coarse, degrading sorcery." His writings about religion (for example, *The Kingdom of God Is within You*) have tremendous force. He felt also the influence of Oriental religions and tried to find the elemental truths that underlie all faiths.

Tolstoy was possibly the greatest prophet of the pre-World War I era; he captured the world's imagination and visitors came to his Russian estate from all over the world to do homage. A member of the Russian landlord nobility, Tolstoy ferociously denounced the corruption of this class and its European counterpart, and proposed a return to a simple life pared of all artificialities, rather like Rousseau or the American sage Henry Thoreau. Denunciations of war and of all forms of coercion made him a hero of the peace movement and in political terms an anarchist; the state, he thought, was the enemy of mankind. The principle of nonresistance to evil, which Tolstoy could not always obey himself, was the cornerstone of his political belief. The Russian government, the most despotic perhaps in the world, did not dare touch him, though he advocated anarchism, pacifism, and noncooperation with government. The affair of the Dukhobars was one astonishing example of his worldwide reputation. He set out to save this sect of Christian communists from brutal persecution by the tsarist government, and succeeded in raising a worldwide fund for the transportation of the Dukhobars *en masse* to Canada.

Tolstoy gave away the money from his literary works and eventually renounced all his wealth (to the great dismay of his wife). His most prominent disciple was to be the great Mohandas (Mahatma) Gandhi, legendary saint and father of the modern Indian nation. Countless others throughout the world acknowledged him as a seer. The American political leader William Jennings Bryan was one who made the pilgrimage to Yassnaya Polyana. The philosopher Ludwig Wittgenstein, sustained through the battles of World War I by reading Tolstoy's scriptural commentary, tried after the war to become a village schoolteacher on the Tolstoy plan. It did not work, and one may suspect that the gap between Tolstoy and the peasants was greater than Count Leo thought. But his role and reputation was a remarkable phenomenon. He provides an extreme example of the prestige a writer could acquire in the nineteenth century, making him a major world force through his influence on popular opinion.

Before about 1886 Russian literature scarcely existed for western Europe, the only exception being Turgenev who proved the rule by living almost all his life outside Russia. Its vogue after that owed much not only to Tolstoy, but to the antinaturalist reaction, the "turn inward" to explore psychological depths. Here the key figure was Dostoyevsky. The greatest of all psychological novelists, whom Freud was to name along with Shakespeare and Goethe among the real founders of psychoanalysis,[2] Dostoyevsky was widely viewed as getting his inspiration from the Russian soul, supposedly more profound than others. But in fact his literary debt was overwhelmingly to European writers: Shakespeare, Rousseau, Byron, Scott, Dickens, Goethe, Balzac, Hugo, and also to the pioneer Russian writers Pushkin and Gogol. Born in 1822, Dostoyevsky's passionate temperament is reminiscent of Baudelaire; he too had been a socialist in his youth and, arrested in 1849, spent

---

[2]The three greatest oedipal dramas were *Oedipus Rex*, *Hamlet*, and *The Brothers Karamazov*. From the next generation Freud might well have added D. H. Lawrence's *Sons and Lovers*.

four years in a Siberian prison camp. Dreadful as it was, the experience supplied him with much material for his novels. He came out no longer a radical and an atheist, but a conservative and a believer.

Between 1866 and his death in 1881 a series of stunning novels, from *Crime and Punishment* to *The Brothers Karamazov*, left their mark not only on literature but on philosophy, religion, and psychology. Dostoyevsky was the most successful of all writers at dramatizing serious ideas. If Freud labeled him a pioneer of psychoanalysis, Nietzsche borrowed the superman from him and Sartre credited him with the origins of existentialism. Nietzsche's "death of God," and the sense of a terrible crisis this meant, was also found in the work of the Russian writer. History, a character in *The Brothers Karamazov* says, is divided into two parts: from the gorilla to the annihilation of God, and from the annihilation of God to the transformation of the earth.

Dostoyevsky adopted a belief in the potential mission of the Slavic peoples to redeem decadent Europe because they were still capable of religion, uncorrupted by materialism. He joined Tolstoy among the predecessors of the post-1914 Christian revival, those Nicholas Berdyaev called "forerunners of the era of the spirit." Dostoyevsky's modernity inheres more in this philosophical dimension than in any novelties of style.

SHAW AND THE EDWARDIANS

George Bernard Shaw was another great writer who adhered to traditional modes of expression. Though far from a conventional thinker, he chose not to cloak his ideas in an obscure style. Defender of Ibsen, proponent of Wagner and Nietzsche, expounder of Marx, feminist and vegetarian, Shaw's mission was to force novel ideas on provincial Britain. For this very reason he could not afford to seem other than heartily straightforward in his manner. His plays often borrowed the familiar structure of melodrama or farce, the difference being that Shaw filled them with daring ideas. A flair for the drama of ideas and a Voltairean wit marked this versatile transplanted Irishman. He went to London as a young man, and there he met socialists, visionaries, feminists, and Hyde Park orators in the ferment of the 1880s.

Some of Shaw's plays exposed social evil or hypocrisy, in the socialist spirit; others reflect his fascination with Nietzschean and vitalist ideas then so much in the air. Bertrand Russell saw Shaw as the British counterpart to Sigmund Freud (they were exactly the same age), "dispelling humbug" about sex and family relations. Most of Shaw's plays shocked the Victorians but amused them so much that they swallowed the insults. Like Voltaire, Shaw became a "licensed lunatic" privileged to criticize the idols of the tribe because he did so in such a scintillating manner.

Bold, free spirits stride through Shaw's plays, knocking down the proprieties and teaching people to assert their individuality. Following a suggestion of Nietzsche's, Shaw had his Don Juan find that the best people are really in hell, not heaven. The common rules are reversed: women drink brandy and smoke cigars, while men are cringing and cowardly; honorable professions are dishonorable, and vice versa: Mrs. Warren's profession (the oldest) is really no worse than a respectable businessman's. Shaw's Caesar is a Nietzschean superman, action controlled by reason, beyond good and evil. *Back to Methusaleh* popularized the theory of creative or emergent evolution, a favorite theme of the influential Paris philosopher Henri Bergson, and indeed the "life force" was a persistent Shavian theme. Colin Wilson observed that Shaw's plays "are all about the same thing: the obscure creative drive of the 'Life Force' and the way it makes people do things they find difficult to understand in terms of everyday logic."

Man and Superman, written in the same year as Freud's *Interpretation of Dreams*, has as its hero a modern Don Juan, but the real victor in the play is a Donna Juana, the New Woman; Shaw's plays, John Simon wrote, "perceived women as predators, but also as basically healthier and more sensible than men." In this as in most of his plays, Shaw's range of ideas was amazingly wide, embracing socialism, Darwinism, sexual emancipation, feminism, vitalism, and new esthetic creeds. In his more than fifty active literary years Shaw wrote more than fifty plays as well as a great deal of other prose including notable music criticism. His heyday was between 1895 and 1917. He participated in the Fabian Society's political work and once served as an elected vestryman on a Borough Council. He stands with other Edwardians like H. G. Wells and Bertrand Russell as a tribute to the amazing intellectual energy of that age. But, as we noted, he was not a literary modernist, presenting few of those barriers to popular communication that the avant-gardists did. Only his ideas were modern.

Herbert George Wells was even more amazing in his energy. He wrote well over a hundred books.[3] Spread over fifty years, this comes to more than two books a year, in addition to which he wrote an immense number of magazine articles and reviews. This alone would hardly gain him immortality, for a number of writers of low-grade fiction have surpassed this in sheer quantity of published words. But Wells was a quality writer, whether in fiction or nonfiction. Like Shaw, he was not a stylistic innovator, preferring to make himself comprehensible to the common reader, and in his later years he made a point of aggressively criticizing writers with any pretense to stylistic novelty. But his early novels received high praise. A 1912 poll among literary authorities voted him second best among all living British novelists, surpassed only by Thomas Hardy, who had by then long since ceased writing novels. On the basis of a series of social satires written between 1900 and 1910, Wells was freely compared to Dickens; "a writer of sparkling humor, a caustic wit, brimming with invention," a representative 1906 review pronounced. These novels, such as *Tono-Bungay* and *The History of Mr. Polly*, were sharply etched representations of real people in England, chiefly London, not the rich and power-

---

[3]The 1966 bibliography by the Wells Society found 156 separately published items, though some were pamphlets of only a few pages. Warren Wagar in his *H. G. Wells and the World State* listed 108 titles, some of which, like the popular *Outline of History*, had more than one volume.

ful but the little people. The tales had a biting edge; "the sordid hopelessness of the life of the lower middle classes," their limited horizons and their pathetic fantasies stood revealed.

As is well known, Wells was simultaneously creating another literary genre, of which he was the virtual inventor—science fiction. He was the author of *The Time Machine* and *The Invisible Man, The First Men on the Moon* and *The Island of Dr. Moreau*, and others. They established the model for all the horror shows, space voyages, and futurology of later days, and were themselves made into early movies. Though "sci-fi" has a few scattered earlier pioneers, it was Wells who put it on the map and was its acknowledged master. More recent practitioners owe their basic debt to him.

The son of a household servant and a small-time professional athlete turned unsuccessful shopkeeper, Wells came by his knowledge of the little people honestly. He never went to Oxford or Cambridge. He once worked as an apprentice in a clothing store. But he got to the university by way of science, parlaying a lean scholarship at South Kensington Normal School into a B.Sci. degree at the University of London (1889). He had by then fought his way through a serious accident (suffered in a football game) and a disastrous first marriage. A kind of mad exuberance marked the volcanic career of this volatile life-force. It seemed to be a custom of the times. The biographer of Wells' friend and contemporary Annie Besant titled the first volume "The First Five Lives of Annie Besant." Besant began as an atheist disciple of Charles Bradlaugh, the man who became famous in 1885 for refusing to take the parliamentary oath; was a pioneer feminist and advocate of birth control as well as free love; joined Shaw as a charter member of the Fabian (socialist) Society, taught science classes, helped organize trade unions and strikes, and then after falling under occult influences went to India and started the Indian nationalist movement (preceding Gandhi as president of the India National Congress). A rather normal Victorian-Edwardian life!

One can similarly identify at least five Wells in this late Victorian era. He had become a socialist, listening to George Bernard Shaw, William Morris, and Henry George in his youth in the 1880s. The Darwinian spirit of evolutionary science deeply influenced him at the same time. Wells wrote a number of books dealing with the subject indicated in the rather wordy title of a 1902 publication: *Anticipations of the Reaction of Mechanical and Scientific Progress upon Human Life and Thought*. He had a special talent, related to his science fiction bent, for predicting coming technological developments and their consequences. Aviation, atomic energy (and perhaps atomic wars), prefabricated housing, suburbanization, huge cities, any number of such things soon to happen to the human race Wells foresaw in a way that if not exactly uncanny was certainly impressive. In 1902 the Wright brothers had not yet launched their pioneer air flight, and radioactivity had barely been discovered. On these and other subjects Wells showed himself up to date on the latest science news and able to imagine what technological change would mean for human life. Futurology, which has since become a somewhat dubious science, owes its beginnings to Wells.

Like Shaw, Wells lived to a ripe old age and never stopped writing, but eventually became an anachronism; his finest hours were before 1914. His success in producing both fiction and nonfiction of high intellectual quality yet readable by the masses was a rare one, perhaps impossible in later times. His postwar *Outline of History* became the all-time best seller for a serious work of history. It might be added that Wells, whose 1910 novel *Ann Veronica* shocked even his socialist friends in daring to present sympathetically a "liberated woman," probably did more to advance women's emancipation than any of the great Edwardians, even Shaw and Russell.

THE BIRTH OF MODERNISM IN THE 1900S

On the Continent, a bolder, more daring, more experimental style in the arts had been growing; it scarcely affected Britain until near the end of the decade. Virginia Woolf once declared that "human character changed" toward the end of the year 1910; among other things she was thinking of the post-Impressionist painting exhibit that opened in London at that time, and that caused immense public controversy.

The revolution had been underway in Europe for some time. A compilation of esthetic "manifestoes" printed between 1890 and 1910 turned up no fewer than 730 of them. The Fauves were a remarkable school of painters headed by Matisse and Dufy; the Cubists followed. We may see in Expressionism and Cubism, Germanic and Gallic respectively, the emotional and the rational wings of modernist painting. The Cubists with their geometric analyses differed from the Expressionists and their subjective symbols; the common denominator was a drastic experimentalism that departed from conventional realism to seek in abstract forms or inner visions a deeper reality. "There is an inherent truth which must be disengaged from the outward appearance of the object," Henri Matisse explained. "Exactitude is not truth." "Objects hinder my meaning," declared another great painter, Vasily Kandinsky, whose first abstract painting belongs to the year 1910. "Away from the Thing, away from Matter, back to Spirit" was the motto.

There was here a serious intellectual quest for deeper truths, and for salvation of humanity from a prison of scientific rationality, but the ordinary person was inclined to dislike the new art intensely. Its anti-realism was one reason; people could not "recognize" anything in the painting or sculpture and suspected these artists of poking fun at them—in which there was a grain of truth. These artists were in rebellion against a world of bourgeois mediocrity and popular philistinism, of bureaucracy, mechanization, triviality. The public reaction was usually one of shock and outrage; the more so as modernist art usually featured a bolder eroticism. Viewers threw things at exhibitions of modern art in London and New York. The emperor Franz Josef struck a Kokoschka painting with his riding whip! The Irish, not to be outdone, rioted for a week over a play by J. M. Synge, *The Playboy of the Western World*, today considered a classic. This was the most extreme break with tradition since the Romantic movement, probably an even sharper one than that, and it was too much for people just getting accustomed to the earlier one. Studies of attitudes toward the arts throughout the nineteenth century, such as Percy Schramm's account of nine generations in Hamburg, reveal a steadily widening gulf between artists and general public, popular and avant-garde taste.

It might seem perverse of the bourgeoisie, which fomented constant change in technology and believed in "progress," to reject anything new in the arts, but they did. A century later, they would pay millions of dollars for paintings derided or ignored at this time, by Van Gogh, Picasso, Matisse, Klee, Mondrian. The revolution extended to the other arts, of course. Music was a scene of furious controversy. The Paris Academy ejected Maurice Ravel in 1903, and Gustav Mahler did furious battle with the Viennese musical establishment, but this was nothing compared to the reception of the more drastic novelties that came a few years later. Wagner and Debussy had tampered with the diatonic scale, but Arnold Schoenberg rejected it entirely in favor of a twelve-tone one, and his "serialism" invented a new kind of musical structure. The Viennese rioted against the offerings of Schoenberg and Alban Berg in 1913, following a more famous disturbance in Paris that greeted Igor Stravinsky's violent rhythms and dissonant chords in his *Rites of Spring*.

A similar outcry arose against the new architecture. The Viennese architect Adolf Loos, whose "international style" had been much influenced by the United States, became a storm center in 1910 when his building on the Michaelerplatz, the Looshaus, caused "a storm of indignation...which has remained unique in Vienna for its violence." This break with architectural tradition, whereby the styles of the past, classical Greek, medieval (resurrected by romanticism), Renaissance or Baroque, formed the basis of all building aspiring to the status of Art, owed much to the influence of Darwinism, as the case of pioneer modernist Louis Sullivan shows. Must not every mode of human culture adapt to new conditions as society evolves? Nothing was more exciting than the frontiers of architectural modernism just before 1914 as revealed in the work of the American Frank Lloyd Wright, the Swiss Le Corbusier, and other young rebel-geniuses of the building world.

It was a brilliant generation. Most of its recognition lay ahead, in the years after World War I, and will be further discussed in that chapter. Foreshadowing a revolution in the novel, James Joyce, D. H. Lawrence, Virginia Woolf, Franz Kafka, and Marcel Proust were serving their apprenticeship as writers just before the war. The fuel for this explosion of art and literature came in good part from philosophical and scientific ideas just then emerging, which we will discuss next. Such were the intuition of Henri Bergson, the Dionysian spirit of Friedrich Nietzsche, Freud's unconscious mind, and the revolution in physics associated with Albert Einstein. ("Time and space died yesterday!" the Futurist Manifesto cried.) At the same time, the ferment of political and social thought continued.

There was enough in Europe to fill the mind to overflowing, one would think. And yet a significant feature of artistic modernism was a reaching out to exotic lands. "Europe bores me," André Gide declared. Paul Gauguin had fled a Brussels bank to find subjects for his paintings in the South Seas. Robert Louis

Stevenson, a perpetual traveler, finally settled in Samoa. An extraordinary number of the writers and artists of the *fin de siècle* generation were almost constantly in motion; of more than Rainer Maria Rilke it could be said that they "had neither a particular place nor a particular direction in which to go." Included in the specific influences on art were some from Japan, so recently and dramatically drawn into communication with the West and surveyed by writers like the American Lafcadio Hearn. "The Orient was in the air" in France in the 1900s. Ezra Pound, the American expatriate who functioned as the leader of modernism in England, drew on the Japanese *haiku* form in his Imagist poetry. Soon, African sculpture made an equally deep impression on European avant-garde art.

THE IRRATIONALISTS

The art and literature of the end of the century interacted closely with philosophical currents, as references to Nietzsche and Bergson have already suggested. For these philosophers made art the chief avenue to truth. They were postscientific and to some extent antirational. The deepest truths elude our merely logical analyses, they believed. With French novelist-politician Maurice Barrès they would say, "Our intellect—what a very small thing on the surface of ourselves!" Our logic, itself a construction of language, is surely not capable of exhausting the infinite abundance of experience. Life is far larger than thought.

In France the poets influenced by the philosopher Henri Bergson, who taught an inner flux of freedom radically different from the public conventions of time and space, seemed to the critic Georges Guy-Grand to exhibit a kind of lyrical insanity in their "orgies of subjectivism." "Bergson brought us poetry and mystic intuition, vindicated freedom and idealism, freed the stream of consciousness," Enid Starkie wrote in recalling the impact of the Paris philosopher on her generation. His lectures at the University of Paris in the 1890s were likened to those of Abelard in the Middle Ages for the sensation they created, and he was soon being compared to Descartes, Rousseau, and Comte as the master of an intellectual generation. Bergson's first notable work appeared in 1889 when he was thirty. Like Nietzsche, Bergson's great gifts of style assured him of an audience; using metaphor and poetic imagery freely, because he believed that conceptual thought does not best communicate the nature of reality, Bergson was a writer's philosopher, with close affinities to the symbolist movement.

Bergson sharply distinguished between the rational, conceptualizing intellect and the intuitive understanding. The former is a practical tool, concerned with useful knowledge, but not truth-giving because reality may not be so divided up and conceptualized. The point is similar to Kant's phenomenal-noumenal distinction. Reality is a continuum, to be grasped by the intuiton. It flows through immediate experience as the "life force" that is in all things. Intuition (defined as instinct become self-conscious and reflective) takes us to "the very inwardness of life," much more so than the intellect, which deals with the surface of life. Bergson said that he began his philosophical speculations by considering what is meant by *time*, and found himself led to conclude that the clock time of everyday life or of the physicist is a convention very different from the real time of experience. The intelligence that analyzes and divides things has given us the former conception, which is useful but not true to experience.

When we grasp immediate experience by intuitive means, what we find is an indivisible continuum, a "duration" that we can scarcely describe save in poetic imagery. So it is in other things. Science tells us that the sound of a bell is a series of vibrations, but we experience it as a whole. A melody is not a series of notes, it cannot be described; we intuit it. Science, as Wordsworth had said, "murders to dissect." Reality is indivisible and hence unanalyzable; insofar as we do analyze it, as for convenience's sake we must, we falsify it. "Science consists only of conventions, and to this circumstance alone does it owe its apparent certitude; the facts of science and, *a fortiori*, its laws are the artificial work of the scientist; science therefore can teach us nothing of the truth; it can only serve as a rule of action."[4] Science, as Nietzsche would put it, is basically a myth.

Critics of Bergsonian or pragmatist indictments of the "conceptualizing" process as conventional only pointed out that these philosophers themselves could not escape the use of conceptual or intellectual language. To do without it would be to abolish thought. It was generally agreed that concepts and reality are not the same thing. Ernst Mach, the Austrian scientist-philosopher who influenced Einstein, was forcefully pointing out the same thing at this time (the 1890s). Conceptual knowledge does not exhaust reality or constitute the only method of dealing with it. But the implication that the two realms are utterly divorced, and that science tells us nothing at all about reality but only about its own arbitrary signs and symbols, went too far. Still, the persuasively conducted Bergsonian counteroffensive against science made an impact; its chief result was to vindicate and rehabilitate forms of "immediate experience" such as literature, religion, and various mystic or nonrational experiences. The Bergsonian message broke through the ban on religious or metaphysical speculations decreed by the positivist regimen. "For the first time since Comte and Kant, metaphysics had waged war against scientific determinism on its own ground and won it," Etienne Gilson wrote in his recollections of what Bergson meant to his generation. Charles de Gaulle spoke of Bergson as having "renewed French spirituality."

Bergson proposed a vitalistic evolutionary theory, arguing in a widely read work opposing Darwinian mechanism that life has within it some purposive forces, without which evolution cannot be explained (*Creative Evolution*, 1908). Doctrines of "emergent evolution" received the support of a number of thinkers at this time, the leading British example being Samuel Alexander. Nature creates itself gradually, rather than existing from all eternity; life evolves new and unpredictable forms. We participate in a universe that is not finished and we help in the making

---

[4]R. B. Perry, *Present Philosophical Tendencies* (1912), pp. 230–31.

of it. A striking idea and, as Bergson noted, a new one in the Western tradition, "creative evolution" turned the rather somber mechanistic atheism of the Darwinists into a feeling for the wondrous freedom of a world in growth.

Among Bergson's disciples in France was the editor and writer Charles Péguy, a nondogmatic Christian, a democrat and a socialist, who was one of the most influential voices in pre-1914 France. Péguy said that Bergson's was "the philosophy of the immediate.... It is a question of quite another thing than the insufficiency of scientific reason; it is a question of a pretention to direct contact with the essence of the living, moving thing." This strongly moved Péguy ultimately in a mystical direction. To Bergson too, novelists owed the idea of presenting an unedited "stream of consciousness." We have mentioned his influence on Shaw.

A friend of William James, Bergson had close affinities to the "pragmatism" of the American philosophers James and John Dewey. They broadly agreed in their attack on intellectual or conceptual knowledge. As Dewey put it, "there is an experience in which knowledge-and-its-object is sustained, and whose schematized, or structural portion it is." Immediate experience, in other words, is deeper and forms the matrix within which the knowing process takes place. As Nietzsche put it, we must reject the dogma of immaculate perception. Bergson and the pragmatists somewhat resemble the founder of phenomenology, Edmund Husserl, then more obscure than they, who around the turn of the century used the term phenomenology to mean the systematic study of how things and concepts are given to the mind directly, prior to their conceptualization in language.

The Englishman F. C. S. Schiller and the Italians Papini and Prezzolini represented pragmatism in Europe, where it was less important than in the United States. Papini subsequently became a fascist, indicative perhaps of pragmatism's tendency to take on the color of its surroundings and embrace any active creed—something also alleged of Bergsonism. The "creative evolution" idea, or the "life philosophy" fashionable in Germany (Max Scheler is a good counterpart of Bergson) had this weakness: they tended to greet every fashionable novelty as a manifestation of the life force or the spirit of history, hence to be welcomed. The strange fixation of the intellectuals on war in 1914 owed much to this syndrome. It happened, it was amazing; ergo it must be virtually divine. Reason could not judge it, for life stands above reason.

FRIEDRICH NIETZSCHE

In Germany people spoke of the revival of metaphysics, citing Hartmann, Lotze, and Eucken, as well as Scheler. But the greatest figure in Germany near the end of the century, with his influence spreading widely throughout Europe, was Friedrich Nietzsche. He had burst on the scene in the 1880s with a series of electrifying books, quite unlike anything ever written, using the German language in a new way to bear the freight of a number of startling ideas. The writing was so unusual that it took a few years for Nietzsche to become known; but by 1900, more than a decade after he had fallen dumb from a stroke at the age of only 45, he was the rage of intellectual Europe. (The term "intellectual" was just beginning to be used to describe a certain kind of temperament; in France it was said to date from a "Manifesto of the Intellectuals" issued during the uproar over the Dreyfus Affair in 1898.)

The young artists and intellectuals of Europe frequently exclaimed that Nietzsche expressed exactly what they felt but could not say; "the influence of Nietzsche preceded with us the appearance of his work; it fell on soil already prepared," as André Gide remarked. From William Butler Yeats in Dublin to Franz Kafka in Prague, the imaginative writers especially responded to Nietzsche. But his was a manifesto for all the different ones, the spiritual minority, the enemies of the crowd, those who hated with a total disgust the newspaper-reading masses. He was, in fact, the enemy of European civilization as it stood; one could only wipe it out and start over. "I saw a great sadness come over men. The best were weary of their work.... All is empty, all is indifferent, all was."

In his prophetic work, *Thus Spake Zarathustra*, Nietzsche resorted to a lyrical form derived from the ancient Greek hymn to Dionysus. He had begun as a precocious scholar, a classical philologist who received his Ph.D. at the age of twenty-four and became a professor at Basel. A part of Nietzsche's story was his clash with the new academic professionalism, technical and arid, which criticized his *Birth of Tragedy* (1872) for being too speculative. Max Weber referred to "specialists without spirit," which was Nietzsche's complaint; they thought him reckless and inaccurate. As a professor Nietzsche was not a success, and he soon resigned from the university complaining of ill health.

The Birth of Tragedy was nevertheless a remarkable book which contained the germ of most of Nietzsche's thought. Nietzsche saw the genius of the ancient Greeks as stemming not primarily from joyous optimism, as the Romantics had suggested, but from tragic suffering; it consisted less in philosophical rationalism and science than in primitive emotionalism tempered by reason and "sublimated" into art. Dionysus, lower-class god of music, tragic drama, and drunken orgies, became for Nietzsche a symbol of this primitive force, without which people cannot be truly creative. It was what overly rationalized modern European man had lost. The Greeks had been great because they had Dionysus as well as Apollo. Apollo's "measured restraint, wise serenity," his plastic formalism, must work dialectically with the imageless rhythmic frenzy of Dionysus, as it does in Greek tragedy, to create the highest art. "We must understand Greek tragedy as the Dionysian chorus discharging itself constantly in an Apollonian world of images." The Greeks had not been merely rationalists, but were infused with the will to live. Their greatest age was the time of the early philosophers and dramatists, of Heraclitus and Œschylus. Plato and Euripides already mark their decadence, which Western civilization inherited more than their grandeur.

This electrifying reversal of perspectives was typical of Nietzsche's sharply iconoclastic thought, his "transvaluation of values." Among his rejections were organized Chrsitianity (a life-denying religion, suitable for slaves), and traditional

Friedrich Nietzsche. Unsurpassed as a master of the modern mind, Nietzsche was the author of *Thus Spake Zarathustra* and *Beyond Good and Evil*. (Presse-und Informationsamt der Bundesregierung)

morality ("the most pernicious species of ignorance"). The supermen needed to rescue a decadent civilization must be beyond morality, "without pity for the degenerate." The most celebrated of Zarathustra's aphorisms announced that "God is dead": Europeans had killed him; a compelling faith no longer existed. Nietzsche's scornful rejection of (Pauline) Christianity resembles Marx's at times: a "Platonism of the people," a "fatal and seductive lie." Yet much more than Marx he wanted new gods, new myths at least; the death of God accompanies a terrible crisis the cause of which is an emptiness of the spirit.

Having seen through all myths (Nietzsche's great skeptical book was *Human, All Too Human*, 1878) there remains nothing to believe in except life itself; we must have the courage to accept life as it is, in all its meaninglessness, just because it is. We can affirm our own life force by living and striving to become what we are, realizing our own unique qualities. We can accept Dionysus after rejecting Christ. The general spirit that emerged from Nietzsche's exciting prose was a proud assertion of individuality against the mob, against the powers that be, ultimately against the universe itself. The existentialists learned from him that the utterly free human consciousness has the power to assert and thus create values in an amoral world. "Having killed God, must we not become gods to be worthy of the deed?"

Those who influenced Nietzsche most deeply were Schopenhauer, Richard Wagner, whom he met in Switzerland early in his career, and Darwin, whom he read in 1864 along with Schopenhauer's essays. The latter's sense of "life as will," not reason, permeated both Wagner and Nietzsche, though Nietzsche came to reject the great pessimist's gloomy denial of life as pointless; the *amor fati* of Zarathustra is the reply to Schopenhauer. We embrace life even though we see its irrationality.

Irrationalist strains were not altogether new. Late in his life (1837) the philosopher Schlegel startled his listeners by suggesting that the truest thought is not rational at all but intuitive-mythic. "Consciousness," Schopenhauer announced, "is the mere surface of our minds, of which, as of the surface of the earth, we do not know the inside but only the crust. Under the conscious intellect is the conscious or unconscious will, a striving, persistent, vital force, a will of imperious desire." Schopenhauer's distinction between Will and Reason, the former being fundamental, could be seen also in Darwin's scheme of nature in which the intellect is only a tool of survival, a part of the whole organism that struggles to adapt to its environment. As Nietzsche was fond of saying, if we make any sense of the world at all, this is because those who couldn't do so failed to survive.

The Saxony-born Nietzsche, who declared that "I have written my books with my whole body and life," was more than a technical philosopher; all of his thought was urgently directed toward life problems. Total disgust with the existing state of Europe, and especially with a Germany swollen with pride and prosperity after the 1870 victory over France (in which young Friedrich served for a time), was his basic feeling. To his delighted readers among restless turn of the century youth, Nietzsche communicated a lofty contempt for all the presently living miserable human specimens. Democracy, socialism, capitalism, nationalism, the mass man as well as economic man all came under his scornful attack. The only chance he saw was to begin again on the basis of a tiny saving remnant of the absolutely uncorrupted. This invitation to wipe out the existing human race and create an *Übermensch*, would prove a dangerous idea in the hands of a Hitler; but Nietzsche was neither a racist nor a nationalist, breaking with his one-time idol Wagner over these points. He called himself "a good European," and anti-Semitism disgusted him.

Nietzsche was a shrewd psychologist, who bequeathed much to Sigmund Freud and Carl Jung. The dark, uncivilized id force in human nature (Nietzsche used the term *das es*, the "it," which Freud borrowed perhaps by way of Georg Groddeck; it has usually been rendered into English as "id") lurks in the unconscious; it can be sublimated into creativity. This "Dionysian" element is partly sexual, and Nietzsche charged that Christian morality had grievously damaged Western civilization by endowing the sexual instinct with a bad conscience. "He who thinks he has killed his sensuality is wrong, for his sensuality lives on in an uncanny vampire form, and torments him in hideous disguises." Writing in aphorisms, Nietzsche threw out ideas the psychologists would develop more systematically. And indeed he was an almost endless source of stimulating, novel ideas.

His political influence worked in more than one direction, like that of all great writers. Atheist, radical critic of conventional religion and morality, friend of the free spirit, this most unconventional of thinkers held a natural appeal to the left, and many socialists or anarchists claimed him for revolutionary activism. He was the darling of the avant-garde, the bible of the bohemians. Some of the Russian Bolsheviks adopted him along with Marx. On the other hand, Nietzsche scorned both democracy and socialism, which to him were descendants of the slave morality of Christianity—teaching meekness, equality, mediocrity. He preached the inequality of men and could be cited on behalf of imperialism, despotism, and war. Benito Mussolini turned from left-wing socialism to fascism in part because of Nietzsche's influence; Hitler and the Nazis glorified him, even if they obviously misunderstood him.[5] During the 1914–18 world war, the Allied governments linked Nietzsche to the Prussian war machine. (H. L. Mencken, an American literary admirer of Nietzsche, related that one day after the American entry into the war the police questioned him about his connections with "the German monster, Nitzschke"—who had of course been dead for seventeen years by then.) But anyone who knew Nietzsche's writings found this as absurd as most war propaganda.

More recently his corrosive skepticism, in pointing out that all human statements are simply unproven assertions emanating from the will-to-power, has helped inspire "deconstructive" criticism. There are as many truths, he liked to say, as there are people with points of view. In brief, Nietzsche's fire flashed in many directions and struck tinder in all kinds of unlikely places. What is undeniable is its power. "I am dynamite," the sage of Sils St. Maria had said; it was true. Virginia Woolf, reading Coleridge, remarked on ideas that "explode" and give rise to all sorts of others. Nietzsche was one who had this effect. *Thus Spake Zarathustra* has been read all over the world (there was a popular Japanese edition, for example), has been set to music (by Richard Strauss and Gustav Mahler), and ranks as one of European literature's great philosophical poems, joining those of Lucretius, Dante, and Goethe on a select list.

In the end Nietzsche's revolt against intellectualism seems his most significant feature. It was part of a much wider tendency in this direction. The symbolist poets shared it (Richard Wagner was a common source, and 1884 was the year of

---

[5]Edited tendentiously by his pro-Nazi sister, who had custody of his papers, Nietzsche was made to seem far more congenial to Hitlerism than he was; only in recent decades has a full and accurate edition of his works made it possible to evaluate him fairly and fully, a process that is still going on.

both *Zarathustra* and the birth of the symbolist movement). Martin Buber, the Jewish religious philosopher and Zionist, discovered in Jewish folklore of the Hasidic school "a primitive vitality, an unreflective openness to immediate experience, which had largely vanished from the over-sophisticated West." (Ritchie Robertson) Objective reason, product of man's fallen nature, reifies and obscures; the myth-creating process is a better route to truth than the conceptual one. (See the Russian philosopher-theologian Nicholas Berdyaev, *The Meaning of the Creative Act*, 1914). The Austrian Robert Musil, who deserted science for the novel because he thought only the latter could find the inward truth, referred to a conflict between *Hirn und verlängerten Mark*, intellect and depth. In France, Georges Sorel popularized a neo-primitivist return to barbarian myth, before sound instinct had been corrupted by too much reason. There are many other examples. The feeling that Western society was dying, and that the chief cause of its death was overrationalization or too much intellect, too much science and abstract knowledge, loss of contact with nature, with myth and symbol, with true religion and speech, was one of this era's leading convictions.

"Human reason was tired," Romain Rolland's hero in *Jean Christophe* reflects in the last book of this 1913 epic novel. "It had just accomplished a mighty effort. It surrendered to sleep.... Even science manifested signs of this fatigue of reason." Weariness does not seem the right word for this pre-1914 creative explosion, but no one can miss the note of unreason. "I have always considered myself a voice of what I believe to be a greater renaissance," wrote the great Irish poet W. B. Yeats in 1892, "the revolt of the soul against the intellect—now beginning in the world."

FREUD

Born in the same year as Shaw, Sigmund Freud was only twelve years younger than Nietzsche, from whom he learned much, and just a little older than Henri Bergson. Freud was one of a remarkable number of creative Jewish artists and scientists (usually lapsed from the ancestral religion) who were born in the Moravian or Czechoslovakian portions of the Austro-Hungarian Empire and came to Vienna at an early age, or whose families had done so; others in this category included Gustav Mahler, Ludwig Wittgenstein, Edmund Husserl. Arriving in the capital city at the age of three, Freud spent the rest of his life there, until driven out by Nazi persecution in the last year of his life. He earned his medical degree at Vienna's university in 1881, and later lectured there as a professor. He carried on a famous psychoanalytical practice at the Vienna address he occupied most of his life, now a shrine. But he never really liked the city, and the movement he created was an international one, whose first president was a Swiss, Carl Jung of Zurich. His close friends Sandor Ferenczi and Karl Abraham carried the word to Budapest and Berlin, respectively. It spread to have branches in all the major cities, doing best perhaps in London and New York. People came from all over the world to study with Freud, and he often lectured abroad, most notably in 1909–10 when the International Psychoanalytic Association was just being launched. Earlier, Freud had studied in Paris under Dr. Charcot.

Freud was a physician and a hard-headed, almost positivistic scientist by nature, out of the Darwin-Pasteur stable. He disdained religion and he often disparaged art; these are crutches of fantasy that the neurotic personality leans upon. Freud's general spirit was averse to metaphysics, mysticism, or anything except the empirically verifiable hypotheses of scientific method. If he studied the unconscious mind with its strange symbols and myths, he did so in order to understand it and in so doing to tame if not abolish it. ("Where Id was, there shall Ego be.") On the other hand, a key to Freud's genius is his deep grounding in Western literature. His own persuasive pen drew on the European classics for many of his leading concepts: Oedipus complex, narcissism, catharsis. He exerted a mighty influence on literature and the arts. Freud was a remarkable combination of scientist and artist, a balance that was often precarious, landing him in trouble with both camps, but was the basis of his enormous appeal.

Another Viennese physician, Anton Mesmer, just a century earlier had popularized what by Freud's time was called hypnosis, and used as a means of therapy in cases of "hysteria," a form of "nervous disorder" marked by symptoms of paralysis, tremors, and other physical problems that had no apparent physiological causes.[6] Watching Charcot use hypnosis, Freud thought he observed that the cure did not come from the hypnosis as such, but rather from retrieving a buried memory. In Vienna, as a young practitioner looking for a promising field, Freud made such cases his specialty and experimented in ways of bringing repressed experiences to consciousness. The notion that there was an "unconscious" part of the mind was an old one, recently featured in a book written by the Schopenhauerian Eduard von Hartmann (*Philosophy of the Unconscious*, 1869). We have already mentioned Freud's debts to Schopenhauer, who had discussed childhood sexuality and repression, as well as to Nietzsche.

Indeed, Freud dealt with matters about which there had always been speculation, because they are such elemental parts of human experience: the sexual drive, family relationships, dreams, the stray thoughts that run through our minds, secret shameful desires and language. Novelists and poets had probed these matters, folklore sometimes touched on them, but no one had ever tried to deal with them systematically and scientifically. Or at least no one had tried to see them as connected, as parts of a single whole, the human personality. Psychology itself was a new discipline, as such; the first psychological laboratory is said to have been set up in 1879 by Wilhelm Wundt. Of course the great writers, whose priority Freud freely acknowledged, were psychologists before the letter. Students of Dickens, Hardy,

---

[6]Mesmer called this force "animal magnetism" and believed it was carried by an invisible fluid, rather like the "pneuma" of the ancient Stoics. But it soon became clear that no such physical substance existed, though the psychological force did.

and almost every nineteenth century novelist and poet now tell us that these writers anticipated Freud.[7] Dickens, who discovered that he possessed mesmeric or hypnotic powers, aroused his wife's extreme jealousy in 1844–45 by applying mesmerism at all hours of the day and night to a friend's wife who suffered from muscular contractions and convulsive seizures, which were alleviated under hypnotic trance. While she was in a trance Dickens questioned her about her dreams and nightmares, seeking to learn more about the "phantom" that she said threatened her.

Freud drew together an amazing amount of data and threw over it the blanket of general theory. He continued to draw on literature as well as clinical data. The "free association" method of getting at the patient's suppressed memories, discovered independently by Carl Jung, may have been suggested by Dujardin's 1886 "stream of consciousness" novel, *Les lauriers sont coupés*. In 1879 Darwin's cousin Francis Galton devised a word association test.

Freud wrote interesting if controversial essays on writers and works of art—*Hamlet*, the Mona Lisa, Dostoyevsky—in which he tried to show that suppressed sexual conflicts shed light on the peculiar quality of masterpieces. He thus was himself the founder of the Freudian school of literary criticism. Additionally, Freud bequeathed to literature and art new themes and subject matter. The startling, once forbidden matter of incest, homosexuality, infant sexuality, and various "perversions" had been brought into the open, not only by Freud. The Viennese physician Richard Krafft-Ebing published a much-discussed *Psychopathia Sexualis* in 1886, the year Freud began his practice. (Another pioneer sexologist was the Englishman Havelock Ellis.) But Freud tied these deviant manifestations of the sexual impulse to a dramatic picture of conflict within the soul between instinctive urges and social taboos. Torn apart by the opposing demands of id and superego, the ego becomes a battleground. Here was a new version of tragedy, which playwrights and novelists quickly learned to exploit.

Rather obscure before 1914, psychoanalysis had its major impact in the 1920s, and we will discuss it again in that context. Still, Freud's most creative period was in the first decade of the twentieth century. His single most substantial book, *The Interpretation of Dreams*, a product of his own self-analysis after a kind of midlife crisis when he turned 40, was published in 1900. The Oedipus complex here made its debut. Having decided that the neurosis-causing repression is usually sexual, Freud now located the traumatic sexual experiences in early childhood. He initially hypothesized a sexual assault on or seduction of the child by an older person; but he soon came to believe that in fact sexual desire is present from the earliest years. (Via dream analysis, Freud claimed to have found sexual jealousy of his father in himself at 2 1/2 years.) Here was a shocking assault on the myth of inno-

---

[7]See also Rosemary Sumner, *Thomas Hardy: Psychological Novelist* (Macmillan, 1981), and Ekbert Fass, *Retreat into the Mind: Victorian Poetry and the Rise of Psychiatry* (1989). Stendhal was another novelist who often seems to anticipate depth psychology.

cent childhood, especially dear to the Victorians, which earned Freud disapproval and even ostracism. This did not deter him from pressing on with his bold theory, which became the cornerstone of psychoanalysis, that the male infant—as early as the age of two—may be sexually attracted to his mother and jealous of his father, with all kinds of resulting complications. (One may be homosexuality, which Freud rescued from the status of "physical abnormality" to view as a quite understandable personality deviation.)

It is in one's earliest years that basic personality traits are shaped, Freud believed. By 1905 he added other previously unmentionable details of early sexual development, tying these to character traits appearing in maturity. These were the oral, anal, and genital stages. Freud meanwhile wrote up a series of his cases, destined to much fame and some debate, which he explained in terms of his theories: Anna O., Dora, The Wolf Man, Little Hans, and others.

From the beginning Freud was challenging, controversial, distinctive. He attracted a remarkable, sometimes bizarre collection of disciples and colleagues, who showed a tendency to enact the Oedipal drama by breaking with their spiritual father to go their own theoretical way. The International Psychoanalytical Association took on some of the features of a professional scientific organization, but in other respects was more like a religious sect, marked by theological disputes and heretical secessions. Already by 1913 the first and greatest of the schisms had occurred, when Freud's younger colleague Carl Jung of Zurich, who had helped found the IPA, quarreled bitterly with him and left to set up his own branch of psychoanalysis.

Was psychoanalysis a science, a pseudoscience (as many claimed), a humanistic religion, an ideology like Marxism? One might suggest that it was primarily a branch of literature. Not only was Freud an accomplished stylist, with an obvious interest in world literature, but the kind of therapy for which he became famous, a long dialogue between analyst and patient, was a telling of life stories and an unraveling of plots. In 1910 the great composer and conductor Gustav Mahler became disturbed in spirit and sought an interview with his fellow Viennese, Dr. Freud. Freud told him, in effect, better I should come to you. A Mahler symphony is much like a Freudian analysis, in which a troubled soul revisits its past, exhumes strange memories, and finally achieves a triumphant integration. Another Viennese, Arthur Schnitzler, also Jewish and also a doctor, chose to present his studies in psychology in the form of plays. Freud might just as well have done so, and many a writer was to make literature out of the id-ego-superego triangle, the Oedipus complex, and other psychodramas Freud wrote about. He thought of himself as a scientist only because of the kind of temperament he had.

6

Social and Political Thought
at the End
of the Nineteenth Century

THE CONTINUING CAREER OF SOCIALISM

Though Marx's theories strongly affected socialism, they did not by any means monopolize the socialist movement. Taking the term in its broadest dimensions, it ranged from a rather conservative right wing, including Christian socialists and welfare-state reformers, to a revolutionary far left that by the 1880s had come to be designated "anarchism." In between lay many species in rich variety. The soil on which socialism grew, of course, was a pronounced disappointment with the existing socioeconomic order, which Marx had named "capitalism."

Marx's contemporaries included Mikhail Bakunin, the Russian revolutionary, with whom he did many a battle and whose ideas lived on for a time, especially in Russia; the terrorist tactics of his disciples, brilliantly satirized by Dostoyevsky in his novel *The Devils (The Possessed)*, eventually discredited Bakunin. Proudhon's authority in French socialism at least equaled Marx's, from whom he differed on important points. The American Henry George (*Progress and Poverty*) exerted an extraordinary influence in Britain and parts of the Continent, being one of the main sources of the remarkable Fabian Society of which Wells and Shaw were members. The Fabians appropriated much of Marx's rhetoric but rejected his economic theory in building a more eclectic brand of reformist socialism. William Morris, poet and craftsman, disciple of Ruskin as well as Marx, popularized "guild socialism," a return to the traditions of the medieval artisans.

Meanwhile Marx's heirs argued about his meaning and divided into a left and a right. This remarkably rich socialist scenario might be discussed in terms of national preferences (British Fabianism, French Proudhonism, German Marxism), but is better handled from the perspective of a right-to-left spectrum. In 1889 a British peer, Lord Harcourt, declared that "we are all socialists now." He meant that practically everybody, except a few fanatics of the Non-Interference Union, had given up dogmatically defending pure private capitalism with no interference by the state except to enforce contracts and punish crime. Earlier we mentioned the role of the Hegelian philosopher T. H. Green at Oxford in the 1880s as a stimulator of this mild revolution.[1] "Gas and water" socialism, or public ownership of utilities, emerged from cities like Birmingham, where the Tory politician Joseph Chamberlain noted that public health agencies were an urgent necessity in modern cities. Within the rival political party, a "new liberalism" began to be discussed in the 1880s and had virtually taken over the party by 1910. The new liberalism differed totally from the old in looking upon poverty as a social, not a private, question.

It would be hard to think of a more conservative personage than the creator and long-time leader of Imperial Germany, Otto von Bismarck, but the iron chancellor was a pioneer of government-administered and partly financed social insurance (health, old age, unemployment). In 1890 the new German emperor, Wilhelm II, having just fired Bismarck and repealed the antisocialist laws, called an international conference to consider "international labor legislation." Italy's almost perennial prime minister between 1900 and 1914, Giolitti, who according to Denis Mack Smith "had studied *Das Kapital* with application and profit," agreed that concessions to the workers would keep them from following lunatics into violent revolution. A certain kind of Tory socialism, based on traditions of stewardship and solidarity, has previously been noted.

In France, following the turmoil of the Dreyfus Affair, some democratic parties, calling themselves Radicals or Radical Socialists, flirted with socialism; statesmen like Aristide Briand and Georges Clemenceau were prepared to tax big property for the benefit of small, and the budget of expenditure on welfare rose sharply. The *Solidarisme* of politician-intellectual Leon Bourgeois found nature as well as society filled with cooperation and interdependence more than cutthroat competition. At the same time, these bourgeois radicals showed no sympathy toward anarchist violence and used troops to break strikes.

In 1891 the new Roman Catholic pope, Leo XIII, attacked capitalistic greed and materialism in a famous encyclical, *De rerum novarum*. This much-discussed call for a new social ethic inspired a renewal of Christian socialism. Christian

---

[1]"When I went up to Oxford [in the early 1870s]," Lord Milner recalled, "the *laissez-faire* theory still held the field.... But within ten years the few men who held the old doctrines in their extreme rigidity had come to be regarded as curiosities."

Social parties appeared in Austria and Germany in the 1890s. Social Christianity was by no means new; following Lamennais (see p. 67), Albert de Mun and La Tour du Pin in France interested themselves in the corporatist economics of the Middle Ages. The Mainz priest W. E. Ketteler tried to bring the working class to the attention of political leaders in Germany. Such people were politically conservative; they hoped to convert the upper class rather than revolutionize the lower. But they opposed modern capitalism and called for a fundamental reorganization of economic life to correspond to Christian principles. In France, Germany, and Italy Catholic trade unions came into existence, and there were individual examples of capitalists (like Leon Hormel) moved to experiment with "the Christian factory."

So important an avant-garde writer as Charles Péguy in France might be called a Christian socialist, insofar as one could classify his social thought. There was a significant revival of Christian socialism in Britain at the end of the century too. The prominent Edwardian *litterateur* G. K. Chesterton, along with his friend the popular poet Hilaire Belloc, formed an energetic party of their own; both Roman Catholics among a people traditionally suspicious of papists, they preached a kind of Christian socialism or anarchism and their wit and wisdom gained them an audience. Chesterton, a friend and debating partner of Shaw, was one of the liveliest of the Edwardians, contributing to its vein of satire and also to the rising genre of the detective story. But Belloc's *The Servile State* indicated the hostility of these "distributists" to state socialism; their ideal was neither the nationalized industry nor the welfare state, but widespread distribution of property among many small producers.

FABIAN SOCIALISM

In the center of socialism we might place the Fabians. Their rhetoric was far from mild. The Fabians emerged from the chrysalis of something called the Fellowship of the New Life, founded in 1882 by a remarkable Scotsman named Thomas Davidson, and they were looking for a new faith. The Fabian Society broke away from Davidson's group in 1884; Shaw joined it the next year. Aware that the marginal utility revolution had discredited Marx's labor theory of value, the Fabians soon decided that "abstract economics" was not of much value. For a more empirical economics they drew on Fabian founder Beatrice Potter Webb's mentor Charles Booth, author of an exhaustive pioneer study, *Life and Labour of the People of London* (9 vols., 1892–97). "The *a priori* reasoning of political economy, orthodox and unorthodox alike, fails from want of reality," Booth wrote. Influenced by the German historical school (Gustav Schmoller, Adolf Wagner), Booth led the Fabians to an economics mainly factual and descriptive.

The chief works of Sidney and Beatrice Webb were massive historical studies of local government, trade unions, and poor relief. Problems should be solved with the aid of thorough factual documentation, they believed. But, more rhetorical than historical, the pamphlets in which the society specialized were often bitterly critical of bourgeois society. The Fabians were in fact not of one mind; a collection of temperamental literary personalities, they were notoriously given to family feuds. But the talent of the industrious Webbs, the brilliant Shaw, joined at times by H. G. Wells and featuring a number of other notable scholars, made the society a memorable circle.

The Fabians did not doubt that socialism was a higher form of human society, the next rung on the ladder of social evolution. Something of their missionary spirit is suggested in what C. E. M. Joad, writing in 1951, recalled of it:

> England before 1914 was a land of gross social and economic inequality, in which the poverty and misery of the many were outraged by the luxury and ostentation of the few. Under Socialism we believed that poverty and misery would disappear and that inequality would be rectified. This was the first, fresh springtime of the Fabian Socialism, and we saw ourselves marching in irresistible procession with Shaw, Webb, and Wells—slightly out of step—in the vanguard, to the promised land of State ownership of the means of production, distribution and exchange which we believed lay just around the corner.

In their early days the Fabians were not too scholarly to harangue working-class audiences. On November 13, 1887, the police roughed up Shaw, William Morris, Annie Besant, and other intellectual socialists at a demonstration at Trafalgar Square. After that they chose the path of gradual change by parliamentary means, their task being to furnish the politicians with the facts of industrial life so fully that even a politician could not do otherwise than recognize the need for social legislation. Their most successful application of this principle was probably the Webbs' 1909 minority report to a far-ranging official investigation of the Poor Laws. Often considered the most significant expression of the new philosophy of economic welfare, it argued that prevention of poverty is the responsibility primarily of government, not of individuals.

Two years after the Webb report a Liberal government secured passage of the National Insurance Act, which a leading newspaper called "the greatest scheme of social reconstruction ever attempted" in Britain. Modeled on the German system, it allowed the government to administer and contribute to a fund for insurance against unemployment. To pay for this and other rising expenses of government, an income tax went through Parliament in the same year amid scenes such as that body had not seen for two hundred years. Its foes declared the tax to be contrary to basic individual rights, the first act of a veritable social revolution. Some of them asserted a parallel with the illegal taxes of King Charles I. But the Fabians persuasively presented the case for a "collectivism" that, they said, was the inevitable result of modern industrial society with its vast enterprises, its complex interdependencies.

Between this intellectual socialism and the practical affairs of industrial workers, marked by trade unionism, there was something of a psychological gap. One gets a picture of it in the uncomfortable workers William Morris invited to his elegantly furnished home to discuss the esthetics of labor. Socialism, George

Orwell wrote, was always a creed of the intellectuals, not the workers. The Fabians were an intellectual elite; Beatrice Webb once said that in moments of depression she remembered that she was the cleverest member of the cleverest class of the cleverest nation in the world. Trade union leaders in France as well as Britain were apt to scorn the socialist intellectuals who preferred theoretical argument to "practical work inside the labor movement." Nevertheless the Fabians did much to help the unions gain legal recognition and the right to strike, including exemption from damage suits, between 1871 and 1906. They watched the great growth of labor organization with mixed feelings.

Some Marxists deplored the "opportunism" of trade unionists who aimed only at getting some workers a bigger slice of the rewards without "changing the system." Trade unionism is the capitalism of the proletariat, Lenin declared. French "syndicalists" dreamed of accomplishing the revolution by one great general strike, and held that the spontaneously growing unions were "the units upon which the future society will be built." But Georges Sorel, the leading syndicalist theorist, later lost faith in the unions as a force for social renewal. In any case they had indeed arisen independently of the socialist thinkers, produced their own leadership and their own special culture—marked more by the pub, the music hall, and the football match than by political meetings and revolutions[2]—and constituted a separate force, sometimes but not always cooperating with the socialist parties.

Some syndicalist theories advocated staying out of politics altogether. Practical unionists were inclined to seek support from political parties of whatever flavor. In Great Britain, the parliamentary Labour party was born in 1900, owing something to the eccentric Marxism of H. M. Hyndman as well as to the Fabians. But it gained less than 10 percent of the seats in the House of Commons, and did not adopt a socialist program until 1918. The organized workers generally preferred to work with the older parties, especially the Liberals, quietly indoctrinating them with practical trade union goals. This was good Fabian method.

Socialism was the wave of the future, the Fabians thought. But it would come gradually, was coming every day, rather than all at once in one great revolution. Parliamentary democracy and other institutions of self-government would ensure its peaceful adoption. The Fabians placed great stress on local government; contrary to a common opinion, they did not at this time (before 1914) propose the nationalization of all industry, but hoped that the recently established county and borough councils would own and operate a great deal of it. They did believe in public ownership as a panacea that, by driving the landlords and capitalists out of business, would increase the workers' share and lead to an era of plenty for all. In this they were often quite naive.

---

[2]"Despite all attempts at indoctrination by socialists...British workingmen for the most part continued to prefer the public house conviviality and football game excitement to choral-singing fellowship and elevating educational classes." Lillian Lewis Shiman, reviewing Chris Waters, *British Socialists and the Politics of Popular Culture, 1884–1914* (Stanford University Press, 1990). The first music halls appeared in the 1850s; by 1900 there were more than fifty of them in London. "The vast majority of the working class" looked to them for recreation and entertainment.

MARXIAN SOCIAL DEMOCRACY

The picture in Germany was rather different. There, a Marxist party developed by far the strongest socialist organization in Europe. The German Social Democrats first won prestige by surviving Bismarck's efforts to destroy them. While trying to alleviate the poverty and alienation of workers with Europe's first state-administered social welfare system, the wily chancellor outlawed the socialists in the 1870s and 1880s. But the SPD (*Sozialdemokratische Partei Deutschlands*) survived the persecution, developed able leaders, and after being legalized in 1890 (save for one brief period) went on to become Germany's largest political party by 1912; it was also the dominant force in the Second International. The latter world organization mounted impressive international congresses and annual May Day demonstrations. It counted 12 million members by 1914; World War I destroyed it.

Entering into close association with the trade unions, the Social Democratic leaders accepted the possibility of overthrowing capitalism by peaceful, democratic means, a position approved by Friedrich Engels, who lived on into the 1890s (Marx died in 1883).[3] At the Second International meetings they opposed the radicalism of the anarchists and preached the inevitability of socialism on the basis of Marx's theory of the self-destruction of capitalism. Unlike the Fabians, however, they did not view socialism as coming piece by piece, but awaited the Great Day when the capitalist system would crumble. For this reason they normally refused to collaborate in governments with the "bourgeois" parties.

They were a well-disciplined mass organization publishing their own newspapers and magazines, led by educated Germans of the caliber of August Bebel, Wilhelm Liebknecht, Eduard Bernstein, and Karl Kautsky—men who had known Marx personally and were, so to speak, his annointed successors, even though Marx had seldom agreed with any of them. The SPD also developed a popular socialist culture of songs, parades, and picnics, catering to the German love of festivals. Unlike the French and British, the German trade unionists accepted the Social Democrats as their political arm.

It would be difficult to deny that Marx himself had bequeathed to them the doctrinal disputes that enlivened their meetings. "Reform or Revolution?" was the most persistent of these. At the end of the 1890s Marx's old friend Eduard Bernstein touched off a storm when he opted for the first of these in a way that seemed to "revise" Marx substantially. Bernstein believed that Marx's prophecies about the decline of capitalism and the increasing misery of the proletariat had proved false. The middle class had not disappeared, but was increasing; workers were better off, not worse; the class struggle had become less acute rather than more so. Bernstein's conclusions led him to a position very like that of the English Fabians.

---

[3]"The time of revolution carried through by small minorities at the head of unconscious masses is past" was Engels' best known dictum on this point.

"In all advanced countries," he urged, "we see the privileges of the capitalist bourgeoisie yielding step by step to democratic organizations."

That political democracy made it possible to establish socialism via the vote rather than the barricades was not Bernstein's key point; though he believed this, so did most other Social Democrats. The majority, however, thought that this victory would come all at once; socialism and capitalism do not mix, and the job of good socialists was to keep alive the proletarian spirit until the day of victory. To be drawn into the politics of compromise would weaken class consciousness. The party refused to accept Bernstein's gradualism and class collaboration; the majority of Social Democrats almost read him out of the party. Yet they remained committed to a revolution achieved by legal, democratic, parliamentary means.

Similar issues agitated the French Socialist party which, rent by schisms, managed to achieve unity in the 1900s but not unanimity. In 1899, after the socialist Millerand accepted a post in a government headed by a left-republican, the French socialists earnestly debated this action. It was the occasion for exchanges between their two outstanding leaders, Jean Jaurès and Jules Guesde. Jaurès, not a dogmatic Marxist, argued like the Fabians that it was good to penetrate bourgeois positions in this way, for the capitalist regime would fall little by little; but how could it fall if its outposts were never occupied? But Guesde carried the day by a narrow margin with an eloquent exposition of Marxist orthodoxy. (One of Guesde's chief lieutenants was Marx's son-in-law Paul Lafargue.) Like those who opposed Bernstein in Germany, he stressed the class struggle, the solidarity of the working class, the utter incompatibility of capitalism and socialism. Like its German counterpart, the French socialist group before 1914 refused to take ministerial posts in any government in which it would share power. Right-left tension continued to exist, however. The French socialists were weaker than the German, though stronger than the British; in 1914 the party won about one-sixth of the seats in the national legislature.

They were also less united; strong traditions other than Marxism existed. If Guesde, "Torquemada in lorgnettes," was a rigid Marxian dialectician, the great scholar and critic Jaurès was a civilized humanist who drew from many other sources than Marx. For him, Leon Blum later wrote, socialism was "the summation, the point of convergence, the heritage of all that humanity had created since the dawn of civilization." Other French socialists were descendants of Proudhon's "mutualism," with its suspicion of the state, its tendencies toward localism and anarchism, its passionate love of individual liberty.[4] One of Proudhon's fol-

---

[4]In his colorful prose, Proudhon had written that

> To be governed is to be kept under surveillance, inspected, spied upon, bossed, law-ridden, regulated, penned in, indoctrinated, preached at, registered, evaluated, appraised, censured, ordered about by creatures who have neither the right nor the virtue to do so.... It is, under the pretense of public benefit...to be requisitioned, drilled, fleeced, exploited, monopolized, extorted, squeezed, hoaxed, robbed...then at the slightest resistance to be squelched, corrected, vilified, bullied, hounded, tormented, bludgeoned, disarmed, strangled, imprisoned, shot down, judged, condemned, deported, sacrificed, sold, betrayed....

lowers, Jean Charles-Brun, was a crusading regionalist who spent his life combatting centralization of all sorts; the cure for social ills was to root people in the soil of a concrete, living community. This was directly opposed to a Marxist bent for centralization.

Similarly in Italy, reformist, revisionist socialists, for example Filippo Turati, argued that democracy had rendered revolution obsolete, but found opponents on the left to whom this was dangerous heresy. There was a lively Marxist discussion in Italy. The great philosopher Benedetto Croce had shown strong interest in Marx, though finally rejecting him as too dogmatic. Within the Marxist camp, Professor Antonio Labriola's distinctions on the materialist conception of history, somewhat too subtle for popular consumption, were countered by Achille Loria's crudely positivistic determinism.

In Russia, the Marxist debate took a not dissimilar turn. Marxism entered Russia via the remarkable G. V. Plekhanov, a self-educated man who, exiled like so many politically conscious Russians, lived and wrote for many years in Switzerland. In the 1870s the main political faith of revolutionary Russians was populism, based on a belief in the uniqueness of Russia's communal peasant institutions. The "big three" of earlier Russian socialism had been the Hegelian Belinsky; Bakunin, the anarchist rival of Marx; and Alexander Herzen, a powerful writer who participated in the June Days of the 1848 Paris revolution and expressed bitter disillusion at its failure. With the aid of a German historian, these pioneer Russian socialists discovered in the *mir* or Russian peasant village an allegedly natural foundation for Proudhonian mutualism. Subsequently somewhat discredited, Bakunin and Herzen nevertheless deeply influenced the populist movement, of which the political offshoot was the Social Revolutionary party.

The tsar's government repressed the *mir* socialists in the 1860s, though they were not a violent group. Chernyshevsky and Pisarev were imprisoned, Moscow University closed in 1868. The result was the remarkable "To the People" pilgrimage of young idealists in the 1870s, which suffered rude disenchantment and resulted in the arrest of hundreds. Then, in desperation, after this unsuccessful attempt of educated youth to make contact with the peasants (they lived in totally different mental worlds), came a wave of revolutionary terrorism. This too led nowhere. In opposition to the excesses of this populism turned violent, which climaxed in the killing of Tsar Alexander II in 1881, the cool, analytical approach of Marxism was welcome. Marxism in Russia in the 1890s had the effect of turning minds from illegal revolutionary pamphlets to the systematic study of economics, sociology, and history. Some Marxism was even legal in Russia, a remarkable tribute to its apparent moderation. The young Lenin was able to publish a book on the principles of economic development. One could accept on Marxist grounds the progressiveness of capitalism for backward Russia. Marxism was a weapon against both agrarian populism and revolutionary terrorism.

Plekhanov himself, a civilized, even fastidiously esthetic intellectual, counseled waiting for a democratic revolution which would come about only after Russia went through a capitalist phase. But those with more activist temperaments were less inclined to wait. In 1903, Lenin proposed the creation of an elite of professional revolutionaries, trained to seize power. To Plekhanov's orthodox Marxism this was heresy, and the majority of the Russian Social Democratic party agreed with him. Lenin's *bolshevik* group was in fact a small minority most of the time, the *mensheviks* a more numerous and prestigious faction. (Both together constituted but a tiny minority in Russia.) Victory and fame would come surprisingly to Lenin in 1917; prior to that he was thought to have departed widely from Marxian orthodoxy and, living in exile mostly in Switzerland, was isolated at the far left of the socialist spectrum (on Lenin, see pp. 193–95).

To sum up the Marxist debate: On the Continent, though not in England, Marxism prevailed as the reigning orthodoxy in the socialist or social democratic parties, which were well organized and gaining adherents on the eve of 1914. But within the parties sharp controversy centered on the issue of whether class struggle, revolution, and the complete destruction of capitalism at one stroke had not become an obsolete program in the era of democratic politics, which had developed in most countries in varying degrees, and of trade unionism. The usual answer was to refuse to abandon Marxism for Fabian gradualism and opportunism (as Bernnstein proposed); but also to reject stress on violent revolution through illegal or conspiratorial means, advocated within Marxism only by a few Russians.

The majority of socialists held to their faith in an apocalyptic revolution that would change the entire system, but thought this could come peacefully as soon as their party won a majority of the electorate—something that theory, if not experience, told them was inevitable—and they refused meanwhile to share power in a coalition with the nonsocialists. This compromise was an uneasy one, giving rise to a degree of internal tension. Between the left and the right within the socialist camp, between, say, Albert Thomas and Jules Guesde in France, Eduard Bernstein and Rosa Luxemburg in Germany, Plekhanov and Lenin in Russia, there was a considerable difference of ideology and temperament. This ambivalence can be traced to unresolved dilemmas at the heart of Marxist doctrine, particularly between voluntarism and determinism, elitism and democracy, revolution and evolution. On the one side there was the call to action on behalf of the downtrodden; on the other, the belief that objective laws of historical development were fast preparing the way for the triumph of democratic socialism. The latter, seemingly more scientific and Marxist position, could lead to a kind of passivity, which Lenin derided as "requiem socialism," content to sit back and wait.

ANARCHISM

Whether to classify the anarchists as socialists is a semantic technicality. The old strife between Marx and Bakunin went deep; anarchists could not stomach the Marxist willingness to use the state, having captured it by political action of some sort, to install the revolution. For though Marx and Engels expected the state to "wither away" (Engels' term) after the revolution, they advocated seizing it and using it in the interlude between the revolution and the final achievement of communism, during which a "dictatorship of the proletariat" might be necessary. With considerable accuracy the anarchists predicted that the Marxists would be corrupted by the state as they used it. The revolution, in the anarchist view, must be made outside the state and must immediately destroy the monster, replacing it by an association of free communes.

Anarchism was weak in Germany (though sometimes spectacular; it was a German anarchist who allegedly threw the bomb in Chicago's Haymarket Square that touched off a famous episode in American history). As "anarcho-syndicalism" or direct action through the trade unions it was stronger in France, and stronger yet in Italy and Spain, perhaps for reasons of national temperament. An anarchist might be a peace-loving enemy of centralization, a friend of liberty and cooperation; but in the 1880s and 1890s a much more familiar type resorted to assassination and other violent actions. They all disbelieved in the value of political action through elections and parliaments.

Some of them were partial Marxists; what they had learned from the master was that economics determines all, that representative legislatures are a sham, and that capitalism owns the state and always will until smashed in the proletarian social revolution. After the revolution there will be no more parliaments or states; there will be the pure freedom of the classless society—no government at all. Most anarchists were so far out on the voluntarist wing of Marxism as to be beyond the pale of party orthodoxy. They stressed the freedom of individuals to change their situation by acting; nothing is predetermined. They might go so far as to decide that socialism is simply a myth, a religion, not a science at all. Marxian scientism was bourgeois! It was the ideology of the intellectual class. A good example of this opinion within socialism is Arturo Labriola, the Italian anarchist; and later the Belgian Henri de Man. The best case is Georges Sorel, discussed below.

Many varieties of anarchism existed, and indeed by their very nature these individualistic radicals could not share any one creed. Significant numbers of them tried to foment revolution by exhortation, or better, by action. Ultra-anarchists engaged in a wave of assassinations in the 1890s that shocked not only the bourgeoisie, but the social democrats, who denounced them furiously. Terrorists assassinated a tsar of Russia, a president of the United States, the empress of Austria, the king of Italy, and a president of France between 1880 and 1901; they continued into the 1900s, killing among others the enlightened Russian prime minister, Stolypin. On July 4, 1914, three anarchists died in New York when a homemade bomb intended for John D. Rockefeller blew up. Just a month before, young Gavrilo Princip and his Bosnian friends, who might best be described as anarchists, had touched off World War I by assassinating the heir to the Austrian throne.

It was not merely the great who were targets. The famous French terrorist Ravachol, who bombed the Chamber of Deputies, had several politically motiveless murders attributed to him. In 1894 a twenty-two-year old French anarchist named Emile Henry tossed a bomb into a railroad station café in Paris, killing two persons and wounding twenty in an assemblage of workers, small shopkeepers, and civil servants, none of any political prominence; reproached at his trial for killing innocent people, he proudly replied "Everyone is guilty!" Another French militant set out in 1881 to murder the political leader Leon Gambetta; not finding him, he shot the first bourgeois he met as a reasonable equivalent. These believers in the "propaganda of the deed" simply wanted to get the public's attention, to dramatize what they felt to be monstrous injustice perpetrated by public authority.

It would be wrong to identify anarchism with these disturbed types. Tolstoy's Christian anarchism was nonviolent. The destruction of the state would take a long time, he knew, because it involved a basic change in human nature; "The transition from state violence to a free, reasonable life cannot happen suddenly. Just as the state took thousands of years to take shape, so it will take thousands of years to disintegrate." To reply to its violence with counterviolence would only prolong the cycle. Another well-known philosophical anarchist was another Russian, Prince Kropotkin.

Popular around the turn of the century was Max Stirner's book, translated as *The Ego and Its Own*. Stirner had been a member of Marx's *Doktorclub* at Berlin; Marx later caricatured him along with other Young Hegelians. Stirner had gone all the way on the road toward particularizing Hegel's World Spirit. Feuerbach made it into Humanity, Marx into the Proletariat; Stirner ended with just the individual, Me. It is from my mind that all these categories derive; the only ultimate reality is the particular human being. The only thing that counts, then, is the freedom of the individual. People make their own reality and should have their own morality. This sort of anarchism connected closely to the sexual revolution that was going on, seeking release from the constraints of social regulation of morality. Freud's id-superego conflict essentially mirrored this rebellion against Victorian morals. Nietzsche's demand that each of us must "become what we are" was a part of this liberation feeling at the end of the century. The only political credo worth the attention of the avant-garde artists was anarchism.

Georges Sorel was one of the major political thinkers of Third Republic France, often ranked as one of the top three along with socialist Jaurès and right-wing publicist Charles Maurras. To classify him as an anarchist would be to oversimplify a complex intellect. But a hatred of the state and all authority stood very close to the heart of Sorel's temperament. Through a number of often contradictory political ideas runs a core in hostility toward the "centralised Jacobin state" and toward what Sorel—an intellectual outsider—saw as its intellectual leadership in the universities. He never joined an organized political party; he wished education to be free from state control. Anything bureaucratic, organized, directed, not spontaneous Sorel despised.

This gadfly, who spent his life swimming against the flow, was a powerful and strikingly original thinker. Originally a Marxist, he came to feel that the orthodox socialists had become bureaucratic and respectable. (Sorel distanced himself not so much from Marx as from Marxism, the mechanical dogmas of the disciples; he was aware that Marx himself was much more subtle.) They were wrong, too, in their scientism. Socialism was really an apocalyptical religion. Everyone lives by myths; what modern Europe needed was a vital one. Sorel spoke of the "myth of the revolution," or of the general strike, with approval; these were faiths comparable to that of the early Christians. Much of Bergson's and Nietzsche's irrationalism entered into Sorel, though apparently less as a direct influence than a parallel development. He was in fact most powerfully affected by the eighteenth-century Italian Vico, whose thought he helped revive. James Joyce was to pick up on this and weave Vico's *corso, ricorso*, the great cyclical ebb and flow of historical epochs, into his mighty novels. A barbarian age must come to renew the energy of a society exhausted by too much civilization and democracy. The need for a profound moral and cultural renewal underlay Sorel's belief in "myth" and the unspoiled proletariat. "The popular soul must return to a primitive state where everything is instinctive, creative, and poetic."

How it was to accomplish this was less clear—perhaps, as Joyce thought, by the total renovation of language. Sorel fathered the idea of a revolutionary elite violently sweeping away bourgeois civilization in the name of a new myth or religion. *Sorelismo* was to get into Italy and into Mussolini's fascism. (Sorel lived long enough to greet the Italian *duce* enthusiastically, but he also hailed Lenin—anything to shake up the stodgy status quo.) In his later thought Sorel turned away from proletarian socialism to embrace the myth of nationalism, obviously, it seemed, an even more potent force. He grew disillusioned with the trade unions, which turned out to be as materialistic and bureaucratic as the business corporations, and by 1910 drew close to Maurras's "integral nationalism." Originally a defender of Dreyfus, Sorel also eventually turned on the victorious Dreyfusards. Indeed Sorel seemed determined to agree with no one, and his political thought was "a series of volte-faces." Its consistent theme was a moral criticism of modern civilization much in the spirit of Rousseau, for its corruption, superficiality, and decadence.

DEMOCRACY

One of the few consistencies in Sorel's thought over the years was a dislike of democracy. Democracy had many critics, but none perhaps hated it so cordially as he. In part this was a function of his hatred of the state. It does not matter whether the tyrant is one man or a multitude, it is still a tyrant; the belief that somehow government is less onerous when based on parliaments deeply irritated Sorel. "Each of us," he noted, "is one ten-millionth a tyrant and every bit a slave!" In the same spirit, Herbert Spencer declared that the divine right of popularly elected assemblies should be resisted just as much as the divine right of kings if it threatened liberty. But to Sorel, also, democracy stood for the last decadent stage of society before the Vichian thunderbolt signals a reversion to barbarism; it was what remains after the destruction of values and of social order. Democracy is corrupt and degenerate because it corresponds to a stage of society marked by these qualities. Leadership and hierarchy prevail in the uncorrupted stage.

Democracy had indeed come into its own in the last decades of the century, in both the political and social senses of the term. "I regard as one of the greatest dangers with which the country can be threatened," *The London Times* editorialized in 1867, "a proposal to...transfer power from the hands of property and intelligence, and to place it in the hands of men whose life is necessarily occupied in daily struggles for existence."[5] Extension of the suffrage, Thomas Carlyle agreed, was like "shooting Niagara," a desperate gamble. But in 1867 and again in 1884, Great Britain took steps toward full manhood suffrage; by 1910 women were aggressively demanding the vote. France never actually lost universal suffrage after 1848, but under the Second Empire it was manipulated in a way that deprived it of much meaning; after 1874, however, the Republic came back. Imperial Germany had a Reichstag elected by universal suffrage though it lacked responsible powers. "An assembly of 350 members cannot in the last instance direct the policy of a great power today," Chancellor Bismarck thought. Perhaps it could not, but the system of a government by a cabinet drawn from and responsible to the elected legislature found success in England, and at least managed to survive in France.

Elements on both left and right previously hostile to parliamentary government "rallied" to its support by the 1890s. The frustrations of democratic politics pushed France close to another military dictatorship in 1889, but this time the threat failed and the antidemocratic impulse mostly subsided. "The conversion of the mass of French peasants to faith in a democratic republic" came in the years 1871–1876, according to the historian of French democracy David Thomson. So did the conversion of liberals who had previously been certain that, as Thomas Macaulay declared, universal suffrage would lead to a new despotism "utterly incompatible with the very existence of civilization." More typical now was the idea expressed in Prévost-Paradol's *Nouvelle France*, that checks on the majority will could prevent abuses of universal suffrage and lead to a workable "liberal republic."

All governments had to pay more attention to public opinion—which might or might not be a good thing, critics noted, depending on how enlightened public opinion was. Those unconverted to democracy complained not only of ignorant and emotional electorates, but of undignified electioneering methods, of political "machines" and bosses, of cheaper politicians driving out finer in a kind of Gresham's law of politics. But very few discerning people thought that the rule of the few in politics and society was any longer possible. Driven by the thought that "we must educate our masters," countries established public school systems and compelled attendance at primary schools. Illiteracy was still extensive in southern and eastern Europe, but had all but disappeared in western Europe by 1900. The rise of cheap popular newspapers, often marked by the lowest of intellectual standards, became a scandal among the better educated. The dynamic nineteenth century had

---

[5]As Disraeli's *Tancred* observed, "I do not believe the public ever think. How can they? They have no time."

displaced millions from the traditional village environment to the suddenly swollen great cities, where a new kind of popular culture was in the throes of creation.

"The democratic principle has gone forth conquering and to conquer, and its gainsayers are few and feeble," one of its critics, Henry Maine, conceded. Its triumph was "universally recognized." Yet this feeling of "case closed" coexisted oddly with an almost equally strong opinion, among the thoughtful and critical-minded element of society, that democracy was either a failure, a disaster, or a fraud. Intellectuals deplored this rise of democracy, or worried about it, more than they hailed it. Tocqueville and Mill mistrusted democracy because they feared the degradation of intelligence and quality. (Mill's strongest argument for it was that it could be a process of education, gradually elevating the masses. At the end of the century it was hard to see that this was happening.)

In his essay *Democracy*, first published in 1861 and reissued in 1879, Matthew Arnold wrote: "Our society is probably destined to become much more democratic; who or what will give a high tone to the nation then? That is the grave question." A society is of real value not simply because large numbers of people are active and free; it is valuable insofar as it produces quality people. America's sage, Walt Whitman, poet of democracy, spoke in similarly chastened tones after 1865. This question of quality, of "high tone," runs through all the diatribes against democracy *qua* mass culture that litter the nineteenth century. "The mass is the enemy of the spirit," Marx's friend Bruno Bauer had thought. Dr. Stockmann in Ibsen's play *An Enemy of the People* proclaimed that "the minority is always right."

"It is a question," cried Edmond Scherer, a French writer of the 1880s, "of knowing whether in traversing this crisis humanity will not lose everything of genius, beauty, grandeur; it is a question of knowing whether, in this tragedy of mediocrity, in this sullen and terrible adventure of the peoples, there is one which will not disappear from history." The defiantly antisocial path that literature, the arts, and even philosophy took was a response to the flagrantly democratic urban culture rising in the later nineteenth century. Bertrand Russell, though in most moods a radical and a socialist, exclaimed in 1902 that "This respect for the filthy multitude is ruining civilization!" In fact it was the consciousness of the literate minority as much as the "stupidity" of the tabloid-reading, sloganizing masses that caused this hostility. The long tradition of European culture had created a body of thought and artistic expression intoxicatingly rich; it was now organized and available, in affordable books, journals, museums, concert halls that were part of that very urban, technological society the intellectuals affected to despise. Many people formerly outside the boundaries of this high culture could now enter it. This "civilized consciousness of Europe," as D. H. Lawrence called it, constituted a separate world in which those able to unlock its doors might live surrounded by endless delights of the mind and senses. But it was not "real" and it failed to match the world of producers and consumers, buyers and sellers, engineers and workmen, barkeepers and politicians, to all of whom, as Yeats wrote, "We and all the Muses are things of no account."

Much of the modern age has been filled with the rise of the intellectuals and their encounter with mass culture. At the end of the nineteenth century this confrontation was at a peak, perhaps because both phenomena had just arisen. Modern European literature, Lionel Trilling remarked in *The Liberal Imagination*, has been dominated by "men who are indifferent to, or even hostile to, the traditions of democratic liberalism as we know it." It is an extraordinary contradiction in the modern world, its foremost "double bind," this dynamism that simultaneously produced cultureless masses and alienated artist-intellectuals.

"But this I know, I hate the crowd!" Walter Savage Landor's credo was a motto for almost the entire late nineteenth-century intelligentsia."Every instinct of my body is anti-democratic, and I dread to think of what our England may become when Demos rules absolutely." George Gissing, writing this at the end of the century, observed that it was not a matter of class; upper and lower are alike in being "blatant creatures" when they are *en masse*. This "blatancy" of the masses, the noisy dwarfs as Nietzsche called them, the newspaper reading "last men" of a sterile, trivializing culture, grated on the sensibilities of the few whose intelligence, they thought, marked them off from the mass. Such people, defined by their sensibility, might come from almost any class. Gissing was a typical literary outcast leading a disreputable life in "Bohemia" or "grub street."

This "scream of horror" from the civilized minority when confronted with the democratic culture was not entirely confined to alienated artists. Scientists too sometimes recorded their mistrust of popular mentality. Here was another lofty goal of the intellect, requiring the highest quality of intelligence. Henry Maine, the Victorian legal historian, in his much-quoted 1885 attack *Popular Government*, declaimed that universal suffrage "would have prohibited the spinning jenny and the power loom, along with the threshing machine," would have preserved the Gregorian calendar and barred vaccination, in effect would have vetoed scientific progress. H. G. Wells, prophet of the scientifically efficient organization of society, who believed that "democracy must pass away inevitably by its own inherent contradictions," saw the chief of these as its being based not on "any process of intellectual conviction," but on the vagaries of a largely ignorant public opinion. There was considerable discussion about the conflict between scientific truths (like Darwinism) and democratic values. While some argued that science is inherently democratic ("the steam engine is republican," Gambetta declared), the opposite view was also expressed. The French sociologist C. Bouglé, in his 1904 book *Le démocratie devant le science*, cited T. H. Huxley on the absurdity of saying men are born free and equal, and noted that foes of democracy such as Charles Maurras and Paul Bourget claimed to be the true heirs of the scientific spirit.

As we have noticed, socialists were ambivalent about democracy. Many of them scorned "bourgeois democracy" as a fraud, a trick designed to divert the workers from their true goal, social revolution. The institutions of democracy are a part of the bourgeois "superstructure," consciously or unconsciously connected to its exploitative strategy. If the working class did capture a majority and try to change the system, the fraud would become apparent. Real decisions in any case are not made by the lawyers and speechmakers, the "parliamentary cretins" as Engels called them. Democracy mirrors the class structure of society, but cannot change it. The ultimate goal, in any case, must be socialism; democracy can only be a means, and perhaps it is not the best means.

Numerous such ruminations, including Lenin's, could not quite eliminate a feeling that democracy was after all a present force, and socialists should use it. Did they not best represent the aspirations of the masses? Yet the refusal of the dominant socialists to take any part in parliamentary governments, preferring to wait for the final collapse of the whole system—after which, certainly, there would be some kind of democracy, but a quite different kind—indicates the depth of socialist suspicion of democracy in its guise of elected legislatures.

Needless to say, right-wing thought contained antidemocratic strains. It is true that many conservatives came over to the democratic side upon seeing that universal suffrage was not going to mean chaos or communism. French industrialists and bishops alike "rallied" to the Republic they had once reviled. A notable strain of French conservatives, represented by Charles Renouvier and Jacques Prévost-Paradol, turned toward liberal democracy as an alternative to the revolutionary or "jacobin" type. This line of thought led to a decidedly low-key version of the case for democracy, in which so far from being a utopia, it was almost the exact opposite—a remedy for utopias. Georges Clemenceau decided that democracy is "the least intolerable of the various frightful evils." There was a sharp reversal of meanings here in the discourse of democracy.

French conservative nationalists criticized parliamentary democracy as corrupt, weakening, divisive, incapable of effective policy, a recipe for national ruin. But Mme. Adam's *La Nouvelle Revue*, an organ of patriotic nationalism, departed from this norm in arguing, rather like Benjamin Kidd in England, that the republican spirit could strengthen the nation for a war against Germany better than the monarchical. Meanwhile the formidable Charles Maurras had launched his Action Française movement, probably the most dynamic one of the 1900–1914 years, one which certainly caught the attention of university youth. It put out a well-known newspaper, and from Maurras's tireless pen flowed a stream of books and pamphlets. Here was a reaction in the name of order against the whole liberal-democratic ethos, calling for a revived monarchy and appealing to the French tradition of classicism and rationalism.

Maurras inherited Comte's dislike of social anarchy. A prominent theme of his thought was the need for leadership by an intelligent minority. Among other ideas his movement bequeathed to the postwar fascist ideology was the "corporate state," borrowed from the Catholic social movement—a return to the medieval conception of society as a hierarchy of groups rather than an assemblage of equal individuals. Violently hostile to the Republic in the 1900s, the Action tended to rally to its support after 1912 with war clouds on the horizon, for it was militantly patriotic and fiercely anti-German. Nationalist, traditionalist, anti-Semitic, antidemocratic, Maurras carried on a war against the liberal parliamentary state, and looms as a forerunner of the "revolutionary conservatism" of the postwar period— what came to be known as fascism.

Gustave Le Bon was another who thought that democracy had become a mortal danger to the state. The brilliant amateur psychologist was the author of a famous study of mob psychology, *The Crowd (Psychologie des foules)*, first published in 1895 and still in print after innumerable editions; it influenced Sigmund Freud as well as Adolf Hitler. In *Psychologie politique* (1912), Le Bon bitterly reproached the elected representatives, who are ruled by "the basest interests of the multitude," dream only of reelection, and do not consult the national interest. He thought democracy had led to a desperate crisis of authority in the modern state, and in urging the respectable middle class to fight back in *le defense sociale*, he too anticipated fascism.

Finally, some of the brilliant group of sociological theorists who sprang up in this era argued that democracy is really not democratic. Paradoxically, it results in just a different form of elite rule. "Everywhere, whether within or outside democracies, politics is made *by the few*," as Max Weber put it. Weber's friend Robert Michels announced an iron law of oligarchy. Political parties, "children of democracy," are necessary in order to mediate between the voters and the electoral process; but in fact as they grew larger they inevitably fell under the control of a small minority. The more voters, the more party organization; oligarchy advances apace with democracy. The paradox was worthy to rank with Marx's alleged discovery that in the process of making profits capitalism destroys private property; democracy creates oligarchy through the operations of its own instrument, the mass political party, whose very size forces it into an elitist structure. An "invisible government" of political bosses controlled politics in the United States, studies such as M. Ostrogorski's *Democracy and the Organization of Political Parties* pointed out. Michels' book *The Iron Law of Oligarchy* was based on a study of the German Social Democratic party; ironically, the most ideologically democratic of parties came to be tightly managed by a small group of insiders.

Two Italians, Gaetano Mosca, the Sicilian author of a famous study of *The Ruling Class* (first published in 1896), and Vilfredo Pareto, were in the forefront of elitist theory, having observed what happened in Italy to deflate the high expectations of the *risorgimento*. Pareto said of one Italian head of government that he was "the leader of a syndicate of speculators ruling the country and robbing the state."

THE RISE OF SOCIOLOGICAL THOUGHT

This tendency to look beneath the surface of formal structures and officially proclaimed goals to find the real practices of social institutions was a feature of the new study of society known as sociology (originally Auguste Comte's term). This could be compared with Freud's insight that under the outer façade of personality things are much different. It can be interpreted as the product of a profound disillusion; sociology, according to historian Fritz Ringer, was "a heroic ideal of rational clarification in the face of tragedy." A steely pessimism does flavor the thought of Max Weber, Vilfredo Pareto, and others of this brilliant generation of social theorists. Following in the footsteps of Marx and Comte, they refined and deepened the earlier ideas, yet retained considerable scope and dramatic power in their writing. They had not yet become narrow specialists. The years from about 1890 to 1920 were indeed the golden age of sociology.

The status of sociology as a refuge of the disenchanted may be seen in Weber's career. Son of a prominent politician of the Second Reich, Max Weber wanted to take part in political life, but the intellectual inheritance he received from his mother by way of Heidelberg blocked him; he rejected the vulgarity of his father's circle. He suffered a nervous breakdown that totally incapacitated him for several years, from which he emerged, like Freud (and at about the same time) to become a powerful thinker, writer, and lecturer. It is not surprising that "the disenchantment of the world" is a prominent Weberian theme. Probably the leading social stimulus to the development of sociology was rapid change from a rural to an urban social environment, from traditional to modern society, something that took place with unusual rapidity in Germany. But a contributing factor was also the mood of disillusionment that followed the failure of Romantic idealism in politics; nowhere was this felt more keenly than in Germany, where the realistic diplomacy of Bismarck achieved what the revolutionaries of 1848 could not.

Social transformation occurred with peculiar abruptness in Germany after the achievement of unification in the 1860s. But what Maurice Barrès, the French novelist, called "deracination" was evident in France as well. To pass from a small, close-knit village community to the large city was to experience cultural shock. The leading sociologists had experienced it in their own lives. Emile Durkheim felt isolated as a student at the Sorbonne, and spent much of his brilliant sociological career writing about what he called *anomie*, the uneasy state of those who have lost the guidance of secure social norms. The leading pioneer of German sociology in the 1880s, Friedrich Tönnies, immortalized a distinction between *Gemeinschaft* and *Gesellschaft*, community and society—the small, cohesive, tightly integrated community, such as most people had always lived in, and the "great society" of the modern city or state, vast and complex, in which the individual felt freer yet uneasier. Georg Simmel, who had also experienced cultural shock in coming from village to city, wrote a celebrated pioneer essay on the effect city living had on people's minds: "The deepest problems of modern life derive from the claim of the individual to preserve the autonomy and individuality of his existence in the face of overwhelming social forces." In the city the individual had greater freedom, more opportunity, greater mental stimulation, but also confronted loss of social ties, rootlessness, disorientation.

In the hands of a Weber or Durkheim or Robert Michels (who indeed referred to "political sociology"), the boundary between sociological and political studies was not sharp. As the scientific or detached study of social phenomena, sociology could be applied to all manner of things; the sociologists of this period were much inclined to direct it toward politics. Weber studied the forms of political authority and the origins of the Western economic order; Michels examined the structure of political parties. Graham Wallas's *Human Nature in Politics*, the work of a Fabian socialist, broke fresh ground in arguing that political science had always dealt more with abstractions than with real people. When one looks at the reality, Wallas thought, one sees the fallacy of assuming that people act rationally; "Most of the political opinions of most men are the result, not of reasoning tested by experience, but of unconscious or half-conscious inference tested by habit." There had been a decline in rationality, Wallas suggested, because of the "de-localizing" of people uprooted from the village to be thrown into the mass anonymity of the huge city.

Durkheim stressed the loss of social solidarity, as he called it, and thought sociology could help modern humanity find its way to some higher form of solidarity, having lost the primitive kind. "Profound changes have occurred in the structure of our societies in a very short time," Durkheim wrote. "Our faith has been troubled; tradition has lost its sway; individual judgment has been freed from collective judgment.... The new life that has emerged so suddenly has not yet been completely organized."[6] Close to the German "socialists of the chair," he viewed the power of state as a protection against the disintegrating effects of modern capitalism. A Sorbonne intellectual luminary, Durkheim (of Alsatian Jewish ancestry) was also a prominent member of the Third Republic's government, the administrator of the highly centralized French educational system. Perhaps the socialist-sociologist using the democratic state could restore that lost solidarity which gives the individual guidance. Such faith in the bureaucrat as a substitute for the priest or patriarch may have been misplaced; Durkheim was more effective in diagnosing the unhappiness of modern man than in providing a remedy.

The greatest of the sociologists was undoubtedly Max Weber. A scholar whose vast range and productivity is reminiscent of Freud and Jung, Weber, a professor at Heidelberg most of his career, suffered intermittently from illness and died in 1920 at the age of fifty-six. During that time he produced a body of writing of amazing scope and acuteness, ranging over societies from ancient and Oriental to European, in pursuit of themes such as the relation between religion and economics, and the modes of political authority. His best-known work was the essay "Protestantism and the Spirit of Capitalism," which spawned an entire industry of commentary. (Zygmunt Bauman wrote several years ago that "the 'protestant ethic' debate...has long reached the stage when the sheer volume of facts and views it has produced makes it no less moot and bottomless than the subject matter it purports to clarify.") Weber's thesis, often oversimplified, was that religious ideas interact with worldly activities to produce a characteristic "style of life," and that Protestantism and capitalism so interacted, the former giving rise to a "thisworldly asceticism" in which working and saving took on sacred qualities.

---

[6]Some idea of the rapidity of urbanization in the nineteenth century may be judged from the fact that in 1801 England and Wales, the most urbanized part of Europe, had less than 10% of their population in cities of 100,000 or more, whereas by 1901 this had risen to over 35%, with 58% living in cities of 20,000 or more. It should be borne in mind that the absolute figures were greater, since total population in Britain nearly tripled in the nineteenth century.

An incredible versatility marked Weber's approach to society. Like all historians, he discovered that in order to understand anything you have to understand everything. He was historian, economist, legalist. Sociology was only just becoming recognized as a discipline; the German Sociological Society was founded in 1909, and Weber held a chair specifically called sociology only in the last months of his life. His first publication, in 1892, was on the history of medieval trading companies, followed by a study of ancient Roman agriculture in its relation to law. He then undertook a survey of rural farm workers in contemporary eastern Germany which was published as part of a series on "social politics." In his mature years Weber turned to a massive synthesis, *Economy and Society*, which is comparable to Marx's *Capital* in its scope—and like that book never finished, being edited for publication after his death from a miscellany of fragments. Some of Weber's inspiration stemmed from Marx, whose central conception of a scientific approach to social, economic, and political phenomena he shared.

His analysis of cities in society across the globe is a classic. Throughout, Weber like Marx was interested in explaining European capitalism. Unlike Marx, he saw it not as one phase in the life cycle of all societies, but as a unique thing created over the centuries in western Europe, owing something to ancient Judaism as well as to Christianity. It did not emerge out of feudalism as a wholly different entity; it was always present in some degree, as feudalism still is. It is a question of a gradual change in the proportion of the same components. (One may construe Marx as saying something similar, using "bourgeois" to mean not so much a social entity as a principle working through history to "abolish all feudal, patriarchal, idyllic relations" in favor of "naked self-interest," as he put it in *The Communist Manifesto*.)

Weber seems to say that rationality and efficiency grew relentlessly and irreversibly from early seeds of Western civilization. Weber's foremost interest was in what he called *rationalization*, meaning the tendency of things to get organized and subjected to rules and orderly processes. What his friend Michels saw happening to the Social Democrats in their path toward bureaucracy, Weber saw as a basic principle in European history, perhaps a universal principle in human history. Beginning in romance or magic, institutions or forms settle into a stable routine. ("Everything begins in *mystique* and ends in *politique*," Charles Péguy once observed.) Music, for example, becomes a science. Government evolves from the king's family to bureaucracy. In this process spontaneity is lost, there is "disenchantment" (*Entzauberung*, in Weber's term, deprival of magic), the pedantic expert takes over from the free spirit; certainly there is a great loss as well as gains in efficiency.

This dislike of modern capitalism because of its depersonalizing and bureaucratic features may be found also in the socialists. It was especially strong in one of Weber's contemporaries, Werner Sombart. But Weber turned into a foe of the socialists in pointing out that collective ownership will do nothing to reverse rationalization, disenchantment, and "alienation." Modern society is essentially the same, whether "capitalist" or "socialist." Divison of labor, bureaucracy, professionalization, discipline, efficiency, the essential features of industrial society are not touched by the question of whether ownership is vested in the state or large business corporations. Indeed, socialists usually proposed an even greater degree of centralization and rationalization. Any sort of advanced technological society will experience the same problems of alienation and anomie.

Hence Weber's rather gloomy outlook, often a stoical injunction to "bear the fate of our times" with steely resignation and expect no miracles. (Here again he resembles the late Freud.) Locked in the "iron cage" of rationalization, modern humanity is not likely to be very happy, and there is little we can do about it. Weber poured his scorn on the inventers of new religions as well as academic prophets. Students should not look to professors for advice on how to live! If we cannot endure a sodden reality, we can go back to the old religion:

> To the person who cannot bear the fate of our times like a man, one must say: may he return silently, without the usual publicity build-up, but simply and plainly. The arms of the old churches are opened widely and compassionately for him.

So no message of salvation came from these sociologists, only an illumination of our predicament. Weber's influence on subsequent sociology, of course, was enormous. His vocabulary became a permanent part of it. Especially influential was the Weberian analysis of the modes of political authority—patriarchal, patrimonial, bureaucratic, charismatic. In our times, when bureaucracy has taken over from more personal sources of authority based on the family, there are reversions to the type of leadership Weber called "charismatic," one of his additions to our vocabulary. For rule-based, impersonal authority has one notable weakness, that it cannot cope with emergencies. Confront the bureaucratic mentality with a new situation and it is helpless. The great individual arises, for good or evil, compelling allegiance by the peculiar force of his personality. Napoleon displayed charisma as much as Caesar had two thousand years earlier. Ahead lay Mussolini and Hitler.

Certainly there was no lack of prophetic figures in the late nineteenth century, from Tolstoy and Stefan George to Mary Baker Eddy and Mme. Blavatsky, exercising leadership in mysterious ways. As if to endorse Weber's complaint about the ending of magic, a host of magicians arose, usually associated with the marginalized literary avant-garde, who flocked to join the Hermetic Society and other occult cults.

Among other notable sociologists, the Italian Vilfredo Pareto, a brilliant and versatile social and economic theorist (he was also an engineer and a mathematician), shared Weber's pessimism. He thought human political thought essentially irrational. He said of his *Trattato di Sociologica Generale* that if he thought it would have many readers, he would not have written it! Marx was mistaken in predicting a future classless utopia; the struggle for power between groups and classes never ends. If Marx's "proletariat" did win, it would become a new ruling class against which others would eventually rebel—an accurate prediction of what did happen in Russia and other Communist states. (Pareto was said to have given Lenin more sleepless nights than any other social theorist.)

In his disabused reduction of all ideals to selfish power struggles Pareto is reminiscent of Hobbes, or his famous Italian forbear Machiavelli. Liberty, Pareto thought, is best served when we are aware of the delusions lurking in ideals, aware of the realities of power and thus able to establish checks on power as far as possible. We should aim at a circulating elite, one able to coopt potential revolutionaries into the circle of power. But in general Pareto did not prescribe, he only described, and he was not optimistic about the state of the existing European governing class. An interesting feature of his sociology was the attempt to classify the basic emotional determinants of ideas, in his terminology the "residues" that underlie intellectual systems, and which resemble Jungian archetypes, or Weber's "modes of authority" in being the real, often unconscious determinants of rational doctrines.[7] Few more ruthless exposers of ideals and ideologies have ever written.

Though enormously learned and often motivated by a disinterested quest for knowledge, these sociologists were far from uninvolved or value-free. They all tended to see a crisis. Durkheim "spoke of sociology with the moral fervor of a prophet" and thought it could save us by explaining how to achieve solidarity and avoid "anomie." Weber, at times hauntingly eloquent, is one ancestor of existentialism: Karl Jaspers was his student. Pareto, apparently the most objective, was the most embittered, and it is plain that what forced him into detachment was his disenchantment. If you have really given up all belief in fairies, to endure life you must stand off and laugh at it all from an Olympian distance. Sociology was patently a strategy for rejecting or satirizing society. The device of pretending to be a stranger in order to say, "See what odd customs these queer people have! And what absurd things they do!" was an old stratagem of satire, used by Swift and Montesquieu in the eighteenth century. Certain sociologists did the same thing.[8] Someone defined sociology as the village atheist studying the village idiot. Sociology itself is subject to sociological interpretation. In this era it joined the alienated artists, the socialists, and other outsiders in criticizing mass democracy, the "bourgeoisie," the philistines, and other enemies of the spirit.

THE RELIGIOUS CRISIS

Sociologists located the crisis of society in the loss of an integrated community with an integrating faith. Durkheim saw religion's chief role as providing the cement of social solidarity; a real community must have some kind of shared value system, consecrated in ceremonies and rituals. (His *Elementary Forms of Religious*

---

[7]Pareto named six "residues," but these seem to boil down to two main ones, the "instinct for combinations" and the "persistence of aggregates." By these he seemed to mean something close to the modernized, pluralistic society and the integral, organic one—Tönnies's *Gesellschaft* and *Gemeinschaft*. The foxes who deal in combinations are capitalists and wily politicians; the lions are feudal, heroic, perhaps in Weber's sense charismatic.

[8]One of the most obvious and most celebrated of this type was the savage caricature of small-town USA written by American sociologists Robert and Helen Lynd which they called *Middletown*. It was popular in the 1920s along with the novels of Sinclair Lewis, which aimed at the same target.

Life, 1912, was probably his best book.) It was widely believed that the ancestral faith of Christianity no longer filled such a function. Long since divided into often mutually hostile churches and sects, it had come under general attack from rationalists, skeptics, agnostics, humanists, positivists, socialists (who charged with Charles Péguy that it was the religion of the rich), scientists, historians. Darwinism, as we know, had dealt blows to religious orthodoxy. Nietzsche had announced "God is dead" (we killed him). Freud was an atheist. Charles Péguy dated the end of the Christian era (for the first time, "a world without Jesus") at 1881. The prestige of scientific positivism was never greater, and books like Ernst Haeckel's *The Riddle of the Universe*, a turn-of-the-century favorite, claimed on behalf of "monism" that religion no longer had a role in knowledge, since science was in possession of all the answers, or soon would be.

It is true that this tendency to write off religion was found more among the educated minority than the ordinary populace—even though attempts to establish mass religiosity, such as a poll of London churchgoing in 1900, generally found some falling off. At the same time, as compared to midcentury there was a notable countertrend among intellectuals seeking to recover or redefine religious faith. We have already noted that such sages of the epoch as Tolstoy and Bergson powerfully reinforced religion, even if it was an unorthodox kind. Spiritual impulses tended to be diverted to non-orthodox, even non-Christian varieties of religion.

Stress on the value of religious experience *qua* experience could be found in Bergson and in William James's famous lectures *Varieties of Religious Experience*, which developed his position that what is important is the will to believe. Religion, if not true, is psychologically valuable; at least it is very interesting. What is most interesting is to see that the various conceptualizations in which religions are objectively embodied are all the outward expressions of an instinct to believe. Emmanuel Mounier remarked a few years later that a century ago everyone was either a Christian or a rationalist opposed to all religion, whereas now there are not many of either sort. There were, instead, a rich variety of more or less exotic neo-religions. One might even, like Yeats, invent a private mythology.

There was a Catholic Revival among French men of letters and even some British ones. George Santayana's attraction to the "splendid error" of the Roman Catholic faith indicated the special sophistication of these conversions; nobody really thought this faith was "true," in a literal sense, but it is a shallow person who thinks religion disposed of when this is pointed out. There was unquestionably some weakness in treating religion as not true but useful, or nice to believe. Simone Weil later complained that Bergson presented religious belief "like a pink pill of a superior kind, which imparts a prodigious amount of vitality." But the turning to religion in this self-conscious way, treating it as poetry or myth, was typical of the fin de siècle vanguard. Many of them did it just to be perverse, in the spirit of the painter Burne-Jones, who said that "the more materialistic science becomes, the more angels I shall paint." For an outcast poet to turn Catholic in England, as Ernest Dowson and Francis Thompson did, was to shock respectable people rather more than turning Communist would in the next generation.

Freud's colleague and then enemy Carl Jung differed from his rival psycho-analyst chiefly in welcoming religion as a cure for neurosis, something Freud ruled out of hand. The Zurich psychiatrist, influenced by Nietzsche, originally turned to psychology because it seemed to combine religion and philosophy with science. Jung attached less importance than Freud to sexual repression and infantile experi-ences as sources of mental disturbance. They shared a belief in the unconscious as a psychic determinant, and in dreams as a key to the content of the unconscious. But to Jung the unconscious was a source less of savagely antisocial impulses than of nourishing myths or "archetypes" in a "collective unconscious." The problem was one of curing dissociation, the divided self, by integrating this unconscious mythic material into the conscious social self. The collective unconscious appears in myths, fairytales, in art and poetry, as well as in dreams. Its archetypes are found in all the great religions. A fabulous scholar himself, Jung cast his net wide-ly over civilizations past and present in his search for the archetypes. In this respect he was a forerunner of the structuralist anthropologists; his disciples tended toward comparative mythology as well as the analysis of art and poetry in terms of its thematic elements.

The fully mature or "individuated" personality must dissolve the "persona," Jung's term for roughly what Freud meant by "ego"; it is our social role, the part society expects us to play, a mask of artificial personality. It must learn to absorb portions of the unconscious mind in the interest of individuation and creativity. Jung obviously took aim here at the age's foremost psychic predicaments, the schizophrenic gap between inner and outer world. His famous classification of per-sonality types into introverts and extroverts (with subdivisions) clearly related to this problem.

Religion appears here as a psychic need, nourishing and enriching, because it is connected to the whole race's storehouse of inner experience. Religion is a fun-damental human need. The great "myths," expressing as they do the language of the mind at its deepest level, with roots in the collective life of humanity, satisfy basic instincts. Without them, human nature shrivels. Being cut off from this realm, he thought, caused immense damage. "The dynamism and imagery of the instincts together form an *a priori* which no man can overlook without the greatest risk to himself," Jung wrote in *The Undiscovered Self.* The forces latent in the unconscious will break forth in wildly irrational ways if they are not understood and administered to. Modern man lives too much, he thought, in a realm of rational concepts, ignoring the underlying emotional determinants. Jung echoed Niet-zsche's conviction that the modern individual is overly rationalized and needs to regain contact with some healthy primitivisms. "The great gains made by the evo-lution of human society…are made at the price of enormous losses."

Like Freud, Jung (the younger man by twenty years) had a long and amaz-ingly creative life. Though he wrote with less clarity and precision than Freud, he could convey the importance of myths, symbols, and mystic experience. World War I moved Jung deeply and pushed him toward a mysticism always congenial to his temperament. Yet he remained a professional psychiatrist, convinced that "The psychiatrist is one of those who know most about the soul's welfare, upon which so much depends in the social sum." His "school" flourished less than Freud's, but the great brought their troubles to him. The troubled offspring of one of the wealthiest American families, Paul Mellon, built him a house and established a publication series in Jung's name.

Over the door of his home, the Swiss sage inscribed a Latin slogan the meaning of which is "Recognized or not, the god is present." We cannot, as Freud thought, avoid the need to choose a faith. (Freud, he said, brought back, as the superego, the god he had expelled.) Jung unlike Freud was inclined to tell a patient "find something to believe in." He did not, of course, presume to dictate the form of the faith; it could be an Eastern mysticism or a primitive animism just as well as a "higher religion," for the value lies in the archetypal roots rather than the formal structure. Simone Weil would have detected another "pink pill," and in fact Jung was (to Freud's chagrin) more than a little indebted to Henri Bergson.

In a powerful essay called "A Free Man's Worship" (1903), young Bertrand Russell, agnostic, anti-Christian, skeptic, philosophical anti-idealist as he was, nonetheless voiced in almost agonizing terms the need for a faith. Russell had lost his belief in God to Mill and Darwin when a teenager, and abhorred the suffocating

Lasting almost a century, Bertrand Russell's life stretched from the Edwardian to the atomic era and was involved at almost every stage with controversy. The notable philosopher ended as a militant political activist famed for his leadership of the Campaign for Nuclear Disarmament. (Caricature of Bertrand Russell by Jack Rosen, caricaturist of world figures; courtesy of the Bertrand Russell Archives, McMaster University)

Victorian piety in which he was brought up. Like Tolstoy his pet aversion was "the organized churches of the world." Yet also like the Russian sage Russell thirsted after religion. "I have never found religious satisfaction in any philosophical doctrine that I could accept," he later wrote. But he never stopped trying, because he thought that "in order to value life it is necessary to value something other than mere life...some end outside human life." The dilemma of the "humanist" is that the attempt to worship just human nature leaves you with no criteria by which to eliminate the obviously wicked things people do (of which Russell was acutely conscious). In "A Free Man's Worship" the young philosopher, destined to live nearly a hundred years and become one of the century's most famous people, eloquently invoked the ability of the free spirit in a cruel and pointless world, "undismayed by the empire of chance, to preserve a mind free from the wanton tyranny that rules his outward life." Faced with the fact that they are only tiny, fleeting accidents in the vast impersonal cosmos, that all their achievements are destined to be "buried beneath the debris of a universe in ruins," humans can take comfort only in the freedom of the mind to formulate a faith, a "vision of the good." Russell hurls Promethean defiance back at a cruel fate.

So the religious spirit was abroad, but the winds of doctrine were various and confusing. The British scholar J. N. Figgis, writing just before 1914, in *Civilization at the Crossroads*, expressed dismay at the babel of voices—Nietzsche, Bergson, James, Tolstoy, Russell—preaching atheism, skepticism, intuitionism, the life force, the "will to believe," the will-to-power.

Russia was alive with esoteric faiths. The composer Scriabin, who upheld the artist's role as messiah and announced himself as the chosen one, and the poet Ivanov, who preached the mystical union of Christ and Dionysus in "ecstasy for ecstasy's sake," were part of a mood in which "every kind of new religion and superstition proliferated" (Martin Cooper). At the other end of Europe, James Joyce in Dublin encountered the Hermetic Order and the Theosophical Society, where Madame Blavatsky, Annie Besant, and other modern mystics were read. There was serious interest in supernormal psychical phenomena, such as spirit messages, clairvoyance, poltergeists; among others the Cambridge professor of philosophy C. D. Broad lent his name to it, and it became quite fashionable to belong to the Society for Psychic Rsesearch. The turn-of-the-century years produced some bizarre occultist fringe figures, such as Frederick Rolfe (Baron Corvo) and Aleister Crowley (magician, eroticist, diabolist). Among others who made a religion of sex was the Freudian castoff Otto Gross, once regarded by Freud as his leading disciple but written out of the psychoanalytic record after his life turned scandalous.

Nikolai Berdyaev mentioned Tolstoy and Dostoyevsky among those he called "forerunners of the era of the spirit"; others this Russian existentialist mentioned were Solovyëv, another Russian, and two Frenchmen, Leon Bloy and Charles Péguy. The latter, initially a Dreyfusard and a socialist, edited prewar France's most influential intellectual journal, *Cahiers de la Quinzaine*, which opened its pages to all kinds of expression. Though a Catholic in his own way, Péguy was essentially a free spirit. Like Tolstoy he was in revolt against all that was false and shoddy and sought to affirm the value of the human soul by preaching integrity, devotion to the spiritual and intellectual life, social justice, dedication to art.

A secondary figure may show the trends of the times even better than the major ones. As an example, A. R. Orage, friend of Shaw and Wells, edited a journal called *The New Age* (1907–1922), probably the leading avant-garde literary organ in London. The Leeds-born Orage had begun as a Fabian socialist, and later became an enthusiast for something called Social Credit, one of the leading economic panaceas of the day. But in the end he came under the influence of the Greek-Russian magician, or charlatan, G. I. Gurdjieff, who along with Mme. Blavatsky was the most fashionable occultist of the hour. Gurdjieff claimed to teach a secret spiritual discipline derived from the religious sages of all times and places, an esoteric theosophy. Among the many he influenced were Yeats and the American architect Frank Lloyd Wright. Gurdjieff was the forerunner of many a guru from the East who would fascinate bored and restless Western youth in later decades.[9] The spiritual hunger of Europe was mirrored in such episodes.

NATIONALISM AS A RELIGION

For some, socialism was a substitute religion; for others, art or science. Popularly, the most obvious value system with accompanying symbols and ceremonies was nationalism. The intellectuals did not entirely ignore it. One of Péguy's notable literary achievements was his promotion of Joan of Arc as a French national symbol. Joan had been very little known in France until the nineteenth century. Interested in anything medieval, some of the Romantics resurrected the story of the fifteenth-century Maid Of Orleans, martyr and heroine of the wars against the English. The great nationalist historians of midcentury, especially Jules Michelet, depicted Joan as the mother of the French nation. Her legend grew. Not only Péguy but Charles Maurras made much of her; yet conservatives were not alone in this. Socialists and liberals, anticlericals as well as clericals rallied around Joan as a symbol of national unity.

The left had its own heroes of the French past, its own version of the French mission to humankind. German Social Democrats, puzzling about the relation between socialism and nationalism, decided that after the revolution national differences would not disappear but would be purified; the *Sonderleben*, or special life of nations, would continue, on a higher plane. The bourgeoisie could not expropriate the German past! Marx himself tended to think that, rescued from the bourgeois state, the nation might well be the natural form of community for socialist man.

World War I was to show how much stronger the appeal of nationalism was

---

[9]Just before 1914 the Bengalese poet and sage Tagore made a sensation on the first of a number of visits to Europe.

than a hypothetical internationalism—emphatically not least to intellectuals (see the next chapter). The persistence of ethnicity as the basis of social life is a surprising fact. United politically with the English for the past two centuries on the island they shared, the Scottish people had never learned to be at home spiritually in Great Britain (and still have not). A Briton never came into existence. Practical necessity perpetuated the union but never secured it a place in the hearts and minds of the people. The same was true of the Welsh.

Literature, at least, had to recognize this fact. Among the more notable literary nationalisms was the Celtic revival in Ireland, using Irish folk themes and even seeking to resurrect the ancient Gaelic tongue as a literary medium. Possibly the greatest poet of the century, William Butler Yeats, emerged from this Irish renaissance. Another prominent figure was Mistral, the poet of a revived *langue d'oc* in Provençe.

In 1896 Theodor Herzl's book, *Der Judenstaat*, laid the foundations of a Jewish cultural revival and aimed at the establishment of a modern Jewish state in the ancestral land of Palestine. The Zionist congresses began in 1897. A less political brand of Zionism interested young Franz Kafka and other Jewish writers in Prague. The Dreyfus affair in France and persecution in Russia, as well as anti-Semitic stirrings in Germany and Austria, brought home to the Jews the fact that Europe was again in the grip of intolerance. But Zionism at this time was mostly an affair of intellectuals and writers.

Largely "assimilated" Jews shared in the literary inheritance of their country; a remarkable group of such partly de-Judaized Jewish writers, musicians, and artists contributed powerfully to European culture in the late nineteenth and early twentieth centuries. Such a list would include Marx, Freud, Einstein, Gustav Mahler, Ludwig Wittgenstein, Kafka, Bergson, the half-Jewish Marcel Proust, and many others. Many of them turned to Zionism as a gesture of dissatisfaction with existing European civilization, and as a means of finding their own identity. A theologian like Martin Buber preached the saving grace of a rooted Jewish nationalism in much the same accents as other "integral nationalists" like Maurras, Barrès, Wagner. The larger history of Zionism of course lay ahead; its origins were in the intellectual ferment of this turn-of-the-century period, so remarkable for its quest for new values.

Nationalism rose to an almost frenzied peak just before 1914. Gabriele D'Annunzio, famous Italian writer, whose perversely erotic novels and lifestyle made him a leader of the "decadents" in the 1890s, became a fierce nationalist about 1909, calling for Italy to sharpen her sword on Africa and then advance on the world. (The Italians responded by trying to seize Tripoli from the Turks, thus putting in train a sequence that had much to do with the outbreak of major war in 1914.) The *Alldeutscher Verband*, or Pan-German League, entertained fantasies of German domination of all Europe. In France, Maurras's patriotic, militantly anti-German *Action Française* was popular among students. Jaurès tried to rally the socialists against an extension of military service in 1911, but without success, a premonition of the pacifist collapse in 1914. Various versions of pan-Slavism flourished in Russia, where Danilevski had argued that the Slavs' turn to dominate world history would come next, the Latins and Nordics having had their turn. At any rate Russia must either advance to the Adriatic or retire behind the Urals, the Pan-Slavist Fadayev declared; it was Russia's manifest destiny to unite all the Slavic peoples of eastern Europe. Books about the British imperial destiny were equally rife in London, where according to the historian Esmé Wingfield-Stratford, "the Press reeked with blood and reverberated with thunder."

That international life is an arena in which those nations not prepared to compete in the struggle for power will deservedly perish was a legacy of Darwinism quite widely shared around the turn of the century. It swept the United States in the Teddy Roosevelt era and was entertained by quite sophisticated minds (Roosevelt himself was certainly one of the most intellectual American presidents.) For example, the British poet John Davidson, a Nietzsche disciple, held that "the universe is immoral" and enthusiastically supported British imperialism, which he along with Rudyard Kipling regarded as having a sanction to rule and rule vigorously over the lesser breeds. "Those swarms of black, and brown, and dirty-white, and yellow people," socialist H. G. Wells explained, will have to go; "it is their portion to die out and disappear."

Such themes had much to do with the great war that erupted in 1914 to end the Victorian era and usher in a new phase of world history. The men of ideas made no slight contribution to them.

7

The West in Trouble: World War I and Its Aftermath

INTELLECTUAL ORIGINS OF THE WAR

Few need to be reminded that the breakdown of international order in 1914 was to dominate a good part of the twentieth century. Out of four years of mass slaughter came red revolution in Russia, black revolution in Italy and Germany, and a general loss of confidence throughout Europe. The war proved scarcely less demoralizing to the victor states than to the losers. During the war, propaganda took over and truth suffered as never before. Out of the war emerged a new kind of cynicism, a loss of faith in human values, such as Europe had never experienced before in modern history. The second world war of 1939–1945, an even worse disaster, was a direct outgrowth of the first.

It is tempting to find some parallels between this crisis of the political order and the crisis of thought and culture that seemed to exist as of 1914. Historians customarily describe the origins of the 1914 war in terms of diplomatic and political history, and quite properly so: the clash of national interests, the alliances between states, the military plans, the conferences and confrontations. But ideas also entered in. The rise of nationalism was an obvious cause of the war. Now and again politicians could be heard declaring, in a Darwinian spirit, that struggle, competition, and force are the laws of life. Democracy forced officials to take account of a public opinion that was often belligerent and narrow-minded, as well as fiercely patriotic. Diplomacy does not function in a vacuum; politicians are people of their age, sharing its prevalent ideas. Historians need to "reconstruct the unspoken assumptions of the men they are studying" and "re-create the climate of opinion in which political leaders operated," James Joll has argued in the thoughtful lecture *1914: The Unspoken Assumptions.*

The unspoken assumptions of 1914 included a distinct eagerness for war, shared by writers and intellectuals—something a later generation found hard to understand, but very much a part of the spirit of the "August days" at the beginning of the war. The war was extremely popular in all countries at the start. Resisting the war spirit in Britain, Ramsay MacDonald was aware that he was pitted against "the most popular war in British history," a fact to which the incredible rush of voluntary enlistments bears witness. And in the van of this rush to enlist were the young poets, artists, university students, intellectuals. The story was not different in France, in Germany, in Russia, and soon in Italy.

It is difficult to find leaders of the intellectual community who held out against this martial spirit. Romain Rolland, one of the few who did try to resist it, cried that "there is not one among the leaders of thought in each country who does not proclaim with conviction that the cause of his people is the cause of God, the cause of liberty and of human progress." The list of these who blessed the war as a holy cause is a lengthy one and includes most of those discussed in the previous chapter, those of them who were alive in 1914. Bergson, Durkheim, Péguy, Weber, Freud (who "gave all his libido to Austria-Hungary"), poets and novelists such as Thomas Mann, Stefan George, and Arnold Bennett were as prominent as historians and sociologists. The socialists forgot their theoretical antiwar principles and rallied to the cause of their country, in the beginning with very few exceptions. In England the idol of the hour was the young poet Rupert Brooke, who marched off proudly to die along with so many others who gave their lives as a willing sacrifice to the Moloch of war. To be sure, Rolland exaggerated when he said "not one," but the small minority who tried to resist were all but swamped in 1914 in the rush to jump on the war wagon.

The reasons for this extraordinary belligerence—strong enough to justify Freud's wartime discovery of a "death wish"—led back into pre-1914 themes. Among the more obvious ingredients were (1) a desire for excitement, adventure, and romance, growing out of boredom with a drab, materialistic, bourgeois civilization; (2) a feeling that the war offered an opportunity for a spiritual renewal through its break with the past and its outpouring of unselfish idealism; (3) exultation at the recovery of community feeling, healing the divisions between classes and individuals; and (4) a sort of apocalyptic, Nietzschean mood which saw in the unexpected catastrophe an awful judgment on a doomed civilization but also the necessary prelude to rebirth; a "cleansing fire" or flood. Clearly all these attitudes involved prewar intellectual themes.

The third, possibly, was both the strongest and the most obviously connected to prewar thought. Alienated intellectuals saw a way to rejoin the human race on honorable terms. They thrilled at what Karl Vossler, writing to Benedetto Croce, called "the magnificent drama of the exaltation of a nation of 70 million people, all without exception...living for all, for the Fatherland." Sophisticated minds such as Max Scheler had come to have as their chief concern "a quest for unity and community in a pluralistic society." A surprising number saw the war as a remedy for anomie, for deracination; an achievement of *Gemeinschaft*, of "integral nationalism." The men in the trenches developed feelings of close solidarity in this war which placed them in dependence on each other; many of them even after they came to hate the fighting valued this experience and hoped to carry it over into their lives after the war.

Anyone who has studied the mood of 1914 knows that a strange *mystique* goes far to explain the incredible support for the war through years of agony; and that this spirit existed above all in the young, those of poetic temperament, the idealists and restless ones. (Never was the cliché about old men sending young ones out to fight their wars more mistaken. The young clamored to fight and accused the old of holding back.) War, still seen romantically in 1914, came as a welcome relief from years of pettiness and greed. In France, the period from 1905 on witnessed a revival of what Eugen Weber, who studied it carefully, summed up as "Discipline, Heroism, Renaissance, *Génie National*." The conversion of Charles Péguy from socialism to nationalism in 1905 was a landmark; thereafter the former Dreyfusard wrote as a patriot, an antipacifist, a fervent prophet of the coming war against Germany. An inquiry into the mood of French university youth in 1913 found that Péguy was the leading influence, along with Barrès and others of the same type. One of them was Paul Claudel, whose plays and poems radiated a blend of heroism and religion and French traditions.

In Germany, the years just before the war gave birth to a youth movement whose fierce idealism subsequently fed into the war. The *Wandervögel* of the *Jugendbewegung* were in revolt against their elders, filled with a Nietzschean spirit of drastic spiritual renewal accompanied by apocalyptical violence. Poets like Stefan George indulged in visions of a purifying war. That the war would bring "the moral regeneration of Europe" so relatively mild a philosopher as Henri Bergson held. "Happy are they who die in a just war," sang Péguy before he went off to be killed on the Marne in its early days.

This frenetic war spirit had much to do with the coming of the war. Not that the poets and intellectuals deliberately contrived war; it came out of the blue, totally unexpected by the vast majority. Only a few professional diplomatists had known how serious the crisis was. But for that very reason it seemed almost a divine omen.

The young Bosnians whose assassination of Archduke Franz Ferdinand provided the spark that set off the flames were themselves aflame with the restless radicalism of pre-1914 Europe. Their idols included Gorki, Andreyev, Whitman, Wilde, amd Ibsen. They had learned tyrannicide from 1848 romanticism (Mazzini,

"William Tell"); they lived in an atmosphere of youthful literary romanticism, fed by exciting writers of the hour, with considerable symbolist and decadent influences. They were in touch with the international anarchist movement.[1]

That the war was a just one, of course, each side believed, alleging that it had been attacked by the other. The socialists rationalized their support by arguing that if they did not fight, their country would be destroyed and with it their movement. The Germans further pointed out that a victory for Russia would be a victory for the most reactionary of European powers. The French similarly believed that a German conquest would wipe out social gains made in France. The working class everywhere was strongly patriotic, and the intellectual socialists were not prepared for the way the war came. The Second International had often rhetorically vowed that the workers of the world would never fight each other in a war their capitalist rulers forced on them; but this war did not happen like that. The great majority knew only that their country was under attack and must be defended. A small minority of the socialists and labor leaders in Great Britain, Germany, and Russia thought otherwise but abided by party discipline. Within a fairly short time Karl Liebknecht in Germany, and Lenin among the exiled Russian Bolsheviks, went into opposition to the war and Ramsay MacDonald resigned the Labour party leadership in Britain, but these were voices crying in the wilderness for several years.

Intellectuals participated in the war to a striking degree. They went off and fought in it, of course, some volunteering at the age of forty or fifty; they wrote poems to it, hailed it as a regenerating process, celebrated its *mystique*. Many of those who did not serve in the trenches lent their talents to propaganda. Arnold Bennett, one of England's leading literary figures, became a director of British propaganda; distinguished historians fashioned handbooks proving the eternal wickedness of the foe (this material has to be seen to be believed) and authenticating stories of barbarous atrocities, which were usually untrue. Many writers, artists, and intellectuals died in the war. A sampling of the notable talent sacrificed could include the British poets Rupert Brooke, Wilfred Owen, Isaac Rosenberg, Charles Sorley, Edward Thomas; Ivor Gurney went mad. The brilliant painters Franz Marc, Egon Schiele, August Macke, Raymond Duchamp-Villon, and Umberto Boccioni were slain; the poet Georg Trakl and the sculptor Wilhelm Lehmbruck committed suicide. Of 161 students of the famous French elite school, the *École Normale Supérieure*, from the years 1911, 1912, and 1913, 81 died in the war and another 64 were wounded. A French anthology of writers killed in the war contained 500 names, among them Péguy, Alain-Fournier (the Rupert Brooke of France), and Psichari. The list might go on and on.

The heaviest casualties in the terrible slaughter on the western front were among the junior officers, where typically one found educated youth. One is led to

---

[1]See Vladimir Dedijer's article, "Sarajevo Fifty Years After," *Foreign Affairs*, July 1964, and his book, *The Road to Sarajevo* (1966).

wonder what potentially earth-shaking achievements were buried with the tens of thousands of brilliant youth killed—what *Ulysses* or relativity theory or *Waste Land* was not created by some even more talented Joyce or Einstein or Eliot who happened to fall in battle. On the other hand, the war stimulated a great amount of creative writing and thinking.

Disenchantment soon set in. "One week in the trenches was sufficient to strip war of its lingering traces of romance," Herbert Read recalled. As the war dragged on and the slaughter mounted, protest inevitably arose. In the end, most of those who survived were ashamed of having been taken in. Yet it is well to remember that this was not so in August 1914, when a generation of rebels found their great crusade. "We were all flame and fire," Isadora Duncan remembered. The student of intellectual history finds much to connect this state of mind with the ferment of ideas in the preceding generation.

If the war was initially popular, it eventually gave way to sometimes bitter disillusionment, a mood that tended to endure and flavor the postwar perspective. "War is hell, and those that institute it are criminals," Siegfried Sassoon wrote from the trenches. The progress of disenchantment may be followed in the poetry, of which this war produced much of high quality. It remained a writer's war all the way and even in its disappointment gave rise to splendid literature. No other war can compare with it. The initial "visions of glory" faded to sorrow and pity and ended in bitterness. The wretchedness, the terror, the nerves tortured by waiting for death, the gassed soldiers, the obscene wounds, even the lice were what the front-line poets wrote about:[2]

> In winter trenches, cowed and glum,
> With crumps and lice and lack of rum.

Soon they began to scorn the people at home who could have no notion of what the war was really like. A comradeship of suffering and death drew the soldiers close together and sometimes drew them closer to other victims of war in the opposite trenches than to the smug ones at home—or to their own senior officers. Soldier-poets wrote of the scarlet majors at the base who "speed glum heroes up the line to death" and would themselves toddle safely home to die in bed. Those who did not die in the first battles but, like the great Wilfred Owen, lived through almost the whole war (he was killed within hours of the armistice) could feel nothing but the horror, the pity, the futility of war. The romance had gone from war forever and abhorrence of the very thought of war was to flavor the postwar era—aiding, ironically, the coming of the next one, since a pacifist-minded public opin-

---

[2]There was a good deal of leisure to write behind the lines in the interludes between fighting; not all a soldier's time was spent in water-logged trenches. There were also the mademoiselles from Armentières, giving rise to severe problems of social disease.

ion in the victor countries permitted a revenge-minded Germany to overturn the peace settlement and the balance of power.

RESULTS OF THE WAR: SOVIET COMMUNISM

The war that claimed such an astounding toll of human life ended not in a brave new world, but in a fog of disappointment. The Austro-Hungarian monarchy was dissolved, replaced with a confusion of small, new states with uncertain boundaries. In Great Britain, the war wrecked the old Liberal party forever and caused a great increase in the Labour party, which now adopted a socialist platform. The great peace conference at Paris in 1919, to which the president of the United States came, left the defeated Germans with a sense of keen injustice and the victorious Allies divided. Most people saw it as having failed to provide a morally exhausted world with a new sense of purpose. The League of Nations, chief symbol during the war around which hopes for a brighter future clustered, managed to struggle into existence in 1919 amid much controversy, but the refusal of the United States to join it reinforced the view that it would prove a major disappointment.

The only gleam of hope seemed to come from the Russian revolution of November 1917, whose leaders during the "ten days that shook the world" swept aside the old ruling class, denounced the entire international political order as well as the reigning economic system, and called for a world revolution. Its leader seemed a man of genius, the only one visible.

Vladimir Ilyich Ulyanov, known better to history by his *nom de revolution* of Nikolai Lenin (many history books and encyclopedias for some reason conflate these and call him V. I. Lenin) began as an orthodox Marxist but was from the beginning a dominating and restless personality. That the tsar's government inflicted the death penalty on his brother and expelled Vladimir from Moscow University did little to calm his revolutionary temperament. Despite the cool rationality of his intellect, his interest in economic theory and philosophical questions (often beyond his depth), Lenin was a romantic revolutionary who, deeply influenced by the populist Chernyshevsky's prison-written *What Is To Be Done?* (1863), committed himself to the life of a professional revolutionary. This, as Chernyshevsky had explained, entails total and lifelong commitment without thought of any other goal, and without any moral compunctions in the ruthless war against the established order. Revolution in Russia was by now a venerable tradition; as Lenin said, his was the fourth generation of revolutionaries, dating back to the futile but heroic Decembrists of 1825. Revolution had matured into a fine art, practiced chiefly by conscience-stricken upper class Russians, the "repentant nobles" who burned with shame at their country's backwardness.

If not exactly a noble, Lenin was far from a proletarian, being the son of a moderately elevated provincial bureaucrat (he shared this status with Adolf Hitler) who gained university admission. The elitist element in Marx's thought, which saw intellectual leadership as necessary for the unsophisticated workers, became extremely pronounced in him; as Adolf G. Meyer remarks, Lenin "conceived a proletarian revolution as the product of great minds, who, conscious of inexorable trends, would create order and progress out of chaotic elements by organizing the raw materials of history in a rational fashion." There was some Nietzschean influence among Lenin's Bolshevik faction, stressing this element of creative will even more. The situation in Russia almost compelled this position. No proletariat existed, the country had barely begun to industrialize, it was questionable whether there was even a middle class. One could not wait hopefully for the self-destruction of capitalism on the morrow; capitalism had barely begun. Ridiculing the "requiem socialism" of the Second International Marxists, Lenin sought a justification on Marxist terms of an activist elite party, looking toward early revolution and a revolutionary dictatorship.

Together with Leon Trotsky (the son of a landowner), Lenin developed theories of this sort. Doubtless it was un-Marxian to claim that Russia could pass directly from agrarian backwardness to socialism, but one could argue that it was the weakest link in world capitalism, therefore the place where the revolution might begin, to spread subsequently over the globe. Precisely because it was so backward, Russia might offer the best chance for a successful revolution that would then become an international one. To train a small, disciplined party for illegal seizure of power might make Marxist sense in the long run. Lenin opted for such a "vanguard" party led by "the revolutionary socialist intelligentsia" who would act in the name of the workers. Lenin did not entirely stick to this position, but he continued to look for ways to reconcile Marxism and revolutionism. In 1903 he split the party, but his Bolshevik faction actually was in a small minority in the (already small) Russian Social Democratic party. Spending most of the years between 1900 and 1917 abroad, chiefly in Switzerland, Lenin theorized and drew around him a small number of loyal disciples, captivated by his charismatic personality. But he did not seem an important figure on the world Marxist scene, which was dominated by west Europeans.

Lenin was one of the few who opposed the 1914 war almost from the beginning. Even most of the Bolsheviks saw no alternative to defending their country from German attack. Lenin was no pacifist; what he advocated was turning the war between nations somehow into an international civil war between classes. His position attracted very little support; an overwhelming majority of European socialists stayed loyal to their governments. After the first Russian revolution of March (new style dating) 1917, Lenin returned from Switzerland on the famous sealed train which the Germans let through to Petrograd because they thought Lenin would help take Russia out of the war. He did immediately call for an end to the war, reversing Bolshevik policy, but the new government, encouraged by European socialists among others, fought on, only to see conditions steadily deteriorate. The circumstances that led up to the Bolshevik coup of early November and, as it turned out, to a dictatorship under Lenin's leadership are a notable part of world history. Again, Lenin alone had pushed for a Bolshevik seizure of power.

Illegal seizure of power, the terrorizing of opposition groups, the organiza-

tion of a secret police to silence dissent did not begin with Josef Stalin but constituted his inheritance from Lenin, which he only improved upon after the latter's
death in 1924. But the word went out that the system based on public enterprise
worked. Why did the capitalist countries seek to overthrow the Bolshevik regime
by blockade and armed intervention if they did not fear for their profits? Here was
the planned production for abundance that represented the economy of the future.
Led in France by Marie Curie's friend Paul Langevin, Western intellectuals signed
up to protest antibolshevism and hail its martyrs.

The new Communist government of the Soviet Union received significant
support from Western intellectuals quite early. "In this muddy age its ten years
shine," wrote the American liberal magazine *The Nation* in 1927, on the tenth
anniversary of the Bolshevik Revolution. In that year of the Sacco-Vanzetti agitation[3] this was probably a representative view on the left, though during the horrors
of the civil war in Russia, 1918–21, and the ensuing confusion amid terrorism and
persecution, there had been less sympathy for Lenin's dictatorship. Visiting Russia
in 1921, Bertrand Russell thought Lenin the most repulsive person he had ever
met. Romanticization of the 1917 Bolshevik seizure of power began early, with the
American journalist John Reed's *Ten Days That Shook the World*; but the ghastly
civil war, during which the Red dictatorship developed its secret-police system of
terrorizing all opponents (including moderate socialists), was followed by a retreat
toward capitalism (the New Economic Policy). After Lenin's death, a confused
debate about policy accompanied a struggle for power among his heirs in the party.
Only after 1929, amid depression in the West and the emergence of Josef Stalin as
the Soviet strong man, did a major rallying of support for the new Russia develop
among Western intellectuals.

FASCISM IN ITALY AND GERMANY

Nowhere was there greater bewilderment and disillusionment than in Germany.
The end of the war came as a shock; few Germans had realized they were so close
to defeat, and few could easily accept the fact that they had been wholly defeated.
There was no taste of defeat via invasion; during the entire war German troops
stood on enemy soil. Now suddenly the government was suing for peace, then
accepting stern conditions for an armistice; the kaiser abdicated, and within
months the Germans found themselves forced to accept what seemed a Carthagin-
ian peace treaty, amid humiliations the victors inflicted on them. Meanwhile a

---

[3]Communists led a worldwide protest against the execution in the summer of 1927 of the two
Italian-born American anarchists for a murder they allegedly committed during a robbery in 1920 at
South Braintree, Massachusetts. The case became perhaps the greatest of all *causes célèbres*, surpassing
even the Dreyfus Affair (to some extent its model), as liberals and leftists charged a frame-up. Decades
later, scholars were inclined to think that at least one of the "dago martyrs" was guilty after all, but for
long it was the first article of the liberal faith that they had been victims of anti-Red hysteria. The irony
is that the Soviet regime itself savagely persecuted anarchists.

strange new government, a republic with a Social Democrat at its head, replaced the kaiser's regime, as revolution broke out in a number of places, including Adolf Hitler's adopted home town of Munich. With soldiers returning home, confusion and chaos reigned.

Hitler's lament, as subsequently recorded in his autobiographical *Mein Kampf*, found an echo in many hearts (not only in Germany): it had all been futile. The years of hardship and heroism, the two million dead, the countless wounded— "it had all been in vain." Only a few years before, a powerful and prosperous Germany had dominated Europe. Now there was hunger and civil strife, as a defeated and leaderless people contended with bolshevism and mutiny. The tsar's abdication in Russia had opened the way for the Bolsheviks. Would this also be Germany's fate? Lenin was certain of it; it was the basis of his big gamble. Local Communist regimes momentarily surfaced in Munich and in Budapest. Even Hitler seems to have accepted the Munich soviet for a time. A sizable number of Germans voted for the Communist Party in the 1920s. Yet most Germans looked with horror on the barbarities they heard were going on in Russia.

Hitler, a failed artist and strange misfit who had found himself in the army during the war, emerged as an effective rabble-rouser in disturbed Munich in 1919, and helped found the National Socialist German Workers party of which he would become the absolute commander. He denounced Marxism, politicians, modern immorality, traitors, and especially the Jews, whom he made a scapegoat. But his was only one of a number of discontented groups milling about in the postwar confusion, and it did not achieve much prominence until near the end of the decade. Next door, Italy was already falling into the hands of a new movement, calling itself fascism, which stressed restoring order and regaining national strength by eliminating the weakening forces. The people must rally around a strong leader who embodies the national will and acts ruthlessly to destroy the poisons that corrupt peoples. Mussolini was less certain than Hitler that this poison was the Jew; Italian fascism displayed little anti-Semitism. But Hitler could agree with the Italian *duce* that not only Marxism and class war but parliamentary democracy, a degenerate system crippling the government for decisive action, had to be purged from the body politic.

Benito Mussolini, a talented left-wing socialist, broke away from the majority of his party on the issue of Italy's entrance into the war in 1915, which he supported. Free to launch ideological ventures of his own after this, he fell under the influence of Nietzschean and Sorelian ideas and emerged in the troubled days after the war as leader of the new movement known as fascism. The troubles in Italy resembled those in Germany. Though nominally one of the victors, Italy suffered humiliations both military and diplomatic (at the hands of its allies at the peace conference, Italians thought) and had trouble coping with the adjustment to a peacetime economy. Parliamentary democracy worked badly, and Italian pride suffered frustration.

The spirit of the war, which Hitler carried on by naming his followers "stormtroopers" and organizing his party like an army, found an echo in postwar

Italy in the superman figure of Gabriele D'Annunzio, the poet and novelist who had become a war hero in his fifties. It is D'Annunzio who must be given credit for inventing much of the *mystique* of Italian fascism, borrowed by Hitler for his political pageantry. D'Annunzio put himself at the head of some ex-soldiers and marched into the disputed city of Fiume in 1919, accompanying his seizure of it with flamboyant gestures soon copied by Mussolini—the uniformed private army, parades and mass meetings, the leader addressing crowds from the balcony as they roared slogans back at him. Admirer of Wagner (like Hitler) and Baudelaire, author of decadent novels, D'Annunzio turned from a literary prodigy in the 1890s to political activist and adventurer. "For Italy's younger generation," writes Ernst Nolte, "he was Nietzsche and Barrès rolled into one." He was an airplane pilot in the war and lost an eye in battle. No one better exemplified the "Leonardist" spirit that was Italy's version of the Nietzschean will-to-power, the Bergsonian *elan vital*. D'Annunzio was a fertile source of slogans, one of them being that Italy was a proletarian nation which should wage class war as a united people against the plutocratic states (a rather novel and disconcerting use of Marx!).

This attempt to invoke will and enthusiasm as a solution to political problems was a distinctive ingredient in fascism and one that clearly leads back to the prewar ideas. Both Mussolini and Hitler were intellectuals of a sort—self-taught, reading widely but promiscuously in search of what Hitler called his *Weltanschauung*, his world-view. They picked up, in a superficial way, many of the prewar irrationalisms. Fascism had no coherent doctrine, but regarded this as a virtue; intuition was superior to intellect. The prewar ideas showed up also in fascism's frank preference for elitist leadership, the charismatic "great man" or *Führer, duce*. And from the Nietzschean canon too it took the concept of a total revolution of values; Fascists and Nazis wanted to destroy the whole democratic-liberal-pluralist order and replace it with another. With what, was less clear. An order, certainly, that was organic and integral.

Mussolini approved the idea of a corporate state, prominent in Charles Maurras's *Action Française*, a strong influence on Italian fascism, and married it to a Hegelian conception of the state. (The neo-Hegelian philosopher Giovanni Gentile was prominent in the Fascist brain trust.) This statism, a legacy of Rousseau and Hegel, combined incongruously but effectively in fascist thought with the revolutionary dynamism that came from Nietzsche and Sorel. Some anarchist-syndicalists on the left supported Mussolini, at least initially. Fascism claimed to oppose materialistic capitalism as much as materialistic socialism; it would use the collective will of the people, represented by the State and its Leader, to compel cooperation between capital and labor.

Whether because of its ideas, the charismatic personality of its leader (and initially Mussolini was a dynamic person), or as is most likely, the bankruptcy of the old order, fascism was a hit in postwar Italy. Italians were sick of a corrupt and impotent parliamentary system; they became equally fed up with a socialism that brought disruption but no coherent program. A Lenin-type dictatorship failed to develop in Italy; it was probably not possible there, and at any rate the Italian socialists looked in an anarchist direction (local workers' control, not a leviathan state). Fascism seemed to offer vigorous leadership, a fresh start, a new faith. It converted the king of Italy, while the Pope himself (Pius XI) believed Mussolini was "a man sent by God." For a while Italy's most distinguished intellect, Benedetto Croce, approved of fascism because of its dynamism and revival of national morale. An impressive number of notable Italian writers, artists, musicians praised the new regime. Almost all became severely disillusioned within a few years after 1922. For "the lie of universal suffrage" Mussolini strove to substitute a vigorous, heroic elite; he only succeeded in putting Italy under the heel of a corrupt oligarchy. Quite a few of Italy's better minds went into exile. Others, like the great writer Ignazio Silone, were turned into Communists who fought the fascist tyranny underground as best they could.

Shaping Italy into a "totalitarian" community was something fascism pro-claimed as a goal but in practice scarcely achieved. By comparison with Stalin and Hitler, Mussolini was a mild dictator, imprisoning a few and killing almost none. Nevertheless he invented the concept of the intolerant racial or national community, which had room for no minorities or dissenting intellectuals, and which controlled the press and education in order to stamp a single culture on everybody. In this way, he thought, Italy could overcome its weakness and regain its ancient glory.

The term "fascism" was applied to Hitler's National Socialism (of which we will say more in the next chapter) and to a variety of other movements that appeared in Europe and North America in the interwar years. There were Belgian Rexists as well as several French Fascist leagues, of which the Cross of Fire became the largest; in February 1934 the Fascists mounted a huge demonstration in Paris. An Austrian fascism, the *Heimwehr*, predated the Nazis who destroyed it after taking over Austria in 1938. In Rumania, the Iron Guard preached return to ancestral customs, rejection of modernism, hatred of Jews as the symbol of capital-ism and modernism, and also a radical program of land distribution to aid the peas-antry. In Britain, the man regarded as the most brilliant young Labour leader, Oswald Mosley, tried to create a British Fascist party.

All these movements had enough in common to justify a common term, though they varied in details of doctrine (not a significant point, since all fascisms showed doctrinal inconsistencies.) Fascism was a response to the collapse of order and authority and integral community. It could be a popular mass movement, since the masses felt the loss of order as deeply as anyone (more so than the classes). Being inherently an emotional reaction, led by rather ignorant people, fascism was wildly erratic, irrational, and violent. But its significance as a reaction to the psy-chic distress that accompanied pluralistic modernization should not be overlooked. What is puzzling and interesting about fascism is that it did draw on a body of important and profound thought, half-understood by the Mussolinis and Hitlers who had skimmed and misunderstood, but were deeply moved by, the Nietzsches and Maurras' and Sorels and Le Bons of the prewar period.

POSTWAR LITERATURE AND THOUGHT

It must be admitted that dominant strains of thought in other countries, which could be called "fascist" only with the loosest use of that elastic term,[4] disparaged democracy. One of the leading tracts of the times, the Spanish philosopher Ortega y Gasset's *Revolt of the Masses*, found modern democracy a menace to historic Europe. In Oswald Spengler's influential *Decline of the West*, Europe's decay culminates in democracy, which is the detritus left behind by the decay of organic civilization. Like Georges Sorel, George Bernard Shaw admired both Lenin and Mussolini—any foe of democracy was his friend. H. G. Wells called for a new "samurai" class of governing experts, as did the American Walter Lippmann, in such widely read books as *Public Opinion* (1922) and *The Phantom Public* (1925). Democracy, D. H. Lawrence thought, was unnatural; any sound society finds its natural leader and lets him rule. "The thing must culminate in one real head, as every organic thing must." Though Lawrence never approved of Mussolini as meeting his standards in Caesarism, Ezra Pound did. Evelyn Waugh approved of Mussolini and later Franco's right-wing dictatorship in Spain. Among other intellectuals who were pro-Fascist, the noted avant-garde artist, Salvador Dali, was attracted to Hitler and then became a supporter of General Franco's regime. We have named some of the 1920s leading literary and intellectual figures.

Weimar Germany produced whole schools of neo-conservatives who lamented *The Rule of the Inferiors*, title of a 1927 book by the romantic reactionary Edgar Jung (later killed by Hitler, who tolerated no rivals in antidemocratic thought); Jung, a Lutheran, was close to the Austrian Catholic advocate of a return to the Middle Ages, Othmar Spann. Robert Brasillach and Drieu de la Rochelle joined the older figures Charles Maurras and Maurice Barrès, still active, among French intellectuals who were at least semi Fascist. On the other wing, those who embraced Soviet communism of course yearned for a stern dictator in their own country to smash the capitalists and install socialism.

The 1920s were nevertheless, on the whole, non- or apolitical. The rather bizarre events and personalities in dismal Russia and far-off Italy were not compelling enough to sway the mainstream intellectual circles of western Europe, while their own dismal politicians provoked only scorn; it was the age of Stanley Baldwin, Calvin Coolidge, Edouard Herriot, and a constant flux of obscure coalition-jugglers in Germany's Weimar Republic. "I don't remember if I voted in those years—certainly not for whom," Ludwig Marcuse recalled. Thomas Mann's *Considerations of an Unpolitical Man* was a characteristic reaction: "I hate politics and the belief in politics, because it makes men arrogant, doctrinaire, obstinate, and

---

[4]Some recent students of fascism have doubted the utility of a term that, like democracy, liberalism, etc., is used to mean so many different things that it is "without value for serious analytical purposes." One may sympathize with this view without altogether sharing it.

inhuman." The political mood reflected a wary suspicion of all lofty ideals, after the shattering disillusion of the war.

On the other hand, there was a brilliant feast in literature and the arts. One of the landmark books of the 1920s was Julien Benda's *Treason of the Intellectuals (Trahison des clercs)* in which the French critic and commentator charged the intellectuals with betraying their mission to uphold the eternal verities. One should avoid serving political -isms of whatever sort. The "lost generation" was too lost to believe in anything, except perhaps sex and drink. Virginia Woolf's Mrs. Dalloway cannot endure her life as the wife of a leading politician; the political scene bores her, kills her spirit, and she seeks refuge in the cultivation of sensibility in purely private ways.

It is difficult to think of any of the great writers of this period—D. H. Lawrence, André Gide, Ernest Hemingway, James Joyce, T. S. Eliot—who did not reject the civilization in which they lived, though it is true that in most cases this rejection antedated the war. They were marked wanderers; the American "expatriates," who joined Hemingway and Gertrude Stein in Paris, had a counterpart in Lawrence, who hated his native England and lived at various times in New Mexico, Mexico, and Italy; or Joyce, a refugee from Ireland who moved to Trieste, Zurich, and then Paris. There were, of course, Russian refugees from communism, Italian ones from fascism, and subsequently German from nazism. Physical flight from the homeland went along with imaginative flight from Western civilization, expressed in Lawrence's admiration for the Etruscans or the Aztecs, in Ezra Pound's importing of Chinese or what he imagined to be Chinese literature. True this alienation had existed in the previous generation too; but a severe gap separated the war from the prewar generation. Evelyn Waugh thought it actually the first significant estrangement between old and young in English history. It was in fact a three-way division: between the older pre-1914 "establishment" that had largely not fought in the trenches; those who fought, and managed to survive; and those who having been born about 1900–1905 just missed the military experience. But by all accounts a sharp difference in manners and morals emerged in the early 1920s between university students and their elders. "Before and after 1914 differed absolutely," Kafka's friend Max Brod remembered—only nominally on the same earth.

"An old bitch, gone in the teeth"—such was Pound's verdict on European civilization, while the usually optimistic H. G. Wells (who had coined the phrase "war to end wars" during the war) thought that "this civilization in which we are living is tumbling down, and I think tumbling down very fast." To reproduce all such comments would be an endless task. The classical statement, perhaps, was Spengler's *The Decline of the West*, which the German schoolteacher had written just before 1914 but which was published in many translations at the end of the war. Like Wells's even more popular reassessment of the past, *An Outline of History, Der Untergang des Abendlandes* was the work of an inspired amateur calculated to make professional historians wince; a literary classic which provided an overview of European history cast in the somber tones of Nietzschean cultural pessimism. Its perspective on Europe as having declined from its zenith in the Middle Ages became a fashionable one. The D. H. Lawrence based character in Aldous Huxley's *Point Counter Point* sees reverse evolution: our ancestors were giants, we are puny dwarfs. In a 1920 book Britain's "gloomy dean," William Inge, saw the idea of progress as "the working faith of the West for about a hundred and fifty years," and found it a fraud. A greater historian than Spengler, Arnold J. Toynbee, began his vaster comparative historical study of the rise and fall of societies in the 1920s, publishing the first three volumes in 1934 and the next three, the best, on decline, in 1939. The war itself, from which an illness excluded him, impelled the brilliant Oxford fellow to undertake possibly the most impressive work of historical synthesis the twentieth century has produced. In the end, he thought the failure a spiritual one.

Ortega y Gasset's *Revolt of the Masses* conveyed a similar theme of European decay from want of creative leadership. Paul Valéry's essay on the European crisis ("the mind is in fact cruelly stricken") and T. S. Eliot's even more famous poem, *The Waste Land*, expressed the same idea. It would be difficult to find a literary classic of these years that did not. A disgust with the absolute corruption of the world may be found in the brilliantly witty novels of Evelyn Waugh, the first of which was significantly titled *Decline and Fall*, and in the subtle psychological probings of French novelist François Mauriac. Marcel Proust's novels chronicled the decay of French society. The 1920s echoed with dirges for the passing of the European age.

Eliot's poem, a bombshell of the early twenties, was on every undergraduate's bookshelf; with its modernist style borrowed from the French symbolists and its fashionable message, it drew attention as few "highbrow" works have ever done. It began with a quotation from Petronius, "We yearn to die." "April is the cruellest month" because it no longer brings forth new life, Europe has lost its creativity. Using all the devices of symbolist technique, the American-born philosophy Ph.D. and quondam bank clerk found images to express the futility of religion and love: "Here is no water but only rock." The energizing springs that had fertilized culture in the past had dried up, leaving fear and timidity. "I show you fear in a handful of dust." The great tradition ends not with a bang but a whimper. It is now thought Eliot was registering an acute personal crisis more than he was recording the downfall of the West, but the two levels fused perfectly; his readers accepted the latter meaning all too readily.

Eliot soon sought refuge from the modern world in seventeenth-century Christianity. The gesture was a popular one. A significant group led by Jacques Maritain in France returned to medieval Thomism, while even more notable was the neo-Calvinism of Karl Barth and Emil Brunner in the German world. The collapse of liberal beliefs in secular progress led these "neo-orthodox" theologians back to original sin and a fallen world. In some ways these much-discussed theologies were not orthodox, for they usually "de-mythologized" the Bible, perhaps drew on Jungian and other modern conceptions to interpret Christianity as existentially true—true to the human condition—rather than literally true. But they were antidotes to the shallow optimism of prewar Christians as well as liberals and socialists who had believed in fulfillment in this world. Christ became less a preacher of humane ethical precepts than an apocalyptic or "eschatological" prophet who announced the end of the world and asked people to choose between God and the world. What had brought Western man low was the sin of pride in glorifying human nature. "It is essential not to have faith in human nature," historian Herbert Butterfield wrote. "Such faith is a recent heresy and a very disastrous one."

Barth's 1919 *Epistle to the Romans* commentary marked a sharp break with the previously prevailing liberal and idealist German theology, which under Hegelian influence had seen the course of human history as in large part a fulfillment of God's plan. This liberal theology almost blended with the secular idea of progress in seeing God's purposes as realized in this world. Regarded quite widely as the greatest theologian of his time, Barth fiercely denied this. There is no synthesis uniting God and humanity; the two are almost utterly estranged, humanity is incomplete, needing God for its fulfillment but unable to find him except in the one tenuous revelation contained in Scripture. The apparently quite reactionary features of the new theology (variously called "Crisis," "Dialectical," "Kerygmatic")—back to original sin and Luther's hapless human creatures in need of rescue by divine grace—actually made it seem revolutionary. One rejected a corrupt world and refused to accept a vapid, institutionalized Christianity (or its secular equivalents) that compromised with that world. Here Barth drew on the nineteenth-century Danish religious thinker, Søren Kierkegaard, in whose revival he notably assisted (see the next chapter,"Existentialism").

The same general features could be found in Martin Buber's Jewish theology and in N. Berdyaev's voice from the Russian Orthodox religion. Berdyaev, initially a Communist, fled from Lenin's police state to Berlin and then Paris in the 1920s. Buber's influential *I and Thou*, distinguishing between a person's relation to other persons and to things, with God as the "eternal Thou" to be encountered in a dialogue, appeared in 1923. These were exciting voices, some of them far less "orthodox" than Barth. Barth's close associate Rudolf Bultmann mediated the message for more modernist minds by his "demythologizing," which meant that the language with which the Word is expressed in the Bible is a mere husk containing the kernel of essential, true-to-life statements.

A revulsion against popular culture reinforced the intellectuals' feeling that culture was decadent. As the age of mass media dawned, a civilized minority rooted in the traditional high culture of Europe was more and more alienated. During the 1920s the "people" seemed more interested in sporting events, airplane flights, detective novels, crossword puzzles, movie stars, mah-jongg, bridge, and Mickey Mouse than serious ideas or good literature and art. The gulf between high and low, elite and popular culture—weeds and wildflowers, the American critic Van Wyck Brooks called them—became a chasm. The common man was a sad joke, cultural democracy the last absurdity of an expiring civilization. The "shopgirl mentality" and the common man as "boob" (H. L. Mencken) were familiar sneers.

Mencken's own United States was a favorite scapegoat, since it was the most obvious source of the new mass media, though by no means were they unwelcome in Europe. A series of European critics called it "America the menace," the subtitle of one French book of the era. A land without art or culture, home of philistines, the conformist American culture was hostile to freedom; Bertrand Russell repeated Tocqueville's point of a century earlier: "It is obvious that, in such a community, freedom can exist only *sub rosa*." But no one castigated American civilization more furiously than American intellectuals themselves. Europeans embraced American literature as never before, partly because Americn writers like Sinclair Lewis savagely satirized their own country. American literary rebels who contributed to the savagely critical symposium *Civilization in the United States* in 1922 soon fled to Paris.

FREUD IN THE TWENTIES

These years of the twenties felt the full force of deeply subversive ideas developed just before 1914. Freud now became widely known. Walter Lippmann, discovering him in 1915, wrote that the great Viennese psychologist "has set up a reverberation in human thought and conduct of which few dare yet to predict the consequences." His fellow Viennese Ludwig Wittgenstein did not discover Freud until 1919, surprised to find a psychologist "who had something to say." Freud contributed to the pessimistic mood of the 1920s. He had grown more pessimistic, perhaps because of age and a painful illness. The war caused him to add aggression to sex as a basic drive and write of the death instinct as well as the life/love drive, the erotic force. Humans are naturally aggressive creatures who will exploit, rob, even torture and kill others if not forcibly restrained. "Who has the courage to dispute it in the face of all the evidence in his own life and in history?" Freud wrote to Einstein. His books of the 1920s, such as *Civilization and Its Discontents*, leave the reader feeling that the battle between the individual and society has no satisfactory solution and will never end. Ordered society demands that the "id" impulses be suppressed, but to do so frustrates the individual. "The price of civilization is neurosis." The slow progress of science remains a faint hope; religion, the collective neurosis, he scorned as much as ever (*The Future of an Illusion*). But in an essay on Freud, Reinhold Niebuhr related him to the pessimism of the Barthians, in that he viewed the human being as a tragic figure, torn by conflicts. Of course, it was hard not to see Freud as chipping away at the boundaries of the rational mind, pointing to "the cobra-filled jungle of the unconscious" (Chad Walsh) as the real determinant of human conduct.

With widening fame, and the expansion of psychoanalysis into a great industry, particularly in the United States, despite illness and further schisms in his movement, Freud remained both amazingly creative and enormously influential until his death in 1939 (driven from Vienna to London by the Nazis in his last year.)

Sigmund Freud. (London, BBC
Hulton Picture Library)

Then the poet W. H. Auden wrote that "To us he is no more a person/Now
but a whole climate of opinion." There was some irony in the way this "climate of
opinion" was understood. Freud was commonly identified with the sexual revolution and eroticism. But in fact he was all his life a man of austere probity in his
personal life, never, so far as can be established, unfaithful to his quite traditional
wife Martha. He did not think that uninhibited sexual freedom brought happiness;
in fact, he thought that by making sexual love more common it devalued it and
thus diminished human happiness. ("In times during which no obstacles to sexual
satisfaction existed, love became worthless, and life became empty.") Certainly the
1920s in literature and life featured a frankness about sex and an openness in practicing it that struck many as unprecedented. (One wonders how much they knew
about the eighteenth-century upper class or the Victorian streets. In any case, the
pre-1914 generation had led the way.) But though Freud had pioneered in placing
sexual impulses and habits on the agenda of research, he did not sanction freeing
them from all moral and social restraints.

Freud's was a conservative temperament in many ways. He was deeply skeptical of claims that a socialist restructuring of society could abolish the conflict
between individual and society. Communism was as much an illusion as traditional
religion. The basic truths of psychoanalysis transcended any kind of social order.
Yet some deviant psychoanalysts like the eccentric Wilhelm Reich tried to marry

communism and psychoanalysis (incurring the displeasure of both authoritarian creeds; Reich got thrown out of both the churches). In the minds of many young radicals, Marxism and Freudianism both appeared to be corrosive skepticisms, "acids of modernity" as Walter Lippmann called them, undermining traditional values. But they mutually deconstructed each other, too. Freudians saw the social radicals as driven by neurotic personalities; Marxists claimed that Freud was a product of capitalist decadence.

The exciting new literature and art of the 1920s drew heavily on Freud; but Freud thought art a neurotic illusion also, an escape into fantasy substituting for mature adjustment to reality. Of this more in a moment. Meanwhile Freud loomed generally as one of the intellectual masters of the postwar decades. The other, in the 1920s, was Albert Einstein. It is more than time to discuss the great upheaval in the physical sciences that struck with explosive force just as the postwar decade began.

EINSTEIN AND THE REVOLUTION IN SCIENCE

The new scientific revolution went back to the last years of the nineteenth century, coinciding in time approximately with the other startling changes of those years in literature, psychology, social doctrine. It was less widely noted, because it was obscure and difficult. Only in the 1920s did continuing debate among the physicists about questions that went to the root of science's very nature command popular attention. It then became one the chief sensations of the 1920s, making Albert Einstein a household name.

Newspaper headlines about Einstein's theory of relativity stole the front page from the Treaty of Versailles in late May and June of 1919. It is true that a Vienna newspaper in 1912, just catching on to what Einstein had proposed in 1905, headlined **THE MINUTE IN DANGER: A Sensation of Mathematical Science.** This was in reference to the so-called special theory of relativity, resolving, or perhaps further mystifying, questions about the objective existence of time and space that scientific research had raised. The brilliant German-born Jewish scientist was in the forefront of a considerable number of researchers whose collaboration reflected the increased international organization of science. He drew on the ideas and experiments of (to name only a few) Ernst Mach of Austria, the Dutchman H. A. Lorentz, the German Heinrich Hertz, the Polish-born Nobel prize winner (1903, 1911) Marie Curie, working in Paris; and the French mathematician and philosopher of science Henri Poincaré, who wrote on relativity three years before Einstein's 1905 paper. Einstein's own teacher at the Zurich Technological School, Herman Minkowski, who unfortunately died young, was in the mainstream of this ferment of novel ideas among the young scientists of Europe.

Einstein's four great immediate predecessors were Mach, Poincaré, Lorentz, and Planck. In his 1905 paper on light as particles (photons) rather than waves, which he regarded as the most important of the three papers published in that year, Einstein picked up the still obscure quantum theory of the older German physicist Max Planck, dating from 1899–1900, and gave it greater notoriety. Planck in turn was an early and enthusiastic supporter of relativity, though he did not initially accept all of Einstein's ideas. Quantum theory was to be no less a revolutionary concept than relativity. "I have made a discovery as great as that of Newton," Planck had thought in 1900; posterity has agreed. We will return to this a little later.

The unraveling of long-accepted scientific ideas began, according to the usual account, in an experiment innocently conducted by two Americans wholly unaware that they were about to stumble onto a new era in physics. The Michelson-Morley experiment of 1887, designed to determine the exact speed of the earth by measuring the time it takes light to travel with, as compared to against, the direction of the earth's motion, seemed to disclose the mystifying fact that no "ether" or other substance exists for the earth and other bodies to move through. The Michelson-Morley experiment had been suggested by James Clerk Maxwell, the brilliant Scottish theorist whose 1867 electromagnetic equations may well be regarded as the crucial beginning point for modern phsyics. Maxwell questioned Newtonian action-at-a-distance and spoke of relativity. But behind him was the Dane Hans Joseph Oested, who has been credited with laying the foundations of electromagnetic field theory as early as 1820.

There is, in effect, no surrounding atmosphere. It was found that the velocity of light does not change regardless of whether it is moving with the earth or at right angles to it—rather as if a person walking on a conveyor belt (such as you find in airports) was found to be moving at the same speed as a person walking at the same pace on the floor off the belt. If no "ether" existed, all sorts of revisions had to be made in physics. Light and electricity were both supposed to act like waves (recent work by Foucault had seemingly proved that light is a wave, not particles). What if there is no medium for the waves to pass through? A positively existing space that formed the stable backdrop of the universe was necessary as a measuring rod for space and time. Without it, space and time ceased to be absolutes, and varied with local conditions. It could be different times for people in different parts of the universe. A sequence of events might seem to occur in a different order to different observers, one perceiving *a* before *b*, another the reverse. There was no single cosmic time, rather as if the clocks in university classrooms told different times and each was right for its locale; no one correct time existed for the entire campus. More spectacularly, a person who traveled a great distance around the cosmos would return to find he was younger than he or she had been, compared to friends who had stayed at home; time slows down for a body in motion relative to another that is not.

These paradoxes of time much caught the public imagination in the 1920s. One of Einstein's three epochal papers (published when he was twenty-six and had yet to gain an academic appointment; he was then working in the Swiss patent office at Bern) addressed itself to this question, explaining the equivalence of inertial systems and offering his theory of a four-dimensional space-time continuum to replace the old space and time absolutes.[5] But Einstein's big headlines (**SPACE CAUGHT BENDING!**) were reserved for the observations of May 29, 1919, conducted all over the world amid considerable publicity, that seemed to confirm his second or general theory of relativity, offering a superior replacement to Newton's venerable theory of gravitation. Listening to Einstein talk about the curved geometry of space-time as a better explanation of gravity than Newton's, many eminent physicists had muttered "bloody nonsense" as they stalked out. Now it seemed that the nonsense was true.

Gravitational force, Einstein postulated in his theory, is not a mysterious instantaneous attraction or "force" such as had long been believed. Indeed, relativity precluded it, for "at the same time" had lost its meaning; there is no "same time" throughout the universe, but many local times. Nor, of course, is there any medium like the ether through which such a "force" might be transmitted. Einstein thought that gravity consists of waves like electromagnetic waves, moving at the speed of light along the geodesics of space-time, and according to non-Euclidean geometry. (Pure mathematicians such as Lobachowski, Riemann, and Gauss had shown that systems other than Euclid's could be created, based on different postulates, curved or hyperbolic rather than straight lines, equally consistent internally. What was to them a logical game turned out to fit the universe of Planck and Einstein better than Euclid's.) These gravitational waves should be affected by fields of matter. Einstein's theory predicted that light from a distant star would be bent as it passed through the sun's gravitational field on its way to earth. As it happened, a rare total eclipse of the sun in May 1919 offered an opportunity to test the theory. The verdict of the observations was in favor of Einstein. Other evidence has since confirmed this.

It was amazing to find Newton's law overturned, or at least amended, and mind-boggling to try to think of the world in the new terms. "The very fabric of the physical universe" changed. The general relativity theory has been called "the most original conception that the mind of man ever created." It was only part of the profound revolution in science going on, which called into question laws thought certain, worked out by scientists in the seventeenth, eighteenth, and nineteenth centuries. Another stupefying revision of familiar scientific landmarks concerned the inner world of the atom, a subject that exploded in the 1920s. Again the beginnings of the revolution went back to just before the turn of the century, that moment when the entire old "paradigm" seemed to fall apart. Where to begin? In

---

[5]Pressed by busy and ignorant journalists for a quick summary of relativity, Einstein later was accustomed to say: "Before me it was thought that if everything was taken out of the universe, space and time would remain. I showed that if everything was taken out, nothing would remain."

1896 the German scientist Wilhelm Röntgen discovered X rays. A month later, the French physicist Henri Becquerel accidentally found that the salts of uranium emit rays that penetrate matter like X rays. He had stumbled upon what would be called "radioactivity," a word actually coined shortly thereafter by Marie Curie, the transplanted Polish scientist working with her husband Pierre in Paris. A crowd of rays or "waves" had emerged, predicted by Clerk Maxwell's equations on electromagnetism. Heinrich Hertz, the brilliant German scientist who died young, had found radio waves in 1885. In 1897 J. J. Thomson was repeating a Hertz experiment at Cambridge University when, after devising a cathode-ray tube (which later evolved into a television picture tube), he discovered "electrons," or negative units of electricity. He did not then identify them with atomic radiation.

A few years later Ernest Rutherford was to show that electronic particles can pass right through atoms, an astonishing thing because atoms had always been thought to be the smallest units of matter (the Greek word itself means that). Like Newton's particles, they were supposed to be "solid, massy, hard, impenetrable." As such, they had formed the solid basis of chemistry ever since John Dalton reinstated them early in the nineteenth century. The chemists' world revolved around these atoms, of different weights each representing an "element," and combining to form molecules. Now it seemed that, far from being solid, they were largely hollow shells, containing a nucleus (responsible for most of the weight, but small in size) surrounded by negative electrical charges. Ernst Mach began to doubt that they existed at all—perhaps they were a linguistic illusion.

Rutherford, the brilliant New Zealand-born experimental physicist working in England (first at Manchester, then at Cambridge's Cavendish Laboratory) used "alpha particles" obtained from radioactivity. These particles represent the spontaneous disintegration of atoms—something never before thought possible, almost a contradiction in terms. Some of the atoms of some of the heavier elements are unstable, and gradually break up—very slowly indeed, as human time is measured, but steadily. The particles that make up their atomic structure escape. Gradually it became evident that atoms (if they exist at all) consist of a small, heavy nucleus made up of protons (later, neutrons were found to be there too), balanced by the negatively charged electrons in a relationship that puzzled physicists in the 1920s. The Newtonian laws of motion and gravity, always assumed to be absolute, did not work inside the atom at all, and a new mechanics had to be found. Within something that had been thought irreducible there was a whole new world of complex forces. Holding atoms together was a force so powerful that to disintegrate atoms could unleash a source of energy far beyond anything previously known.

In one of the 1905 papers Einstein had deduced this force, producing the famous formula $E = mc^2$. Matter and energy are aspects of the same thing; matter is highly concentrated energy. (Why should this connection involve the speed of light?) Others were on the same track. Historians find Einstein's claim to have first discovered this celebrated equation justified, though it has been disputed, and "several people participated" in the development of the formula relating mass to energy.[6] Frederick Soddy produced almost the same equation as Einstein's in 1904. Pierre Langevin, a close friend of Marie Curie's, arrived at it in 1906 without knowing that Einstein had already figured this out.

In 1919 Rutherford split the atom. In 1914 he had pointed out in a popular lecture that the potential energy stored inside atoms was now, after Einstein, known to be incredibly great: "many million times greater than for an equal weight of the most powerful explosive." Already the science fiction writer H. G. Wells had foreseen its use. Interrupted by the war, during which he worked on submarine detection, Rutherford, one of the greatest of all experimental physicists, pecked away in odd moments until he finally succeeded in making alpha particles (which were helium atoms) break up nitrogen atoms, resulting in hydrogen and oxygen. But the possibility of tapping this source by "causing a substance like uranium or thorium to give out its energy in the course of a few hours or days, instead of over a period of many thousands or millions of years," in other words to speed up radioactivity, "does not at present seem at all promising," Rutherford thought.

"If I have disintegrated the nucleus of the atom," he wrote in June of 1919, "this is of greater significance than the war." But Rutherford's achievement led to no immediately sensational results, and was overshadowed by the Einstein gravity observations of that same date. Thirteen years later, Rutherford's student and colleague James Chadwick would discover the neutron, a particle within the atom having neither positive nor negative charge, something Rutherford had earlier predicted. This was to lead to atomic energy, because the neutron—as heavy as a proton—is able to approach the nuclei of larger atoms without being repelled, and thus can be used to split them. (This story belongs to the 1930s and to World War II.)

Meanwhile a furious, compelling, and much noted debate about nuclear physics erupted among the top physicists in the 1920s. Initially, it was supposed that inside the atom was a miniature solar system, with the nucleus like a sun around which the electrons performed planetary motions. But this view had to be abandoned, since the laws of mechanics would not support it. (On their principles, the electrons would quickly have crashed into the nucleus.) The laws of motion for the solar system do not apply at all within atoms. Thus the Newtonian laws, so long regarded as certain, broke down first at the macro level and now at the micro. What did apply seemed to be the quantum principle Max Planck had discovered early in the century. Working in the area of thermal physics, he discovered that heated bodies emit energy discontinuously, in spurts, thus violating another of Newton's laws of motion. Heat causes electrons to make sudden jumps from one energy level to another. The constant number that Planck found to be the ratio

---

[6]See W. L. Fadner, "Did Einstein Really Discover 'E=MC^2'?" *American Journal of Physics* 56 (1988), 114–22.

between energy and frequency of radiation applied in atomic physics to relations between the mass, velocity, and wave length of electrons (it having become necessary to consider electrons as being both waves and particles.)

Einstein, who had made contributions to quantum theory himself as he joined Max Planck in Berlin from 1913 on, emerged in the 1920s as an opponent of the new theories of quantum mechanics. At a series of international conferences, a new generation of physicists and mathematicians seemed to attack such venerable principles of science as determinacy and certainty. This was too much for Einstein's faith in an intelligible universe (God will challenge us but not deceive us, according to his famous motto). There was piquancy in a younger generation, all in some sense Einstein's children, now rebelling against their father—rather like the Freudian scene. Einstein was now approaching fifty; the new crop of scientific geniuses was amazingly young. Werner Heisenberg was twenty-three, Dirac was twenty-three, and de Broglie about the same age when they leaped to the center of the stage. The Danish wizard Niels Bohr had studied under Planck and Rutherford. Einstein, upsetter of the universe in the popular view, was now a conservative! Refusing to accept the finality of indeterminacy, Einstein used his famous imagination to devise thought experiments embarrassing to quantum mechanics.

It was the heroic age of modern physics, an era of extreme brilliance and crucial revision. Unutterably strange phenomena at the extreme limits of matter led to an array of intepretations. Electrons seemed to have the properties of both particles and waves, something seemingly impossible. Scientists spoke of "wavicles" and "wave mechanics." Two electrons can be in the same place at once. Even more disturbingly, it was impossible to know both their position and their velocity. Nobody before quantum theory, as Bertrand Russell observed, ever doubted that at any given moment a physical body is at some definite place and moving with some definite speed. But the more accurately you determined the place of a particle, the less accurately could you measure its velocity, and vice versa. In fact, we know only certain equations of which the interpretation was obscure. These apply to statistical probabilities for large numbers of electrons over periods of time; the individual ones elude exact prediction. An anarchic universe, Russell suggested, filled with a nonconformist minority. For example, quantum mechanics can calculate the proportion of a radioactive material that will decay over a stated period of time— 10 percent in the next thousand years, say—but how long it will be before the next alpha particle is extruded or which one it will be defies prediction.

Like the paradoxes of relativity, this was not just a deficiency in research that might in the future be overcome; it is an absolute limit set by the nature of things. One reason for this is that we reach the limits of observation because we must use particles (gamma rays, the shortest ones of all) to observe other particles, and in so doing we interfere with them. Scientists cannot stand outside what they are observing; they are a part of it. Interesting, and perhaps encouraging to the poor humanist or social scientist, but alarming to the whole scientific tradition; science reaches a frontier it cannot cross, and it must give up the quest for certainty.

Broglie and Schrödinger visualized a kind of chamber filled with peculiar wave movements—waves of what? Of probability, was one mystifying answer. Some thought it a mistake to attempt to visualize a physical model comparable to everyday human experience; the world is best thought of as a set of mathematical equations. If we free ourselves from such earthbound prejudices, we can imagine all sorts of things—a *fifth* dimension, or a dozen of them.

To mathematicize the world, however, risks not only making it incomprehensible to the vast innumerate majority, but also mystifying it in a way that destroys the very premises of modern science. And our mental limitations may be built into our mathematics. Mathematics itself experienced doubts about its status; the dismantling of one-time certainties had gone on here also. The path from Hilbert, 1900, to Gödel, 1931, in mathematical philosophy was comparable to that from Planck and Einstein to Bohr and Heisenberg in physics, one of increasing doubts about objectivity and consistency. Mathematics, like language (of which perhaps it was only a branch), seemed to be not a mirror of nature, but a human invention telling us more about the human mind than about physical nature.

Matrix algebra, amazing even Einstein, was introduced to deal with hypothetical "waves of probability." The battle flared at the 1927 Solvay Congress in Belgium, when Einstein offered objections to "indeterminacy" which Bohr and Heisenberg countered. Most of the top scientific brains at this distinguished assembly sided against Einstein. One had to accept the limitations of human knowledge, the radically different nature of subatomic behavior, the inability to attain more than theoretical probability (statistical laws only, not predictions of specific

Albert Einstein. (Yerkes Observatory Photograph, University of Chicago, Williams Bay, Wisconsin)

events). Attempts to conceptualize this impasse took several forms. Perhaps the world itself is unclear, fuzzy; complementary, Niels Bohr speculated, ambivalent, each thing having also its opposite. Or perhaps the external world is clear, it is our human minds that are flawed, unable because of some inherent limitation to get the world in focus. Either nature or the human mind seemed flawed, or something in the way they fit together. The paradox defied solution, or at least "common sense."

But of course, as Einstein had reminded people in regard to relativity, common sense is only the layer of prejudices our early training has left in our minds; in time, the new science would become as familiar as the old. But it seemed far more difficult, less graspable and less human. A long-familiar picture of the world had been laid waste, creating a sense of confusion and dismay. "Very little of the nineteenth-century picture of the world remains today," the editor of a survey of twentieth-century thought observed a few years ago. In 1930 Einstein traveled to California, where he dined with Charlie Chaplin and Upton Sinclair (the great scientist had intermittent and rather simplistic political interests). He visited the Mt. Wilson observatory, which had the biggest telescope in the world, and where in 1929 Edwin Hubble had observed other galaxies moving away from us with speed relative to distance. Einsteinian relativity had predicted a dynamic universe, just as it predicted atomic energy (and lasers, based on Einstein's view of light as particles, "photon" bullets). Now his theories were being confirmed. A Belgian priest, the Abbé LeMaitre, theorized about a primeval egg, an incredibly dense and hot object no bigger than a baseball that was the universe when it began in an explosion some dozen billion years ago, still going on—indefinitely, or until an eventual contraction back into the egg? (Today we are told that the universe began as the size of an *atom*, though it grew in a billion-billionth of a second to grapefruit size.)

These strange cosmic explosions heightened the sense of a universe weird beyond the wildest science fiction. Science had ceased to exist as a bulwark of stability; the "last certainty" was gone. For several generations science had appeared to the average person much as the scientists saw themselves: lifting the veil of mystification in which ignorance and superstition had always kept matters to reveal simple, clear truths. C. T. R. Wilson, a prominent physicist of the early twentieth century, believed that scientific laws could be made understandable even to a barmaid. For in the end it was only common sense. Now all the solid realities of matter, together with their media of space and time, had vanished. Matter, according to Bertrand Russell, had become a formula for describing what happens when it is not. Writing in 1925 in his *Science and the Modern World*, distinguished philosopher Alfred North Whitehead remarked that

> The eighteenth century opened with a quiet confidence that at last nonsense had been got rid of. Today we are at the opposite pole of thought. Heaven knows what seeming nonsense may not tomorrow be demonstrated truth.

Science was still an exciting adventure of the mind, indeed more exciting than ever; but it had ceased to be something that one placed in the opposite corner from mystics and poets. Scientists themselves now readily spoke of "the mysterious universe" and sought the aid of religion. The German physicist von Weizsaecker studied Indian religion in search of scientific insights. Wolfgang Pauli and Carl Jung tried to collaborate on a study of parapsychology. Pauli's famous "exclusion principle" was indeed as strange a magic as anything claimed by the occult. Science, Pauli knew, had emerged from mysticism in the time of Kepler; now it seemed to be returning to it. A historian of witchcraft (Charles Hoyt) suggests that contemporary physics is not irrelevant to his subject! The rigid boundaries between art, religion, and science tended to dissolve.

Amid the intolerant political ideologies of the postwar world, science was also being politicized. In 1933 Einstein renounced his German citizenship upon Hitler's taking power in Germany, eventually settling in the United States. The Nazis denounced Einstein as a degenerate Jewish Bolshevik and refused to accept his scientific theories. Worse, some reputable German scientists, including Nobel Prize winner Johannes Stark, accepted National Socialism's thesis that science is subservient to nationalism. Nor did Stalin's Soviet Union recognize these "bourgeois modernist" theories. Marxist science, the Communists held, was different from capitalist science. For many years the charlatan biologist Lysenko terrorized Russian scientists on behalf of Lamarckian genetics, ideologically congenial to Soviet Marxism.

IDEAS IN THE LITERATURE OF THE 1920S

Tinged as it was by despair, the writing and art of the postwar years had a brilliance seldom matched, for it marked the stylistic maturity of the whole modernist movement. The literary revolution whose roots lay in the prewar period burst upon the general public in the 1920s. In the English-speaking world, such names as Joyce, Pound, Eliot, Lawrence, and Virginia Woolf came to the fore after the war, though they had begun their careers just before it. Typically they had been born in the early 1880s. D. H. Lawrence's first major novel, *Sons and Lovers*, was completed in 1913; he wrote *The Rainbow* and *Women in Love* during the war. Joyce had *Ulysses* ready to launch on a world almost as astonished by it as by Einstein's theory; he had worked on it during the war in Zurich and finished it in Paris in 1920.

Elsewhere too, buds of the prewar years burst into bloom. Paul Valéry and Marcel Proust in France are examples. The latter's great symphony of novels, translated as *Remembrance of Things Past*, appeared between 1913 and 1927, though Proust died in 1922 at the age of fifty-one. The German master Thomas Mann reached the peak of his reputation in the 1920s, as did the Frenchman André Gide and the Irish poet W. B. Yeats. Another destined to join this group of modernist immortals, Franz Kafka of Prague, did not become widely known until the end of the decade, several years after his death from tuberculosis (a disease that was also to claim Lawrence in his forties).

Moreover, the new art and music, associated with such names as Picasso, Kandinsky, Klee, and Stravinsky, predated the war but received major recognition once the guns were silenced. The same is largely true of architecture. The paintings produced by cubists and other avant-garde experimentalists were, with few exceptions, little more than the obscure eccentricities of certain social outcasts before 1914. After the war conditions became more favorable for the reception of anything new and startling. In Paris in 1919, writers and artists launched the new age under the name of Dada (a nonsense word); its conception took place in a Zurich café near where Joyce and Lenin had lived. Dada held public meetings, advertised by postfuturist posters, at which people made nonsensical speeches. Tzara, a Hungarian-Swiss who was one of Dada's founders, wrote poems by clipping words from a newspaper article, putting them in a sack, shaking them up, and then taking them out one by one.

This savagely nihilistic spirit was a thing of the hour; Dada led to more constructive esthetic theories, especially surrealism. Something of Dada's wish to derange meaning deliberately (borrowed from Rimbaud) appeared in the surrealists, also some of its violent political protest (the surrealists flirted with left-wing politics).[7] Surrealism borrowed from Freud and Jung the idea that in dreams and semiconscious states, or under the influence of drugs, the mind is freed from the tyranny of the rational and can produce fresh, authentic symbols. "Psychic automatism" produced poetry by suspending thought and letting the words come. Surrealism may be regarded as a continuation of prewar symbolism with Freudian (and Marxian) additions. It was a mode for both literature and painting, resembling in that respect the German *Bauhaus*, domiciled at Weimar and then Dessau, which linked art and architecture in the task of creating a new esthetic for the modern age.

Freud indeed was a pervasive influence throughout literature. It swarmed with Freudian motifs—Oedipal complexes, illicit love, unconscious motivations, such as for example filled the plays of the great American dramatist Eugene O'Neill. It was said that Freud had restored the possibility of tragedy, with id and ego standing for the classic powers of fate and free will, the individual against the cosmos. Often the alleged dependence on Freud was more a case of independent discovery, however. Lawrence wrote his great Oedipal novel *Sons and Lovers*, about a young man struggling to release himself from love of his mother that inhibits his relations with other women, when the twenty-seven-year-old son of a coal miner had not read Freud; later he did, finding much to admire but criticizing Freud's scientific positivism. A few years earlier Marcel Proust had begun writing the long autobiographical series of novels destined to become another twentieth-century classic; his "search for vanished time" (*A la recherche du temps perdu*)

---

[7]André Breton, founder of surrealism in 1924, joined the Communist Party in 1927, but broke with it when the party line turned against surrealism in favor of "socialist realism." In 1938 Breton collaborated with the exiled Leon Trotsky in a manifesto against party control of the arts. But Louis Aragon broke with surrealism to become a Communist militant in 1932.

was based on the recovery of childhood memories in order to integrate his fragmented life by a kind of literary dialogue, and it is full of sexual themes. But Proust did not then know Freud either.

Kafka was directly influenced, though perhaps more so by Nietzsche and Dostoyevsky (who also influenced Freud). Mann said he would not have written his *Death in Venice* but for Freud. But the American writer Sherwood Anderson was amazed to find himself classified as a Freudian when he had never heard of the man. Freud and Jung had some impact on James Joyce—he sent his daughter to Jung for treatment—but must take their place among a number of at least equally important intellectual sources of *Ulysses* and *Finnegans Wake*, ranging from Dante and Vico to Wagner and Ibsen. (In psychology, the American explorer of the multiple personality, Morton Prince, affected Joyce as well as Jung.) The age, the climate of opinion, was bigger than Freud; he merely became its chief sign. A set of vaguely Freudian tendencies including subjectivity, removal of sex taboos, and problems with the self in a pluralistic society, were endemic in the whole modern situation.

Freud's onetime colleague and now rival within psychoanalysis, Carl Jung, also extended his reputation. The extensive use of myth in the literature of the 1920s owed much to Jung, an esteemed postwar sage. T. S. Eliot used myth in his *Waste Land*, pillaging Frazer's *Golden Bough*; Joyce filled his novels with it. Eliot saw it as a weapon against the chaotic confusion of modern life, "a way of controlling, or ordering, of giving a shape and a significance to the immense panorama of futility and anarchy which is contemporary history." Classics of the 1920s like the American expatriate F. Scott Fitzgerald's *The Great Gatsby* depend for their enduring appeal on their mythic overtones; the bootlegger and his girlfriend somehow stand for the plight of all men and women. Myth represents the recurring repetitive motifs in the human condition, the Jungian "archetypes," poetically (metaphorically) expressed. Yeats asked

> How can the arts overcome the slow dying of men's hearts that we call the progress of the world, and lay their hands upon men's heart-strings again, without becoming the garment of religion as in old times?

Myth provided the answer. In a book about Yeats and Jung, James Olney (*The Rhizone and the Flower*) documented the remarkable parallel in the thought of these two great figures, who worked in different genres and scarcely knew each other, yet talked in different accents about the same things.

Joyce above all made use of myth. One day in the life of one man on one June day in 1904 became an allegory of the human condition, or a summation of the history of Western civilization; Leopold Bloom is the modern Ulysses. Though a vividly realized individual given local habitation in Dublin, surrounded by its sights, sounds, and events, he is also Everyman. This mythic quality is indicated by making the episodes in Bloom's day correspond to adventures of Homer's Ulysses

(Joyce does not name them in chapter titles, you have to know them, a foretaste of the mystification he was to raise to greater heights in *Finnegans Wake*). There is birth, death, eating and drinking, marriage, all the events of life in this one day which is the life of all humanity. This is made evident in many other ways. There is explicit reference to recurrence. Molly is scornful of Leopold using big words she cannot even spell; the leading example is "metempsychosis" ("that word met something with hoses in it and he came out with some jawbreakers about the incarnation....") So Bloom is Ulysses and Elijah and the Wandering Jew and, as one passage puts it,

> Sinbad the Sailor and Tinbad the Tailor and Jinbad the Jailer and Whinbad the Whaler and Ninbad the Nailer and Finbad the Failer and Binbad the Bailer and Pinbad the Pailer and Minbad the Mailer and Hinbad the Hailer and Rinbad the Railer and Dinbad the Kailer and Vinbad the Quailer and Linbad the Yailer and Xinbad the Phthailer.

Molly is an archetypal woman, a great earth mother or goddess, if not (as many have thought) the Life Force itself. Then in the dream language of *Finnegans Wake* Joyce ransacked history to illustrate original sin, family and social conflict, the dualism of public and private spheres, the endless repetitions of life. Its thesis was the Jungian one that the individual unconscious contains the whole of human experience; the night's sleep of one Irish barkeeper could recapitulate everything in history.

Einstein's influence on the arts was equally pervasive though less easy to pinpoint. There was general agreement with Ortega y Gasset that the theories of relativity were "the most important intellectual fact that the present time can show," but less agreement on just what they meant. "'Tis only one great thought the less" was the refrain of old Thomas Hardy's "Drinking Song," lamenting a series of human deflations from Copernicus through Darwin to Einstein:

> And now comes Einstein with a notion—
>   Not yet quite clear
>   To many here—
> That there's no time, no space, no motion,
>   Nor rathe nor late
>   Nor square nor straight,
> But just a sort of bending-ocean.

This impression that all had been thrown into confusion might be cause for depression. We "weep for the lost ages," Auden wrote, "before Because became As If, or rigid certainty/ The Chances Are...." But in the iconoclastic mood of the twenties people just as often found it exhilarating to think that science was as zany as everything else, on a par with the Keystone Cops, Joyce's prose, and the stock market.

"I like relativity and quantum theories," D. H. Lawrence mused, "because I don't understand them, and they make me feel as if space shifted...and as if the atom were an impulsive thing, always changing its mind." Bertrand Russell's popular attempt to explain Einstein (*The ABC of Relativity*) agreed that the individual electron's indeterminacy gave the universe a pleasantly anarchist flavor.

All the old rules had been obliterated and the arts stood open to endless experimentation. Already in 1909 the Futurist Manifesto had exulted that "time and space died yesterday!" Cubism and other forms of abstract or expressionist art owed something to relativity.[8] In 1929 the architect Eric Mendelsohn built an Einstein Tower. Completely new systems in music, like Schoenberg's twelve-tone scale and serialism, derived from the thought that the rules are arbitrary, not fixed in eternal truth, and one may make up new ones—something immensely stimulating to the composer, if immensely confusing to the average listener. "Of the notable family named Stein," ran a limerick of the times,

> There's Gert and there's Ep and there's Ein.
> Gert's prose is the bunk,
> Ep's sculpture is junk,
> And no one can understand Ein.[9]

Thus did the common person register amused skepticism about the strange pathways of thought and expression in the 1920s.

The relation between Joyce and Einstein appears in a Paris magazine founded in the 1920s by Joyce admirers, *transition* [sic], which announced its goal as "a pan-symbolic, pan-linguistic synthesis in the conception of a four-dimensional universe." Comparison between the two has often been made; "Writing as we know it is unimaginable without him; imagine physics without Einstein!" exclaims distinguished Joyce student Hugh Kenner. Joyce knew as little of nuclear physics as Einstein did of literature (though there is a little geometry in *Finnegans Wake*)—as little as Freud and Einstein knew of each other's work.[10] But their styles seemed to parallel each other. Joyce was remaking language as Einstein had just reshaped the fabric of the universe and Freud the topography of the mind. A physicist would later choose a word from *Finnegans Wake* to bestow on a sub-particle, the "quark."

---

[8]A recent monograph, of the sort much needed to illuminate the connections between the arts and scientific ideas, finds the cubists of 1907 not aware of Einstein, but they knew Henri Poincaré who had written on the concept of relativity in 1902. See Linda Dalrymple Henderson, *The Fourth Dimension and Non-Euclidean Geometry in Modern Art* (1983).

[9]Gertrude Stein, of course, the American in Paris, wrote notably experimental prose. Jacob Epstein, also American-born but working chiefly in England, was one of the first controversial modernist sculptors; he did a portrait of Einstein.

[10]"I spent two hours chattering away with Einstein," Freud wrote in a 1927 letter. "He is merry, self-assured, and amiable. He understands as much of psychology as I do of physics, and so we had a very good talk."

FIGURES OF THE LITERARY RENAISSANCE

Joyce's great novel outranked all other literary events of the 1920s. It was born amid controversy; portions of *Ulysses* were first printed in 1920 in the American avant-garde magazine *Little Review*, a publication banned in Britain after a judge pronounced it incomprehensible as well as immoral (though it is difficult to see how it could have been both). The 1922 edition published in Paris by another obscure American enterprise, Sylvia Beach's Shakespeare & Co., was soon an eagerly sought-after collector's item. Except for small printings in 1922–23, most copies of which were confiscated, Joyce's legendary novel found no publisher until 1934, when Random House brought it out in the United States after receiving a special exemption from the ban on indecent literature. *Ulysses* enjoyed the unique status of being hailed as the greatest novel ever written and yet being an underground book, the more exciting for being obscure.

Joyce's attempts to expose the private unedited thoughts of Leopold and Molly Bloom, as well as the speech of Dublin barflies, certainly did include quite prominently those parts that are normally unprintable. But of course this account of a modern Ulysses was much more than just a salacious book (though Shaw claimed it only proved that Dubliners were as dirty-minded now as they were when he was a lad). It contained some of the most brilliant prose ever written in the English language, and gave promise of the philosophical depths that were to appear in *Finnegans Wake*. It reflected the wide and deep reading of this Irishman who had wanted to go to medical school (in which case he might have succeeded Freud) but couldn't afford it. Among other modernist devices in *Ulysses* was the Wagner-influenced one of scattering the plot through recurring themes, "nodally," rather than narrating it directly in the boring old manner. *Ulysses* had the effect of making all previous novels passé, and all previous writing flat and dull. Despite the frequent outrage that greeted it (characteristic judgments included "morbid and sickening," "the foulest book that has ever found its way into print"), *Ulysses* was immediately recognized by the more perceptive as "the most important expression which this age has found" (T.S. Eliot), or in American critic Edmund Wilson's words, "a work of high genius which has the effect of making everything else look brassy."

After finishing *Ulysses* Joyce spent virtually the rest of his life, from 1922 to 1939, working on the linguistically even more adventurous book eventually published as *Finnegans Wake*. The "Work in Progress," as it was initially known (portions of it being printed in *transition* from time to time) aroused excitement among a small band of devotees but mystified everyone else, and continued to do so for a long time. It is best discussed later.

Ulysses' companion in scandal in the 1920s in England and America was D. H. Lawrence's *Lady Chatterley's Lover*, also widely banned or censored. Lawrence was much more the "priest of love" than Joyce, who like Freud recognized the power of sex more than he celebrated its glories. Lawrence said that "I always labor at the same thing, to make the sex relation valid and precious, instead of shameful." "My great religion is a belief in the blood, the flesh, as being wiser than the intellect," he had declared (very much in the spirit of the times).

To Lawrence, return to a healthy sexuality was important not in itself, but because he thought people who know how to love know how to live. Sex to him was the key to creativity; taproot of all energies, it is the source of beauty, religion, of everything wonderful and vital. Lawrence castigated the effete intellectualism as well as the timid bourgeois conventionality of the modern European world, feeling acutely the need for something more sincere, more real. This neo-primitivism sent him back to the Etruscans and the Indians, or Mediterranean peasants. Lawrence had a good many disciples in the 1920s (like the young W. H. Auden and his friends). In Aldous Huxley's brilliant and sophisticated novels of ideas (*Antic Hay*, *Those Barren Leaves*, *Point Counter Point*, 1923–28), which probe the failure of all the old values and role models, the only hopeful face is an artist modeled on Huxley's friend D. H. Lawrence. (Lawrence also painted, and wrote some often marvelous poetry.) Perhaps by a return to healthy instincts one might make one's way out of the desert.

The integrity and "committedness" of Lawrence, along with his tremendous creative vitality, made him one of the age's chief seers. As much as Joyce, though by different means, Lawrence could get at the inner mind in all its irrational complexities. A Lawrence novel takes us immediately into its characters and makes us be them as they struggle with their lives and problems. This engagement with the interior life was a hallmark of the new novel. In a famous essay Virginia Woolf accused the older novelists, such as Arnold Bennett, of depicting only the external aspects of people; in wanting to see them from within, as their minds actually work from minute to minute, she was squarely in the center of 1920s writing. The Italian master of the theater, Luigi Pirandello, exposed the baffling ways in which illusion and reality mingle in human affairs—object indistinguishable from subject, as in the new physics. Woolf's fascinating novels are usually poised somewhere tantalizingly between a dream world and the real world.

Huxley's *Brave New World* (1932) was probably the most widely read satire on modern civilization's shallow materialism and hedonistic values ever written. It was an example of the dystopia or reverse utopia in which the imagined future society was not, as formerly, an ideal to be aspired to, but a horror to be avoided. In the 1930s Huxley, transplanted to California, began to find consolation in withdrawal and mysticism, not to say mescalin. Huxley was a subtle prober of values and a sensitive barometer of the moods of his day among sophisticated Europeans who felt themselves in a dying culture and searched often in vain for a firm intellectual anchorage for their lives. In the next decade hosts of them would flock into the arms of Soviet communism. A similar case of searching for some kind of oasis in the wasteland was Thomas Mann's notable *The Magic Mountain* (1924), in which figures representing the modern mind include a scientific rationalist, a Dostoyevskian irrationalist, a pagan sensualist, and others. Set in a Swiss tuberculosis

A leading figure among the vanguard novelists of the brilliant postwar generation, Virginia Woolf was also an essayist, diarist, critic, and feminist—one of the twentieth century's greatest literary personalities. (National Portrait Gallery, London; photo by C. S. Beresford)

sanitarium, the allegory exudes images of death; in the end Hans Castorp, the hero, almost dies in a snowstorm but rouses himself by a great effort of the will, an evident anticipation of existentialism.

James Joyce's brother Stanislaus observed that "In our world today, serious literature has taken the place of religion. People go, not to the Sunday sermon, but to literature for enlightened understanding of their emotional and intellectual problems." The Viennese author Robert Musil (*The Man without Qualities*) had initially tried his hand at being an engineer, then wrote a dissertation on Ernst Mach and was offered a post under the distinguished philosopher Alexius Meinong. But Musil came to feel that only through creative writing, through the "novel," could he come to grips with the whole of modern experience, and thus by understanding it change it. D. H. Lawrence had the same insight about the same time in England, and Marcel Proust in France: The novel is "the one bright book of life," as Lawrence said, capable of dealing with humanity in its entirety rather than in bits and pieces, and concretely rather than abstractly. Proust once compared himself to Casaubon in George Eliot's *Middlemarch*, who searched for "the key to all mythologies." The great modernist novelists were psychologists like Freud (they were all more or less obsessed with sex), but their methods were literary rather than scientific. Their interest was the human personality in a problematical society.

When Franz Kafka died from tuberculosis in 1924 at the age of forty the

Prague writer left behind unfinished manuscripts of *The Castle* and *The Trial* *(Der Prozess)*, remarkable allegories of the modern situation which were published a few years later and widely read in the 1930s, when the "nightmare world" they seem to describe became an even more vivid reality. In the 1920s the mood was perhaps not tragic in the deepest sense. There is a sunset charm about the dying culture, talk is brilliant, ideas richly abundant, there are marvelous books to read. What literate person could be really unhappy in a decade that produced Joyce, Lawrence, Proust, Huxley, Mann, and a parade of other stunning commentators on the sickness of civilization? A funeral that attracted so many distinguished pallbearers had its compensations. "Though the great song return no more/There's keen delight in what we have," Yeats wrote. The civilized upper class to which Yeats and Proust and Huxley belonged still existed, if it had gone slightly to seed. If this decade was not the pre-1914 *belle époque*, neither was it yet the time of nazism, communism, depression, and war. The 1930s and 1940s brought these things.

8

From Depression to War in the 1930s

GERMANY'S NATIONAL SOCIALISM

The 1930s opened ominously, with economic depression, spreading from the great American stock market crash of October 1929, throughout the capitalist world. By 1931, which historian Arnold Toynbee labeled "annus terribilis," rising unemployment, bank failures, and the collapse of governments signaled the panic stage. A Labour government fell in Great Britain. In the USSR, Stalin hardened the Communist Party dictatorship while introducing the first Five Year plan, a program of planned economic development to transform backward Russia that some in the West viewed as a beacon of hope. Germany floundered through parliamentary crises as Adolf Hitler's National Socialist party grew stronger; in 1933 Hitler would take power, while fascism seemed on the rise also in France, and the French Communist Party increased its strength significantly. The sound of crumbling democracies could be heard from Spain to Austria, and even the United States decided to grant newly elected president Franklin Roosevelt unprecedented emergency powers in 1933 amid a severe banking crisis.

Intellectuals in the 1930s often felt themselves squeezed between the conflicting "totalitarian" ideologies of German nazism and Russian communism, as the democracies seemed helpless to cope with the economic ordeal. There was a sudden change in the climate of opinion, from the estheticism of the 1920s to political activism and social realism. "Drop those priggish ways forever, stop behaving like a stone," young Auden admonished other writers. "Start at once to try to live." ("They say life's the thing but I'd rather read," Logan Pearsall-Smith had declared in the 1920s.) Come down from the ivory tower and march in a protest parade or join a picket line. The new mood, George Orwell recalled, was suddenly more like a Boy Scout camp than a poet's corner. It was another swing in the cycle from political idealism to disenchantment, out of and back into the ivory tower, that may be traced from 1848 to 1914 and after. Julien Benda, famed for his advice in the 1920s to the "clercs" to stand above politics, by 1937 had become a *compagnon de route* of the Communists and would later demand death for right-wing intellectuals. He followed the trend here as before.

If a considerable number of Europe's free minds were to choose communism in the 1930s, nevertheless some did opt for fascism. "It is a myth that the Nazi movement represented only the mob," George Lichtheim observed. "It had conquered the universities before it triumphed over society." Though this judgment may go too far, there is a good deal of evidence to support it. A recent study found that 64 percent of the faculty at Hamburg joined the Nazi party. For every Einstein who refused to stay in Hitler's state there was a Stark who stayed; if the average was better among the humanists, led by Thomas Mann and Stefan Zweig, there were plenty of artists like Emil Nolde who joined the Nazi party, or who like the great philosopher Martin Heidegger at least gave it a friendly pat. Echoes of the ambivalence with which reputable intellectual figures greeted the Nazis were heard as late as 1988, with the discovery that top literary theorist Paul de Man had written pro-Nazi editorials during World War I in France. Philosopher Max Scheler, and possibly the world's greatest living musical composer Richard Strauss, are samples of those among the very top German cultural leaders who were pro-Nazi, or at least not anti-Nazi. Carl Schmitt, called "the most respected political scientist of the Weimar era," was an early and steadfast Hitler supporter. Admirers of the famous Viennese Jewish writer Karl Kraus—a satirist and scourge of the stuffy— have to explain his silence about the Nazis. Einstein's old collaborator Max Planck remained silent too, though he later regretted this, and his son became a martyr in the resistance to Hitler. The honeymoon phase of the Nazi government in 1933–34, indeed, brought almost all Germans to its side for the time being, in an emotional surge of solidarity reminiscent of 1914. Universities, churches, intellectuals joined the masses in heiling Hitler.

We shall look further at the German situation in a moment. An example of a French writer whose sheer disgust with the human race evidently led him to fascism was Louis-Ferdinand Céline, author of *Le voyage au bout de la nuit*, a 1932 novel which had a considerable vogue. This physician's voyage to the end of night ended in anti-Semitism, nazism, collaboration with the German conquerors of France during World War II. There were other French intellectuals who went fascist. Robert Brasillach and Drieu de la Rochelle followed in the footsteps of perhaps the leading forerunner of the postwar fascisms, Charles Maurras' Action Française, and of the novelist-politician Maurice Barrès, one of the leading literary figures of the 1890–1920 era. As we know, they had considerably affected Italian fascism, the close ideological relative of German national socialism.

What were the Nazi ideas, and how much did they contribute to the National Socialist victory in Germany? Hitler's little group of disaffected Bavarians attempted without much success to expand their organization throughout Germany in the 1920s, and as late as 1928 won the votes of less than 3 percent of all Germans. Hitler had established his creed years before, and never wavered from it; a remarkable rigidity was his chief characteristic, one that could be either a strength or a weakness. He had decided that the whole liberal-democratic system must be destroyed and replaced with one based on unanimity and leadership—*ein Volk, ein Reich, ein Führer*; a process that entailed ruthlessly eliminating all incongruent and weakening elements, such as modern ideas and art, intellectuals, Jews, and other unassimilated ethnic elements. (The Nazis were to pursue the gypsies as ferociously as the Jews, also murder the mentally ill, forcibly sterilize mulattoes.) To this end Hitler would head not an ordinary political party, but a kind of church organized like the army, which he had found so admirable during the war. "Our purpose must be to create not an army of politicians but an army of soldiers of the new philosophy." Hitler believed the law of life to be the power struggle: "Nature...confers the master's right on her favorite child, the strongest in courage and industry.... Mankind has grown great in eternal struggle, and only in eternal peace does it perish." Thus spake Adolf in his 1924 *Mein Kampf*.

Many studies of the hard-core Nazis who joined Hitler in the early days and, unless he destroyed them in internecine party power struggles, survived to be numbered among the Nazi elite, stress their marginality, "their ambiguous personal and social status" (John Haag). They have been called "alienated intellectuals"; "the armed intellectuals" (Konrad Heiden); "truants from school" (Thomas Mann). Jean Baechler notes that "all [of the Nazi leaders] without exception experienced a major setback that prevented them from realizing their life ambition": Hitler the failed architect and artist set the pace. Peter Merkl found "a childhood of poverty and frustrated upward mobility in the city" a prominent factor in the lives of the most militant Nazi activists. At the first meeting of the German Workers party that Hitler attended, the forty-five members ranged from a doctor, two engineers, a chemist, a pharmacist, to writers, painters, students, but also a judge, businessmen, artisans—a cross-section of society, bound together, it seems, chiefly by their interest in (simple) ideas. Among the would-be intellectuals in the early Nazi party were a poet and folklorist, an amateur economist, the founder of a pagan religion. Probably posterity would have remembered them as little as it remembers hundreds of other cranks, misfits, and would-be philosophers, except for their finding a leader of Hitler's caliber in the abnormal times after the war.

For in normal times Hitler would never have found a political career through the usual boring channels; but he could fish in the troubled waters of postwar Germany, where the old order had fallen and everybody was groping for a new one. Having settled on his program, Hitler showed considerable skill in devising ways of presenting it. His talent for publicity owed something to American advertising as well as to grand opera. Yet the first of the great party rallies at Nuremberg, which became famous for their elaborate pageantry, did not occur until after the party had begun its upward ascent, and hence was able to attract money from wealthy donors. In 1926 a rally in Weimar at which Hitler wore his leather-belted raincoat and army boots, while saluting his uniformed followers in the manner of Mussolini, impressed most observers as a dreary affair. Not until the Great Depression brought down the precarious Weimar Republic did Hitler's luck change.

His unwavering adherence to a single program was unquestionably a source of strength. Ian Kershaw in his study of *Der Führer* observes that "Hitler's quasi-messianic commitment to an 'idea,' a faith which brooked no alternatives, gave him a strength of will-power which in his presence was difficult to resist." It also made him an effective mass orator. It enabled him to devote his entire attention to the techniques of gaining power without having to worry about the goals. The price was rigidity and a set of terribly simplistic ideas. Hitler claimed to have learned from Gustave Le Bon that emotion not reason sways people *en masse*, and that slogans incessantly repeated sink into the mass consciousness. Nevertheless it is a mistake to see him as cynical; the key to Hitler's success was that he actually believed his slogans. His sincerity was manifest and was what kept him devoted to the cause through years of struggle.

The racialist ideology dominated all else in Nazi propaganda. The Nazis denounced capitalism,[1] communism, the traitors who had allegedly caused the defeat of Germany, the pacifists and liberals who continued to weaken the nation, intellectuals who undermined moral values, degenerate modernist styles in the arts and literature (and even science), internationalisms of all sorts. Linking all these manifestations of weakness and disunity was the universal villain, the Jew, an entirely mythical creature with features drawn from bankers, socialists, newspaper publishers, department store owners, artists, writers, Zionists.

Anti-Semitism was much more prevalent in eastern Europe than in Germany, where a small Jewish population seemed well assimilated into German culture. Other Germans had called for national unity without invoking racialism. In the 1920s a group of neo-conservatives that included Oswald Spengler and Moeller van den Bruck wrote of the need for strength of will, national resurgence, and a leader capable of embodying the people's will. All weakening forces, such as democracy (alien to the "Prussian style"), liberalism, and class conflict, they thought must be eliminated if Germany was to climb back from the ashes of defeat and regain its place in the sun. Moeller and Spengler were evan tagged as "conservative revolutionaries" who would use revolutionary means to reach a nationalistic goal. Hitler may have borrowed from these writers of the 1920s, but they were not racists and they despised Hitler as a disreputable rabble-rouser. He persecuted this group as relentlessly as others after coming to power.

---

[1]Some Marxists tried to make the Nazis out to be capitalists, but this is a bizarre interpretation. Nazi ideology featured an almost manic hostility to bankers and financiers. Its first discussion topics were about how to eliminate "capitalism."

Hitler in his youth as a down-and-outer in Vienna is supposed to have found repellent the Polish Jews who were then flocking to Vienna; more relevant, however, was his exposure to the anti-Semitic ideas of Austrian populist Georg von Schoenerer, and the anti-Semitic mayor of Vienna (for a short time), Karl Lueger. Schoenerer, the idol of young Hitler, was the son of an industrial baron who turned against his father and attacked capitalism, becoming a militant spokesman for the agrarian class. Though mutterings about Jewish financiers were not entirely absent from American Populism, and Anthony Trollope's novel *The Way We Live Now* had featured a British Jew as the symbol of capitalistic corruption,[2] Schoenerer added a great deal more of this to his ideological brew.

In "international Jewish bankers" such as the Rothchilds he saw the "vampire that knocks at the narrow-windowed house of the German farmer." Lueger also inveighed rhetorically against "financial cliques" and monopolies. This anti-Semitism of the left associated Jews with rich bankers and manipulative speculators (rather strangely in view of the extreme poverty of the Jewish immigrants from the East). So also did the anti-Semitism of Edouard Drumont that accompanied the Dreyfus Affair in France at this same time (1898). But Lueger suggested little more than restrictions on immigration from Poland, taking as his model the Chinese Exclusion Act passed in the United States in 1881. (His Christian Social party owed something to the influence of Pope Leo XIII's famous 1891 encyclical, *De rerum novarum.*)

Systematic racialist doctrines came to Hitler, oddly enough, from a Frenchman and an Englishman. We previously mentioned Gobineau's pseudoscientific views on the inequality of the races (see p. 100). Houston Stewart Chamberlain further developed these in his *Foundations of the Nineteenth Century* (1901), an inspiration in turn for the Nazi ideologist Alfred Rosenberg's *Myth of the Twentieth Century*. Chamberlain, a by no means uninteresting English spiritual pilgrim of the Fabian generation, became a Wagnerian, moved to Bayreuth, and married Wagner's daughter; he was a friend of Kaiser Wilhelm II and in his last years met Hitler, also a devoted Wagnerian. This strange lineage of ideas found the key to world history in alleged racial traits and saw in the "Aryan" race, represented by pure Nordics, a uniquely creative strain. Talk about the "Nordic race" and its superiority may be seen in England's Cecil Rhodes, whose Anglo-American scholarships, still awarded annually and considered a high honor in the United States, were established for the purpose of knitting together "the Nordic race." The prominent American political scientist John W. Burgess was among the believers in Nordic superiority.

This has perhaps been overrated as a source of Hitler's world-view. But Rosenberg, though not a very influential Nazi, was widely recognized as the Third Reich's quasi-official philosopher. Rosenberg's *Mythos* identified the Jew with

---

[2]"Fifty years ago anti-Semitism was a political force in England that respectable people supported and with which honourable people sympathized," Henry D'Avigdor-Goldsmid wrote in 1964 (*History Today*, April issue).

intellectualism, relating it to internationalism—both degeneracies to be set off against the sound instincts of a cultural people. Christianity had been corrupted by both Judaic and Mediterranean elements, but there is a sound "Aryan Christianity," Rosenberg claimed, which should be encouraged. An Aryan Christian Church actually did arise in Hitler's Germany. A myth indeed. But then, was it not intellectually fashionable to say that everything is a myth?

Nazi propaganda made much of the *Bauer*, the German farmer, full of Nordic virtues and uncorrupted by modernity—a line especially developed by Walther Darré, Hitler's agricultural expert. Yet none of the Nazi founders had tilled the soil, and the party seems to have appealed to farmers least of all the social strata. Hitler's mind was filled with archetypes of rural rootedness versus urban corruption, of course. His biographer Joachim Fest numbers among Hitler's "phobias" big cities and (American) technology, unrestricted industrialization, business corporations, and "the morass of metropolitan amusement culture."

These ideas were common currency in conservative thought.[3] On the other hand, Hitler as well as Mussolini cultivated an image of modern speed, riding on motorcycles and descending from airplanes, and Hitler wanted to design a new city of Berlin, capital of the world, with a population of 10 million (a supermegalopolis by the standards of that time). Possibly his most constructive action was a great superhighway system and automobiles for the masses, the *Volkswagens.* Here were some of the paradoxes and inconsistencies of a mind that functioned by the power of fixed images and stereotypes, rather than rational logic.

There was no coherent Nazi economic program; claiming to stand for a kind of non-Marxian, Germanic socialism, Hitler purged the Strasser brothers, prominent in the early party, for pushing socialism too hard. Hitler's plans for coping with the depression were rather like President Roosevelt's in being ad hoc—exchange controls, public works, agricultural price supports, appeals for self-sacrifice. The depression seems to have run its course in about the same way regardless of the kind of government—British conservatism, the American New Deal, French parliamentary anarchy, Italian and German authoritarianism all had about the same measure of success.

COMMUNISM AND THE WESTERN INTELLECTUALS

Nazism had limited appeal to intellectuals looking for a hopeful cause, though, as we pointed out, there were exceptions. Among the reasons for this were Nazism's contempt for intellectuals ("When I hear the word 'culture' I reach for my gun," Goebbels is supposed to have said), and especially for modern art and

---

[3]Martin Buber, the Zionist philosopher, talked about the mystic brotherhood of blood, the folk-soul, and an agrarian, soil-rooted society, in a way that can sound like Hitler or D. H. Lawrence. If blood, soil, and *volk* are considered to be fascist ideas, then the new Jewish nation according to its chief theologian would be fascist.

literature; its atavistic views on race, expressed chiefly in violent anti-Semitism; and above all the aggressive tone Hitler's foreign policy took after 1936, making blustering demands for territory and threatening war. The Nazis engaged in an orgy of book-burning, destroyed Kafka manuscripts and Klimt paintings, banned modern physics along with modern art and literature. All this was hard indeed for cultured people to swallow. Yet it must be admitted that the Stalin regime in Communist Russia, to which they were strongly attracted, was guilty of many of the same practices.

Certainly the Communist Party line condemned most modernisms in the arts. (It was curious that Fascists and Communists denounced modern art for exactly opposite reasons, the one calling it Communist and the other capitalist.) This position dates from about 1932, along with the Stalinization of all phases of Soviet life at that time. Writers and artists were forced to submit to Party control of their work; as soldiers in the class war they had to produce what was required of them, which was chiefly propaganda. Until this time, though many Russian artists and intellectuals had migrated to Paris and other Western cities (Rachmaninoff, Stravinsky, Berdyaev are examples), and others had died or committed suicide (like the great poet Mayakovsky, unable to live with his role as Party propagandist), Soviet literature and art retained considerable prestige.

But the rejection of artistic modernism (called "formalism") and the adoption of "socialist realism" as the principle of Communist art, under political tutelage, meant that the supposed land of the economic future was esthetically backward, and soon ceased to be of much interest to the outer world. The only literature and art acceptable to Stalin was hackneyed political propaganda glorifying the USSR, while abstract art, Kafka, Joyce, surrealism, anything innovative in architecture, everything exciting that had appeared since the turn of the century stood condemned as reactionary. With few exceptions the great artists who stayed in Russia were destroyed, as the poet Osip Mandelstam was for writing an (unpublished) poem against Stalin, or like Boris Pasternak kept silent. But one of the greatest living writers in the world, Maxim Gorki, was an enthusiastic supporter of the Soviet regime in the 1930s. (Stalin had him murdered later, as he did so many millions of other Russians.) A genius of the silent cinema, Sergei Eisenstein, added luster to Soviet culture for some years until his own demise. The great composers Sergei Prokofieff and Dmitri Shostakovich avoided an open break with the regime.

Western artists and intellectuals convinced themselves that a new era was being born, however roughly, in this strange and violent east. The mystique of communism spread amid the woes of the West in the early 1930s. Picasso said he went to communism as to a spring of fresh water. Writers and artists who flocked to the hammer and sickle knew little of the realities of Soviet life. Stephen Spender, the British poet, at one time at home among the young university communists, said "I never met any who had the slightest interest in any side of Russia which was not Stalinist propaganda presentation." In 1932 the venerable Fabian socialist scholars, Sidney and Beatrice Webb, who had always stood for political democracy and personal liberty, went to Russia and produced a book that heaped praise on Soviet communism as a "new civilization." It was the first and probably most influential of many uncritical accounts published in the West in the 1930s. Eventually it was revealed that the Webbs spent just three weeks in Russia, used materials supplied them by the Soviet government, and allowed Stalin's officials to read and correct the manuscript. Lauding especially the Russian "abandonment of the incentive of profit-making, its extinction of unemployment, its planned production for community consumption," the Webbs' *Soviet Civilization* also approved "liquidating the landlord and the capitalist." Stalin's ruthless war on the peasants, driving them into collective farms, which cost millions of lives and virtually destroyed Soviet agriculture for years, was then underway. But the Webbs declared the Soviet system to be more democratic than the Western ones. Others hailed it for introducing a "new era in civil liberties" (Louis Fisher), a "new democracy."

Extremely popular, going through numerous editions, was the totally uncritical account of *The Soviet Sixth of the Earth* by the "red dean" of Canterbury, Hewlett Johnson. George Bernard Shaw visited the USSR to lavish praise on Stalin. This virtual abdication of critical intelligence by people eager to find hope in the Russian Revolution later seemed as unbelievable as the rush into war in 1914. Nothing did more to discredit the intellectuals. The list of distinguished writers, artists, and thinkers who became either party members or "fellow travelers" was so long as to include, it seemed, almost everyone of note. Poets like W. H. Auden and C. Day Lewis, former surrealists like Louis Aragon in France, the leading novelists John Dos Passos, André Malraux, Henri Barbusse (who found time to write an extravagantly adulatory biography of Stalin) and Ignazio Silone, along with the German playwright Bertolt Brecht—these were only the tip of the iceberg. (Most of the above luminaries had indignantly abandoned communism by the end of the decade, but others never did.)

Even Virginia Woolf could be found writing for the Communist organ, *The Daily Worker*. Karl Radek, a top Soviet leader (soon to be liquidated by Stalin in the great "purge" of 1937–38) boasted that "in the heart of bourgeois England, in Oxford, where the sons of the bourgeoisie receive their final polish, we observe the crystallization of a group which sees salvation only with the proletariat." More celebrated, because of a subsequent spy scandal, was the group of students at Cambridge that included Guy Burgess, Kim Philby, and Anthony Blunt. It appears that between 1932 and 1934 virtually every intellectually alive undergraduate there was a Red sympathizer, and a number joined the Party. One may say with little exaggeration that an entire generation of inquiring young people at the universities underwent the Communist experience either during the 1920s or, more frequently, the depression-ridden next decade.

At Cambridge a Marxist economics professor, Maurice Dobb, demonstrated to admiring students the superiority of the "planned" Soviet economic system. (Students may have taken Dobb's course because mainstream economics, represented by Alfred Marshall, had become heavily mathematicized; no innumerate could understand it at all.) The distinguished biologist J. B. S. Haldane was an avowed Communist. In France Pierre Langevin, close friend of Marie Curie and

Nobel prize winner in physics, was prominent among the French sympathizers with Russia. Mme. Curie's son-in-law, Frederic Joliot-Curie, joined the Party. These scientists believed that in the Soviet Union science, released from its bondage to capitalism, was better off than elsewhere.

Nathaniel Weyl, who participated in this experience in the United States, claimed that "During the popular-front and war-alliance years, 1935–1939 and 1941–1945, many New Dealers regarded communists as heroes, members of a dedicated elite of uncompromising social revolutionaries," adding that he knew of one high government official, "a man with access to the White House," who pleaded to be allowed to join the Party but was told he was not worthy of membership. Kim Philby said that he regarded it as a great honor to be selected by the Party. Distinguished British historian Hugh Trevor-Roper in his book *The Philby Affair* (1968) remarked that "it would never have occurred to me, at that time, to hold Philby's communist past against him."

Bertrand Russell, who though a socialist was rather consistently a critic of Moscow from his 1920 *The Practice and Theory of Bolshevism* on, wavered in the early 1930s when he expected and on the whole welcomed what he saw as the coming triumph of communism (see *Education and the Social Order*, 1932, pp. 145–46). John Strachey, an Englishman of impeccably aristocratic lineage, predicted this victory in a book of the hour, *The Coming Struggle for Power* (1932), foreseeing wars between the capitalist nations over declining profits (the United States would fight Great Britain, while communism would triumph in Germany). As Hitler's militant brand of anti-bolshevism gained control of Germany, while the democracies languished and dithered, a kind of apocalyptical feeling grew that a showdown loomed between the only two active faiths, communism and fascism; one must choose sides in the final struggle:

> Singing I was at peace,
> Above the clouds, outside the ring....
> None such shall be left alive:
> The innocent wing is soon shot down,
> And private stars fade in the blood-red dawn
> Where two worlds strive.
>
> (C. Day Lewis)

Several reasons may be offered for this strange desertion of the Western intellectuals to Soviet communism. Of course, economics ranked foremost. While the democracies struggled almost hopelessly against the depression in the 1930s, in Russia things went forward with vigor and drive, at least according to Stalin's propaganda machine and guileless foreign sympathizers).[4] The first of the great Five-

---

[4]The Webbs turned to the Soviets in good part because of disappointment with their Fabian solutions; "we went seriously wrong...in suggesting that we knew how to prevent unemployment," Mrs. Webb reflected. "We did not." John Maynard Keynes' answer in his *General Theory* was not published until 1936.

Year plans aimed at industrializing Russia was launched in 1929. "There is no unemployment in Russia!" The explanation might be that there was economic slavery, but in the grim atmosphere of the jobless 1930s even that might seem preferable. Books by friends of the Soviet Union claimed that something like a paradise for the workers was being created.

Next, the Communists profited from the unpopularity of war in the 1930s. Lenin was one of the few who had rejected the war in 1914; the Bolsheviks had taken Russia out of it soon after the October Revolution and called for peace; they had published the secret treaties and denounced the whole European state system. Lenin provided a Marxist explanation of the war, caused by capitalistic imperialism, and socialists alleged that universal peace would follow the extinction of the capitalist system. Then in the 1930s some thought only the Soviet Union consistently opposed Hitler's drive toward mastery of the continent.

In the Spanish civil war of 1936–39, Stalin sent some help to the anti-Fascist side while the democracies did not. The latter seemed to take the lead in the "appeasement" of Hitler during his demands on Czechoslovakia in 1938, excluding the USSR from the Munich pact allegedly because of a desire to use Germany as a foe of Bolshevism. This might be a considerable oversimplification of the events, but it had some plausibility. Communists did fight nazism and fascism courageously in Italy and Germany. Communism was, after all, the peril constantly denounced by Hitler and Mussolini. Like André Gide, some might love Soviet Russia for the enemies it made.

The Communists became more approachable after 1934 when the party line changed to the "popular front" strategy. Prior to that, Communists had denounced socialists as "social fascists" or "traitors to the working class," and refused to cooperate with them. In Russia the Bolsheviks banned and persecuted the former Menshevik Social Democrats. Some of the fiercest polemics of the 1920s passed between the old socialists and the new Communists, who had split off from the Second International to create the Third, directed from Moscow. Recognizing after Hitler's triumph in Germany that they had gravely erred in not forming an anti-fascist front (they had seriously underestimated Nazism), the Communists on orders from Moscow now tried to make friends with other left-wing groups to form a united front. They did not always do this sincerely, and much mistrust remained, but the Popular Front was popular for a time; headed by socialist intellectual Leon Blum, a Jaurès disciple, a Popular Front government headed France in 1936–37.

In the last analysis the drama of the Western intellectuals and communism lay in the fact that they were looking for a faith. Edward Upward wrote that "I came to [communism] not so much through consciousness of the political and economic situation as through despair." Arthur Koestler, one of the most articulate analysts of "the god that failed" after he left the Party, commented on "the intellectual comfort and relief found in escaping from a tragic predicament into a closed system of beliefs that left no room for hesitation and doubts." "The strongest appeal of the Communist party was that it demanded sacrifice," Louis MacNeice recalled. "You had to sink your ego." The apparent gullibility of the converts stemmed from a kind of will to believe that caused them to refuse to credit anything ill said of the Soviet Union. (This was the work of the capitalist devil, trying to sow confusion among the faithful.) *Certus est quia impossible est.* The Party was, indeed, infallible. The keys of the kingdom had descended from Marx to Lenin to Stalin, carried in the body of the Party/Church and certified by the holy writ of Marxist-Leninist writings. (Of course, inconvenient passages from Marx and even Lenin were suppressed, something the Christian Church also is alleged to have done. Before his untimely death in 1924 Lenin had warned against Stalin, but this material remained a closely guarded secret for more than thirty years.) Of the major Western figures who embraced communism, Brecht perhaps carried furthest this urge to "sink into the mud" and "commit any vileness" in order to advance the good cause, becoming "blank sheets on which the Revolution will write its orders."

Koestler described his own rather horrifying experience within the Party as a "spiritual discipline" he would not wish to see expunged from his past, though he came to regard it as an intellectual error. (See *The Invisible Writing* and *Arrow in the Blue*.) In his great novel *Darkness at Noon* the German writer (one-time journalist, like Ernest Hemingway) depicted the self-destroying psychology of the Communist who had given his mind and soul over to the Party.

Artists who thought, rather selfishly, that communism would unleash their creativity usually found the opposite. The vast majority, by nature individualists if not egoists, could not sustain a sacrifice that required them to serve as apologists for Stalin's increasingly enormous crimes. The spectacular "purge" trials of 1937 in the USSR marked a turning point; then came the 1939 agreement with Hitler, with the party line abruptly changing. If they stayed, Party members and "fellow travelers" had to assume an increasingly ignominious role, which American ex-Communist Eugene Lyons described as providing "alibis for the killers and insults for the killed." Only a handful could stomach it. These included some like Kim Philby who had committed themselves too far by becoming secret Soviet agents, spying for Stalin.

THE FLIGHT FROM COMMUNISM

The one-time Communists wrote a great deal about their exodus in and out of the Party. The path usually led them away from Marxism altogether, though they could plausibly claim that Stalin had perverted Marx. A possible rallying point was Leon Trotsky, Lenin's chief lieutenant in the revolution and a scintillating theorist; he became a martyr after being assassinated by Stalin's agents while in exile in Mexico. Trotsky accused Stalin of betraying the revolution by the errors of bureaucratization and the cult of personality. But Trotsky's own views did not seem distinctively different; he accepted the Leninist doctrine of the elite vanguard party, and was himself implicated in terrorist tactics practiced during the civil war.

Harold Laski, left-wing theoretician of the British Labour party, was typical of ex-fellow travelers in reacting eventually against the moral creed of the party, "deception, ruthlessness, contempt for fair play, willingness to use lying and treachery...dishonesty in the presentation of facts." Hard-boiled party members regarded such scruples as mere bourgeois sentimentality. George Orwell's disenchantment with communism came in Spain, where he like so many other left-wing intellectuals went in 1936 to defend the Spanish Republic against the "fascist" rebels (right-wingers backed by Mussolini and Hitler). The future author of *Animal Farm* and *1984*, those devastating satires on Stalinism, saw his friends among a minor socialist party arrested and killed, as well as lied about, not by the fascists but by the Republican government under Communist influence. Returning from Spain to write about his experiences, Orwell found few on the left prepared to accept his indictment, and had some trouble getting *Homage to Catalonia* published (1937–38). Orwell wrote as a democratic socialist now convinced that Soviet totalitarianism was on a par with fascism, and an enemy of real socialism. This was heresy among pre-1939 intellectuals. A manifesto by 400 prominent American writers on August 14, 1939, denied that the Soviet Union had anything in common with "totalitarianism."

The mystique of the Russian Revolution died hard, so deeply had it sunk into the consciousness of some people. Italian peasants were said to have hung pictures of Stalin alongside Christ in their cottages. A few never gave it up. One example: Sylvia Townsend Warner, a second-rank but quite well known British fiction writer, became an enthusiastic Communist who wanted to get Stephen Spender purged from the party for his lack of sufficient orthodoxy. Her communism seemed to have nothing to do with her art. Her stories depict the specifics of personal life—they have nothing to do with Marxist theory, which one is sure she could not have wanted for a moment to study. Yet she defended Stalinism for the rest of her life, into the 1970s. Perhaps what kept her firm in the faith was simple inertia, the trouble it would be to find a new framework of thought, in effect forge a new identity, find new friends.

Many a family experienced the trauma of a generation revolt in reverse in the 1950s and 1960s, as mama and papa, loyal Communists, were shocked by the children turning against them. "Fascist! McCarthyite!" they had to yell at the kids, who could not understand how their parents could defend a mass murderer and idealize a slave system. This poignant tragedy appears in a number of autobiographies, novels, and plays (like the Arnold Wesker trilogy of plays, 1958–60). British publisher Victor Gollancz suffered a nervous breakdown when Stalin, his surrogate father, turned out to have been a monster.

But the decade was not all pink. Evelyn Waugh complained with some justice that Auden, Spender, and their friends "ganged up and captured the decade," leaving behind the impression that everyone had gone far left. Waugh himself was a leading novelist who converted to Catholicism; like C. S. Lewis, he made his way back to "mere Christianity"—spiritually more profound than these upstart creeds, which Orwell called "smelly little orthodoxies," of fascism and communism. T. S. Eliot's writing of the thirties was far less bitterly iconoclastic than formerly; the *Waste Land* poet announced himself a convert to Anglo-Catholicism, classicism, and monarchy (there was no small amount of Charles Maurras influence here). Eliot edited a journal, *Criterion*, which sought to rally the defense of traditional values against both fascism and communism—which he saw as debased rival religions, successful only if Christian culture failed to assert its message. His later poetry was deeply meditative and religious. In France there were many right-wing intellectual journals; Georges Bernanos and Emmanuel Mounier are examples of deeply committed, rather unorthodox, but in some ways highly reactionary leaders of thought. The Christian revival associated with Jacques Maritain's neo-Thomism continued, as did the neo-Protestant theology of Karl Barth and Rudolf Bultmann in Germany; Reinhold Niebuhr and Paul Tillich carried it to the United States. At times this current blended with the far left's eschatological visions.

By the end of the decade W. H. Auden, probably the greaest poet of his generation, who in his student days was a drillmaster of the leftward march—"Wystan, lone flyer, birdman, my bully boy!" as Day Lewis hailed him—had become a Christian. Others of the ex-Communists opted for a more democratic socialism, or a more sophisticated, non-Stalinist Marxism. Chief source of the latter was the Frankfurt Institute for Social Research, to which belonged such German social theorists as Max Horkheimer, Herbert Marcuse, and Theodor Adorno. Thrown out of Germany by Hitler in the early thirties, the group ended in New York City as part of that great cultural migration of German scholars, scientists, philosophers, architects, and writers that so altered American intellectual life, bringing it closer to European themes. This "critical" Marxism made its biggest impact after World War II; indeed in one of the many odd twists of intellectual history, Marcuse as an old man was to become a hero of the youth movement of the 1960s.

In the interwar years the Frankfurt School studied Marx's little known early writings, rejected Stalinism as a simplistic perversion of Marx, and experimented with Freudian, existential, or phenomenological graftings onto Marxism. There were other non-Communist left-wing groups in Germany during the Weimar years, all of course destroyed by the Nazi revolution, which did not pause to distinguish between shadings of Marxism, the more so since these circles tended to be heavily Jewish (this was certainly true of the Frankfurt School).

Varieties of socialism milder than Moscow's total centralized state planning found vigorous support in the 1930s. The Great Depression discredited capitalism. That "planned production for use, not profit" was superior to capitalism's chaos and greed, all right-thinking, i.e. left-thinking, intellectuals accepted in principle, if not necessarily in the Russian practice. Such views came not just from Marxists, but from such anti-Communists as Albert Einstein (see his "Why Socialism?") and Bertrand Russell, paladins of thought. The latter's hostility to Soviet communism was entirely based on its lack of democracy and intellectual freedom, which he attributed not to socialism itself, but mainly to Marxian dogmatism. "Private ownership of land and capital" he thought indefensible not merely on grounds of social justice, but "on the ground that it is an uneconomical way of producing what the community needs." Compare George Bernard Shaw's many lectures on this theme. The whole Western socialist tradition, rooted in Fabianism more than Marxism, took for granted the greater efficiency of socialism. The only concern was whether this efficiency might be bought at too high a price in liberty.

If socialism was too tainted a term, "collectivism" could be effectively substituted. "The intelligentsia worked with great success to establish collectivism as the conventional wisdom for all thinking people," Paul Addison remarks. "Collectivism" meant "social security," the "welfare state," strong trade unions, heavy regulation and high taxation of "big business"; perhaps some nationalization. But increasingly the leading rationale for government action to counteract the depression came from the brilliant Cambridge economist John Maynard Keynes—onetime Bloomsburyite, friend of some of the undergraduate communists, but himself impatient with Marxian economics, which he regarded as hopelessly obsolete, along with its close relative, classical Ricardian economics. Keynes, who had challenged conventional public finance methods in the 1920s, in the next decade put his views in the form of a general theory, published in 1936.

Keynes argued that contrary to established economic theory, there is no automatic tendency toward equilibrium and full employment in a free economy (Say's Law); rather, there can be stagnation and unused human resources. This is because, among other things, the community's total savings are not necessarily invested in capital equipment. The interest rate, which is supposed to provide the mechanism for insuring the investment of savings (the rate of interest falling as savings rise), may not function effectively because liquidity preference (desire to keep funds in cash or some form easily converted to cash) causes savers to accept a lower return on their money. Keynes stressed the propensity to oversave and underinvest in a mature capitalist economy. The result can be economic stagnation.

The economy cannot be counted on to right itself, as the older theorists believed; it may need the stimulus of government intervention. Formerly the approved government policy for dealing with a depression, which was thought to be a temporary fluctuation around an equilibrium point, was to pare expenditures and balance the budget. Governments did this during the early stage of the 1930s depression, with ineffective (and sometimes politically disastrous) results. The new economics, as advocated by Keynes along with some others, especially a Swedish school, called for an unbalanced budget, for the government to throw its financial weight into the economic stream to break the logjam. (Keynes never intended to institutionalize budget deficits. A temporary deficit would be recovered on the upswing.) A multiplier effect insured that this spending would stimulate the private sector many times more than the amount provided.

In other ways, too, government could regulate the economy, by manipulating interest rates, raising and lowering taxes—in general, using its great fiscal resources as a balance wheel according to the needs of the economy at any given time. The whole of this program cast the public sector in a new and much more active role, though it was not "socialist" in any usage of the term, since private ownership and the market economy remained intact, though subject perhaps to the higher taxes deficit financing and social welfare measures might entail.

The Keynesian view tended to prevail, soon becoming the new orthodoxy as the older theorists retreated in confusion. The depression's persistence had shaken the neo-classical establishment. In 1937 notable British mainstream economist A. C. Pigou, who at first rejected Keynes's arguments, recanted to a considerable degree in his *Socialism and Capitalism*. The great names of pure free-market theory were literally driven into obscurity. A student of Ludwig von Mises has recalled how in the 1940s the distinguished Austrian economist, who had sought to demonstrate the unworkability of socialism, couldn't get a university post and was reduced to teaching part-time at a New York City business school.[5] The University of Chicago and other universities also rejected Mises' student and fellow Austrian Friedrich von Hayek, who would receive a Nobel prize in 1975.

Unmitigated free-enterprise capitalism was relegated to the dark ages of human society; Karl Marx's predecessor and teacher Adam Smith became a byword for folly. In *The Road to Serfdom*, Hayek bravely presented his view that the welfare state and Keynesian economics no less than outright nationalization would prove disastrous. But few were listening. Most thought that Keynesianism, the American New Deal, the Swedish "middle way," perhaps the French "popular front," provided hopeful democratic alternatives to Russian communism as a means of dealing with the terrible economic blight, though it must be said that prior to 1939 the results were not spectacular.

Of many other notable economic ideas the depression brought forward, from the wildest amateur ones to intricate professional analysis, the work of Joseph Schumpeter is worth mentioning. Transported to Harvard University from Austria, where he once served as a minister in the government, Schumpeter was notable for casting the study of economics in a wider context than the narrowly economic (a serious flaw in most professional analysis). His sympathies were probably with the other Austrian anti-socialists Hayek and Mises, but Schumpeter believed that the future lay with socialism. Though an admirer of capitalism (as generator of wealth), Schumpeter thought it was destined to perish. His reasons were less economic than sociological. The entrepreneurial spirit of the nineteenth-century capitalists fades; faceless bureaucrats become managers, while the off-spring of capitalists are intellectuals. The family, that great stimulator of the desire to accumulate, Schumpeter also saw weakening. No more Buddenbrooks! Capitalism itself, as it succeeds in creating wealth, undermines thrift and family values. Here was a version of Marx's "self-destruction of capitalism" thesis, but with very different overtones, more Spenglerian than Hegelian, more pessimistic than optimistic. In that respect, perhaps, it matched the mood of the times better than did the Marxists.[6]

The figures strongly suggest that it was mainly the intellectuals who defected

---

[5]Richard Cornuelle, "New Work for Invisible Hands," *TLS*, April 5, 1991.

[6]Compare James Burnham's *The Managerial Revolution* (1940): "Capitalism" is doomed, but what replaces it is not "socialism," but rule by a managerial elite, a new class that rises to power in both the USSR and the West. Other students of the Stalinist economy were to notice that it was in fact an odd combination of socialism, capitalism, and feudalism.

to the left. Amid the rise of the Left Book Club and other suggestions of a mass conversion, there were evidently just 1,376 British CP members in 1930 and only a little over 15,000 by 1939. Most of them must have been at Cambridge! True, the situation was rather different on the Continent; the Paris Communist newspaper *L'humanité* rose to have the largest circulation of any daily. But everywhere the majority found more relief from depression woes in the escapist fare of the increasingly popular movies. The 1930s was the era of popular culture, carrying on from the twenties with fuller development of radio, cinema, even the dawning of television. More people by far probably knew the names of Garbo and Dietrich than Stalin and Hitler.

Both dictators were aware of the propaganda value of this new medium; Leni Riefenstahl's *Triumph of the Will*, celebrating National Socialism's victory, may have been the most powerful propaganda movie ever made. Despite some Hollywood stars who went modishly Red, popular entertainment culture was temperamentally hostile to political ideology. Perhaps Noël Coward, the fabulously successful British entertainer, is a fair example. In fact Coward, like Charlie Chaplin, came close to bridging the gulf between popular and elite culture; but unlike Chaplin, this actor-playright-composer of modest birth had no respect for the commies. "I wish the intellectuals, The clever ones, Would go to Russia," he wrote. To be sure, his review of British history called *Cavalcade* (1931) had ended with "The Twentieth Century Blues":

> In this strange illusion,
> Chaos and confusion,
> People seem to lose their way.
> What is there to strive for,
> Love or keep alive for?

THE REVOLUTION IN PHILOSOPHY

The Vienna-born Ludwig Wittgenstein, an aeronautical engineer turned philosopher under Bertrand Russell's influence just before the war, published his *Tractatus Logico-Philosophicus* (as it was titled when translated into English) in 1922, at about the same time as *Ulysses* and *The Waste Land*. It joined them as a manifesto of modernism, a cult book, as obscure and exciting as the literary masterpieces redolent of postwar intellectual and moral crisis. The *Tractatus* too was a kind of literary masterpiece; trenchant, compressed, gnomic, its 20,000 words could be read in an afternoon, but puzzled over for years. Begun in often acerbic debates with Russell and G. E. Moore at Cambridge, labored on in solitude in a Norwegian hut in 1914, carried around with him on the battlefield during the war (in which he fought bravely as a private in the Austro-Hungarian army), the *Tractatus* had as romantic a provenance as one could want; and the strange, intense Wittgenstein was as charismatic as a philosopher of genius could be. As it turned out, it was the only book he ever published in his lifetime, though he wrote a great deal in the 1930s that was published after his death in 1951. Obeying its conclusion that philosophy can say nothing about the important problems of life, Wittgenstein dropped out of philosophy during the 1920s. He had deconstructed his own subject: "We had better be silent about that of which we cannot speak." Cold comfort, perhaps, in his belief that fully explaining a problem makes it go away. "There are then no questions left, and this itself is the answer. The solution of the problem of life is seen in the vanishing of the problem."

In 1926–28 Wittgenstein held conversations with the so-called Vienna Circle, authors of a manifesto announcing a revolution in philosophy styling itself logical positivism. They were admirers of the *Tractatus* as they understood it, but in talking to Wittgenstein they discovered that in fact he was not so close to them. He did not even want to talk about logic, the passion of his earlier days in England, but about literature and religion, subjects rather abhorrent to philosophers such as Rudolf Carnap and Moritz Schlick of the science-minded *Wiener Kreis*. Nevertheless until the 1950s, Wittgenstein was usually thought of as a logical positivist. He seemed to be saying, as they did, that there are external states of affairs to which language must be made to correspond. At this stage Wittgenstein appeared to accept Russell's "logical atomism," according to which the world consists of separate, discrete facts or states of affairs, to which basic statements can be matched. And he agreed that "the business of philosophy is not to establish a set of propositions but to make other propositions clear."

In common with others of the Vienna school, Wittgenstein held that philosophy ought not to build theories or systems, or even, as such, search for Truth; its purpose is strictly a logical one, to clarify those confusions into which people fall when they attempt to think. It is "a struggle against the bewitchment of our intelligence by language." Philosophy finds no knowledge of its own, there are no metaphysical truths; finding knowledge (true propositions) is the province of the sciences. "Philosophy gives no picture of reality and can neither confirm nor confute scientific investigations." "The reason why philosophical problems are posed at all is owing to a misunderstanding of language." "Most of the propositions and questions to be found in philosophical works are not false but nonsensical." The function of philosophy is thus a dual one: to show the futility of most that has previously passed for philosophizing (attempts by verbal trickery to answer unanswerable questions); and to help the natural and human sciences methodologically, by demystifying and clarifying their terminology.

Logical positivism originated with a group of philosophers and mathematicians active at Vienna University from about 1920 until Nazism and war dispersed them in the 1930s. Then some of them went to Great Britain and the United States, where they exerted considerable influence while mixing with native traditions akin to them in spirit (British empiricism, American pragmatism). They owed something to Ernst Mach's prewar "empirio-criticism" and to a preoccupation with the formal structure of language found in turn-of-the-century linguistics. (Note the symbolist poet Mallarmé's decision to "surrender the initiative to words," to recognize the priority of language not as a tool of thought but as its creator, an autonomous realm quite other than the "reality" with which it has occasional and adventitious encounters.) To Carnap and his friends, though not to the later Wittgenstein, the task was that of devising a new language, or reforming the old one, to make it match the realm of observable phenomena that empirical science reveals. Languages as they are tend to be untrustworthy guides; created for purposes other than rational thought, they disguise and distort. Perhaps a language using mathematical symbols is necessary for scientific purposes.

As we know from our encounter with Einstein, the new scientific revolution pointedly raised the question of how words like "atom," "electron," "force," "matter," are related to the real world. Obviously they are not the *same* as it. Nor are they a direct copy of it. The words we employ to transcribe sense data into language belong to another order, which tries to correspond with the real world but sometimes succeeds badly in this, perhaps even becoming an obstacle. "Atoms are not things, electrons are no longer things in the sense of classical physics.... When we get down to the atomic level, the objective world in space in time no longer exists, and the mathematical symbols of theoretical analysis refer merely to possibilities not to facts" (Werner Heisenberg). The hard, precise, "real" physical world seemed to dissolve into "nothing more than a shadow of our imagination" (Mara Beller). "The frank realization that physical science is concerned with a world of shadows," Arthur Eddington, in his widely read *The Nature of the Physical Universe*, called the most significant of modern "advances."

At Cambridge before the war, the young Wittgenstein had become involved with Russell's attempt to express mathematical principles in logical form. Russell's 1905 paper "On Denoting" was part of his intense early preoccupation with making language more exact and logical. In seeking like the Viennese logician Gottlieb Frege (also an influence on the Vienna Circle) to establish arithmetic on secure logical foundations, Russell tried to demonstrate that the purely logical notions of identity, class, class membership, and class equivalence suffice for constructing the series of natural numbers. His "theory of types" was designed to overcome obstacles in the way of this goal, notably the paradox of "the class of classes that are not members of themselves."

So Russell, Mach, Frege, science, logic, mathematics, linguistics all milled around in the philosophy revolution. In the mid-1930s, the British logical positivist A. J. Ayer presented it provocatively. There was some connection between this revolution and the leftish mood of the decade. The Vienna Circle looked moderately leftward, and one of its members, Otto Neurath, had been a part of the short-lived revolutionary regime in Munich in 1919. Ayer said that "Philip Toynbee almost, but not quite, persuaded me to join the Communist Party." Logical positivism was an iconoclastic doctrine; "the old men were outraged," Ayer recalled with glee. One has only to read the first sentence of his "manifesto," *Language, Truth, and Logic* (1935) to sense this mood: "The traditional disputes of philosophers are, for the most part, as unwarranted as they are unfruitful." Much of what traditional philosophy concerned itself with was absurd—questions about God, freedom, spirit, the purpose of life, morals. If attempts to discuss these are not just confused terminology, they are simply projections of the feelings of the philosopher, "emotive" statements about which there can be no useful disputation. Insofar as one cannot reduce a question to empirical, testable statements, it must be dismissed as so much empty wind.

Someone remarked that theologians who were accustomed to being told they were wrong found themselves speechless at being told they were not saying anything at all! Applied to morality, logical positivism might be extremely subversive. Statements of value not being empirically verifiable, they become mere expressions of preference. "I think adultery is wrong" is the same sort of statement as "I hate spinach" or "I dislike modern art." Logical thought can supply no sanctions for behavior; we must look elsewhere for values. It is open to us to find them in religion or social utility. But the frank equation of moral tastes with other kinds of personal taste might be construed as an invitation to libertinism. Presumably I should choose my conduct in the same way I choose my neckties—all a matter of personal taste. (The Bloomsbury Circle had found in G. E. Moore's teachings at Cambridge a somewhat similar support for liberation from conventional morality.)

This revolution in philosophy may be characterized by saying that philosophy ceased to be a "search for wisdom" or a quest for absolute values and became instead just the logic of science or the clarifier of scientific methods and concepts. The new philosophy, with its search for perfect clarity, reflected something of the professionalism that was taking over all branches of thought. The "men of letters," the amateurs, or the kind of people who inhabited universities before their modern transformation, had indulged in bold and broad-ranging but often not very rigorous thinking. The new professionals wanted to be "scientific," to be competent, to do work of high technical caliber. Knowledge must be exact. The logical positivists put forward the verification principle (true statements must be verifiable in sense experience), combining it with the careful examination of language. To those who protested that philosophy was abdicating its chief function, thus leaving modern humanity, which never needed help with its values so badly, high and dry, the new philosophers answered briskly: "Sorry, not our business. Go ask some poet or theologian if you really need help. We're scientists."

The acute analytical methods of professional philosophy eventually caught up with logical positivism. Someone asked, "How do you verify the verification principle?" Wittgenstein himself shifted to a more skeptical position. Drawn back into philosophy in 1929, he continued his philosophical investigations. In 1932 he said, "I used to think there was a direct link between language and reality. I no longer think so." How could we know? We cannot get outside our language; we are its prisoners. In what except language could we talk about the relation between language and the world? How can I picture the relationship between a picture and reality? Something like Heisenberg's interference principle appeared here to set a limit to knowledge. Rather than language mirroring the world, it may be that the world mirrors language: its structure, its rules constitute a self-contained system that largely determines the way we see the world. Words derive their meaning less from their correspondence to objects in the external world than from the way they are used in a system of language. "A name functions as a name only in the context of a system of linguistic and non-linguistic activities."

This and other Wittgenstein remarks were to have a powerful influence on philosophy mostly after 1953, the year of the postmortem publication of his *Philosophical Investigations*, containing the core of his later thought. So, though he had formulated them in the 1930s, these ideas belong essentially to later intellectual history. *Philosophical Investigations* was derived from material he dictated between 1933 and 1935—clearly the moment of Wittgenstein's greatest creativity, when he was in his mid-forties. He had ceased being silent; that he published nothing to speak of was owing to his inability to produce anything systematic. The numerous volumes published since his death are in the form of notebooks, "remarks," conversations, lecture notes, or transcripts. This was in accordance with his temperament, and also with the character of his new direction. He had given up the attempt to devise a new, perfectly logical language. No language can escape being just another language with the same limitations. So we must make do with the tangled one we have. The philosopher can help us untangle it, but this is a matter of particular cases.

The astringent and professional spirit of analysis appeared also in English literary criticism. F. R. Leavis was in fact a friend of the rather unclubbable Wittgenstein at Oxford in the 1930s; he edited the journal called *Scrutiny*, encouraging what its title suggested, a meticulous, line-by-line examination of poetry, in reaction against the rather relaxed sort of armchair chat about literature that had passed for criticism in Victorian times. Clear literary standards must be established—and defended. The Scrutinizers thought of themselves as cutting away large husks of sentimental dross with the keen razor of critical analysis in order to get down to the solid core of real literary value. Like the analytical philosophers, they were to be accused of aridity. But they introduced what seemed like a bracing scientific expertise in the examination of the arts. For Leavis at least, this task was not an end in itself, but part of a kind of Matthew Arnold-like project of discovering the true masterpieces of "the great tradition." (He liked D. H. Lawrence, didn't like James Joyce.)

Science commanded great respect. Progress went on in numerous areas, though sometimes it was rather ominous progress. After Chadwick's discovery of the neutron in 1931 in England, continental physicists—Otto Hahn, Lise Meitner, Leo Szilard, Enrico Fermi—took the lead in developing controllable uranium fission, the source of atomic energy. The Hungarian Szilard filed for a patent on a chain reaction in 1934, the same year Fermi caused a uranium atom to split by bombarding it with neutrons. Fermi, "the Italian explorer," was to join Einstein and Szilard in the United States, where he supervised the creation of the first atomic reactor under the football field at Chicago University. The Austrian Meitner, another pioneer who along with Einstein's old friend Hahn and her nephew Otto Frisch had perfected Fermi's experiment in 1938–39, also fled Nazi intolerance to settle in the United States. Frederic Joliot-Curie, Marie Curie's son-in-law, helped keep the Germans away from the atomic bomb during World War II, and in the process became a devoted Communist. Such were the vicissitudes of science and politics in the totalitarian era.

Positivistic psychology tended to be more influential among professional academicians than Freud's psychoanalysis. J. B. Watson, the American behaviorist, whose main treatise appeared in 1913, joined the Russian Pavlov in eschewing any effort to analyze interior states of mind as quite unsuitable for exact treatment; they stuck to measurable observations of external behavior, and tended to prefer rats to humans as subjects. Behaviorism in its more dogmatic moods was inclined to insist that human nature is determined by its environment in a mechanical way, that life is made up of a series of conditioned reflexes, and that mind, as such, does not exist, there being only a pattern of electrical reactions in brain tissue. This heritage from the eighteenth-century materialists would be carried on in the next generation by B. F. Skinner. Here was the same horror of "metaphysics" as the logical positivists exhibited.

"Scientific humanism," a term popularized by Julian Huxley, among others, was presented as a faith of progress through science, with heavy overtones of hostility to traditional religion. Another Huxley, Aldous, satirized the scientific civilization in one of the decade's most popular books, *Brave New World* (1932), of which nearly three million copies had been sold by 1970. In the Year of Our Ford 632, dehumanized people have been conditioned to think alike, indeed they are genetically engineered alike (Huxley was very prescient here); they are kept submissive through being entertained by the "feelies" and free public sex.

Thus continued a long argument between scientists and artists about whether technology was liberator or enslaver. But with the abdication of philosophy, it was to the imaginative writers that serious people looked for values and a message of salvation.

LITERATURE IN THE PINK DECADE

The infatuation of creative writers with social issues in the 1930s left behind some remarkable literary deposits, now out of date but remaining as landmarks for the historian to contemplate. Some of them were awe-inspiring in their sheer magnitude. Jules Romains, the French social novelist, wrote ten thousand pages in his mammoth multivolume novel of social realism, *Men of Good Will*, outdoing Marcel Proust in length if not in quality, and intended to rival Balzac's *Human Comedy* as a picture of the social world. Politicians, capitalists, industrialists, as well as intellectuals seeking to set the world right fill these pages. The Englishman Robert Briffault and the American Upton Sinclair wrote similar panoramas of social history. More impressively, John Dos Passos wrote his *USA* trilogy, combining social realism with some symbolist and surrealist techniques. John Steinbeck's *Grapes of Wrath*, a moving saga of poor farmers in the American West, was the hit of the decade. There were many other examples.

Critics complained that these social realists had little knowledge of real capitalists and politicians, much less workers, but produced stereotypes of what Marxist theory required them to believe about such individuals. Social realism could be wildly unrealistic. It could also be dreary, sermons flavored with melodrama. Romains' huge opus is nevertheless a tribute to the moral earnestness of the writers of the 1930s and their desire to bring life back into the scope of art and intellect. Among the curiosities of 1930s "social realism" was the "Mass Observation" poem attempted in England, originating among those who wanted to be both surrealist and Communist. Thousands of people all over the country were supposed to send in their literary reports on a single event, the coronation of King George VI, from which a composite poem would somehow be created. Predictably, the result was not impressive.

The great war of 1914–18 continued to inspire many novels, plays, and also memoirs—recollections of life at the front of the sort exemplified by Robert Graves's *Goodbye to All That* and Edmund Blunden's *Her Privates We*. Romains's epic paused for a whole volume at the battle of Verdun. Hemingway had immortalized Caporetto in *Farewell to Arms*. Most celebrated of all, perhaps, was the poignant *All Quiet on the Western Front (In Westen Nichts Neues)*, by the German writer Erich Maria Remarque (published just before Hitler, made into a memorable motion picture, as was Hemingway's story). A play by an English insurance agent R. C. Sheriff, called *Journey's End* (1929), set in the trenches, became an international hit. Such writings appeared most frequently around the end of the twenties and the early thirties. They coincided with and fed the swell of hostility toward war that rose in the 1930s, accompanying the leftward, activist trend. Usually they emphasized the horror and futility of war, or at least the mood of the thirties read this into them. Hemingway's title summed it up: farewell to war. *Nie wieder Krieg*. In England young people took the Oxford Oath, vowing never again to fight for king and country.

Later in the decade both Ernest Hemingway and André Malraux wrote impressive novels about the Spanish civil war; Malraux, later a bitter foe of Soviet communism, hired warplanes for the Loyalists. The great French writer wanted to be a man of action; his urge was toward a union of literature and life, above all in military or revolutionary action. The restless quest led him to revolution in China, civil war in Spain, in and out of communism, and finally to the service of a World War II war hero.

A dramatic clash between conflicting emotions, hatred of war and of Nazism, marked the last two or three years of the decade. Perhaps the fervent pacifism induced by antiwar novels, plays, rallies, tracts, had something to do with the coming of World War II. It encouraged Hitler to believe that the democracies would never fight. The tragic irony of this generation was that it had to go back to war, which it hated, in order to destroy fascism and Nazism, themselves products of the first war's brutalization of humanity.

The greater literature of the 1930s was left over from the 1920s. Franz Kafka had died in 1924, but his unfinished novels *The Trial* and *The Castle* only entered the consciousness of most of Europe after 1930, when they were translated into many languages. Before his death a few had recognized Kafka as a modern master, but about all he was known for outside his native Prague was the remarkable *Metamorphosis (Verwandlung)*, about the government worker who turned into an insect. A minor bureaucrat himself, this son of a Jewish businessman lived only to write, and the stress of his attempt to live in two worlds probably brought on his early death. His two great novels are parables on the ambivalent and stress-ridden human condition (written in a detached, clinically exact prose describing a Freudian dream world) which are best related to Sartrean existentialism. In the 1930s they seemed to record in an uncanny way the "nightmare world" of totalitarian tyranny and the shadow of war.

The Nazis burnt Kafka's books in 1933, and the Gestapo destroyed a number of his manuscripts. Stalin's Communists made him a symbol of the "formalism" it condemned, calling it "bourgeois decadence." The enormous irony of this appears when we think of how totally Kafka rejected "bourgeois" values, if by that much-abused term one means the business-success outlook of his father, or the mechanical rationality of a society oriented toward economic efficiency at the expense of freedom and creativity.

Writing in the 1930s, Walter Benjamin declared that "Kafka's world...is the exact complement of his era which is preparing to do away with the inhabitants of this planet on a considerable scale." To many others in the troubled 1930s, Kafka had caught the flavor of a "nightmare world" of depression, Nazism, communism, and the drift toward World War II; or perhaps they read this mood into his cryptic fables. Benjamin could have had no idea of how many of earth's inhabitants would perish in Hitler's holocaust, Stalin's terror, the immense battles and aerial bombings of 1940–45. Kafka's writings seemed to expose the grotesque logic that made such things possible. One of his stories, indeed, "In the Penal Colony," was about the sadistic yet impersonal torture of prisoners. (Kafka's three sisters were to perish in Hitler's murder factories.)

There is a dreamlike quality about almost all of Kafka's stories. His characters act and talk in that bizarre yet strangely pseudorational way that people do in dreams. Virginia Woolf's fascinating novels are usually tantalizingly poised somewhere between a dream world and the real world. We may explain the retreat to dreams as flight from an intolerable reality, or the search, in positive terms, for an alternative world. Joyce's sequel to *Ulysses*, titled *Finnegans Wake*, finished in 1939 not long before his untimely death at the beginning of the war, was about a dream; its attempt to write a dream language that was simultaneously the dream of the human race ("the untireties of livesliving being the one substance of a streamsbecoming," in Joycespeak) produced probably the most ambitious literary experimentation of all time, one that most readers initially pronounced incomprehensible. The translation and reception of this myth-laden masterpiece is still going on (producing a vast literary industry).

FW is a continuation of *Ulysses*; it is the same titanic effort to unify the whole of a complex inheritance and society in one literary work, exhibiting a

James Joyce. The Dublin born author of the notorious *Ulysses* left his *Finnegans Wake* as a fantastic riddle for an anxious world to solve. (National Portrait Gallery, London)

remarkable range of knowledge. Perhaps its foremost theme is a contrast between the daytime world and the dream world, which also stands for the dualism of real and ideal, life and art, this world and the next, bourgeois and intellectual, reality principle and pleasure principle (also spirit and body, Oriental and Western, yin and yang, the dualism in Giordano Bruno's thought). "There are two signs to turn to, the yest and the ist, the wright side and the wronged side, feeling aslip and wauking up, so an, so farth." As a sheer *tour de force* of verbal mastery (in many languages) Joyce's masterpiece stands unrivaled, a fit counterpart to Einstein's physics. What it meant to humankind was less clear. Perhaps that art can rise above life, but only at the price of impenetrability. Trying to comprehend everybody[7]

---

[7]The sleeping hero of *Finnegans Wake* is generically known as HCE, which among many other things stands for Here Comes Everybody.

(*Ulysses* and *Finnegans Wake* celebrate popular culture as much as the literary elite), this Dubliner of humble birth was condemned to become the focus of a new elite, the most exclusive of all: those who could understand him.

He died at the start of World War II, as did Freud, William Butler Yeats, and Virginia Woolf, among other distinguished representatives of the brilliant generation just ending. Lawrence and Proust and Kafka were long since gone, dying young, but their works took center stage. Thomas Mann and Albert Einstein died in 1955, well after the peak of their genius. Bertrand Russell lived to almost one hundred, his most famous years still ahead of him in 1945. But his younger and even more brilliant protégé Ludwig Wittgenstein departed in 1951. Malraux was also to play an extraordinary role in postwar politics. They all belonged essentially to the years *entre deux guerres*, a period that had thought of itself as lost and lamented the good times before 1914, but was itself to be looked back to as the golden age of modern art, literature, science, and philosophy.

SARTRE AND EXISTENTIALISM

A novel called *Nausea*, destined to be regarded as possibly the most significant of the decade, received relatively little attention outside France upon its publication in 1938. Its author, Jean-Paul Sartre, a young *lycée* teacher who had been a *normalien* (student at one of the "great schools" that select the cream of the cream among French youngsters), leaped to fame during and just after the war, becoming the acknowledged leader of a generation of intellectuals; his qualifications for this role included an extraordinary versatility, for he was philosopher, psychologist, dramatist, and political activist as well as novelist. Under the rubric of Existentialism, his Parisian school of thought became the leading fashion of the postwar decade, and so might be deferred to the next chapter. But Sartre drew heavily on a strain of philosophy that can be located in the period between the wars. He was deeply indebted to the German philosophers Edmund Husserl and Martin Heidegger, whose thought he brought vividly alive in plays and novels, and also gave his own interpretation in his 1943 philosophical work *Being and Nothingness*.

Heidegger's *Being and Time* (1927) was a seminal and quite influential book in Germany.[8] He had been a student of Husserl, the founder of "phenomenology" (a term taken from Hegel), in 1901. Born in Moravia about the same time as Freud, this German-Jewish philosopher was also interested in the inner self, though his explorations took a different form than Freud's. He sought to study pure consciousness scientifically, by somehow "bracketing out" all content—rather like taking all the merchandise off the shelves in order to disclose their shape. These original states of consciousness remind us of Kant's categories of the understand-

---

[8]See the striking passage in Hans-Georg Gadamer, *Philosophical Hermeneutics*, trans. David Linge (1976), pp. 133–39, testifying to its impact on young Germans looking for new answers amid the postwar wreckage.

ing, but on a deeper level (our Logic, like other ideas, is an invention of the mind; what lies behind it?). The search proved elusive, probably impossible; that consciousness cannot stand outside consciousness is rather like Wittgenstein's discovery that there is no metalanguage in which we can talk about language.

Heidegger added moral relevance to the austere scientism of Husserl. Inside consciousness lurks that Being with which modern European humanity has lost touch. The German philosopher, who never published the promised second volume of *Sein und Zeit* (he got hung up on Being, one might say), and who fell silent in the Nazi years after an initial sympathy with Hitler that was to compromise his standing, like Wittgenstein left behind a large body of writing upon his death in 1976, on the basis of which he has been widely regarded as among the greatest thinkers of the century.[9] There were differences between Husserl, Heidegger, and Sartre; in fact, each rejected the others. But they shared the same deep thirst for the strange reality that lies behind all ideas, all thought, at the very basis of consciousness. What lies there, as pure receptivity, anterior to all objects?

Consciousness must have objects, it is that form of being that responds to or "intends" objects. In Sartre's exciting version, phenomenology becomes bitterly pessimistic though tinged with a dash of desperate hope. Sartre radicalized Heidegger's concept of the self by depriving it of any essence or transcendence; consciousness is a nothingness, a "hole in being," "a great wind blowing toward objects," a radically different kind of being from everything in the objective world. It is totally free and undetermined. It demands objects, and must objectify other people. Existential or phenomenological psychology was to become an exciting subject; it had already been pioneered by Heidegger himself and by Ludwig Binswanger and Karl Jaspers. Sartre's powerful imagination was to bring it vividly alive in novels and plays. He had a rare ability to fuse literature and philosophy, something learned in part from his early mentor Alain, and done better, perhaps, only by his idol Dostoyevsky.

The Husserlian hero of *Nausée*, Roquentin, has been stripped down to bare existence indeed; he has no job and no home, he loses his girl and is friendless; his only task is finishing his doctoral dissertation in history, which he abandons as meaningless and dishonest. He is reduced to pure consciousness, his bare humanity. In this state of pure freedom—released from being determined by others—Roquentin first experiences nausea (at his own face in the mirror, his flesh, his "facticity") and a schizoid sense of his outer self being an inert object. Roquentin was an appropriate metaphysical hero for our time, when our plight is indeed so often loneliness, anomie, uncertain identity.

Roquentin finally is partly rescued from his anxiety at the absurdity of existence and his insecure identity by realizing that his consciousness, just because it lacks any determinate structure, is infinitely free. It can choose any-

---

[9]Not to the other school of philosophy. A. J. Ayer's *History of Philosophy in the Twentieth Century* (1982) devotes only a few dismissive lines to Heidegger.

thing it likes and fashion its own being. There is no Self, but consciousness can manufacture one.

The war about to break out caught Sartre up in it along with all other French people, forced him into new roles, and surprisingly made him into a national hero as well as a literary sensation. He was to persevere in an amazing project of writing and living—writing about his life, living his writing, fusing the so often incompatible worlds of art and experience as few other moderns have ever done. His greater fame and the bulk of his writing came after 1940, a year that saw Hitler's tank columns slice through France to begin five years of European horror and heroism.

An important source of what came, rather loosely, to be called Existentialism (and there were many; it was a sort of "perennial philosophy," marked less by a doctrine than an attitude) was the mid-nineteenth-century Danish clergyman Søren Kierkegaard. Discovered in the twentieth century (not translated into English until 1938, though known in Germany earlier in the century), Kierkegaard was an influence on Kafka, among others: the sense of a nameless generalized fear that runs through most of Kafka's works is Kierkegaard's *Angst.* "The Kierkegaard renaissance is one of the strangest phenomena of our times," F. Heinemann remarked in the 1950s. Kierkegaard died in 1855 at forty-two, a poor unknown. His intense personalism and demand for total commitment, his hatred of the crowd, institutions, phony external substitutes for inward experience, reminded many of Nietzsche, but unlike the latter, the Danish Lutheran pastor was deeply religious. "Existence is prior to essence," Kierkegaard declared. The point seems to resemble Marx's, that one must start with concrete human beings, not Hegelian ideas; and indeed it was Hegel that both reacted against. But Marx had ended with another abstraction, the proletariat. Only individual consciousness exists. What Kierkegaard bequeathed to existentialism was his vivid exposition of the soul's journey from anxiety and dread to the "leap" of faith; the individual chooses and wins existence by reaching out to a transcendent Being who is not "understood" but is encountered.

It was this kind of desperate faith, "on the far side of despair," that Europe was to have need of during the dark days that followed.

9

World War II and Its Aftermath

REPEATED SHOCK

"The historian should compare the pictures of August 1, 1914, and September 1, 1939, carefully," Ludwig Marcuse wrote in his memoirs. "War beginning and war beginning are not the same." One major difference was that the second world war, unlike the first, began with no tremulous excitement and hymns in praise of battle, no hosannas to war. A great majority of intellectuals and almost everybody else had spent the last two decades renouncing war and vowing never to fight again. Forced to do so to combat a terrible threat, people in the Western democracies went to war more in a spirit of glum distaste than exuberant adventure. (This was also true in Germany.) Though Hitler was a much more obvious evil than Kaiser Wilhelm, and much more arrant an aggressor, public opinion in 1939 was less unanimous than in 1914. "It is strange," T. S. Eliot mused, "that in 1914 we did not expect war and were not confused when it came. Now we have been expecting war for some time but are confused when it has come."

Confusion stemmed partly from the reluctance of a pacifist-minded public, distracted by other problems, to face the Nazi menace resolutely. Writing in 1936 (*Which Way to Peace?*), Bertrand Russell faced the issue with his usual clarity, and perhaps with his usual perversity decided that surrender to Hitler was preferable to making war against him. In the end not even he could abide by that. Most intellectuals welcomed the Munich cave-in to Germany with relief ("a thousand times right!" Simone Weil declared), but the mood swung sharply after that as Hitler increased his demands and seemed bent on mastering the continent. Politicians shifted abruptly and after selling out Czechoslovakia, decided to fight for indefensible Poland. There was considerable underestimation of the threat: Hitler was a paper tiger, the bizarre National Socialist regime would collapse quickly, perhaps even without war. The Nazi-Soviet pact of August 1939, forced the Communists into opposing war against Germany; they were soon trying to organize strikes against military production in France.

Failure to resist Hitler's demands from the start, which Monday quarterbacks later argued should have been done, owed something to an uneasy conscience about the last peace settlement. The interwar years had witnessed a large-scale battle of historians over the causes and origins and blame for the 1914 war, often semantically confused but with massive intrusions into the archives. The result was mainly a victory for the "revisionists," who argued against sole German guilt or responsibility. Germany was no more to blame than Russia and France; perhaps one might blame the "system," whether economic, political, or human. Most of the British public wondered if Hitler's demands for the return of the Rhineland and the Saar to full German sovereignty, even the annexation of Germans in Austria and the fringe of Czechoslovakia, were not just ones. Prime Minister Neville Chamberlain declared in March 1939 that, "however much we might take exception to the methods," all of Germany's gains up to then might be defended, "whether on account of racial affinity or of just claims too long resisted." Later excoriated as a craven, the "appeaser" prime minister was in fact quite in step with public opinion.

This war turned out to be quite a different one from the last in almost all respects except its terrible destructiveness. Prepared for a defensive struggle like the last time, the French watched the German *Panzer* divisions slice through their lines and race around to outflank them in a war of dazzling movement. As Hitler's temporary ally Stalin took the Baltic states and attacked Finland, while sharing Poland with the Germans in another partition of that unhappy land, the German legions overran France and the Low Countries in six weeks.

The hero of Jean-Paul Sartre's autobiographical novel *Death in the Soul* (one of series called collectively *Roads to Liberty*) died defiantly fighting the Germans; in real life Sartre was quietly captured after all his officers had surrendered. Thus does fiction repair the failures of life. Sartre's actual experience was all too typical of France's dismal collapse. His dramatic existentialist ethic would have it that the German occupation forced stark choices on French people: to collaborate or to resist. Many brave people did go underground and work as Allied agents, though to a surprising degree business (and pleasure) as usual prevailed; it is a bit startling to find Sartre's friend Simone de Beauvoir on a skiing vacation in the last months of the war. Albert Camus, another Existentialist, edited the Resistance organ *Combat*. He joined the Communist Party for a time.

During the war the Communists won a great deal of prestige by their loyal work in the anti-Nazi cause. In the French Resistance, two oddly different groups came to the fore: Christians and Communists. Both had enough faith to meet the dangerous demands of the underground. Both produced heroes like those of Camus and Sartre. After 1945, the Communist Party (in France and Italy) and the Christian Democratic or Christian Social parties (in France the MRP, Popular Republican Movement) emerged from the war as the leading political groups. In both defeated countries, Germany and Italy, the Christian parties, which had scarcely existed before, dominated postwar politics. The few who had dared to defy Hitler in Germany were mainly committed Christians, like the brothers Bonhoeffer.

Propaganda in World War II was a feeble thing compared with that of World War I. "Democracy" took on a new aura; the virtues of the free society might be tawdry ones, but they looked good compared to Hitler's tyranny. "None of the evils that totalitarianism claims to remedy is worse than totalitarianism itself," Camus declared. *Democracy Marches*, Julian Huxley announced in 1941. American vice-president Henry A. Wallace proclaimed it *The Century of the Common Man* (compare C. J. Friedrich, *The New Belief in the Common Man*, 1942), and composer Aaron Copland wrote a "Fanfare for the Common Man" (whoever he might be). A collection edited by a Marxist literary critic, Bernard Smith, was titled *The Democratic Spirit*. But these were mainly Americanisms.

So abhorrent was the Nazi regime that few in the United States and Great Britain opposed the war, though there were far more "conscientious objectors" than in 1914–18. Nevertheless, indiscriminate, virtually terrorist aerial bombing of German and Japanese cities (even before the use of the atomic bomb on Japan in August 1945) elicited some protests. The man who was to become probably the USA's greatest poet, Robert Lowell, wrote President Roosevelt a letter in August 1943 declining his invitation to serve in the armed forces because of the bombing and the Allied policy of demanding "unconditional surrender" from the German government. FDR proving unsympathetic, the poet spent some not unpleasant months in jail.

Such gestures were rare. The left, formerly so pacifist, had been converted wholeheartedly to all-out war against fascism at the side of Soviet Russia. No one is so bloody-minded as a radical turned patriot, it had been said; something like that was the case here. Relations between hardline Communists and those fellow travelers put off by the Nazi-Soviet pact improved dramatically after June 1941; once again, all left-liberal factions could unite in a popular front against Hitlerism. Though conservatives worried about the alliance with Russia, few saw any alternative to prosecuting the war on an all-out basis. Disagreement tended to focus on the "unconditional surrender" policy as insuring the total destruction of German power and thus leaving a vacuum the Soviets were bound to fill. Soviet sympathizers within the Allied governments worked to prevent a compromise peace.[1] The question of whether cooperation with anti-Hitler elements (especially

---

[1]The famous Soviet spy Kim Philby, a high-ranking British intelligence officer, helped block connections to anti-Nazi groups in Germany during the war to prevent any compromise short of Germany's total destruction.

in the army) might not have averted or shortened the war, reaching back as far as a missed opportunity at the time of the Munich pact in 1938, became a major postwar controversy.

The question of the Holocaust, the Nazi slaughter of the Jews, came up later as a serious criticism of Allied policy—could they have done more to halt it? But during the war the issue barely existed. There was initially a reluctance to believe the horror stories, partly because World War I atrocity tales so often turned out to have been deliberately manufactured as propaganda. (World War I British civil servants spent the interwar years confessing their lies.) It is a remarkable fact that few in the Allied countries, even Jewish leaders there, believed the stories of mass extermination of Jews as late, certainly, as the summer of 1942. The evidence became overpowering enough to force its way into public consciousness only in 1944. Allied leaders avoided publicizing it, thinking it would somehow impede the war effort. Only in the latter days of the war did the murder camps at Auschwitz, Majdanek, and Treblinka attain their frightful notoriety. Those who wanted to blame the greatest of historic crimes on the German people had to face the fact that non-Germans had long refused to credit these stories.

At the war's end, invading American soldiers received orders not to talk to Germans or be kind to them; General Eisenhower said that Germans were beasts. One of the century's greatest composers, Anton Webern, was killed when he left his home to buy a bottle of wine. An American historian has recently claimed that hundreds of thousands of German war prisoners died of cruel treatment and neglect. But mistreatment of the Germans did not last long. Camus said that "revenge is sour," and argued that the taint of Nazism was one that all Europe might share. The revenge taken against "collaborators" or Vichyites (supporters of Marshall Petain's subservient government which Hitler allowed to govern a portion of France until 1944) was surprisingly mild. It has been estimated that about 12,000 were killed, 100,000 arrested.

In England, the psychology of a beleaguered people bravely holding off a powerful and ruthless foe worked throughout the war to draw the nation together. The brotherhood born in London during the air raids of 1940–41 created an atmosphere of hope for a new era of economic equality. Successful management of the war economy encouraged an optimism about the chances of using this power for peacetime purposes. As a participant later recalled, "There was in the air an eagerness and vigour, a belief that change was not merely desirable but actually possible." The cake of custom had been broken, the chance existed for a fresh start. The sad days of life on the dole in the thirties must not recur. To William Beveridge, author of the famed wartime report in Britain *Full Employment in a Free Society*, the price of economic planning had always before seemed too high, in loss of freedom, and he did not accompany his friends the Webbs on their journey into Stalinland. But during the war, as his biographer José Harris records, Beveridge "had become convinced that some form of planning was no longer an option but a sheer necessity." His book set forth the Keynesian program of government directing the economy toward full employment by wise fiscal management, as well as making the case for expanded social services.

Edward Hulton's *The New Age* (1943) was the book of a conservative convert who financed the popular progressive paper *Picture Post*. This euphoric mood, which did not long survive postwar realities, accounted for the unexpected Labour party election victory of 1945, which unseated the government of Winston Churchill that had led Britain to victory in the war.

Jean Monnet, the French prophet of "planification" (as well as European union), believed that "The same cooperation, the same mobilization of material and human resources" could supply the energy to turn France's stagnant economy around and push it toward modernization. "Modernization or downfall" was Monnet's slogan. It seems clear that the shock of defeat and military occupation brought something of a revolution in France, marked by new ideas and new leaders. The war wiped out old political parties, brought former political enemies together, and produced a new vision of France, "a new France competing in growth, vigor, and material power with her neighbors" (Robert Paxton).

For the Germans, defeat, humiliation, the ruin of most of their cities from air bombardment, constituted a disaster so great that only a completely new beginning was possible. Those who survived the horrors often testified to a strange exhilaration from the shock of losing every material possession, from living with danger and fear. It produced something akin to Sartre's picture of humanity pared of everything except its bare humanity, its elementary consciousness. Life was given more value by being made precarious; simple objects acquired value. What Karl Jaspers called "boundary situations" brought people up against elemental human values, and served as a kind of purgative, a cure for shallowness and complacency. Sartre caught this spirit when he said, "Never were we so free as when enslaved" in a prison camp.

The war stimulated technological progress, of the sort that might (or might not) prove useful in the future. Often this was a matter of European brains mating fruitfully with American technology. European scientists worked in the United States to help develop the atomic bomb, first successfully tested on July 16, 1945, and used on Japan soon thereafter. The father of electronic computers is said to be a German, John von Neumann; but Alan Turing brought the digital computer into effective being at Bletchley Park in England, where thousands of people worked deciphering intercepted German wireless messages during the war. Further computer development took place in the United States, supported by the government for military reasons.

At the beginning of the war a desperate British push to create a workable "radar" system to provide warning of German air attacks saved the country; an eventual outgrowth of radar was the transistor revolution, leading to the microchip revolution. The war gave a crucial boost to the most important medical advance of the century, the discovery of penicillin. (Developed at Oxford just before the war by the Australian Florey and a Jewish refugee from Hitler, Ernst Chain, it languished from lack of support until the U.S. government stepped in during the war.) Aircraft design was another area where wartime needs stimulated significant technology. Prof. A. P. Speiser has written that during World War II "the groundwork was laid for U.S. leadership in such fields as electronics, communications, computer technology, aircraft construction, satellite technology, atomic energy...." France was to build the finest railroad system in the world on the base of wartime ruins.

Victory in the "wizard war" of high-tech military and intelligence operations went decidedly to the Allies. That Germany was years behind the U.S.–Great Britain team in development of the atomic bomb owed something to the latter's spectacular success in the intelligence area. The British pulled off the war's greatest coup by cracking the German code and then manipulating German agents in Britain. Werner Heisenberg may have sabotaged the German atomic effort; it is certain that Frederic Joliot-Curie in Paris smuggled out important information to England. A pioneer in "heavy water," the kind containing the rare isotope of hydrogen needed for a successful atomic explosion, the French scientist helped to keep a supply of this from the Germans. Later, with the aid of their intelligence network, the British sank a crucial shipment of heavy water, a key factor in slowing the pace of German progress toward the A-bomb. They also contrived the escape of ace atomic physicist Niels Bohr from Denmark.

In a short space we cannot come close to doing justice to this mighty historic panorama; we can only suggest a few themes. The war, a vast convulsion that shook the entire world (it was much more a "world war" than the 1914–18 one) was a bizarre mixture of good and evil—unbelievable bloodshed and devastation, immense crimes, population upheavals, but also a remarkable creativity stimulated by its needs, and by the destruction that leveled bad as well as good things, including city slums and outmoded attitudes.

POSTWAR PERSPECTIVES

The continent of Europe stood devastated and stunned at the war's end, as indeed did the whole of what Winston Churchill called "an outraged and quivering world." Gabriel Marcel, the French Existentialist, wrote of "the more than physical horror and anxiety I experienced in walking among the ruins of inner Vienna in 1946, or more recently in Caen, Rouen or Würzburg." Germany's major cities were all heaps of rubble, in proportions ranging from 60 to 95 percent (Berlin). A vast area of Russia had been totally ravaged, the Polish capital of Warsaw was nearly gone, Yugoslavia's casualties were proportionately greater than even Germany's or Russia's. These physical ruins were manifestations of the moral ruins displayed in Hitler's extermination of the Jews.

Marcel went on to note that for many, the corollary was a rejection of the European heritage (*The Decline of Wisdom*, 1954). A number of books of 1946 fitted Marcel's generalization: Old H. G. Wells wrote *Mind at the End of Its Tether*, and Max Weber's brother Alfred, *Farewell to European History (Abschied von der Bisherigen Geschichte)*. *The Passing of the European Age*, title of a notable historical work, seemed evident; power had passed to the Americans, the Russians, perhaps to the Chinese, who were dividing the world among them. Arnold J. Toynbee's mordant volumes (IV–VI of *A Study of History*) on civilizations in decline and disintegration had come out in 1939, after an inquest that started in the 1920s; they struck the post-1945 mood as just right. Toynbee's ultimate judgment cast blame on a spiritual decay stemming from the poison of materialism: "We are betrayed by what is false within." A faint ray of hope remained, however, since nothing human is wholly determined.

A shattered and exhausted Europe was occupied by Soviet and American soldiers, both of whom some Europeans looked upon as barbarians from outside. It quickly became evident that the Russians intended no liberation, but a new enslavement to communism. Most West Europeans soon came to look upon the Americans as allies against the menace of Soviet power, and many were glad to clasp hands with the democratic land of the New World. The fact remains that quite a few bearers of European culture regarded Russia and America as the same, basically, as Heidegger put it; "the same dreary technological frenzy, the same unrestricted organization of the average man" (*An Introduction to Metaphysics*, trans. 1959). This apart from a Communist minority that, especially in France and Italy, sided with the Soviets in the Cold War that quickly broke out as the two victors quarreled over the spoils.

The years immediately after 1945 were disappointing to those who had expected that the end of the war, the purging of Nazism from the German system (symbolically performed at the Nuremberg trials of 1946), the establishment of the United Nations, would bring brighter days. The quarrel between the Soviet Union, led by a confident and intransigent Stalin (sure that capitalism was now on its last legs), and the Western alliance led by the United States threatened a renewal of war—another in a self-perpetuating cycle, "wars in a chain reaction," as French writer Raymond Aron titled a book. By 1954 far more destructive nuclear weapons were available than the ones that had wiped out the Japanese cities of Hiroshima and Nagasaki at the end of World War II, guaranteeing that the seemingly inevitable next war would put a finish to much of the world.

EXISTENTIALISM

In France, and in a large degree throughout the western world (Albert Camus is said to have been the most popular French literary figure ever to visit the United States), Existentialism supplied the immediate postwar period's most impressive and widely known philosophy or ideology.

Up to 1940 Sartre was a pure intellectual, thinking only of his writing, the only possible route out of the trap of inauthentic being. But "The war taught me that one must be engaged, committed." A prisoner of war for nearly a year after June 1940, Sartre found solidarity with people of all sorts in the prison camp. He wrote a play for the people of Stalag XII, a parable on the theme of resisting oppression. After contriving his release from the camp, he played some part in the underground resistance movement as editor and writer. In 1943 the Germans allowed his play *The Flies* to be presented in Paris, though its message of resistance to tyrants (and their abettors) was transparent enough. In this version of Eschylus's ancient Greek tragedy, the Furies who pursue Orestes and Electra, after the brother and sister have killed their mother to avenge their father, become the eponymous flies; harmless creatures, like their master Zeus, if you choose not to believe in them.

Sartre had published his philosophical treatise *Being and Nothingness (L'etre et le néant)* in 1943 also. Upon the liberation of Paris in 1944, his most famous play, *No Exit*, was the first to be performed. He had become overnight a remarkable kind of national and intellectual hero. Sartre's fellow Frenchman, the Algerian-born novelist and essayist Camus, joined him in leadership of "the second lost generation" after 1945. Existentialism's fashionable ethic, spreading from the cafés of Montmartre, combined disillusioned pessimism with a pinch of desperate hope in just the right proportions. Camus, the handsome ex-athlete who rose to fame with equal rapidity during the war, was an eloquent speaker and activist as well as writer of novels and essays. It has been claimed that his rise was "unparalleled in the history of French literature."

Unlike the decidedly bourgeois Sartre (brought up by a professor grandfather), Camus was authentically working class, raised in poverty in Algiers by his illiterate Spanish mother after his father died on the Marne when Camus was a year old; he shared with Sartre this fatherlessness. He studied philosophy at the University of Algiers between 1932 and 1936. The hero of his first novel (1942), *The Stranger*, strikingly resembles Sartre's Roquentin in being a man whose objective existence is alien to him. Camus' 1943 parallel to *Being and Nothingness, The Myth of Sisyphus*, made the Nietzschean, Existentialist point that we must strive in spite of the absurdity of existence. It is a slighter work than Sartre's. Camus had little of Sartre's theoretical brilliance, but in many ways he offered a more attractive intellectual personality. He was to win a Nobel Prize at the age of forty-four, before dying in an accident in 1960 when he was only forty-seven. His novels of the 1950s, *The Plague* and *The Fall*, matched Sartre's brilliant succession of plays. Ultimately he quarreled with Sartre on the question chiefly of communism. But Camus had belonged to the Party at one time.

We previously noted the roots of Existentialism in the thought of the philosophers Husserl and Heidegger, as well as Kierkegaard and Nietzsche. In one of the war's many intellectual adventures, Husserl's manuscripts were rescued from the Nazis and carried to Belgium, where they now repose. Heidegger lived on to enhance his reputation, though like Wittgenstein the bulk of his writing would be published only after his death. They were not the only forbears of Sartre and

Camus, and of their colleague Maurice Merleau-Ponty, who joined them in editing *Les temps modernes*. The German philosopher Karl Jaspers, who was forced out of teaching by the Nazis and narrowly escaped the concentration camp, lived in Switzerland after the war, refusing like Einstein to return to his homeland. He was a very prolific and popular writer. He had begun his career in medicine, moved to psychology, and hence to philosophy; influenced by Nietzsche and Max Weber, his path crossed those of Husserl, Freud, and Jung. An early (1913) book pioneered phenomenological psychiatry. After World War I Jaspers obtained a philosophy chair at Heidelberg but encountered hostility from more traditional philosophers until in 1932 his *Philosophy* stamped him as an exciting proponent of the *Existenzphilosophie*. (Like almost all of those identified with Existentialism, Jaspers eventually denied that he was an "existentialist.") His most famous work, *Man in the Modern Age* (1931) was translated into sixteen languages and read by millions—a seminal book of the thirties fit to place side by side with *Brave New World* and *Nausea*. It called for a recovery of essential selfhood in an era when the human personality stood in danger of extinction.

It is of the nature of the human being to be unique, a concrete particular not to be understood by membership in a class or group, like other objects. True, insofar as people are flesh they partake of objective being, subject to its laws and determinism; moreover, society is always at work trying to make them into stereotyped objects. My own past, insofar as I look at it as something vanished and dead, is being of this sort. But human consciousness, as it exists in our minds every moment, is a radically different kind of being. In Sartre's vocabulary, ultimately derived from Hegel, the *pour-soi* or for-itself is human consciousness, while *en soi* or being-in-itself is objective being. The *pour-soi* is really not being at all, but a receptivity, a kind of "hole in being"—a negativity, with the capacity to respond to objects. In contrast to other forms of Existentialism, which posited either a God or some sort of metaphsyical Being (Heidegger and Jaspers), Sartre's was defiantly atheistic. There can be no God, for consciousness submits to no generalization, there can be no *pour-soi* in general, only distinct pieces of what Heidegger called being-there, *Dasein*. As Kingsley Amis put it, "The unaided and self-constituted human spirit [is] the final proof of the non-existence of God."

In his leading works, especially the early ones by which he became known, Sartre seemed to deny that there can be happy relations with other people. The human situation is an impossible one because we want to have objective being, grounded in necessity, yet we are condemned to be the other kind of being, one that has no objectivity or necessity. When we are constituted in the eyes of other people, they make objects of us, which is humiliating and inauthentic; they must do this, as we do to them, because consciousness can respond only to objects. People both need and resent this objectification; it gives them their role in society, but at the cost of inner integrity. In sum, we are condemned to try to reconcile radically different and irreconcilable modes of existence. "Man is a useless passion"; "a being who is what he is not and is not what he is."

"Hell is other people," as Sartre put it in his best-known play, *No Exit*. The worst is that we cannot do without this hell. At the end of this absorbing psychological-metaphysical drama, the three people who are torturing each other have a chance to leave the room in which they have been condemned to coexist; but they do not take it. Sartre was especially good at describing the frustrations of love, a "game of mirrors" in which lovers torment each other, attempting the impossible task of avoiding objectification, capturing the other's *pour-soi*. It was a game, however, that he himself never ceased to play.

SARTRE AND COMMUNISM

Sartre, Camus, and Merleau-Ponty moved on to intellectual leadership of the postwar decade. Their organ *Les temps modernes*, a title Sartre borrowed from Charlie Chaplin, became the world's foremost serious magazine. It featured their quarrels as well as their agreements. The dramatic clash between Soviet communism and American-led resistance to it made for immense excitement amid the sense of dismay at a new conflict. The Marshall Plan, the North Atlantic Treaty Organization, tightening Soviet control over Eastern Europe, Yugoslavia's clash with the Soviets, the Berlin blockade, the emergence of China's Communist regime followed by the Korean war, all these episodes of the Cold War forced people to choose sides again. The choice was painful for many European intellectuals. They were instinctively anti-American, and they had been pro-Soviet, but more and more stories about the death of millions in Soviet labor camps disquieted them. Like accounts of the Holocaust, such tales initially were not believed, but the evidence gradually became overwhelming.

Sartre's struggles with Marxism and communism led him back and forth. Camus had once been a Communist but left the Party. So too had Malraux; shocked by revelations about Stalin, he asked the Russian tyrant "What have you done with our dream?" More than a few noticed the chameleon-like quality of the Existentialist ethic, which asked only total sincerity in making a choice based on one's particular situation. (To those who applied to him for advice, Sartre was inclined to say, "Make up your own mind, just be sure you are totally sincere and do not lean on rules made by others.") Politically, the result might be a quasi-conservatism, hostile to all ideologies, those "smelly little orthodoxies," as George Orwell called them, including communism as well as Nazism, that had poisoned the interwar years.

Sartre felt this way for a time after the war. He had never shown much interest in Marxism, and his 1945–47 writings dismiss official Marxism as a debased philosophy with harmful effects: "The policy of Stalinist Communism is incompatible with the honest exercise of the literary profession." He associated himself with an anti-Stalinist "Socialism and Liberty" group. He founded a brief-lived Rally for Revolutionary Democracy which included some ex-Trotskyites, and he supported

Yugoslavia's dissident Communists in their tilts with Stalin. The Communist Party denounced him. His popular play *Dirty Hands (Les mains sales)*, which he later tried to suppress, seemed to rebuke the bad faith of those who surrender their will to the Party.

His friend and fellow Existentialist Albert Camus, like George Orwell in England, became almost obsessively convinced that the "concentration camp socialism" into which Russian communism had degenerated was a monstrous fraud from which true socialism needed to be rescued. Sartre himself was not far from this position between about 1946 and 1950, the years of the democratic rally against the USSR that gave rise to the Marshall Plan and the NATO alliance. On the other hand, the Communist Party had earned credits by valiant service in the wartime Resistance. Sartre had met and learned to respect Communists in the underground. He wished not so much to oppose communism as to rescue it from the dead hand of Stalinism. A mechanical materialism actually destroys the possibility of revolution, he observed, since it neglects the all-important subjective side; robots do not rebel, the decision to rebel takes place in a consciousness.

The discovery at this time of another Marx assisted this line of thought—the Kremlin had distorted and misused Marx's authority, critical students were finding. Sartre presented himself as a better Communist than the Soviet rulers—more royalist than the king! His offer to help them out by supplying a more up-to-date philosophy and psychology naturally did not please the Kremlin priests. This bohemian with his pessimistic subjectivism and his ties to Heidegger impressed them as even sinister. French Communist intellectuals who later apologized to Sartre called him a fascist at this time. But Sartre's popularity with young French radicals could hardly be dismissed.

Sartre swung far over toward communism between 1951 and 1955. He visited Russia and China. He accused the Americans of practicing biological warfare in Korea. He also underwent psychoanalysis in 1953 and wrote his autobiography of childhood, the fascinating *Les Mots* (The Words), a kind of session on the couch. (Begun in 1953–54, the book was laid aside and not finished until later; it was published in 1963.) He broke again with the Party in 1956, but would approach it once more in the sixties—a love-hate relationship with the surrogate father. Camus, meanwhile, went in the other direction. He remained true to Existential personalism. A Christian feeling of guilt appears in *The Fall* (1956), as the problem of evil haunted *The Plague*; both novels featured Existential heroes who do their best to alleviate suffering while knowing that like suffering itself, such efforts are pointless, absurd. "Beware both nihilism and utopianism" was the message of Camus' study *The Rebel*; the worship of abstractions is the danger. Revolutionaries end by creating tyrannies worse than those they rebel against, Camus thought. As Yeats had written, the beggars change places, but the lash goes on.

A hostile review in *Les temps modernes* of *L'homme revolté* marked the beginning of the Sartre–Camus split; Camus' low-key spiritual nonconformist was very different from the violent political revolutionary Sartre was beginning to favor. Camus, a genuine proletarian, accused Sartre and his friends of being armchair revolutionaries, in which there was much truth. He soon quarreled bitterly with Sartre over the Algerian war as well as communism.

Raymond Aron told Sartre he could not be the heir of both Marx and Kierkegaard, but Sartre thought he could. The "new" Marx, rescued from the Kremlin bureaucrats, in Sartre's hands turned out to look like an Existentialist. Men make their own history by their free choices; their subjectivity interacts with an ossified social order that is the product of past struggles with a niggardly nature. In choosing to revolt they overcome alienation and forge real bonds of interpersonal communication.

Sartre came to believe that Marxism, of this existentialized sort, is the necessary, basic philosophy for modern individuals: "our thoughts, whatever they are, can take shape only upon this humus." The assertion struck many as bizarre. By 1951 Sartre had evidently passed over to orthodox communism; though he never joined it, he was saying that one must not criticize the Communist Party even if it is wrong, that the USSR is a free society, or even—if we read his play *The Devil and the Good Lord* this way—that ruthless tyrants are necessary. In 1954 (the year after Stalin's death, but before the 1956 repudiation of him by Nikita Khrushchev) Sartre was an honored guest in the USSR, drinking so much vodka he had to be hospitalized upon his return. Merleau-Ponty accused him of "ultra-bolshevism," inconsistent with Existentialist belief in freedom.

When Soviet tanks crushed the Hungarian revolution in 1956, Sartre denounced the repression and along with numerous other intellectuals and Party members was disgusted with the French Communist Party for defending it. His reaction was to attempt a massive work of social theory, *The Critique of Dialectical Reason*, of which the first volume was published in 1960. The second volume never appeared, though portions of it were printed after Sartre's death and one part came out separately in his lifetime as *The Ghost of Stalin*. He wanted to rescue Marx from the Kremlin, with the aid of the newly discovered writings, and create a Marxian theory of history that would come to terms with real human beings rather than abstract conceptualizations. In the end, Sartre ceased to think of himself as a Marxist, remarking that Marx was all right for his own day but irrelevant now. But the *Critique* played some part in the revival of left-wing revolutionary ideas in the 1960s, dealt with in the next chapter.

While his friend Raymond Aron wrote of "the end of the socialist myth," Sartre became one of the chief prophets of a new wave of radicalism. One of his greatest plays, translated as *The Condemned of Altona*, performed in 1960, contains elements of his profoundly interesting depth psychology, but was widely construed as a commentary on the alleged use of torture in the Algerian revolution then going on. Angry French Algerians bombed Sartre's apartment, and thousands of veterans marched through Parisian streets shouting "Kill Sartre!" He had become a public personage, a political symbol.

THE DECLINE OF COMMUNISM

During the war communism did well in many parts of the war-ravaged continent, where the Red Army was now the leading opponent of Hitler's Germany and Communists took the lead in organizing anti-fascist resistance movements. This was the case not only in France but in Yugoslavia, where Tito's Partisans proved the ablest fighters against the Germans and were able to surmount that multi-ethnic country's disunities. One example of a French convert was the distinguished scientist Frederic Joliot-Curie, son-in-law of the famous discoverers of radium and husband of another great woman physicist. The Joliot-Curies stayed in France to play a dangerous game with the Germans, who hoped to get help from them in building an atomic bomb. He discreetly avoided that while tipping off the Allies. By 1943 he had come to believe that the Communists were the best leaders of the Resistance, an opinion he shared with many others. He became a quite uncritical and obsessive believer in Stalin's USSR, not the only example of scientists' political gullibility. Joliot-Curie implied that he would not fight for France in a war against the Soviet Union. His enthusiastic pro-Soviet position led him to visit the USSR to accept a Stalin prize and to attend the world peace conferences the Soviets sponsored in the postwar years as they attempted to slow the pace of Western armament while they were building their own bomb.

There is no evidence that Joliot-Curie helped the USSR build its bombs, the fission "atomic" bomb in 1949 and then the much more powerful fusion "H-bomb" a few years later, but Bruno Pontecorvo, one of his former colleagues at the Radium Institute and a dedicated Communist, did. Pontecorvo went to the United States after the fall of France. In 1943 the Italian scientist took his atomic expertise to Canada where he worked on heavy water research along with another Communist, the Cambridge-trained Alan Nunn May. Pontecorvo later went to England to work on the British atomic bomb at Harwell; then in 1951 he defected to the Soviet Union to give valuable aid to the USSR's H-bomb project.

The surprisingly rapid Soviet development of nuclear weapons owed much to a plentiful supply of information they received from devoted European and American Communists. Nunn May and later (1950) another European scientist, the German Klaus Fuchs, confessed to passing nuclear secrets to Russia. Both had had abundant access to the Manhattan Project, where the first atomic bomb was assembled during World War II. The most sensational revelations of spying for the Soviets began to unfold in May 1951, when two highly placed British intelligence officers fled to Russia. The story led back to Cambridge in the 1930s, and eventually implicated a number of others, including celebrated art historian Anthony Blunt, custodian of the queen's own art collection. From key positions in British diplomatic and intelligence service Guy Burgess, Douglas Maclean, Kim Philby, and Blunt passed valuable information to Moscow up to at least 1951. The story of the generation that defected to Marxism and sometimes spied for Russia inspired a notable literature (and has continued to do so). Rebecca West's *The Meaning of Treason* stood out in this category. (She included some British defectors to Germany during the war.)[2]

Shocked reactions to spy revelations in the atmosphere of the Cold War were often extreme. A witch hunt against suspected spies made every liberal a potential traitor. "McCarthyism," a term derived from the particularly paranoid American senator, helped turn Sartre and others against the anti-Communist camp. Ethel and Julius Rosenberg, American Communists involved in passing atomic secrets to Russia, went to the electric chair in 1951, year also of the jailing of suspected Communist Alger Hiss after a sensational trial for perjury. Hiss was a high U.S. State Department official who had advised President Roosevelt at the Yalta Conference. The Hiss case became a kind of Dreyfus Affair or Sacco-Vanzetti case ranging left against right in bitter ideological confrontation.

A European counterpart was the Kravchenko affair in Paris. Victor Kravchenko was a Soviet defector, author of a book titled *I Chose Freedom*, which a French Communist Party publication called a pack of lies. Kravchenko sued for slander, and during the case Communist officials denied that purges or prison camps existed in the USSR. From this the Party emerged considerably discredited. "The Kravchenko affair sealed the PCF's isolation," as historian Irwin Wall remarks. Maurice Thorez, leader of the PCF, said that in the event of war with Russia, the French people would welcome the Red Army as liberators. "Whoever is anti-Soviet is also anti-French," the party's counsel declared at the Kravchenko trial. The Communist Party was driven into isolation after 1948 as it opposed the Marshall Plan, the NATO alliance, the Yugoslav revolt against Kremlin domination, the defense of West Berlin, and other actions denounced by Stalin's regime as "capitalist imperialism," but seen by most Frenchmen as a necessary reply to the Soviet Union's assault on free institutions.

Isolated they might be, but the Communists retained a solid core of fanatically dedicated followers. In 1951 they gained 21 percent of the vote in elections to the national legislative assembly—more, actually, than any other party, non-Communists being divided among Socialists, two kinds of Gaullists, the Christian MRP (Popular Republican Movement), and miscellaneous other small parties. ("The largest party of all," someone said, consisted of those who did not vote.) Just after the war, the Communists had won 28 percent; they were to continue in slow but steady decline. In general, they held their old faithful, forged in the 1930s and in the war, but they failed to gain new ones. The PCF was made up of true believers for whom the Party was infallible. Perhaps their most extreme fanatic was a woman, Jeanette Vermeersch. This was their strength as well as their weakness: they stood apart from all other politicians as a "countersociety," a beleaguered but

---

[2]She might have included the former king, the abdicated Edward VIII, whose pro-Nazi sympathies were well-known; there is a story that a hold Anthony Blunt had over the royal family was his knowledge of Nazi documents proving Edward's outright treason.

defiant minority. What really defeated them was the growing success of the mainstream society.

History, the history they counted on to vindicate them, was not on their side. The point about Stalin's misdeeds became moot in 1956, when the Soviet leadership itself admitted them. Nikita Khrushchev's sensational "secret speech" shook the world Communist movement to its foundations. In this same year, Russian intervention against attempted revolution in Hungary forced Sartre and most French intellectual Communists to break with Moscow. The post-Stalin Soviet leaders began a difficult struggle to escape a dilemma: how to "liquidate the harmful effects of Stalin's cult of personality" without "undermining the bases of Marxist-Leninist theory" which legitimized the whole Soviet regime (to quote the Central Committee's orders to the leading Soviet historical journal.)

Such a dilemma led the party in the Khrushchev era (1956–64) to vacillate between thaw and refreeze, seeking some degree of honesty and international respectability while fearing to undermine their own authority. That authority was, after all, based on the Stalin regime which they had served and whose structure and basic principles remained unimpaired. The "cult of personality" line, arguing that Stalin was right up to a point but finally became megalomaniac, was a tortured one. Why had no one questioned this trend when it was happening? Not until 1961 was the late dictator's grave removed from Lenin's side on Red Square and his name from place names all over the country. Censorship continued to exist, and "socialist realism" remained the literary standard. Khrushchev continued to support the quack Lysenko, who terrorized reputable Soviet scientists and did great damage to Soviet agriculture. The new Politburo leadership was by no means prepared to license unrestrained freedom of expression.

Nevertheless, faced with a more hesitant and less inhumane repression, a series of attractive dissidents arose in the USSR and soon gained a hearing in the West. Official control of literature and thought had reached a peak in the immediate postwar years, when such great Soviet artists as composers Shostakovitch and Prokofieff and cinema director Eisenstein received rebukes from the party. "Our so-called statesmen lay down the law on what kind of books we are to write and what kind of pictures we are to paint," complained prominent Soviet writer Ilya Ehrenburg. The official position was that "A historian is not an impartial narrator who sets down the facts and arranges them, albeit in a scientifically based scheme. He is a fighter whose aim is to bring the history of the past to the service of the struggle for Communism." George Orwell's famous satire *1984* hardly did justice to the requirement that history must be altered to fit the current Party line. (Condemned to savage imprisonment for approving Russian nationalism in his history of the Napoleonic invasion, Eugene Tarle was released when Stalin changed his mind about Russian nationalism in the later thirties; historians whose mistake it was to have condemned Ivan the Terrible and Peter the Great took his place in the prison camp.)

Now a courageous group of writers claimed a right to do something else than parrot the official government line. It was to be a long hard struggle. When a 1956 thaw following the secret speech produced Vladimir Dudintsev's withering satire on time-serving bureaucrats (*Not by Bread Alone*), Khrushchev threatened to shoot writers and forced abject apologies on them. In 1958 he abused Boris Pasternak and forced him to refuse the Nobel Prize for his novel *Dr. Zhivago*, which this great Russian writer had had published in Italy after it was rejected in the USSR. The novel attracted great international attention and soon become a notable American-made movie. Sartre refused to sign a protest about the treatment of Pasternak French intellectuals sent to the Kremlin, and he was himself to refuse the prize in 1964. But he would subsequently protest the persecution of the Soviet scientist Andrei Sakharov.

The arrest and trial of Daniel and Sinyavsky, two writers who had ventured to offer criticisms of Soviet culture, leaked out and became front-page news in the West. Shaken by this adverse world reaction, Khrushchev fired his cultural advisers and decreed a new thaw in 1961, but this one fizzled out too. In 1962 Khrushchev, muttering obscenities, personally closed an exhibiton of abstract art by the great sculptor Ernst Neizvestny. Visiting Moscow in 1963, Sartre found the Russian leader surly and suspicious. Khrushchev now agreed with Maurice Thorez, the French Communist boss, that Sartre was a dangerous reactionary. In Prague later that year for a writers' conference, Sartre responded that to brand Freud, Kafka, and Joyce as "decadent," the official Soviet line, was to preclude a dialogue. Khruschchev was soon to fall from power, but his successors proved even less liberal.

At this time exhaustive research by Western scholars like Robert Conquest (*The Great Terror*) and by Russian dissidents like Roy Medvedev was beginning to dig out the full story of the Stalin era, and to reveal an inhumanity that surpassed even Hitler's. Stalin's successors no longer cared or dared to use illegal brutality to repress dissent. But they were to resort to the sinister device of sending nonconformists to mental institutions. Perhaps more important, they had none of the great tyrant's charisma. Stalin at least was a true believer; that is why he could send millions to death. They were opposing the march of history and the triumph of truth. Those who followed Khrushchev were faceless bureaucrats, with a tendency toward corruption, trapped in a system they no longer really believed in but couldn't escape. The last vestige of the *mystique* attached to the Russian Revolution had faded. Not even the charisma of Lenin was safe from the corrosions of time and reality. If Stalinization debased it, the post-Stalin era completely destroyed it.

THE END OF IDEOLOGY

If Lenin's communism was the last of the great ideologies, its demise was greeted with considerable relief. Ideologies, like intolerant religions, are creeds teaching hate and leading to slaughter. This was the dominant mood of the 1950s. It was

Camus who had announced "the end of ideology." Substituting logic for human realities had led people to slaughter each other in the name of -isms. The writer whose books almost dominated the British 1950s, George Orwell, expressed the same horror of ideologies, and retreated to concrete personal experience. You cannot kill or torture a real human being, he said, but ideology can condemn whole classes and races as abstractions. After experiencing all those "cruel or fierce political ideologies [which] have played havoc with human welfare," wrote Polish-British historian L. B. Namier, the mature political community learns to do without them altogether.

The retreat to personalism, to concrete realities, was almost forced by the very magnitude of world events. In the concluding statements to his book *Poetry of This Age* (1959), J. M. Cohen remarked that "events have dwarfed all possible comment" on public affairs and driven the poet to purely personal statement. "All that he can hope to rescue from an ever-imminent disaster will be a moment of love or insight or a clear conception of truth, which, having once been, can never be destroyed." One might have replied that the threat of death is nothing new, every person's life always has been contingent every moment; or that earlier generations lived under the threats of starvation, disease, and other afflictions from which modern Europeans by comparison are almost free. In terms of the totality of human life, the modern world with its massive and longer-lived populations would be far ahead of any previous age even if it experienced a thermonuclear war. Nevertheless, the possibility of centuries of progress being extinguished in a few moments, which might even be the result of an accident, hung over a decade that saw the development of intercontinental nuclear missiles while the Cold War raged, occasionally becoming hot, as in Korea (1950–53), or Algeria, or Indochina. The worst nuclear confrontation of all lay just ahead, in 1962.

"There is a tired lull in British politics, and argument on general principles has largely died," philosopher Stuart Hampshire wrote in the late fifties. "Both political parties are now in this sense conservative, tied to day-to-day expedients." The Labour victory of 1945, in which so much socialist idealism had been invested, ended in 1951 in an atmosphere of considerable disenchantment. The Conservatives returned, to hold office from 1951 to 1964. They now accepted the welfare state, Keynesian economics, and the managed economy; one might say, in an old metaphor, that they had stolen Labour's clothes. The latter party split badly into left and right, but the more moderate group prevailed; the Labour leader of the late fifties and early sixties, Hugh Gaitskell, spoke for an abandonment of socialist dogma in favor of a more flexible program. Someone coined the word "Butskellism," linking the liberal Tory R. A. Butler with Gaitskell. There was not really much difference between the parties; "consensus" was the word. The model of a successful economy, a mixture of free enterprise and government direction, was almost the same for a majority of both political parties. Labour theorist W. Arthur Lewis opted for a more vigorous kind of entrepreneurial capitalism. In Germany, the Social Democrats—once archetypically Marxist—ceased to be a socialist party!

Behind this consensus, and the desire not to rock the boat too much, lay the fact of economic recovery. By 1948, with American aid and the work ethic of a generation reacting from the trauma of war—especially notable in Germany—the revival had begun. By 1963, Raymond Aron could write: "In 1945, Western Europe was a mass of ruins; today it is one of the most prosperous regions of the world." It was truly a *Wirtschaftswunder*, an economic miracle, to many who after looking on the ruins of 1945 had said that it would take a thousand years to rebuild Germany. The formula, whatever it was, seemed to work marvelously well. Western Europe's leaders put their trust in the market, drawing on the advice of such free-enterprise economists as Jacques Rueff, Wilhelm Röpke, Luigi Einaudi, Lionel Robbins, and Friedrich von Hayek. (Such a group met at Pilgrim Mountain in Switzerland in 1947 to foment a sort of conspiracy to bring back capitalism.) But it was called a "social market," and the role of government in guiding the economy was important—this apart from the social security and welfare provisions now considerably expanded to protect workers against the worst buffets of the competitive order. The French word was *dirigisme*: the direct-ed economy, basically free enterprise but steered in the right direction. Probably it worked because Europe had to be rebuilt, the Americans had capital, and people were willing to work.

A symbol of hope came from the idea of European economic unification. The 1957 Treaty of Rome, establishing the goal of a common market, abolishing tariffs and other obstacles to trade between the German Federal Republic (West Germany), France, Italy, and the three Low Countries (Belgium, Netherlands, Lux-emburg), grew from the nucleus of a Franco-German coal and steel community, which in turn had roots in a long tradition of cooperation between German and French industrialists in the Rhineland zone, where economic realities transcended political boundaries. The vision belonged to people like Jean Monnet, who saw national sovereignty as an anachronism in the modern era and a hindrance to eco-nomic progress. The old idea of a United States of Europe was reborn.

The European Economic Community owed its initial success, however, more to the new balance of power in Europe than to idealism. It was a way of gaining West Germany's economic strength without allowing it full independence. World War II and the Cold War had, more by accident than design, brought about the division of Germany. West Germany, purged of Nazism, became a valued member of the Western alliance, though still not fully trusted. Germany needed France, and France needed Germany. The old enemies clasped hands (officially in 1963) on the common grounds of resistance to the Soviet threat, economic necessity, and equali-ty of strength: a divided Germany represented no such threat as formerly. For its part, the Federal Republic looked toward eventually rescuing eastern Germany from Soviet domination.

In flight from ruinous dictators, there was in general a return to democracy, but more by default than with enthusiasm. "It can hardly be denied that democra-cy no longer inspires the same enthusiasm as it inspired in Rousseau or the men of the French Revolution," Bertrand Russell observed in 1952. This latest apotheosis of democracy presented it in the guise of moderation and common decency against the overwrought idealism which had plagued the world. The idea of democracy shaped by clashes with totalitarian creeds of both left and right was a subdued one. It stressed the inevitable imperfections of any political society. It conceded democracy's defects. Democracy was seen not as an "ideology," but as the opposite: "There can be no ideology of democracy," wrote Christopher Martin, in an article entitled "In Praise of Political Apathy." The lack of reformist activity that so disgusted young people of the next decade seemed a positive virtue to the fifties; the world-savers had turned out to be world-destroyers. Two cheers for democracy, not three, a well-known essay by E. M. Forster proposed (1951). It is a bent world, never to be entirely straightened out; the troubles are from eternity and will not fail.

CONSERVATIVE DIRECTIONS

The conservative theorizing of Michael Oakeshott, prestigious in England in the postwar years, saw "rationalism in politics" as a delusion. "Every claim in the sphere of human affairs to an absolute truth," Hannah Arendt argued, "strikes at the very roots of all politics and all governments." This seemed to be a return to Edmund Burke. C. S. Lewis said that he was a democrat because of original sin: men are "too wicked to be trusted with more than the minimum power over other men." Alfred Weber went so far as to argue that the best weapon against the rule of the masses is "freedom and democracy"—pluralist democracy as a safeguard against the rule of the "people" in a totalitarian manner. This mistrust of power may be found in one of the decades most distinguished political writings, Bertrand de Jouvenel's *Du Pouvoir* (On Power), which found the most significant aspect of political evolution to lie not in forms of government, aristocratic or democratic (which in any case turn out to be much the same thing), but in the steady growth of the apparatus of coercion, regardless of who exercises it—the growth of power. Bertrand Russell's study of the same subject argued that power was an independent variable, not just a function of economics. A gloomy fear that, as J. B. Priestley put it ("The Gentle Anarchists," 1955), "personality is losing all along the line against power," liberties are being lost, the younger generation "takes regimentation for granted," usually accompanied this low-key approval of democracy as, in Winston Churchill's phrase, "the worst form of government that has ever been tried except all the rest."

The study of power was indeed a notable interest of postwar political and social thought—a natural enough consequence after Hitler and Stalin. "We have all become intensely aware of power as the major phenomenon in all societies," Raymond Aron wrote. In addition to Jouvenel's brilliant book, the work of the Heidelberg sociologist A. Rüstow, writing in the shadow of the great Max Weber, might be instanced among numerous studies of "power elites." Political scientists dwelt on "pluralism" as a competition of elites in a "polyarchical" order of power.

Lewis Namier and his disciples among historians focused on the location of real power. Weber himself now became at least as much studied as Marx; the point that modern society's bureaucratic organization is the source of alienation, and will persist under socialism as well as capitalism, suited the mood of rebellion against Marxist ideology.

The preoccupation with power carried over into the novel. That "nothing is so corrupting as power" was the basic theme of the carefully crafted novels of Ivy Compton-Burnett, widely read in the 1950s. Her works, like those of Sartre's sparring partner François Mauriac, are usually set in a family household. (Child abuse, incest, domestic violence are hardly discoveries of the most recent period.) *The Lord of the Flies*, a novel by William Golding published in 1954, possibly the most esteemed serious novel of the decade in England, is a kind of Hobbesian study of isolated children in a "state of nature," exhibiting the raw realities of power in a primeval situation. (A Swedish parallel is Stig Dagerman's *Island of the Doomed*, written in 1946.) But the hit of the decade was George Orwell's *1984*, published in 1948 not long before this engaging author's untimely death. As a "dystopia," a reverse utopia, depicting the scientifically organized society of the future not as a paradise but as a hell, the book bears comparison with Huxley's *Brave New World*[3] and, among others, with Eugene Zamyatin's *We*, written in Russia soon after the revolution.

It was most obviously aimed at the Soviet Union (compare Orwell's devastating satire *Animal Farm*), but there are echoes in it of Hitler's state too, as well as the author's own experiences as a bureaucrat in the war; and of the Cold War. Perpetual war, or the pretense of it, exists between three great empires that divide the world and are all evidently run in the same way. (The British have perhaps unluckily ended as a branch of the American superstate.) A small ruling elite, fanatically disciplined, blindly obedient to Big Brother, prepared to say $2 + 2 = 5$ if ordered to, keeps the great majority in poverty and oppression. This suggests the Stalinist state; but those who made *1984* a perennial bestseller in the West evidently recognized in it all too many features of their own society. Endemic in 1984 was the pessimistic view, so prevalent among liberals as well as conservatives, that the world is inevitably headed toward statism and loss of individual liberty. Power, in Orwelliana, is a function of the elite's control over language, largely; the ruling group invents "Newspeak" in order to make people believe that slavery is freedom, war is peace, ignorance is strength. This deception is easier because too many intellectuals, Orwell claimed, "worship power and successful cruelty." He could never forget their abdication to Stalinism, and even to fascism.

Orwell himself, like so many others, looked back nostalgically on a vanished rural society; he could have been a happy parson if born a few centuries earlier, he sighed. He shared with D. H. Lawrence, whom he admired (and whose fate in

---

[3]Huxley updated his classic in 1952 as *Brave New World Revisited*, finding its prophecies all too accurate.

dying young of tuberculosis he shared) a dislike of the whole modern industrial society. But he had no doubts about the futility of that hope; "whether we like it or not, the trend is toward centralization and planning." This sort of disenchanted realism marked the conservative thought of the 1950s, a notable and often distinguished genre. It was literate and sophisticated. Its scorn was directed toward the arrogance of the modern liberal, with his naive belief in progress. Is it plausible, R. G. Collingwood asked, that sixty generations of thinkers have wasted their time, and that ours is the first to be right? Is it rational to suppose that the human dilemmas and tragedies of war, injustice, and inhumanity for which those sixty generations vainly sought remedies are now to be solved? We have in fact less wisdom than our ancestors; modern "social science" with its simpleminded belief that scientific technology can be applied to human affairs is far less rewarding than Shakespeare, Montaigne, Voltaire, or Coleridge.

"On balance life is suffering, and only the very young and the very foolish imagine otherwise," Orwell observed in his essay "Lear, Tolstoy, and the Fool." It was the very young who soon assailed this gloomy outlook. They accused it of being a kind of reactionary conspiracy against progress, but the conservatives thought it wisdom, and held that the naive idealist ends by doing far more damage to the human race than the cautious meliorist. Seeking eternal peace in one leap, he stumbles into all-out war. Seeking utopia through terror, he ends with only the terror, and a fearful one.

In the 1950s France struggled with problems of government; it is surprising, and perhaps a tribute to the irrelevance of politics, that it did so well economically. The Fourth Republic that emerged after the war was approved by a minority and boycotted by General Charles de Gaulle, hero of the Resistance. It suffered numerous changes of government as precarious coalitions rose and fell. It lacked the capacity to make firm decisions, and colonial wars in both Indochina and then Algeria plagued it. Between 1951 and 1962, French interest in politics was incredibly low. In May 1958, after an army revolt in Algeria, the Fourth Republic collapsed, as the assembly asked de Gaulle to preside over an interim government to frame a new constitution.

When completed, the Constitution of the Fifth Republic bore the mark of the man a considerable majority of the French (not including Jean-Paul Sartre) respected as a national hero. It granted the president a much stronger role, and tried to weaken the legislature's power. The French people approved the new constitution by an overwhelming majority and de Gaulle became the first president; he was reelected by popular vote in 1965, in an election that set an all-time high of 85 percent voter participation. The Gaullists presented this as a superior form of democracy, permitting strong and responsible government while avoiding the weakness and corruption of the party system. The general would have liked to do away with political parties altogether, in favor of a kind of plebiscitary caesarism, his foes charged. But de Gaulle was no fascist. He was an authentically great figure, and he attracted the support of some leading intellectuals who, after leaving the god that failed, looked for a new idealism. The most important of such figures was André

Malraux, possibly France's foremost living novelist, who became de Gaulle's minister of culture.

The Gaullist *mystique* included the vision of a new France, modernized, strong, united, regaining its historic place as the center and incarnation of European civilization. The vision included a strong feeling for the whole of this European civilized tradition, and for a Europe standing together from the Channel to the Urals, a union, however, of sovereign states—not a single superstate. Such a Europe, France of course at its head, should offer leadership and aid to the whole world. De Gaulle's greatest political achievements were decolonializing the French empire and healing the quarrel with Germany. He himself was a man of culture and dignity, caring much for French culture and knowing much about it. He did not succeed in eliminating France's notorious political divisions; he once remarked that it is not easy to govern a country that has 350 kinds of cheese. In his years (1958–70) the French economy and social structure underwent rapid transformation—ironic perhaps in view of the general's nostalgia for an ancestral culture.

Gaullism was thus hardly a new ideology. De Gaulle, offering a policy based on flexibility and realism, shared the civilized disenchantment of the times. "I am like Hemingway's Old Man of the Sea, I have brought back a skeleton," he sighed at the end. He endured until 1970 when a new spirit, represented by angry and rebellious university students, caused his departure. They too in a sense were in revolt against "ideology"; but they rejected the conservative quietism of the 1950s.

SOME INTELLECTUAL CURRENTS OF THE POSTWAR DECADES

The disabused, personalist, apolitical mood of the 1950s appeared notably in its thought and literature. Sartre's activist and radical kind of existentialism was not typical. Other so-called Existentialist philosophies that flourished tended to be introspective, meditative, politically disillusioned. The Kierkegaard renaissance continued unabated, and there was a certain Nietzsche renaissance; the great German was rescued from Nazi appropriation and, with the aid of new materials as in the case of Marx, given fresh interpretations. Edmund Husserl left behind a large body of mansucripts. His last major work, *The Crisis of European Sciences and Transcendental Phenomenology*, made it clear that he disapproved of Heidegger and of Existentialist irrationalism; phenomenology must be "a rigorous science of philosophy," if a different kind of science from the positivist sort. But the categories of the mind turn out to be lacking in system, not reducible to any order. They are numerous and ambiguous.

Martin Heidegger's quest was broadly religious, though it did not involve a personal god, and in 1946 (*Existentialism Is a Humanism*), Sartre situated Heidegger's with his own as an atheistic and humanistic sort. The two thinkers were actually very different, diverging from a common set of ideas (the two different modes of being, the interest in human subjectivity, the crisis of despair or anxiety, authentic and inauthentic existence). There was a religious aura about Heidegger's reverence for being—not a personal God, but something transcendent that is the root of all meaning, from which European humanity has been cut off, and with which we must try to regain contact. Sartre saw no such transcendent Being, only the ideas invented and acted on by individual human consciousness. The two had very different literary and life styles. Heidegger's was quietist, conservative, hostile to modern technology, profoundly archaist, fleeing to the forest and listening to nature—something that made him eventually a hero of the environmentalist "Greens" of a later day.

The search for lost Being leads us to rethink all our words and categories, and return to an ancient time when language—"the house of being"—was in close contact with Being. With Nietzsche, who deeply influenced him, Heidegger would return to the pre-Socratic philosophers, before intellectualism caused words to lose their original magic. Art, especially poetry, is a means of regaining this contact with Being. A notable interpreter of literary works, Heidegger offered an exciting esthetic that viewed art as not just an imitation of the world, but as a drawing out of deeper meaning, a partial revelation of Being. There were affinities with Oriental mysticism in Heidegger's "listening to the music of Being." (One major physical scientist, Weizsaecker, found value in this message that science should listen, not appropriate. Phenomenological psychiatry differed from Freud in wanting just to listen to the disturbed person's problems and understand them, not impose some preconceived theoretical framework on them.) "Man is the shepherd of Being." Heidegger's vocabulary teems with metaphors of tending, shepherding, caring, listening, always in search of that transcendent mystery that lies beneath the phenomenal world. The man who said that all philosophy is a form of homesickness was perhaps trying to return to his childhood in a small Baden town. He was a philosopher of the village community, not the urban megalopolis.

Wittgenstein's later thought, widely known only with the publication in 1953, soon after his death, of *Philosophical Investigations*, was deeply skeptical in seeing no way of connecting language (or mathematics, logic, any form of expression) with the external world. "The desire to understand the world is an outmoded folly." We are the prisoners of our language, and can know only it. (There is no point in trying to invent another language, we would still be its prisoner. The philosopher should take language as it is.) This language is indeed a confused tangle of all sorts and levels of usages, and if we want to think clearly about any question we must untangle it. But it is useful to do that. We can (in his term) play consistent language games, thus avoiding confusion, and the flawed communication (hence flawed human relations) that goes with it. We can examine the problems that bother people, problems small and large, and show that they almost always rest on some inconsistent use of language. The value of straightening out these verbal tangles was more a human, psychological one than a natural science one to the later Wittgenstein.

Our speech contains a "prodigious diversity," Wittgenstein says, of overlapping languages, within the larger one, like a rope made up of tightly wound fibers.

Confusion is engendered by "category errors" in jumping from one to another—as if a bridge player should call out "I'm going to castle" instead of leading a card, or "check" instead of "double." The problem with our attempts to think straight, according to Wittgenstein, is something like this: Everybody thinks there is one big game going on, with a single set of rules, whereas in fact the universe of human communication is made up of many smaller games, each with somewhat different rules; and people keep moving about constantly and at random from one table to another. When the difficult task of untangling this confusion is performed, we normally find, Wittgenstein insisted, that the difficulty disappears. Most arguments are really nonarguments, seen to be meaningless when terms are defined. The student might try this out on some typically heated question people argue about, such as "Is abortion murder?" or "Is capitalism unjust?"

Wittgenstein turns out to be a deeply religious thinker, as concerned as Heidegger about a realm of meaning that lies outside the world of facts, of appearances. "The sense of the world must lie outside the world." The world is a collection of facts, neither good or bad in themselves, just as they are; "in the world everything is as it is." (Time will say nothing but I told you so, W. H. Auden put it in a beautiful poem.) The marvel, Wittgenstein said many times, is not *how* things are in the world, but *that* the world as a whole exists. The meaning of this must lie outside the world. If it lay within the world, it would be just another part of that collection of contingent facts; self-evidently, he thought, "If there is any value that does have value, it must lie outside the whole sphere of what happens and is the case."

In his relation to religion Wittgenstein was not far from the Existentialists, often taken to be his direct opposite. The similarity is suggested by Wittgenstein's remarks on an old theological argument, whether God is bound by a preexisting reason, or created that reason arbitrarily—whether God necessarily wills what is good, or the Good is what God willed it to be. Wittgenstein thought the latter position the more profound; he aligned himself,in medieval terms, with the voluntarism of Ockham rather than the rationalism of Aquinas. Sartre, the Existentialist, also saw an arbitrary, unconditioned will as the source of values, in his case the human will rather than God's. This position saves the omnipotence of God—or humans—at the cost of some apparently embarrassing implications: if God (or humans) had chosen to declare torture, murder, disloyalty, etc. to be good, would they have been? Both Wittgenstein and Sartre stand here in the shadow of Nietzsche, whose insight was the irrationality of a world that simply *is*, in itself without meaning or explanation, a blind struggle between competing energies.

Wittgenstein's bequest to professional, academic philosophy was the "ordinary language" school. It was often the target of criticism for concerning itself with minute trivialities. Bertrand Russell, no longer sympathetic to his old protégé, exclaimed that this kind of philosophizing was only concerned with "the different ways silly people can say silly things." But common discourse, while often confused, raises existentially significant questions. And our thinking can never get anywhere unless we start by clarifying each individual proposition. The "absence of any dogma, any universal method, any claim to finality" tied the Oxford school to the postwar *Zeitgeist*. Its air of modesty (or perhaps false modesty) was expressed in J. L. Austin's characterization of his work as "something about one way of possibly doing one part of philosophy." "Doing" philosophy, the fashionable way of putting it, connoted the limited goals—no question of finding or making great truths—as well as the brisk professionalism of an academic exercise. Here, of course, the analytical philosophers sometimes differed drastically from the Existentialists, and there were famous uncomprehending confrontations of the two schools when they met at international congresses in the 1950s. But analytical and phenomenological philosophy in fact had numerous points of contact.

They both inquired into unique, concrete human meanings. So did the postwar novel, for the most part. Stunned, as it were, by *Finnegans Wake*—who could go beyond that?—writers of the 1950s tended to eschew vast symbolic canvasses in favor of plain lives carefully described. Literature turned away from social realism, but it also tended to reject "modernist" experimentation. The title of a survey of the English novel in the 1950s (by Rubin Rabinovits) is "The reaction against experiment." What Iris Murdoch described as the "crystalline" novel, "small, clear, self-contained," as opposed to "large, shapeless, quasi-documentary" novels gained favor. A prominent French literary school called itself *chosiste* (thing-ist): dedicated to the full exploration of objects *qua* objects, the thing for its own sake, not seen as a symbol of anything or as part of any logical scheme. *Tel Quel* was the title of a leading French literary journal—just that, such as it is. "Against interpretation," against depth was the word. The French *nouveau roman*, practiced by such as Alain Robbe-Grillet and Nathalie Sarraute, was indeed highly unconventional in method, but the goal was to break the traditonal novel's illusion of order, imposed by the godlike, omniscient narrator, and bring literature closer to the fragmented, multileveled nature of actual experience, or of fantasy.

Such highly esteemed novelists as Graham Greene, Angus Wilson, Evelyn Waugh, and François Mauriac presented a gloomy view of human nature derived from traditional Christianity, as did the older T. S. Eliot, whose brilliant modernist delineation *The Waste Land* had given way to the Christian humility of *Four Quartets*. So also the later Auden, a great poet now of the everyday and commonplace, who went back and censored the poetry of his revolutionary youth. "Wild Kierkegaard, Williams, and Lewis guided me back to belief," Auden wrote, after Hitler and Stalin had "forced me to think about God." He referred to the remarkable return to "mere Christianity" of the brilliant critic C. S. Lewis and his disciples at Oxford.

In a comment on British poetry of the 1950s, John Wain (in the 1959 symposium *Declaration*) explained that "a deliberate, conscious, limited, cautious poetry of experiences, carefully chosen and rationally explored, is inevitable today." The Swiss dramatist Friedrich Dürrenmatt, whom some thought the greatest German-language playwright of his generation, radiated the religious intensity of neo-orthodox Lutheranism. Joyce's friend Samuel Beckett, an Irishman transplanted to Paris, wrote *Waiting for Godot*, a play of the early fifties that came close to being

T. S. Eliot: A Caricature by David Low. (Cartoon by permission of *The Standard*)

the theatrical event of the decade, in a style accurately described as "highly distinctive, despairing, yet strangely exhilirating." It was often associated with what was called the Theater of the Absurd. The Romanian playwright Eugene Ionescu and Sartre's friend Jean Genet were among others in this group. Their plays brilliantly portrayed the themes of human isolation in a dehumanizing society, apocalyptic intimations of the end of everything, the absurdity of existence, the desperate hope of finding a meaning that would come from some inner strength. Waiting for Godot was waiting for the end, or just possibly for God.

The end was indeed thought to be near in years that saw the advent of the awesomely destructive nuclear bombs, mounted in missiles soon capable of hitting targets thousands of miles away. Among the most widely read books of the decade, Neville Shute's picture of atomic war, *On the Beach*, joined Orwell's *1984* and Golding's *Lord of the Flies*. Students asked professors to give their last lecture: What would you say just before the final big bang? Underlying the political quietism of the fifties was certainly not complacency, but the opposite—a stunned realization that the human plight was so terrible it was ludicrous to imagine it could be cured by some political nostrum. "At a time when all the future holds in store is atomic and other catastrophes, a deep gloom pervades our thinking," a young Frenchman remarked in an issue of the magazine *NEF* on the theme of "Mal du Siècle."

The return to plain existence and the return to religion found expression in a poem of Philip Larkin's that struck a unique response in the readers of this English poet, one of the decade's leading voices. "Church Going" is the glance of a sophisticated and disillusioned modern at the curious spectacle of ordinary people going to church; maybe there's something here we've overlooked.

"And what remains when disbelief has gone?" Perhaps the old faith: "And that much never can be obsolete." The outlook was typical of this decade; it was that of the jaded modern intellectual, who has seen everything, known everything, turning away from this impossibly complicated labyrinth of words to put his feet on the ground of common humanity. A rough American equivalent of Larkin was Howard Nemerov, who admired the English poet.

The realm of knowledge was indeed out of control. Orwell's vision of a populace kept ignorant by close control of its reading matter was strangely at odds with what actually happened. There was an explosion of education. The British, for example, built seven new universities, in sites ranging from East Anglia and Kent to Lancaster and York; several new technical universities, and new Scottish universities. By 1970 there were some 450,000 university students in Great Britain. A similar rapid expansion of higher education occurred in all Western countries; in France, there was an increase between 1940 and 1970 from about 80,000 to 600,000 university students. It was at one of the new universities built in the Paris suburbs, branches of the old Sorbonne, that the student revolution of 1968 began.

One significant result of this educational expansion was that all branches of knowledge came more under the domination of professors. There were now so many of them that they dominated publication; they created specialist associations and learned journals and set up a competition for professional advancement based on in-group standards of excellence. This process, which was to advance remorselessly, began in the postwar years. Even creative writers were now more likely to nest in some university fellowship than in Bohemia or Grub Street. There were protests against this professionalization, especially in the humanities, but in vain. British novelist Kingsley Amis memorably satirized the provincial university academic type in *Lucky Jim* (1954), but there was to be no stopping him or her.

The charmed circle of Europe's literati increased at least tenfold. Never were there so many books, magazines, movies, ideas. About 1970 someone calculated that more books had been published since 1945 than in all the previous history of printing. Intellectually at least, it was with a bang and not a whimper that the world was ending. It was being gorged, not starved. For both technology and democracy marched relentlessly on. The terrible war had greatly advanced both. There were, in fact, beginning to be so many books, so many "movements" and trends, that any generalization about a period became dangerous; the river with certain identifiable currents in it was becoming more like a sea in which countless waters mingled in confusion.

10

Rebellions and Reactions, 1968–1980

THE NEW LEFT AND THE RADICAL SIXTIES

Despite difficulties in detecting trends, no one could miss the turn toward radical activism in the 1960s. Climaxed in the great student riots and revolts, it dominated this decade as much as communism had the 1930s. A poem of Donald Davie's, written in the 1950s, called "Remembering the 'Thirties," noted how the scene of just a few years ago can seem like "worlds more remote than Ithaca or Rome." In 1954 John Wain wondered "will the Sixties think us as silly as we think the Thirties?" He could have guessed they would.

The source of this change was in part, of course, just a new generation's urge to be different, to make its own statement, to rebel against its parents. This generation effect (speeded up by the pace of modern communication; a "generation" now might be only a few years) was the reponse of those who had come of age since the war, knowing not its heroes and villains; Hitler and Stalin were to them as remote as Pericles and Caesar. A little of this had appeared even in the fifties, among Britain's "angry young men," who took their name from John Osborne's curiously significant 1956 play, *Look Back in Anger*. A debate about whether literature ought to be more "committed" and socially relevant enlivened the later fifties. What the Angries were angry about was not altogether clear—it seemed more nearly just the natural rebelliousness of a new generation searching for its identity. A "rebel without a cause" made his appearance among teenagers. Few writers dared to say a word for social realism, which raised memories of the dreary propaganda tracts of the 1930s. But a novelist like Alan Sillitoe (*Saturday Night and Sunday Morning*, made into a notable movie) managed to present persuasively an authentic world of proletarians without illusions.

All this was mild compared to what was to come. Among the leading stimulants to a revival of activism was the decline of the old left, leaving space for a new and much less disciplined one. By 1965 the Russian-dominated Marxian communism of the thirties was in disarray. For a moment in the 1950s it might have looked as if the future belonged to Marx and Lenin. China went Communist, and the newly independent countries of Asia and Africa, seeking a quick path of Western-style "development," were attracted to the Soviet more than to the Western model. Despite a sudden and rapid dismantling of their empires in the sixties, Western countries were after all associated with a hated colonialism in the eyes of newly liberated peoples.

Heroes of rebellion against European "imperialism" like Indochina's Ho Chi Minh, Cuba's Fidel Castro, perhaps Nigeria's Nkrumah or Algeria's Ben Bella, burst into the consciousness of young people. Though Yugoslavia's Tito tried to organize them as a third force of the "unaligned," belonging to neither of the two great power blocs, a good many of these "Third World" countries were listening to Soviet advice and seemed about to join that sphere of influence, even if they were not already enthusiastically Marxist. Castro announced himself a convert to Marxism, Ho Chi Minh already was. Castro's ideological mentor Che Guevara, a hero of the New Left, was roaming the South American countryside seeking whomever he could revolutionize.

But the world Communist movement soon became a scene of dissension. The breakup had begun in 1948, when Yugoslavia's highly militant and once loyally Stalinist Communist Party, now governing Yugoslavia, quarreled spectacularly with the aging Soviet dictator. It continued with the even more spectacular rift between China's new Red regime and Stalin's successor Khrushchev. When the Communists captured a major country, they wanted to declare independence and embark on their own course, whereas the Kremlin bosses assumed that all other Communists took orders from Moscow, which usually meant serving Soviet Russia's interests. Communism as well as capitalism had its "contradictions." The most damaging blow to Moscow's prestige, from which it never really recovered, took place in 1956, when Soviet tanks appeared in the streets of Budapest to shoot down Hungarian workers.

The discrediting and then the splitting up of world communism opened the way to a freer development of the left. The death of Stalin was a little like the death of Queen Victoria, which it was said lifted a great paperweight from people's minds. With his subsequent fall from grace, and the struggles of his hapless successors, the old believers were thrown into despair or isolation. But there were new models for a new left. Some, as we noted, came from splinters of the old revolutionary monolith. Like Yugoslovia's Tito, China's leadership, having quarreled with the Kremlin on matters of pride and power, proceeded to create another version of Marxian philosophy, in some ways more up-to-date than the Kremlin's now creaky model. Mao Tse-tung's ideology in many ways resembled the reinterpretations of Marx going on in Europe, a large enterprise to which the Frankfurt School "critical theorists," the Italian Antonio Gramsci, and Sartre himself had contributed. So had some of Tito's ideological advisers; the Belgrade journal *Praxis* became a virtual bible of the neo-Marxists.

The sources of the New Left were in fact numerous. A bewildered Soviet publication of 1973, trying to identify all the "revisionists" who had seduced Western youth away from the true faith, named Scheler, Husserl, Unamuno, Heidegger, Jaspers, Camus, Garaudy, Adorno, Horkheimer, Marcuse, Fromm (notably omitting Sartre). Some of these were Existentialists, others were members of the Frankfurt School; Erich Fromm was a deviant Freudian, while Roger Garaudy had left the French CP to seek "a dialogue between Catholicism and Communism," a goal which, encouraged by the remarkable Pope John XXIII, was popular also in Italy. The Italian Communist Party, Gramsci-influenced, had moved away from Moscow's domination to become a much more open-minded organization after 1956.

So the New Left had an almost prodigal abundance of new ideas on which to draw for a credo of revolution, much more active-minded in many cases than the old one. (Moscow showed very little desire to cause serious trouble for the Western democracies in the post-Stalin years. Khrushchev hobnobbed with Presidents Eisenhower and de Gaulle, to Peking's great annoyance. He disappointed Castro by backing off from confrontation with the United States over Cuba in 1962.)[1] In fact, the student radicals often expressed a disdain for all ideological "positioning." They were heavily existentialized, and they preferred action to talk. They might call themselves "situationists." The black flag of anarchy was more in evidence than the red one. Indeed, student activists often were innocent of any serious social thought at all. The editor of a compilation of student revolutionary materials from this era comments that the movement "owes more to Marinetti, Dada, Surrealism, Artaud, the Marx Brothers, than to Lenin or Mao." The Marx they knew was more likely to be Groucho. What they felt most keenly was a dislike of the rationalized, bureaucratic society they were being trained to join, and a craving for adventure—shades of 1914, only this time directed toward "the system" within, not the enemy abroad.

Material values had preoccupied the immediate postwar generation to a degree their children found repugnant. That West Germany probably produced the first and most radical student rebels was a tribute to the special strength of the

---

[1]Mao once alarmed Khrushchev by observing that if a nuclear war killed two hundred million people on both sides, there would be few Americans left but lots of Chinese. He didn't mention how Russia would stand. Withdrawal of Russian aid for the Chinese nuclear program was one prominent factor in the Sino-Soviet rift.

"work ethic" in that country after 1945 among those who came, often as refugees from the east, to rebuild the shattered land—as they did with spectacular success, making it the richest of European countries by 1970. As usual, the rebellious young people were from the upper middle class, often the offspring of professional people. They were spoiled, their critics claimed; certainly in any previous epoch they would have been at work in field or factory, not attending universities. Numbers had diluted the quality of education—"more is worse," Kingsley Amis claimed. The new students tended to study sociology, producing a considerable overproduction in this field. The immense and relatively sudden expansion of the universities created conditions of overcrowding; students complained of being processed at the education mills, in Sartrean terms, serialized.

When all the social and psychological causes of university youth's profound malaise in the 1960s have been noted, it remains true that ideas enabled them to channel this discontent, and that ideas were extremely important despite the tendency to shy away from heavy doses of theory. At the peak of the Paris student revolution of May 1968, ten thousand students packed a theater to hear Sartre. Books like Frantz Fanon's *The Wretched of the Earth*, with a preface by Sartre, sold a million copies, as did Regis Debray's account of Guevara's revolutionary adventures. *The Thoughts of Chairman Mao*, the "little red book," was in every student's pocket. Many of them knew Herbert Marcuse's *One-Dimensional Man* and other writings by this veteran Frankfurt School social theorist turned radical demagogue after being translated to the heady atmosphere of California. The student movement was international; it spread from California to West Germany, appearing in British, Italian, French, Dutch, and even East Zone European universities. Its chief model was the Chinese "great cultural revolution," which Chairman Mao had encouraged in order to "raise consciousness" by taking over the universities from the old fogies. Fanon was a West Indian doctor who had migrated to North Africa. The common link in the student international was a set of ideas or intellectual attitudes, whose dispersal jet-age aviation facilitated.

The attitudes transcended formal doctrine. Most of these came from a youth culture that was connected to a new music and a new freedom of conduct. The latter owed something, at least in the English-speaking world, to a relaxation of censorship. A much-discussed landmark of cultural history was the 1960 British court case which, after hearing testimony from a battery of distinguished writers and critics, adjudged D. H. Lawrence's *Lady Chatterley's Lover* not obscene. The decision opened the gates to a flood of "pornography." (Much of it, singularly, consisted of reprints of Victorian tales of men and maids, heretofore not legally publishable.)[2] A similar landmark in France overturned the conviction of the pub-

---

[2]The Obscene Publications Bill of 1857 had been the response to a widely perceived problem of scandalous literature. Walter E. Houghton observes that "the major reason why sex was so frightening to the Victorians was the glaring fact...that sexual license in England not only existed on a large scale but seemed to be increasing."

lisher Pauvert for printing the works of the Marquis de Sade, who had become a hero of the existential left. If it was not quite true, as Philip Larkin wrote (ironically) that:

> Sexual intercourse began
> In nineteen-sixty-three,
> Between the end of the Chatterley ban
> And the Beatles' first LP

many young people thought so. The so-called sexual revolution coincided with the birth of rock music. Among the slogans the students produced in abundance, one was "We fear nothing, we have the Pill." They had yet to encounter AIDS.

The ideas of the New Left were associated with a new kind of Marxism. A revised and existentialized Marx, who might or might not have been recognizable to the master himself, talked less of economic impoverishment than of "alienation," the alienation of the individual in a false society. Indeed, the new Marxists tended to admit what was obvious, that "capitalism" was all too successful in material terms. It had bought off the workers, who were evidently all too willing to be seduced, with automobiles and television sets, but at the cost of human values. Herbert Marcuse accused capitalism of producing not too little but too much, thus corrupting the working class. (The poor capitalists were in a no-win situation.) Affluence more than poverty became the target of criticism; a fashionable American economist flayed "the affluent society." Bureaucracy, "the technological society," "consumerism" all came under fire. The real "contradictions of capitalism" were cultural. Its very material success, theorists pointed out, breaks down social discipline, leads to an extreme enhancement of individual consciousness, yet at the same time imposes a straitjacket of corporate conformism and bureaucratic regulation. The usual position of the "liberal," demanding ever more individual cultural liberty and ever more government economic regulation, was a characteristic contradiction.

The new Marxists were almost all critical of Soviet Marxism as well as Soviet society, the two being linked. The Soviet Union's alleged Marxism-Leninism was a sad misunderstanding of both Marx and Lenin. A monstrous state bureaucracy suppressing dissent and dehumanizing labor was clearly not what the founding fathers of communism had intended. Stalinism had debased Marxism into a crude economic determinism which led to an elite ruling stratum, in effect a new ruling class. The Chinese Communists added their voice to the charge that Russian "dialectical materialism" had distorted Marx and led to an elite dictatorship. This was the result of an actually undialectical Marxism, which made the mistake of regarding ideas and culture as mechanical results of economic conditions. "Who sees in ideologies the mechanical, passive product of…economic processes," declared George Lukacs, "understands absolutely nothing of their nature and growth, and holds not Marxism but a caricature of it." Lukacs, the Hungarian literary critic and philosopher who like his friend Bertolt Brecht had long clung to the

Communist Party while trying to save it from Stalinism, finally abandoned Moscow after 1956.

Drawing heavily on modern psychology or phenomenology, Western critical Marxism was often subjectivist and at times almost irrational. Frankfurt theorists tended to see "instrumental reason," production and technology, as corrupting all phases of modern life, leading to bureaucracy and disenchantment. (There was a Max Weber influence here.) Some of the Frankfurt School writings assailed "science" as a product of bourgeois culture. Lukacs's "reification" of consciousness, allegedly a product of capitalism, results from an excess of what Weber had called "rationalization." Walter Benjamin, in a well-known essay, shuddered at mass production of art objects, as Adorno deplored jazz and Marcuse despised "one-dimensional" popular culture—a strain of cultural elitism in these thinkers that allowed the Kremlin to brand them "bourgeois decadents." But Moscow, condemning rock music, long hair, drugs, and sexual freedom, was very much out of step with college youth in the 1960s.

Some stressed the democratic side of Marx, who had seldom sanctioned revolutionary conspiracies. Gramsci declared that before the working class makes a political revolution, it must first conquer in the cultural domain. "Politics is only the means, the end is culture," Lukacs agreed. When, in the 1968 Prague Spring, Slovakian Communist Alexander Dubcek asserted that "it is not possible for a small minority to introduce and maintain socialism," a heresy which quickly earned him armed intervention from Moscow, he reflected the influence of a new breed of humanist Marxists in the East European countries subject to Communist control since 1945. "Socialism with a human face" drew on the Czech Karl Kosik's 1963 *Dialectic of the Concrete*. Other East European philosophers such as the Poles Kolakowski and Schiff contributed to the humanizing of Marx. From the viewpoint of the Soviet satellites, a less dogmatic Marx who saw humanity as making its own history could support the idea that no one socialist system fits all peoples, that each country must work out its own model, and develop its own brand of socialist ideology and literature. As boldly as they dared, these East European Marxists used Marxist humanism as a weapon against the Soviet model to which they were forcibly yoked. They argued that an open, progressive Marxism was truer to Marx than a dogmatic kind, a logic unlikely to gain converts in Moscow.

In his *Critique de la raison dialectique*, Sartre explained how the realm of the "practico-inert," the body of reified, alienated institutions, originally born of human needs, has grown ossified and now, as "worked matter," frustrates these needs and escapes from human control. Arnold Toynbee had identified "the idolization of an ephemeral past" as one of the causes of that failure of creativity which marks social decline. Other sociologists had spoken of "social lag." But Sartre presented these clichés with a more vibrant accent. "Seriality," another of his terms, is the mechanical, artificial form of human association, an accidental grouping of people like the bus queue.

Beginning in scarcity, feeding on the struggle for existence, seriality and the practico-inert have prevailed through human history, frustrating *praxis*, the true,

creative interaction between individual and group. The "group in fusion," a spontaneous and organic community which overcomes this conflict between individuals
and society, is found especially in revolutions. No matter that Sartre later decided
"I cannot see how it is possible to resolve the problems which are brought about by
any institutionalized structure," something most people already knew. Young people eagerly accepted the proposition that although the system had engulfed almost
everybody, revolution might come from those completely outside the system, such
as students and the guerrilla bands of the colonial world.

Seizing university buildings from bewildered deans in campus uprisings, the
revolutionary students hoped to set off further revolts throughout the society,
which they held to be linked together as a single system. Total negation, rejecting
the society *in toto*, they saw as the key to drastic social change, after which all
would live happily somehow in sexual and esthetic fulfillment. All "structures of
authority" must be abolished, the self-motivating individual left free to find self-
realization. This mixture of fantasy, utopia, and negation contained echoes of
almost every strain of radical social thought over the past two centuries—not only
Marx and Nietzsche and Freud but the early socialists, the anarchists, Trotskyists,
Existentialists. It all came to a glorious explosion in the campus revolts of 1967
and 1968, climaxed by the Paris Spring of 1968, when for a moment it looked as if
the students would indeed bring down the established order.

"Politics outside the system" in Britain reached back to the protests organized by the Committee for Nuclear Disarmament in 1959–61 with the goal of
getting Britain to scrap nuclear weapons and perhaps declare neutrality in the
Cold War. Inspired originally by the octogenarian philosopher Bertrand Russell,
the CND organized huge rallies which initially were non-violent but began in
1960 to use provocative tactics of blocking entrances and occupying buildings.
Russell and his wife got themselves arrested. He may be credited with doing more
than anyone to introduce the aggressive "civil disobedience" that became the
stock in trade of student revolutionaries in the 1960s. Mohandas Gandhi had used
these methods earlier, learning them from Leo Tolstoy, who found the idea among
other places in Henry David Thoreau, and so on back (Russell himself mentioned
the early Christians).

Impatient with the Labour party's caution and pragmatism, the *New Left
Review* searched for new roads to socialism. Later in the decade, disappointment
with the Labour governments elected in 1964 and 1966 brought more violent
protests; radical students "sat in" at the London School of Economics in March
1967. A radical wing of Labour spoke of the "new politics" as one of "confrontation" and "direct action." A mob of Cambridge students disrupted a minister's
speech, something unheard of in that domain of English civility. By that time the
Vietnam war, which Prime Minister Wilson (under American pressure) defended,
provided a focus for protest. As we know, Sartre had earlier assailed the French
authorities who were attempting to put down nationalist rebellion in Algeria; after
president Charles de Gaulle secured an end to the war and France granted independence to Algeria in 1962, Sartre turned his attention to Vietnam. Though he could

hardly reproach de Gaulle for this war, he turned his wrath on the Americans whom he implored the USSR to bomb, and whom he again charged with war crimes, joining with Russell in an attempt to stage a war crimes trial of the United States. Meanwhile in Germany the veteran existentialist Karl Jaspers wrote a long and bitter polemic against the West German Republic, charging that it was plotting new wars and leading to another Nazi dictatorship (*Where Is the Federal Republic Heading?* 1965). Joining him as a critic of Germany's bourgeois values was the outstanding novelist Günter Grass.

THE DECLINE OF THE LEFT

The student uprising foundered on its inconsistencies, contradictions, and divisions. The goals were vague, diverse, and utopian. The basic contradiction was between the claim to be democratic ("Students for a Democratic Society" was the leading American radical activist group, "power to the people" a leading slogan) and, on the other hand, the claim that a small minority of outsiders could change the whole system by revolution. This would lead logically to an elite dictatorship like that of the Soviet Union. But the New Left abhorred that, and talked of a totally free, decentralized society. One might have asked, how can a better society emerge spontaneously from the existing one if the latter is as corrupt as it is said to be? Only a miracle could bring this to pass.

The new Marxists who accused capitalism of too much abundance estranged themselves from the working class, which revelled in the materialism. The reviewer of a book by Michael Harrington, a popular American neo-Marxist, noted that "he is denouncing values held by a large majority of the working class, and he is calling them dupes for holding these values." Back to Orwell's point that socialism was always a creed of middle-class intellectuals. No wonder the Paris students and the Paris workers turned out to be poor collaborators. Some of the latter had more sympathy for the police assailed by the students, a case of working people versus spoiled sons of the bourgeoisie.

In some ways, the revolt was surpassingly silly, rather like the pranks bored college students were long accustomed to play in the spring. American students had overturned cars and conducted panty raids. There was, in fact, a long tradition of "student stirs" in European universities. A large majority of French people were appalled at the students' violence and *outré* behavior, and the trade unionists who seemed for a moment to coalesce with them in revolt were really from a totally different world. No doubt Sartre's "group in fusion" materialized in one moment of revolutionary ecstasy, but one cannot live in revolution, the real world was still there. Having had their fun the students left school or went back to it, leaving behind some educational reforms but no totally negated society.

The repercussions from this abortive rebellion included some reactions against the existentialized Marxism with which it was associated. Kurt Sontheimer, in *Das Elend Unserer Intellektuellen* (The Misery of Our Intellectuals, 1976), reproached the German left-wing intelligentsia for having egged the juveniles on to mindless violence. He was answered by Jürgen Habermas, who claimed the student movement had done lasting good by taking democracy and culture out of the hands of the professionals. But in fact the lasting results were not very significant. Most of the prophets of 1968 faded rapidly from the center of the stage. A debate between Sartre, Garaudy, and Louis Althusser about the meaning of the dialectic could still draw a huge crowd in Paris, but hardly anywhere else.

Sartre turned to the Maoists, joining the editorial staff of a Maoist newspaper titled "The Cause of the People." In 1970 President Charles de Gaulle, remarking that "You don't arrest Voltaire," refused to have the philosopher detained for selling illegal Maoist pamplets; the world was fascinated by this encounter. De Gaulle was about to retire, a victim in part of the student revolt. But Sartre was really too busy with his Flaubert biography to give politics his full attention. The Chinese soon failed him; Mao's death in 1976 led to a return to "pragmatism" in Communist China. Sartre spent most of his later intellectual energies on an enormous psychobiography of Gustave Flaubert. Flaubert was really Jean-Paul Sartre, the alienated bourgeois writer; Joyce's Dedalus/Shem. He finally became totally pessimistic about the political situation: "No political party offers any hope at all," he declared (*Situations X*, 1977). Still advocating a vague "libertarian socialism," he found no revolutionary potential any longer in a proletariat which had let itself be "serialized."

Sartre defended the so-called Baader-Meinhof gang of West German terrorists. In the aftermath of 1968, some of the young radicals turned to terrorist activity resembling that of the late nineteenth century anarchists (a more recent model was Latin American urban guerrillas). Children of the bourgeoisie resorted to bombings, assassinations, and kidnappings, notably in Italy and Germany, with a recrudescence of terrorism too among the Irish Revolutionary Army. Ulrike Meinhof was the daughter of a theologian and the former wife of a pacifist who published a pornographic magazine. Her trial, along with three other members of the "gang" in West Germany in 1975, was an international sensation. Italian Red Brigades kidnapped and murdered a former prime minister of Italy in 1978. Such extremism inevitably further discredited the New Left, and at the end of the decade it subsided. Its desperate rage registered a kind of intellectual bankruptcy.

Meanwhile, in another reaction, Althusser led a new Marxist turn, rejecting the sentimental "humanism" of the existentializing and psychologizing school to preach a return to objectivism and science, though hopefully not to Stalinism. For a while in the early seventies he was the hero of the hour, seeking to revive the French Communist Party while being sufficiently subtle to attract the intellectuals. Althusser was no "Euro-Communist" like the Italian Party, which hoped to bring communism back to the democratic fold by rejecting Soviet Russian leadership. He defended the Soviet repression of Prague's 1968 attempt to humanize its socialist regime (a rather ironic accompaniment to the Paris Spring), and tried to keep the PCF tied to Moscow. Althusser strove to establish a new orthodoxy, released from the crudities of Stalinism yet no less dogmatic, and to make the theorist (himself) the dominant figure in a revived Communist Party. (For this he was to be attacked by other Marxists for the heresy of bourgeois idealism.) Althusser married Marxism to newer structuralist fashions. In the end this proved too much for him; he shot his wife and went mad.

Marxist disputes, conducted mostly by university philosophers, became so difficult that few except experts could follow them. British Marxist scholar David McLellan complained that Althusser was incomprehensible ("large parts of the book [*Reading Capital*] are virtually unintelligible"). Marxism had become an arcane science, light years away from plain people or those earlier Marxists whose simple faith was now scorned as "vulgar." The neophilia of the professional intellectuals here clashed head on with the actual world Marxism was supposed to address. The intellectuals themselves frequently expressed despair at their inability to contribute anything helpful to practical politics.

And the world Communist cause continued to decline. Sartre had to complain about his old friend Fidel Castro's persecutions as well as the Soviet Union's attempts to terrorize and intimidate a growing band of dissidents. The arrest and brutalizing of the poet Heberto Padilla in 1971, which he survived to tell about (living on in Cuba for a number of years, after he publicly confessed his "errors" in the customary Stalin-style ritual) was a curiously significant episode in the story of the left's increasing disenchantment with communism—following as it did closely on the Czech drama of 1968. Sartre protested the arrest of the famous nuclear physicist Andrei Sakharov, one of the best known of the Soviet dissidents who called for greater freedom and an open society.[3] *Samizdat* or self-published clandestine magazines and newspapers in the USSR could no longer be effectively suppressed. In the 1970s many in the West got a spiritual lift from the brave and eloquent dissenters in the USSR who spoke out with increasing boldness, braving persecution that was milder than Stalin's terror but hardly inconsequential.[4] The world was inspired by the example of Poland's Solidarity movement, challenging the Communist regime's ban on free labor unions. Millions all over the world read Alexander Solzhenitsyn's moving record of the slave labor camps, *The Gulag Archipelago*.

The dissidents all wanted an end to the corrupt and degenerate Brezhnev regime, they all wanted freedom, an end to censorship, release from the tyranny of crude Marxism enforced by state power. But they did not agree on a positive program. Sakharov opted for Western-style freedom and democracy; in 1972 the father of the Soviet atomic bomb told an American interviewer that he no longer considered himself a Marxist-Leninist, but a liberal. The Medvedev brothers want-

---

[3]See his 1968 *Progress, Co-Existence, and Intellectual Freedom*. Unlike Solzhenitsyn, the Medvedev brothers, V. I. Chilidze, and other Russian critics of the regime, Sakharov did not emigrate but stayed in the Soviet Union to endure harassment until almost the end of his life.

[4]The Medvedevs wrote an account of Zhores's commitment to a mental institute, from which he was finally released in 1970 after an international campaign of protest, which was published as *A Question of Madness*.

ed a reformed socialism; the great Solzhenitsyn appeared to wish a return to Orthodox Christianity and the Slavic folk soul. (These modern Russians recapitulated the old battle of Slavophiles and Westernizers.)

More important, lagging Soviet productivity and technology clearly foreshadowed the economic collapse of the late 1980s. Students of the Soviet Union label 1976 as the year of a final withdrawal of public confidence in the regime, whose corruptions became manifest and whose excuses had run out. The title of a popular Soviet song told the story: "I Don't Believe in Promises Any More." The title of a book by the dissenter Andrei Amalrik, *Will the Soviet Union Survive until 1984?*, appeared at the time a rhetorical exaggeration, but it turned out to be sober truth. It earned the young historian an involuntary journey to Siberia, but he survived to become a famous refugee. The last of the Communist tsars had lost the will to destroy their enemies, or did not dare risk the international outrage that greeted news of persecution of scientists, scholars, and artists. Increasingly after 1974, when they deported Solzhenitsyn, the harried Kremlin bureaucrats preferred to permit or encourage the dissenters to leave the country. (More and more the famous ones escaped anyway by defecting during trips abroad, which it was extremely embarrassing to deny to Soviet artists and scientists.) In exile, they functioned as symbols of Soviet intolerance and continued to emit a torrent of revealing books, such as Roy Medvedev's massively documented history of Stalinism, *Let History Judge*, published in 1971 in England.

That Marxism is "a self-refuting system" the deconstructing John Gray (reviewing a season's crop of fourteen new Marx books in 1983) found evidenced by the Marxist societies themselves. "Its most spectacular victories in the real world have afforded the most devastating criticisms of [Marxism's] fundamental tenets." Successful socialist revolutions had given rise to wholly unsocialist and nonrevolutionary regimes. Perhaps the most authoritarian elite, and the most conservative, that ever existed ruled the major land of Marxian socialism. Moreover, with a fine irony this self-described Marxist order illustrated the points that Marx most denied, including the autonomous power of ideas. It had produced an "ideology" in the sense that Marx applied to the old regimes, supposedly absent in the new one. Further, this regime exemplified the primacy of politics rather than of economics, as Marx taught. The world's most privileged ruling class in the USSR owed its awesome power to purely political modes of domination. And while capitalism was dynamic, progressive, revolutionary, the land of socialism stagnated. An exact reversal of roles: Marx's worn-out social order, "a fetter on production," culturally sterile, suffering under the rule of a selfish privileged class—this was a perfect description of the regime that claimed to be Marxist.

The Third World countries which had once looked hopefully to the land of communism lost faith when it failed to deliver the goods. The competitive free market mounted an impressive economic comeback. The recipe for economic success seemed to lie here, not in Marxian economics, and even the Soviet area began to use it. Meanwhile Euro-communism, hopeful for a moment in the 1970s, lost its glamour too as it failed to yield much in the way of a new politics or society.

In his *Marxism and the French Left* (1986), Tony Judt placed between 1973 and 1978 the time "when Marxism lost its stranglehold upon the intellectual imagination of France." While 1956 and 1968 had mortally wounded the PCF, it kept the loyalty of an aging clientele who had acquired their faith in the 1930s and kept it the rest of their lives. (According to one calculation, by 1975 they were above the average in income, a function of their age no doubt.) This generation was now dying out. Separated from Moscow, Marxism had taken a new lease on life via Sartre, the Critical Marxists, the new Hegelianized or humanized Marx, and finally Althusser's desperate foray into structuralism. When these faded, Marxism largely expired as a vital option. Marx's analysis was more and more irrelevant to modern society and economics as the "proletariat" diminished in size and significance, outmoded along with the smokestack industries, the old-style factories, in a changing technology. "A myth is shattered—the myth of the revolutionary potential of the working class," Ludwig Reichhold declared in 1972 in his *Abschied von der Proletarischen Illusion* (End of the Proletarian Illusion). The revolutionaries of the new era came, in fact, largely from an academic and technological intelligentsia.

There were exceptions, for Marxism died hard; it had been the classical ideology of the intellectuals. But in 1986 Sunil Khilnani, reviewing Cornelius Castoriadis's *Domaines de l'homme* (The Estate of Man),[5] remarked that "Marxism, the reference point for almost all French intellectual activity between 1945 and the mid-1970s, has all but ceased to be a subject of serious discussion." Intellectuals found new amusements in later, more sophisticated ideas, now produced in profusion by academia. Some of these might make use of Marxist elements, but in such eclectic combination with neo-Freudian, structuralist, deconstructionist ones as to deprive Marxism of its independence. And this claim to be separate and unique was an essential part of Marxism's ascendancy; it could not survive amalgamation.

The contradiction in Marxism was that while it had to be a separate and self-contained body of thought, it could not refuse the challenge of new ideas. Marxist *praxis* claimed to meet the evolving world and interact with it. It was difficult to make Marxism a closed system. The "revisionists" who argued that true Marxism is open to change could find much to support their view in Marx's own life and thought. A real problem for Marxists was whether to reject a new strain of thought as bourgeois corruption or welcome it as scientific advance. In trying to avoid backwardness, one might fall into it. In the end, one was likely to give up any attempt to be "Marxist." One used Marx as one used every other thinker, taking what fitted the situation and rejecting what didn't. A study of neo-Marxism,[6] seeking common denominators in the divided Marx family, found that the only one with much substance was simply a reverence for Marx's "sacred aura." In the end, a book called *Marxism and Deconstruction* (by Michael Ryan, 1982) decided that rejecting "monolithic" and "authoritarian" Marxism leaves one free to select from "a plurality of struggles"—make up your own Marx.

---

[5]Founder of the review *Socialisme ou Barbarie* in 1949, Castoriadis was a kind of French Orwell, akin to Camus or Raymond Aron in France, who attacked Soviet communism as antirevolutionary and antisocialist.

[6]Robert Gorman, *Neo-Marxism: The Meanings of Modern Radicalism* (1982).

The neo-Marxists thought they could translate Marx's old-fashioned Victorian speech into a hip modern lingo. But why go this roundabout route? Why not simply address modern issues directly in a language appropriate to them? This vocabulary might retain some phrases from the one-time master, along with gleanings from other masters old and new. But it would not be "Marxian" any more than Weberian, Freudian, or Wittgensteinian. The only reason for hanging onto a privileged Marx is a religious one: he becomes a mythical figure, an icon, father and God, surrogate deity for the disinherited mind.

Something similar, of course, had happened to Freud. The Freud family continued to divide. In London during and just after World War II, Anna Freud carried on a terrible but obscure war with Melanie Klein and her disciples, jealously guarding her father's legacy against what she saw as subversive revision. Klein, who had been trained in authentically Freudian circles,[7] argued that the true spirit of Freud was progressive; he himself had not stayed the same, and would have expected his successors to refine his ideas. Anna, on the other hand, tended to see heresy in straying beyond the boundaries of the strict Freudian creed. The debate resembled that between orthodox and revisionist Marxism, and was equally fierce. Had these women had the power, they might have persecuted each other as fiercely as Stalin and Trotsky. The issues centered on formation of the ego or self in earliest infancy, a subject Freud had touched on in his "narcissus" image, but was now deepened. Both Anna and Melanie were experts in child psychology. The latter had invented a method of deciphering children's secret anxieties and phobias by watching them play with toys. Along with the Scottish psychologist W. R. D. Fairbairn, Klein developed the "object-relations" theory and speculated about the infant's differentiation between herself and the outer world, her formation of a self-image, rage against the mother as well as fixation on her. It was fascinating material; the fury with which these heirs of Freud fought over evidently trivial differences (in any case quite unprovable) continued the intensity of the earlier Freud circle.

Again, in the end Freudian and post-Freudian theories dissolved in a larger mix of ideas. The most noteworthy Freudian revival, in France in the 1960s, involved a synthesis of Freudianism with structural linguistics. Since the ghosts of both Marx and Freud interacted significantly with structruralism, it is time to introduce this intellectual fashion.

STRUCTURALISM

As a fashion in ideas in France, structuralism tended to be the successor to existentialism. In its name, anthropologist Claude Lévi-Strauss issued an explicit challenge to Sartre late in the 1950s. In its basic traits structuralism positioned itself at

---

[7]The Vienna-born Klein had undergone analysis with the old Freudian Sandor Ferenczi in Budapest, later in Berlin with Karl Abraham, before settling in England in 1926 to become a dominant figure in the British Psychoanalytic Society.

opposite poles from existentialism; it was cool, detached, objective, and impersonal. It did not see humanity as creating the world's meaning out of undetermined subjectivity, but the reverse: mathematical structures creating humanity.

The roots of structuralism were in linguistics. In the beginning—or almost—there had been Saussure. Of the same generation as Freud and Husserl (born in 1857), the Swiss Ferdinand Saussure studied at Leipzig, where Nietzsche had studied philology only a few years earlier, then taught in Paris and Geneva until his death in 1913. Saussure replaced philology, the historical study of language, with linguistics, an analysis of its formal structure. Published from his lectures, the *Course of General Linguistics* (1915) presented language as a system of signs, arbitrarily assigned—words have no logical connection with their referents. Meaning is in the system of signs, not in the thought of the subject; in the signifier (the word) rather than the signified. This system of signs, *la langue*, is a structure whose parts can be understood only in terms of the particular system as a whole. Wittgenstein and the logical positivists, it will be recalled, held similar views. But the science of linguistics remained largely confined to academic specialists until Lévi-Strauss applied structuralist methods to anthropology (myths, kinship systems); it soon became a tool of literary criticism, and then was adopted by Marxists, Freudians, sociologists, and historians, as a way of looking at things that might be used almost anywhere. It transcended specialized subjects to become a unifying force, able to exert a general intellectual appeal.

Structuralism was a rationalism. One does not discover the hidden harmonies or patterns by amassing empirical evidence, but by means of abstract mental constructs. A homely analogy is the newspaper: what interests the structuralists is its "layout," which largely determines the content. The layout is found to be arranged in a grammatical manner, like a sentence. The content is less interesting; Lévi-Strauss affected to be uninterested in the content of the hundreds of North American myths which he classified, tabulated, and found to be logically related according to their components.

The brilliant Lévi-Strauss, of a French-Jewish family, more than anyone else put structuralism on the map. He borrowed the idea from the linguistic scholar Roman Jakobson, who had migrated from Moscow via Prague to the United States, bringing with him the insights of Russian "formalism." Lévi-Strauss's dazzling demonstrations of the hidden order behind kinship systems and myths among primitive peoples subsequently came under attack for leaving out some of the data, as perhaps every grand social theory must. He was more a surrealist poet than a scientist, some have thought; certainly he wrote with a beautiful mastery of style, seeking like Wittgenstein to make his treatises resemble musical compositions. His friend and inspirer Jakobson also was a modernist literary personality who had been close to the poet Mayakovsky and others of the pre-1917 Russian *avant-garde*. It was this esthetic component that gave structuralism its appeal in the 1950s and 1960s when it was in high vogue, influencing the novel and film. But its claims to scientific precision were to be called into question. The obvious bias of Lévi-Strauss in favor of the "cool" world of these primitive peoples who lived in a timeless present rather than in the feverish pace of change, Western-style, was a criticism of European progress and technology.

A younger American scholar, Noam Chomsky, also influenced by Jakobson, made something of a sensation in 1957 with his book *Syntactic Structures*. Chomsky found a "deep structure" underlying the surface forms of sentences, a structure expressible in mathematical symbols; a built-in human capacity to understand basic grammatical principles and transform these into language as it exists. It was a kind of linguistic Kantianism, a critique of linguistic reason. But the structuralists did away with the subject. The structures that determine language and, by extension, all culture, are determinants which use individuals, as Hegel's "cunning of reason" had done. Hegel's agent had been the World Spirit, working through human history. Structuralism's was a hidden harmony of things, generating languages, patterns of culture, ideologies, and institutions.

This antihumanism was the most shocking part of structuralism. Humanity has been abolished; it was an invention now seen through. History is a process without a subject, its formations imposed on people by a "hidden mechanism," just as language forces us to think in certain ways. In literary criticism, the author was declared irrelevant to a study of his or her work; it is simply not important what pen was responsible for putting together this particular sequence of verbal formations. Historical treatments, including social background and cultural context, gave place to some sort of formal analysis. Structuralist historians rejected "historicism" in favor of a new paradigm for studying the past as social process rather than as a continuity of events. They joined other structuralists in seeking "emancipation from history." Human culture, leading structuralist critic Roland Barthes claimed, is an "untiring repetition."

Closely related to structural linguistics was the even more ambitious program of semiotics, or the science of signs in general—not just words, but gestures, pictures, clothing, anything that bears a message. Semiotics aspired to code the rules and signification processes in all cultural manifestations. Saussure defined "semiology" as "a science which studies the life of signs at the heart of social life.... It would teach us what signs consist of and what laws govern them." Linguistics was only one part of this general study. Traced back as far as John Locke, and especially to the American logician Charles Peirce in the later nineteenth century (Peirce's term was "semeiotics"), the new science of semiotics had a lofty philosophical pedigree, intersecting with symbolic logic. But almost anyone could use it to show that, for example, Shakespeare and the comic strips made use of the same communicative patterns. Umberto Eco, Italian high priest of semiotics, in an essay on semantics drew examples from Leonardo, *Finnegans Wake*, Felix the Cat, and Mandrake the Magician. It quickly became fashionable among literary scholars, always hungry for novel methods.

A prestigious group of scholars associated with the French journal *Annales d'histoire économique et sociale* (later *Annales: économies, societés, civilisations*) made fashionable a new kind of structural social history. The *Annales* historians, led initially by Lucien Febvre and Marc Bloch, the latter a hero and martyr of

World War II, disparaged narrative, political, "event" history, preferring to analyze the structure of society at any given time and place (they favored the medieval and early modern periods, the Mediterranean world) thus cutting across traditional national boundaries as well as conventional time units like "the Renaissance." With heavy use of statistical data processed by computers, they also drew on new material from local archives. They searched for a "total history," a full picture of the social scene surpassing older accounts that allegedly dealt only with "elites." Social history of this sort often consorted with left-wing politics; a number of the leading French social historians, including E. LeRoy Ladurie, began as Communists. But its more professionally researched findings diverged significantly from orthodox Marxism. An interesting debate broke out among Yugoslav Marxists about structuralist history. Structuralist Marxism clashed with the humanist variety. Louis Althusser thought that to view humans as making their own history is a myth of the historians, a "bourgeois" prejudice. People are puppets moved by laws of language and behavior that essentially do not change.

If one wished to make a political statement, one could say that the structures of authority, resting on discourse, serve the interest of the ruling class, and may perhaps be overthrown when this hidden unconscious logic of power is uncovered and exposed to view. Structuralist Marxists found history to be determined, not made by conscious individuals; the unconscious determinants, however, were not so much economic as psychological or linguistic. Cultural factors appear far more important than socioeconomic ones as modes of domination. A structuralizing Marxist of Frankfurt School lineage was Jürgen Habermas, who made Marx's ignoring of the psychological dimension his starting point, stressing the role of language in modes of domination, or what Habermas called "functionalist reason" as opposed to "instrumental reason," and eventually (1983) producing two ponderous volumes called *Theory of Communicative Action (kommunikativen Handelns)*.

A more controversial theorist was Michel Foucault, who established a considerable reputation or notoriety in the 1960s and 1970s before dying of AIDS in 1986. Foucault's books on the archaeology of knowledge and the structure of cultural change were marked by inconsistencies and shifts of ground (until in the end he laughed at himself), but also by brilliant historical theorizing apparently based on extraordinary research. Foucault was no coffeehouse dilettante, but a Sorbonne professor of the highest rating. Many of his arresting generalizations turned out to be wildly inaccurate.[8] This did not prevent them from having considerable visibility, so very scintillating were they. Foucault proposed a view of social change as consisting of sudden total shifts in the basic structure of language and knowledge,

---

[8]Foucault's early, perhaps best-known work, *History of Madness in the Age of Reason (Folie et déraison, 1961)* is based on the view that insanity did not exist until, beginning in the eighteenth century, people began defining it; also that alleged mad people were confined then because industrial society demanded it as a form of rationalized work discipline. But Roy Porter in his *History of Madness in England* (London, 1987) finds very little confinement before 1800, and this done not by the State; nor any correlation with industrialization. Moreover, the notion of mental illness existed long before the psychiatric profession appeared.

the *episteme*; in the words of another structuralist historian, Thomas S. Kuhn (*The Structure of Scientific Revolutions*), a "paradigm shift."

Like other structuralist Marxists, Foucault offered a kind of epistemological rather than economic determinism. His view of the great change that brought in capitalism or "bourgeois civilization" was more like Weber's than Marx's; principles of rationality, discipline, efficiency had taken over society's ways of classifying and dealing with crime, madness, sickness, illiteracy. Not only factories but prisons, asylums, clinics, schools regimented the masses for work and production. Foucault saw all this as linked in one great process, of which the common denominator was a new system of language and meaning.

This was stimulating, but not reducible to any easy system. "There is no Foucault system; one cannot be a Foucauldian" as one can be (still?) a Marxist or Freudian," Alan Sheridan remarked in his 1980 book about Foucault. "The Subversion of Intellect" was the subtitle of another study of the French theorist. In the end he reduced all theorizing to a rhetorical game. Here he impinged on deconstruction, discussed in the next chapter. At its edges, structuralism tended, oddly, to slide into deconstruction. It had begun by assuming there is a definite meaning to writing, history, society, though not the same kind of meaning usually found, or not found by the same kind of method; it has to be "decoded" (a cult word). Structuralism ended in doubts about whether there is any single meaning.

Lévi-Strauss had presented structuralism as an answer to historical relativism, a "science of the permanent," a new principle of certainty; also a unifying perspective tying together the various parts of the sundered body of humane studies, applicable to literature, sociology, history, popular culture, art. (*The Hidden Order of Art* was a notable structuralist title.) Though admittedly their origin is mysterious, these hidden mechanisms, these deep structures printed in the human mind and showing up in all human culture, constitute a fundamental reality. But evidently in their search for this logic printed into the nature of things the structuralists, like many other social scientists before them (like the first of them, the "ideologue" Destutt de Tracy), discovered the irrational more than the rational. An opening to "deconstruction" lay in the structuralist claim that the individual's intellectual self does not matter; he or she is determined by words, "inhabited by language."

Like all the grand structuralist theorists, Foucault was difficult to understand. To be more or less incomprehensible became a *sine qua non* of grand theory. In French high intellectual culture the rule seemed to be the more obscure, the more prestigious. To be at all formidable a writer must, as someone said of Julia Kristeva, "play wilfully at the edges of unintelligibility." The prime example was Jacques Lacan, French Freudian-structuralist who became a fabled cult figure in the world of intellectual high fashion. Someone described Lacan as "Freud crossed with structural linguistics and strained through some of the most harrowing French since Mallarmé." Lacan's celebrated lectures paid tribute to his theory that the unconscious, realm of the outrageous and absurd as well as the obscene, must be unleashed. "Lacan does not lecture, he produces resonances," it was said. Dressed in outrageous costumes, "he speaks in a wavering, syncopated, or thundering voice, spiced with sighs and hesitations," trying to mimic the unconscious.

Early in his career Lacan was the leading figure in a notable Freud revival in France, where in fact Freudianism had never done as well as elsewhere in Europe (despite the notable presence of Princess Marie Bonaparte in Freud's own circle). Predictably, the orthodox psychoanalysts threw him out for miscellaneous heresies. In fact Lacan drew on an amazing variety of intellectual sources. He was influenced by Saussure, Jakobson, and Lévi-Strauss, also by Wittgenstein (there is no metalanguage, we cannot know language, only *be* it). Lacan had a remarkable facility for threading these different modern perspectives together; his thirst for an all-embracing synthesis rivals that of Joyce or Toynbee, except that he performed on the theoretical level. Few could fail to be excited by the way he wove structural linguistics into psychoanalysis, relating the unconscious and the Oedipus complex to the child's entrance into the "symbolic order" of public discourse.

Lacan had also absorbed the symbolic logicians, Frege, Cantor, Boole, Russell; ideas of infinity and empty sets appear in his complex thought. So did the Hegel whom French philosophers Kojéve and Hyppolite had revived and reinterpreted. Lacan seemed to offer a synthesis of all that was going on in the 1950s and 1960s, if one could only understand him. But, Lacan said, it would take at least ten years for anyone to do that. "I don't have a doctrine, I have a style. " Perhaps his arcane vocabulary and deliberate mystifications, put forward as the language of the unconscious, were only a massive put-on. A consummate showman, was he really a profound thinker? His role among the 1968 students was to provide the sportive, prank-playing side a status in high theory, going along with Marxism of the Harpo variety, a type of inspired insanity later translated to the television screen by "Monty Python."

All the structuralists expressed a profound alienation. Lévi-Strauss had used it to esteem primitive peoples above modern civilization. Barthes (*Mythologies,* 1957) called himself a "mythologue" or professional demythologizer, whose relationship to the world was a sarcastic one. Understanding is seeing-through. Structuralism joined Freudianism as a subverter of apparent meanings. In leading on to its apparent opposite, deconstruction, much of structuralism was preserved, not least this urge to undermine conventional truths and apparent realities.

THE FEMINIST REVOLUTION

Feminism was a term in common use during the very lively agitation by women in Edwardian England, a crusade which some bewildered men joined and many uncomprehending women rejected; the chief goal of the embattled women, mostly upper-class, who used "civil disobedience" methods that would have put the CND to shame, was legal equality, especially the right to vote. These goals were so far achieved (in Britain, at least; women won the vote in France only after World War II) that the issue was widely regarded as settled.

Nothing showed the gap between the fifties and the next decades more than the woman question. It scarcely existed in the former years. "Gone are the days of vigorous feminism and antifeminism," the eminent British anthropologist E. E. Evans-Pritchard remarked in a 1955 lecture. "Surely these are...'issues which are dead and gone.'" The generation of the Pankhursts and Virginia Woolf had resolved them. The New Woman who had made her debut in the 1900s settled in during the 1920s and was now a permanent resident. In 1956 an ad for a book on women's education in a British journal of sociology referred to "the emancipation which they have achieved in recent decades." No crystal ball was ever more clouded than Pritchard's. But the postwar decade, to the chagrin of later feminists, featured women happily married to a Dream Man, raising children amid cosy domesticity. Geoffrey Gorer's inquiry into women's magazines in Britain in the 1950s found an "incredibly chaste" fiction, with none of the frank discussions about sex and how to be sexier that came later. The sexual revolution was only just about to begin. The time of militant "women's liberationists" outraged at patriarchal repression was years down the road.

Jean-Paul Sartre's close companion Simone de Beauvoir did indeed write a book often hailed as a harbinger of the future; at that time (1948) she denied, however, being a "feminist." *The Second Sex* was a remarkable existential study in the life-meaning of being a woman, the ways in which, for example, girls saw their future differently from boys and had their choices restricted. In her later years Beauvoir campaigned actively for women's rights. Sartre was far from a supporter of female equality; the usual Existentialist view was like that of D. H. Lawrence, cherishing the polarity between the sexes and seeing woman as representing an entirely different principle of life—better, perhaps, than the male, but only insofar as it stood totally apart from the masculine realm of power and politics.

Male intellectuals had their own version of the "separate spheres" concept. The literary, symbolist, Nietzschean avant-garde had typically seen women as non-rational creatures, erotic and sensuous, "natural" as opposed to the artificiality of civilization; their metier was not thinking. The early modernists—Apollinaire and the Futurists are examples—were antifeminist if by this is meant they held a separate sphere for women. Marinetti, for example, supported divorce in cases of incompatibility but thought, like Lawrence, that the sexes should be educated separately and deplored the effects of women's entrance into the work force during the war. ("Marriage and the Family," in *Futurist Democracy*, 1919.)

The feminists, indeed, found little support in the mainstream of the radical tradition. Marx had been a card-carrying male chauvinist, the Russian Revolution a masculine club (the rare woman Bolshevik, like Alexandra Kollontai, felt uncomfortable and was shunted to the fringes.) Class came first, as the Social Democrats explained to those who raised the *Frauenfrage*; women should stand behind their husbands in solidarity against the class enemy. Time enough after the revolution to think about other issues. Prominent Social Democratic women like Clara Zetkin and Rosa Luxemburg on the whole accepted this logic, though there were tensions and "contradictions." Soviet Russia proved to be far from a par-

Simone de Beauvoir. Associated in the popular mind with Jean-Paul Sartre, Madame de Beauvoir was herself a prolific writer and, among other things, a pioneer feminist. (Gilles Peress/Magnum Photos)

adise for women, who continued except for some tokenism to be excluded from the highest citadels of power, and who found themselves having to serve both as factory workers and homemakers.

Nietzsche was notorious for some of his apparently misogynist expressions; and as for Freud, his views affronted the feminists mightily. Though a surprising number of Freud's closest friends and disciples were women (among others, his own daughter Anna, Princess Marie Bonaparte, Karen Horney, Melanie Klein,

Helene Deutsch, Lou Andreas Salome), classical Freudianism, noting the failure of the female to participate in the great Oedipal drama (the comparable jealousy of her mother by a girl they considered not so strong a force), found here an explanation for woman's allegedly weaker creative power. Envying the male his sexual organ, she learns to think of herself as inferior. Freud's own life reflected a belief in the traditional role of woman as wife and mother, staying in the home. It is true that, moving with the times, he had changed somewhat by 1932. Still, most feminists, initially at least, placed him well inside the camp of male chauvinists. It is significant that Melanie Klein's revisions of Freud included a much greater role for the mother in the child's emotional development.

Some radical feminists of the 1970s were reacting against the masculine arrogance typical of the 1960s rebels. Fidel Castro wondered who would do the cooking and washing if women took to politics. New Left radicals tended to be "macho" in their attitude toward women in a way feminists thought offensive. Sartre himself, especially in his early writings, is strongly misogynist. Sexual liberation, some feminists believed, had created an atmosphere in which women became objects to be exploited. In any case, a wave of radical feminism emerged after 1968, featuring the fervent if naive writings of such prophets of the movement as Gloria Steinem, Shulamith Firestone, and Germaine Greer. The movement was stronger in Great Britain and the United States than in France.

In its simpler form, this revolutionary faith resembled basic Marxism with the Woman substituted for the Worker as the forlorn creature who, oppressed through all previous history, was now at last rising up to claim freedom. The enemy oppressor was "patriarchy" rather than "ruling class." It is interesting that this revolution confronted the same divisive dilemma as the proletarian one: was it to be a total revolution drastically changing all previous society, or a gradual and peaceful one arising within the old society and preserving its progressive features? The more radical feminists regarded all previous forms of society and all modes of knowledge and discourse as tyrannical. If a woman enters this patriarchal environment she becomes corrupted by it; the equivalent of embourgeoisment was anthropization. The woman revolution must create a wholly different culture. The very language must be altered. There would have to be feminine institutions of all sorts, replacing the existing ones—anti-universities, publishers, journals—for all the old ones were tainted by patriarchalism. The stain discredited all Western thought from the Greeks on down; one would have to start all over! "A feminist reading of the history of logic" (Andrea Nye, 1991) found that its masculine provenance had discredited the very process of thinking. Lacan held that the very structure of language, not just its words, is masculine. "The phallus is the first signifier."

Among the growing number of women scholars, those who wrote sympathetically about notable women of the past, or dug up overlooked women of distinction, or even found that most women had not been unhappy with "separate spheres" (leaving power and politics to the men), were accused of condoning patriarchal domination. They were "gender collaborationists." By the same token, the radicals downgraded previous heroines, reading Virginia Woolf out of the Party because, on close inspection, she was found wanting in faith, too inclined to write about and for men, too interested in other matters like literature. (Her *Night and Day* had actually made fun of the humorless suffragettes.)

On the other hand, a historicist dilemma confronted these revolutionaries. From where did the women's revolution come, if not out of the old order? There must have been something good in patriarchalism, since its environment conceived feminism and nurtured it. If the heritage was entirely patriarchal, how could it have produced feminism? Why, after so many centuries, had the feminist fruit finally ripened? Moderate feminists asked only that the present society be opened to more female participation, and that the old thought be reinterpreted and corrected, not condemned and abandoned. They did not demand a dictatorship of women, but an "androgynous" regime with men and women sharing power as equals. These issues proved divisive; at international conferences, feminist leaders quarreled as bitterly as socialists had. A great 1982 convention proved a disaster.

The greatest achievement of organized women was to open up careers from which women previously had been largely excluded. Though this was uneven, and women continued to complain of inequality, progress was startling in many places. By 1990 women constituted 40 percent of the civilian work force in Western Europe, a third of the doctors in Britain and Portugal were women, and women made up 31 percent of Denmark's parliament, though the female component in the sciences and engineering still seemed to lag. This was part of a momentous revolution in the family. Marriage became less common, divorce much more so, single-parent families widespread. Nearly a quarter of all babies were born out of wedlock in 1990, rising from 5 percent in 1960. "We have simply ceased to live in these respects as all previous societies have lived," historian-demographer Peter Laslett remarked. This is a significant factor in recent history; its causes, as usual in such great happenings, reveal an intimate intersection of ideas and technology, intellectual and social history.

In many ways, the ideas of the women's movement and even its activities were not all that new. The opinion of some visionary feminists that the whole thing began in 1968 (which one of them named Year One of the new age) stood in glaring opposition to the fact that there had been significant waves of feminism in the past, from the Hellenistic age of ancient Greece through the Renaissance, the Enlightenment, and the Edwardian suffragette crusade. One proposed model saw cycles of feminist revolt, followed by relapse into patriarchy, occurring all through history. Brigid Brophy noted cynically that "Women have achieved social emancipation almost as often as the working class, each time with universal amnesia of its ever having happened before." (A similar case of cultural amnesia was the rediscovery of the American Indian every generation in the United States.) This most recent uprising actually drew on the works of many past women, including Mary Wollstonecroft in the eighteenth century, Harriet Martineau, George Sand, Harriet Taylor, Josephine Butler, and a crowd of others in the nineteenth, and Virginia Woolf and others in the twentieth (A lively fifteenth-century discovery was Christine of Pisa, who seems to have used most of the arguments for women's liberation found among the Greers and Firestones.)

Still, no one could doubt the vigor of the 1970s epiphany of feminism. Its magnitude owed much to a female invasion of the universities, now the chief center of intellectual activity, at least of the published variety. From one angle, feminism could be viewed as another quest for novelty in the neophiliac world of competing scholars in the humanities, offering the possibility of reinterpreting almost everything. To look at things from the woman's perspective was to challenge established verdicts and canons. "The intellectual interest of this subject is extraordinary," Evelyne Sullerot declared. "You have the impression of discovering a country in all its dimensions, different from that which is usually presented." The French Revolution had been endlessly combed and reinterpreted, but almost no one had seen it as a victory for male domination; the Jacobins had not been remembered for forcing the women to stay silent and for executing the author of a Declaration of the Rights of Woman.

Almost every great historical event, and every literary figure or movement, looked different when viewed from the distaff side. The new social historians' "history from the bottom up" received a new twist most of them had not thought of. "Women's studies" soon became the greatest academic industry of them all, producing a volume of literature requiring enormous bibliographies to keep track of it. The immense flow still continues; every event of the past, every writer has to be done over again from the female perspective. Of course, every generation had always found *some* excuse for this repetition.

Second-generation feminist critic-scholars, by the laws of academic neophilia, had to do something different than the first, and the generations seemed to change every few years. This caused subtle changes in the style of feminist criticism. It became more fashionable to show that celebrated figures were really feminist than to expose their sinister patriarchalism. Too naive, the older sisters had thought that Shakespeare and Conrad were sexist pigs; they should have seen that, rescued from "masculine ownership," these great writers really ennoble women or at least offer them opportunities for "empowerment." It all depends on how you read the text, which, as everyone was learning, has no determinate meaning. Freud, once seen as an arch-sexist, now became interesting to many feminists; indeed Kate Ford, reviewing several books on the subject in 1990, declared that "the *rapprochement* of feminism and psychoanalysis is one of the great modern intellectual adventures." (This would seem to be a case of one of those mergers of enterprises as common in the intellectual world as in the financial; two theoretical competitors find that after all they have much in common and much to gain by sharing the market.)

In this respect feminism intertwined with academic specialization, discussed in the following chapter. One problem was that the competitive pressure for university jobs and promotion made for a kind of subtlety which cut off the academic feminists from the general public. It also involved them in complex disputes with each other. The mystifications of high theory à la Lacan, Foucault, Derrida, and such other favored theorists as Kristeva and Bakhtin invaded the militant feminist cause, often with detrimental effects. Germaine Greer, one of the original founding mothers, complained in 1988 (*TLS* June 3–9, p. 629) that feminist academic literary critics change their jargon monthly, and "any critic who falls behind and uses outdated 'concepts' or, worse, no jargon at all forfeits all claim to serious consideration." "The mastery of the jargon has become more important than the understanding of the text."

Such frenetic in-house novelty-hunting, the product of academic competition and hyperspecialization, grew amazingly in the 1980s. Feminism had been coopted as a part of the academic game. Feminists liked deconstruction because it enabled them to show the implicit patriarchal structure of the work in question, not merely in its choice of words and figures, but in its very syntax. Among the most vocal feminists were literary theorists writing in a way that few of their sisters outside the academic professional world could understand at all—and (students complained) refusing to talk to anyone except the few who shared their esoteric vocabulary. Their belief that they were leading a great revolution while earning their academic tenure was astonishing.

Visible also were feminine scholars bogged down in the familiar endless details of specialized research: one who began with the goal of re-creating women's spirituality might find herself spending the rest of her life editing the poems of Christina Rossetti (perhaps as she settled comfortably into tenure and lost her initial enthusiasm).[9] This is to push the picture ahead a few years, and is not meant to deny the vitality of the first wave of feminist scholarship. It was like discovering a new land. But from the beginning it was hard to find any specific theory of feminism, while the sisterhood was always deeply divided within itself, between pragmatists and utopians, reformers and revolutionaries. Women who asked for a greater share in the existing society conflicted with those who called this selling out to the enemy.

Leading feminists proved uncertain of their position. Greer herself eventually left behind a large number of followers disillusioned by her shifts, which included a turn toward chastity after preaching sexual emancipation. Advance toward the latter goal, it occured to some, might mean regression rather than advance for the majority of women who, not equipped to understand Kristeva, had to live in the world as it is. They might leave the relative security of marriage for the right to compete in the employment market, while sacrificing parenthood or trying the difficult role of single parent. Juliet Mitchell in 1971 (*Woman's Estate*) feared that "the new national liberation of sexuality and laxity of marriage most often frees women only into insecurity, economic as much as emotional." In a

---

[9]Howard Nemerov's poem "A Full Professor" described the humanist as careerist:

Surely there was, at first, some love of letters
To get him started on the routine climb
That brought him to this eminence in time?
But now he has become one of his betters.

1982 book, pioneer feminist Betty Friedan seemed to call for a truce in the war between men and women.

Like other revolutions that began with high hopes, feminism inevitably experienced some disenchantment. Much evidence indicated that "liberation" did not bring most women happiness, but new anxieties and uncertainties. In the 1990s feminist books were still complaining that nothing much had changed, women were still unhappy. Men were too, it was occasionally noted.

Ironically, the leading female political personality of the 1980s aroused little feminist enthusiasm. Mrs. Margaret Thatcher, the Conservative prime minister of Great Britain who set a record by winning three consecutive elections, never found much support among her sisters. Feminists who had expected a female messiah to rescue the human race from the monstrous regiment of men did not think much of her; they were usually of the left, and revealed their primary loyalty to a (male-invented) political ideology rather than to pure feminism— cheering for any woman. Here again other values and other causes intruded to hamper feminist solidarity.[10]

It might be argued that for most feminists, liberation was an individual matter; they wanted to be free personally, to create and achieve fame and fortune. Solidarity with other women against the whole of the male tribe was a feeling without much real substance. In the competitive professional world they entered, some of their enemies or rivals were women, some of their allies men. They wanted equality for women only in the sense that individual women must not be penalized for their gender.

One problem with any emancipation movement like feminism was that it had to compete with numerous others. Homosexual males arose to demand their rights to be accepted as equals, treated with respect, and not discriminated against; again, history and literary criticism had to be rewritten to take account of a once suppressed component. Blacks and other racial minorities filed similar claims. Black feminists felt estranged to a degree from white ones. There was a black lesbian as well as a white lesbian identity; no doubt some distance separated black lesbians from white gays. An Indian woman announced herself a "third-world Marxist feminist"; it sounded formidable, but one wonders how in any real poltiical situation she could sort out the conflicting claims of race, sex, and class. (In the case of Islamic women, a strong antifeminist impulse emerged, registering their attachment to the fundamentalist movement so strong in the Middle East; they chose nation and religion over gender, a choice that required them to accept fiercely patriarchal values.)

Feminist commitment and academic neutrality might clash uncomfortably.

---

[10]Freud and psychology could subvert the women's movement as well as other crusades by revealing how palpably personal unhappiness bred the role of public rebel. For an example, see Steven C. Hause, *Hubertine Auclert, The French Suffragette* (1987). Kate Millett's memoir, *The Loony-Bin Trip* (1991), disclosed the depths of personal instability in one of the first and most brilliant feminist scholars.

Was it bad faith to put gender loyalty over critical judgment, or disloyalty to the cause ever to admit that a male writer was better than a female? (Amy Lowell a better poet than Yeats, and Virginia Woolf a better novelist than Joyce, were examples of feminist opinions that would raise eyebrows.) The female reviewer of a raft of feminist literary criticism (*TLS*, March 11–17, 1988) reproached several British women critics for arriving at their own judgments without attention to the collective cause. As it happened, these were the most distinguished authors. A woman of real professional and critical stature was likely to be a person of independent judgment unwilling to follow any Party line, even that of feminism (who would set it?) So quarrels inevitably arose between women within the movement.

All of this made for many books, many controversies, innumerable conferences, whose noise fills the contemporary world. But as society dissolved into its constituent elements, the world of knowledge and of history lost its unity, became a cacophony of different voices, and ceased to be comprehensible as a whole. Feminism was just one cause, one theoretical strategy among many.

A NOTE ON THE LOSS OF INHIBITIONS

Despite some rear-guard skirmishing, the path after the *Lady Chatterley's Lover* case led steadily away from any censorship of published matter on moral grounds. In the twelve years since the Lawrence trial under a new Obscene Publications Act, C. H. Rolph remarked in 1972, "the development of 'literary frankness' and pictorial nudity has been almost incredibly swift." It still had some way to go. By 1980 all European countries had given up prosecutions for obscenity. This unprecedented process, needless to say, did not go unchallenged. Along with much approval of this release from repression and hypocrisy, an occasional voice protested against "a horrible epidemic...that threatens our country's psychic health" (British author and educator David Holbrook, in 1972). But ten years later virtually no one among the intellectuals defended censoring anything. Julian Symons's estimate of the British situation in 1982 was that "almost anything may be published without risk of prosecution, and anything short of closely simulated sex acts is permitted on films or stage." After that there was even more progress, with hard-core sex films readily available on VCR and television. In the 1960s and 1970s sex shops and X-rated movies were likely to be confined to special areas where the "counterculture" flourished, such as Copenhagen's famous "free city." Not so a decade later. A number of painstaking attempts to mediate the issue—public commissions and committees, assemblies of the learned—usually ended in a characteristic failure to agree on anything: What is pornography? Is it harmful? If so, is there any way of suppressing it that is not even more harmful?[11]

---

[11]See Gordon Hawkins and Franklin E. Zimring, *Pornography in a Free Society*, and Susan Gubar and Joan Hoff, eds., *For Adult Users Only: The Dilemma of Violent Pornography* (both 1990).

The only protest with any force came from those embattled feminists who believed pornography degrading to women. "The whole pattern of pornography is one long woeful saga of female degradation," Jill Tweedie observed. Earlier feminists had generally thought free love and sexual promiscuity antifeminine. In 1992 a writer observed that though his bookseller displayed Salman Rushdie's famous *Satanic Verses*, on which Iranian Islamicists had passed a death sentence, he could not buy a novel that Andrea Dworkin and her group had boycotted.[12] In 1992 a prominent British woman was leading an effort to get a new and less permissive law enacted. But such feminists as Dworkin, who attributed the pornographic debasement of women to male compulsion, ignored the fact that liberated women freely posed for pictures in *Playboy* (and innumerable other magazines of this sort), and performed in X-rated films, the market for which was extensive. And some feminists took the "hard core" revolution to heart, arguing that women should exploit it for their own purposes.[13]

The shock effect of using the forbidden words and displaying the forbidden acts proved a bonanza for writers, particularly dramatists. The London stage in the 1960s was enlivened by scenes of babies being stoned to death, soldiers burned alive, as well as explicit sexual scenes, including homosexual rape. It could still outrage the citizenry. Joe Orton, subsequently murdered by his homosexual lover, observed that "Sex is the only thing that infuriates them. Much more fucking [on stage, in one of his plays] and they'll be screaming hysterics in next to no time." The diminutive Spaniard Fernando Arrabal, whose childhood had been traumatized by the civil war, became a Parisian favorite in the 1970s; his themes included "sadism, masochism, matricide, necrophilia, scatology, perversion, and stage nudity" (Francis Donahue).

But the shock effect eventually wore off. By 1969, the liberal *New York Times* was commenting that "the insensate pursuit of the urge to shock…is bound to achieve its own antidote in total boredom." And casting a considerable pall on the sexual revolution—even *Playboy* finally could not ignore it—was the AIDS epidemic of the 1980s. The "joy of sex" became a little less hilarious in light of this modern plague, which seemed to be associated with sexual excess.[14] The real winners in the sexual revolution, wrote British author John Ryle, "have been the viruses and bacteria that exploit the new vectors created by widespread promiscuity and unusual sexual practices."

If the physical consequences of sexual liberation were appalling, some also

---

[12]Review by John Sutherland in *TLS* of Edward de Grazia's whimsically titled history of censorship in the United States, *Girls Lean Back Everywhere* (1992).

[13]See Linda Williams, *Hard Core*, and Lynne Segal and Mary McIntosh, eds., *Sex Exposed: Sexuality and the Pornography Debate* (both 1992).

[14]"The epidemic had broken out in American homosexuals not because they had 'sinned against nature,' but because, as a group, they had been more prone to promiscuity than heterosexuals…. The current AIDS pandemic was released when a series of circumstances coincided, facilitating the transmission of the highly virulent strains of an old virus, namely sexual contacts of a quantitatively new type…. " Mirko D. Grmek, *History of AIDS* (trans. Maulitz and Duffin, 1990), pp. 168, 158.

questioned the mental ones. The argument of Celia Haddon in *The Limits of Sex* (1983) that liberation leads to more anxiety and guilt than it appeases repeated a view held by Freud himself. Yet of course the opposite view remains; "the sexual fix" (Stephen Heath) has its loyal following.

THE GREEN REVOLUTION

Joining feminism as a leading "cause" in the last decades of the century, winning the allegiance of devoted acolytes, was environmentalism. Both at their extremes were tinged with a deep negativism, at bottom resting on a bitter rejection of the main values by which Western civilization had lived virtually since its beginning. They contemplated some vague total revolution or apocalypse. The prophet of the "Greens" might be Heidegger, to whom even building a bridge was an unwarranted interference with the natural order. Or William Blake:

Kill not the moth or butterfly,
For the Last Judgment draweth nigh.

Destroying a single link in the great chain of being impairs the whole balance of nature. Voices from the mystic East persuaded uneasy Westerners that every particle of being had a soul.

The Greens came to be the leading counter-Establishment political organization in many parts of Europe, not least West Germany, and including even the USSR, where a popular filmmaker like Vasily Shukshin expressed nostalgia for an older rural society. An archetypal pastoralism inhabited the Green mystique, but very practical matters of technology and of economics were involved. The early stages of environmentalism connected chiefly to dislike of atomic energy, on vaguely moral as well as health and safety grounds. Later, atomic energy might seem preferable to burning the oil and coal responsible for the global warming caused by an excess of carbon dioxide in the upper atmosphere. At first too, critics of unrestrained industrial development thought scarce sources of energy were being used too rapidly, a disservice to posterity. Less was heard about this later, more about questions of ozone depletion, of global warming (the "greenhouse effect)," of acid rain and deforestation.

Fashionable doomsayers in the 1980s replaced nuclear extinction with these other enviromental perils, though the catastrophe at the Soviet nuclear plant at Chernobyl near Kiev in 1986, sending clouds of radioactive gases around the world, did little to ease the former fear. An example is Günter Grass's novel *Die Rättin* (The Rats, Munich, 1986). *Der grosse knall* will doubtless get us in the end, but if it doesn't ozone depletion or acid rain will, determined pessimists such as the famed German novelist not implausibly argued. As the underdeveloped world—at least 80 percent of the total population—advanced on modernization with determination if often frustration, one wondered how the world would fare when everybody consumed energy and produced waste and contaminants in the way a minority now does.

So environmentalism was an attractive ideology, combining Romantic nature worship with hostility to the cheap values of a materialist, "consumerist" society, and offering to save humanity from ecological disaster. The "green" appeal was surprisingly popular. In 1992 the *Economist* grumbled, "So effectivly have environmentalists greened public opinion that it takes an unashamed reactionary to question the wisdom of becoming ever greener and cleaner." This leading news journal did, citing the enormous cost of existing or proposed legislation, and the law of diminishing returns applying to the quest for hyper-cleanness of air, water, and soil. Was environmentalism the new anticapitalism, replacing Marxism? The ultimate contradiction of capitalism was not an impoverished proletariat or inadequate consumption, but pollution. The system choked on the waste products of its own hyperproductivity.

The Greens also split ideologically into realists and purists, those willing to work gradually "within the system" for more conservation, parks, purer air and those who rejected the entire technological-consumerist society, even if it was not clear how its destruction was to be accomplished.[15] Lost young souls from Europe and the United States roamed the roads of India in search of Nirvana, even as India itself was engaged in a struggle to modernize. A type of literature also flourished in which Americans gone native, perhaps discovering an ancient Native American identity, recounted their ramblings over the western countryside, much as the Beat poets of the 1950s had done, but usually on motorcycles and in search of a bestseller.

The underdeveloped world had in general little sympathy with the environmentalist opponents of economic development. The USSR itself was an ecological disaster area. Poor countries seeking exports to pay for technological modernization were the worst offenders in cutting down forests, which enhanced the greenhouse effect by removing consumers of carbon dioxide.

Such contradictions between various "counter-hegemonic" causes were legion. The established order, if such a thing exists—fashionably put, the "hegemonic discourse"—is safe enough because the numerous dissenters go in different directions and contradict each other.[16] Radical feminists hate all men including the left-wing ones. Freudians and Marxists deconstruct each other. Environmentalists clash with advocates of greater economic development. Antitechnology led one feminist writer to argue tortuously that women have been "smothered by technology"; they were better off in the good old days before electric washing machines. In

---

[15]An example of the split is Martin Lewis, *Green Delusions: An Environmentalist Critique of Radical Environmentalism* (1992), in which one who calls himself a sane environmentalist argues that the extremist policies, if carried out, would cause more ecological damage than they would prevent.

[16]Conservatives think that the left dominates the realm of discourse; "in every branch of the American media the same kind of political orthodoxy obtains," Hilton Kramer asserts—an orthodoxy shaped by "the left-liberal politics of race, class, and gender." *TLS*, January 17, 1992.

other corners, gays crusade for their own version of sexual emancipation while a host of other creeds, ethnic and religious, shout their slogans. The abortion issue bitterly divides those who call abortion freedom and those who detect in it a dehumanizing disregard for life.

In the cacophony of international urban culture, radical protest falls victim to the pervasive pluralism. Instead of one great movement that might have some chance of success, a dozen or more "counter-hegemonic discourses" cancel each other out. They all gain a hearing, they all have their devotees, but they are simply pieces of the huge, formless social mass that is the contemporary world, far too big and too unintegrated to submit to total change. Its only successful common principle is the free market in which they all compete, and where none may gain a monopoly.

11

The Deconstructive 1980s

THE DECLINE OF THE EAST

Among many memorable changes in the 1980s, the downfall of the Soviet Communist order must rank as the foremost. The age of Lenin drew to an end; a presence that had virtually dominated the European and world scene for most of the century, deeply affecting thought both by attraction and repulsion, suddenly ceased to exist. The collapse of the Soviet economy came rather swiftly in the 1980s; that so few among a distinguished corps of Sovietologists predicted it said something about the state of the historians' art, and may have contributed to the next decade's cynical anti-intellectualism.

A specialist symposium published in 1983 titled *The Soviet Economy: Toward the Year 2000*[1] included such judgments as a prediction that the USSR's gross national product would continue to grow at an annual rate of better than 3 percent to the year 2000, and that the odds were "overwhelmingly against" any fundamental economic reform. In reviewing this book, Soviet expert Alec Nove, while suggesting a possible system crisis added that "It would indeed be wrong to

---

[1]Edited by Abram Bergson and Herbert S. Levine; New York and London, 1983. Reviewed *TLS* August 5, 1983.

suggest that the Soviet Union is in any danger of collapse or disintegration." This was typical of professional judgment. A review of books about the Soviet economy in September 1983 thought there was no reason to believe that "the current disorder of the Eastern economies is more profound than that of the Western economies." Yet at that time disintegration was well underway. It is true that the end came in a series of spectacular events in 1989 and 1990, which left the world gasping. But a serious illness was in evidence from at least 1976 on.

In *Les empires contre l'Europe* (1985), Regis Debray, the one-time Castroite and Guevarist, pointed out to French intellectuals that the Soviets were no longer even a threat, having lost the competition with America in every area including the cultural: "the inhabitants of the most remote Siberian village hum California rock music." But the cultural decay of a Soviet Union which had long ceased to produce anything interesting in the arts was not the same as economic collapse, and few expected it. It came as only the last in a long series of twentieth-century surprises. (Very few had expected World War I, Hitler's rise to power, the Great Depression, the recovery of Europe after 1945, the microchip revolution, and most other epochal events.)

In 1922 the Viennese economic theorist Ludwig von Mises alleged that only the market can provide a rational system of allocating resources. A planned economic system has no way to determine real costs of production. The attempt to decide on prices by administrative fiat can only lead to confusion and breakdown. "The motive force of the whole process which gives rise to the factors of production is the ceaseless search on the part of the capitalist and entrepreneur to maximize their profits by serving the customer's wishes." Likewise there was a fatal flow in divorcing managerial performance and managerial reward. The most effective answer to von Mises' charge that a socialist economy was simply unworkable came from the Polish-born University of Chicago economist Oskar Lange, who stipulated the necessity of "market socialism," with considerable decentralization of planning. Another line of theory saw the answer in simulation of a market by elaborate mathematicization.

Such ideas, however, were never implemented in the USSR. The remarkably rapid disintegration of the old order in the USSR and throughout Eastern Europe in 1989–90 could be explained by the simple fact that, having failed miserably, one whole economic system had to be replaced by another one. Between a system based on commands from central planning offices and one based on freely negotiated contracts, between bureaucratic allocation and a market determination of production and prices, there could be no middle ground. *Tertium non quid.* The changeover was bound to be agonizingly painful, but was best done as quickly as possible. The new capitalists were now found in the lands of communism.

It is too early to appraise the outcome of the Communist overturn in the former Soviet Union.. "The past five years have seen a renaissance in Russian writing comparable to that immediately before and after the Revolution," Sally Laird remarked in 1991. Catching up with the past absorbed much of the scene: works written long before but unpublishable, authors with underground reputations now able to come forward, memoirs of the long terror, exposures of countless crimes from the hideous past mingled with attempts to catch up with a half century of literary isolation from the West. All this filled magazines and books eagerly absorbed by a public starved for anything other than the wooden official propaganda it had been fed for so long. Literature had always been peculiarly important in Russia; no other country so valued its great writers. At the same time, the agonizing difficulties of the attempt to replace one economic system with another, and the accompanying political turmoil, complicated the picture. One typical compilation of Russian writing, appropriately named *Dissonant Voices*, included an account of revolutionary terror from the 1930s, posthumous works of writers from the 1960s and 1970s, a story from a soldier on the Afghanistan front, and several different ideological statements. With the breakup of the erstwhile Union into a number of ethnic units, eager to assert their separate cultural identities, complexity is compounded, and it would be a brave person who would venture any generalization about the intellectual state of the Russian zone except that it is seething with change.[2]

The recession of revolutionary Marxism could also be discerned in the new Chinese leadership's repudiation of Maoism and approaches to a market economy, especially in peasant agriculture, even if it clung grimly to political power at the cost of repression. Shocks from the breakdown of the two great models of communism in power spread rapidly to the already languishing Communist Parties of Western Europe. Italy's once successful Communist Party, Western Europe's most adaptable and least Sovietized one, had in fact moved up sharply in the 1976 elections, when it won about a third of the popular vote. It declined in 1979 and continued to slip back, to under 22 percent in 1988 municipal elections. After 1988 the new Party leader, Achille Occhetto, sought to lead the PCI away from "communism" altogether to join social democracy, strengthening ties to Europe's socialist parties and finally dropping the name "Communist"—as it had already dropped "Marxist."

But it was not just communism, with its aroma of repression and tyranny, that suffered collapse. The trouble with the Soviet Union was primarily its economic system, which had failed to deliver the plentiful goods that had been promised. The planned economy had failed, and this in some measure implicated even the moderate socialists. The flight from any socialist model was in evidence throughout the world. In Great Britain, a Labour government suffered almost as ghastly a fate as the Communist Parties of Eastern Europe. In the aftermath of a winter of uncontrolled strikes, the Conservative Party led by Mrs. Margaret Thatcher won the election of 1979 and began an antisocialist restructuring of the British economy, looking toward the restoration of a free market and competitive capitalism, as the Labour Party split in two and the power of the trade unions

---

[2]Victor Erofeyev's erotic modernist novel, translated as *Russian Beauty* (1992), was one straw in the wind: see also his essays, *In the Labyrinth of the Cursed Questions*(1990).

declined—truly a capitalist revolution. Suddenly, after decades of disgrace, capitalism was not a nasty word.

The embattled leader of the revived and renovated Conservative Party is the only British prime minister, it has been noted, to have an -ism named after her; but Thatcherism was only another word for free enterprise capitalism. When Labour emerged from the shock of defeat in three successive elections, it opted for a more moderate stance on most issues, seeking to shed its reputation as the party of socialism. Margaret Beckett, a Labour politico who in 1980 had been on the party's left, urging unilateral disarmament, withdrawal from the European Community, extension of public ownership, in 1990 had reversed all these positions. "The world has moved on, it's an entirely different place," she said in October 1990. The new technology of computers and robots and electronics had revolutionized the nature of production. Most workers were now white collar, not blue; the service sector had overtaken the manufacturing one; small business had revived.

"Socialism," wrote the ex-Marxist Leszek Kolakowski, if defined as the abolition of private ownership and elimination of the market, "has invariably resulted in abysmal failures...and has brought about political tyranny, economic inefficiency and stagnation, poverty and cultural disasters." The "overwhelming experience of the twentieth century," historian Peter Jenkins wrote, is "the moral failure of socialism." Political scientist John Dunn added that "Virtually every socialist policy of any ambition that has ever been implemented in practice is acknowledged to have major limitations and...no confident model for the socialist organization of society at any stage of development survives with its credibility intact." So much for a cause in which nineteenth and twentieth century political idealism had invested most of its capital.

It is no wonder that habitual left-wingers, a category embracing most of the intellectuals in the humanities and social sciences (economics perhaps excepted), were reluctant to give it up. A crowd of anxious old friends gathered around the socialist body searching for some signs of life, or hoping for a miraculous resurrection. Some were inclined to try keeping the term while redefining its methods, and to some extent its goals; aiming at "a strongly egalitarian, liberal, and anti-individualist political morality" (Steven Lukes) on an ad hoc basis, not very clearly defined. But in the 1980s, at least, they were swimming against the tide. The Reagan years in the USA coincided with the desertion of socialism in practice by French President François Mitterand, and by Spanish Prime Minister Felipe Gonzales Marquez, nominal socialists who presided over a vigorous revival of enterprise capitalism.

The renaissance of classical economics struck even at Keynes; "Keynes's lasting impact on political economy is in some doubt," wrote Michael Prowse in reviewing a new biography of the great Cambridge thinker and activist in 1991. Keynes's basic analysis had been wrong. He had denied that the economy tends under free market conditions automatically to adjust itself, and alleged that aggregate demand might be insufficient to secure full employment and use of resources. This was true only if impediments to the movement of prices existed, in the form of trade unions or monopolies. Government intervention had outlasted its time, after several decades when the need for it to prevent disequilibrium had scarcely been questioned. Like successive doses of a stimulant, deficit spending finally ceased to work, bringing, paradoxically, inflation without fuller employment—neither having your cake nor eating it. (Again one must note that Keynes never recommended perpetual deficit spending.) It is true that economics was in considerable disarray on this and other points (see further below); but Keynes had at least ceased to be the acknowledged master of macroeconomics, and on the whole the discipline settled back into a classical mold. The approved policies were those of the free market with as little intervention as possible, and as much consistency of rules as possible.

The story of the 1980s was the victory of capitalism over communism. The Soviet system collapsed not only because of its own defects, but because of the Western economy's success in producing an increasingly affluent society. "All socialist utopias come to grief on roast beef and apple pie," Werner Sombart had written long ago. The modern pie was BMWs, VCRs, PCs, vacations on the Riviera. If these amenities were not the lot of everyone, they had become remarkably widespread. Figures for the mid-1980s for western Europe showed about one automobile for every four people, a television set (probably color) for every two; 25 percent owned video recorders, 10 percent personal computers, with these figures increasing annually. Sixteen million Britons took holidays abroad. Critics who might sniff about "consumerism," mass-produced art, and the decline of rural solitude risked setting themselves apart from the mass of people as a snobbish elite who did not even practice what they preached, for few did without their TVs or word processors, while growing numbers of writers and artists found profitable employment in the mass media. If they were successfully modish university professors, they certainly did not eschew jetting to international conferences equipped with audiovisual and simultaneous translation features.

The 1980s introduced young people who, reacting against their parents of the sixties generation, were unbearded, nonradical, success-oriented. "Yuppies" or cynics were more in evidence than urban guerrillas or flower children. In 1988, the *New Statesman & Nation*, leading journal of the intellectual left for 75 years in Great Britain (with a wide international leadership), ceased publication after suffering severe subscription decline and according to many a notable falling off in quality of writing; likewise an identity crisis, marked by a large difference in the tone of the political first half and the literary second half of the magazine. Once integrated around a socialist theme, the political and cultural components had come schizophrenically apart. This classic organ of the left, beginning as Fabian socialism, had gone a long way toward Stalinism in the 1930s, though its pacifism aided in the "appeasement" of Hitler. It seemed to recapitulate all the political left's errors and defects, as well as its occasional triumphs. The *New Statesman* shared in the Labour victory of 1945–51, then suffered from Labour's subsequent schisms. Revived somewhat by the New Left of the 1960s, it finally fell into mortal illness in the Thatcher era. Its demise was an important sign of the times. That it was absorbed into a rather pedantic sociological organ seems equally significant.

THE UNIVERSITIES AND THE FRAGMENTATION
OF KNOWLEDGE

For, as Daniel Bell wrote in the 1970s, the university had become the key institution of "post-industrial society," one of the alleged characteristics of which was that brains had replaced brawn. The "communications revolution," the electronic media, computerization, microchips and satellites, space-age technology, all this invaded private life (entertainment, leisure activities) as well as business. The key to it was science, pure and applied. Universities became places where engineers and doctors and programmers trained for lucrative jobs in hi-tech corporations. Or they might study to become one of the lawyers such corporations demanded in droves. Even if they stayed in the humanities, it might be to seek a job in business, which required more literacy than it used to (ability to write memos, grant proposals, publicity brochures).

Today the intellectual is a college professor if he or she is not a hireling of the communications media. The erstwhile denizen of artists' cafés now holds a research chair. We may regret this, perhaps, but the decline of the intellectual (the "man of letters" in Victorian times) is a facet of the growing professionalization and specialization of modern life.

University expansion certainly included the humanities and social sciences as well as the hard sciences and professions. A surprisingly strenuous debate raged in the 1960s between the "two cultures," in which the scientists (led by novelist C. P. Snow) took the offensive and tended to suggest that antisocial poets and novelists might be superfluous. But the latter were more than able to hold their own. The transfer of literature to the university could be dated from the 1950s. Before that a few *universitaires*, most of them by recent standards quite unspecialized, exerted some influence, but critics like Edmund Wilson, Virginia Woolf, Malcolm Cowley, T. S. Eliot made the running; these were writers from outside the professoriate, "men of letters" in an old-fashioned sense, participants in a literary culture centered in magazines and books accessible to the general public. Such a type now became an endangered species.

As mass higher education multiplied the number of teaching posts and intensified competition for grants and promotions, an enormous increase in specialization resulted. Ambitious scholars searched for new ways of research and writing, new "methodologies." Ever more extreme specialization led to loss of contact with other fields and with the general public. "Literature today is fragmented.... Scholarship is fragmented too; so is life." Thus lamented a distinguished British scholar in 1968. The situation was to get steadily worse.

A veteran literary critic, Graham Hough, had spoken of enormous gains in "technical competence" at the cost of range and substance, a "loss of authority." The 1980s brought authority at the price of intelligibility, and removal from literature itself to the ground of theoretical debates among critics. This move was connected with Deconstruction, discussed in the next section. To "play the academic game," displaying knowledge of all the modish methods and prestigious names in the field became a necessity. "A dreadful Logo-kit terminology has become the vocabulary of much recent criticism," John Coggrave remarked in a review of a 1991 issue of the *James Joyce Quarterly*. There were many of these arcane schools of interpretation. Leafing through the 1,000 pages of *The Year's Work in English Studies* for 1988 (published in 1991; it is a herculean labor to keep abreast), Giles Foden commented that "the varying approaches one sees...show critical yardsticks splintered, and sects in hot dispute."

Most publication in the specialist quarterlies was the occasion for a display of knowingness about fashionable names and critical doctrines. Students interested in just knowing James Joyce and Joseph Conrad as writers who might have something to say to them as human beings would profit little from all this; its usefulness was purely in-house professional. "Talking among themselves," as Chris Baldick titled a 1987 review, "schools of literary critics have no common ground left between them and are falling away centrifugally into mutually incomprehensible salons, each conducting dazzling conversations in a patois which automatically excludes all the others." The professional literary critics could not understand each other, much less could outsiders understand any of them.

Much of the voluminous work published in specialized journals and books could readily be judged bad. Charles Martindale, reviewing a batch of Milton books (*TLS* February 5–11, 1988) found this academic writing "opaque, windy, with frequent neologisms." "It is a worrying thought that few ordinary educated persons interested in Milton would be likely to want to read any of these books." All but a very few undergraduate university students would find them incomprehensible. Very high quality work did appear, but the bulk of this kind of publication bore a taint of bad faith. It strained to invent a new interpretation for no reason except self-promotion. In general, the effect of this tortuously difficult (to the outsider) professional critical discourse was to narrow and dessicate the works examined. Form got far more attention than content; the stress was not on the mysterious places and strange people Conrad's imagination conjured up, for example, but on his "narratological strategies," his "rhetorical tensions." If content was involved, it was the author's patriarchial prejudices or his neurotic symptoms, something concealed before that must be exposed with the aid of a high-powered critical lens.

In an essay "The Man of Letters in a Closed Shop,"[3] the veteran literary scholar and editor John Gross complained that "you have to submit to a new language, with a dozen different dialects. You have to train yourself to see the world in terms of metonymy and semioclasm, marginalization and aporia, *jouissance* and *difference* [Lacanian terms], and misprision as a mode of partial recuperation...." Hegemonic, agonistic, dialogical are deceptively familiar adjectives that turn out to have baffling meanings. Gross concluded that "The body of theory that has accumulated over the past few years, taken as a whole, seems to me a monstrous excrescence, a vast distraction, a paltry substitute for the experience of literature

---

[3]From the afterword to a new edition of his *The Rise and Fall of the Man of Letters* (1991). See also Bernard Bergonzi, *Exploding English* (1990).

itself." A similar diatribe from Michael Tanner, reviewing a pretentiously obscure book about opera, asked "Why has a gifted critic produced so laborious and unhelpful a book? I find the most plausible answer profoundly depressing: the academic establishment is now (still) in the hold of people who will only respect those who speak its jargon, who want to be dazzling in their employment of a set of moves whose expression hovers on unintelligibility, so that those who understand can feel flattered, and never need to raise the question why the great works they talk about are great, why they matter otherwise than as fodder for endless discussions at desirably located conferences" (*TLS* November 1, 1991).

As long ago as 1929, Martin Heidegger in one of his searching criticisms of modern civilization wrote that "the scientific fields are far apart. Their subjects are treated in fundamentally different ways. Today this hodgepodge of disciplines is held together only by the technical organization of the universities and faculties and preserves what meaning it has only through the practical aims of the different branches." Each of the innumerable units of academic specialization becomes a small, highly organized world of its own, the intellectual lives of its members focused on their meetings and conferences, their specialized journals and collective scholarship. By a variation of the familiar law about committees, the more research published, the more there is to do. Working largely in isolation, such groups develop their own subcultures. The older general organizations, such as the American Historical Association, which encompassed all professional historians, faded in importance compared to increasingly specialized groups, such as Eighteenth Century Studies or Society for the History of American Foreign Relations. Literature was even more finely divided, around a single author—the Joyce or Johnson or Shaw or Dickens society. Each of the units forms a microcosm in which all the great issues may be raised, but are discussed largely in ignorance of perhaps comparable debates going on in another part of the room. In fact, each of these coteries appears faintly ridiculous to everyone except itself.

Literature was only an extreme case of what was true pretty much throughout the traditional university departments. They all suffered in various degrees from neophilia, from hyperspecialization perhaps, from excessive subtlety cutting them off from communication with others ("talking to themselves"), from publication for publication's sake, and from fragmentation, dissolving into a multitude of subdiscourses. They are discussed further below. Meanwhile we should mention the leading new school of literary theory, deconstruction, for it not only contributed to the obscurity of literary criticism but, like its parent, structuralism, spread to become a method applied in other areas.

DECONSTRUCTION

As a major fashion in thought, challenging if not replacing structuralism as the latter had done to existentialism, deconstruction flourished in the 1980s, related perhaps to the political turn previously discussed, and contributing much to the departure of academia toward regions of inscrutability light years away from the ordinary person's perceptions. The deconstructors, led by the brilliant Jacques Derrida, who tended to succeed Foucault and Lacan in the role of Parisian star intellectual, retained and even intensified the structuralist abolition of the person, unmasking the "metaphysics of presence" that causes us to assume a person behind the text. No such essential author exists; we have only the text. When we write, we do not "express" ourselves, we enter a domain of words dominated by the modes of language and by an impersonal culture of public discourse. The view that *I* am writing, having transferred *my* mental state into words, is a "logocentric fallacy." The biography of an author has nothing to do with his work. Neither, it would seem, have the social context and historical events of his time.

But the structuralists assumed that there is a single meaning to the text, which must be decoded but can be determined, placed firmly within some logical structure. The structuralists were neo-Kantian in seeing a basic structure that reflected given features of all minds (so were the Jungian archetypists). Now it was argued that texts have no implicit meaning, for every reader will take the work differently; text changes its meaning from time to time and place to place. (A dialectical relationship between reader and text draws out further meanings in both during the reading process.) It is vain to ask which of these innumerable construals is the true one. We are in an Einsteinian universe; we have no ultimate yardstick, in Wittgenstein terms, no metalanguage in which to evaluate language. There can be no single, privileged intellectual perspective, capable of grasping the totality of things.

In the end we have only the irrational realm of language, a magnificent disorder in which, with Nietzsche or Joyce, we may bathe ourselves, rejoicing in life's plenty without thought of plan or unity to it all. The attraction of deconstruction for the literary critic was that it allowed him or her to put almost any interpretation on a text—the more bizarre the better, provided only it was done with sufficient skill in detail and a knowing awareness of theory. For such outrages one group of highly esteemed American academics won the appellation "hermeneutical Mafia." The most prized method was to reveal suppressed, hidden meanings, deduced from what the author left out, presumably because of inhibitions either social or personal—"holes in the discourse," Lacan called them. "It isn't so much what he said," a Henry James character had remarked in *The Golden Bowl*, "as what he didn't say"; and very often of course in life what people don't talk about is a pertinent fact. It remained for the deconstructers to elevate it to a critical principle. Absence or deferral is just as much involved in writing as presence.

The point of most deconstructive criticism was that the text bears no relation to anything except itself. *Madame Bovary* is about Flaubert writing a novel, it has nothing to do with the bourgeoisie or French society or romanticism. Conversely, nature and history are texts to be read, rather than objective entities to be apprehended. There is nothing that is not a text, in a Derrida statement.

Preoccupation with the technique of literary creation, with the way the threads of a tapestry are woven rather than with the scene they emblazon, considerably antedated deconstruction; it was found in the "new criticism" of the 1950s, and reflects a basic general tendency in modern times, the result of the disintegration of cultural unity. In a pluralistic culture, one becomes conscious that things once taken for granted are conventions. Historians discovered this quite a while back (later nineteenth century). The assumption that a work of history tells the truth "exactly as it happened," which would be the same for everybody, came to seem naive to historians well before 1914. This assumption was possible only when almost everybody substantially shared the same experiences, traditions, and values, as the literate classes in nineteenth-century England did.

Different historians writing in different places and times find very different things worthy of attention and perceive them in very different ways. This is because they intrude all kinds of culturally conditioned factors, woven into the very language, into the framework of selection and evaluation they must use in writing about "the past." At the extreme case, how would an African write the history of the last century compared to a European? The "facts," which are in any case infinitely numerous and must be selected—*what* facts?—are a small part of any historical narrative, which contains a rhetoric, "interpretation," arrangement, focusing, to make the facts meaningful and intelligible. And this part is "subjective" or at any rate nonfactual, nonscientific—noncognitive.

Literary criticism discovers the same thing about the classic novel. The naive reader assumes that its characters are "real," an imitation of life; that the narrator is rendering them as a neutral photographer does. The reader is unaware of narrative strategies. How much in fact depends on special conventions becomes clear when someone from a different culture tries to read them, or even when an English reader reads French or Russian novels, to the degree that these cultures are a little alien. (Anthropologists tell us that even movies, which we might think directly and simply mimetic, bewilder primitive peoples watching the screen for the first time; they can make no sense of them.) In any case, modern critics become self-consciously interested in all the conventions that make a novel. They are interested only in the question of why the writer put it together the way he or she did. They discuss narrative strategies (the omniscient author, the personal narrator, interior monologue). They point out that the characters in a novel, which seem so real, are in fact the creations of a special imagination. It is not that Dickens gave us matchlessly accurate pictures of Victorians; he created the Victorians' image of themselves (as they occasionally realized with some discomfort). These characters are mediated by the narrator or author (the two may be different) who has intruded his or her own sensibility, perhaps at two removes. (The author creates a narrator persona who is not exactly her- or himself.) Moreover, they take on different meanings to different readers, who bring to them their own sensibility. Novelists themselves began to write novels about writing a novel, or if this game palled, more complex variations: novels about novelists writing a novel. Andrea Canobbio, *Vasi cinesi* (Chinese Vases, 1990), for example, features the multiple identities of a man (or several) imagined by a novelist who is a character in the novel.

Literature professors searching for constant novelty in the game of academic competition found a large opening in the deconstructionist annihilation of stable meanings. If there is no inherent, fixed meaning in a text—no one "real" *Hamlet* or *Paradise Lost*—then any interpretation is possible. The only thing legitimizing a critic's viewpoint is his or her ability to bring it off by sufficient skill. A kit of conceptual tools obtained from every sort of modern theory—sociological, political, psychological, linguistic, philosophical—along with the dialectical skill to apply them to some helpless author of the past might result in a mystifying discourse, called perhaps demystifying (establishing what the author ought to have meant but didn't). If cleverly done, and something new, it meant an edge in the struggle for academic surivival. One could also shamelessly indulge one's prejudices.

The reckless nihilism of this was evident at times even to the deconstructors themselves. It led to the subversion of all meaning, hence of all rational debate, "the closing down of any critical forum and the elimination of any common criteria of evidence, judgment, or relevance," as Christopher Baldick noted. It could scarcely escape notice that deconstruction itself could be deconstructed; Derrida said his writings were meaningless. No deconstructer could claim a privileged position, enabling her to write the truth; her formulation will in turn be deconstructed from some other equally valid perspective.

Philosophically, Derrida and deconstruction liked to show that every system of thought rests on some unexamined premise, and assumes that which it is explicitly rejecting. Marx, for example, can be shown to assume all the bourgeois values he purports to reject. What purports to be based on logical argument is simply rhetoric, style—an irrational affirmation of the will (much of this from Nietzsche). The scientist is no different from the artist! As Nietzsche had noted, the metaphor is primary in cognition. Any system of thought which insists upon clarity and certainty does so at bottom by sheer force, the violence of totalitarian terror; the only authentic kind of thinking is ambivalent and amorphous. The wordplay of *Finnegans Wake* would seem to be one of the few kinds of novels deconstructionists could approve. Books in the various disciplines began to appear called "The Rhetoric of...." Donald N. McCloskey, *The Rhetoric of Economics* (1985) was part of a series on the rhetoric of everything, including accounting and medicine as well as (obviously) law.

Such exercises sought to show that even the most pretentious of sciences really consist of arbitrary assertions, situated in one particular framework of language and culture. Sociology and philosophy of science produced a body of thought arguing that science itself is a mode of discourse without much to do with external reality. (See, for example, Alan G. Gross, *The Rhetoric of Science*, 1991.) Scientific judgments contain much more than experimental evidence analyzed by "reason"; a great deal of rhetoric and nonscientific discourse goes into them. Science varies accoding to the culture in which it is embedded, and the European scientific tradition can claim no privileged position. Thus, for example, there are non-European mathematics that use an entirely different language but are equally valid. (See George Gheverghese Joseph, *The Crest of the Peacock: Non-European Roots of Mathematics*, 1991).

The obvious glee with which highly adept professionals undertook such operations suggest Ernest Jünger's remark about the joy of setting the intellect to destroy Intellect. Freudians and Kleinians would no doubt detect an underlying sadism.

There was a tendency to show very little patience with the clods who had not mastered Lacan, Bakhtin, Kristeva, Derrida, et al. Plain readers were scornfully dismissed. University professors were not writing for the general public; they were in effect writing for each other. The object in publishing a book was to pass a kind of obstacle course on the road to a permanent academic job. It was judged by other professors on its technical skill, seen as the ability to manipulate all the reigning theories in a convincing manner. Increasingly and inevitably, the competitive game led to ever new and more sophisticated theories, outmoding yesterday's heroes and allowing the candidate to display up-to-the-minute, state-of-the-art intellectual weaponry. The result was much jargon-ridden and pretentious rubbish; often, however, it was very subtle, clever skating on the outer limits of meaning. Pity the poor National Endowment judges; it was often hard to tell the frauds from the geniuses. In either case, it was formidably difficult for all except those adept at the game. This arcane discourse, incidentally, contradicted the postmodernist claim to have eliminated the gap between high and low culture; on the contrary, the gap had greatly increased. Authoritative books about Shakespeare, for example, were no longer comprehensible to the vast majority of people.

Typically, such exercises strove to be as shockingly irreverent as possible; the feminists assailing some masculine reputation were not the only ones to go for the jugular. Anyone was fair game; John Keats becomes a Cockney creep. Daring what only George Bernard Shaw had previously gotten away with, young academics sought to debunk Shaksepeare. Iconoclasm mixed with clouds of obscurantism and a few unusual insights was the common recipe. The genre was extremely rationalist, usually an exercise in analysis that disdained anything as simpleminded as the imagination or the emotional effect of the whole work. Logical inconsistencies were pointed out, hidden meanings disclosed. What excitement there was came from the sense of a complex code being deciphered. No author, it was assumed, says exactly what he or she means; it is what he or she hides that is interesting.

The (disguised) political tendency of deconstruction was on the whole trendily leftward, the natural bent of humanist intellectuals—left over, as it were, from the age of Marx. Authority was being attacked. Without an obvious target or focus following the spectacular decline of communism and socialism in recent decades, and in any case wanting to be much more subtle than ancient radical simplicities allowed, deconstructers could still subvert traditional verities. They might not want to be too radical, for they were well-paid and grant-endowed—not suffficiently in their own opinion, to be sure, and some of this tended to erode. A considerable battle roared in Britain as in most countries between affronted academics and outraged politicians over the level of public support to be given to the arts and humanities. Mrs. Thatcher, a grocer's daughter, was no friend of aristocratic left-wing professors. Oxford University refused to grant her an honorary degree! When

Belgian theorist Paul De Man was found to have written pro-Nazi essays in his youth, the scandal was considerable and this world-class deconstructer went somewhat out of style. If he had written pro-Stalinist ones, few would have cared.

A "new right" or "redefined conservatism"[4] was a rather strong presence in the eighties; intellectuals as distinguished as Britain's Roger Scruton and France's André de Benoist aroused the conventional left but scarcely converted it. "Since the campus violence in 1968 gave the New Left an illiberal name," wrote a reviewer of Arthur Seldon (ed.), *The New Right Enlightenment: The Spectre That Haunts the Left* (1986), "the most impressive young intellectuals in America have been on the political New Right." The same was almost true of Britain in the mid-eighties. By the end of the decade, as Thatcherism lost some of its allure, most intellectuals seemed very anti-Thatcher, anti-Reagan, anxious to position themselves somewhere on the left but uncertain about the exact site. (See John Dunn's rather hysterical view of Roger Scruton, one of the British neo-conservative or "new Right" thinkers, *TLS* April 4, 1986.)

In February 1989, the *New York Times* contained a story about militant Dartmouth University students interrupting classes and leading protests, with roles reversed: these were right-wing students rejecting liberal professors who had probably led protests and interrupted classes in the 1960s and now represented the Establishment. This New Right in good part was a New Liberalism, praising the free market's victory over economic serfdom and cheering for privatization of the state's huge and inefficient economic sector. On the issues of sexual liberation, feminism, freedom from censorship, legalization of drugs, questions which lie close to the heart of the contemporary social scene, conservatives were divided. Their hatred of state controls and moral absolutes clashed with an instinct to fight the corrosive effects of cultural modernization. The paradox was often noted that in modern times liberals have voted for statism in economics and individualism in morals, while the reverse is true of conservatives: each one is inconsistent.

Alasdair MacIntyre's argument in *Whose Justice? Which Rationality?* (1988), that there are no universally valid principles of morality, which must be situated in a specific cultural tradition, fitted into conservatism in a way reminiscent of David Hume's radical skepticism during the Enlightenment: if reason is powerless to tell us how to act, we must fall back on custom and habit. A mistrust of the feeble and fallible contrivances of human reason was the basis of Edmund Burke's classic conservatism. Here, it seemed, "postmodernism," which really was not that new, showed an affinity to conservatism. Of course, even if critical theory undercut truth claims from the "traditional" or "hegemonic" culture, it did the same to all the "counter-hegemonic" discourses, which could only be applauded because they were better fun.

Though deconstruction truly looked like the end of the road, its nihilism something that comes *After Everything*, in the title of one book about modern intel-

---

[4]See Charles Covell, *The Redefinition of Conservatism*; A. de Benoist, *Vu de droite* (Paris, 1979); J. David Hoeveler, *Watch on the Right: Conservative Intellectuals in the Reagan Era* (1991).

lectual culture, yet in most of its qualities, it was far from new. Skepticism, after all, is as old as Sextus Empiricus; revived in the Enlightenment, it had seldom been out of sight since then. Good biographers and historians have always corrected myths and misunderstandings about their subjects; what was called "debunking" in the 1920s now became "deconstructing"—just the latest word for critical analysis or iconoclasm. Stressing how much of what we believe about an era or a person comes to us from some literary invention was also an old truism. (Historians were accustomed to say that Michelet invented the Renaissance, literary scholars that Dickens invented the Victorian age.) A new set of words simply replaced older ones that meant much the same thing.

POSTMODERNISM

Closely related to deconstruction, "postmodernism" was a buzz word of the 1980s. Its exact meaning was hard to pin down (that itself was postmodern). The fragmentation of thought appeared in a tendency for the various disciplines to mean different things by postmodernism. They all wanted to use the term, as a rather desperate principle of integration; there should be a postmodernist economics and sociology as well as architecture and poetry, even science and technology. Everyone took it to mean a loss of unity and of synthesis; multiple discourses, not commensurable with each other, different "language games" and life worlds.

As an inheritance from structuralism and deconstruction, postmodernists spoke of eliminating or "decentering" the individual in favor of discursive realms, an antihumanism. Eclecticism in style, a "premeditated chaos," was a notable feature of architectural postmodernism: pillage the past in any way you choose, make up arbitrary combinations. This proved especially controversial. Rejection of "systems," belief in the relativity of truth, and, in general, discontinuity, fragmentation, irrationality, volatility (truth can change from moment to moment as well as from person to person, circle to circle) was postmodern. Everybody agreed that postmodernism in some sense rejected, negated, or transcended "modernism." But there was little agreement about what modernism was or had been. An economist, Paul Wendt, thought it meant neo-classical economics, essentially the staid old Victorian orthodoxy.[5] Was Keynes, then, already a postmodernist? Or was he the modernism postmodernism was reacting against? Modernism in the arts certainly meant the revolutionaries of the early part of the century, the Cubists, Expressionists, Futurists; this association was too strong to be obliterated. But these esthetic revolutionaries had not by any means all been alike, except in their experimentalism and rejection of older forms.

Postmodernism tended to focus on their attempts to synthesize, to integrate, which it rejected; but antiscientific, irrationalist, subjectivist strains had been

---

[5]See I. Amariglio, "Economics as a Postmodern Discourse," and commentary, in Warren J. Samuels, ed., *Economics as Discourse* (1990).

strong among the early modernists, who were of course by no means all alike. In this the modernists seemed to resemble the postmodernists (who often admired and quoted, for example, Nietzsche and Joyce). The two things in fact tended to get muddled up together; confusion compounded. For the modernists had in a sense been postmodernist, if one chose to identify modernism with the mainstream society often associated with "modernization," a term much used by historians and sociologists. A book by a prominent social theorist on "the consequences of modernity" sounds like a description of postmodernity.

Other alleged postmodern features included anti-elitism, taking the form of claiming that pop culture is as good as traditional, but this was not consistently adhered to. The classical modernists, like the first symbolists, were assumed to have abhorred mass culture; most of them did, but this hardly applies to the futurists or Joyce. The veteran Marxist Frederic Jameson thought postmodernism very like "capitalism," that other catchall term (*Postmodernism, or the Cultural Logic of Late Capitalism*. He cannot quite decide whether to join postmodernism or go into opposition.) Christopher Norris also saw in postmodernism an alarming loss of faith in the old Marxist politics (*What's Wrong with Postmodernism?*, 1991). But some theologians in *Varieties of Postmodern Theology* (1989, ed. D. R. Griffin, W. A. Beardslee, and J. Holland) thought Marxists (among others, including Pope John Paul II) postmodern.

"After us the savage god," Yeats had written. The great modernists with all their rebellions had clung to the great traditions of European culture, the "civilized consciousness": a set of quotations, allusions, references, memories, reaching back to the ancients and extending down through the great writers of medieval and early modern history, from Homer through Dante to Cervantes and Shakespeare; a precious body of noble expression they did not want to lose. In the 1920s, intellectuals contemplated the breakdown of the Western tradition with alarm, sometimes with deep pessimism, but they still wanted to talk about it, as if they might yet stem the tide of barbarism or, failing that, rally a civilized minority to keep the flag flying in one small but distinguished corner. It was at least still a scandal, a shocker. Dean Inge, for example (borrowing a term from Barrès) had written that

> The industrial revolution has generated a new type of barbarism, with no roots in the past.... A generation is growing up, not uneducated, but educated in a system which has little connexion with European culture in its historical development. The Classics are not taught; the Bible is not taught; history is not taught to any effect. What is even more serious, there are no social traditions. The modern townsman is *deraciné*.

Books about the universities such as Abraham Flexner's appeared at this time, deploring the collapse of a great humane tradition into vocationalism. A whole battery of European mandarins crossed the ocean to register their horror at "Americanism." Meanwhile the whole course of literature blazoned the message that while the inheritance might be ill, it could still inspire masterpieces, if rather bizarre ones—from Mann, Joyce, Proust, Woolf, Kafka, Malraux.

The postmodernists gave up on the tradition. They fully accepted, or pretended to accept, the situation described by John Elsom as one in which "there exists in the West no set of artistic, cultural, or social standards so sacrosanct that they are not constantly under attack nor any standards readily at hand to replace them" (*The Erotic Theater*). One might continue to admire the great tradition of Western literature and claim membership in it while, as Richard Rorty wrote, "considering all attempts to supply it with an extra-logical legitimation a waste of time." Knowledge is validatable only within its own community and tradition; there is no universal basis for rationalism. Even science had to accept this; certainly the social sciences did.

Europe was now a part of the world, open to currents from Asia and Africa. Civilizations met and mingled, fusing a new culture in the melting pots of great cities, or preserving a multitude of cultures in a "pluralistic" society, becoming, in Joyce's language, a "Europasianized Afferyank." Was there any longer a single tradition, even in Western countries? A sign of the times was the decision of Stanford University in 1988, after a heated debate, to turn the western civilization course into a kind of world civilization survey with Black, Hispanic, and Asian ingredients. (A somewhat similar argument among historians raged in England in 1990, over the content of a new National History Curriculum.) While some denounced this as surrender to confusion and political pressure, others saw no alternative. Professor Gertrude Himmelfarb, a noted European intellectal historian, protested that we should privilege, if not Western civilization, "the best that has been thought and said." But who is to decide what is best, and by what standards? In Matthew Arnold's time and place, one might have hoped for a consensus, but in late twentieth-century California? Historians have grown aware that "the landmarks of history" are simply the favorite vistas of the articulate members of a particular community. If it is no longer the case that most people belong to the European cultural community, we can hardly justify requiring the study of it.

Technology, after all, was knitting the world closely together in a kind of cosmic popular culture. Back in the 1920s a "modernist," Wyndham Lewis, spoke of "cosmic man," denationalized and made into a common mold, which in a manner typical of the times he related to the dread of "Americanization." This fear of the machine and mass culture decivilizing the Europeans persisted. One of the most widely read serious books of the 1970s in France was *The American Challenge*, by the politician-journalist Jacques Servan-Schreiber; it now seems rather quaint. The Americans invented neither modern technology nor democracy, it only happened that these forces made their appearance in the United States a little in advance. Television and the cinema, global communications via satellites, jet airplane travel and other modern miracles are "cosmic" forces knitting the world together culturally as well as commercially. Zen Buddhists or devotees of African art may just as readily be found in Boston or Munich as in India or Mali. And this is apart from the universal pop culture of rock music and sports, blue jeans and miniskirts. It may be depressing to witness the extinction of local cultures in favor of a flavorless international style, for example to watch Tokyo change from a Japanese city to a kind of exotic imitation of New York. But ideas intermingled in a way reminiscent of something that happened once before in history, at the time of the Alexandrian and then the Roman empires. Perhaps out of this vast process of syncretization a new civilization will emerge, as happened when Western Europe emerged from the twilight of the ancient world.

In any case, it was strange to describe as postmodern something that had been gestating in the modern world ever since Galileo, and which had come of age in the nineteenth century. Yet welcoming the age of laser beams and giant TV was definitely a switch from those modernist intellectuals who had deplored the whole enterprise of Western science. Like deconstruction, its near relative, postmodernism seemed to subvert itself constantly, turning into its opposite and making itself disappear. Was feminism postmodern? There were now postfeminist feminists, arguing for a return to "family values." Sexual license? But the postmodern disease seemed to be AIDS. Environmentalism? *Glasnost* and *perestroika*? Or their debunkers?

Perhaps postmodernism is the inevitable fate of a civilization that has seen so many once potent systems of thought and value destroyed. The relentless advance of fashions and techniques devours past creations. One-time rages are forgotten or consigned to the waste heap. Romanticism is no longer possible (in its pure state), but neither is logical positivism or Marxism. Fascism and communism, riding high for a while, were eventually blown out of the water. Freudianism faded away; Sartre's existentialism, once so cherished, is no longer considered of much intrinsic interest. The 1960s have been largely forgotten, by intellectuals as well as politicians. New fashions have arisen, but do any of them stand a chance of lasting more than a season? Science itself succumbs to mutability. The absence of an ultimate standard, a Master Umpire in the Sky, "is just as characteristic of mathematics and science as it is of ethics and esthetics" (Hannah Pitkin, *Wittgenstein and Justice*). And so nothing is left except the thought that humanity likes to think, and will probably always spin webs of ideas destined to be blown away with the next gale. All we can do is enjoy the game while refusing to take it quite seriously.

Writing in 1919 on "The Crisis of the European Mind," Paul Valéry forecast that European culture would end as "an infinitely rich nothing," the diffusion of knowledge advancing to the point where no distinctive forms could emerge; "a perfection of disorder." Cultivated minds would contain a hodgepodge of unrelated ideas. Postmodernism seems to be the fulfillment of his prophecy. In his 1987 *Shapes of Culture*, Thomas McFarland visualized the collapse of cultural forms into disconnected blobs. This was rather like one of the age's chief diseases, the disassociative Alzheimer's.

SOME OF THE BLOBS

The separate arenas of expertise that arose with fragmentation of knowledge were housed administratively in the traditional departments such as literature, philosophy, history, psychology, sociology, and physics. These old units proved surprisingly stable. Many and sometimes bizarre were efforts to establish new units, or amalgamations of the old ones in some kind of "interdisciplinary" study. Professional organizations sometimes more or less successfully crossed boundaries, usually on the basis of a restricted subject matter: eighteenth-century studies brought together historians, literary scholars, musicologists, art historians and others interested in the Enlightenment. Failures occurred, however; a joint enterprise between science and literature foundered on what each group regarded as the invincible ignorance of the other about its subject. Mathematicians usually scorned what philosophers of mathematics had to say about their subject; in general, the project of analytical philosophy to supply aid to all the empirical sciences did not work out very well. The extreme specialization and in-group vocabulary impeded communication—often between members of different schools within the same department, this being especially true in literature, but even more so between departments.

We need hardly repeat that it is impossible to do even summary justice to the huge contemporary output of knowledge. It may be itself a significant historical fact that for the first time in human history, full knowledge has ceased to be even a possibility. (We do not know what is happening to us, as Ortega y Gasset wrote, and that is what is happening to us.) The Grail or Atlantis do not exist even as dreams. What David Knowles called "a single reasoned and intelligible explanation of the universe on the natural level, and a single analysis of man and his powers...valid for all men and final within its sphere" had never been free from skeptical attack, even in the Middle Ages about which Knowles wrote. And yet, as he adds, this skepticism "was never wholly victorious, and never finally accepted." European thought clung to its dramatic belief in an ultimate knowledge accessible to the enlightened mind. Despite Hegel and Darwin, the great Victorians continued to believe in the unity of knowledge and the individual's ability to grasp in a general way this *totum scibile*, the sum of the knowable.[6] As late as the 1920s Beatrice Webb recorded in her diary her shock at the thought that no absolute truth exists. Today it is accepted, it no longer shocks us. If no integrating intellectual personality any longer exists, then we are at the end of individuality, the "dissolution of man" has occurred; the future must lie with "artificial intelligence," a leading study of our times: human beings replaced by computers.

Bertrand Russell wrote in 1914, in *Our Knowledge of the External World*, that the great syntheses of the past were breaking down, "making our own age one of bewildered groping where our ancestors walked in the clear daylight of unquestioning certainty." Yet in the next breath he welcomed this as an advance in philosophy toward precision rather than "large untested generalities." The old generalities had satisfied a large public; the new precision, ever more precise and ever more complex, they could not understand at all. Professional philosophy was increasingly cut off from the larger public to be immersed in a specialized subcul-

---

[6]For a note on this ideal as a nineteenth-century scholar felt it, see John Sparrow, *Mark Pattison and the Idea of a University* (1967). In his last, unfinished novel, *Bouvard et Pécuchet*, Flaubert records the efforts of two retired office workers to make an inventory of all human knowledge. They reappear "satirically" in Sartre's *Nausée*.

ture, with incentives to be original, be clever, perhaps invent a new thesis. It proliferated into all sorts of combinations during the 1960s and 1970s in the burgeoning universities. There were phenomenological sociologists (Schütz, Gadamer, perhaps Sartre's *Critique of Dialectical Reason*), linguistic psychoanalysts. Based on linguistics, structuralism arose as an important new tendency. A 1975 assessment of philosophy (Charles J. Bontemps and S. Jack Odell, eds., *The Owl of Minerva: Philosophers on Philosophy*, 1975) found such diversity, from Zen Buddhists to logical positivists, from revolutionary activists to austere analysts, as to defy the judgment that this is a single subject.

Philosophers were usually absorbed in the intricacies of one small segment of philosophy, dissecting a problem that was only one of innumerable possibilities, developed because of some accident of professional achievement. Occasionally one of these problems achieved a wider notice, but then it would fade out as the debate exhausted itself; it was seen through, the fly was let out of the bottle, in Wittgenstein's phrase. One such nine days' wonder stemmed from John Rawls' *A Theory of Justice* (1971), which argued for the justice of inequality (of access to public goods) if such additional privileges helped the least advantaged, a theme that related to ongoing social changes. But a decade later little interest remained; Rawls had been refuted, or at least talked to death, after a rash of books and articles took up the question. Other points replaced it, destined in their turn to run their course. The frightening efficiency of academic analysis devoured every such riddle, chewed it up into tiny pieces and then spat it out, ready for some other morsel. Of all this the general public, or almost anyone outside the professional philosophers' circuit, was blissfully unaware.

One cause of the student revolt was their bewilderment at a world of knowledge that was disunited and seemingly irrelevant to real life. Social theory itself, academic style, showed this lack of relevance. A reviewer of Anthony Giddens and Jonathan Turner, eds., *Social Theory Today* (1988) observed that "the juxtaposition of so many radically different designs under one roof is as likely to confuse as it is to enlighten the uninitiated." The range was from "unreconstructed behaviourism" to Frankfurt School critical theory, the Weberian persuasion of Talcott Parsons and his successors, mathematical models, and structuralism. Faced with such a "disparate disarray one is soon rendered incapable of making a rational choice." Perhaps in desperation, the anthology included such low-key relative empiricisms as Ralph Milliband's simpler Marxism and Immanuel Wallerstein's "world system." Only these seemed to have any connection at all to the real world.

Reviewing recent political philosophy in a section called "The State of Philosophy" (*TLS*, July 3, 1992), John Gray remarked on "the strange death of an older tradition" (surely not strange in the light of current academic culture) in which political philosophy overlapped with economic theory and history, as with Adam Smith and John Stuart Mill; it has come to be "dominated by a school that prides itself on its insulation from other disciplines," and which is also distanced from real life. The same might almost be said for economic theory. Economics certainly was in disarray, as the title of a book asserted (Peter Giles and Guy Routh, ed., *Economics in Disarray*, 1984). Some discontented economists thought that "disrespect for fact" is the main problem: failure to see how the real world diverges from the highly theoretical one of reigning economic theory. Feelings of isolation from the real world as well as from other fields of study was in evidence in such books as William N. Parker, ed., *Economic History and the Modern Economist* (1986) and Amiya Dasgupta, *Epochs of Economic Theory* (1985).

Latching on to the postmodernist, deconstructive *Zeitgeist*, books such as *Economics as Discourse* (edited by Warren J. Samuels, 1990) sought to deflate the discipline's pretensions to "science." It is "ideology," it is "rhetoric," it pretends to be scientific only in order to gain the advantage of a blessed word. The idea of an autonomous economic science standing apart from any special context is a fantasy adopted either for self-promotion or for easing the burden of commitment ("acts as an anxiety-reducing mechanism"). This symposium by some young Turks in the profession, obviously taking rather self-interested aim at the older professoriate, reprinted the great mathematical-marginalist Walras just to show how strange those old fellows were, thinking that economics was as much a science as mechanics. In their analysis a popular textbook like Paul Samuelson's turns out to be a bag of rhetorical tricks. These "deconstructive" economists were, of course, aware that their own savage attacks on the received traditions were subject to the same subversive criticisms. It's all a game; points are awarded for cleverest demolition job.

Economics demonstrated to a startling degree the theme of expanding technical mastery with diminishing range and utility. Dazzling theoretical virtuosity leads to conclusions ever more remote from the real world, or to no conclusions at all: the realm of uncertainty. Experts were of little value to politicians who must have definite prescriptions. As long ago as 1977, a veteran economist was quoted as saying "Our craft is bankrupt." No wonder, despite professional disapproval, as one writer (Frank Hahn) complains, "the pronouncements of amateur economists...and of non-economists...command at least as much and probably more respect than those of professional economists...." He was reviewing the collected papers of Kenneth J. Arrow (1986).

Called one of the greatest pure theorists of the century, but hardly a household name like Schumpeter or Keynes, or even Hayek or Friedman, Arrow like other advanced theorists offered models that do not pretend to describe any actually existing economy. They drift farther and farther away from that reality as they find "no invariant laws...no certainties" (Hahn). Their theories were not without applications, but these were difficult and in any case limited ones. Totalizing systems, of course, whether socialist or capitalist, are much too simplistic. Essentially this was a discourse among themselves by highly intelligent chess players, enjoying the game.

So urgent an issue as the economics of free market versus state intervention was by no means something on which experts agreed. (Give me one-handed advisers, Harry Truman once cried!) They disagreed on very basic things: "whether in theory there are likely to be persistent market failures of a sort that would call for government interference if high levels of employment are to be achieved or, if intervention is called for, what the appropriate monetary and fiscal policy instruments are...." Such reflections on the state of an art that, in technique, was almost as intricate as nuclear physics suggest its limitations for practical purposes. Take your pick of economists. The guru of Harold Wilson's unfortunate last Labour government was the Hungarian-born Nicholas Kaldor who, says Christopher Johnson reviewing Anthony Thirlwall's 1988 study of him, appeared to practical people as an eccentric professor, but "to many academics he was the political controversialist." Margaret Thatcher chose Keith Joseph. A volume titled *The State and Economic Knowledge: The American and British Experiences*, published in 1991 (ed. Mary O. Furner and Barry Supple), seemed to show how little politicians understood, or listened to, economists.

One of the last attempts at a total synthesis of human history came from Arnold J. Toynbee, whose popularity in the 1950s we have mentioned. His vast probe into the rise and fall of civilizations was strangely old-fashioned in its positivist framework of "laws," its "philosophy of history" in the nineteenth-century sense, though the range of erudition of this classical scholar turned director of the Royal Institute of International Affairs was far greater than that of his predecessors, Comte or Buckle or Marx. His quest for the secret of Western civilization's sickness was more in the spirit of Spengler's pessimism. And he wrote in a meditative, deeply allusive style that set him apart from most other historians and stamped him as the last of the great Romantic ones.

There were many delights in this leisurely ramble through twenty-one different civilizations in search of their common patterns of growth and decay, but other historians found little validity in its pretense to discover "laws," or indeed in the claim to have isolated separate civilizations for comparison, like so many types of trees. Toynbee's massive work, an attempt as he said to "drink the ocean," testified to the global perspective and the technical resources of the modern historian, as well as to perennial interest in the great question, whither humankind? But he scarcely provided an answer. After an initial impact, Toynbee's reputation faded badly. Like *Finnegans Wake*, *A Study of History* was a terminus; no one was likely ever again to undertake such a task. A total synthesis had become too much for the powers of a single human brain.

The structuralist turn of the French social historians has been mentioned. Historians, professionalized and specialized like other disciplines, tended to follow the fashions in theory featured in deconstruction and postmodernism. Even the intellectual historians, who are supposed to keep track of all this, succumbed to their own, largely methodological specialization, producing theoretical debates quite incomprehensible to anyone except a few insiders. For like most thoughtful historians they had decided that no true or certain understanding of the past exists; history is only the special subjectivity of one time-bound, discourse-restricted historian. Wondering how historical knowledge is even possible, they drifted into intricate analyses of the rhetoric or structure of historical writing, treating it as just another literary genre, which of course can have no inherent or stable meaning.

Some of the old-guard historians held out stoutly for traditional history, but inevitably seemed like old fogies. G. R. Elton (*Return to Essentials*, 1991) in a tirade similar to an earlier one by Harvard's Oscar Handlin, complained of social science jargon, half-baked theorizing, deconstructionism, those who would fictionalize history. Sir Geoffrey agreed with Hannah Arendt and Michael Oakeshott that there are no theories of human political behavior. And the State, he thought, in a defense of old-fashioned political history, is the only possible focus of a history that has any unity. Agreeing with him on many of these points, social historian Lawrence Stone nonetheless in reviewing the book accused Elton of "bad-tempered and ill-informed abuse of...most of the influential figures over the past fifty years in history, the social sciences, literary criticism and philosophy."

Foucault, Derrida, the feminists, the Marxists, the *Annales* school, indeed practically all Frenchmen—all these the distinguished British historian denounced for fakery and pretentiousness. His was a voice crying in the modern wilderness on behalf of the old-fashioned virtues of hard digging and careful criticism of the facts. Against this cult of the facts stood most scientific methodologists; facts do not speak for themselves, we are guided selectively to the facts we see by some built-in "theory"; new theories lead to seeing new facts and seeing old ones in different ways. Peter Munz (*The Shapes of Time*, 1977) was closer to the modern mood in his subjectivism: "Our historical knowledge is of historical knowledge, not of what actually happened." And "All discussions of historical truth are discussions about different ways of writing history."

For the scholar, whether historian, anthropologist, or sociologist, such extreme "reflexivity" or methodological self-consciousness threatens paralysis. Thinking too much about what it is you are doing, the athlete knows, is likely to induce failure through self-consciousness. Someone asked what might happen to the centipede if it started consciously trying to position each foot as it walked. Historians and anthropologists began to write about the process of themselves writing; they began a study by a whole volume setting forth their presuppositions and prejudices, their "methodology," and became paralyzed by "a sort of epistemological hypochondria."[7]

Sociologists complained that more than a half dozen schools, including functionalists, structuralists, phenomenologists, behavioralists, Marxists, existentialists, and symbolic interactionists, disputed the mastery of their terrain in complicated methodological quarrels that left students bewildered before they could begin. They were invited to choose their basic metaphor from among the organism, the computer, the logical equation, the market, the theater, and others, with no guidance about which was the best—just different "perspectives." This was similar to the study of literature, where it was noted that students now began not with the text of a work, but with various theoretical approaches to it. In *The Coming Crisis of Western Sociology* (1971), A. W. Gouldner proclaimed his intention to write several other volumes detailing "a systematic and generalised sociologi-

---

[7]See Clifford Geertz, *Works and Lives: The Anthropologist as Author* (1988).

cal theory about social theories." When others do the same, one can envisage a theory about the theories of social theories—and so *ad infinitum*. Robert Friedrichs had written *A Sociology of Sociology* in 1970. The prominent French sociologist and Parisian intellectual Pierre Bourdieu held that the sociologist must begin by studying her- or himself, to discover all his or her special prejudices and predilections; whether he or she would ever escape from this "reflexive" enterprise to do sociology was unclear.

A history of British social anthropology now was not, as used to be the case, about how these investigators, inspired by Darwin and Comte, went forth in search of a science of human development; it was about how, secretly inspired by imperialism and misogyny, or perhaps suppressed homosexuality, they went out to discharge their frustrations on hapless natives.

Psychologists were separated at the extremes between behavioralists, who seek rigorously to exclude anything subjective, and existential "humanists" interested only in deep subjectivity. This polarization between *Within/Without*, the title of a book of readings in psychology, did not exhaust the diversities. According to one psychiatrist, the multiplication and constant revision of mental disorders threatens "differentiation into separate languages." The standard manual of classification swelled from 60 disorders in 1952 to more than 250 in the 1987 edition, with an even more massive tome slated for 1992. To the dismay of practitioners, psychiatry changes every few years. But then according to the wisest ones, every case is different, so there can be no general science.

In an age of widespread anxieties and depression, when it had become almost an oddity *not* to have had a nervous breakdown or psychiatric sessions (health care insurance paid for mental health treatment, figures showed that 25 percent or so at some time had it), no subject was more popular than psychology. Psychoanalysis was a link between popular and intellectual culture; every movie star had his or her "shrink." Marilyn Monroe had helped subsidize Anna Freud's Hampstead clinic. Whenever something strange happened, a bizarre murder for example (an everyday occurrence in most American cities), the authority reporters sought out for helpful comments was certain to be a psychologist, not a priest or a poet. The pervasive influence of psychologism appeared in terms commonly used to describe cultural phenomena: the "culture of narcissism," for example.

RELIGION

Ever since the crisis of Christianity in the nineteenth century, the search for a substitute religion, something to believe in, had gone on without success. "The fatal word NOT has been inscribed in all our creeds," a character in Shaw's play *Too True to Be Good* cried. The quest had led Western intellectuals to communism in the 1930s, to existentialism's nothingness in the 1940s, to a kind of quiet resignation in the 1950s, to revolutionary hysterics in the 1960s. But there were always signs of wanting to return to the traditional churches. The second world war, like the first, had quickened interest in religion. The great Italian writer Ignazio Silone, once a Communist, declared in 1946 that "the rediscovery of a Christian heritage in the revolution of our time remains the most important gain that has been made in these last years for the conscience of our generation." Other distinguished elder statesmen of the literary world who returned to Christianity included Auden, T. S. Eliot, Graham Greene, and François Mauriac.

The Oxford and Cambridge scholar C. S. Lewis, one of the most brilliant writers of his generation, had found his way to "mere Christianity," and together with others of his "Inklings" circle, J. R. R. Tolkien and Charles Williams, set about creating a new religious mythology for modern people. Appalled by his intellectual friends abasing themselves before a great tyrant, the British writer and television personality Malcolm Muggeridge redisovered Jesus (*Jesus Rediscovered*, 1969). Arnold Toynbee concluded his massive and widely read comparative study of civilizations (*A Study of History*, 1934, 1939, 1954; abridged in two volumes by D. C. Somervell, 1947, 1957) with the advice to return with a contrite heart to the bosom of religion; he saw higher religion as the leading goal of the historic process. Roger Garaudy deserted the French Communist Party in the 1960s in order to conduct a dialogue between communism and Christianity. These were some of the many straws in the wind of postwar doctrine.

Others: Carl Jung, who lived on to his late eighties as a revered sage, was increasingly interested in the universal symbols and archetypes underlying religious experience. Scholars engaged in a massive exploration of comparative religions. Never was there greater interest in historical and theological studies of the Christian past; and the same could be said of Judaism, stimulated by world Jewry's post-Holocaust recovery of ancestral traditions. The thriving study of theology produced great figures like the Heidegger-influenced Karl Rahner (d. 1984). Sartre's atheistic existentialism was by no means the only kind; among those described as Christian Existentialists, heirs of Kierkegaard, were Gabriel Marcel and Paul Tillich; Martin Buber was a prestigious Jewish one. Sixty years of persecution in the Soviet Union had not destroyed the Russian churches, which persisted underground, and the great dissident writer Solzhenitsyn reaffirmed the Orthodox creed in his crusade against Stalinism. The Roman Catholic Church was a bulwark against total communization in Poland even before a Polish pope galvanized the Polish revolt of 1980 and after.

It could be said of this persistent religious impulse that it suffered from fragmentation as much as other fields. A much-publicized ecumenical movement in the Christian world sought to break down the walls between sects and churches, which had increasingly proliferated ever since the Reformation; but the many conferences and books did not get very far. The modern world bred ever greater fissiparous tendencies. New Christian sects and theologies appeared in abundance. Some of them virtually bracketed out any specific Christian content. Controversial in the sixties was "secular theology," with its goal of making the Church "relevant." The position popularized in Britain by the Bishop of Woolwich (*Honest to God*) prided itself on being liberated from anything specifically Christian in the way of formal creed or liturgy. Leaning on "situation ethics," the church could bypass conventional Christian morality; it could even talk of atheistic or religionless Christianity.

Similarly, a crisis marked by criticism from left-wing theologians like the Swiss Hans Küng, and by conservative resistance to modernizing the traditional church services, shook the Roman Catholic Church. The Latin American wing led one portion of Catholicism into left-wing politics. What all this seemed to say was that Christianity either had to adapt to the modern secular world or perish; but if it adapted, it not only betrayed its inheritance and alienated the faithful, but ran the danger of liquidating itself. The papacy itself wavered on these issues.

One obvious danger for the adapting church was losing anything recognizably Christian, as in those split-level Unitarian churches, satirized by the American novelist Peter De Vries, which were indistinguishable from pinkish political clubs. While "Jesus freaks" among the rebellious young in the 1960s held to little that was recognizable in Christian orthodoxy (they thought the Savior a pot-smoking enemy of the Establishment), learned theologians "demythologized" the Word. But opposition to this appeared in, for example, the rigorously conservative theology of Professor Pannenberg of Mainz.

But increasingly in the cosmopolitan minglings of the modern urban world, religious impulses escaped entirely from the old Christian or Judaic molds. A host of cults ranging from Scientology (an Australian invention) and the Unification Church, one of many Oriental imports, testified eloquently to the need for faith at the popular level. All sorts of mixtures of Eastern and Western religions flourished. Harvey Cox, holder of a chair of theology at Harvard University, claimed in his 1978 *Turning East* that "within twenty blocks of the intersection of Massachusetts Avenue and Boylston Street forty or fifty different neo-Oriental religious movements thrive." California of course surpassed Boston in this regard, and these religious fads spread to European cities. A wave of religious fundamentalism swept in from the Islamic world in the 1970s and 1980s. People from all over the world could be found in London and Paris as well as in New York and Los Angeles.

There were visionaries like John Michell in London who received messages from beyond the earth portending the end of an age and the beginning of another marked by a new "expansion of consciousness." Code words of this sort appeared in the places where dropouts from conventional society congregated. Here was a counterpart of the religious ferment that had marked the declining days of the ancient world. Apocalyptic themes appeared everywhere; even children's literature, according to a German report, changed from the traditional happy endings to preoccupation with "psychic catastrophes, violence, injustice, unmerited destruction" (*Stimmen der Zeit*, November 1976). Apocalypses abound in science fiction, that most popular of literary genres, whose celebration of scientific marvels now turned toward visions of the extinction of this planet, or this galaxy, or this universe—"waiting for the end."

The stresses of modern society breed massive demands for the consolation and direction that religion can bring. Such a strange variety of spiritual phenomena had not been seen since the age of the Reformation. But this new "religious consciousness" in the end seemed to mean little except that modern humanity is disturbed. The indices of mental illness, suicide, crime, divorce, and drug addiction are symptoms of anomie and anxiety. If the function of religion is to provide a core of values that all can share, uniting and stabilizing the community, then these numerous crazes flitting through the heated urban world do not function as religion, but are rather signs of its absence. The vast process of secularization, so basic a part of modernization, has continued on; the very nature of modern society is nonreligious.

SCIENCE

Like Scientology, many of the new religious cults overlapped with science, fictional or real, serious or popular. A reputable physicist, Fred Alan Wolf, author of a book explaining quantum mechanics to the ordinary person, wrote *The Eagle's Quest: a Physicists's Quest for Truth in the Shamanic World* (1992). He went to Santa Fe for instruction in an urbanized Native American shamanism! Shamanism, druidism, magic, witchcraft were peddled commercially as alternative religions or perhaps psychotherapy; popular psychology, classified in bookstores as "self-improvement," shaded into both pseudoscience and offbeat religion.

A satisfying integration of knowledge also escaped the ever-proliferating domain of science. Intellectual synthesis in post-Einstein physics remained elusive. A pluralistic universe, as we will recall, had been indicated in the failure to find a single kind of force. Einstein, clinging to his faith in an orderly cosmos, spent his last years (he died in 1955) working on a unified field theory, attempting to unite his special and general relativities, electromagnetism and gravity, by postulating that ultimate physical reality consists not of particles but of fields—areas of influence, like knots in a string. In 1945 Einstein published a general theory of this sort, but few scientists accepted it.

The future seemed to lie with the particles, more and more of which were identified until the number reached some 200, their relation to each other uncertain. Neutrinos, muons, gluons, several kinds of "quarks" (bearing adjectives like "strange" and "magic") were only the leaders. Quarks and leptons seemed to be the basic building blocks of the cosmos. There now appeared to be not two but four basic forces; added to electromagnetism and gravity there was the "strong force" binding atoms together, and a "weak force" that holds together protons and neutrons. Hope was held out for eventually finding a formula to link some of these forces, but no one was sure. Billions in public money went to build giant cyclotron accelerators capable of smashing protons and neutrons to reveal their subunits. At the end of the 1980s, the latest theory tended toward the idea that the weak force and electromagnetism are two parts of a single force, "electro-weak." Above a certain energy, the difference vanishes. At very high (unobtainable) energies, the strong force and the electro-weak may merge—true perhaps in the first moments after the beginning of the universe.

In one theory, the five dimensions had increased to eleven. Some of the sub-atomic particles lived less than a billionth of a second, others apparently occupied no space at all. At the other extreme, radio telescopes revealed literally billions of galaxies, each containing billions of stars like our own solar system, and also turned up quasars, pulsars, black holes—the gravitational collapse of large stars leading to the trapping of light, a sensational confirmation of Einstein's theory. Further exciting light was shed on the theory of the original "big bang" with which the universe began, and the stages through which it evolved from this moment. When space vessels made possible the discovery of a vast amount of radiation impossible for earth-bound instruments to detect, this cosmic wave background cemented the victory of the "big bang" over "steady state" cosmic models; these emissions must have been produced by the original explosion. In 1968 the discovery of pulsars, the pulsations emanating from neutron stars, testified further to a remarkably dynamic universe.

The primeval egg or baseball became much smaller. The original universe was now believed to have been the size of an atom, though it grew in a billion-billionth of a second to grapefruit dimensions. Quarks and leptons existed a second after creation. Quarks then gathered to make protons and neutrons, which in turn (when cool enough) fused to form atomic nuclei. Next, electrons clung to nuclei. Leptons became neutrinos. Gravity then appeared. All this reconstruction was so imaginative, and hypothetical, that the ordinary person might be excused some skepticism. The Big Bang theory itself came under criticism, yet data from telescopes on a spaceship were said to reconfirm it in 1992. One proof of the Big Bang is that theories based on it predict the proportion of the various elements that occur in the universe. Unexplained, however, was the grouping of the galaxies in spirals, rather than in even distribution throughout the universe. Those who tried to keep up with these amazing frontiers of physics might suspect a total divorce of language from reality. One should not confuse these instrumental words and formulas with ontological reality, with which they have no logical connection. The debate between realists and antirealists went on.

Rivaling if not surpassing the nuclear physicists and astronomers in disclosing marvels were the molecular biologists who searched for the secret of life in the miracles of genetics. Discovery of the hereditary molecules, the DNA, that pass from parents to their children carrying elaborately coded instructions for growth, was one of the most exciting scientific events of the 1950s. Genetic engineering became a growth industry in the 1980s, when synthetic genes began to serve as cures for human ailments and as creators of improved vegetables and livestock. In the next decade, expensive projects were underfoot; the biologists' answer to the particle accelerator, estimated to cost the taxpayer several billions of dollars over the next fifteen years or so, was an undertaking to sequence the human "genome" or DNA set. Each of the two sets of DNA everyone inherits, one from each parent, is said to contain some 3,000,000,000 nucleotide units. A complete record of these would probably turn up many previously unknown genes. As in the case of atom smashing, what this might mean either in practical terms or as contributing to a fuller understanding of the nature of reality was not clear. But the quest went on, a quest the scientists sometimes compared to the old search for the Holy Grail. Was it likely to be found in the intricate chemical language with which nature transmits its information about life? If so, what would it mean?

None of these projects would be possible, of course, without computers, the miracle invention of the last half of the twentieth century. The microcomputer could store, process, and transmit "data" at speeds and reliability so far outdistancing previous modes as to constitute a multiple quantum leap. It could perform mathematical calculations previously out of the question because they would have taken centuries. It could picture or model relationships between vast amounts of data to open up whole new realms of knowledge. Every few years, faster computer chips were produced. The computer screen could display three-dimensional maps of the cosmos, and simulate a completed building for the architect to check. Computers could beat all but a few humans at chess, calculating the best move from millions of possibilities, but they could not plan a strategy. Artificial intelligence was a subject of great interest to the "cognitive scientists." But computers could also "simulate reality," so that real people (it was conjectured) might have a future if they made love via computers, among other forms of communication.

All this and many other wonders opened up in the age of Turing. Michael Shallis, in *The Silicon Idol* (1984), declared the microchip revolution dehumanizing. But, as he realized, it was only an extension of what the telephone had begun. At that time he had yet to confront the Fax revolution. This determined flat-earth-society mentality (which had distinguished precedents in Tolstoy and other antimaterialists) arouses our admiration along with our amusement. Mr. Shallis probably wrote his book on a computer, while listening to music on his laser disk, and retrieved his information with the aid of library electronics; interrupted perhaps by visits to dentists and doctors made far more comfortable by the progress of medical technology. Few are likely to reject all these modern conveniences. Culturally, they mean the ability to bring movies, plays, concerts, and operas as well as sports events into homes in virtually living form via VCRs and television, vastly increasing the audience for high culture as well as low.

THE ARTS

What is one to say of the contemporary art scene? Immense profusion, total fragmentation, commercialization, grotesquerie, vitality are among the words that spring to mind. Writing of the contemporary avant-garde in the 1960s, Ken Baynes declared that "the artist's brave cry of freedom has turned into the shout of a buffoon." One view of the art scene was this one, that it had dissolved into a series of publicity stunts. Nietzsche had predicted the "dissolution of art" once it had cut loose from the discipline of classical rules and boundaries. The first generation of experimenters experienced an exhilarating freedom; but, in the words of Stephen Spender, "to go further would lead to a new and completer fragmentation, utter obscurity, form (or rather formlessness) without end." The search for ever fresh novelties leads to ever more grotesque inanities threatening the death of serious art.

Art in recent decades featured a series of fads, each one of which seemed more bizarre than the preceding one. "Conceptualizing" artists did not paint at all, they invented the ideas for a painting and sold them as do-it-yourself kits. In the 1950s "Pop" artists painted cans of soup and tubes of lipstick. Minimalism had its counterpart in giganticism, such as the Bulgarian-born artist Christo's much-publicized wrapping of the Rocky Mountains or Biscay Bay (he had apprenticed in 1962 by merely wrapping the Chicago Museum of Contemporary Art). But each year brought the promotion of a new style.

All this was an easy target; already in 1956 a character in Noël Coward's *Nude with Violin* says: "I don't think that anyone knows about painting anymore. Art, like human nature, has got out of hand." In *The Use and Abuse of Art* (1974) Jacques Barzun, the distinguished Columbia University humanist, agreed with the famous British satirist that "what we are witnessing in all the arts…is the liquidation of 500 years of civilization." Never was there so much art. It was subsidized, publicized, advertised, invoked as a talisman of power and prestige. (One of the stranger publications in the burgeoning academic discipline of art history, which came into its own in the postwar decades, was a study by a young art historian turned sixtyish left-winger, or vice versa, which stated that the post-1945 transfer of art fashion leadership to New York from Paris was a Cold War plot, engineered presumably in that well-known home of connoisseurs, the CIA. The book stands as a monument to the desperate search for connections.)[8]

Art like religion is needed to counteract the rationalized, bureaucratic society—the dullness of work, the boredom of leisure time, the soul-killing practicality of science as well as business. Art stands against a profoundly anti-esthetic mainstream, which it criticizes and presents an alternative to, or provides relief from—amusement for the masses, the opium of the people in a godless society. Views of art as radical criticism faced the awkward fact that outrageously avant-garde art became big business, almost the biggest; capitalists from New York to Tokyo and Abu Dhabi put their money into art as the best investment. Investors paid millions of dollars for paintings the early modernists, such as Van Gogh and Picasso, could not sell at all. Governments, often to the dismay of their citizens, stuck modern art conspicuously in public places. (A whole series of skirmishes matched outraged citizens against pieces of sculpture inflicted on their space as well as their pocketbooks.)[9]

Efforts to make some sense of all this themselves approached the bizarre. A London critic, Robert Hewison, attempting to generalize, announced the end

---

[8]Serge Guilhaut, *How New York Stole the Idea of Modern Art* (1983). It is true that the promotion of Jackson Pollock and Abstract Expressionism in New York was conducted with the aid of a publicity campaign involving noted art critics and *Life* magazine.

[9]Hilton Kramer memorably described one such encounter in "A Plaza Taken Hostage," *TLS*, November 8, 1991.

of modernist art, the beginning of something else; he wrote gropingly of a "network of pluralisms" (messengers between the blobs), a purely personal art of self-image, but also "social surrealism" (*Future Tense: A New Art for the Nineties*, 1990). "Beyond the avant garde" might mean almost anything. Reaction against the high modernists, with their abstract designs and portentous symbolism, even brought acceptance of older forms of realist painting; formerly ridiculed middle-brow painting of the nineteenth century was worth an exhibition (Paris, 1978). Las Vegas architecture, in postmodernist ideology, should not be relegated to the trash, nor punk culture unjustly condemned. Toleration was not usually extended to television, though, its commercial images being considered "corporate" and corrupting.

Art in the widest sense expresses the spirit of an age better than anything else. Nietzsche, who thought it the highest human task, held art to be highly communal, being related to religion. "Our literature, like our politics, has been fragmented into warring interest groups," the noted art critic Hilton Kramer observes. The fragmentation of art reflects the cultural condition today in the West. From this fragmentation the artist has suffered more than anyone else. The tragic lives of modern poets and dramatists and painters reveal this. The conflict between individual sensitivity and public culture was perhaps most acute in the United States, where a series of personal horror stories encompassed the insanity, the alcoholism, the suicides and shortened lives of such great artists as Hart Crane, Robert Lowell, John Berryman, Tennessee Williams, Jackson Pollock, and too many others to mention. But Europe was not a whole lot better off; compare such cases as the periodic mental breakdowns and eventual suicide of Virginia Woolf, and of the great German-language poet Paul Celan (Paul Antschel) as well as Malcolm Lowry, or the disturbed life of Anthony Burgess as related in his autobiography.

There is not enough space to discuss literature. There are as many novels as the leaves in a forest, an abundance of poetry, theater, biographies, histories. In 1927 Virginia Woolf foresaw the shape of modern fiction as taking the mold of "that queer conglomeration of incongruous things, the modern mind." It has certainly done so. Increasingly it has, as Roger Fry said of modern art, sought not to imitate life, but to find an equivalent for it—alternate realities.

One might risk the generalization that of all the serious genres, the one that flourishes the most today is literary biography. Individual lives never cease to fascinate; the lives of the notable writers, usually both tormented and spectacular, scandalous and successful, are best of all. Modern scholarship boosted by electronic aids can accumulate and organize mountains of material. The insights of psychology may be spiced with a dash of high literary theory; all the methodological novelties with which modern thought swarms can be focused on a single object. The barriers and inhibitions that used to protect private affairs from prurient curiosity increasingly have broken down (writers and actors freely write about their own agonies and sins). The biographer can celebrate an ideological hero(ine) or cruelly deflate an enemy; display the sins of society or examine the guilt of the individual. There is no need to justify doing a subject written about many times before; everyone knows that each study will be different, but not any the less true, and a kind of cultural amnesia wipes out the memory of a biography written a few years ago. The diminished gap between elite and popular culture means that one can extend the range of subject matter; a movie star will do as well as a literary giant. She or he can be subjected to the same semiotic analysis, if need be.

Above all, the individual life is manageable, whereas the whole culture or nation or city has become too big; and the individual, it is widely felt, alone is real. Structuralist attempts to depersonalize have not succeeded; never was there so much interest in these prisoners of discourse. Even if some biography is anti-biography, it still uses the individual person as the object of study. The atomization of culture is perfectly illustrated in this popularity of biography, memoir, autobiography, or novels which are barely disguised biography or autobiography. If, as some recent writers have thought, we are at the "end of history," we are left with just a vast ocean of individual lives.

Conclusion

There was pessimism about the very survival of the civilized Western tradition as the twentieth century approached its end. Lynne Cheney, chairman of the National Endowment of the Humanities, in her report to the Congress of the United States on the state of the humanities, noted that in 37 percent of American colleges and universities it is possible to earn a degree without taking a single history course. You could do so without taking any literature course at 45 percent, and without a philosophy course at 62 percent. Even if they take a Lit course, complains Hilton Kramer in a 1992 article on the "grim scenario" of American letters, students may watch movies or read comic books rather than the classics. ("An American undergraduate today is more likely to be familiar with the work of Alice Walker than with the novels of Thomas Hardy or Henry James, which, if studied at all, will probably be examined for their retrograde views of race, class, and gender." They might read high theory, to their utter mystification, about low culture.) The situation in Europe was only marginally better. Urban popular culture induced among youth a frenetic now-ism that bred contempt for anything old.

Yet such complaints had always been heard. "One no longer reads, one no longer has time. The spirit is called from too many directions at once, it must be addressed quickly or it passes. This acceleration of movements which does not permit continuity or meditation...will entirely destroy human reason." This sounds like a recent complaint, but it came from Lamennais in 1819. Matthew Arnold repeated it in his comments on the sick hurry and divided aims of a populace subjected to the repeated shock of change and the destruction of old values. Kierkegaard, 150 years ago, spoke of minds "confused by too much knowing." The intellectuals have almost always regarded their own age as culturally debased. We have to take the current complaints with a few grains of salt; high culture is always the privilege of a few.

Never before have so many been educated, and never have so many cultural products of all sorts been available as today. In the 1980s in any school year more than two million people in the United Kingdom were taking some kind of advanced educational courses; there were 300,000 full-time university students. More than 25 percent of the population had received a higher education. One might compare this with the fraction of 1 percent that attended universities in 1900; at that time only about 1 percent of the working class even reached secondary school. (The "working class" itself, if defined as unskilled or semiskilled manual laborers, had decreased from about 70 percent to 30 percent.)

It would seem that for a growing minority, serious art, literature, music, drama, and thought are increasingly important. These are all big businesses, whether we look at symphony orchestras paying conductors salaries not too incommensurate with those earned by football players and rock musicians, the worldwide star status of an opera singer like Luciano Pavarotti, the sale of paintings for millions of dollars, or the vast royalties earned by successful novelists who are not all purveyors of trash. Far more leisure time exists, of course, than formerly; medical advances have added another third onto life, usually postretirement time.

Many people obviously live in the worlds created by the great creative writers. Some years ago Virginia Woolf remarked that "the life which is increasingly real to us is the fictitious life." It is reported that 6 million copies of Proust's *A la recherche du temps perdu* have been sold in French editions. People take tours visiting the important places in the novel. In 1982 thousands of people from all over the world descended on an amazed Dublin on "Bloomsday" to celebrate Joyce's one hundredth anniversary year by reenacting scenes from *Ulysses*, which to them were obviously more real as well as more interesting than anything in real life. Television productions of *Sons and Lovers*, *Buddenbrooks*, Wagner's *Ring*, Dickens's *Nicholas Nickleby*; the memorable movie of *Little Dorrit*, scores of other movies now brought into the home as a regular household feature via VCRs, have made the classics of literature available to millions. Serious thinkers such as Marx, Freud, Nietzsche, Sartre, Wittgenstein, Einstein, and Derrida became almost as much cult figures as the writers of fiction or poetry. It is impossible to deny that with all its anti-intellectual crassness (its highest-paid heroes, after all, are athletes and popular music stars), contemporary mass society also consumes culture as humanity never consumed it before.

The whole vast process of social modernization contributes to this forcing of the individual into a fantasy world. Until very recent times, the strongly familial society provided a network of human relations surrounding most people—not only the middle and upper classes—with affection, care, and ceremonial activities from childhood to old age. Today the individual is more likely to be alone, or with few close human contacts; there are fewer children, less family life, and more dispersal of people over vast distances. People are more likely to seek emotional outlets in books, movies, television programs.

It will not have escaped attention that one of the most significant changes in intellectual life, accompanying modernization, has been the creation of a separate class of intellectuals, separated from the rest of society in many ways. A student of the mid-nineteenth-century Positivists remarks on the fact that these critics of their society were only semi-rebels, and never thought of themselves as constituting a countersociety. Gadfly and naysayer that he was, Bertrand Russell was struck by the way in which the generation of the 1920s differed from his in being much more bitterly estranged. They had given up on the tribe; he had spoken as a member of it. Ever since then, through communism and existentialism and deconstruction, we can say with little exaggeration that the intellectual community has gone its own way. We can, of course, trace this rejection of the real world back to the symbolists of the 1880s, if not further (in some ways the first modern writer was Cervantes, whose Don Quixote cannot understand why the experienced world is not like his books). The emergence of the term "intellectual" to mean a separate and different order of people belongs to the *fin de siècle*.

It has never been absolute, however. Ralf Dahrendorf, in *Reisen nach innen und aussen* (Journeys Inward and Outward) (Stuttgart, 1985), by a noted sociologist who got into public life, mentions Raymond Aron and Henry Kissinger—scholars, historians, intellectual journalists—who achieved a significant public role, not without paying a price in the disparagement of jealous academic colleagues as well as the scorn of practical politicos as eggheads in politics. Aron, Dahrendorf remarks, was "too near to power to influence ideas and too far from power to influence action." Yet such figures at least come close to bridging the mighty gulf between thought and action, intellectual and popular spheres. Economists as different (ideologically) as Milton Friedman and John Kenneth Galbraith manage to be both well known and intellectually respectable. A serious scientist such as Stephen Jay Gould writes best sellers. These are not unique examples. A few succeed in straddling the ground between serious scholarship and popular history or biography, despite the difficulties. In a strange way the public seems to honor both charlatans and real geniuses.

Demand for cultural products should have a function as the remedy for a host of social pathologies raging today. Alarming rates especially among young people of suicide, madness, drug abuse, and crime arouse dismay. Irving Kristol among others stands bewildered at the fact that although since 1945 "the average citizen has achieved a level of economic affluence and economic security that would have been regarded, at the time, as visionary," making this the most remarkable half century in world history, "this economic progress has been accompanied by an unforeseen tidal wave of social disintegration and moral disorientation," exemplified by "an incredible increase in criminality," in teenage pregnancy, drug addiction, and abortions. In Europe, the centers of such cities as London and Zurich have recently featured scenes of grotesquely dressed youths stoned on drugs or alcohol, aiming to live probably short lives on a continual "high."

"Unforeseen" is an odd adjective here; the social crisis of modernity called forth anxious diagnoses from Weber, Tönnies, Durkheim, Le Bon, Sorel, and practically every other serious social thinker at the end of the last century, which anyone familiar with the history of ideas would know. Following Weber's identification of this "iron cage" in which uprooted, urbanized, disenchanted modern humanity is imprisoned, there was much discussion of the "double bind" in which individuals are caught: their consciousness enriched beyond anything previously known, they are free to choose from a bewildering number of options, but the economic system demands that they conform to a hyperspecialized, extremely complex organism—to be cogs in an immense machine. And this professional specialization invades even the realm of knowledge, which becomes fragmented into a horde of almost unrelated divisions.

Amid the proliferation of bewildered professional psychotherapists and much political demagoguery, little attention seems to be paid to the need for an education that will feed the disinherited minds hungry for a meaningful world of culture. The inaccessible, inbred, elitist world of academic thought now does little for most of them. The hungry sheep find their own trash. From prison, a man who belatedly discovered intellectual history writes me that "I feel sick to think that instead of reading Sidney Sheldon I could have been reading Thomas Mann."

The Jesuit Teilhard de Chardin named the realm of the mind and all its products the "noösphere." He as well as Julian Huxley suggested that this vast realm, consisting (Huxley) of "the daring speculations and aspiring ideals of men long dead, the organized knowledge of science, the hoary wisdom of the ancients, the creative imaginings of all the world's poets and artists," is presently unorganized, most of it "lying around unused." Today it is a victim of a cultural Alzheimer's disease, existing in segments almost totally unconnected. In attempting to deal with urgent social problems, we do not use a vast amount of relevant analysis.

A century ago Ernest Renan said that from the present debased age he found refuge in the past; "all that has been of the beautiful, the civilized, the true, the noble." Within this "enchanted garden of his thoughts" he felt secure against misfortunes. Perhaps we must come back to this theme as the chief surviving reason for visiting the words and thoughts of the past.

Suggested Readings

Of necessity, the following bibliography must be extremely selective; a complete list, including all the individual figures mentioned, would compete in length with the Library of Congress printed catalog. Some idea of its potential dimensions may be suggested by the quantity of writings on a single figure: *D. H. Lawrence: An Annotated Bibliography of Writings about Him*, compiled and edited by James C. Cowan (1984) contained 4,627 entries up to 1975, before the major inundation of academic scholarship. At least a hundred other major figures can boast the same attention. Lawrence, Proust, Dickens, Hardy, Shaw, and other literary figures now have their own specialized journals (e.g., *The James Joyce Quarterly*). English Ph.D. students write dissertations consisting of an annotated bibliography of the Hardy literature, say, for just a few years. And this is only the field of literature. The Marx, Freud, Nietzsche industries are as big as any others. We face not only the multitude of subjects, but the vast proliferation of professorial work emanating from the expanded universities.

Of course undergraduate students do not need any such wealth of references; advanced students will presumably have consulted their guiding professors. Listed below are a few of the most useful reference works, some general studies, and a sampling of more specific studies, critical and biographical. The stress is on more recent publications.

Reference:

The Cambridge "Companion to" books, begun in 1991–92, published by Cambridge University Press, focus a formidable expertise on a series of notable thinkers; the *Freud* volume is edited by Jerome Neu, the *Kant* by Paul Guyer, the *Marx* by Terrell Carver. The *Oxford Companion to English Literature*, edited by Margaret Drabble (5th edition, 1985) is part of a useful series from Oxford University Press that includes a *Companion to French Literature* and a *Companion to German Literature*. There is also an *Oxford Companion to the Mind* (1987), and to *Twentieth Century Art* (1981), as well as an *Oxford Dictionary of the Christian Church* (1974). Other reference works: Elizabeth Devine, et al., ed., *Thinkers of the Twentieth Century* (1983); *Dictionary of Scientific Biography* (1973); *International Encyclopedia of the Social Sciences* (1968–79).

Some Bibliographic Aids:

Bibliographies, such as Alistair Davies, *An Annotated Critical Bibliography of Modernism* (1983), quickly become obsolete. They may be updated by the annual or periodic surveys of the "work" in a field, such as *Studies in English Literature 1500–1900* (Rice University), though these may suffer from having the survey written by a jargon-ridden or theory-haunted academic, reviewing the same sort of thing. The history of science bibliographies published annually in the journal *Isis*, and sometimes gathered together in a cumulative volume (Cumulative Bibliography for 1966–75, 1980; for 1976–85, 1989), are standard for that field; *Bibliography of the History of Medicine* (National Library of Medicine, Washington, DC) can also help in finding sources in the sciences, including psychology. *Philosopher's Index* is valuable for its field. So also *Historical Abstracts, Sociological Abstracts, Repertoire Internationale de Literature d'Art*. The basic academic journals in history of ideas include *Journal of the History of Ideas, Isis, Eighteenth Century Studies, Victorian Studies, Journal of European Studies, History and Theory, Mind*.

General Surveys:

Henry William Spiegel, *The Growth of Economic Thought* (1983); Albert S. Lindemann, *A History of European Socialism* (1984); Geoffrey Hawthorn, *Enlightenment and Despair: A History of Social Theory* (1987); Roger Scruton, *From Descartes to Wittgenstein: A Short History of Modern Philosophy* (1987); Frederick Copleston, *History of Philosophy* (7 vols., 1960–63); John Herman Randall, Jr., *The Career of Philosophy* (2 vols., 1965); Hugh Lloyd-Jones, *Blood for Ghosts: Classical Influences in the Nineteenth and Twentieth Centuries* (1983);

René Wellek, *A History of Modern Criticism, 1750–1950* (7 vols., 1955–1992; L. Pearce Williams and Henry John Steffens, *A History of Science in Western Civilization* (3 vols., 1977–78); David Knight, *Ideas in Chemistry: A History of the Science* (1992); Thomas S. Kuhn, *The Structure of Scientific Revolutions* (1970); Owen Chadwick, *The Secularization of the European Mind in the Nineteenth Century* (1976).

The Enlightenment and the French Revolution:

Emmet Kennedy, *A Cultural History of the French Revolution* (1989): William Doyle, *Origins of the French Revolution* (2nd edition, 1988); Franco Venturi, *Utopia and Reform in the Enlightenment* (1970); Alan C. Kors, *D'Holbach's Coterie* (1976); Robert Darnton, *The Literary Underground of the Old Regime* (1982); Roger Chartier, *The Cultural Uses of Print in Early Modern France* (trans. Lydia G. Cochrane, 1988); Norman Hampson, *Will and Circumstance: Montesquieu, Rousseau, and the French Revolution* (1983); Keith M. Baker, *Condorcet* (1975); Lynn Avery Hunt, *Politics, Culture, and Class in the French Revolution* (1984); Gary Kates, *The Cercle Social, the Girondins, and the French Revolution* (1985); John Lough, *The Philosophes and Post-Revolutionary France* (1982); Carol Blum, *Rousseau and the Republic of Virtue: The Language of Politics in the French Revolution* (1985); Emmet Kennedy, *A Philosophe in the Age of Revolution: Destutt de Tracy and the Origins of "Ideology"* (1978); F. P. Lock, *Burke's Reflections on the Revolution in France* (1985); John P. Clark, *The Philosophical Anarchism of William Godwin* (1977); Mark Philip, *Godwin's Political Justice* (1987); J. L. Talmon, *Origins of Totalitarian Democracy* (1960); Claire Tomalin, *The Life and Death of Mary Wollstonecraft* (1974); J. F. C. Harrison, *The Second Coming: Popular Millenarianism 1780–1820* (1979); John O. Lyons, *The Invention of the Self: The Hinge of Consciousness in the Eighteenth Century* (1978); Charles Taylor, *Sources of the Self: The Making of the Modern Identity* (1992).

Kant and German Philosophy:

Roger Scruton, *Kant* (1983), one of the series "Past Masters" published by Oxford University Press; Bentham, Hegel, Kierkegaard, Marx, Mill, Bergson, and Wittgenstein are others covered in this series. W. H. Walsh, *Kant's Critique of Metaphysics* (1975); Howard L. Williams, *Kant's Philosophy of Religion* (1983); Patrick Riley, *Kant's Political Thought* (1983); Donald W. Crawford, *Kant's Aesthetic Theory* (1974); Gordon S. Brittan, *Kant's Theory of Science* (1978); René Wellek, *Kant in England* (1931); Ermanno Bencivenga, *Kant's Copernican Revolution* (1987); Tom Rockmore, *Fichte, Marx, and the German Philosophical Tradition* (1980); F. M. Barnard, *Herder's Social and Political Thought* (1965).

Romanticism:

Meyer H. Abrams, *The Mirror and the Lamp* (1953); Northrop Frye, *A Study of English Romanticism* (1968); Geoffrey Hartman and David Thorburn, ed., *Romanticism: Vistas, Instances, Continuities* (1973); Jerome J. McGann, *The Romantic Ideology: A Critical Investigation* (1983); Paul de Man, *The Rhetoric of Romanticism* (1984); G. P. Thompson, ed., *The Gothic Imagination: Essays in Dark Romanticism* (1974); Leslie Marchand, *Byron: A Portrait* (1970); Michael Foot, *The Politics of Paradise: A Vindication of Byron* (1988); Peter L. Thorsley, *The Byronic Hero* (1962); William A. Veeder, *Mary Shelley and Frankenstein* (1986); Herbert F. Tucker, *Tennyson and the Doom of Romanticism* (1988); Jonathan Wordsworth, Michael C. Jaye, and Robert Woof, *William Wordsworth and the Age of English Romanticism* (1987); Fred Kaplan, *Thomas Carlyle, A Biography* (1984); Philip Rosenberg, *The Seventh Hero: Thomas Carlyle and the Theory of Radical Activism* (1974); Theodore Ziolkowski, *German Romanticism and Its Institutions* (1990); Nicholas Boyle, *Goethe: The Poet and His Age* (vol. 1, 1991); William Vaughan, *German Romantic Painting* (1980); Ronald Taylor, *Robert Schumann: His Life and Work* (1982); S. S. Prawer, ed., *The Romantic Period in Germany* (1970); D. O. Evans, *Social Romanticism in France 1830–1848* (1951); D.G. Charlton, ed., *The French Romantics* (2 vols., 1984); Chris Baldick, ed., *The Oxford Book of Gothic Tales* (1992).

Political Ideologies:

Richard A Lebrun, *Joseph de Maistre: An Intellectual Militant* (1988); René Remond, *The Right Wing in France from 1815 to De Gaulle* (1965); George Armstrong Kelley, *The Humane Comedy: Constant, Tocqueville, and French Liberalism* (1992); Klaus Epstein, *The Genesis of German Conservatism* (1966); John Stuart Mill, *On Bentham and Coleridge* (reprinted 1950); Richard Bellamy, ed., *Victorian Liberalism* (1990); J. W. Burrow, *Whigs and Liberals* (1988); Boyd Hilton, *The Age of Atonement: The Influence of Evangelicalism on Social and Economic Thought* (1989); Mary P. Mack, *Jeremy Bentham: An Odyssey of Ideas* (1962); Ross Harrison, *Bentham* (1984); Douglas Long, *Bentham on Liberty* (1977); Bhiku Parekh, ed., *Bentham's Political Thought* (1973); William Thomas, *The Philosophical Radicals* (1979); Nancy L. Rosenblum, *Bentham's Theory of the Modern State* (1978) and *Another Liberalism: Romanticism and the Reconstruction of Liberal Thought* (1988); Frederick Rosen, *Jeremy Bentham and Representative Democracy* (1983); A. Sen and B. Williams, ed., *Utilitarianism and Beyond* (1982); O. H. Taylor, *The Classical Liberalism, Marxism, and the Twentieth Century* (1960); William D. Grampp, *The Manchester School of Liberalism* (1960); Jack Lively, *The Social and Political Thought of Alexis de Tocqueville* (1962); James J. Sheehan, *German Liberalism in the Nineteenth Century* (1978); Harold

Silver, *The Concept of Popular Education: A Study of Ideas and Social Movements in the Early Nineteenth Century* (1965).

Political Economy:

William Letwin, *The Origin of Scientific Economics* (1963); Terence Hutchinson, *Before Adam Smith: The Emergence of Political Economy 1662–1776* (1988); Patricia H. Werhane, *Adam Smith and His Legacy for Modern Capitalism* (1991); Richard F. Teichgraeber, *"Fair Trade" and Moral Philosophy: Rethinking the Sources of Adam Smith's Wealth of Nations* (1986); Istvan Hunt and Michael Ignatieff, eds., *Wealth and Virtue: The Shaping of Political Economy in the Scottish Enlightenment* (1984); Lionel Robbins, *Theory of Economic Policy in English Classical Political Economy* (1953); D. P. O'Brien, *The Classical Economists* (1975); Marc Blaug, *Ricardian Economics* (1958); William Peterson, *Malthus* (1979); Ronald Meek, *Smith, Marx, and After* (1977); Pedro Schwarz, *The New Political Economy of John Stuart Mill* (1973); R. D. Collinson Black, A. W. Coats, G. D. W. Goodwin, eds., *The Marginal Revolution in Economics* (1973); Gertrude Himmelfarb, *The Idea of Poverty: England in the Early Industrial Age* (1984); Margaret Schabas, *A World Ruled by Number: William Stanley Jevons and the Rise of Mathematical Economics* (1990).

Socialism:

George Lichtheim, *Origins of Socialism* (1969); R. B. Rose, *Gracchus Babeuf* (1978); J. F. C. Harrison, *Quest for the New Moral World. Robert Owen and Owenism in Britain and America* (1969); Jonathan F. Beecher, *The Utopian Vision of Charles Fourier* (1987); Keith Taylor, *The Political Ideas of the Utopian Socialists* (1982); Frank E. Manuel, *The New World of Henri Saint-Simon* (1956); Christopher H. Johnson, *Utopian Communism in France: Cabet and the Icarians, 1839–1851* (1974); Robert L. Hoffman, *Revolutionary Justice: The Social and Political Theory of P.-J. Proudhon* (1972); James T. Billington, *Fire in the Minds of Men: Origins of the Revolutionary Faith* (1980); Martin Malia, *Alexander Herzen and the Birth of Russian Socialism* (1961); Noel W. Thompson, *The People's Science: The Popular Political Economy of Exploitation and Crisis, 1816–1834* (1985); Peter Stearns, *Lamennais: Priest and Revolutionary* (1968); A. M. C. Waterman, *Revolution, Economics, and Religion: Christian Political Economy 1798–1833* (1991); Edward Norman, *Victorian Christian Socialists* (1987); Friedrich A. Hayek, *The Fatal Conceit: The Errors of Socialism* (1988); George Crowder, *Classical Anarchism: The Political Thought of Godwin, Proudhon, Bakunin and Kropotkin* (1992); Peter Marshall, *Demanding the Impossible: A*

Political History of Anarchism (1992); Jean H. Quataert, *Reluctant Feminists in German Social Democracy 1885–1917* (1979).

Hegel:

Michael Inwood, ed., *Hegel* (1985); Peter Singer, *Hegel* (1983); George A. Kelly, *Idealism, Politics, and History: Sources of Hegelian Thought* (1969); David Lamb, ed., *Hegel and Modern Philosophy* (1987); Jean Hyppolite, *Genesis and Structure of Hegel's Phenomenology of Spirit* (trans. 1974); Michael Rosen, *Hegel's Dialectic and Its Criticism* (1982); B. M. G. Reardon, *Hegel's Philosophy of Religion* (1977); Bernard Cullen, *Hegel's Social and Political Thought, An Introduction* (1979); George D. O'Brien, *Hegel on Reason and History* (1975); Burleigh T. Wilkins, *Hegel's Philosophy of History* (1979); Charles Taylor, *Hegel and Modern Society* (1979); L. S. Stepelevich and David Lamb, ed., *Hegel's Philosophy of Action* (1983); William J. Brazill, *The Young Hegelians* (1970); Edward J. Brown, *Stankevich and His Moscow Circle 1830–1840* (1967); Michael S. Roth, *Knowing and History: Appropriations of Hegel in Twentieth Century France* (1988).

Comte:

D. C. Charlton, *Positivist Thought in France 1852–1870* (1959); Walter M. Simon, *European Positivism in the Nineteenth Century* (1963); John Stuart Mill, *August Comte and Positivism* (reprinted 1961); T. R. Wright, *The Religion of Humanity: The Impact of Comtean Positivism on Victorian Britain* (1986); Christopher Kent, *Brains and Numbers: Elitism, Comteanism and Democracy in Mid-Victorian England* (1978); J. B. Bury, *The Idea of Progress* (1920); Christopher Lasch, *The True and Only Heaven: Progress and Its Critics* (1991); Peter J. Bowler, *The Invention of Progress: The Victorians and the Past* (1989).

Marx:

David McClellan, *Karl Marx, His Life and Thought* (1973); L. Kolakowski, *Main Currents of Marxism* (2 vols., 1978–80); R. H. Hunt, *The Political Ideas of Marx and Engels* (2 vols., 1974–84); Jon Elster, *Making Sense of Marx* (1985); N. Scott Arnold, *Marx's Radical Critique of Capitalist Society* (1990); Peter Calvert, *The Concept of Class* (1982); P. N. Furbank, *Unholy Pleasure; or the Idea of Social Class* (1985); Frank Parkin, *Marxism and Class Theory: A Bourgeois Critique* (1979); Terrell Carver, *Marx and Engels: The Intellectual Relationship* (1983); Thomas Sowell, *Marxism, Philosophy, and Economics* (1985); M. C. Howard and J. C. King, *The Economics of Marx* (1976); G. H. R. Parkinson, ed., *Marx and Marxisms* (1982); Leonard Wessell, *Prometheus Bound: The Mythic Structure of Karl Marx's Scientific Thinking* (1984); S. W. Prawer, *Karl Marx and World Liter-*

ature (1976); Paul Thomas, *Marx and the Anarchists* (1980); Shlomo Avineri, *Moses Hess: Prophet of Communism and Zionism* (1987); Richard B. Saltman, *The Social and Political Thought of M. Bakunin* (1983); Anthony Giddens, *Capitalism and Modern Social Theory* (1971); Robert J. Antonio and R. M. Glassman, eds., *A Weber-Marx Dialogue* (1985); David W. Lovell, *From Marx and Lenin: An Evaluation of Marx's Responsibility for Soviet Authoritarianism* (1984).

Darwin and Darwinism:

The fullest biography is *Darwin: The Life of a Tormented Evolutionist*, by Adrian Desmond and James Moore (1991). Bentley Glass, ed., *Forerunners of Darwin* (1959); Roy Porter, *The Making of Geology: Earth Science in Britain 1660–1815* (1977); Pietro Corsi, *The Age of Lamarck* (1988); Maureen McNeil, *Under the Banner of Science: Erasmus Darwin and His Age* (1987); John Langdon Brooks, *Just Before the Origin* (1984); Arnold C. Brackman, *A Delicate Arrangement: The Strange Case of Charles Darwin and Alfred Russel Wallace* (1980); David Hull, *Darwin and His Critics* (1973); Michael Ruse, *The Darwinian Revolution* (1979) and *Darwinism Defended: A Guide to the Evolutionary Controversies* (1982); William Irvine, *Apes, Angels, and Victorians* (1955); David Kohn, ed., *The Darwinian Heritage* (1986); Stephen J. Gould, *Ever Since Darwin* (1977) and *The Panda's Thumb* (1980); Bryan Leith, *The Descent of Darwin: A Handbook of Doubts about Darwinism* (1982); Alan Grafen, ed., *Evolution and Its Influence* (1989); Thomas F. Glick, ed., *The Comparative Reception of Darwinism* (1974); Alfred Kelley, *The Descent of Darwin: The Popularization of Darwin in Germany 1860–1914* (1981); Alexander Vucinich, *Darwin in Russian Thought* (1989); Daniel Todes, *Darwin without Malthus: The Struggle for Existence and Russian Evolutionary Thought in the Nineteenth Century* (1989); Peter J. Bowler, *Theories of Human Evolution: A Century of Debate 1844–1944* (1986).

Social Darwinism:

Robert C. Bannister, *Social Darwinism: Science and Myth in Anglo-American Thought* (1978); Greta Jones, *Social Darwinism and English Thought* (1980); D. P. Crook, *Benjamin Kidd: Portrait of a Social Darwinist* (1984); Paul Heyer, *Nature; Human Nature, and Society: Marx, Darwin, Biology and the Human Sciences* (1982); Richard P. Alexander, *Darwinism and Human Affairs* (1979); Linda L. Clark, *Social Darwinism in France* (1984); J. G. Kennedy, *Herbert Spencer* (1978); George W. Stocking, *Race, Culture, and Evolution: Essays in the History of Anthropology* (1982); Murray J. Leaf, *Men, Mind, and Science* (1979); Michael P. Banton, *The Idea of Race* (1977); Michael D. Biddiss, ed., *Images of Race* (1979); Geoffrey Field, *Evangelist of Race: The Germanic Vision of Houston Stewart Chamberlain* (1981); Redmond O'Hanlon, *Joseph Conrad and Charles Darwin* (1984).

Victorian Religion:

John Durant, ed., *Darwinism and Divinity* (1985); Mary Midgley, *Evolution as a Religion: Strange Hopes and Stranger Fears* (1985); B. M. G. Reardon, *Religious Thought in the Victorian Age* (1980); M. A. Crowther, *Church Embattled: Religious Controversy in Mid-Victorian England* (1970); A. O. J. Cockshut, *The Unbelievers: English Agnostic Thought 1840–1890* (1966); Ian Bradley, *The Call to Seriousness: The Evangelical Impact on the Victorians* (1976); K. J. M. Smith, *James Fitzjames Stephens: Portrait of a Victorian Rationalist* (1985); J. Hillis Miller, *The Disappearance of God* (1963); Owen Chadwick, *The Spirit of the Oxford Movement* (1990); Lawrence F. Barmann, *Baron von Hügel and the Modernist Crisis in England* (1972); Josef L. Altholz, *The Liberal Catholic Movement in England 1848–1864* (1960).

Victorian Literature and Thought:

John Stuart Mill, *On Liberty and Other Essays*, ed. John Gray (1991); Gertrude Himmelfarb, *Victorian Minds* (1968); Alan Horsman, *The Victorian Novel* (1990), part of The Oxford History of English Literature; Grahame Smith, *The Novel and Society: Defoe to George Eliot* (1984); William Myers, *The Teaching of George Eliot* (1984); Barbara Smalley, *Eliot and Flaubert* (1974); F. B. Pinion, *Thomas Hardy: Life and Thought* (1977); Trygve Tholfsen, *Working Class Radicalism in Mid-Victorian England* (1977); Martha Vicinus, *The Industrial Muse* (1974); P. J. Keating, *The Working Classes in Victorian Fiction* (1971); Myron Magnet, *Dickens and the Social Order* (1987); Fred Kaplan, *Dickens* (1988); Jeffrey L. Spear, *Dreams of an English Eden: John Ruskin and His Tradition in Social Criticism* (1984); P. D. Anthony, *John Ruskin's Labour: A Study of Ruskin's Social Theory* (1983); Edward Alexander, *Matthew Arnold, John Ruskin, and the Modern Temper* (1973); Bernard Semmel, *John Stuart Mill and the Pursuit of Virtue* (1984); John M. Robson, *The Improvement of Mankind: The Social and Political Thought of John Stuart Mill* (1968); M. W. Taylor, *Men Versus the State: Herbert Spencer and Late Victorian Individualism* (1992).

Realism and Naturalism:

Peter Morton, *The Vital Influence: Biology and the Literary Imagination 1860–1900* (1984); Harry Levin, *The Gates of Horn: A Study of Five French Realists* (1963); Richard Terdiman, *The Dialectics of Isolation: Self and Society in the French Novel from the Realists to Proust* (1976); Philip Walker, *Zola* (1985); Brian Nelson, *Zola and the Bourgeoisie* (1983); Michael Bedlow, *The Fiction of Humanity: The Bildungsroman from Wieland to Thomas Mann* (1982); William M. Todd III, *Literature and Society in Imperial Russia* (1980); Joseph Frank, *Dostoyevsky* (3 vols., 1976–86); Edward Wasiolek, *Tolstoy's Major Fiction* (1978);

Richard F. Gustafson, *Leo Tolstoy: Resident and Stranger* (1986); George Steiner, *Tolstoy or Dostoyevsky* (1959).

Nationalism:

Eugene Kamenka, *Nationalism: The Nature and Evolution of an Idea* (1976); Anthony D. Smith, *Theories of Nationalism* (1983); Hans Rogger, *National Consciousness in Eighteenth Century Russia* (1960); Leonard Schapiro, *Rationalism and Nationalism in Russian Nineteenth Century Thought* (1967); M. B. Petrovich, *The Emergence of Russian Pan-Slavism* (1956); Gwilym O. Griffith, *Mazzini: Prophet of Modern Europe* (1970); Luigi Salvatorelli, *Thought and Action in the Risorgimento* (1970); Eugen Weber, *The Nationalist Revival in France 1905–1914* (1959) and *Peasants into Frenchmen: The Modernization of Rural France 1870–1914* (1976), also *The Action Française* (1962); Michael Sutton, *Nationalism, Positivism and Catholicism: The Politics of Charles Maurras and French Catholics 1898–1914* (1983); Marianne Heiberg, *The Making of the Basque Nation* (1989); Peter Brock, *The Slovak National Awakening: An Essay in the Intellectual History of Eastern Europe* (1976); Rosalind Mitchum, ed., *The Roots of Nationalism: Studies in Northern Europe* (1980); W. F. Mandle and Pauric Travers, eds., *Irish Culture and Nationalism 1750–1950* (1983); David Vital, *The Origins of Zionism* (1975) and *Zionism: The Formative Years (1982)*.

Professionalization:

Marie Boas Hall, *All Scientists Now: The Royal Society in the Nineteenth Century* (1985); Mogali S. Larson, *The Rise of Professionalism* (1977); A. J. Engel, *From Clergyman to Don: The Rise of the Academic Profession in Nineteenth-Century Oxford* (1983); A. H. Halsey, *Decline of Donnish Dominion: The British Academic Professions in the Twentieth Century* (1992); George Weisz, *The Emergence of Modern Universities in France 1863–1914* (1983); Charles E. McClelland, *The German Experience of Professionalization* (1991); Nigel Cross, *The Common Writer: Life in Nineteenth Century Grub Street* (1985); Cesar Grana, *Bohemian vs. Bourgeois: French Society and the Man of Letters in the Nineteenth Century* (1964); Ronald Hingley, *Russian Writers and Society in the Nineteenth Century* (1967).

Wagner and Nietzsche:

David C. Large and William Weber, eds., *Wagnerism in European Culture and Politics* (1984); William J. McGrath, *Dionysian Art and Populist Politics in Austria* (1973); Jacob Katz, *The Darker Side of Genius: Richard Wagner's Anti-Semitism* (1986); Elizabeth Magee, *Richard Wagner and the Nibelungs* (1991); Bryan

Magee, *The Philosophy of Schopenhauer* (1983); Robert Solomon and Kathleen M. Higgins, eds., *Reading Nietzsche* (1989); George Stauth and Bryan S. Turner, *Nietzsche's Dream* (1988); Walter Kaufmann, *Nietzsche: Philosopher, Psychologist, Antichrist* (1974); F. C. Lea, *The Tragic Philosopher* (1973); Arthur Danto, *Nietzsche as Philosopher* (1967); Giles Deleuze, *Nietzsche and Philosophy* (1983); J. P. Stern, *The Study of Nietzsche* (1979); Martin Heidegger, *Nietzsche* (1979); Karl Jaspers, *Nietzsche: An Introduction...* (1965); Keith Ansell-Pearson, *Nietzsche contra Rousseau: A Study of Nietzsche's Moral and Political Thought* (1991); R. H. Thomas, *Nietzsche in German Politics and Society 1890–1918* (1983); Herbert W. Reichert, *Nietzsche's Impact on Modern German Literature* (1975); John B. Foster, *Heirs to Modernism: Literary Modernism and Nietzsche* (1981); William D. Williams, *Nietzsche and the French* (1952); Patrick Bridgwater, *Nietzsche in Anglosaxony* (1972) and *Nietzsche and Kafka* (1974); Bernice Glatzer Rosenthal, ed., *Nietzsche in Russia* (1987); Edith W. Clowes, *The Revolution of Moral Consciousness: Nietzsche in Russian Literature, 1890–1914* (1988); Rudolph Binion, *Frau Lou: Nietzsche's Wayward Disciple* (1968); Robert Eden, *Political Leadership and Nihilism: A Study of Weber and Nietzsche* (1983); Frances Nesbitt Oppel, *Mask and Tragedy: Yeats and Nietzsche, 1902–1910* (1987); Colin Milton, *Lawrence and Nietzsche: A Study in Influence* (1987); Timothy Martin, *Joyce and Wagner* (1992); Otto Heller, *Prophets of Dissent* (Maeterlinck, Strindberg, Tolstoy, Nietzsche, reprinted 1968); Erich Heller, *The Importance of Nietzsche* (1988).

Symbolism and Late Nineteenth-Century Literature:

Edmund Wilson, *Axel's Castle* (1936); Mario Praz, *The Romantic Agony* (1954); Philippe Jullian, *Dreamers of Decadence* (1971) and *D'Annunzio: A Biography* (1972); John Porter Houston, *French Symbolism and the Modernist Movement* (1980); Lawrence M. Porter, *The Crisis of French Symbolism* (1990); Jean Pierrot, *The Decadent Imagination, 1880–1900* (1981); Debora Silverman, *Art Nouveau in Fin de Siècle France* (1989); Richard Ellmann, *Oscar Wilde* (1988); Carl Schorske, *Fin de Siècle Vienna* (1980); Edward Timms and Ritchie Robertson, eds., *Vienna 1900* (1990); Roy Pascal, *From Naturalism to Expressionism: German Literature and Society 1880–1918* (1973); Mark G. Ward, ed., *From Vormärz to Fin de Siècle: Essays in Nineteenth Century German Literature* (1986); James West, *Russian Symbolism* (1970); Oleg A. Maslenikov, *The Frenzied Poets: Andrei Biely and the Russian Symbolists* (1952); Hermann Broch, *Hugo von Hofmannsthal and His Time: The European Imagination 1860–1920* (1981); Jonathan Rose, *The Edwardian Temperament 1895–1919* (1985); A. M. Gibb, *The Art and Mind of Shaw* (1984); Robert F. Whitman, *Shaw and the Play of Ideas* (1977); David Smith, *H. G. Wells, Desperately Mortal* (1988); Robert M. Philmus, *Into the Unknown: The Evolution of Science Fiction from Francis Godwin to H. G. Wells* (1975).

Philosophic Irrationalism:

A. E. Pilkington, *Henri Bergson and His Influence* (1976); S. K. Kumar, *Bergson and the Stream of Consciousness Novel* (1963); R. C. Grogin, *The Bergsonian Controversy in France 1900–1914* (1988); J. R. Jennings, *Georges Sorel: The Character and Development of His Thought* (1985); Jack J. Roth, *The Cult of Violence: Sorel and the Sorelians* (1980); Richard Vernon, *Commitment and Change: Georges Sorel and the Idea of Revolution* (1978); John Stanley, *The Sociology of Virtue: Political and Social Themes of Georges Sorel* (1981); Janet Oppenheim, *The Other World: Speculation and Psychic Research in England, 1850–1914* (1985); I. L. Horowitz, *Radicalism and the Revolt against Reason* (1961); Robert A. Nye, *The Origins of Crowd Psychology: Gustave Le Bon and the Crisis of Mass Democracy in the Third Republic* (1975); Graham Hough, *The Mystery Religion of W. B. Yeats* (1984).

Early Twentieth-Century Modernism:

Malcolm Bradbury and James McFarlane, eds., *Modernism 1890–1913* (1976); Roger Shattuck, *The Banquet Years: The Arts in France 1885–1918* (1958); Carl and Ellendra Proffer, *The Silver Age of Russian Culture* (1971); Marjorie Perloff, *The Futurist Moment* (1986); Marianne W. Martin, *Futurist Art and Theory* (1968); Vladimir Markov, *Russian Futurism* (1969); Paul Raabe, ed., *The Era of German Expressionism* (1974); Peter Paret, *The Berlin Secession: Modernism and Its Enemies in Imperial Germany* (1980); Stephen Bronner and Douglas Kellner, eds., *Passion and Rebellion: The Expressionist Heritage* (1982); Donald E. Gordon, *Expressionism: Art and Idea* (1988); Douglas Cooper, *The Cubist Epoch* (1972); Christopher Green, *Cubism and Its Enemies, 1916–1928* (1988); John Golding, *Cubism: A History and Analysis* (1968); Wilfred Mellers, *Caliban Reborn: Renewal in Twentieth Century Music* (1967).

Sociology and Social Thought:

H. Stuart Hughes, *Consciousness and Society: European Social Thought 1890–1930* (1958); Raymond Aron, *Main Currents of Sociological Thought* (2 vols., 1967); Robert A. Nisbet, *The Sociological Tradition* (1966); Arthur Mitzman, *Sociology and Estrangement* (1973); Anthony Giddens, *Studies in Social and Political Theory* (1977); Philip Abrams, *The Origins of British Sociology 1834–1914* (1968); Wolf Lepenies, *Between Literature and Science: The Rise of Sociology* (trans. 1988); Dirk Käsler, *Max Weber: An Introduction to his Life and Work* (1988); Frank Parkin, *Max Weber* (1982); Donald G. Macrae, *Max Weber* ("Modern Masters" series, 1974); Reinhard Bendix, *Max Weber: An Intellectual Portrait* (1960); Bendix and G. Roth, eds., *Scholarship and Partisanship: Essays on Max Weber* (1971); Gordon Marshall, *In Search of the Spirit of Capitalism: An Essay on Max Weber's Protestant Ethic Thesis* (1982); Ronald M. Glassman and Vatro Murvar, eds., *Max Weber's Political Sociology* (1984); Sam Whimster and Scott Lash, eds., *Max Weber, Rationality and Modernity* (1987); Robert A. Nye, *The Anti-Democratic Sources of Elite Theory: Pareto, Mosca, Michels* (1977); Steven Lukes, *Emile Durkheim: His Life and Work* (1973); William Logue, *From Philosophy to Sociology: The Evolution of French Liberalism 1870–1914* (1983); Fritz Ringer, *The Decline of the German Mandarins* (1969); Rudolf A. Makreel, *Wilhelm Dilthey: Philosopher of the Human Studies* (1975).

Late Nineteenth-Century Socialism:

William Maehl, *August Bebel* (1980); Vernon Lidtke, *The Alternative Culture: Socialist Labor in Imperial Germany* (1985); Mark F. Blum, *The Austro-Marxists, 1890–1918: A Psychobiographical Study* (1985); Gary P. Steenson, *Karl Kautsky, 1854–1938* (1978); Peter Gay, *The Dilemma of Democratic Socialism: Bernstein's Challenge to Marx* (1952); J. P. Nettl, *Rosa Luxemburg* (1966); Harvey Goldberg, *Jean Jaurès* (1962); George Lichtheim, *Marxism in Modern France* (1966); F. F. Ridley, *French Syndicalism* (1970); Patrick H. Hutton, *The Cult of the Revolutionary Tradition: The Blanquists in French Politics 1864–1893* (1976); Temma Kaplan, *Anarchists of Andulasia, 1868–1903* (1976); Willard Wolfe, *From Radicalism to Socialism: Foundations of Fabian Socialism, 1881–1889* (1975); Norman and Jeanne MacKenzie, *The Fabians* (1977); Ian Britain, *Fabianism and Culture* (1982); J. W. Hulse, *Revolutionists in London: A Study of Five Unorthodox Socialists* (1970); Peter D'Arcy Jones, *The Christian Socialist Revival in England* (1968); Stanley Pierson, *English Socialists* (1979); Norman Dennis and A. H. Halsey, eds., *English Ethical Socialism: Thomas More to R. H. Tawney* (1989); Lillian P. Wallace, *Leo XIII and the Rise of Socialism* (1966); Peter Stansky, *Redesigning the World: William Morris, the 1880s, and the Arts and Crafts* (1985).

The Intellectuals and World War I:

Roland N. Stromberg, *Redemption by War: The Intellectuals and 1914* (1982); Paul Fussell, *The Great War and Modern Memory* (1975); Robert Wohl, *The Generation of 1914* (1979); J. D. Ellis, *French Socialists and the Problem of War 1904–1914* (1967); Georges Haupt, *Socialism and the Great War: The Collapse of the Second International* (1972); Peter Vansittart, *Voices from the Great War* (1981); Jon Silkin, *Out of Battle: The Poetry of the First World War* (1977), and (ed.), *The Penguin Book of First World War Poetry* (1981); Bernard Bergonzi, *Heroes' Twilight* (1964); Robert Giddings, *The War Poets, 1914–1918* (1988); George Parfitt, *Fiction of the First World War* (1988); Kenneth Silver, *Esprit de Corps: The Great War and French Art 1914–1918* (1988); Paul Delany, *D. H.*

Lawrence's Nightmare: The Writer and His Circle during the Years of the Great War (1979); Frank Field, *Three French Writers and the Great War* (1975) and *British and French Writers of the First World War* (1991); John Cruickshank, *Variations on Catastrophe: Some French Responses to the Great War* (1982); William T. Starr, *Romain Rolland and a World at War* (1956); F. L. Carsten, *War against War: British and German Radical Movements in the First World War* (1982); Jo Vellacott, *Bertrand Russell and the Pacifists in the First World War* (1981).

Freud:

Ekbert Faas, *Retreat into the Mind: Victorian Poetry and the Rise of Psychiatry* (1989); Harry F. Ellenberger, *The Discovery of the Unconscious* (1970); Marthe Robert, *The Psychoanalytic Revolution: Sigmund Freud's Life and Achievement* (1966); Ronald W. Clark, *Freud: The Man and the Cause* (1980); Peter Gay, *Freud: A Life for Our Time* (1988) and *Reading Freud: Explorations and Entertainments* (1991); W. J. McGrath, *Freud's Discovery of Psychoanalysis* (1986); M. Kanzer and J. Glenn, eds., *Freud and His Patients* (1980); Sara Kofman, *The Enigma of Woman: Women in Freud's Writings* (1985); Paul Ricoeur, *Freud and Philosophy* (1970); Frank J. Sulloway, *Freud, Biologist of the Mind* (1979); Harry Trossman, *Freud and the Imaginative World* (1985); Steven Marcus, *Freud and the Culture of Psychoanalysis* (1984); Marie Balmary, *Psychoanalyzing Psychoanalysis* (1982); Marshall Edelson, *Psychoanalysis—A Theory in Crisis* (1988); Erich Fromm, *The Crisis of Psychoanalysis* (1970); H. J. Eysenck, *Decline and Fall of the Freudian Empire* (1985); Gerald N. Izenberg, *The Crisis of Autonomy: The Existentialist Critique of Freud* (1976); B. A. Farrell, *The Standing of Psychoanalysis* (1981); Martin J. Kalin, *The Utopian Flight from Unhappiness: Freud against Marx on Social Progress* (1974); Morris Lazerowitz, *The Language of Philosophy: Freud and Wittgenstein* (1977); T. S. Szasz, *Karl Kraus and the Soul Doctors* (1976).

Other Psychoanalysts:

Robert S. Steele, *Freud and Jung* (1982); Walter Kaufmann, *Freud versus Adler and Jung* (1980); Paul J. Stern, *Jung, the Haunted Prophet* (1976); Harold C. Coward, *Jung and Eastern Thought* (1985); James Olney, *The Rhizome and the Flower: Jung and Yeats* (1980); Andrew Samuels, *Jung and the Post-Jungians* (1985); Bettina L. Knapp, *A Jungian Approach to Literature* (1984); Charles B. Hanna, *The Face of the Deep: The Religious Ideas of Carl Jung* (1967); Paul Roazen, *Freud and His Followers* (1971); E. J. Lieberman, *Acts of Will: Life and Works of Otto Rank* (1985); Phyllis Grosskurth, *Melanie Klein, Her World and Her Work* (1986); Judith M. Hughes, *Reshaping the Psychoanalytic Domain* (1989; the British school including Klein, Fairbairn, Winnicott); Elisabeth Roudinesco, *Jacques Lacan & Co.: A History of Psychoanalysis in France 1925–1985* (1990); Richard Lichtheim, *The Production of Desire: The Integration of Psychoanalysis into Marxist Theory* (1982).

Lenin and Bolshevism:

Philip Pomper, *The Russian Revolutionary Intelligentsia* (1970); Franco Venturi, *Roots of Revolution* (1970); James H. Billington, *Mikhailovsky and Russian Populism* (1958); Andrej Walicki, *The Controversy over Capitalism: Studies in the Social Philosophy of the Russian Populists* (1969); Tibor Szamuely, *The Russian Tradition* (1974); Paul Avrich, *The Russian Anarchists* (1967); Samuel H. Baron, *Plekhanov: The Father of Russian Marxism* (1963); Vera Broido, *Apostles and Terrorists: Women and the Revolutionary Movement in the Russia of Alexander II* (1977); Robert Service, *Lenin: A Political Life* (1985); A. J. Polan, *Lenin and the End of Politics* (1984); A. B. Ulam, *Lenin and the Bolsheviks* (1965); R. H. W. Theen, *Lenin: Genesis and Development of a Revolutionary* (1973); Alain Besançon, *The Rise of the Gulag: Intellectual Origins of Leninism* (1981); Z. A. Sochor, *Revolution and Culture: The Bogdanov-Lenin Controversy* (1988); Joel Carmichael, *Trotsky* (1975); Curtis Stokes, *The Evolution of Trotsky's Theory of Revolution* (1982); Stephen F. Cohen, *Bukharin and the Russian Revolution* (1973); Robert C. Williams, *The Other Bolsheviks: Lenin and His Critics 1904–14* (1988) and *Artists in Revolution: Portraits of the Russian Avant-Garde 1905–1925* (1977); Edward J. Brown, *Mayakovsky: A Poet in the Revolution* (1973); Barbara Evans Clements, *Bolshevik Feminist: The Life of Aleksandra Kollontai* (1979).

Einstein and the Scientific Revolution:

P. M. Herman, *Energy, Force and Matter: The Development of Nineteenth Century Physics* (1982); Lewis Pyenson, *The Young Einstein: The Advent of Relativity* (1985); Elie Zahar, *Einstein's Revolution: A Study in Heuristic* (1989); Russell McCormmach, ed., *Historical Studies in the Physical Sciences*, vol. 7 (1976); Arthur Miller, *Einstein's Special Theory of Relativity: Emergence and Early Interpretation* (1981); also his *Frontiers of Physics 1900–1911* (1986); Christa Jungnickel and Russell McCormmach, *Intellectual Mastery of Nature: Theoretical Physics from Ohm to Einstein* (2 vols., 1986); Stephen Kern, *The Culture of Space and Time 1880–1918* (1983); Jed Z. Buchwald, *From Maxwell to Microphysics* (1985); Don Howard and John Stachel, eds., *Einstein and the History of General Relativity* (1989); L. Pearce Williams, ed., *Relativity Theory: Its Origins and Impact on Modern Thought* (1968); Bertrand Russell, *The ABC of Relativity* (1959); Lincoln Barnett, *The Universe and Dr. Einstein* (1964); Nigel Calder, *Einstein's Universe* (1979); Stanley Goldberg, *Understanding Relativity* (1984);

Albert Einstein, *The Meaning of Relativity* (latest edition, 1988); Robert M. Wald, *Space, Time, and Gravity* (1977); Arthur Fine, *The Shaky Game: Einstein, Realism, and the Quantum Theory* (1986); Bruce R. Whcaton, *The Tiger and the Shark: Empirical Roots of Wave-Particle Dualism* (1991); John Hendry, *The Creation of Quantum Mechanics and the Bohr-Pauli Debate* (1984); Michio Kaku and Jennifer Trainer, *Beyond Einstein: The Cosmic Quest for the Theory of the Universe* (1987); Arthur Eddington, *The Philosophy of Physical Science* (1939); James Jeans, *Physics and Philosophy* (1942); Milic Capek, *The Philosophical Impact of Modern Physics* (1961); Alan J. Friedman and Carol C. Donley, *Einstein As Myth and Muse* (1985); Thomas F. Glick, *Einstein in Spain: Relativity and the Recovery of Science* (1988); Harvey R. Brown and Rom Harré, eds., *Philosophical Foundations of Quantum Field Theory* (1988); a life of Heisenberg called (what else?) *Uncertainty*, by David C. Cassidy (1992); Helge S. Kragh, *Dirac: A Scientific Biography* (1990); Walter J. Moore, *Schrödinger: Life and Thought* (1989); John Honner, *The Description of Nature: Niels Bohr and the Philosophy of Quantum Physics* (1988); David Wilson, *Rutherford: Simple Genius* (1983); Larry Laudan, *Science and Relativism: Some Key Controversies in the Philosophy of Science* (1990).

Fascism:

Renzo de Felice, *Interpretations of Fascism* (1977); Stein Ugelvik Larsen, Bernt Hagvet, Peter Myklebust, eds., *Who Were the Fascists?* (Oslo, 1982); Stanley G. Payne, *Fascism: Comparison and Definition* (1980); Hannah Arendt, *The Origins of Totalitarianism* (1966); Denis Mack Smith, *Mussolini* (1981); Adrian Lyttleton, ed., *Italian Fascisms from Pareto to Gentile* (1975); David D. Roberts, *The Syndicalist Tradition and Italian Fascism* (1979); Walter Struve, *Elites against Democracy* (1973); Andrew Cox and Noel O'Sullivan, eds., *The Corporate State: Corporatism and the State Tradition in Western Europe* (1989); Peter Pulzer, *The Rise of Political Anti-semitism in Germany and Austria* (revised edition, 1988); George L. Mosse, *Toward the Final Solution: A History of European Racism* (1977); Werner Maser, *Hitler: Legend, Myth, and Reality* (1974); Eberhard Jäckel, *Hitler's Weltanschauung* (1972); Ian Kershaw, *The Hitler Myth: Image and Reality in the Third Reich* (1987); Joseph W. Bendersky, *Carl Schmitt: Theorist for the Reich* (1983); Robert Soucy, *French Fascism: The First Wave 1924–33* (1985) and *Fascism in France: The Case of Maurice Barrès* (1973); Zeev Sternhall, *Neither Right nor Left: Fascist Ideology in France* (1986); W. F. Mandle, *Anti-Semitism and the British Union of Fascists* (1968); A. D. Beyerchen, *Scientists under Hitler* (1977); Robert R. Taylor, *The World in Stone: The Role of Architecture in National Socialist Ideology* (1974); J. M. Ritchie, *German Literature under National Socialism* (1983); Peter Hoffman, *History of the German Resistance 1933–1945* (1977); Ian Kershaw, *Popular Opinion and Political Dissent in the Third Reich: Bavaria 1933–1945* (1983).

Literature and the Arts between the Wars:

Graham Hough, *Image and Experience: Studies in a Literary Revolution* (1960); Leon Edel, *Bloomsbury: A House of Lions* (1979); C. K. Stead, *Pound, Yeats, Eliot and the Modernist Movement* (1986); Hugh Kenner, *The Pound Era* (1971); Ronald Bush, *T. S. Eliot: A Study in Character and Style* (1984); Louis Menand, *Discovering Modernism: T. S. Eliot and His Context* (1986); Stanley Sultan, *Eliot, Joyce and Company* (1987); Richard Ellmann, *James Joyce* (revised ed., 1982); Frank Budgen, *James Joyce and the Making of Ulysses* (reissued 1989 with introduction by Clive Hart); Clive Hart, *Structure and Motif in Finnegans Wake* (1962); Colin McCabe, *James Joyce and the Revolution of the Word* (1979); Hugh Kenner, *Ulysses* (revised ed., 1987); John Bishop, *Joyces's Book of the Dead* (1986); Quentin Bell, *Virginia Woolf* (1972); John Worthen, *D. H. Lawrence: The Early Years 1885–1912* (1991, first of projected 3-volume biography); Anthony Burgess, *Flame into Being: The Life and Work of D. H. Lawrence* (1985); Gamini Salgado and G. K. Das, eds., *The Spirit of D. H. Lawrence* (1988); Valentine Cunningham, *British Writers of the Thirties* (1988); Michael O'Neill and Gareth Reeves, *Auden, MacNeice, Spender: The Thirties Poetry* (1992); Joseph G. Brennan, *Three Philosophical Novelists* (1964; Joyce, Gide, Mann); Ernest Pawel, *The Nightmare of Reason: A Life of Franz Kafka* (1984); Ritchie Robertson, *Kafka: Judaism, Politics, and Literature* (1985); Frederick G. Peters, *Robert Musil: Master of the Hovering Life* (1978); Herbert S. Gershman, *The Surrealist Revolution in France* (1968); Roger Shattuck, *Marcel Proust* (1974); J. M. Cocking, *Proust: Essays on the Writer and His Art* (1982); J. E. Rivers, *Proust and the Art of Love* (1980); Keith Bullivant, ed., *Culture and Society in the Weimar Republic* (1978); Anthony Phelan, ed., *The Weimar Dilemma: Intellectuals in the Weimar Republic* (1985); Dagmar Barnouw, *Weimar Intellectuals and the Threat of Modernity* (1988); Alan Bance, ed., *Weimar Germany: Writers and Politics* (1982); Uwe Westphal, *The Bauhaus* (1991); Reginald Isaacs, *Gropius* (1991); Peter Blake, *The Master Builders* (1976); H. Allen Brooks, ed., *Le Corbusier* (1987).

Logical Positivism, Philosophy:

Leszek Kolakowski, *Positivist Philosophy* (1972); Osward Hanfling, *Logical Positivism* (1981); Gustav Bergmann, *The Metaphysics of Logical Positivism* (1967); Arno Naess, *Four Modern Philosophers* (1965); Klaus Christian Kohnke, *The Rise of Neo-Kantianism* (1991); David F. Lindenfeld, *Alexius Meinong and European Thought 1880–1920* (1980); Michael Dummett, *Frege, Philosopher of Language* (1973); Paul Levy, *G. E. Moore and the Cambridge Apostles* (1979); Peter Hylton, *Russell, Idealism, and the Emergence of Analytic Philosophy* (1990); Brian McGuinness, *Wittgenstein: A Life*, vol. 1 (1988), and (ed.), *Wittgenstein and His Times* (1982); P. M. S. Hacker, *Insight and Illusion: Themes in the Philosophy of Wittgenstein* (1987); David Pears, *The False Prison: A Study of the Development of Wittgenstein's Philosophy* (vol. 1, 1987); A. C. Grayling, *Wittgenstein* (1988); Friedrich Waismann, *Wittgenstein and the Vienna Circle* (1979); Gordon Baker, *Wittgenstein, Frege, and the Vienna Circle* (1988); Jorn K. Braman, *Wittgenstein's "Tractatus" and the Modern Arts* (1985); John W. Danford, *Wittgenstein and Political Philosophy* (1978); Henry Staten, *Wittgenstein and Derrida* (1984); Ray Monk, *Ludwig Wittgenstein: The Duty of Genius* (1990).

Soviet Communism and Stalinism:

Robert A. Maguire, *Red Virgin Soil: Soviet Literature in the 1920s* (1968); Alexander Erlich, *The Soviet Industrialization Debate 1924–1928* (1961); Adam B. Ulam, *Stalin: The Man and His Era* (1973); Robert C. Tucker, *Stalin in Power, 1928–41* (vol. 2 of a projected three, 1991); Robert H. McNeal, *Stalin: Man and Ruler* (1988); Walter Laqueur, *Stalin: The Glasnost Revelations* (1991); C. Vaughan Jones, *Soviet Socialist Realism: Origins and Theory* (1975); Robert C. Tucker, ed., *Stalinism: Essays in Historical Interpretation* (1977); G. R. Urban, ed., *Stalinism: Its Impact on Russia and the World* (1983); Robert Conquest, *The Great Terror: Stalin's Purge of the 1930s* (1971; revised ed., 1990); Sheila Fitzpatrick, ed., *Cultural Revolution in Russia, 1928–1931* (1984); Graeme Gill, *The Origins of the Stalinist Political System* (1990); Nadezhda Mandelstam, *Hope against Hope* (1970); Victor Serge, *Memoirs of a Revolutionary 1901–1941* (1965); George S. N. Luckyj, *Literary Politics in the Soviet Ukraine 1917–1934* (1990).

Communism and the Intellectuals:

David Caute, *The Fellow Travellers* (revised ed., 1988); Neal Wood, *Communism and British Intellectuals* (1964); R. H. S. Crossman, ed., *The God That Failed* (1950); Raymond Aron, *The Opium of the Intellectuals* (1952); Arthur Koestler, *The Invisible Writing* (1954); Samuel Hynes, *The Auden Generation* (1977); Humphrey Carpenter, *W. H. Auden: A Biography* (1981); Bernard Crick, *George Orwell: A Life* (1980); Stanley Weintraub, *The Last Great Cause* (1968); Frederick R. Benson, *Writers in Arms: The Literary Impact of the Spanish Civil War* (1967); Irwin Wall, *French Communism in the Era of Stalin* (1983); Michael Scriven, *Paul Nizan: Commmunist Novelist* (1989); Sudhir Hazareesingh, *Intellectuals and the French Communist Party: Disillusion and Decline* (1992); Lee Congdon, *The Young Lukacs* (1983); Arpad Kadarkay, *Georg Lukacs: Life, Thought, and Politics* (1991); Andrew Sinclair, *The Red and the Blue: Cambridge, Treason, and Intelligence* (1986); Peter Clarke, *The Keynesian Revolution in the Making, 1924–1936* (1989); G. L. S. Shackle, *The Years of High Theory: Innovation and Tradition in Economic Thought 1926–1939* (1967); Richard F. Kahn, *The Making of Keynes' "General Theory"* (1984); Richard Swedberg, *Joseph A. Schumpeter, His Life and Work* (1992); Norman Ingram, *The Politics of Dissent: Pacifism in France 1919–1939* (1991).

World War II and the Intellectuals:

Robert Hewison, *Under Siege: Literary Life in London 1939–1945* (1977); José Harris, *William Beveridge: A Biography* (1977); George Orwell, *Collected Essays, Journalism, and Letters*, vols. 2 and 3 (1968); Stephen Brooke, *Labour's War: The Labour Party and the Second World War* (1992); James D. Wilkinson, *The Intellectual Resistance in Europe* (1981); H. R. Kedward, *Resistance in Vichy France: A Study of Ideas and Motivation in the Southern Zone* (1978); Andrew Shennan, *Rethinking France: Plans for Renewal 1940–1946* (1990); Gerhard Ritter, *The German Resistance: Carl Goederler's Struggle against Tyranny* (1958); Klemens von Klemperer, *German Resistance against Hitler* (1992); Wilhelm W. Schutz, *Pens under the Swastika* (1971); T. E. J. de Witt, *Hitler's War and the Germans: Public Mood and Attitudes during the Second World War* (1977); Ilya Ehrenburg, *The War 1941–1945* (1964); Milovan Djilas, *Wartime* (1977); Donald Fleming and Bernard Bailyn, eds., *The Intellectual Migration: Europe and America 1930–1965* (1969); H. Stuart Hughes, *The Sea Change: The Migration of Social Thought 1930–1965* (1975); Lawrence L. Langer, *Versions of Survival: The Holocaust and the Human Spirit* (1982); Sidra G. Erzahl, *By Words Alone: The Holocaust in Literature* (1980); Linda M. Shires, *British Poetry of the Second World War* (1985); Holger Klein, John Flower, Eric Homberger, *The Second World War in Fiction* (1984).

Sartre and Existentialism:

Luc Ferry and Alain Renault, *Heidegger and Modernity* (trans. 1990); Annie Cohen-Solal, *Sartre: A Biography* (1987); Ronald Hayman, *Writing Against: A Biography of Sartre* (1986); Paul Schilpp, ed., *The Philosophy of Jean-Paul Sartre* (1981); Dominick LaCapra, *A Preface to Sartre* (1988); Christina Howells, *Sartre: The Necessity of Freedom* (1988), in the series "Major European Authors," Cambridge University Press; Mark Poster, *Existential Marxism in Postwar France* (1976); Raymond Aron, *History and the Dialectic of Violence: An Analysis of Sartre's Critique* (1973); Howard Davies, *Sartre and "Les Temps Modernes"* (1987); Maurice Merleau-Ponty, *Adventures of the Dialectic* (1973); Ronald Aronson, *Sartre's Second Critique* (1987); Thomas R. Flynn, *Sartre and Marxist Existentialism* (1986); Gila J. Hayim, *The Existentialist Sociology of Jean-Paul Sartre* (1980); Hazel Barnes, *Sartre and Flaubert* (1981); Betty T. Rahv, *From Sartre to the New Novel* (1974); William Plank, *Sartre and Surrealism* (1981); Betty Cannon, *Sartre and Psychoanalysis* (1991); Germaine Bree, *Camus and Sartre* (1972); Patrick McCarthy, *Camus, a Critical Study of His Life and Work* (1982); Herbert Lottman, *Albert Camus* (1979); Mary Evans, *Simone de Beauvoir, a Feminist Mandarin* (1985); Deirdre Bair, *Simone de Beauvoir: A Biography* (1990); Tony Judt, *Past Imperfect: French Intellectuals 1944–56* (1992).

Other Existentialists and Phenomenologists:

Joseph Fell, *Heidegger and Sartre* (1979); Leszek Kolakowski, *Husserl and the Search for Certitude* (1975, 1988); Zygmunt Bauman, *Hermeneutics and Social Science* (1978); Hans-G. Gadamer, *Philosophical Hermeneutics* (1976); Joseph A. Kotarba and Andrea Fontana, *The Existential Self in Society* (1984); Thomas Sheehan, ed., *Heidegger: The Man and the Thinker* (1981); John Sallis, ed., *Radical Phenomenology: Essays in Honor of Martin Heidegger* (1978); R. Bubner, *Modern German Philosophy* (1981); Karl Jaspers, *The Philosophy of Existence* (1971); Leonard H. Ehrlich, *Karl Jaspers: Philosophy and Faith* (1975); Rudolf Bultmann, *Existence and Faith* (1960); John O'Neill, *Perception, Experience, and History: The Social Phenomenology of Maurice Merleau-Ponty* (1970); Hugo Ott, *Martin Heidegger: An Intellectual and Political Portrait* (trans. Allan Blunden, 1992).

Neo-Marxism and the New Left:

Dick Howard, *The Unknown Dimension: European Marxism since Lenin* (1972); Raymond Guess, *The Idea of Critical Theory* (1981); Martin Jay, *The Dialectical Imagination* (1973); Jack Lindsay, *The Crisis in Marxism* (1981); John O'Neill, ed., *On Critical Theory* (1976); Gillian Rose, *The Melancholy Science: An Introduction to the Thought of Theodor Adorno* (1979); David Held, *Introduction to Critical Theory: Horkheimer to Habermas* (1980); Julius Sensat, *Habermas and Marxism* (1979); Walter L. Adamson, *Hegemony and Revolution: Antonio Gramsci's Political and Cultural Theory* (1980) and *Marx and the Disillusionment of Marxism* (1985); Neil McInnes, *The Western Marxists* (1972); J. G. Merquior, *Western Marxism* (1986); Paul Piccone, *Italian Marxism* (1983); Robert Gorman, *Neo-Marxism: The Meanings of Modern Radiculism* (1982); Eugene Lunn, *Marxism and Modernism* (1984); John Roemer, ed., *Analytical Marxism: An Anthology* (1986); Maurice Cranston, ed., *The New Left* (1971); Douglas Kellner, *Herbert Marcuse and the Crisis of Marxism* (1984); Arthur Hirsh, *The French New Left: An Intellectual History from Sartre to Gorz* (1981); B. Marie Perinbaum, *Holy Violence in the Thought of Frantz Fanon* (1981); David Caute, *The Year of the Barricades* (1988); Alex Callinicos, *Althusser's Marxism* (1976); Klaus Mehnert, *Moscow and the New Left* (1976).

Russia and Eastern Europe after 1953:

Joshua Rubenstein, *Soviet Dissidents* (1980, 1987); Alec Nove, *Stalinism and After* (1981); Michael Meerson-Aksenov and Boris Shagrin, eds., *The Political, Social, and Religious Thought of Russian "Samizdat": An Anthology* (1977); Loren Graham, *Science and Philosophy in the Soviet Union* (1972); Stephen F. Cohen, ed.,

An End to Silence: Uncensored Opinions in the Soviet Union (1982); Geoffrey Hosking, *Beyond Soviet Realism: Soviet Fiction since "Ivan Denisovich"* (1980); Oleg Chukhontsev, ed., *Dissonant Voices: The New Russian Fiction* (1991); Norman Stone and Michael Glenny, *The Other Russia* (1990); Michael Bourdeaux, *Gorbachev, Glasnost, and the Gospel* (1991); Gerson S. Sher, *Praxis: Marxist Criticism and Dissent in Socialist Yugoslavia* (1977); N. Markovic and Robert S. Cohen, *Yugoslavia: The Rise and Fall of Socialist Humanism* (1978); Osker Gruenwald, *The Yugoslav Search for Man: Marxist Humanism in Contemporary Yugoslavia* (1983); A. Hegedus, A. Heller, N. Markus, and M. Vajda, *The Humanization of Socialism: Writings of the Budapest School* (1976); Vladimir Kusin, *Intellectual Origins of the Prague Spring* (1971); Vaclav Havel, *Living in Truth* (1990); Timothy G. Ash, *The Polish Revolution: Solidarity 1980–1982* (1984); Janos Kornai, *The Road to a Free Economy* (1990).

Structuralism:

Howard Gardner, *The Quest for Mind: Piaget, Lévi-Strauss, and the Structuralist Movement* (1981); Edith Kurzweil, *The Age of Structuralism* (1980); John Sturrock, ed., *Structuralism and Since: From Lévi-Strauss to Derrida* (1979); Fredric Jameson, *The Prison House of Language: A Critical History of Structuralism and Formalism* (1972); Thomas G. Pavel, *The Feud of Language: A History of Structuralist Thought* (1990); Roland Barthes, *Mythologies* (1972); Alan Sheridan, *Michel Foucault: The Will to Truth* (1980); Mark Poster, *Foucault, Marxism, and History: Mode of Production versus Mode of Information* (1984); Gary Gutting, *Michel Foucault's Archaeology of Scientific Reason* (1989); Joseph H. Smith and William Kerrigan, eds., *Interpreting Lacan* (1983); Sherry Turkle, *Psychoanalytic Politics: Freud's French Revolution* (1978); Stuart Schneiderman, *Jacques Lacan: The Death of an Intellectual Hero* (1983); Samuel Weber, *Return to Freud: Jacques Lacan's Dislocation of Psychoanalysis* (1991); Malcolm Bowie, *Lacan* (1991); John Sturrock, *The French New Novel* (1969).

Deconstruction and Postmodernism:

John Sallis, ed., *Deconstruction and Philosophy: The Texts of Jacques Derrida* (1987); Christopher Norris, *Deconstruction: Theory and Practice* (1982); Jonathan Culler, *On Deconstruction: Theory and Criticism after Structuralism* (1982); Bice Benvenuto and Roger Kennedy, *The Works of Lacan: An Introduction* (1986); Gianni Vattimo, *The End of Modernity: Nihilism and Hermeneutics in Postmodern Culture* (1989); Allan Megill, *Prophets of Extremity: Nietzsche, Heidegger, Foucault, Derrida* (1985); Fredric Jameson, *Postmodernism, or the Cultural Logic of Late Capitalism* (1991); Jean-François Lyotard, *The Postmodern Condition* (1984); Jonathan Arac, ed., *Postmodernism and Politics* (1986); Pauline Marie Rosenau, *Post-Modernism and the Social Sciences* (1992); Anthony Giddens, *The Conse-*

quences of Modernity (1991); John Gross, *The Rise and Fall of the Man of Letters* (1991); Bernard Bergonzi, *Exploding English* (1990); John Lechte, *Julia Kristeva* (1990), one of a series on Critics, general editor Christopher Norris, including Lacan (by Juliet Flower MacCannell), Leavis (by Michael Bell), Barthes (by Mary Bittner Wiseman); Geoffrey Hartman, *Saving the Text: Literature, Derrida, Philosophy* (1981); Allen Thiher, *Words in Reflection: Modern Language Theory and Postmodern Fiction* (1984).

Recent Philosophy:

Charles J. Bontemps and S. Jack Odell, eds., *The Owl of Minerva: Philosophers on Philosophy* (1975); Anthony Giddens and Jonathan Turner, eds., *Social Theory Today* (1988); Kenneth Baynes, James Bohman, Thomas McCarthy, eds., *After Philosophy: End or Transformation?*; A. J. Ayer, *Philosophy in the Twentieth Century* (1984); Paul Franco, *The Political Philosophy of Michael Oakeshott* (1990); Will Kymlicka, *Contemporary Political Philosophy: An Introduction* (1991).

Recent Science:

Robin Herman, *Fusion: The Search for Endless Energy* (1990); James S. Trefil, *From Atoms to Quarks: An Introduction to the Strange World of Particle Physics* (1981); Fred Alan Wolf, *Star Wave: Mind, Consciousness, and Quantum Physics* (1985); Yuval Ne'eman, *The Particle Hunters* (1986); Herbert Friedman, *The Astronomer's Universe: Stars, Galaxies, and Cosmos* (1991); Alan G. Gross, *The Rhetoric of Science* (1991); Robert Shapiro, *The Human Blueprint* (1992).

Recent Psychology and Sociology:

Mitchell G. Ash and William R. Woodward, eds., *Psychology in Twentieth Century Thought and Society* (1988); Anthony Clare, *Psychiatry in Dissent* (1979); G. E. Zuriff, *Behaviorism: A Conceptual Reconstruction* (1985); Charles C. Lemert, *French Sociology since 1968* (1981); A. W. Gouldner, *The Coming Crisis of Western Sociology* (1971); Pierre Bourdieu, *In Other Words: Essays toward a Reflexive Sociology* (trans. 1991).

Recent Economics:

Warren J. Samuels, ed., *Economics as Discourse* (1990); Peter Giles and Guy Routh, eds., *Economics in Disarray* (1984); Eamonn Butler, *Hayek: His Contribution to the Political and Economic Thought of Our Time* (1984); Donald N. McCloskey, *The Rhetoric of Economics* (1985); Walter Eltis and Peter Sinclair, eds., *Keynes and Economic Policy: The Relevance of the "General Theory" after Fifty Years* (1989); Robert Skidelsky, ed., *Thatcherism* (1989); J. F. Shackleton and Gareth Luksley, eds., *Twelve Contemporary Economists* (1981).

Recent Arts:

Robert Hughes, *The Shock of the New: Art and the Century of Change* (1991); Charles Russell, *Poets, Prophets, and Revolutionaries: The Literary Avant-Garde from Rimbaud through Postmodernism* (1991); Christopher Butler, *After the Wake: An Essay on the Contemporary Avant-Garde* (1980); Malcolm Bradbury, ed., *The Novel Today* (1977); Anthony Thwaite, *Poetry Today: A Critical Guide to British Poetry 1960–1984*; Peter Austin Jones and Michael Schmidt, eds., *British Poetry since 1970* (1980); Christopher Innes, *Modern British Drama, 1890–1990* (1992); Maurice Valency, *The End of the World: An Introduction to Contemporary Drama* (1980); Ronald Hayman, *Theatre and Anti-theatre: New Movements since Beckett* (1977); J. Mordaunt Crook, *The Dilemma of Style: Architectural Ideas from the Picturesque to the Post-Modern* (1989); Daniel Wheeler, *Art since Mid-Century* (1990); Hilton Kramer, *Abstract Art: A Cultural History* (1992); Sandy Nairne, *The State of the Art: Ideas and Images in the 1980's* (1988).

Recent Religion:

David Ray Griffin, *God and Religion in the Postmodern World* (1988); R. J. Reilly, *Romantic Religion: A Study of Barfield, Lewis, Williams, and Tolkien* (1971); Paul L. Holmes, *C. S. Lewis: The Shape of His Faith and Thought* (1977); Daniel Cohen, *Waiting for the Apocalypse* (1983); Warren Wagar, *Terminal Visions: The Literature of Last Things* (1982); Hans Küng, *Does God Exist? An Answer for Today* (1980); Helmut Thielicke, *Modern Faith and Thought* (trans. 1991); David F. Ford, ed., *The Modern Theologians: An Introduction to Christian Theology in the Twentieth Century* (vol. 1, 1989); James P. Mackey, *Modern Theology* (1987); Julian N. Hartt, Ray L. Hart, and Robert P. Scharlemann, *The Critique of Modernity: Theological Reflections on Contemporary Culture* (1987).

Feminist Perspectives:

Marlon B. Ross, *The Contours of Masculine Desire: Romanticism and the Rise of Women's Poetry* (1989); Anne K. Mellor, ed., *Romanticism and Feminism* (1988); Margaret Homans, *Bearing the Word: Language and Female Experience in Nineteenth Century Writing* (1986); Elaine Showalter, *A Literature of Their Own: British Women Novelists from Brontë to Lessing* (1976); Barbara Taylor, *Eve and the New Jerusalem: Socialism and Feminism in the Nineteenth Century* (1983);

Barbara Caine, *Victorian Feminists* (1992); Irene Calder, *Women and Marriage in Victorian Fiction* (1976); Martha Vicinus, *Suffer and Be Still: Women in the Victorian Age* (1972); Jane Nardin, *He Knew She Was Right: The Independent Woman in the Novels of Anthony Trollope* (1989); Richard J. Evans, *The Feminists: Women's Emancipation Movements 1844–1920* (1977); Richard Stites, *The Women's Liberation Movement in Russia, 1860–1930* (1980); Brian Harrison, *Separate Spheres: The Opposition to Women's Suffrage in Britain* (1978) and *Prudent Revolutionaries: Portraits of British Feminists between the Wars* (1987); Sheila Rowbotham, *The Past before us: Feminism in Action since the 1960s* (1989); Bonnie Kime Scott, *Joyce and Feminism* (1984); Germaine Greer, *The Obstacle Race* (1979); Jean Grimshaw, *Philosophy and Feminist Thinking* (1986); Hester Eisenstein, *Contemporary Feminist Thought* (1983); Shari Benstock, ed., *Feminist Issues in Literary Scholarship* (1987); Elaine Showalter, ed., *The New Feminist Criticism* (1985); Nancy J. Chodorow, *Feminism and Psychoanalytic Theory* (1990); Margaret W. Ferguson and Jennifer Wicke, eds., *Feminism and Postmodernism* (1992); Pnina G. Abir-am and Dorinda Outram, eds., *Uneasy Careers and Intimate Lives: Women in Science, 1789–1979* (1987); Terry Lovell, ed., *British Feminist Thought: A Reader* (1990); Lorna Sage, *Women in the House of Fiction: Postwar Women Novelists* (1992).

Other Books about Recent Thought and Culture:

Christoper Booker, *The Neophiliacs* (1970); Matei Calinescu, *Five Faces of Modernity* (1987); Barry Cooper, Allan Karnberg, and William Mishler, *The Resurgence of Conservatism in Anglo-American Democracies* (1988); Roland N. Stromberg, *After Everything* (1976); Robert A. Nisbet, *The Twilight of Authority* (1975); M. Ashley Montague and F. Watson, *The Dehumanization of Man* (1983); Raymond Aron, *In Defense of Decadent Europe* (1979); G. Santoni, ed., *Contemporary French Culture and Society* (1981); Irving Howe, ed., *1984 Revisited* (1983); John Sutherland, *Offensive Literature: Decensorship in Britain, 1960–82* (1982); John Carswell, *Government and the Universities in Britain: Programme and Performance 1960–1980* (1986).

Index

NAMES

Abelard, Peter, 148
Abraham, Karl, 155
Acton, Lord John, 20, 99
Adam, Mme. Juliette, 174
Adler, Mortimer, 4
Adorno, Theodor, 234, 278, 281
Aeschylus, 151, 256
Agassiz, Louis, 110
Alain (Emile Chartier), 247
Alain-Fournier, Henri, 191
Alexander, Samuel, 149
Alexander I of Russia, 37, 39–40, 45
Alexander II of Russia, 166
Althusser, Louis, 284–85, 287, 291
Amalrik, Andrei, 286
Amis, Kingsley, 257, 275, 279
Anaximander, 104
Anderson, Sherwood, 215
Andreyev, Leonid, 190
Anquetil-Duperron, Abraham, 37
Apollinaire, Guillaume, 294
Aquinas, Thomas, 83, 116, 201, 234, 272
Aragon, Louis, 214, 229
Ardigo, Robert, 85
Arendt, Hannah, 267, 327

Aristotle, 7, 25, 72
Arnold, Matthew, 49, 88, 92, 129–31, 172, 337
Arnold, Thomas, 49
Aron, Raymond, 225, 260, 266, 267, 339
Arrabal, Fernando, 302
Arrow, Kenneth, 325
Auclert, Hubertine, 300
Auden, W. H., 94, 134, 204, 216, 219, 223, 229,
   272, 273, 329
Augustine, St., 1
Austen, Jane, 128
Austin, J. L., 273
Aveling, Edward, 118
Ayer, A. J., 239–40, 247

Baader, Franz von, 40
Baader-Meinhof group, 284
Babeuf, François, 17, 65
Baer, Karl von, 110, 116
Bagehot, Walter, 88
Bakhtin, Mikhail, 9, 299
Bakunin, Mikhail, 73, 93, 159, 166–67
Baldick, Chris, 312, 316
Baldwin, Stanley, 199
Balfour, Arthur J., 101
Balzac, Honoré de, 12, 32, 43, 48, 53, 67, 93,
   132, 242

CONCEPTS